SEXUALITY AND GENDER IN THE ENGLISH RENAISSANCE

GARLAND STUDIES IN THE RENAISSANCE
VOLUME 10
GARLAND REFERENCE LIBRARY OF THE HUMANITIES
VOLUME 2011

Garland Studies in the Renaissance
Raymond B. Waddington, *Series Editor*

Our Accustomed Discourse
on the Antique
*Cesare Gonzaga and Gerolamo
Garimberto, Two Renaissance
Collectors of Greco-Roman Art*
by Clifford Malcolm Brown, with the
collaboration of Anna Maria Lorenzoni

Mapping *The Faerie Queene*
*Quest Structures and
the World of the Poem*
by Wayne Erickson

Reading the Renaissance
Culture, Poetics, and Drama
edited by Jonathan Hart

Rubens and the Roman Circle
Studies of the First Decade
by Frances Huemer

The Mirror of Confusion
*The Representation of French
History in English Renaissance
Drama*
by Andrew M. Kirk

Renaissance Humanism
at the Court of Clement VII
Francesco Berni's *Dialogue
Against Poets* in Context
Studies, with an edition and translation
by Anne Reynolds

Low and High Style
in Italian Renaissance Art
by Patricia Emison

Sexuality and Gender
in the English Renaissance
*An Annotated Edition
of Contemporary Documents*
edited by Lloyd Davis

Sexuality and Gender in the English Renaissance

An Annotated Edition of Contemporary Documents

Edited by
Lloyd Davis

LONDON AND NEW YORK

First published 1998 by Garland Publishing, Inc.

Published 2018 by Routledge
2 Park Square, Milton Park, Abingdon, Oxon OX14 4RN
52 Vanderbilt Avenue, New York, NY 10017

First issued in paperback 2018

Routledge is an imprint of the Taylor & Francis Group, an informa business

Copyright © 1998 by Lloyd Davis

All rights reserved. No part of this book may be reprinted or reproduced or utilised in any form or by any electronic, mechanical, or other means, now known or hereafter invented, including photocopying and recording, or in any information storage or retrieval system, without permission in writing from the publishers.

Notice:
Product or corporate names may be trademarks or registered trademarks, and are used only for identification and explanation without intent to infringe.

Library of Congress Cataloging-in-Publication Data

Sexuality and gender in the English Renaissance : an annotated edition of
  contemporary documents / edited by Lloyd Davis.
      p.   cm. — (Garland reference library of the humanities ; vol. 2011)
  (Garland studies in the Renaissance ; vol. 10)
    Includes bibliographical references and index.
    ISBN 0-8153-2452-9 (alk. paper)
    1. Sex—England—History—Sources. 2. Gender identity—England—
History—Sources. 3. Sexual ethics—England—History—Sources. 4. Sex in
literature. 5. Gender identity in literature. 6. English literature—History and
criticism. 7. Women—History—Renaissance, 1450–1600. 8. Renaissance—
England.   I. Davis, Lloyd, 1959–   . II. Series. III. Series: Garland reference library of the humanities. Garland studies in the Renaissance ; vol. 10.
HQ18.G7G45   1998
305.3'0942—dc21   97-29382
                                                                               CIP

ISBN 13: 978-1-138-86434-4 (pbk)
ISBN 13: 978-0-8153-2452-2 (hbk)

For Charlotte

"The Bridling, Saddling, and Riding of a Rich Churl," reprinted from the title page of the book *The Bridling, Saddling, and Riding of a Rich Churl in Hampshire by the Subtle Practice of One Judeth Philips, a Professed Cunning Woman or Fortune Teller* (London, 1595), courtesy of the University of Queensland Library, Queensland, Australia.

Contents

Acknowledgments   xi

Introduction   xiii

Sermons and Homilies

1. *Certain Sermons or Homilies Appointed*   3
   to Be Read in Churches

       A Sermon against Whoredom and Uncleanness   5

       A Homily against Excess of Apparel   16

       A Homily of the State of Matrimony   24

2. *A White Sheet, or a Warning for Whoremongers*   37
   Richard Cooke

Moral and Religious Tracts

3. *An Apology for Women*   63
   William Heale

4. *Of the Lawfulness of Marriage upon a Lawful Divorce*   89
   John Rainolds

5.	*A Treatise against Painting and Tincturing of Men and Women* Thomas Tuke	107
6.	*The Answer of a Mother unto Her Seduced Son's Letter* Ez. W.	133
7.	*The Honor of Chastity: A Sermon* John Featley	145

Marriage and Household Manuals

8.	*The Order of Household: Described Methodically out of the Word of God, with the Contrary Abuses Found in the World* Dudley Fenner	165
9.	*A Godly Form of Household Government: For the Ordering of Private Families* Robert Cleaver	183
10.	*A Discourse of Marriage and Wiving* Alexander Niccholes	213
11.	*The Mother's Blessing: Or, the Godly Counsel of a Gentlewoman, not Long since Deceased, Left behind for Her Children* Dorothy Leigh	231
12.	*A Bride-Bush: Or, a Direction for Married Persons* William Whately	245

Midwifery

13.	*The Birth of Mankind* Eucharius Roesslin	277
14.	*Childbirth, or the Happy Delivery of Women: Wherein Is Set Down the Government of Women* Jacques Guillimeau	291

Ballads and Chapbooks

15. Ballads — 309

    A Proper New Ballad Expressing the Fames, Concerning a Warning to All London Dames — 311
        Steven Peele

    The Contented Cuckold, or a Pleasant New Song of a Newcastle Man, Whose Wife Being Gone from Him, Showing How He Came to London to Her, and When He Found Her Carried Her back again to Newcastle Town — 313

    A Merry Dialogue betwixt a Married Man and His Wife Concerning the Affairs of This Careful Life — 318

16. Chapbooks — 323

    A Miraculous and Monstrous but yet Most True and Certain Discourse of a Woman (now to be seen in London) of the Age of Threescore Years, in the Midst of Whose Forehead (by the wonderful work of God) There Groweth out a Crooked Horn of Four Inches Long — 324

    The Bridling, Saddling, and Riding of a Rich Churl in Hampshire by the Subtle Practice of One Judeth Philips, a Professed Cunning Woman or Fortune Teller — 328

Witchcraft

17. *A Discourse of the Damned Art of Witchcraft: So Far Forth as It Is Revealed in the Scriptures and Manifest by True Experience* — 341
    William Perkins

18. *The Admirable History of the Possession and Conversion of a Penitent Woman* — 351
    Sebastien Michaelis

Law

19. *The Law's Resolutions of Women's Rights: Or, the Law's Provision for Women*   371
    T. E.

Works Cited   407

Index   413

Acknowledgments

Numerous people have helped me in bringing this project to completion. Most important were the tremendous efforts of three excellent research assistants—Bruce Parr, Glen Thomas, and Anna Bemrose. Various people at the University of Queensland also helped in supplying leads and information for the annotations as well as with Latin and Greek translations: Tony Glad and Martin Duwell of the English Department; Robert Milns, Suzanne Dixon, and Michael Apthorp from the Classics and Ancient History Department; Michael Lattke and Philip Almond of the Studies in Religion Department; and Spencer Routh of the University of Queensland Library. I am very grateful to all.

As editor of the Garland Publishing Studies in the Renaissance series, Raymond Waddington has offered much advice and many helpful suggestions on assembling the collection. Phyllis Korper, Tania Bissell, and Laurel Stegina of Garland have also provided great long-range assistance.

Research on the collection was funded by two grants, one from the University of Queensland and one from the Australian Research Council. I am grateful to both institutions.

Julia Duffy and Charlotte Davis deserve my greatest thanks for their constant support and friendship.

Introduction
Lloyd Davis

The texts and extracts in this collection bring into focus a range of issues relating to historical experience and conceptions of sexuality and gender, and the possibilities of theorizing and analyzing them. Together they depict some of the main areas and institutions in Early Modern England where questions of gender and sexuality featured significantly. Included are a broad selection from religious sermons and tracts, moral treatises, domestic manuals and handbooks, midwifery and legal textbooks, ballads, and chapbooks, published between the late years of Henry VIII's reign and the middle of Charles I's. The choice of texts aims to appeal to modern readers, scholars, and students by reproducing important but varied social documents and topics from the period. The initial producers and audiences might deny that the selected texts deal with "gender and sexual relations," insisting, for example, that sermons and treatises only treat religious and moral standards, or that midwifery and legal handbooks concern themselves purely with technical methods. A collection such as this inevitably appropriates texts from various topics and categories and, to a degree, transforms them into an image of its own interests. Stephen Orgel has recently written that "All historical claims, even the most tactful and unpoliticized, are ultimately concerned to make the past comprehensible, usable and relevant to our own interests—to make it, that is, present" (*Impersonations* 64). Relevance to contemporary interests is particularly at issue for controversial topics such as sexuality and gender.[1] Reservations may arise over whether a modern perspective alters or reveals what is "really" at stake in older works. The position that has guided selection of and commentary on these texts is that Renaissance authors and readers were neither oblivious to nor entirely preoccupied with sexual and gendered meanings. Rather, they perceived such meanings in ways that, on the one hand, can vary considerably from how they might be recognized today and, on the other, can "reverberate" significantly with twentieth-century versions.[2] The usefulness and significance of the texts included here are that they highlight what those contrasts and connections are.

Perhaps most striking to modern readers is the continual reference to older works to support and verify attitudes and arguments that are being presented. The most commonly cited book is the Bible, with commentaries and explications of the Scriptures and classical philosophical and ethical works also being frequently mentioned. Reference to traditionally authoritative texts was accepted as the primary means of mounting and defending a case and is used in all genres, from homilies and sermons that faithfully quote the Scriptures to illustrate religious and moral doctrine to the seventeenth-century legal digest, *The Law's Resolutions of Women's Rights*, which cites judicial precedents in explaining women's rights and obligations. This logical and rhetorical method displays a strong reliance on the past, especially the sacred tradition through which God's word offers "authoritative continuity" (Greene 12) on all matters including gender and sexuality, as well as a willingness to apply and, in some cases, adapt traditional views to sixteenth- and seventeenth-century contexts. For example, a number of the texts gathered here, most notably John Rainolds' *Of the Lawfulness of Marriage upon a Lawful Divorce*, address the legitimacy of divorce and remarriage in the aftermath of Henry VIII's separation from Katherine of Aragon which preceded the English Reformation. They associate disagreements in scriptural interpretation with current moral and theological debates between conformist and reformist Protestants in England. In such cases, biblical and classical citations, though not made "heuristically" in Thomas Greene's sense (40-41), or in highly imaginative ways, are used to evaluate and judge current events and viewpoints. The older works are necessarily repositioned in terms of contemporary concerns. In this manner, the Renaissance texts enact a dialogue between past and present values which parallels their relation to modern criticism, research, and attitudes.

The use of biblical and classical authorities to anchor opinions on gender and sexual relations is far different to the way ideas on such matters are presented in late-twentieth-century media of news, film, television, popular fiction and non-fiction. Today, it seems that people either have their own positions on these matters or are trying to work out what their positions are. The issues appear to be highly individual, and the idea that an ancient text might offer definitive guidance seems to contradict the private, first-hand nature of sexual and gender identity. However, through their distance and difference these works reveal that, in its fascination with the personal, that kind of view often conceals other factors that construct and influence people's genders and sexual ties. In the first place, personal revelation and opinion are not natural modes of self-expression. They are effects of genre and convention, the availability and acceptability of writing about oneself in certain ways. In contrast, each of these authors adopts a distinctive public voice and speaks to readers about their situations rather than about his or her own. Forms of personal disclosure may be attempted in poetic and dramatic works from the period (though some critics also question whether "the personal" is actually represented in such texts), and in the diaries and journals which start to proliferate in the late-sixteenth century, but a discourse of psychological revelation is not culturally prevalent. As Bruce R. Smith has emphasized, during the Renaissance "sexuality was not. . .the starting place for anyone's self-definition," and sexual desire was not taken as a key to personal identity (10-12).

Instead, authors offer counsel, information, or instruction, to groups such as the God-fearing parishioners of St. Swithin's church (Richard Cooke in his warning to whoremongers), to the young men of England (Alexander Niccholes in his account of marriage and wiving), or to potentially wayward sons (Dorothy Leigh in her posthumous maternal blessing). Authorial sentiment is directed to instructing one's audience. Such aims do not preclude the expression of emotion, but they do suggest that a private voice and the individual behind it, whose presence modern readers tend to assume almost automatically, are less important to Early Modern authors and readers. They appear to be much more interested in the social character that is being displayed and the kinds of attitudes which playing that role entails.

Generic features which shape authorial voice and audience response also affect subject matter. In this case, where texts function through didactic address, sexuality and gender are primarily connected to public behavior and interaction: how one dresses, whom one marries, what authority one holds, and so on. They signify social relationships and identities rather than personal ones. People in Tudor and Stuart England obviously experienced intimate, loving ties and passionate, erotic longing. Yet texts that discuss and depict states of affection and desire constantly frame and distinguish them with social markers. Literature from the period is filled with instances where such elements intertwine with sexuality and gender: demands of urban life that the speaker of John Donne's "The Sun Rising" and "The Canonization" seeks to repudiate; courtly rivalries and intrigues with which Astrophil and Stella contend in Philip Sidney's sonnet sequence; pressures of sovereign command and desire that rule the lovers in Beaumont and Fletcher's play *The Maid's Tragedy*; feudal, familial enmity dooming Romeo and Juliet; the economic, ethnic, and religious forces that determine the bonds among males and females in *The Merchant of Venice*. Viola's summary of the complications in Shakespeare's *Twelfth Night* conveys an intensity of romantic involvement along with the limited power of individual desire and action to resolve such affairs:

> My master loves her dearly,
> And I (poor monster) fond as much on him;
> And she (mistaken) seems to dote on me.
> What will become of this? . . .
> O time, thou must untangle this, not I,
> It is too hard a knot for me t' untie. (2.2.33-41)

Eventually, the play's confusion of roles and perceptions is cleared up through uncertain collaborations between characters. Even then, any consummate vision of relationships and identities is not entirely shared, with figures such as Malvolio and Antonio noticeably excluded and the clown's closing song suggesting the transience and folly of people's actions and arrangements.

In analogous terms, the texts in this collection depict the ways in which sexual and gender relations are enacted "on the borders of public and private morality" (Ingram 142), with people's convictions and acts always being observed, evaluated, and guided according to social standards. They are subject to enduring notions of religious, political, and ethical obligation, and conditioned by immediate and local events, including doctrinal disputes in the wake of the English Reformation, manipulations of state ideologies as successive sovereigns seek to maintain and reinforce control, and collective scrutiny and debate over responsibilities and entitlements in areas as diverse as household duties, legal status, and physical demeanor and appearance. Authors appeal to audiences to judge the deeds and words of the figures they write about as they would their everyday associates, and move them to monitor and, if necessary, reform their own patterns of behavior. The implicit and explicit message is that sexual and gender roles are never arbitrary or inconsequential but are crucially involved in the affairs of one's family, neighbors, and community. Indeed, such roles emerge as one of the primary ways in which people are made to feel and acknowledge their social existence, since members of a society create "sexual categories and roles within which they act and define themselves" (Padgug 60). All of the texts implicitly emphasize that gender and sexuality do not offer freedom or release from social structures but are elements of identity, experience, and interaction that make individuals accountable to other people and to the community more generally.

Because they are acted out with and before others, gender and sexuality are depicted as practices rather than abstract ideals or permanent states. They are ordered, though not constrained, by cultural norms and remain contingent upon changing situations. For example, Thomas Tuke's *Treatise against Painting and Tincturing* and William Heale's *Apology for Women* present opposing arguments about masculine and feminine behavior. Tuke attacks women's use of fashion and cosmetics as a sign of the sex's corrupt nature and inability to adhere to decent standards of domestic and public conduct. Heale criticizes the treatment of women by the majority of men, who in some cases beat them but more regularly relate to them selfishly and thoughtlessly. In invoking principles of correct behavior, each author reveals that such criteria are being widely infringed and challenged and so may not be predominant at all. Their attempts to shore up standards of sexual behavior simultaneously question the effects of applying norms to interactions which were full of personal value and "could become a staging ground for many forms of social struggle" (Howard, "Sex" 173). Their potential volatility and significance make gender and sexual practices the more liable to be targeted for regulation, yet the less likely to remain subject to control.

One of the main areas of dispute in the period involves power relationships between men and women. Rights of authority and duties of submission were argued across many texts published during the reigns of Elizabeth and James I.[3] The controversy over women's roles in families and society was, however, always equivocal, for it necessarily questioned the naturalization of male superiority and control, hence the hierarchical structures of society itself. As Joan Wallach Scott contends, contests over the meanings of sexual difference are an integral "part of many kinds of struggles for power" (6). Since any sexual code or value has the effect of restricting and producing attitudes and behaviors, gender works as "a primary way of signifying relationships of power" (42). Dominant or prevailing definitions of gender reinforce and are reinforced by these relationships, but they are also open to question and challenge.

Polemical pamphlets in the "woman debate" scored points against each other and sought to establish general principles concerning men and women's social position.[4] In contrast, the kinds of texts included in this volume come from specific institutions and backgrounds and give details about various aspects of everyday life in the Early Modern period, from marriage, household arrangements, fashion, and health to crime, witchcraft, and superstition. Because of men's dominance of public positions and discourse, many of the texts articulate overtly masculinist viewpoints on these topics. Yet the range of activities to which gender and sexuality are seen as germane supports Scott's contention that these relations were frequently at issue, caught up in contests across the social spectrum. As has recently been pointed out, prescriptive dicta provide evidence of adaptation and resistance as well as assertive rule: "The space in which women lived, appeared, and worked, whether they were princesses or peasants. . .was one staked out by norms, prohibitions, and controls; but women devised ways of living within these constraints and even ways to escape from them" (Davis and Farge 4). Occasionally a male voice, puzzled or bridling at the constraints of patriarchal norms, can also be discerned.

While indicating various areas in which gender and sexuality were being debated and contested, the texts also contain their own interpretative complexities. At first the difficulties seem to come from the references and allusions to unfamiliar ancient and Early Modern theological and philosophical authorities noted earlier. There is also a formal denseness to many of the texts, owing either to polemical purposes in which every line of argument needs to be covered, or to specialized subject matter. Even texts written for a much wider public audience, such as the homilies, chapbooks, and manuals, may seem stylistically obscure on first reading. Yet a more significant source of complexity lies in the contentious nature of the issues being written about. The texts are caught amid and play important parts in social struggles for power, authority, and rights that are being waged through and around gender and sexuality. Their direct assertions and points of view are open to dispute, revision, and rejection by both readers and other texts. The authors constantly try to pre-empt or respond to such thematic and ideological inversions by citing and dismissing the claims of others, urging audiences to grant their assent and to ignore their own and others' questionings and doubts.

The disputatious and at times defensive strain that pervades the texts is the strongest sign that no single system of values and rules organized gender and sexual relations in Renaissance England. If they do capture the social and historical circumstances in which these relations were played out, they do so by embodying its contested atmosphere, at one moment fragile and on the verge of radical conflict, at another resolutely static and traditional. And, in portraying the backgrounds which inform the period's famous literary and dramatic works, they not only depict "a context which has its own complex particularity that calls for detailed interpretation" (LaCapra 16) but also bear the traces of lived efforts to adopt, adapt, evade, and challenge the discourses that mold people's understandings and experience of sexuality and gender.

As noted earlier, the texts in the volume are taken from a variety of important institutions and areas of everyday life in sixteenth- and seventeenth-century England. The approximately hundred years covered by their publication sees the continuity of traditional views on gender relations along with the recognition of increasing pressure on these relations from changing cultural, political, and religious circumstances. To convey the diversity of social customs and rituals in which questions of sexuality and gender are debated the works are grouped into seven sections. Within each section, the texts are ordered chronologically to suggest the interplay of continuity and contrast in attitudes to gender relations. Generally, however, disagreement and similarity among the texts have less to do with differences in dates of publication than in generic details such as occasion and motive for producing the texts, their intended audiences, the social position of the authors. Each work is accordingly accompanied by an introduction which offers biographical information about the author, publishing history, and a brief account of its main contextual details through discussing some of the social and historical conditions framing the text and to which it responds. In supplying these details, it often has been necessary to cite and discuss observations from recent historical and critical interpretations of the period; references made in this way are gathered at the end of the volume. The introductory remarks do not aim to provide full textual interpretations, though occasionally comments are made on notable stylistic features and on analogies with other works, including literary texts, from the period. Each introduction tries to offer a number of starting points for different responses to the works, which may concentrate, for example, on the significance of gender and sexual relations in theological heritage and dispute, or social history, or interactions with dramatic and poetic discourses.

The opening section, Sermons and Homilies, comprises four texts, the three homilies, officially recommended for weekly reading in Elizabethan and Jacobean church services, which deliberate on sexuality and gender: "Against Whoredom and Adultery," "Against Excess of Apparel," and "Of the State of Matrimony." Written in broadly accessible style for delivery from the pulpit, the homilies convey prevailing, conservative views on their subjects as well as rehearsing the chief biblical citations that informed much discussion of sexual issues. The other text in this section, *A White Sheet, or a Warning for Whoremongers*, an individual sermon originally delivered in a parish church by the priest, Richard Cooke, aims to castigate a local adulterer and to impress the heinousness of the sin of fornication on the congregation and readers. Unlike the homilies, which convey official attitudes in a public voice, Cooke's sermon sounds a more immediate note of personal and community involvement.

The second section contains extracts from five Moral and Religious Tracts, covering a range of contemporary debates over sexual and gender relations. The opening text is William Heale's *Apology for Women*, which counters traditional anti-feminist claims by appealing to spiritual, moral, and legal equality between men and women. As mentioned above, John Rainolds' *Of the Lawfulness of Marriage upon a Lawful Divorce* argues for the permissibility of a man remarrying, having legally divorced his wife for adultery. Rainolds' argument confronts disagreements among Puritan, Protestant, and Catholic positions on the issue. It also represents the way in which legal and theological perspectives on many moral and personal questions remained intertwined. The following text, Thomas Tuke's *Treatise against Painting and Tincturing of Men and Women*, develops the arguments made in the homily on apparel, stressing the naturalness of divine creation and human appearance and the corrupt nature of cosmetics and fashion, especially as pursued by women.

Chapter 6 contains an impassioned *Answer of a Mother unto Her Seduced Son's Letter*, in which the author, "Ez. W.," pleads with her son to renounce the luxurious embrace of a French harlot, the Catholic Church, and return to her own secure embrace, the spiritual security of the Anglican Church. The letter shows the tensions of Reformation and Counter-Reformation conflicts being translated into near-sensual terms of family romance. The final text in the section is John Featley's sermon, *The Honor of Chastity* which celebrates sexual restraint as a cardinal virtue for male and females.

The following section, Marriage and Household Manuals, reveals many of the abstract positions and viewpoints raised in the sermons and tracts being translated into practical advice for earnest, hardworking, middle-class families. Dudley Fenner's *The Order of Household* underlines the importance of patriarchal authority over wife, children, and servants in maintaining godly harmony and conformity in the home. Whereas Fenner, one of the leading early Puritan theologians, fills his text with quotations from the Bible, later authors of similar manuals tend to present their views in less overtly religious terms though still using the Scriptures for ultimate reference. As suggested by the title of the next selection, Robert Cleaver's *A Godly Form of Household Government*, the maintenance of masculine privilege in the home is frequently seen as guaranteeing political and religious orthodoxy as well as domestic order.

In Chapter 10, Alexander Niccholes provides a contrasting tone to the seriousness of the other essayists. His *Discourse of Marriage and Wiving* presents a skeptical view of personal and sexual relationships similar to those depicted in satirical writings of the time. The gravity of family and gender relations is emphasized once again by Dorothy Leigh's advice on choosing and treating a wife, which she provides to her sons in *The Mother's Blessing*. Finally in this section, the Puritan preacher William Whately aims to reinforce views of the family as a setting for male supremacy and female submissiveness in the published version of a number of his sermons, *A Bride-Bush: Or, a Direction for Married Persons*.

The fourth section on Midwifery introduces two texts from the specialized field of Early Modern obstetrics. As the seventeenth century progressed, numerous English works on midwifery came to be published, but most fall outside the time-span covered by this collection. These earlier works, *The Birth of Mankind* by the German physician Eucharius Roesslin, and *Childbirth, or the Happy Delivery of Women* by the French surgeon Jacques Guillimeau, were both translated into English. Each subscribes to medical authority stemming from the classical period, combining conscientious motives of care with assumptions that reinforce notions of the mysterious nature of women's bodies and the importance of their subjection to traditional male expertise.

The fifth section, Ballads and Chapbooks, contains a number of texts in which official attitudes to marriage, fashion, and crime are presented in popular and often light-hearted contexts. The three ballads, *A Warning to All London Dames*, *The Contented Cuckold*, and *A Merry Dialogue Between a Married Man and His Wife*, reproduce many of the concerns of the tracts and manuals but with humorous tones that may question as much as they endorse more learned, pious, and even sanctimonious views. The other two texts in the section contain tales "stranger than fiction," which aim to offer readers sobering ethical lessons. *A Miraculous and Monstrous but yet Most True and Certain Discourse of a Woman* tells of a horn which grew out of a woman's forehead, a sign connoting all manner of sexual and moral impropriety, in none of which, however, the woman herself appears to have engaged. *The Bridling, Saddling, and Riding of a Rich Churl in Hampshire* recounts the felonies committed by one woman, who seems to embody the chaos of society turned upside down through female dishonesty. In these two texts, sensational and criminal deviance is linked to transgressions against naturalized gender hierarchy and code of behavior.

Threats to social order ignited by gender transgression are also raised in the following section, Witchcraft, which comprises extracts from two of the numerous texts published during the English experience of the Early Modern witch-hunts. *A Discourse of the Damned Art of Witchcraft* by William Perkins is a learned account of the perils of magical temptation that menace men and women. Perkins goes on to underline female susceptibility to satanic snares. Next, the translation of French priest Sebastien Michaelis' *The Admirable History of the Possession and Conversion of a Penitent Woman* offers a graphic, day-by-day account of the rites of exorcism borne by a French nun. Devils, priests, assistants, family and community members, all predominantly male figures, observe and participate in this struggle for a soul, wherein misogynist myths and superstitions are acted out on and through a female body.

The collection's final section on Law contains extracts from the anonymously authored *The Law's Resolutions of Women's Rights*. The text is a vast summary of the legal status of women in mid-seventeenth-century England. Explaining the history of relevant case law and statutes, it is directed to women readers and attempts to furnish them with details of rights, obligations, and provisions (hence it also supplies much information about men's legal standing in the period). The sections chosen here deal with judicial processes regarding marriage, property ownership, rape and ravishment.

The Law's Resolutions provides a suitable if complex conclusion to the anthology. The complicated legal discussion vividly conveys the dense interweaving of Early Modern notions of gender, sexuality, and personal relations with other social codes and systems. The recognition that masculine prerogative is in most cases privileged by precedent and statute reflects the cultural authority and material power of patriarchal tradition. Finally, the textual address to female readers underscores a historically developing sense of women as social actors, whose desires and rights demand and inform representations of both their positions and those of men, along with the sexual and gender relations between them.

Some of the texts included in the collection were very popular with contemporary readers and were republished a number of times. In most cases, republishing seems to indicate regional rather than national regard. For example, a second edition of Dudley Fenner's *The Order of Household* was printed in Edinburgh, where its endorsement of patriarchal control over the family may well have been approved by Presbyterian church elders. Generally, the place of publication was London, which reflects not only its concentration of commerce and population but a complementary urban demand for texts on many different issues, especially controversial ones involving gender, law, religion, and so on. Exceptions to London as place of publication are again illuminating: Fenner's work was first printed in Holland, where he had moved with other strict Puritans to avoid official opposition to religious and social practices; John Rainolds' tract on divorce, whose views contradicted those of the early-seventeenth-century Church of England, was also published in Holland; William Heale's *Apology for Women* was printed at Oxford, where it initially had circulated in disagreement with another paper, delivered at the University, that sanctioned wife-beating. In cases where a text was printed several times, the clearest available microfilm edition has been used as the copy-text and is identified in the introduction to the text by both *Short Title Catalogue* (*STC*) number and reel number from the University of Michigan series, "Early English Books I (1475-1640)."

Because of the length of some of the originals, it has not always been possible to reproduce entire texts. Where some sections of a work have been chosen over others, I have used criteria entailing my sense of what will prove stimulating to modern readers in social, historical, and critical terms. Complete and partially reproduced texts have all been edited in the following ways: punctuation and spelling, including that of proper names, have been modernized, except for old forms whose sense is relatively clear (such as "shew," "saith," or "sayeth"); the spelling of archaic words has been regularized according to the *Oxford English Dictionary*; italics, often occurring profusely in the texts, have been altered to conform with the modern convention of emphasizing words and phrases rather than paragraphs or pages; capital letters, used frequently in the old texts to emphasize words, have been retained; odd subject-verb agreement has also been kept; obvious misprints in the original texts have been silently corrected, but misquotations from the Bible and other sources have not been changed.

In the majority of cases, phrases and statements in foreign languages, such as Greek, Latin, and French, have been translated into English in the text and the original language removed; well-known foreign-language phrases have been left untranslated. The reason for translating in the text is to reduce the number of annotations accompanying each work; for the same reason, parenthetic references for biblical quotations have generally been added at the end of relevant passages even if they were not provided in the original. The general aim of the annotations has been to assist in appreciating and following the authors' discussions. They comprise definitions from the *OED* of archaic or obsolete words and glosses of unusual phrases; details about persons, places, and things mentioned in the text; citations from classical and other texts identified by the authors in sidenotes; where possible, references to classical and other texts cited but not identified by the authors; and finally, comments on interesting allusions, images, or puns. The backgrounds to many of these works are very arcane, representing highly specialized research fields in themselves, and unfortunately I have not always found it possible to trace allusions and citations. It is hoped that these instances do not confuse, mislead, or irritate readers' responses to a point where they efface the more suggestive implications and striking viewpoints which the texts depict and debate on sexuality and gender in the English Renaissance.

NOTES

1. Cf. Phyllis Rackin's comments: "The questions with which we approach the past are the questions that trouble us here and now, the answers we find (even when couched in the words of old texts) the products of our own selection and arrangement. These difficulties are especially troublesome in the case of gender and sexuality—subjects that tend to be occluded in the historical records of the past and are heavily fraught with present concerns and controversies" (68).

2. Cf. Lisa Jardine, *Reading Shakespeare Historically* 6.

3. It has not been possible to include primary texts representing Early Modern English contexts of homosocial, homosexual, and lesbian relations in this one volume.

4. See both of the collections edited by Simon Shepherd and by Katherine Usher Henderson and Barbara F. McManus. Linda Woodbridge offers detailed summary and analysis of the relevant texts.

Sermons and Homilies

CHAPTER 1

Certain Sermons or Homilies
Appointed to Be Read in Churches

It can be difficult for modern-day readers to grasp the overriding importance of religious thought and discourse to everyday life in Renaissance England. Yet as has recently been emphasized, "The Bible remained the central cultural text in England, as in the rest of Europe, through the seventeenth century. . .[and] operated as a synthetic field, the site where the disciplines converge" (Shuger, *Renaissance Bible* 2-3). It was "central to all intellectual as well as moral life in the sixteenth and seventeenth centuries" (Hill, *English Bible* 20). As will be apparent through the many biblical references in the texts collected in this volume, the relevance of the scriptures to issues of sexuality and gender epitomizes the views and practices of what historian Christopher Hill has termed "A Biblical Culture."

Whereas late-medieval Catholicism had been based on visual rituals, Protestantism was "above all a religion of the sermon" (Collinson, "New Religion" 171), and preaching was thought of as a "specifically *protestant* activity" (Hill, *Society* 79). Sermons replaced confession as the primary means of conveying guidance on spiritual, moral, and other social issues including economics and politics. Sermons were also considered the preeminent means of expressing officially accepted views on sexual matters. Social standards thereby received divine sanction and authority, especially in cases where the preacher was conceived as an "inspired impersonation of Christ" (Collinson, "New Religion" 183).

The aim of preaching was to teach, to delight, and to move the audience. Protestant preachers, in an effort "to change the religion of England until it accords with the simplicity of 'the Gospel'" (Blench 142), made use of a more colloquial rhetorical style than did their Catholic counterparts. A highly ornate style was rejected by sacred English rhetoricians, who recommended "the unadorned sanctity of. . .spiritual preaching" (Shuger, *Sacred Rhetoric* 3). This is not to say that Protestant preaching was dry or dull, focusing only on subject matter; rather its practitioners believed that their "passionate plain style" (Shuger, *Sacred*

Rhetoric 109) more authentically and truthfully captured the spirit and meaning of the scriptures.

These views constituted important motives for the publication of the *Book of Homilies* in 1547, the first year of Edward VI's reign and still early in the Reformation process. Eleven Elizabethan editions were subsequently printed. The 1562 edition included a preface explaining the purposes of the homilies. In 1563 a book of additional homilies was released, and in 1623 a folio edition of both books, along with the 1562 preface, was printed for the first time. The versions of the three homilies below are taken from this 1623 edition.

The 1562 preface emphasizes that regular preaching of the homilies would help the people to learn and fulfill religious, political, and social duties. Accordingly, one of the homilies was to be delivered to congregations at least once a week. Their subject matter ranged from what might be thought of as doctrinal and practical aspects of religious life—reading the holy Scripture, good works, repairing and cleaning the church, the perils of idolatry—to topics which clearly defined political obligations such as "An Exhortation Concerning Good Order and Obedience to Rulers and Magistrates" and the "Homily against Disobedience and Willful Rebellion." There were also a number of homilies on moral values, three of which addressed issues of personal, sexual, and gender relations: "Against Whoredom and Adultery," "Against Excess of Apparel," and "Of the State of Matrimony."

Because, as the preface puts it, individual ministers might not have "the gift of preaching sufficiently to instruct the people," the *Book of Homilies* would supply all preachers with a standard text of royally approved doctrines. It has been suggested that the originator of the homilies, Thomas Cranmer, Archbishop of Canterbury under Henry VIII and Edward VI, undertook the project to "deal with problem of disaffected, extravagant and illiterate preaching" (Dickens 212). In this sense, the homilies comprised an important and enduring part of the crown's attempt to impose uniform Protestant doctrine not only on the populace but also on the clergy, thus to counter the "anarchic possibilities of unlimited preaching" (Hill, *Society* 46). The preface repeatedly reminds "Ecclesiastical persons" that they are commanded and charged to read "her Majesty's Injunctions. . .as is in the book thereof appointed." At the same time, the homilies' direct target remained the opinions and beliefs of congregations which, in theory at least, comprised the complete English population: "that all her people, of what degree or condition soever they be, may learn how to invocate and call upon the name of God, and know what duty they owe both to God and man."

The homilies exemplify the stylistic conventions of Protestant preaching noted above. They resound with biblical quotations, paraphrases, and echoes. They use a range of simple stylistic devices, especially different forms of repetition and personal address, which aim to convey the doctrines rhythmically and forcefully to an audience marked by its mix of ages, social classes, and educational backgrounds. The homilies are straightforwardly constructed, usually providing brief topical treatments of the subject matter rather than intricate logic, argument, and divisions: "Their concern is to be direct and forcible, rather than to be subtle and learned" (Blench 87). References to the ancient church fathers and to classical authors such as Plato and Seneca are included but combine with more homely allusions to aspects of everyday life.

Authorship of the homilies is not definitely known, though doubtless they were written by leading figures of the Reformation. Cranmer is credited with writing the majority of sermons in the first book. "Against whoredom and adultery" may have been written by Thomas Becon, a prolific author of devotional and controversial works (Blench 42 n.186), and "Against excess of apparel" by James Pilkington, a Protestant scholar at Cambridge and later Bishop of Durham. No author for "Of the state of Matrimony" is noted, but the sermon is jointly based on a homily by the church father St. Chrysostom and the English translation of an address by the German Lutheran minister Veit Dietrich (Blench 223).

A SERMON AGAINST WHOREDOM AND UNCLEANNESS

Although there want not (good Christian people) great swarms of vices worthy to be rebuked (unto such decay is true Godliness and virtuous living now come), yet above other vices the outrageous seas of adultery (or breaking of wedlock), whoredom, fornication, and uncleanness have not only burst in but also overflowed almost the whole world unto the great dishonor of GOD, the exceeding infamy of the name of Christ, the notable decay of true Religion, and the utter destruction of the public wealth. And that so abundantly that through the customable use thereof, this vice is grown into such a height that in a manner among many it is counted no sin at all but rather a pastime, a dalliance, and but a touch of youth, not rebuked but winked at, not punished but laughed at. Wherefore it is necessary at this present to entreat of the sin of whoredom and fornication, declaring unto you the greatness of this sin and how odious, hateful, and abominable it is and hath always been reputed before GOD and all good men, and how grievously it hath been punished both by the law of GOD and the laws of divers Princes. Again, to show you certain remedies whereby you may (through the grace of GOD) eschew this most detestable sin of whoredom and fornication, and lead your lives in all honesty and cleanness.

And that you may perceive that fornication and whoredom are (in the light of GOD) most abominable sins, you shall call to remembrance this commandment of GOD, "Thou shalt not commit adultery" (Exod. 20.14). By the which word "adultery," although it be properly understood of the unlawful commixtion or joining together of a married man with any woman beside his wife, or of a wife with any man beside her husband, yet thereby is signified also all unlawful use of those parts which be ordained for generation. And this one commandment (forbidding adultery) doth sufficiently paint and set out before our eyes the greatness of this sin of whoredom, and manifestly declareth how greatly it ought to be abhorred of all honest and faithful persons. And that none of us all shall think himself excepted from this commandment, whether we be old or young, married or unmarried, man or woman, hear what GOD the Father sayth by his most excellent Prophet Moses: "There shall be no whore among the daughters of Israel, nor no whoremonger among the sons of Israel" (Deut. 23.17).

Here is whoredom, fornication, and all other uncleanness forbidden to all kinds of people, all degrees, and all ages without exception. And that we shall not doubt but that this precept or commandment pertaineth to us indeed, hear what Christ (the perfect teacher of all truth) sayth in the New Testament, "Ye have heard (sayth Christ) that it was said to them of old time, Thou shalt not commit adultery. But I say unto you, whosoever seeth a Woman, to have his lust of her, hath committed adultery with her already in his heart" (Matt. 5.27-28). Here our Saviour Christ doth not only confirm and establish the law against adultery given in the Old Testament of GOD the Father by his servant Moses, and make it of full strength continually to remain among the professors of his Name in the new law. But he also (condemning the gross interpretation of the Scribes and Pharisees, which taught that the foresaid commandment only required to abstain from the outward adultery and not from the filthy desires and unpure lusts) teacheth us an exact and full perfection of purity and cleanness of life, both to keep our bodies undefiled and our hearts pure and free from all evil thoughts, carnal desires, and fleshly consents. Now, can we then be free from this commandment where so great charge is laid upon us? May a servant do what he will in anything, having commandment of his master to the contrary? Is not Christ our Master? Are not we his servants? Now, then, may we neglect our Master's will and pleasure, and follow our own will and fantasy? "Ye are my friends (sayth Christ) if you keep those things that I command you" (John 15.14).

Now hath Christ our Master commanded us that we should forsake all uncleanness and filthiness both in body and spirit. This therefore must we do if we look to please GOD. In the Gospel of Saint Matthew we read that the Scribes and Pharisees were grievously offended with Christ because his disciples did not keep the traditions of the forefathers, "for they washed not their hands when they went to dinner or supper" (Matt. 15.2). And among other things, Christ answered and said, "Hear and understand. Not that thing which entereth into the mouth defileth the man, but that which cometh out of the mouth defileth the man. . . . For those things which proceed out of the mouth come forth from the heart, and they defile the man. For out of the heart proceed evil thoughts, murders, breaking of wedlock, whoredom, thefts, false witness, blasphemies. These are the things which defile a man" (Matt. 15.11-20). Here may we see that not only murder, theft, false witness, and blasphemy defile men, but also evil thoughts, breaking of wedlock, fornication, and whoredom. Who is now of so little wit that he will esteem whoredom and fornication to be things of small importance, and of no weight before GOD? Christ (who is the truth and cannot lie) saith that evil thought, breaking of wedlock, whoredom, and fornication defile a man, that is to say, corrupt both the body and soul of man and make them, of the temples of the holy Ghost, the filthy dunghill or dungeon of all unclean spirits, of the house of GOD, the dwelling place of Satan.

Again in the Gospel of Saint John, when the "woman taken in adultery" (John 8.3) was brought unto Christ, said not he unto her "Go thy way and sin no more" (Rom. 6.11)? Doth not he here call whoredom sin? And what is the reward of sin but everlasting death? If whoredom be sin then it is not lawfully for us to commit it. For Saint John sayth, "He that committeth sin is of the devil" (1 John 3.8). And our Saviour saith, "Everyone that committeth sin is the servant of sin" (John 8.34). If whoredom had not been sin, surely Saint John Baptist would never have rebuked king Herod for taking his brother's wife. But he told him plainly that it was not lawful for him to take his brother's wife (Mark 6.18). He winked not at the whoredom of Herod, although he were a king of power, but boldly reproved him for his wicked and abominable living, although for the same he lost his head. But he would rather suffer death (than see GOD so dishonored by the breaking of his holy precept and commandment) than to suffer whoredom to be unrebuked, even in a king. If whoredom had been but a pastime, a dalliance, and not to be passed off (as many count it nowadays), truly John had been more than twice mad if he would have had the displeasure of a king, if he would have been cast in prison and lost his head for a trifle. But John knew right well how filthy and stinking and abominable the sin of whoredom is in the light of GOD, therefore would not he leave it unrebuked, no not in a king.

If whoredom be not lawful in a king, neither is it lawful in a subject. If whoredom be not lawful in a public or common officer, neither is it lawful in a private person. If it be not lawful neither in king, nor subject, neither in common officer, nor private person, truly then it is lawful in no man nor woman of whatsoever degree or age they be. Furthermore in the Acts of the Apostles we read that when the Apostles and Elders, with the whole Congregation, were gathered together to pacify the hearts of the faithful dwelling at Antioch (which were disquieted through the false doctrine of certain Jewish preachers) they sent word to the brethren that it seemed good to the holy Ghost and to them to charge them with no more then with necessary things. Among other, they willed them to abstain from idolatry and fornication, "from which (said they) if ye keep yourselves ye shall do well" (Acts 15.29). Note here how these holy and blessed Fathers of Christ's Church would charge the congregation with no more things than were necessary. Mark also how among those things, from which they commanded the brethren of Antioch to abstain, fornication and whoredom is numbered. It is therefore necessary, by the determination and consent of the holy Ghost and the Apostles and Elders, with the whole Congregation, that as from idolatry and superstition so likewise we must abstain from fornication and whoredom. It is necessary unto salvation to abstain from idolatry; so is it to abstain from whoredom. Is there any nigher way to lead unto damnation than to be an idolater? No. Even so, neither is there any nearer way to damnation than to be a fornicator and a whoremonger. Now where are those people which so lightly esteem breaking of wedlock, whoredom, fornication, and adultery. It is necessary, saith the holy Ghost, the blessed Apostles, the Elders, with the whole Congregation of Christ, it is necessary to salvation (say they) to abstain from whoredom. If it be necessary unto salvation then woe be to them which, neglecting their salvation, give their minds to so filthy and stinking sin, to so wicked vice, and to such detestable abomination.

The Second Part of the Sermon against Adultery

You have been taught in the first part of this Sermon against Adultery how that vice at this day reigneth most above all other vices, and what is meant by this word Adultery, and how holy Scripture dissuadeth or discounseleth from doing that filthy sin, and finally what corruption cometh to man's soul through the sin of Adultery.

Now, to proceed further, let us hear what the blessed Apostle Saint Paul sayth to this matter. Writing to the Romans he hath these words, "Let us cast away the works of darkness, and put on the armor of light. Let us walk honestly, as it were in the day time, not in eating and drinking, neither in chambering[1] and wantonness, neither in strife and envying. But put ye on the Lord Jesus Christ, and make not provision for the flesh to fulfill the lusts of it" (Rom. 13.12-14). Here the holy Apostle exhorteth us to cast away the works of darkness, which (among other) he calleth gluttonous eating, drinking, chambering, and wantonness, which are all ministers unto that vice and preparations to induce and bring in the filthy sin of the flesh. He calleth them the deeds and works of darkness not only because they are customably in darkness or in the night time ("For every one that doeth evil hateth the light, neither cometh he to the light lest his works should be reproved" [John 3.20]), "but that they lead the right way unto that outer darkness where weeping and gnashing of teeth shall be" (Matt. 25.30). And he saith in another place of the same Epistle, "They that are in the flesh cannot please GOD" (Rom. 8.8). "We are debtors, not to the flesh, that we should live after the flesh. For if ye live after the flesh, ye shall die" (Rom. 8.12-13). Again he saith, "Flee from whoredom, for every sin that a man committeth is without his body. But whoever committeth whoredom sinneth against his own body. Do ye not know that your members are the Temple of the holy Ghost which is in you, whom also ye have of GOD, and ye are not your own? For ye are dearly bought. Glorify God in your bodies, etc." (1 Cor. 6.18-20). And a little before he saith, "Do ye not know that your bodies are the members of Christ. Shall I then take the members of Christ, and make them the members of a whore?" GOD forbid. "Do ye not know that he which cleaveth to a whore is made one body with her? There shall be two in one flesh (saith he) but he that cleaveth to the Lord is one spirit" (1 Cor. 6.15-17).

What godly words doeth the blessed Apostle Saint Paul bring forth here, to dissuade and discounsel us from whoredom and all uncleanness? "Your members (saith he) are the Temple of the holy Ghost which, whosoever doeth defile, GOD will destroy him," as saith Saint Paul (1 Cor. 6.13, 19). If we be the Temple of the holy Ghost, how unfitting then is it to drive that holy Spirit from us through whoredom, and in his place to set the wicked spirits of uncleanness and fornication, and to be joined and do service to them? "Ye are dearly bought (saith he) therefore glorify GOD in your bodies" (1 Cor. 6.20). Christ, that innocent Lamb of GOD, hath bought us from the servitude of the devil, not with corruptible gold and silver, but with his most precious and dear heart blood (1 Pet. 1.18-19). To what intent? That we should fall again into our old uncleanness and abominable living? Nay verily, but that we should serve him all the days of our life in holiness and righteousness (Luke 1.75), that we should glorify him in our bodies by purity and cleanness of life. He declareth also that our bodies are the members of Christ. How unseemly a thing is it, then, to cease to be incorporate or embodied and made one with Christ, and through whoredom to be enjoined and made all one with a whore? What greater dishonor or injury can we do to Christ than to take away from him the members of his body, and to join them to whores, devils, and wicked spirits? And what more dishonor can we do to ourselves than, through uncleanness, to lose so excellent a dignity and freedom, and to become bondslaves and miserable captives to the spirits of darkness? Let us therefore consider first the glory of Christ, then our estate, our dignity, and freedom, wherein GOD hath set us by giving us his holy Spirit. And let us valiantly defend the same against Satan and all his crafty assaults, that Christ may be honored, and that we lose not our liberty or freedom but still remain in one Spirit with him.

Moreover, in his Epistle to the Ephesians, the blessed Apostle willeth us to be so pure and free from "adultery, fornication, and all uncleanness, that we not once name them among us (as it becometh Saints), nor filthiness, nor foolish talking, nor jesting, which are not comely, but rather giving of thanks. For this ye know (sayth he), that no whoremonger, neither unclean person or covetous person (which is an idolater) hath any inheritance in the kingdom of Christ and of GOD" (Eph. 5.3-5). And that we should remember to be holy, pure, and free from all uncleanness, the holy Apostle calleth us Saints, because we are "sanctified and made holy by the blood of Christ through the Holy Ghost" (1 Cor. 6.11).

Now, if we be Saints what have we to do with the manners of the Heathen? Saint Peter sayth, "As he which called you is holy, even so be ye holy also in your conversation, because it is written, Be ye holy, for I am holy" (1 Pet. 1.15-16, Levit. 19.2). Hitherto have we heard how grievous a sin fornication and whoredom is, and how greatly GOD doeth abhor it throughout the whole Scripture. How can it any otherwise be than a sin of most abomination, seeing it may not once be named among the Christians, much less it may in any point be committed? And surely if we would weigh the greatness of this sin and consider it in the right kind, we should find the sin of whoredom to be that most filthy lake, foul puddle, and stinking sink whereunto all kinds of sins and evils flow, where also they have their resting place and abiding.

For hath not the adulterer a pride in his whoredom? As the Wise man sayth, they are glad when they have done evil and rejoice in things that are stark naught. Is not the adulterer also idle, and delighteth in no godly exercise but only in that his most filthy and beastly pleasure? Is not his mind plucked and utterly drawn away from all virtuous studies and fruitful labors, and only given to carnal and fleshly imagination? Doth not the whoremonger give his mind to gluttony, that he may be the more apt to serve his lusts and carnal pleasures? Doth not the adulterer give his mind to covetousness and to polling and pilling[2] of others, that he may be the more able to maintain his harlots and whores, and to continue in his filthy and unlawful love? Swelleth he not also with envy against others, fearing that his prey should be allured and taken away from him? Again, is he not ireful and replenished with wrath and displeasure, even against his best beloved, if at any time his beastly and devilish request be letted?[3] What sin or kind of sin is it that is not joined with fornication and whoredom? It is a monster of many heads. It receiveth all kinds of vices and refuseth all kinds of virtues. If one several sin bringeth damnation, what is to be thought of that sin which is accompanied with all evils and hath waiting on it whatsoever is hateful to GOD, damnable to man, and pleasant to Satan.

Great is the damnation that hangeth over the heads of fornicators and adulterers. What shall I speak of other incommodities[4] which issue and flow out of this stinking puddle of whoredom? Is not that treasure which before all other is most regarded of honest persons, the good fame and name of man and woman, lost through whoredom? What patrimony or livelihood, what substance, what goods, what riches doth whoredom shortly consume and bring to nought? What valiantness and strength is many times made weak and destroyed with whoredom? What wit is so fine that is not besotted and defaced through whoredom? What beauty (although it were never so excellent) is not disfigured through whoredom? Is not whoredom an enemy to the pleasant flower of youth, and bringeth it not gray hairs and old age before the time? What gift of nature (although it were never so precious) is not corrupted with whoredom? Come not many foul and most loathsome diseases of whoredom? From whence come so many bastards and misbegotten children, to the high displeasure of GOD and dishonor of holy wedlock, but of whoredom? How many consume all their substance and goods, and at the last fall into such extreme poverty that afterwards they steal and so are hanged through whoredom? What contention and manslaughter cometh of whoredom? How many maidens be deflowered, how many wives corrupted, how many widows defiled through whoredom? How much is the public and common weal[5] impoverished and troubled through whoredom? How much is GOD's word contemned and depraved through whoredom and whoremongers?

Of this vice cometh a great part of the divorces which (nowadays) be so commonly accustomed and used by men's private authority, to the great displeasure of GOD and the breach of the most holy knot and bond of matrimony. For when this most detestable sin is once crept into the breast of the adulterer, so that he is entangled with unlawful and unchaste love, straightaway his true and lawful wife is despised, her presence is abhorred, her company stinketh and is loathsome, whatsoever she doeth is dispraised. There is no quietness in the house so long as she is in sight. Therefore to make short work she must away, for her husband can brook her no longer. Thus through whoredom is the honest and harmless wife put away and a harlot received in her stead. And in like sort, it happeneth many times in the wife towards her husband. O, abomination! Christ our Saviour, very GOD and man, coming to restore the Law of his heavenly Father unto the right sense, understanding, and meaning (among other things) reformed the abuse of this Law of GOD. For whereas the Jews used a long sufferance, by custom, to put away their wives at their pleasure for every cause (Matt.19.3), Christ, correcting that evil custom, did teach that if any man put away his wife and married another for any cause, except only for adultery (which then was death by the law), he was an adulterer and forced also his wife, so divorced, to commit adultery if she were joined to any other man, and the man also, so joined with her, to commit adultery (Matt. 19.9).[6]

In what case, then, are these adulterers which, for the love of a whore, put away their true and lawful wife against all law, right, reason, and conscience? O how damnable is the estate wherein they stand! Swift destruction shall fall on them if they repent not and amend not. For GOD will not suffer holy wedlock thus to be dishonored, hated, and despised. He will once punish this fleshy and licentious manner of living and cause that this holy ordinance shall be had in reverence and honor. For surely "Wedlock (as the Apostle sayth) is honorable among all men, and the bed undefiled. But whoremongers and fornicators God will judge" (Heb. 13.4), that is to say, punish and condemn. But to what purpose is this labor taken, to describe and set forth the greatness of the sin of whoredom and the discommodities that issue and flow out of it, seeing that breath and tongue shall sooner fail any man than he shall or may be able to set it out according to the abomination and heinousness thereof? Notwithstanding, this is spoken to the intent that all men should flee whoredom and live in the fear of GOD. GOD grant that it may not be spoken in vain.

The Third Part of the Sermon against Adultery

In the second part of this Sermon against adultery that was last read, you have learned how earnestly the Scripture warneth us to avoid the sin of adultery and to embrace cleanness of life. And that through adultery we fall into all kinds of sin and are made bond-slaves to the devil, through cleanness of life we are made members of Christ. And finally, how adultery bringeth a man from all goodness and driveth him headlong into all vices, mischief, and misery. Now will I declare unto you in order with what grievous punishments GOD in times past plagued adultery, and how certain worldly Princes also did punish it, that ye may perceive that whoredom and fornication be sins no less detestable in the sight of GOD to all good men than I have hitherto uttered.

In the first book of Moses, we read that when mankind began to be multiplied upon the earth, the men and women gave their minds so greatly to fleshly delight and filthy pleasure that they lived without all fear of GOD. GOD seeing this their beastly and abominable living, and perceiving that they amended not but rather increased daily more and more in their sinful and unclean manners, repented that ever he had made man. And to show how greatly he abhorreth adultery, whoredom, fornication, and all uncleanness, he made all the fountains of the deep earth to burst out and the sluices of heaven to be opened, so that the rain came down upon the earth by the space of forty days and forty nights, and by this means destroyed the whole world and all mankind, eight persons only excepted, that is to say, Noah the preacher of righteousness (as St. Peter calleth him [2 Pet. 2.5]) and his wife, his three sons and their wives. O what a grievous plague did GOD cast here upon all living creatures for the sin of whoredom! For the which GOD took vengeance not only of man but of all beasts, souls, and all living creatures. Manslaughter was committed before, yet was not the world destroyed for that (Gen. 4). But for whoredom, all the world (few only except) was overflowed with waters and so perished. An example worthy to be remembered that ye may learn to fear GOD.

We read again that for the filthy sin of uncleanness, "Sodom and Gomorrah, and other Cities nigh unto them, were destroyed by fire and brimstone from heaven, so that there was neither man, woman, child, nor beast, nor yet anything that grew upon the earth there left undestroyed" (Gen. 19.28-29). Whose heart trembleth not at the hearing of this history? Who is so drowned in whoredom and uncleanness that will not now forever after leave this abominable living, seeing that GOD so grievously punisheth uncleanness, to rain fire and brimstone from heaven, to destroy whole Cities, to kill man, woman, and child, and all other living creatures there abiding, to consume with fire all that ever grew? What can be more manifest tokens of GOD's wrath and vengeance against uncleanness and impurity of life? Mark this history (good people) and fear the vengeance of GOD. Do you not read also that GOD did smite Pharaoh and his house with great plagues, because that he ungodly desired Sara the wife of Abraham (Gen. 12.17)? Likewise read we of Abimelech, king of Gerar, although he touched her not by carnal knowledge (Gen. 20.2). These plagues and punishments did GOD cast on upon filthy and unclean persons before the Law was given (the law of nature only reigning in the hearts of men), to declare how great love he had to Matrimony and wedlock and, again, how much he abhorred adultery, fornication, and all uncleanness (Levit. 22.3-7).

And when the Law that forbade whoredom was given to Moses to the Jews, did not GOD command that the breakers thereof should be put to death? The words of the law be these: "Who so committeth adultery with any man's wife shall die the death, both the man and the woman, because he hath broken wedlock with his neighbour's wife" (Levit. 20.10). In the Law also it was commanded that a damsel and a man taken together in whoredom should be both stoned to death. In another place we also read that GOD commanded Moses to take all the head Rulers and Princes of the people, and to hang them upon gibbets openly that every man might see them, because they either committed or did not punish whoredom (Num. 25.4). Again, did not GOD send such a plague among the people for fornication and uncleanness, that they died in one day three and twenty thousand (1 Cor. 10.8)? I pass over for lack of time many other histories of the holy Bible which declare the grievous vengeance and heavy displeasure of GOD against whoremongers and adulterers. Certainly, this extreme punishment appointed of GOD showeth evidently how greatly GOD hateth whoredom. And let us not doubt but that GOD at this present abhorreth all manner of uncleanness no less than he did in the old law, and will undoubtedly punish it both in this world and in the world to come. For he is a GOD that can abide no wickedness (Ps. 5.4), therefore ought it to be eschewed of all that tender the glory of GOD and the salvation of their own souls.

Saint Paul saith All these things are written for our example, and to teach us the fear of GOD and the obedience to his holy Law (1 Cor. 10.6, 11). For if GOD spared not the natural branches, neither will he spare us that be but grafts if we commit like offence. If GOD destroyed many thousands of people, many cities, yea, the whole world for whoredom, let us not flatter ourselves and think we shall escape free and without punishment. For he hath promised in his holy Law to send most grievous plagues upon them that transgress or break his holy commandments. Thus have we heard how GOD punished the sin of adultery. Let us now hear certain laws which the Civil Magistrates devised in their countries for the punishment thereof, that we may learn how uncleanness hath ever been detested in all well ordered cities and commonwealths and among all honest persons.

The law among the Lepreians[7] was this, that when any were taken in adultery they were bound and carried three days through the City and afterwards, as long as they lived, were they despised and with shame and confusion counted as persons void of all honesty. Among the Locrensians[8] the adulterers have both their eyes thrust out. The Romans, in times past, punished whoredom sometimes by fire, sometimes by sword. If any man among the Egyptians had been taken in adultery, the law was that he should openly in the presence of all the people be scourged naked with whips, unto the number of a thousand stripes. The woman that was taken with him had her nose cut off, whereby she was known ever after to be a whore, and therefore to be abhorred of all men. Among the Arabians, they that were taken in adultery had their heads stricken from their bodies. The Athenians punished whoredom by death in like manner. So likewise did the barbarous Tartars. Among the Turks, even at this day, they that be taken in adultery, both man and woman, are stoned straightaway to death without mercy.

Thus we see what godly acts were devised in times past of the high powers for the putting away of whoredom and for the maintaining of holy Matrimony or wedlock and pure conversation.[9] And the authors of these acts were no Christians but the Heathen. Yet were they so inflamed with the love of honesty and pureness of life that for the maintenance and conservation or keeping up of that they made godly Statutes, suffering neither fornication or adultery to reign in their Realms unpunished. Christ said to the people, "The Ninevites shall rise at the judgment with this Nation (meaning the unfaithful Jews) and shall condemn them. For they repented at the preaching of Jonas. But behold (saith he) a greater than Jonas is here (meaning himself)" (Matt. 12.41), and yet they repent not. Shall not (think you) likewise the Locrensians, Arabians, Athenians, with such other, rise up in the judgment and condemn us, for as much as they ceased from the whoredom at the commandment of man, and we have the Law and manifest precepts and commandments of GOD, and yet forsake we not our filthy conversation? Truly, truly, it shall be easier at the day of judgment to these Heathen than to us, except we repent and amend. For though death of body seemeth to us a grievous punishment in this world for whoredom, yet is that pain nothing in comparison of the grievous torments which adulterers, fornicators, and all unclean persons shall suffer after this life. For all such shall be excluded and shut out of the Kingdom of heaven. As St Paul saith, "Be not deceived, for neither whoremongers, nor worshippers of Images, nor adulterers, nor effeminate persons, nor Sodomites, nor thieves, nor covetous persons, nor drunkards, nor cursed speakers, nor pillers, shall inherit the Kingdom of GOD" (1 Cor. 6.9-10, Gal. 5.19-21, Eph. 5.5). And St. John in his Revelation saith that whoremongers shall have their part with murderers, sorcerers, enchanters, liars, idolaters, and such other, in the lake which burneth with fire and brimstone, which is the second death (Rev. 20.14). The punishment of the body, although it be death, hath an end, but the punishment of the soul, which St. John calleth the second death, is everlasting. There shall be fire and brimstone, there shall be weeping and gnashing of teeth (Matt. 13.42). The worm that there shall gnaw the conscience of the damned shall never die (Mark 9.46).

O, whose heart distilleth not even drops of blood to hear and consider these things? If we tremble and shake at the hearing and naming of these pains, oh what shall they do that shall feel them, that shall suffer them, yea, and ever shall suffer, worlds without end. GOD have mercy upon us. Who is now so drowned in sin and past all godliness, that he will set more by filthy and stinking pleasure (which soon passeth away) than by the loss of everlasting glory? Again, who will so give himself to the lusts of the flesh that he feareth nothing at all the pain of hell fire? But let us hear how we may eschew the sin of whoredom and adultery, that we may walk in the fear of GOD and be free from those most grievous and intolerable torments which abide all unclean persons.

Now, to avoid fornication, adultery, and all uncleanness, let us provide that above all things we may keep our hearts pure and clean from all evil thoughts and carnal lusts. For if that be once infected and corrupt, we fall headlong into all kinds of ungodliness. This shall we easily do if, when we feel inwardly that Satan our old enemy tempteth us unto whoredom, we by no means consent to his crafty suggestions but valiantly resist and withstand him by strong faith in the word of GOD, alleging against him always in our heart this commandment of GOD: It is written, Thou shalt not commit whoredom. It shall be good also for us ever to live in the fear of GOD, and to set before our eyes the grievous threatenings of GOD against all ungodly sinners, and to consider in our mind how filthy, beastly, and short that pleasure is whereunto Satan continually stirreth and moveth us. And again, how the pain appointed for that sin is intolerable and everlasting. Moreover, to use a temperance and sobriety in eating and drinking, to eschew unclean communication, to avoid all filthy company, to flee idleness, to delight in reading the holy Scriptures, to watch in godly prayers and virtuous meditation, and, at all times, to exercise some godly travails[10] shall help greatly unto the eschewing of whoredom.

And here are all degrees to be admonished, whether they be married or unmarried, to love chastity and cleanness of life. For the married are bound by the law of GOD so purely to love one another that neither of them seek any strange love. The man must only cleave to his wife, and the wife again only to her husband. They must so delight one in another's company, that none of them covet any other. And as they are bound thus to live together in all godliness and honesty, so likewise it is their duty virtuously to bring up their children and provide that they fall not into Satan's snare nor into any uncleanness, but that they come pure and honest unto holy wedlock when time requireth. So likewise ought all masters and rulers to provide that no whoredom, nor any point of uncleanness be used among their servants. And again, they that are single and feel in themselves that they cannot live without the company of a woman, let them get wives of their own and so live godly together. "For it is better to marry than to burn" (1 Cor. 7.9).

And to avoid fornication, saith the Apostle, let every man have his own wife and every woman her own husband. Finally, all such as feel in themselves a sufficiency and ability (through the working of GOD's Spirit) to lead a sole and continent life, let them praise GOD for his gift and seek all means possible to maintain the same, as by reading of holy Scriptures, by godly meditations, by continual prayers, and such other virtuous exercises. If we all on this wise[11] will endeavor ourselves to eschew fornication, adultery, and all uncleanness, and lead our lives in all godliness and honesty, serving GOD with a pure and clean heart and glorifying him in our bodies by the leading an innocent and harmless life, we may be sure to be in the number of those of whom our Saviour Christ speaketh in the Gospel on this matter, "Blessed are the pure in heart, for they shall see GOD" (Matt. 5.8), to whom alone be all glory, honor, rule, and power, worlds without end. Amen.

A HOMILY AGAINST EXCESS OF APPAREL

Where ye have heretofore been excited and stirred to use temperance of meats and drinks and to avoid the excess thereof, many ways hurtful to the state of the common wealth and so odious before Almighty GOD, being the author and giver of such creatures to comfort, and establish our frail nature with thanks unto him and not by abusing of them to provoke his liberality to severe punishing of that disorder. In like manner it is convenient that ye be admonished of another foul and chargeable excess. I mean of apparel, at these days so gorgeous that neither Almighty GOD by his word can stay our proud curiosity in the same, neither yet godly and necessary laws, made of our Princes and often repeated with the penalties, can bridle this detestable abuse, whereby both GOD is openly contemned and the Princes' Laws manifestly disobeyed to the great peril of the Realm. Wherefore, that sobriety also in this excess may be espied among us, I shall declare unto you both the moderate use of apparel, approved by GOD in his holy word, and also the abuses thereof which he forbiddeth and disalloweth, as it may appear by the inconveniences which daily increase by the just judgment of GOD where that measure is not kept which he himself hath appointed.

If we consider the end and purpose whereunto Almighty GOD hath ordained his creatures, we shall easily perceive that he alloweth us apparel not only for necessity's sake but also for an honest comeliness. Even as in herbs, trees, and sundry fruits, we have not only divers necessary uses but also the pleasant sight and sweet smell to delight us withall, wherein we may behold the singular love of GOD towards mankind in that he hath provided both to relieve our necessities and also to refresh our senses with an honest and moderate recreation. Therefore David in the hundred and fourth Psalm, confessing GOD's careful providence, showeth that GOD not only provideth things necessary for men, as herbs and other meats, but also such things as may rejoice and comfort, as wine to make glad the heart, oils and ointments to make the face to shine (Ps. 104.14-15). So that they are altogether past the limits of humanity who, yielding only to necessity, forbid the lawful fruition of GOD'S benefits. With whose traditions we may not be led if we give ear to St. Paul, writing to the Colossians, willing them not to hearken unto such men as shall say, "Touch not, Taste not, Handle not" (Col. 2.21), superstitiously bereaving them of the fruition of GOD'S creatures. And no less truly ought we to beware, less under pretence of Christian liberty we take licence to do what we list,[12] advancing ourselves in sumptuous apparel and despising other, preparing ourselves in fine bravery to wanton, lewd, and unchaste behavior. To the avoiding whereof it behoveth us to be mindful of four lessons, taught in holy Scripture, whereby we shall learn to temper ourselves and to refrain our immoderate affections to that measure which GOD hath appointed.

The first is that we "make not provision for the flesh, to accomplish the lusts thereof" (Rom. 13.14), with costly apparel, as that harlot did of whom Solomon speaketh, Proverbs the seventh, which perfumed her bed and decked it with costly ornaments of Egypt to the fulfilling of her lewd lust (Prov. 7.16-17). But rather ought we by moderate temperance to cut off all occasions whereby the flesh might get the victory. The second is written by Saint Paul, in the Chapter Seven of his first Epistle to the Corinthians, where he teacheth us to use this world as though we used it not (1 Cor. 7.31). Whereby he cutteth away not only all ambition, pride, and vain pomp in apparel, but also all inordinate care and affection which withdraweth us from the contemplation of heavenly things and consideration of our duty towards GOD. They that are much occupied in caring for things pertaining to the body are most commonly negligent and careless in matters concerning the soul. Therefore our Saviour Christ willeth us not to take thought what we shall eat, or what we shall drink, or wherewith we shall be clothed, but rather to seek the Kingdom of GOD and the righteousness thereof (Matt. 6.31-33). Whereby we may learn to beware, lest we use those things to our hindrance which GOD hath ordained for our comfort and furtherance towards his Kingdom.

The third is that we take in good part our estate and condition and content ourselves with that which GOD sendeth, whether it be much or little. He that is ashamed of base and simple attire will be proud of gorgeous apparel if he may get it. We must learn therefore of the Apostle St. Paul both to use plenty and also to suffer penury (Phil. 4), remembering that we must yield accounts of those things which we have received unto him who abhorreth all excess, pride, ostentation, and vanity, who also utterly condemneth and disalloweth whatsoever draweth us from our duty toward GOD or diminisheth our charity towards our neighbours and children, whom we ought to love as ourselves.

The fourth and last rule is that every man behold and consider his own vocation, in as much as GOD hath appointed every man his degree and office within the limits whereof it behoveth him to keep himself. Therefore all may not look to wear like apparel but every one according to his degree as GOD hath placed him.[13] Which if it were observed, many one doubtless should be compelled to wear a russet coat which now russeleth[14] in silks and velvets, spending more by the year in sumptuous apparel than their fathers received for the whole revenue of their lands.

But alas, nowadays how many may we behold occupied wholly in pampering the flesh, taking no care at all but only how to deck themselves, setting their affection altogether on worldly bravery, abusing GOD'S goodness when he sendeth plenty to satisfy their wanton lusts, having no regard to the degree wherein GOD hath placed them. The Israelites were contented with such apparel as GOD gave them although it were base and simple. And GOD so blessed them that their shoes and clothes lasted them forty years, yea, and those clothes which their fathers had worn their children were contented to use afterward (Deut. 29.5). But we are never contented and therefore we prosper not, so that most commonly he that russeleth in his Sables, in his fine furred gown, corked slippers, trim buskins, and warm mittens, is more ready to chill for cold than the poor laboring man which can abide in the field all the day long when the North wind blows with a few beggarly clothes about him. We are loath to wear such as our fathers have left us; we think not that sufficient or good enough for us. We must have one gown for the day, another for the night; one long, another short; one for Winter, another for Summer; one through[15] furred, another but faced; one for the working day, another for the holy day; one of this color, another of that color; one of Cloth, another of Silk or Damask. We must have change of apparel, one before dinner and another after, one of the Spanish fashion another Turkish, and to be brief, never content with sufficient. Our Saviour Christ bade his disciples they should not have two coats (Matt. 10.10), but the most men, far unlike to his scholars, have their presses[16] so full of apparel that many know not how many sorts they have.

Which thing caused Saint James to pronounce this terrible curse against such wealthy worldlings, "Go to ye rich men, weep and howl on your wretchedness that shall come upon you. Your riches are corrupt, and your garments are motheaten.... Ye have lived in pleasure on the earth, and in wantonness; ye have nourished your hearts, as in the day of slaughter" (Jas. 1-2, 5). Mark, I beseech you, Saint James calleth them miserable notwithstanding their riches and plenty of apparel, forasmuch as they pamper their bodies to their own destruction. What was the rich glutton the better for his fine fare and costly apparel? Did not he nourish himself to be tormented in hell fire (Luke 16.23-24)? Let us learn therefore to content ourselves, having food and raiment as Saint Paul teacheth, lest desiring to be enriched with abundance we fall into temptations, snares, and many noisome[17] lusts "which drown men in perdition and destruction" (1 Tim. 6.8-9).

Certainly, such as delight in gorgeous apparel are commonly puffed up with pride and filled with divers vanities. So were the daughters of Sion and people of Jerusalem whom Isaiah the Prophet threateneth because they walked with stretched out necks and wandering eyes, mincing as they went and nicely treading with their feet, that Almighty GOD would make their heads bald and discover their secret shame. "In that day," saith he, "shall the Lord take away the ornament of the slippers and the cauls and the round attires, and the sweet balls and the bracelets, and the attires of the head, and the slops[18] and the head bands, and the tablets and the earrings, the rings and the mufflers, the costly apparel, and the bails and wimples,[19] and the crisping pin and the glasses, and the fine linen and the hoods and the lawns[20]" (Isa. 3.16-23). So that almighty GOD would not suffer his benefits to be vainly and wantonly abused, no not of that people whom he most tenderly loved and had chosen to himself before all other.

No less truly is the vanity that is used among us in these days. For the proud and haughty stomachs of the daughters of England are so maintained with divers disguised sorts of costly apparel that, as Tertullian an ancient father saith, there is left no difference in apparel between an honest matron and a common strumpet.[21] Yea, many men are become so effeminate that they care not what they spend in disguising themselves, ever desiring new toys and inventing new fashions. Therefore a certain man that would picture every countryman in his accustomed apparel, when he had painted other nations, he pictured the English man all naked and gave him cloth under his arm and bade him make it himself as he thought best, for he changed his fashion so often that he knew not how to make it. Thus with our phantastical devices we make ourselves laughing stocks to other nations. While one spendeth his patrimony upon pounces[22] and cuts, another bestoweth more on a dancing shirt than might suffice to buy him honest and comely apparel for his whole body. Some hang their revenues about their necks, rustling in their ruffs, and many a one jeopardeth his best joint[23] to maintain himself in sumptuous raiment. And every man, nothing considering his estate and condition, seeketh to excel other in costly attire. Whereby it cometh to pass that in abundance and plenty of all things we yet complain of want and penury while one man spendeth that which might serve a multitude, and no man distributeth of the abundance which he hath received, and all men excessively waste that which should serve to supply the necessities of other.

There hath been very good provision made against such abuses by divers good and wholesome laws which, if they were practiced as they ought to be of all true subjects, they might in some part serve to diminish this raging and riotous excess in apparel.[24] But alas, there appeareth amongst us little fear and obedience either of GOD or man. Therefore must we need look for GOD'S fearful vengeance from heaven to overthrow our presumption and pride as he overthrew Herod who, in his royal apparel forgetting GOD, was smitten of an Angel and eaten up of worms (Acts 12.23). By which terrible example GOD hath taught us that we are but worms' meat, although we pamper ourselves never so much in gorgeous apparel.

Here we may learn that which Jesus the son of Sirach teacheth: not be proud of clothing and raiment, neither to exalt ourselves in the day of honor, because the works of the Lord are wonderful and glorious, secret and unknown, teaching us with humbleness of mind, everyone to be mindful of the vocation whereunto GOD hath called him.[25] Let Christians therefore endeavor themselves to quench the care of pleasing the flesh. Let us use the benefits of GOD in this world in such wise[26] that we be not too much occupied in providing for the body. Let us content ourselves quietly with that which GOD sendeth, be it never so little. And if it please him to send plenty, let us not wear proud thereof but let us use it moderately, as well to our own comfort as to the relief of such as stand in necessity. He that in abundance and plenty of apparel hideth his face from him that is naked despiseth his own flesh, as Isaiah the Prophet sayeth (Isa. 58.7). Let us learn to know ourselves and not to despise others. Let us remember that we stand all before the Majesty of Almighty GOD, who shall judge us by his holy word wherein he forbiddeth excess not only to men but also to women.

So that none can excuse themselves of what estate or condition so ever they be.

Let us therefore present ourselves before his throne, as Tertullian exhorteth, with the ornaments which the Apostle speaketh of, Ephesians the Sixth Chapter, having our loins girt about with the verity, having the breastplate of righteousness, and shod with shoes prepared by the Gospel of peace (Eph. 6.14-15). Let us take unto us simplicity, chastity, and comeliness, submitting our necks to the sweet yoke of Christ (Matt. 11.28-30). Let women be subject to their husbands and they are sufficiently attired, saith Tertullian. The wife of one Philo, a heathen Philosopher,[27] being demanded why she wear no gold, she answered that she thought her husband's virtues sufficient ornaments. How much more ought Christian women, instructed by the word of GOD, to content themselves in their husbands?

Yea, how much more ought every Christian to content himself in our Saviour Christ, thinking himself sufficiently garnished with his heavenly virtues. But it will be here objected and said by some nice and vain women that all which we do in painting our faces, in dyeing our hair, in embalming our bodies, in decking us with gay apparel, is to please our husbands, to delight his eyes and to retain his love towards us. O, vain excuse and most shameful answer, to the reproach of thy husband. What couldst thou more say to set out his foolishness than to charge him to be pleased and delighted with the Devil's tire? Who can paint her face and curl her hair and change it into an unnatural color, but therein doth work reproof to her maker who made her? As though she could make herself more comely than GOD hath appointed the measure of her beauty. What do these women do but go about to reform that which GOD hath made, not knowing that all things natural are the work of GOD and things disguised and unnatural be the works of the Devil? And as though a wise and Christian husband should delight to see his wife in such painted and flourished visages which common harlots most do use, to train therewith their lovers to naughtiness, or as though an honest woman could delight to be like a harlot for pleasing of her husband.

Nay, nay, these be but vain excuses of such as go about to please rather others than their husbands. And such attires be but to provoke her to show herself abroad to entice others, a worthy matter. She must keep debate with her husband to maintain such apparel, whereby she is the worse housewife, the seldomer at home to see to her charge and so neglect his thrift by giving great provocation to her household to waste and wantonness, while she must wander abroad to show her own vanity and her husband's foolishness. By which her pride she stirreth up much envy of others which be as vainly delighted as she is. She doeth but deserve mocks and scorns to set out all her commendation in Jewish and Ethnic apparel and yet brag of her Christianity. She doeth but waste superfluously her husband's stock by such sumptuousness, and sometimes she is the cause of much bribery, extortion, and deceit in her husband's dealings that she may be the more gorgeously set out to the sight of the vain world, to please the Devil's eyes and not GOD'S, who giveth to every creature sufficient and moderate comeliness wherewith we should be contented if we were of God.

What other thing doest thou by those means but provokest other to tempt thee, to deceive thy soul, by the bait of thy pomp and pride? What else doest thou but settest out thy pride and makest of the indecent apparel of thy body the devil's net, to catch the souls of them which behold thee? O thou woman, not a Christian but worse than a Panim,[28] thou minister of the devil. Why pamperest thou that carrion flesh so high which sometime doeth stink and rot on the earth as thou goest? Howsoever thou perfumest thy self, yet cannot thy beastliness be hidden or overcome with thy smells and savors, which do rather deform and misshape thee than beautify thee. What meant Solomon to say of such trimming of vain women when he said, "A fair woman without good manners and conditions is like a Sow which hath a ring of gold upon her snout" (Prov. 11.22), but that the more thou garnish thyself with these outward blazings[29] the less thou carest for the inward garnishing of thy mind, and so dost but deform thyself by such array and not beautify thyself?

Hear, hear, what Christ's holy Apostles do write. "Let not the outward apparel of women (saith Saint Peter) be decked with the braiding of hair, with wrapping on of gold or goodly clothing. But let the mind and the conscience, which is not seen with the eyes, be pure and clean. That is," sayth he, "an acceptable and an excellent thing before GOD. For so the old ancient holy women attired themselves, and were obedient to their husbands" (1 Pet. 3.3-5). And Saint Paul saith that "women should apparel themselves with shamefastness[30] and soberness, and not with braids of their hair, or gold or pearl or precious clothes, but as women should do which will express godliness by their good outward works" (1 Tim. 2.9-10). If ye will not keep the Apostles' precepts, at the least let us hear what pagans, which were ignorant of Christ, have said in this matter. Democritus saith, "The ornament of a woman standeth in scarcity of speech and apparel."[31] Sophocles saith of such apparel thus, "It is not an ornament, O thou fool, but a shame and a manifest show of thy folly."[32] Socrates saith that that is a garnishing to a woman which declareth out her honesty.[33] The Grecians use it in a proverb: "It is not gold or pearl which is a beauty to a woman but good conditions."[34]

And Aristotle biddeth that a woman should use less apparel than the law doth suffer.[35] For it is not the goodliness of apparel, nor the excellency of beauty, nor the abundance of gold that maketh a woman to be esteemed, but modesty and diligence to live honestly in all things. This outrageous vanity is now grown so far that there is no shame taken of it. We read in histories that when king Dionysius sent to the women of Lacedaemon rich robes, they answered and said that they shall do us more shame then honor, and therefore refused them.[36] The women in Rome in old time abhorred that gay apparel which king Pyrrhus sent to them, and none were so greedy and vain to accept them.[37] And a law was openly made of the Senate and a long time observed, that no woman should wear over half an ounce of gold nor should wear clothes of divers colors.

But perchance some dainty dame will say and answer me that they must do something to show their birth and blood, to show their husbands' riches. As though nobility were chiefly seen by these things which be common to those which be most vile. As though thy husband's riches were not better bestowed than in such superfluities. As though when thou was christened thou didst not renounce the pride of this world and the pomp of the flesh. I speak not against convenient apparel for every state agreeable, but against the superfluity, against the vain delight to covet such vanities, to devise new fashions to feed thy pride with, to spend so much upon thy carcass that thou and thy husband are compelled to rob the poor to maintain thy costliness. Hear how that noble holy woman Queen Hester setteth out their goodly ornaments (as they be called), when (in respect of saving GOD's people) she was compelled to put on such glorious apparel, knowing that it was a fit stable to blind the eyes of carnal fools (Esth. 5.1-2). Thus she prayed, "Thou knowest, O Lord, the necessity, which I am driven to, to put on this apparel, and that I abhor this sign of pride and of this glory which I bear on my head, and that I defy it as a filthy cloth, and that I wear it not when I am alone." Again, by what means was Holophernes deceived by the glittering show of apparel which that holy woman Judith did put on her, not as delighting in them nor seeking vain voluptuous pleasure by them. But she wore it of pure necessity by GOD's dispensation, using this vanity to overcome the vain eyes of GOD's enemy.[38]

Such desire was in those noble women, being very loth and unwilling otherwise to wear such sumptuous apparel, by the which others should be caused to forget themselves. These be commended in Scripture for abhorring such vanities which, by constraint and great necessity against their hearts' desire, they were compelled to wear them for a time. And shall such women be worthy commendations, which neither be comparable with these women aforesaid in nobility nor comparable to them in their good zeal to GOD and his people, whose daily delight and seeking is to flourish in such gay shifts and changes, never satisfied nor regarding who smarteth for their apparel, so they may come by it? O, vain men, which be subjects to their wives in these inordinate affections. O vain women, to procure so much hurt to themselves, by the which they come the sooner to misery in this world and in the meantime be abhorred of GOD, hated and scorned of wise men, and, in the end, like to be joined with such who, in hell too late repenting themselves, shall openly complain with these words: "What hath our pride profited us or what profit hath the pomp of riches brought us? All these things are passed away like a shadow. As for virtue, we did never show any sign thereof, and thus we are consumed in our wickedness." If thou sayest that the custom is to be followed, and the use of the world doeth compel thee to such curiosity, then I ask of thee whose custom should be followed? Wise folk's manners or fools'? If thou sayest the wise, then I say follow them. For fools' customs, who should follow but fools? Consider that the consent of wise men ought to be alleged for a custom. Now, if any lewd custom be used be thou the first to break it, labor to diminish it and lay it down. And more laud before GOD and more commendation shalt thou win by it than by all the glory of such superfluity.

Thus ye have heard declared unto you what GOD requireth by his word concerning the moderate use of his creatures. Let us learn to use them moderately as he hath appointed. Almighty GOD hath taught us to what end and purpose we should use our apparel. Let us therefore learn so to behave ourselves in the use thereof as becometh Christians, always showing ourselves thankful to our heavenly Father for his great and merciful benefits, who giveth unto us our daily bread, that is to say, all things necessary for this our needy life, unto whom we shall render accounts for all his benefits at the glorious appearing of our Saviour Christ. To whom, with the Father and the holy Ghost, be all honor, praise, and glory, forever and ever. Amen.

A HOMILY OF THE STATE OF MATRIMONY

The word of Almighty GOD doth testify and declare whence the original beginning of Matrimony cometh and why it is ordained. It is instituted of GOD, to the intent that man and woman should live lawfully in a perpetual friendship, to bring forth fruit and to avoid fornication. By which mean a good conscience might be preserved on both parties, in bridling the corrupt inclinations of the flesh within the limits of honesty. For GOD hath straightly forbidden all whoredom and uncleanness, and hath from time to time taken grievous punishment of this inordinate lust, as all stories and ages have declared. Furthermore, it is also ordained that the Church of GOD and his kingdom might by this kind of life be conserved and enlarged, not only in that GOD giveth children by his blessing but also in that they be brought up by the Parents godly, in the knowledge of GOD's word, that thus the knowledge of GOD and true Religion might be delivered by succession from one to another, that finally many might enjoy that everlasting immortality.

Wherefore, forasmuch as Matrimony serveth us as well to avoid sin and offence as to increase the kingdom of GOD, you, as all other which enter the state, must acknowledge this benefit of GOD with pure and thankful minds, for that he hath so ruled your hearts that ye follow not the example of the wicked world who set their delight in filthiness of sin, but both of you stand in the fear of GOD and abhor all filthiness. For that is surely the singular gift of GOD, where the common example of the world declareth how the devil hath their hearts bound and entangled in divers snares, so that they in their wifeless state run into open abominations without any grudge of their conscience. Which sort of men that live so desperately and filthy, what damnation tarrieth for them Saint Paul describeth it to them, saying, "Neither whoremonger, neither adulterers, shall inherit the kingdom of GOD" (1 Cor. 6.9). This horrible judgment of GOD ye be escaped through his mercy if so be that ye live inseparately, according to GOD's ordinance. But yet I would not have you careless without watching. For the devil will assay to attempt all things to interrupt and hinder your hearts and godly purpose if ye will give him any entry. For he will either labor to break this godly knot once begun betwixt you, or else at the least he will labor to encumber it with divers griefs and displeasures.

And this is the principal craft, to work dissension of hearts of the one from the other. That whereas now there is pleasant and sweet love betwixt you, he will in the stead thereof bring in most bitter and unpleasant discord. And surely that same adversary of ours doeth, as it were from above, assault man's nature and condition. For this folly is ever from our tender age grown up with us, to have a desire to rule, to think highly of ourselves, so that none thinketh it meet to give place to another. That wicked vice of stubborn will and self love is more meet to break and to dissever the love of heart than to preserve concord. Wherefore married persons must apply their minds in most earnest wise to concord, and must crave continually of GOD the help of his holy Spirit so to rule their hearts and to knit their minds together that they be not dissevered by any division of discord. This necessity of prayer must be oft in the practice and using of married persons, that oft times the one should pray for the other lest hate and debate do arise betwixt them.

And because few do consider this thing but more few do perform it (I say to pray diligently), we see how wonderful the devil deludeth and scorneth this state, how few Matrimonies there be without chidings, brawlings, tauntings, repentings, bitter cursings, and fightings. Which things whosoever doth commit, they do not consider that it is the instigation of the ghostly enemy, who taketh great delight therein. For else they would with all earnest endeavor strive against these mischiefs not only with prayer but also with all possible diligence. Yea, they would not give place to the provocation of wrath, which stirreth them either to such rough and sharp words or stripes,[39] which is surely compassed by the devil, whose temptation, if it be followed, must needs begin and weave the web of all miseries and sorrows.

For this is most certainly true, that of such beginnings must needs ensue the breach of true concord in heart, whereby all love must needs shortly be banished. Then, can it not be but a miserable thing to behold that yet they are of necessity compelled to live together which yet cannot be in quiet together? And this is most customably everywhere to be seen. But what is the cause thereof? Forsooth, because they will not consider the crafty trains of the devil, and therefore give not themselves to pray to GOD that he would vouchsafe to repress his power. Moreover, they do not consider how they promote the purpose of the devil, in that they follow the wrath of their hearts while they threat one another, while they in their folly turn all upside down, while they will never give over their right as they esteem it, yea, while many times they will not give over the wrong part indeed. Learn thou, therefore, if thou desirest to be void of all these miseries, if thou desirest to live peaceably and comfortably in wedlock, how to make thy earnest prayer to GOD that he would govern both your hearts by the holy Spirit to restrain the Devil's power, whereby your concord may remain perpetually.

But to this prayer must be joined a singular diligence, whereof Saint Peter giveth this precept, saying, "You husbands, deal with your wives according to knowledge, giving honor to the wife as unto the weaker vessel, and as unto them that are heirs also of the grace of life, that your prayers be not hindered" (1 Pet. 3.7). This precept doth particularly pertain to the husband. For he ought to be the leader and author of love in cherishing and increasing concord, which then shall take place if he will use moderation and not tyranny and if he yield something to the woman. For the woman is a weak creature, not endued with like strength and constancy of mind. Therefore they be the sooner disquieted and they be the more prone to all weak affections and dispositions of mind more than men be, and lighter they be and more vain in their fantasies and opinions. These things must be considered of the man that he be not too stiff, so that he ought to wink at some things and must gently expound all things and to forebear.

How be it, the common sort of men doeth judge that such moderation should not become a man. For they say that it is a token of womanish cowardness, and therefore they think that it is a man's part to fume in anger, to fight with fist and staff. How be it, howsoever they imagine, undoubtedly Saint Peter doth better judge what should be seeming to a man and what he should most reasonably perform. For he saith reasoning should be used and not fighting. Yea, he saith more that the woman ought to have a certain honor attributed to her, that is to say, she must be spared and borne with the rather for that she is the weaker vessel, of a frail heart, inconstant, and with a word soon stirred to wrath. And therefore considering these her frailties, she is to be the rather spared. By this means thou shalt not only nourish concord but shalt have her heart in thy power and will. For honest natures will sooner be retained to do their duties rather by gentle words than by stripes. But he which will do all things with extremity and severity and doeth use always rigor in words and stripes, what will that avail in the conclusion? Verily nothing, but that he thereby setteth forward the devil's work, he banisheth away concord, charity, and sweet amity, and bringeth in dissension, hatred, and irksomeness, the greatest griefs that can be in the mutual love and fellowship of man's life.

Beyond all this it bringeth another evil therewith, for it is the destruction and interruption of prayer. For in the time that the mind is occupied with dissension and discord there can be no true prayer used. For the Lord's prayer hath not only a respect to particular persons but to the whole universal, in the which we openly pronounce that we will forgive them which have offended against us even as we ask forgiveness of our sins of GOD. Which thing how can it be done rightly when their hearts be at dissension? How can they pray each for other when they be at hate betwixt themselves? Now, if the aid of prayer be taken away, by what means can they sustain themselves in any comfort? For they cannot otherwise either resist the devil or yet have their hearts stayed in stable comfort in all perils and necessities but by prayer. Thus all discommodities, as well worldly as ghostly,[40] follow this froward testiness and cumbrous fierceness in manners, which be more meet for brute beasts than for reasonable creatures. Saint Peter doeth not allow these things, but the devil desireth them gladly. Wherefore take the more heed. And yet a man may be a man although he doeth not use such extremity, yea, although he should dissemble some things in his wife's manners. And this is the part of a Christian man which both pleaseth GOD and serveth also in good use to the comfort of their marriage state.

Now, as concerning the wife's duty, what shall become her? Shall she abuse the gentleness and humanity of her husband and at her pleasure turn all things upside down? No, surely. For that is far repugnant against GOD's commandment, for thus doeth Saint Peter preach to them, "Ye wives, be ye in subjection to obey your own husbands" (1 Pet. 3.1). To obey is another thing than to control or command, which yet they may do to their children and to their family. But as for their husbands, them must they obey and cease from commanding and perform subjection. For this surely doth nourish concord very much when the wife is ready at hand at her husband's commandment, when she will apply herself to his will, when she endeavoreth herself to seek his contentation[41] and to do him pleasure, when she will eschew all things that might offend him. For thus will most truly be verified the saying of the Poet, "A good wife by obeying her husband shall bear the rule," so that he shall have a delight and a gladness the sooner at all times to return home to her.

But on the contrary part, when the wives be stubborn, froward, and malapert,⁴² their husbands are compelled thereby to abhor and flee from their own houses, even as they should have battle with their enemies. How be it, it can scantly be but that some offences shall sometime chance betwixt them. For no man doth live without fault, specially for that the woman is the more frail party. Therefore let them beware that they stand not in their faults and willfulness, but rather let them acknowledge their follies and say, "My husband, so it is that by my anger I was compelled to do this or that. Forgive it me and hereafter I will take better heed." Thus ought the woman more readily to do, the more they be ready to offend. And they shall not do this only to avoid strife and debate, but rather in the respect of the commandment of GOD, as Saint Paul expresseth it in this form of words, "Let women be subject to their husbands as to the Lord. For the husband is the head of the woman as Christ is the head of the Church" (Eph. 5.22-23). Here you understand that GOD hath commanded that ye should acknowledge the authority of the husband and refer to him the honor of obedience. And Saint Peter saith in that place before rehearsed that holy matrons did in former time deck themselves not with gold and silver but in putting their whole hope in GOD and in obeying their husbands, as Sara obeyed Abraham, calling him lord, whose daughters ye be (saith he) if ye follow her example (1 Pet. 3.5-6). This sentence is very meet for women to print in their remembrance.

Truth it is that they must specially feel the grief and pains of their Matrimony in that they relinquish the liberty of their own rule, in the pain of their travailing,⁴³ in the bringing up of their children. In which offices they be in great perils and be grieved with great afflictions, which they might be without if they lived out of Matrimony. But St. Peter sayth that this is the chief ornament of holy matrons, in that they set their hope and trust in GOD, that is to say, in that they refused not from marriage for the business thereof, for the gifts and perils thereof, but committed all such adventures to GOD, in most sure trust of help after that they have called upon his aid. O woman, do thou the like and so shalt thou be most excellent beautified before GOD and all his Angels and Saints, and thou needest not to seek further for doing any better works. For obey thy husband, take regard of his requests, and give heed unto him to perceive what he requireth of thee, and so shalt thou honor GOD and live peaceably in thy house.

And beyond all this, GOD shall follow thee with his benediction that all things shall well prosper both to thee and to thy husband, as the Psalm saith: "Blessed is the man which feareth GOD, and walketh in his ways, thou shalt have the fruit of thine own hands, happy shalt thou be, and well it shall go with thee. Thy wife shall be as a vine, plentifully spreading about thy house. Thy children shall be as the young springs of the Olives about thy tables" (Ps. 128.1-3). Lo, thus shall that man be blessed (saith David) that feareth the Lord. This let the wife have ever in mind, the rather admonished thereto by the apparel of her head, whereby is signified that she is under covert or obedience of her husband. And as that apparel is of nature so appointed to declare her subjection, so biddeth Saint Paul that all other of her raiment should express both shamefastness and sobriety (1 Tim. 2.9). For if it be not lawful for the woman to have her head bare but to bear thereon the sign of her power wheresoever she goeth, more is it required that she declare the thing that is meant thereby. And therefore these ancient women of the old world called their husbands lords and showed them reverence in obeying them.

But peradventure she will say that those men loved their wives indeed. I know that well enough and bear it well in mind. But when I do admonish you of your duties then call not to consideration what their duties be. For when we ourselves do teach our children to obey us as their parents, or when we reform our servants and tell them that they should obey their masters not only at the eye but as the Lord, if they should tell us again our duties we should not think it well done. For when we be admonished of our duties and faults we ought not then to seek what other men's duties be. For though a man had a companion in his fault yet should he not thereby be without his fault. But this must be only looked on, by what means thou mayest make thyself without blame. For Adam did lay the blame upon the woman and she turned it unto the serpent, but yet neither of them was thus excused. And therefore bring not such excuses to me at this time, but apply all thy diligence to bear thine obedience to thine husband.

For when I take in hand to admonish thy husband to love thee and to cherish thee, yet will I not cease to set out the law that is appointed for the woman as well as I would require of the man what is written for his law. Go thou therefore about such things as becometh thee only, and show thyself tractable to thy husband. Or rather, if thou wilt obey thy husband for GOD's precept, then allege such things as be in his duty to do but perform thou diligently those things which the lawmaker hath charged thee to do. For thus is it most reasonable to obey GOD if thou wilt not suffer thyself to transgress his law. He that loveth his friend seemeth to do no great thing, but he that honoreth that is hurtful and hateful to him, this man is worthy most commendation. Even so think you if thou canst suffer an extreme husband, thou shalt have a great reward therefore. But if thou lovest him only because he is gentle and courteous, what reward will GOD give thee therefore?

Yet I speak not these things that I would wish the husbands to be sharp towards their wives. But I exhort the women that they would patiently bear the sharpness of their husbands. For when either parts do their best to perform their duties the one to the other, then followeth thereon great profit to their neighbors for their example's sake. For when the woman is ready to suffer a sharp husband and the man will not extremely entreat his stubborn and troublesome wife, then be all things in quiet as in a most sure haven. Even thus was it done in old time, that every one did their own duty and office and was not busy to require the duty of their neighbors. Consider, I pray thee, that Abraham took to him his brother's son, his wife did not blame him therefore. He commanded him to go with him a long journey, she did not gainsay it but obeyed his precept (Gen. 13-14).

Again, after all those great miseries, labors, and pains of that journey, when Abraham was made as lord over all, yet did he give place to Lot of his superiority. Which matter Sarah took so little to grief that she never once suffered her tongue to speak such words as the common manner of women is wont to do in these days. When they see their husbands in such rooms to be made underlings and to be put under their youngers, then they upbraid them with cumbrous talk and call them fools, dastards, and cowards for so doing. But Sarah was so far from speaking any such thing that it came never into her mind and thought so to say, but allowed the wisdom and will of her husband. Yea, besides all this, after the said Lot had thus his will and left to his uncle the less portion of land, he chanced to fall into extreme peril. Which chance, when it came to the knowledge of this said Patriarch, he incontinently[44] put all his men in harness and prepared himself with all his family and friends against the host of the Persians. In which case Sarah did not counsel him to the contrary, nor did say, as then might have been said, "My husband, whither goest thou so unadvisedly? Why runnest thou thus on head? Why doest thou offer thyself to so great perils and art thus ready to jeopardize thine own life and to peril the lives of all thine, for such a man as hath done thee such wrong? At the least way, if thou regardest not thyself yet have compassion on me, which for thy love have forsaken my kindred and my country, and have the want both of my friends and kinfolks, and am thus come into so far countries with thee. Have pity on me and make me not here a widow, to cast me into such cares and troubles." Thus might she have said. But Sarah neither said nor thought such words, but she kept herself in silence in all things.

Furthermore, all that time when she was barren and took no pains, as other women did, by bringing forth fruit in his house, what did he? He complained not to his wife but to Almighty GOD. And consider how either of them did their duties as became them. For neither did he despise Sarah because she was barren, nor never did cast it in her teeth. Consider again how Abraham expelled the handmaid out of the house when she required it. So that by this I may truly prove that the one was pleased and contented with the other in all things. But yet set not your eyes only on this matter, but look further what was done before this, that Agar used her mistress despitefully and that Abraham himself was somewhat provoked against her, which must needs be an intolerable matter and a painful to a free-hearted woman and a chaste.

Let not therefore the woman be too busy to call for the duty of her husband where she should be ready to perform her own, for that is not worthy any great commendations. And even so again, let not the man only consider what belongeth to the woman and to stand too earnestly gazing thereon, for that is not his part or duty. But as I have said, let either party be ready and willing to perform that which belongeth especially to themselves. For if we be bound to hold out our left cheek to strangers which will smite us on the right cheek, how much more ought we to suffer an extreme and unkind husband? But yet I mean not that a man should beat his wife, GOD forbid that. For that is the greatest shame that can be, not so much to her that is beaten as to him that doth the deed. But if by such fortune thou chancest upon such a husband, take it not too heavily, but suppose thou that thereby is laid by no small reward hereafter and in this lifetime no small commendation to thee if thou canst be quiet.

But yet to you that be men, thus I speak. Let there be none so grievous fault to compel you to beat your wives. But what say I, your wives? No, it is not to be borne with that an honest man should lay hands on his maid servant to beat her. Wherefore if it be a great shame for a man to beat his bondservant, much more rebuke it is to lay violent hands upon his free woman. And this thing may be well understood by the laws which the Panims have made, which doth discharge her any longer to dwell with such a husband as unworthy to have any further company with her that doeth smite her. For it is an extreme point thus so vilely to entreat her like a slave that is fellow to thee of thy life, and so joined unto thee before time in the necessary matters of thy living. And therefore a man may well liken such a man (if he may be called a man rather than a wild beast) to a killer of his father or his mother. And whereas we be commanded to forsake our father and mother for our wife's sake, and yet thereby do work them no injury but do fulfill the Law of GOD, how can it not appear then to be a point of extreme madness to entreat her despitefully for whose sake GOD hath commanded thee to leave parents? Yea, who can suffer such despite? Who can worthily express the inconvenience that is to see what weepings and wailings be made in the open streets when neighbours run together to the house of so unruly a husband as to a Bedlam man,[45] who goeth about to overturn all that he hath at home? Who would not think that it were better for such a man to wish the ground to open and swallow him in than once ever after to be seen in the market?

But peradventure thou wilt object that the woman provoketh thee to this point. But consider thou again that the woman is a frail vessel, and thou art therefore made the ruler and head over her, to bear the weakness of her in this her subjection. And therefore study thou to declare the honest commendation of thine authority, which thou canst no way better do than to forbear to urge her in her weakness and subjection. For even as the King appeareth so much the more noble the more excellent and noble he maketh his officers and lieutenants whom, if he should dishonor and despise the authority of their dignity, he should deprive himself of a great part of his own honor, even so if thou dost despite her that is set in the next room beside thee thou doest much derogate[46] and decay the excellency and virtue of thine own authority. Recount all these things in thy mind, and be gentle and quiet. Understand that GOD hath given thee children with her and art made a father, and by such reason appease thyself. Doest thou not see the husbandmen what diligence they use to till that ground which once they have taken to farm, though it be never so full of faults? As for an example, though it be dry, though it bringeth forth weeds, though the soil cannot bear too much met, yet he tilleth it and so winneth fruit thereof. Even in like manner, if thou wouldst use like diligence to instruct and order the mind of thy spouse, if thou wouldst diligently apply thyself to weed out by little and little the noisome weeds of uncomely manners out of her mind with wholesome precepts, it could not be but in time thou shouldst feel the pleasant fruit thereof to both your comforts.

Therefore that this thing chance not so, perform this thing that I do here counsel thee. Whensoever any displeasant matter riseth at home, if thy wife hath done ought amiss, comfort her and increase not the heaviness. For though thou shouldst be grieved with never so many things, yet shalt thou find nothing more grievous than to want the benevolence of thy wife at home. What offence so ever thou canst name, yet shalt thou find none more intolerable than to be at debate with thy wife. And for this cause most of all oughtest thou to have this love in reverence. And if reason moveth thee to bear any burden at any other men's hands, much more at thy wife's. For if she be poor upbraid her not, if she be simple taunt her not, but be the more courteous, for she is thy body and made one flesh with thee.

But thou peradventure wilt say that she is a wrathful woman, a drunkard, and beastly without wit and reason. For this cause bewail her the more. Chafe not in anger but pray unto Almighty GOD. Let her be admonished and helped with good counsel, and do thou thy best endeavor that she may be delivered of all these affections. But if thou shouldst beat her thou shalt increase her evil affections. For frowardness and sharpness is not amended with frowardness but with softness and gentleness. Furthermore, consider what reward thou shalt have at GOD's hand. For where thou might beat her and yet, for the respect of the fear of GOD, thou wilt abstain and bear patiently her great offences, the rather in respect of that Law which forbiddeth that a man should cast out his wife what fault soever she be cumbered with, thou shalt have a very great reward and, before the receipt of that reward, thou shalt feel many commodities. For by this means she shall be made the more obedient, and thou for her sake shalt be made the more meek.

It is written in a story of a certain strange Philosopher, which had a cursed wife, a froward and a drunkard. When he was asked for what consideration he did so bear her evil manners he made answer, "By this means (said he) I have at home a Schoolmaster and an example how I should behave myself abroad. For I shall (saith he) be the more quiet with others being thus daily exercised and taught in the forbearing of her."[47] Surely, it is shame that Panims should be wiser than we, we, I say, that be commanded to resemble angels or rather GOD himself through meekness. And for the love of virtue, this said Philosopher Socrates would not expel his wife out of his house. Yea, some say that he did therefore marry his wife to learn this virtue by that occasion.

Wherefore, seeing many men be far behind the wisdom of this man, my counsel is that first and before all things a man do his best endeavor to get him a good wife, endued with all honesty and virtue. But if it so chance that he is deceived, that he hath chosen such a wife as is neither good nor tolerable, then let the husband follow this Philosopher and let him instruct his wife in every condition, and never lay these matters to sight. For the Merchant man, except he first be at composition with his factor[48] to use his interfairs[49] quietly, he will neither stir his ship to sail nor yet will lay hands upon his merchandise. Even so let us do all things that we may have the fellowship of our wives, which is the factor of all our doings at home, in great quiet and rest. And by these means all things shall prosper quietly, and so shall we pass through the dangers of the troublous sea of this world. For this state of life will be more honorable and comfortable than our houses, than servants, than money, than lands and possessions, than all things than can be told. As all these with sedition and discord can never work us any comfort, so shall all things turn to our commodity and pleasure if we draw this yoke in one concord of heart and mind.

Whereupon, do your best endeavor that after this sort ye use your Matrimony, and so shall ye be armed on every side. Ye have escaped the snares of the devil and the unlawful lusts of the flesh, ye have the quietness of conscience by this institution of Matrimony ordained by GOD. Therefore use often prayer to him that he would be present by you, that he would continue concord and charity betwixt you. Do the best ye can of your parts to custom yourselves to softness and meekness, and bear well in worth such oversights as chance. And thus shall your conversation be most pleasant and comfortable. And although (which can no otherwise be) some adversities shall follow, and otherwhiles now one discommodity, now another shall appear, yet in this common trouble and adversity lift up both your hands unto heaven, call upon the help and assistance of GOD, the author of your marriage, and surely the promise of relief is at hand. For Christ affirmeth in his Gospel, "Where two or three be gathered together in my name and be agreed, what matter soever they pray for, it shall be granted them of my heavenly father" (Matt. 18.19). Why therefore shouldst thou be afraid of the danger where thou hast so ready a promise and so nigh a help?

Furthermore, you must understand how necessary it is for Christian folk to bear Christ's cross, for else we shall never feel how comfortable GOD's help is unto us. Therefore give thanks to GOD for his great benefit in that ye have taken upon you this state of wedlock, and pray you instantly that Almighty GOD may luckily defend and maintain you therein, that neither ye be overcome with any temptations nor with any adversity. But before all things, take good heed that ye give no occasion to the devil to let and hinder your prayers by discord and dissension. For there is no stronger defence and stay in all our life than is prayer, in the which we may call for the help of GOD and obtain it, whereby we may win his blessing, his grace, his defence, and protection, so to continue therein to a better life to come. Which grant us he that died for us all, to whom be all honor and praise, for ever and ever, Amen.

NOTES

1. Indulging in lewdness.
2. Robbing and plundering.
3. Hindered.
4. Ill-effects.
5. General good.
6. For further treatment of this issue, see the extract by John Rainolds in this volume.
7. Inhabitants of Lepreum, a town in Triphylia, founded in the time of Theseus.
8. Inhabitants of Locri Epizephrii, a town in the south of Italy, founded in the seventh century B.C.
9. Sexual intimacy.
10. Labors.
11. In this way.
12. Desire or wish.
13. The homily here offers religious support for the numerous sumptuary laws in England which sought to codify fashion according to class and gender norms.
14. Rustles.
15. Completely.
16. Wardrobes.
17. Offensive or disgusting.
18. Jackets or tunics.
19. Women's head cloths.
20. Sheer linen or cotton fabrics.
21. Tertullian, A.D. c.160-c.240, a member of the Carthaginian Church and early Christian author. Reference is to *Defence of the Christians against the Heathens* 6.3.
22. Points and scallops cut at the edges of garments.
23. Cut of meat, diet.
24. In addition to various sumptuary laws, statutes dealing with both poverty and vagrancy were enacted repeatedly from 1531 onwards. Comprehensive acts were passed in 1572, 1598, and 1601. The laws enforced three main measures: a

compulsory poor-rate to be paid in each parish; penalties against beggars and vagabonds; workhouses for the poor.

25. The reference is to the author of the Deuterocanonical book Ecclesiasticus (or Sirach).

26. In such a way.

27. Possibly Philo of Larissa, a Greek philosopher of the first century B.C.

28. Pagan.

29. Sparkling brightness.

30. Modesty.

31. Democritus, 460-370 B.C. Greek philosopher.

32. See Sophocles, *Ajax* 293.

33. Xenophon, *Oeconomicus* 10.2-10.8. The remark is actually said to Socrates by Ischomachus.

34. Plutarch, *Moralia* 2.141-42.

35. *Economics* 3.1

36. Reference is to the response of Spartan women to Dionysius the Elder, the Tyrant of Syracuse, 405-367 B.C., in Plutarch, *Moralia* 3.228-29.

37. Reference is to Pyrrhus, King of Epeiros, c. 307-272 B.C., in Plutarch, *Lives* 9.18.

38. The story is told in the apocryphal Book of Judith.

39. Strokes with a whip or rod.

40. Spiritual.

41. Contentment.

42. Bold or saucy.

43. Labor, that is, childbirth and work.

44. Immediately.

45. An insane man. The term Bedlam derives from the Hospital of St. Mary of Bethlehem in London which, originally founded as a priory, became a hospital for the insane at the beginning of the fifteenth century. It was granted royal funding in 1547.

46. Diminish.

47. The couple are Socrates and Xanthippe; Diogenes Laertius, *Lives of Eminent Philosophers*, 2.5.

48. Agent.

49. An affair or business between two parties.

CHAPTER 2

A White Sheet,
Or a Warning for Whoremongers
Richard Cooke

The subtitle of Richard Cooke's sermon explains its occasion. Delivered on 19 July 1629 at St. Swithin's church in London, it was "appointed by Honorable authority for penance to be done by an inhabitant there for fornication, continued more than two years with his Maidservant." As Cooke reveals later in the sermon, the maid subsequently had died, having already killed her illegitimate child, while the man had been acquitted of involvement in either death, perhaps for lack of evidence.

The title of the sermon invokes one of the main penalties imposed by the Church courts on sexual offenders. The two key forms of punishment were fines or public penance. The man whom Cooke addresses appears to have been fined previously and is now undergoing penance by being the subject of a sermon on adultery while having to wear a white sheet in church and possibly while making a public confession. These forms of social penance were considered harsh penalties in a time when credit and reputation were deemed to be all-important (Amussen 152-53). In the Elizabethan and Jacobean periods, the Church courts were primarily responsible for hearing cases concerning sexual immorality as well as other civil and criminal matters. Sexual immorality included issues such as prenuptial fornication and bridal pregnancy, sex outside of marriage, incestuous marriage, bestiality. There are few records of cases on the latter issues even though they were prominent in folklore (Sharpe 48, Ingram 247).

In Early Modern England, sexuality seems to have been conceived as a form of social behavior rather than a personal preference. This conception provided the motive for legal intervention in people's sexual lives. Courts tended to focus on "notorious cases" within communities (Ingram 239), where the values of a village or parish seemed to be threatened or disrupted by the acts of some of its members. Adultery was a prime instance of such disruption, with frequently drawn analogies between stability in the family and in the community. For example, adultery involving a married woman was regarded as highly immoral in bringing shameful public exposure upon herself and the cuckolded husband. The majority of adultery cases conformed to the one described and denounced in Cooke's sermon: a married man and a single woman, often a servant. Whereas single women in adultery cases tended to be from lower classes, men were from more varied social backgrounds, a contrast which suggests that pressures of wealth and power were often crucial to women's involvement. At the same time, women were more likely to be charged, due to visible evidence through pregnancy and a social bias which might shield the higher-status males (Ingram 267-69).

Cooke presents the sermon on behalf of his parish, where he has lived for over twenty-four years. He asserts that the community has been as much affronted by the accused's actions as was the maid herself. Of course, his warning is also directed to the rest of the St. Swithin's congregation and, after publication (within a few months of its delivery), to a wider reading audience as well. The sermon is noteworthy more for the dramatic immediacy of its address and the mass of biblical, religious, and other citations on sexual immorality than for its stylistic polish. In the printed preface, the parson is quite modest, explaining that friends had urged him to publish the text. He also reveals that since preaching the sermon he has been abused by the man involved, and he calls on the parish to support him. The text thus provides details of various repercussions which might flow from the breaking of social-sexual codes.

The sermon was printed only once, in London in 1629 (*STC* 5676; Reel 1093).

A WHITE SHEET, OR A WARNING FOR WHOREMONGERS

"Whoremongers and Adulterers, God will judge."

(Heb. 13.4)

You will not much wonder, I persuade myself, that I have this day changed mine ordinary and usual Text, while you cast your eye upon this penitentiary spectacle of a black soul in a white sheet, the first of this kind and nature (I thank God) that since my time we ever had. And I hope both we and he also will pray God that as he hath been the first so also he may be the last.

A Spectacle causing I know not whether greater sorrow or rejoicing. In me, I can assure you, it causeth both. If natural parents having children that prove unnatural and disobedient cannot but lament and grieve for them, as for the murdering Cain, a mocking Ishmael, a profane Esau, etc.; but to have in the family a Reuben, climbing up to his father's bed; an Amnon, to defile his sister Tamar; or an Absalom, to lie with his father's concubines, in the sight of all Israel and of the Sun, how can this but cut them to the very heart and soul?[1]

How then can those, whom God hath made to be spiritual Fathers, but mourn as much to have such monsters? God is my witness, this is no pleasing sight to me further than I consider in it *digitum Dei*, the finger of God, in this justly inflicted and imposed punishment upon him. Which I hope, through the mercy of God, may be for the destruction of the flesh that his soul may be saved in the day of the Lord Jesus, which God grant.

It hath been often said that it is a fair flock that hath never a scabbed sheep in it. The fruitfullest fields of corn, when they have been freest, have had some weeds growing as well as grain, tares[2] amongst the wheat. And what Congregation ever was yet so fortunate to have all stand sound and straight amongst them? In the primest times and purest days of the Gospel, the Apostles had an Ananias and Sapphira, an Elimas, a Simon Magus, and the like.[3] In the Church of Corinth, for all Paul's zealous praying for them and preaching to them, there was such a sin break out amongst them that was not named amongst the Heathens, that a man should have his father's wife (1 Cor. 9.12). Yea, Christ himself, amongst those few he had, even of twelve one proved to be a devil (John 6.70).

Sorrow and compassion is never more sweet and seasonable than when God is dishonored, the souls of men endangered, and religion blemished by the foul and filthy sins of ungodly and graceless men.

When Zimri and Cosbi had committed fornication in the camp of Israel, you shall find all the congregation of the people of Israel weeping before the doors of the Tabernacle of the congregation (Num. 25.6). What made David to take on so pitifully for the death of Absalom but for his sins. The main cause of his untimely death, he died a rebel to God and a traitor to his Father. This caused that sorrow (2 Sam. 18.33).

St. Cyprian in his sermon *De Lapsis*, a little from the beginning, testifies of himself that when he saw or heard of any that fell away from the Orthodox faith for fear of persecution, that he could not but shed many tears for them and that he felt himself as deeply wounded with their apostasy as if he had been wounded unto death by the swords or other weapons of cruel persecutors.[4]

When that incestuous person in the Church of Corinth had brought that scandal on the Church and had nothing said or done to him for it, St. Paul went not behind their backs to blame them for it and to tell them they were rather puffed up than sorrowed, that he which had done that fault might be put away from amongst them (1 Cor. 5.2).

It is a masterpiece of religious wisdom in sorrowing for the sins of others to put a difference betwixt their sins and their souls, having compassion (Jude 22), hating them as sinners but loving them as men. And thus and no otherwise stand I this day affected to the sin and the shame of him that stands here before us.

And as I am sorry for the foulness of his sin, so I profess I rejoice and am glad with all mine heart for the execution of justice by those Honorable, Reverend, and Worshipful persons in the High Commission Court[5] that have so justly and worthily inflicted this punishment upon him. No more, I am confident, than law permitted though not so much, I dare say, as his sin deserved. If such a fly had fallen on weak spiders' webs, God knows where he would have light and fly-blowed next.

There is nothing that causeth such boldness and impudence in sin as impunity. "Because sentence against an evil work is not speedily executed, the hearts of men are fully set in them to do evil" (Eccles. 8.11). Saul can no sooner swear to the witch of Endor for her safety at the raising of only seeming Samuel, but she presently falls to her sorcery, which till then she durst not for her life have attempted. Hope of escaping draws men to sin bare-faced and with boldness (1 Sam. 28.9-11). Which made Cato wisely to say that it were better to receive no thanks for doing well than no punishment for doing evil.[6]

We should therefore be so affected when we see the hand of God in the punishment of offenders as the author of them is, who delights not in them as they make his creatures miserable but as thereby his justice is made more conspicuous and glorious. It should not only joy us to see God kind and gracious in his mercies to his own but also to see him terrible and just in the punishment of his enemies. It is no cruelty to rejoice in justice. The foolish pity of men is cruelty in God's esteem.

It was a wise and religious answer of Louis King of France who was styled the Saint,[7] who having signed a pardon for a malefactor and afterward calling it in again, being asked the reason of it replied nothing nor made no other answer to it than with these words of the Psalmist: "Blessed is he that doth judgment and justice at all times" (Ps. 106.3). And I have read of that Isabel of Spain that was wont to say of sour things which she loved to look at.[8] One was this, to see a thief upon the ladder at the Gallows, rejoicing to see the execution of justice.

The Psalmist tells us that the righteous shall rejoice when he seeth the vengeance (Ps. 58.10), a text not to be tentured[9] to private revenge or meant of that joy when men are tickled to see or hear of some mischief to befall their enemies. Such a kind of rejoicing is unchristian and uncharitable, and the contrary is commanded, "Rejoice not when thine enemy falleth and let not thy heart be glad when he stumbleth, lest the Lord see it and it displease him" (Prov. 24.17-18), but of the justice of God when he meets with offenders for their sins.

Metellus Macedonicus and Scipio Africanus were always out with one another and as cross and contrary each to other as might be. Yet when

Metellus heard of the death of Scipio, he ran about the streets and lamentably cried out, "Help neighbors, help, the walls of our city are overthrown."[10] And when Caesar saw the head of Pompey he wept bitterly.[11]

The Joy of the godly never is or ought at any time to be in the hurt or punishment of the wicked, but in this that God hereby is glorified and his justice magnified. As Anselmus well observeth, "We may not rejoice that the wicked suffer, but that their sufferings come from a righteous Judge."[12] And thus and no otherwise I profess myself, and I hope I may promise as much for you all do no otherwise rejoice in this man's shame and punishment this day.

If he hath but so much grace as to do both these for himself, he is a happy man. For though happily[13] he hath hitherto deceived the expectation of the world, who as yet see but small sign of either, yet hereby he may conceive some hope of finding God more favorable in forgiving this that is past, and the world also more friendly to help him by their prayers for mercy and forgiveness at the hands of God if this be wanting. If this be not obtained, what can be expected after these earthly shames and censures but eternal tortures both of soul and body in those easeless and endless flames of fire and brimstone? That very doom which here is denounced against the sin of uncleaness and filthiness, for "Whoremongers etc."

The whole verse as it lyeth in the lump, if you please to consider it as it is compact together, consisteth of these two principal parts and members, a Recommendation and secondly a Commination[14]: the gracing of marriage and then the disgracing of the polluters of marriage; the first honorable, the last damnable.

Marriage is honorable, an honorable testimony of that holy institution of God in the times of man's innocence, when God, seeing that it was not good for him to be alone, out of man made he a help meet for man (Gen. 2.18-22). That forever after, for the avoiding of fornication, every man might have his own and every wife her own husband (1 Cor. 7.2), that such as have not the gift of continency might marry and keep themselves undefiled members of Christ's body, as we have it well in our liturgy of marriage.

But if any such should happily be born that, like wild beasts, would needs be breaking over the pale of this park of God, and like fed horses fall aneighing after their neighbors' wives, as God complains of such in Jeremiah's time (Jer. 5.8). Or that should discover their father's nakedness, or humble her that was set apart for pollution, or committed abomination with his neighbor's wife (Ezek. 22.11), they might know they should do it at their own peril and pay sweetly and dearly for it first or last, for "Whoremongers etc."

Which words, being for the sum and substance of them a definitive and peremptory sentence against unclean and filthy persons, may it please you to take into your observation three several circumstances, whereby it is exemplified and enlarged: first, the sinners to be censured; secondly, the Judge that shall set upon them; and thirdly, the punishment that shall be inflicted.

The persons punishable and to be tried are two ways discovered: first, by the nature of the sin; secondly, by the number of offenders. Whoremongers and adulterers, the Judge before whom they shall be arraigned is God. Whoremongers and adulterers God will judge. The censure and punishment to be inflicted is Judgment, a word of large extent, aggravating the soreness and severity of their punishment for Whoremongers and Adulterers, as Gualter truly hath observed.[15]

Let us first look upon the prisoners at the bar. There are here two sorts of sins and sinners, named Whoremongers and adulterers.

Both apparently peccants and delinquents against that peremptory commandment of God, "Thou shalt not commit adultery" (Exod. 10.14), but not offenders alike. Faulty enough both, and bad is the best. Both condemned, and with these and whatsoever other uncleanness else, by that commandment and law of God, is also interdicted.

I know Divines have well distinguished them. Whoredom to be filthiness and uncleanness committed by those that are at liberty and loose, and therefore called single fornication. The sin of such as be both free, not yet knit together, nor of twain made one by any tie of matrimonial conjunction, such as was the sin of Sheehem with Dinah (Gen.34.2) and of Zimri with Cosbi (Num. 25).

The other kind of this uncleanness is Adultery, which is a plain and a palpable breach of holy marriage. The word *adulterium* some have thought to have been derived of *quasi ad alteram*, of coming to or accompanying with another, which I think is something short. Others better tell us that *adulterium* is *ad alterius thorum accessio*, the climbing up unto the bed of another, as Aquinas defineth it to be the unlawful companying together of them that are coupled together.[16] Such as was the sin of Reuben, David with Bathsheba (2 Sam. 11.4), and of Absalom with his Father's concubines, both which the Apostle tells us God will judge.

Secondly, we have them discovered by their number, Whoremongers and adulterers, meaning not someone but all such, speaking indefinitely and generally in the plural number, aiming at every man and mother's son. God, in cases of justice, being a God of pure eyes that can behold no iniquity (Hab. 1.13), a God that taketh no pleasure in wickedness, neither shall any evil dwell with him (Ps. 5.4). He is neither accepter of places nor persons. He that gave such a strict charge to his delegates and deputies not to countenance a poor man in his cause (Exod. 23.3), and charged them also not to have respect of persons in Judgment but to hear the small as well as the great and not to fear the face of men (Deut. 17.10-11).

This God, I say, thus strict and punctual in his precept unto others that justice might be carried in a right line and level, will not lay heavy burdens on other men's shoulders and not move them himself with one of his fingers, but will be as impartial against all sorts of sinners whose repentance and humiliation after sin committed comes not forth speedily to meet this God as Abigail did David, or the inhabitants of Tyrus and Sidon to pacify Herod displeased with them.[17]

Let no unclean person dream of a dispensation in his sin. I know God never hath nor will grant any. That is enough for *Dominus Deus noster Papa*[18] of Rome (as his base claw-backs and Sycophants blasphemously style him). God scorns to live by so base and beastly rents and comings in. "That soul that sinneth shall die" (Ezek. 18.20). "The Lord will cut off head and tail, branches and rush in one day" (Isa. 9.14). And if happily it should find any favor with men (which God forbid), yet let it hope for none with God. God's purpose is otherwise (if such mend not their manners), for "Whoremongers etc."

The next thing to be handled and dispatched in the text is the Judge before whom they should be tried, and that is God. For Whoremongers and Adulterers God then shall be their Judge, truly termed and styled by Abraham to be the Judge of all the world: "Shall not the Judge of all the world do right?" (Gen.18.15). And surely so he is the only Lord chief Justice of all the world, riding no lesser or shorter circuit than the compass of all the world.

Two ways is God said to Judge, *per se, per suos*, by himself or by some others, immediately or mediately, usually by both and in both together. In taking vengeance and inflicting punishment upon offenders, what or who is it that is not at his command, readily and cheerfully to be at his beck to do his pleasure?

When God goes about the devastation and conflagration of Sodom and Gomorrah by the judgment of hell out of heaven, by raining down "fire and brimstone from the Lord out of Heaven" (Gen. 19.24), God will be their Judge but God's Angels shall be his executioners. When God intends to coop up that blasphemous mouth of Rabshakeh and to take down the pride and insolence of his Master, God will bring it to pass by an Angel and men (2 Kings 19.35-37). Yea, what creature is so mean, despicable, or contemptible which God cannot quickly arm with strength and power enough to avenge the quarrel of God in the confusion and destruction of the proudest offenders? Lice, frogs, caterpillars. Out of the very dust and ashes of the earth can God muster up an army to fight against Pharaoh, when he comes to plague him and his people (Exod. 8.16). By all which or by any of which whatsoever is effected, these are but the instruments. God is *primus motor*, the especial agent and mover. God by these and in these bringing to pass his intended purposes and good pleasure in the punishments of such as shall dare to provoke him by sinning against him.

It is true that usually and most an end God hath put the power of punishing into the hands of subordinate authority, of whom he hath said, "Ye are Gods" (Ps. 82.6), by God appointed to take vengeance of them that do evil (Rom. 13.4). Yet whatsoever these do in courts and causes of Justice justly and sincerely is God's own act. It is he that does it. These are the mouths and hands of God from whom they speak and for whom they strike when offenders suffer.

If any shall ask why the Apostle tells us that God, naming none but God, will have the hearing and handling of such foul matters as these and himself will sit in judgment upon whoremongers and adulterers, I suppose that happily it might be fore these several causes and reasons. First, the church and people at this time being under persecution and dispersion, they could have no public court of Justice nor any law civil or Ecclesiastic to punish this sin. Or secondly, if there were means for the suppressing of it, yet it was not so strictly looked after as was fitting, as may appear by that indulgency which the incestuous person found in the Church and Congregation of Corinth.

But the chief and principal cause, as I conjecture, was for the greater terrifying of such offenders, that all such filthy wretches and beastly livers might be assured that they could neither sin so secretly but they should be discovered, nor after sin committed escape unpunished. If there were none that either would or could look after them yet God himself would plague them for it, for "Whoremongers and adulterers God etc."

Two things amongst many make the wicked bold and presumptuous to fall upon any sin with greediness. Hope that their sin shall not be seen and, secondly, weakness in authority if found out and taken with it. It often happens that, as other sinners, so Whoremongers and adulterers are so close and cunning in their uncleanness that the most vigilant and observant eye of authority can take no notice or knowledge of it. It is a piece of the mystery of their iniquity and a trick in that black Art, if they can be but secret they think they are safe enough.

"The eye of the Adulterer waiteth for the twilight, and saith none eye shall see him, and disguiseth his face" (Job 24.15). And the simple young man, when he goeth to a bawdy house and to meet with his harlot, takes his time in the twilight, in the morning, in the black and dark night (Prov. 7.7-9). Thus indeed they may be too cunning and too crafty for the eyes of men, but they are too young to hide their sins from God. For "There is no darkness nor shadow of death where the workers of iniquity can be hid," as Elihu speaks in Job (34.22). "Can any man hide himself in secret, that I shall not see him? Do not I fill heaven and earth" (Jer. 23.25). The darkness is no darkness with him, but the night is as clear as the day. The darkness and the light to him are both alike. And "all things are naked and open unto the eyes of him with whom we have to do" (Heb. 4.13). "He therefore that made the eyes must needs see, and he that planteth the ear must needs hear, and he that chasteneth the Heathen, shall not he punish?" (Ps. 94.9-10). Yes, surely. And as he never winks at any sin so will he not at this, for "Whoremongers and adulterers God will judge."

The other thing that flesheth[19] men in their filthiness is weakness of authority, when either those that would may not or those that may do not or dare not meddle with them. When these beastly creatures think they can either overlook or overtop authority by being greater or better either by their persons, or places, or purses, than the Magistrate. For this is not always or alone the sin of beggars, as it was wont to be said of drunkenness, as drunk as a beggar. But Erasmus[20] called it long since the sport of great men, and therefore through their greatness know how to deal well enough with Authority, presuming that either by fraud or force or fear to escape well enough by breaking the cords of Magistrates and casting these bonds from them.

'Tis true, it may so now and then fall out that greatness of offenders may manumit[21] malefactors and free them from the force of the stroke of a mortal Magistrate. But they are likely to meet with their match when they meddle with their maker. He neither wants eyes to see nor hands to smite, nor courage to punish the proudest whoremonger or the greatest adulterer when he shall come to sit in judgment. The strongest will be too weak to deal with him. Who will set the briars and thorns against him in battle (Isa. 27.4)? "Do we provoke the Lord to jealousy, are we stronger than he?" (1 Cor. 10.22). What is a pot of earth to a scepter of iron, or the stubble to the fire? "For our God is a consuming fire" (Heb. 12.29). He can tear in pieces and none shall deliver. He can kill "both soul and body in hell" (Matt. 10.29).

And this is that judge which, here the Apostle tells us, shall give this sentence upon these and all other impenitent sinners, Whoremongers and adulterers by name in this text, for "Whoremongers and adulterers God will judge."

The third and the last thing in the trial of these persons is to hear their judgment. For God will judge them.

There is a twofold kind of judging given to God, a judgment of absolution and another of condemnation. The first is grace, the other anger; that comfortable, this other terrible. The judgment of absolution is only for such which, after sin committed, have heartily repented and humbled themselves to God and through Christ have made their peace with God. For whose only sake they have their pardon sealed, and hear no more of them but some sweet words of grace and mercy, like that of Nathan to David, "The Lord hath put away thy sin, thou shalt not die" (2 Sam. 12.13), or as

Christ said to him that he had cured of the palsy, "Son be of good comfort, thy sins are forgiven thee" (Matt. 9.2). So that there is "now no condemnation to those that are in Christ" (Rom. 8.1). For "he that heareth my words, and believeth in him that sent me, hath everlasting life and shall not come into condemnation" (John 5.24). And thus only are the godly judged, and none thus but these.

The other kind of judging is a judgment condemnatory, binding over all remorseless and impenitent sinners to all those temporal and eternal plagues and punishments, which God the righteous Judge hath not only nominated and threatened but undoubtedly shall be inflicted as severely as threatened. And of this kind of judging only is this in the text intended. Thus "Whoremongers and adulterers God will judge."

A terrible saying but a true. A word of astonishment and amazement, like that handwriting which appeared to Belshazzar on the wall, at the very sight whereof, before he knew what it might be or meant, "his countenance was changed, his thoughts troubled him, the joints of his loins were loosed, and his knees knocked one against another" (Dan. 5.6). Little less terrible than Peter's words to Ananias and Sapphira, at the hearing whereof they both gave up the Ghost and died (Acts 5.5). Much amazement well may this word cause in Whoremongers and adulterers to deter them from this sin, for God will judge them.

But if God be purposed to judge such beastly livers, where, when, or how, will some man ask, will God effect it? I answer for the time that is in his own appointing and at his own pleasure. Sooner or later or whensoever he listeth. Only let such know that first or last, at one time or another, God hath appointed a day in which he will judge them. There damnation sleepeth not. It may come suddenly. God's hands are never so bound, never so pinioned, that he cannot punish at his pleasure. If not suddenly, yet certainly. God's punishment comes slow but sure.

Hath not God met with some in the very act of their abominable filthiness? Thus perished Zimri and Cosbi by the hands of Phinehas (Num. 25.7-8). Plutarch reports that Alcibiades was burnt in his bed with his Courtesan Timandra,[22] and Paulus Diaconus[23] that Rodoaldus, King of Lombardy, was slain with a certain Matron even in the action of their concupiscence. But what if present execution be not done, shall they therefore escape scot-free? Will God put it up or pass it by unpunished?

"I have a long time held my peace, I have been still and refrained myself; but I will cry like a travailing woman, I will destroy and devour at once" (Isa. 42.14). What is deferred is not removed. Forbearance with God is no payment. The longer he stayeth, the liker to pay home at the last. The further he fetcheth his blow, the heavier it must needs fall wheresoever it lighteth. But of this let all those be fully assured that whensoever it comes it will be to their cost, whether here or hereafter, now or then, temporally or eternally, it may be in both. "Whoremongers and Adulterers God will judge."

And as for the manner how God will punish them, that also is as he will and how he pleaseth. God never wanteth weapons to wound his enemies, or rods in piss[24] to whip ungracious and rebellious children, fire and brimstone for Sodom and those Cities (Gen. 19.24). When God sees the old world so foul with sin, he knows how to wash it with a flood of waters (Gen. 7.7). He hath a ten-stringed whip for Pharaoh (Exod. 7.8-9); the earth to swallow up Korah and his Company (Num. 16.31); leprosy for Miriam and Gehazi (Num. 12.10 and 2 Kings 5.27); the sword, famine, and pestilence for Israel (Ezek. 6.12); lice and worms for Herod and the like (Acts 12.23). And what not indeed to meet with sinners? Oh, that we could ever think of that after reckoning for sin! Or that we knew the worst or what it would cost us before God hath done with us. Who knows? Who can presage how God may deal with him when by his sins he hath once provoked him?

What punishment originally, and by that first law that God made against Adulterers, you know was no less than death. The mercy of the Gospel in some Churches hath mitigated that severity into more mild and merciful proceedings, not taking away all censures or punishments from that sin but hath left it in the wisdom and power of Authority to have that sin severely and sharply punished, though not with death.[25] God grant this sin may find no hole to hide his head in, nor that there may be no daubing, nor dallying, no dandling of it. We see where this man's sin was lately censured. It hath had but little countenance and less encouragement. The blessing of him that dwelt betwixt the bush[26] reward them seven-fold into their bosom for their singular Justice and Sincerity.

But shall I tell you how this sin hath prospered and what entertainment it usually finds at God's hands? I must tell you then, but them especially that find such pleasure in this sin, that God never gives other than sour sauce to such stolen meat, as will pregnantly appear by those fearful precedents and examples of God's heavy hand in revenging and punishing this sin of uncleanness. What a pitiful massacre followed upon the deflowering of Dinah, Jacob's daughter, by Shechem the son of Hamor (Gen. 34.25)? How dearly did Amnon pay for his incest with his sister when, though full two years after (yet God nor man had not yet forgotten it), he was suddenly murdered by the servants of his brother Absalom as he sat at the table (2 Sam. 13.28-29). What a heavy time was it, what a black day in the Camp and Congregation of Israel for this very sin, when not only Zimri and Cosbi perished by the hand of Phinehas (Num. 25.8), but twenty-and-four thousand of the people besides were swept away suddenly by the hand of God (1 Cor. 10.8)?

Yea, the very heathen have had this sin in such detestation that they thought no punishment bad enough for the committers of this sin. Zaleucus, King of Locris, adjudged them by Law to lose their eyes both man and woman. And so strict was he to see his Law observed that when his own son was taken in Adultery and should have lost both his eyes, the people importuning his Father to forgive him, rather than justice should not be done he commanded that one of his own and another of his son's eyes should be put out, and so they were,[27] as Peter Martyr upon the two Books of Samuel.[28] Nebuchadnezzar[29], hearing that one Acub and Zedekiah, Jews, had committed foulness with two married women, broiled them both to death on a gridiron.

Amongst the Egyptians the man that was taken in Adultery was beaten with a thousand stripes, and the woman had her nose cut off, as Diodorus Siculus reporteth.[30] The Ancient Germans used to set the Adulteress naked before her kindred and to cut off her hair, and then her husband was to drive her before him through the City, beating her with cudgels.

The Cumeans placed the Adulteress in the open market-place upon a stone in the public view of all the people, that she might be derided and scorned of all and then setting her upon an ass to ride through the streets. And she was ever after called in mockage an ass-rider, and that stone she stood on was ever held and abhorred as a thing filthy and unclean, as Plutarch hath related.[31]

And hath God at any time been less friendly or favorable to this sin than so? Hath his sight been weaker that he cannot see or his power wasted that he doth not smite now as of old? His anger is not now turned away, but his hand is stretched out still. We see enough every day to make us believe it. How many fearful sights are daily in our eyes, representing God's justice upon such offenders in their souls, bodies, goods, good name, and in their issue and posterity of these (if any be). For by some of these ever, by many of these often, by all these now and then, God meets with them and pays them home for their beastly living.

Look upon his justice in their souls, what impressions of his wrath he hath left there? By the subtraction of his grace, a plain presager of a Precipitation and downfall into sin. Blinding their understanding, besotting their affections, hardening their hearts, delivering them up to a reprobate sense, and giving them up to uncleanness through the lusts of their own hearts, as St. Paul speaks of the Gentiles (Rom. 1.14). And at last in his justice, suffering them to perish in the vanity of that sin and to carry it with them to the grave from which, while they lived, neither Laws of God or man could possibly reclaim them.

Look upon them in their goods and estate, though fair and great, how God hath blown upon it, and how soon hath it been blasted and brought to nothing.

That which Solomon speaks of another sin, the sin of drunkenness, a companion, I am sure, if not Cousin-German[32] to the sin of filthiness, that "the drunkard and the glutton shall come to poverty" (Prov. 23.21). I am sure he tells us it will be no better with whoremongers, "For by means of an whorish woman, a man is brought to a morsel of bread" (Prov. 6.26). Whores and Jesuits (I may well couple them together), like Simeon and Levi brethren in evil (Gen. 34.25). For those as well as these are, if not carnal, yet spiritual fornicators. Those I say have ever been, wheresoever they come, the only soakers and sinkers of the fairest inheritances. Horseleech-like ever crying give, give. That which Diogenes sometime said of a drunkard's house with a bill on it, to signify that it was to be let. "I thought as much," said the Cynic, "that ere long he would spew up his house also."[33] And so will these do that follow this. It is a thousand to one, if they leave not that that will not leave them worth a gray groat.[34] Misery and beggary will be their end. For if he that followeth vain persons shall have poverty enough, they shall be sure to be beggarly enough that follow this sin. I can give them no comfort, but if their lives be so bad the reward of their sin can be no better, and lasting parsimony will come in the end. To the shame of their faces and in the sorrow of their souls, they shall say we are wise too late. It is too late to spare when all is gone and spent.

Look upon their bodies, more near and dear unto them than all they have besides. How have they been stigmatized by the hand of God? What foul, what filthy, what infectious diseases have lighted, yea, loaded the bodies of such? How many have hereby had the very noses of their faces consumed and eaten off? That that face which could not blush at the sin might carry in it, like Cain's mark, a perpetual stamp both of their sin and shame.

Look upon their credit and their reputation, and how lies all their honor not in the dust but even in a dunghill. The most precious thing that a man hath in this world is a good name. "A good name is rather to be chosen than great riches" (Prov. 22.1), "better then the most precious ointment" (Eccles. 7.1). Whence the Heathen could persuade men to it, labor rather to get a good name than anything. Yet how soon is that precious ointment made to stink by this dead fly of filthiness? "Their remembrance shall perish from the earth, and they shall have no name in the streets," as Bildad speaks in Job (18.17). And when the memory of the just shall be blessed, "the name of the wicked shall rot" (Prov. 10.7).

Lastly, look upon them in their issue and posterity (if any be), and how they are branded with baseness and infamy.

By the law of God they were not to "enter into the congregation" (Deut. 23.2), and by the laws of man a base son cannot inherit. If he hath any right to inherit anything, it is nothing but the fruit of his father's filthiness, shame, and disgrace, like the leprosy of Gehazi shall cleave unto him and his seed forever (2 Kings 5.20-27). And what greater blemish than to be a son of the people, a spurious seed, and who knows whose? For how high soever they may carry their heads and look big upon such as know them not, yet knowing themselves to be no better they must live and die with the shame of bastardy. This is the portion of those wicked filthy livers from God and the heritage appointed unto them from God, as Zophar speaks in Job (20.29). "This is their portion to drink" (Ps. 11.6), accursed in their souls, plagued in their bodies, beggared in their estate, blemished in their reputation, and infamized in their posterity. Thus "Whoremongers etc."

And all this but in this life. God hath two places to keep Courts of Justice, one here below, the other in heaven above. Here he keeps but quarter Sessions, there his general Assizes.[35] Oh, happy were it for Whoremongers and Adulterers if the mountains and hills could fall upon them, or the hills hide them from the terror of their trial at that day!

But alas, alas, it will not be! As it will be terrible to appear, so it will be impossible not to (1 Cor. 5.10). Later we must all appear before the Tribunal seat of Christ. How merry might such wretches be if they might covenant with God by temporal punishments to be dispensed with and exempted from eternal torments? But woe worth the day that ever they were born if they be not born of water and the Spirit. This is not all, the worst is yet to come. All these are but the beginning of sorrows. These are but flea-bitings to that which is behind. As Abner told Joab about his wars, "knowest thou not that it will be bitter in the latter end?" (2 Sam. 2.26). Or as Solomon tells the Drunkard concerning his cups and carousings, that "at the last it will bite like a serpent, and sting like a cockatrice" (Prov. 23.32), so will it be with these before God hath done with them. The latter end of these will be worse than their beginning; it will be bitter at the last: "The lips of a strange woman etc."[36]

What greater bitterness than eternal torments with the Devil and his Angels? What fouler shame than perpetual banishment and everlasting abdication from the glorious and blessed presence of the everlasting God? What is the sorest or the sharpest censure of an earthly Judge to the final and universal judgement of an angry God? What is the paying or parting with a little money to the loss, at the last, of the soul and body? Shame amongst men to the disgrace of Saints and Angels? A white sheet in a Church to the eternal flames of Hell? This and nothing else can such expect unless their repentance and humiliation to God, like another Moses, stand in the breach to stop this gap, to turn away his indignation and displeasure from them. For except they repent they shall surely perish.

To come then, by the way of conclusion, to that which is the life and power of preaching, I mean to application of all that hath been spoken. This Doctrine meeteth first with the cursed and corrupt opinion of our adversary of the Church of Rome, who in their conclusions and propositions concerning this Doctrine of the Apostle are as cross and contrary as Belial[37] to Christ and darkness to light. For it hath been a common and current tenet amongst them that simple fornication is no sin. No sin it may be because they think so, or no sin because so common with them. Custom in the sin blinds them, they think it is no sin.

But if it be no sin, why, I would know of them, hath God so precisely prohibited and so severely punished it?

"There shall be no whore of the Daughters of Israel, nor a whore-keeper of the sons of Israel" (Deut. 23.17) These be the express words of the Law. "Flee fornication," sayth the Apostle (1 Cor. 6.18). "Let us not commit fornication" (1 Cor. 10.8). St. Paul, reckoning up the fruits of the flesh which (I hope) our adversaries will not deny to be sins, nameth Adultery and Fornication first: "The works of the flesh are manifest, which are adultery, fornication, uncleaness, etc." (Gal. 5.19). "Mortify your members which are on earth, fornication first, uncleanness, inordinate affection" and the like (Col. 3.5). "This is the will of God your sanctification, and that you should abstain from fornication" (1 Thess. 4.3). What mean these plain and precise dehortations from it if it were not apparently a sin against God?

St. Augustine proves it thus to be a sin because it is a plain breach of that Law, "Thou shalt not commit adultery" (Exod. 20.14), a commandment forbidding all kind of uncleanness and therefore fornication: "If fornication be not here forbidden, whether it can be found prohibited elsewhere in the Decalogue I cannot tell, but it is most certain that is either forbidden here or nowhere in the moral Law."[38]

The same Father answereth an objection which might seem to defend it, "I am unmarried, and make use of a harlot." St. Augustine answers, "Thou dost sin against God, whose image in thee thou defacest in thy self by thy overflowing lusts. The Lord who knoweth what is best for thee hath granted thee a wife. This he prescribed, thus he hath commanded." It is therefore surely a sin against God.

Tostatus[39] argueth well to prove it a sin. Every natural act not used or employed to the right end is evil. As to eat and drink not to preserve the body but for riot and excess is evil, so to use carnal copulation of lust not for the preserving of the kind by generation, for the which it is appointed, must needs be evil. So it is in fornication.

Reverend H. Latimer[40] maintains it to be a sin against God, out of this text thus. Where we read that God blessed marriage it is easy to gather on the contrary that all other companying of man and woman not in marriage is accursed. And proves it by the words of my text and concludes thus, seeing therefore the sanctity and chastity of marriage is commanded in the Law and the contrary is forbidden, and all other acts of uncleanness whatsoever which are a violation of marriage. Adding also to this reason the testimony of Hosea, "Whoredom and wine take away the hearts" (4.11), and the punishment of the Israelites for their fornication, out of 1 Cor. 10.8.

But we must give these Apes leave to hug their own, and these crows to think their own birds the most beautiful. It is one of the Pope's purveyors that carrieth in his provision? No marvel then if they have so many Champions to maintain it, and so many monstrous whoremongers and adulterers amongst them to practice it. And so they do both act and teach. Who knoweth not this that hath read anything concerning the filthiness of both Popes and Priests in the Church of Rome? Theodoricus of Niem[41] will tell us that in Norway and Ireland it hath been lawful for the Bishops and Priests to keep their Concubines, and when twice a year they visited the Parish Priests that were under them they were wont to carry their Concubines with them. Yea, their Concubines would not suffer them to visit without them. Here was good doing. This was good stuff and singular holiness.

Udulricus, Bishop of Augsburg,[42] reports that when a certain Pope sent to draw a Pond for fishes there were taken up and brought him above six thousand Infants' heads. Alvarius Pelagius[43] complaineth that the Priests live incontinently and wisheth they had never vowed continency. Alvarus Chartier[44]: the ministers of the Church, leaving the use of marriage, follow wandering, dissolute, and unlawful lusts. Nun Bridget[45]: Priests and Deacons keep whores that with their great bellies walk up and down with other women. And Picus Mirandola,[46] to name no more, speaks as broadly and truly of them: "The Priests once lay with the women at the door of the Tabernacle (alluding to the sin of Eli's sons[47]), but in our time they break into the sacred houses, and (Fie for shame) women are to be brought in to satisfy their filthy lusts." And no marvel, then, if it be not sin with such that are such egregious and shameless beasts.

What means their common Stews and open bawdy houses allowed by the Pope and even under his nose. Out of which sin he sucks no small advantage, persuaded that gain is sweet howsoever it comes in, as he said of the ill sent of Urine. Yea, the hire of a whore and the price of a dog, which were had in detestation and held a thing abominable to be brought into the house of God (Deut. 23.18), must not miss his mouth nor shall escape his greasy chops. All that bring such grist come welcome to his Mill, bed and bosom friends, though never so base or beastly, to the Court of Rome and Chamber of the Pope. But leaving these like Swine to wallow in their own mire, or like Boars and Beasts to fatten in their own filthiness, let us in a word or two see how this Commination concerns ourselves.

The use for us may be, in a word, by the severity of the punishment to be deterred from the filthiness of the offence against which it is threatened. Recollect but briefly the particulars already dispatched, and you shall soon see reason sufficient to dissuade you from it. Is uncleanness a sin? Come not near. He that toucheth this sin must needs be defiled. He that cometh too near this fire shall surely be scorched. For the house of a whore is "the way to hell going down to the chambers of death" (Prov. 7.27). Again, will God be avenged of it if nobody else will punish it? Is it that God from whom we cannot hide it, nor from whose power we can not be delivered? Will it light so terrible, first or last, either in our souls or bodies, goods, good name, or posterity, or in one of these? Perhaps in all of these? Are we liable to such deadly strokes of God's hand here, and in danger of eternal torments in hell fire forever, after all the plagues and judgments either by God or men to be inflicted? Shall neither Whoremongers nor Adulterers "inherit the Kingdom of Heaven" (1 Cor. 6.9)? Shall no unclean thing enter into that new Jerusalem (Rev. 21.27)? Shall dogs and sorcerers and whoremongers be without (Rev. 22.15)? Then let him that hath an ear to hear hear what the mouth of the Lord hath spoken: "Flee fornication" (1 Cor. 6.18); "Mortify your members which are upon the earth, fornication, uncleanness, etc." (Col. 3.5); "Fornication and uncleanness, let it not be once named amongst you" (Eph. 5.3); "Know you not, that your bodies are the members of Christ. . .make them not the members of a harlot" (1 Cor. 6.15); "For if any man defile the Temple of God, him will God destroy" (1 Cor. 3.17); "I beseech you therefore brethren, by the mercies of God, that you present your bodies a living sacrifice, holy, and acceptable unto God" (Rom. 12.1); "For this is the will of God, even your sanctification, that you should abstain from fornication; and that every one should know how to possess his vessel in sanctification and honor" (1 Thess. 4.3-4). And as those shall be sure with Psalms in their mouths and Palms in their hands (Rev. 7.9), as conquerors to "follow the Lamb wheresoever he goeth which have not defiled themselves with women but are virgins" (Rev. 14.4), so those that have given themselves over to fornication, in "going after strange flesh" as Jude speaketh, shall suffer "the vengeance of eternal fire" (Jude 7). For "Whoremongers and adulterers God will judge."

And now before we part, I must speak a word or two to you, not long (and yet too late), our unworthy neighbour. I must say to you as Ehud said to Eglon, "I have a message unto thee from God" (Judg. 3.20). But not with a Dagger in my hand to kill you but with good counsel from my heart to keep you that you cast not away yourself.[48] The words of the wise, they are like goads and nails (Eccles. 12.11), not like Jael's nails to be driven into your head,[49] but like St. Peter's nails to be fastened in the heart. And I pray God they may have no worse success than his had, for they were pricked in their hearts and said, "Men and brethren, what shall we do?" (Acts 2.37), sorrowful and ashamed of the evil past and desirous how to learn to go and sin no more.

And while I shall perform this last work of charity to your soul (which God make profitable unto you as my soul desireth), let me entreat this favor from you which Daniel desired of Nebuchadnezzar, let my counsel be acceptable unto you (Dan. 4.27), and suffer a word or two of exhortation. Account me not your enemy because I tell you the truth. Hate me not because I have not used to prophesy good unto you, dealing plainly when I found you faulty. Or (if you do), it shall be all one with me. I will discharge my conscience before God and men, and then your blood be upon your own head. You shall fall or stand to your own master.

You have heard out of this text the foulness of the sin of fornication, and how roundly and tartly God usually proceedeth in the punishment of it. This hath been your sin, and this sin hath brought you to this day's shame. Inasmuch as few are punished and all are afeared, God grant it may do you good and that others by your punishment may learn to be wise. How long you have loved and lived in this sin, your own conscience can tell you best. By your own confession since October 1626, near three years, and that which is worst, to keep a whore under your wife's nose. Too long and too much, if you bethink you well, if it had been less and never so little.

You have heard that "Whoremongers and adulterers, God will judge." If such a thunderclap will not startle and awake you, I may justly fear you have slept your last and that you are not only dead but with Lazarus stink in the grave (John 12.39).

Rouse up yourself. "Awake thou that sleepest and stand up from the dead, that Christ may give thee light" (Eph. 5.14). I have heard of that public protestation that you made where you first did penance, in that Honorable and Worshipful presence at Paul's cross,[50] of an ample and large restitution and satisfaction to such as you had wronged even to threefold. Had you said more you had not promised too much, and had you ever climbed up on a tree to see Christ as Zacheus did and with no worse heart than he, you would have enlarged your tongue whatsoever you would have done with your hands and promised to restore fourfold as he did (Luke 19.4-8).

But words will not carry it. Good trees are known by their fruits and not by their leaves, and good Christians not by their words but by their lives. I will not wonder to see light ears of corn to prick and peer up themselves above all in the furrows or field, nor to hear an empty cask to make the greatest noise. I should think myself a happy man if I might presume to take you at your word. In the meantime, let me tell you what I think, that the world or (wise men at the least) will never believe it till they see it, and till then you shall show some wisdom to say less and do more. Be not verbal in your purposes and protestations but real and royal in your performances.

Let me tell you plain what I think, and that is this. You have run yourself mightily in debt by this your sin, and unto divers, which must be discharged or you must lie by it awhile and die for it at the last. I speak not of your purse or charge before your filthiness was found out, while you lived closely in uncleanness. I have heard then you were base and sordid enough, perhaps so provident as to provide something against a rainy day. I speak not of your expenses in Newgate, or other prisons whither you have been most justly committed by Authority. I know you are not behind hand for paying these scores. These you have cleared.

But some other Creditors have entered actions against you and will be paid before you can be discharged.

What do you think you owe to God, whom you have so highly dishonored in the violation and transgression of that sacred and holy Law of his, peremptorily forbidding the sin of uncleanness. Item, to the world. I mean not by the world such as yourself, such as love filthiness as well as yourself, for I know that birds of a feather will fly together. Those that run with you to the same excess of riot will easily forgive you and not stand with you if it were a greater matter than this. But I speak of those that profess Religion in truth and sincerity, and so cannot but hate this sin wheresoever they find it. Here you have drawn blood, and that will bear an action and must be answered. You have wounded Religion, given just cause to the sons of Shem[51] to laugh at your nakedness, and as Nathan told David, by this deed you have given great occasion to the enemies of God to blaspheme (2 Sam. 12.14). What satisfaction can you ever make to that servant of yours, who by your base and beastly fornication with her came to a shameful and untimely death? Blessed had you both been if you had never seen each other's faces, for had she never known your face nor you her body you might perhaps (I say verily perhaps) have proved a better husband than before, and she lived in time to have been a wife for as good a man as yourself. She lost her life, and living and dying helped to save yours. I dispute not by what means she was wrought and brought to it. The Law was satisfied and I am contented.

What satisfaction can you make to God or the world for the blood of that sweet new born babe, murdered and made away by her by putting it alive, by some secret conveyance, into the house of office (an office fit for a whore and no mother).[52] I do not say nor charge you to be privy to the putting of it into the privy. I shall leave that to God and your own conscience, who (if you were) will not go behind your back when time shall serve to tell you of it. I judge you not. You were acquitted from the Law of man. God grant you may come off as fair with God, that he may never lay this sin unto your charge. Amen.

Last of all, what satisfaction can you make to this place and parish where you lived of late and a little too long? What dishonor have you done us in bringing this disgrace and casting this aspersion on us? What favors have you had successively amongst us? How often have you been invited to our public feastings? How usually called to our councils and meetings? How preferred to several places of offices with us? And after all this, to reward us thus, to cast this filth in our faces, to leave this stink behind you is base ingratitude. It must needs be a bad bird that thus defiles her own nest. We can count you no better you have used us so badly. We shall be willing to pray for your well-doing elsewhere, but not for your dwelling here till you be a little sweeter.

Shall I tell you in a word or two how you may make all well? I would set you this way if I were worthy to be your guide. First, begin with God and make your peace with him. As Elihu said to Job so I can advise you no better, "Acquaint thyself with God and be at peace, thereby shall good come unto thee" (Job 22.21).

And there can be no peace to be had with God but by hearty humiliation and sincere and sound repentance for former sins and unfeigned resolution for future holiness. "There is no peace, saith God, unto the wicked" (Isa. 57.21). "What peace," said Jehu unto Joram, "so long as the whoredoms of thy mother Jezebel, and her witchcrafts are so many?" (1 Kings 9.22). Rebels must lay down their arms if they look for peace or pardon. The best means to obtain remission of sins from God is man's submission for sins unto God. Where God takes the one with the one hand he ever gives the other with the other.

Let it now, I beseech you, be your care to return speedily unto God. Let this day's punishment beat you home to God, and like a sovereign medicine work kindly with you to purge your soul of your sins for the health and recovery of your soul. And when you go about this business, beware how you slight and slubber it over. It must be no easy or ordinary repentance that will serve the turn. Your offence hath been great, your humiliation must not be less. If you make not the plaster as large as the sore it will do you little good.

Cry therefore mightily unto God, and roar for the very disquietness of your heart. "Rend your heart and not your garments, and turn to the Lord" (Joel 2.13). With David make your bed to swim, and water your couch with your tears (Ps. 6.6). With Jeremiah wish that your head were waters and your eyes a fountain of tears, that you might weep day and night for this sin (Jer. 9.1). With Ephraim smite upon your thigh and be ashamed (Hos. 10.6). And with Peter go out and weep bitterly (Matt 26.75).

Eusebius in the Sixth Book of his Ecclesiastical history, chapter eight,[53] reports of one that, having sworn falsely against Narcissus, Bishop of Jerusalem, and seeing God's hand upon two other of his companions for their perjury, wept so abundantly that according to his own imprecation he lost both his eyes. I shall have much ado to persuade you to be so cruelly merciful to your own soul as to weep out but one eye. Yet for your comfort let me tell you that "it is more profitable that one member should perish, and not the whole body should be cast into hell" (Matt 5.29).

If you cannot mourn so much yet do what you may. Blessed shall you be if you thus mourn and that thus sowing in tears you may reap in joy. God send you such weather: a wet time here of sowing and the Sunshine of blessedness at the time of Harvest, when God shall wipe away all tears from your eyes.

And for that satisfaction which will give all the world best content, it will be when they see you prove an honest man. Blind not the eyes of the world with seeming holiness. Satan can (to serve his own turn) seem a Saint by transforming himself into an Angel of light. Judas heard many a good Sermon from his Master's mouth at Church and had many a good admonition in private and yet miscarried. And so may any such whose heart is not upright. Not the hearers but the doers of the Law shall be justified (Jas. 1.22).

To shut up all in a word, let me give you that holy counsel and gracious admonition which Simon Peter gave Simon Magus: "Repent of this your wickedness, and pray God if perhaps the thought of your heart may be forgiven you" (Acts 8.22). I will not add that which follows. I hope you are not in the gall of bitterness nor in the bond of iniquity. God never suffer you to come so near to hell. Turn over a new leaf. Resolve to practice our Saviour's counsel to one that (but changing the sex) was faulty as you are, found and taken in Adultery, "Go and sin no more" (John 8.11).

I have read of a certain Nun that, reading in a book she had, at the bottom of the leaf she found these words written, "it is good to know all things." Whereupon she resolved with herself to know what the carnal copulation of man and woman together might be. But turning over the leaf, the next words were, "but not use it," whereupon she presently changed her mind. So shall you do well to resolve to go from hence with a sealed purpose to become a new man. As it is said of Noah that when he awake from his wine, as Pareus observeth,[54] the good old man awaked from his wine and was very sorrowful for his sin (Gen. 9.25). And as it is said of Judah concerning his uncleanness with Tamar, "He knew her again no more" (Gen. 38.26), so let your repentance testify to the world a perfect detestation not of this sin only but a hearty reformation of all besides.

And as for me, let me promise and profess to you and for you, as Samuel did unto the people, terrified with a terrible tempest of thunder in the time of harvest, desiring Samuel's prayers, "Pray unto the lord for thy servants" (1 Sam. 12.19), whom Samuel comforted thus, "As for me, God forbid that I should sin against the Lord, in ceasing to pray for you" (1 Sam. 12.23). I will, God willing, do no less for you. I would to God with all mine heart I could do so well. And I hope I may promise as much for all here, whose sorrowful faces be dewed with so many tears at this time make me to persuade myself they pity your shame and pray to God for mercy to forgive your sin. Even so, God of mercy, hear and help, and let all here present say, Amen, Amen.

NOTES

1. Cain: murderer of his brother Abel (Gen. 4); Ishmael: son of Abraham by his concubine Hagar (Gen. 16:15); Esau: older son of Isaac (Gen. 25.21-26); Reuben: first son of Jacob, slept with his father's concubine (Gen. 35.22); Amnon: son of David, raped his half-sister Tamar (2 Sam. 13); Absalom: son of David (2 Sam. 15-18).

2. Weeds; cf. the parable of the sower (Matt. 13.18-32).

3. Ananias and Sapphira pretended to sell their worldly goods (Acts 5); Elymas: a magician who resisted Barnabas and Saul (Acts 13.6-11); Simon Magus: a magician who relapsed after his conversion and baptism (Acts 8.9-24).

4. St. Cyprian, A.D. c. 200-258, Bishop of Carthage, in *Treatise of the Lapsed* Ch.4.

5. A court of ecclesiastical jurisdiction, founded by the Act of Supremacy in 1588, abolished in 1641.

6. Cited in Plutarch's *Life of Marcus Cato*.

7. Louis IX, 1214-70.

8. Isabel I, 1451-1504, Queen of Castille.

9. Stretched.

10. Metellus, 183-115 B.C. and Scipio, 185-129 B.C., in Valerius Maximus, *The Memorable Deeds and Sayings* 4.1.

11. Julius Caesar, 101-44 B.C. and Pompey, 106-48 B.C.

12. St. Anselme, 1033-1109, Bishop of Canterbury.

13. Perhaps.

14. Threatening. A commination is included in *The Book of Common Prayer*: "A Commination or Denouncing of God's Anger and Judgments against Sinners."

15. Rodolphus Gualterus, 1518-86, Swiss theologian and reformer. He wrote numerous commentaries on the scriptures.

16. St. Thomas Aquinas, 1224-74, Italian theologian and philosopher; for his discussion of adultery, see *Summa Theologica* 72.2, 73.5 and 7.

17. The story of Abigail and David is at 1 Sam. 25; Tyre and Sidon were ancient Phoenician towns.

18. "Lord God, our Father."

19. Inflames the passions.

20. Desiderius Erasmus, 1466-1536, Dutch humanist and scholar who visited England numerous times.

21. Release.

22. In the last paragraph of his *Life of Alcibiades*.

23. Italian historian, also known as Paul the Deacon, d. 770.

24. Related to the expression, "A rod in pickle": a punishment in store or in reserve (pickle as brine, vinegar, or other salt or acid liquor used to preserve the rod).

25. Cooke here cites Deuteronomy 22 which does, however, prescribe death for adultery at verses 22-24.

26. God, from where he appeared to Moses at Exod. 3.

27. Erasmus also recounts this tale in his *Adages* 2.10.63. He takes it from Valerius Maximus, *Acts and Sayings of Ancient Romans*.

28. Peter Martyr or Pietro Vermigli, 1500-62, an Italian Protestant Reformer, theologian, and academic, who moved to England and then Switzerland. His commentaries on the two Books of Samuel were published in London in 1583.

29. Ruler of the Babylonian empire in the sixth century B.C.

30. Greek historian of the first century B.C., see his *Library of History* 1.78.2.

31. See Plutarch, *Moralia*, "The Greek Questions" 2.
32. First cousin.
33. Diogenes Laertius, *Lives of the Eminent Philosophers*, 6.47.
34. Worth four pence.
35. Quarter Sessions: court sittings held four times a year before justices of the peace. General Assizes: trials held before circuit judges commissioned by the Crown.
36. The quotation, from Prov. 5.3-4, continues, "drop as an honeycomb, and her mouth is smoother than oil. But her end is as bitter as wormwood, sharp as a two-edged sword."
37. Here, a synonym for Satan.
38. St. Augustine, A.D. 354-430, theologian and philosopher, Bishop of Hippo. One of his many texts on adultery was published in London in 1550.
39. Possibly Tossanus, 1541-1602, a Protestant divine and author of numerous commentaries on the Bible and defenses of Reformation doctrine.
40. Bishop of Worcester and chaplain to Henry VIII, 1490-1555.
41. Medieval bishop and surgeon, d. 1298.
42. St. Ulrich, c. 890-973.
43. British monk, author of commentaries on the Pauline epistles, d. after A.D. 419.
44. Possibly Jean Chartier, French monk and historiographer to Charles VII, d. 1462.
45. Founded first nunnery in Ireland, d. 524-28.
46. Pico della Mirandola, 1463-1494, Neoplatonist scholar and philosopher.
47. 1 Sam. 2.22.
48. After addressing Eglon thus, Ehud slays him.
49. Jael murdered Sisera by nailing his head to the ground (Judg. 4.21)
50. A pulpit in the old St. Paul's Cathedral.
51. One of Noah's three sons; the legendary forefather of Semitic peoples (Gen. 10.21-31).
52. House of office: a privy or latrine.
53. Bishop of Caesarea, A.D. 260-340.
54. David Woengler de Pareus, 1548-1622, German Protestant theologian, author of many Biblical commentaries and exegeses.

Moral and Religious Tracts

CHAPTER 3

An Apology for Women
William Heale

Disputes over women's roles in personal, social, and family relationships were waged vigorously throughout the Elizabethan and Jacobean periods. The content of many anti-feminist texts recycled claims and images from classical and biblical sources, while defenses of women tended to "call for praise and gratitude toward women rather than for change in women's roles" (Henderson and McManus 30). William Heale's *Apology for Women* falls into this second category, defending the rights of women and wives in a way that reinforces subordination to males. As Linda Woodbridge notes, "The Renaissance found the concept of marital equality incomprehensible because its view of order was hierarchical" (76). Nonetheless, at certain points in his tract Heale challenges the logical, legal, and rhetorical premises of the main current in misogynist texts.

Heale was probably born in 1581. He studied at Oxford and was appointed chaplain-fellow of Exeter College in 1608, before becoming a vicar in a local parish in 1610. He died in 1627. His single published work is the *Apology*, which was printed at Oxford by the University printer in 1609. Its subtitle provides details of the background and motivation for Heale's efforts: "An Opposition to Mr. Dr. G. his assertion. Who held in the Act at Oxford, 1608, That it was lawful for husbands to beat their wives." The title page also cites Colossians 3.19 in support, "Husbands love your wives, and be not bitter unto them."

Heale's opponent was William Gager, a Latin dramatist and poet at Oxford University (fl. 1580-1619). In the early 1590s, Gager had been in dispute with John Rainolds, defending the moral and religious validity of stage plays. No printed version of his 1608 thesis on husbands and wives is recorded. It seems that Gager's viewpoint was to carry more weight in the Oxford community than Heale's response, for the University historian Anthony Wood (his *Historia et Antiquitates Univ. Oxon.* appeared in 1674) sums Heale up as "always esteemed an ingenious man, but weak as being too much devoted to the female sex." This is also the note on which the short *Dictionary of National Biography* entry on Heale concludes. *An Apology for Women* thus sets the seal on its author's place in history.

Heale's self-deprecating preface is dedicated to a female patron, the "Lady M. H." While conventionally calling into question the work's effectiveness, it underlines "the strength of so good a cause." The six chapters introduce the subject "that it is not lawful for a husband to beat his wife," and then seek to prove and confirm it by "reasons drawn from Nature," "rules of morality or civil policy," "the Civil and Canon Laws," and "the law of God." The following extracts comprise chapters three and four of the *Apology*, on morality and law, and the conclusion.

In the common law of the period a husband was allowed to beat his wife, though not to such a degree that her health or life was endangered (Ingram 183). If her well-being was threatened, other people in the community or parish might intervene and the husband could be brought before the church courts. The preferred solution to such problems was, however, reconciliation, with neighbors, clergy, and court officials offering advice to this end.

As noted above, Heale criticizes the notion that wives are entirely subordinate to husbands. He uses a range of logical, rhetorical, and legal arguments to defend women's rights in marriage and to point out the hypocrisy and failings of the kind of case that Gager must have presented. To support his position, Heale constantly cites other authors, mainly classical (probably to counter the allusions of the classicist Gager) along with some references to the Bible and to various Renaissance authors including Petrarch, Vives, and Sidney.

The conclusion exemplifies Heale's position. It envisions harmony between husband and wife on the basis of his due authority and her due obedience. To this end, Heale recommends forms of discipline more moderate than beating: "admonition," a kind of gentle advice proceeding from the husband's patient love; and "reprehension," a more direct, verbal amendment of faults. Heale also emphasizes the importance of the example set by the husband, which provides a model for the wife's actions and responses. Hence as well as arguing for more equitable and humane treatment of women, the *Apology* reproduces the social implications of plays such as Shakespeare's *The Taming of the Shrew*, "conscientously modelling a series of humane but effective methods for behavioral modification" for women (Boose 198), even as its criticisms of the misogynist arguments are strongly made.

An Apology for Women was published only once, at Oxford in 1609 (*STC* 13014; Reel 725).

The Same Confirmed by the Rules of Morality or Civil Policy

Marriage of all human actions is the one and only weightiest. It is the present disposal of the whole life of man. It is a Gordian knot that may not be loosed but by the sword of death.[1] It is the ring of union whose poetry is Pure and endless. In a word, it is that state which either emparadiseth a man in the Eden of felicity or else exposeth him unto a world of misery. Hence it is that so mature deliberation is required before such an eternal bond be united. The mutual affection of each party, the consent of parents, the approbation of friends, the trial of acquaintance, besides the especial observance of disposition, of kindred, of education, of behavior. Now then, if a man solemnize marriage upon these due respects he can hardly make his choice amiss because he is guided by virtue which never faileth her followers. But if not, he may well be styled a fool because he is carried away with passion, which easily empoisoneth the best designs. The man therefore that is truly wise cannot but choose a virtuous wife, and so by consequent live quietly with her. And if any take a vicious woman it argues his own folly, and so by good reason may patiently endure her. For now he hath but that which before he desired, and he desired that which then he fancied, though indeed not from the informance of a true judgment but by the inducement of a giddy affection.

And yet in this unfortunate case, it is the greatest folly of all follies for a man to aggrandize his own misfortunes by quarreling with his own choice. For that dissension taketh away the very end and use of marriage, debarreth from all comfort and utility thereof, banisheth its joy and felicity, no man is so ignorant but he may well know, none so obstinate but he must needs acknowledge. What wife is there, so absolutely void of all passionate spleen, who will so lovingly perform her marriage rites, so carefully bring up her children, so providently order her house, so diligently direct her servants, for a disagreeing as for a loving husband? Who will buy blows as dear as she will pay for love? Or what husband is there, so clear without gall, that will so intentively augment his patrimony, so warily employ his stock, so heedily follow his affairs, so well in all things use all his diligence, for a wife whom he loatheth as for her whom he loveth? Who will be as devout a beadsman to the Saint he fancieth not as to him whom he chiefly adoreth? So that indeed, neither (as they should) caring for the other, both receive an infinite damage to themselves and for their posterity leave it most unfortunate. Unfortunate in their birth, for fear their dissentious parents derived to them their dissentious spirits. Unfortunate in their education, for fear their backward parents hindered their instruction. Unfortunate in their estate, for fear their careless parents diminished their portions. Unfortunate in their credit, unfortunate in all, for fear lest all their parents' faults redound unto the children's pain. When as in agreeing matches, where man and wife make up the sweet harmony of mutual love in a reciprocal consent and union, ye may observe a heaven of government, the husband intent on his business, the wife employed in her house, their children brought up religiously, their attendants, their servants, every one (as Virgil's commonwealth of Bees[2]) busied in his place. Whence towards the autumn of their years, they gather in the fruitful harvest of true friendship, of competent riches, of good estimation, of self-content.

But let us discard those utilities a while. And suppose thy wife not as thy wife but as a woman only. Tell me then, I pray (since every action of man must be tutored by some virtue or other), what appearance of virtue can it be for a man to beat a woman? It is not valor, because that demands equality of combatants. It is not wisdom, because that depends on a staid carriage. It is not justice, because that requires a serious deliberation. Not temperance, because that wants unsettled passion. And if none of these then no virtue at all, for all other virtues are comprised under them as some lesser dignity under a more ample style. Tell me likewise to what end should men attempt such violence? If a woman be perverse, she thereby amendeth not; if gentle, she deserves it not. If you seek praise thereby, you shall merit laughter; if reward, you shall be sure of shame. Whereas, therefore, you are guided by no virtue nor directed unto any end, who but stony hearts will lay their violent hands on a woman, the pattern of innocence, the Queen of love, the picture of beauty, the Mistress of delight? Who could with blows deface those rich ornaments of nature? Who could quarrel with her cheeks so purely mixed with Lilies and Roses? Who could violate those eyes, the spheres of light and lodestars of affections? Who could wrong those lips, such rubies of value and rivers of delight? Who would not imagine those ivory arms fitter for embracing than buffeting? And who but think those snowy hands more apt for a seamster's needle than a fencer's cudgel.

> Beauty must not acquaint her with the wars,
> And therefore hates such men as love such jars.[3]

And howbeit all women are not beautiful, neither hath nature bestowed all perfections on every wife. Yet a true-loving husband must imagine them all in his truly beloved wife. For love esteems not a thing beloved as in itself it is, but as it appears in the lover's eye. And therefore a woman that is not fair may yet make a fair wife in regard of her husband, as if she be only fair in her husband's thought. For he sees her with his own (not with others') eyes, loves her only with his own heart, enjoys her only to his own content. In her, then, whom need he to please but himself? So that if thy wife be not fairer to thyself than other women are, thou lovest her not truly.

And if thou lovest her not, why didst thou accept a loathed companion? Why didst thou dissemble with God before whom thou professedst love? Why didst thou lie unto Man in whose presence thou promisedst love? Or if she be (as indeed she should be) fairer in thine own eye because dearer to thine own heart, with what art canst thou turn rebel unto love and whom before thou lovedst presently hate her? Or remaining constant, with what face canst thou look upon thy beloved and instantly beat her? No, no. Heaven may as soon sink into hell as perfect love turn into hatred, and whole rivers of water may as well spring out of flames of fires as violent blows proceed from fervent love. In a word, therefore, if thou lovest not thy wife thou hast played the hypocrite, and so with shame maist beat her. But if thou lovest her thou hast performed thy vow, and so with due respect must honor her.

Neither may it be thought a small reason to deter all husbands from such violence to forecast the dangers that may ensue thereof. For diverse women being of a diverse stature, strength, complexion, and disposition, there must needs fall out a diverse event[4] of such an action. As for other men I dare not speak, and for Mr. Dr.[5] I know not what may befall. But if I should chance to marry with a stout and valiant woman, such as either Penthesilea was amongst the Amazons, or the Lady Parthenia of Greece, or the Empress Livia in Rome,[6] or some other of far less valor, and after a while from Cupid's wars fall unto Martial arms, I doubt my learning would not save me from some unlearned blows. If I should accept of a weak and feeble wife such a one whose courage is daunted with a word, whose innocence is her defense, whose yielding her resistance, and yet play the Tyrant still and so dispatch her, I am sure my law will not free me from the tribunal of heaven howsoever it clear me from the judgment of man. Suppose I should marry a modest matron, whose speech, gate, carriage, and behavior are as clear as Crystal, all without blemish, and yet all please me not without some civil wars. How should I live, offensive to my friends, upbraided by mine enemies, of most men hated, beloved of none? Lastly, if I should light on a light housewife who yet being civilly entreated might civilly demean herself, but being trodden upon (as every worm) will turn again, how justly might I wear Vulcan's nightcap[7] on fools' holidays and in sad devotion do perpetual homage unto the new moon. Now therefore, a far safer course it is for us to lay aside our weapons and rest in terms of love than to venture ourselves in so doubtful a jeopardy. And let our wives be what they be, it is our wisdom now to love them since it was our fortune first to have them.

And as the private event of this action must needs be inconvenient unto ourselves, so the public example thereof is dangerous unto the commonwealth. For whatsoever in this kind is committed within our own family is acted (as it were) on an open theater where we have store of spectators: our children, our servants, our neighbors, sometimes our nearest kindred, oft times our dearest friends. Who perchance (as most men are), being ready to follow the ill example of others, may prove by little and little the very abstracts of impiety. Especially when in this case we have experience of so many cruel and execrable murders. Some through open tyranny, as of Pompeia by Nero; some through secret villainy, as of Apronia by Sylvanus.[8] Some through strangling, some through poisoning, some through false accusing, too many through pining away at their husband's unkindness. Withal which kinds I could have wished that this our white Albion had never been bespotted. Now, in those heinous crimes, though thyself perchance abhorrest to be an actor, yet to teach the principles which breed these conclusions or to be the exemplary cause which bringeth forth these effects will appall any moral man and touch a Christian's conscience. For faulty is he that gives the occasion as well as he who commits the action, seeing men are as greedy to catch at opportunity as a fish to leap at the hook, especially when the one hath a pretense of law as the other a show of bait.

Besides, it is a main hindrance to any public preferment. For how can he be thought fit to manage the affairs of a commonwealth who is not able to keep orders in his own house? How can he well preserve peace among the unconstant many who is at daily strife in his own family? Gorgias the Rhetorician made an oration unto the Grecians, being then in some civil broils, to persuade them unto concord. And having generally won the hearts of both sides, Melanthius his adversary replied, "O ye foolish Grecians, is this fellow fit to persuade you concord who lives himself in perpetual dissension? Can he rule the whole city (think you) in peace, where are so many diverse minds as there are diverse men, and was yet never able to govern his house in quiet where are none but his wife and himself?" Which speech of his to this effect so possessed the people that what before they were fully persuaded of they now but faintly believed, and so by degrees falling into a perfect relapse of discord. Whereas at the beginning they entertained him with good applause, in the end they hissed him from the bar with this acclamation: "Gorgias rule thyself first at home, then after rule us at Olympia." Neither was this Gorgias his fortune only, but it is a common brand of infamy to all his followers, who always by their ill private carriage draw unto them suspicion of their like public government.[9]

Wherefore antiquity hath been very provident herein. When as the chief guests at their marriage-feasts used to offer sacrifice for those that were married, but before they came unto the altar they purified their oblation from its gall and spiced it with fragrant odors. A custom in my sense not so ceremonious as judicious, whose moral is given by the best moralist to pretend a duty of man and wife, that in them should be no gall or bitterness but the sweet relish of pleasing love. They themselves should be as Virgil's vine and elm, the tenderness of the one supported by the other's strength.

Their hearts as Leda's twins both interchangeably embracing each other. Their house as Plato's city, wherein nothing must be called mine or thine but all things common unto them both.[10] Nothing peculiar to the husband, nothing proper to the wife, which upon either's occasion is not to be imparted to the other. And if those singular pairs and parallels of friends (whose fame with golden wings flies throughout the world) nothing was singular, all things mutual: in prosperity mutual joy, mutual sorrow in adversity, in adventures mutual aid, mutual triumph in victories, in all things mutual love, the mother of all this mutuality, what less can we expect in marriage, a stronger bond than friendship, where to the present fruition of a friendly mate is added the hopeful expectation of future issue?

Now, we never read nor heard of any of those friends who gave a blow unto his friend, either moved thereunto on violent passion or otherwise induced by any occasion. Why then should husbands sue for a toleration to beat their wives to whom, as they are in society more nearly linked, so in love more dearly engaged than to their dearest friend? Many are the friendly offices of thy friend, many more of thy wife. She sits at thy table, she lies in thy bosom, she shares of thy grievances and lessens the burden, she participates thy pleasures and augments the joy. In matters of doubt she is thy counselor, in case of distress thy comforter. She is a co-partner with thee in all the accidents of life. Neither is there any sweeter taste of friendship than the coupling of souls in this mutuality either of condoling or comforting, where the oppressed mind finds itself not altogether miserable since it is sure of one which is feelingly sorry for his misery. And the joyful spends not his joy either alone or there where it may be envied, but freely sends it to such a well-grounded object from whence he shall be sure to receive a sweet reflection of the same joy and, as in a clear mirror of sincere goodwill, see a lively picture of his own gladness. For which cause especially (as I conceive) Isocrates condemns him for most lewdly disposed who, by his fair speech and close demeanor hath wooed a virgin and in pomp and joviality married her his wife, will yet through anger or folly live at variance with her. Seneca terms the brawls in marriage worse than divorce from marriage. Cato plainly calls it sacrilege for a husband to beat his wife.[11] Such as is the soul (saith Plutarch) in regard of the body, such is the husband in respect of his wife: both do live in union, in disjunction both do perish. True love is the best amatory or chief medicine to breed true love. And therefore if thou look truly to be beloved of thy wife, first love her truly. For else how canst thou require that for thyself of her which thou affordest not from thyself unto her. She may in this case answer thee as L. Crassus the Senator replied on L. Philippus the Consul: "How should I show myself a Senator unto you, whereas you behave yourself not as a Consul towards me?"[12] How should a wife prove loving unto her husband when as her husband proves not loving unto her? For both in love and friendship the demand of Martial unto his Marcus stands with good reason:

> If Pylades thou wilt me have,
> Then (Mark) I'll thee Orestes crave.
> And not in words thou must it prove;
> Wilt be belov'dst then thou must love.[13]

Love is a relation and must have two subjects for its residence, as well the husband as the wife. If it find not good entertainment with one it departs from both. Both therefore must be like Crateres and Hyparchia, who were said to see with double eyes because in mutual love they acquainted one the other with passage of all things that concerned them.[14] So that as the Prophets in Israel were sacredly entitled Seers because they had a double sight of nature and from God (1 Sam 9.9), so was Crateres in Athens jestingly termed a Seer because he used a double sight, his wife's and his own.

And howsoever we exclaim against women, that they are unworthy of such respect by reason of the multiplicity of their supposed infirmities, such words often flash forth indeed but from the pregnancy of wit not from the soundness of judgment, spoken either from a prejudicate opinion, which ever miscarrieth, or from particular example, which never concludeth. For instance, we may hold them unconstant in their resolutions, shallow in their judgment, lavish of their tongue, and with so many weaknesses beweaken this weak sex as that we may revive that old theorem hissed long ago from off the stage of virtue:

> Of womankind found good there's none:
> And if perchance there be found one,
> I know not how it comes to pass,
> The things made good that evil was.

A flat impiety against the all Creator's all-sufficiency, who when he had built this world's fair house looked in every corner thereof and saw that all was good. Yet they in the fairest room of all have found that all is naught. And if you fly from their first unspotted creation unto their now corrupted disposition, what privilege have men beyond women? They are both made of one metal, cast both in the same mold. All are not good, nor the most best. But if any might challenge pre-eminence it should seem the woman might, whose complexion is purer, which argues a richer wit; whose passions are weaker, which pretend a more virtuous disposition. In fine, therefore, dislike of them we cannot whom nature hath every way so curiously framed, unless we more dislike of ourselves who are the monuments of her rougher workmanship.

Yet for your pleasure's sake, suppose women to be as bad as you would have them. Say they are past all virtuous modesty. Swear they are beyond all hopeful recovery. Be it so. I demand then, wherefore should they be beaten? None but final punishment is there to be inflicted where the person punished cannot be amended. Women (say you) are past amendment, and therefore (say I) they are past punishment. It is an axiom in Philosophy that where the cause is taken away, the effect perisheth, and it is again as firm a position in humanity[15] that amendment is the chief (if not sole) cause of every such punishment. There being then no hope of the one, there ought likewise be no exaction of the other. Now, that women will never be amended, it is as common a phrase in our adversary's mouth as "what lack ye" in the Exchange.[16] So that it was grown long since unto a proverb:

They wash a jeat[17]
To make it white as snow,
Who women beat
To make them vice forego.

Lastly, Aristotle (whose words are maxims in Philosophy, and his *ipse dixit*[18] an authentical proof) seemeth herein to soar above himself, and leaving his wonted school of humanity to speak from out the sacred chair of divinity. The divine providence (saith he) so framed man and woman that they of necessity must be of one society, otherwise how could they perpetuate the world by their offspring's succession, since neither man without woman, nor woman without man can have any issue? Wherefore they were made both like and yet dislike. Like in specific nature, their bodies of the like feature, their souls of the same essence. Dislike in the individual, the one hotter and drier, the other colder and moister, that out of this disagreeing concord of a divers temper should proceed the sweet harmony of agreeing love. The one stronger, the other weaker, that the stronger in love should demean himself more royally, the weaker for fear should behave herself more courteously. The one valiant and laborious in the fields, the other mild and diligent within the doors, that what the one had painfully gotten abroad the other might carefully conserve at home.[19] The one fairer and as a delightsome picture of beauty, the other more stern and as a perfect mirror of manhood. The one more deeply wise, the other of a more pregnant wit. Both which being by the sacred power of marriage made but one, the first condition of their Union is that no wrong should be done by either to the other. For by the Pythagoreans' law of hospitality it was decreed that none who entered into another's house should for the time of his abode there suffer any kind of injury upon any occasion. A husband taketh his wife from her friends, disacquainteth her with her kinfolks, debarreth her her parents' sight, and estrangeth her from whomsoever was dearest unto her. He takes her into his own hospitality, receives her into his own protection, and himself becomes her sole Guardian. Wherefore then to beat and abuse her is the greatest injury that can be against the law of hospitality.

This law (we read) was so religiously observed of Antiquity that had anyone come under their roof (though he were their mortal enemy) yet dared they do no other but entertain him with fair language and send him away with safe conduct. And hence it was that Themistocles,[20] being banished from Athens and pursued by the Athenians, was forced to fly for rescue unto the house of that citizen who had ever been his mortal enemy and at that present the present cause of his banishment. Whereinto nevertheless being entered, he was courteously received and delivered forth in friendly manner. Should then a Christian deal more roughly with his wife than the heathen would with their enemy? Surely the world will condemn us for men of little wisdom, or else it would never have commended them for their laudable custom. Let me join unto Aristotle a follower of his, a worthy philosopher and famous Doctor, whose opinion is that wives are to be persuaded by reason not compelled by authority, led on by persuasion not drawn by compulsion, induced by lenity not constrained by severity. For they are one flesh, one mind, together with us. Howbeit then this mind be troubled with perturbations and this flesh be wounded with affections, yet should we seek some cordial to heal them not a Corrosive to afflict them. For by afflicting them we afflict ourselves. But to pass this easier combat and to enter the lists with you in your own school, give me leave to ask counsel of the Law in this case.

The Same Discussed by the Civil and Canon Law
And as the law in general is generally held the groundwork and foundation of a commonwealth, in whose bosom justice is seated the sole preserver of good government, so the Canon and Civil of all other the species are by most approved (yet how justly I cannot tell) the chiefest forms thereof.[21] Whether it be for its largeness and universality, because observed in almost all our Christian world, or for its plainness and perspicuity because applied well near to each particular case of each several estate. Nevertheless in these also, by my slender observation, I have found a certain kind of strictness and obdurity against no condition more than against the estate of wives. For instance, it decrees a wife shall lose her dowry for giving a lascivious kiss. That a wife is legally bound to follow her husband wandering at his pleasure from city to city, be it from one land into another region, be it from her own country into banishment itself, especially if it be in pilgrimage unto the holy land. That the wife is only dignified by the husband, and not any ways the husband graced by the wife. That the husband's suspicion of his wife's lightness may be the wife's expulsion from her husband's company. Lastly, if a wife play the Adulteress (a fault indeed

deserving no excuse), her husband may then produce her into public judgment, deprive her of her promised dowry, and expose her to perpetual divorcement. But if the husband commit the like offence, though it were as open as the sun and as odious as hate itself, yet the wife may not in public as much as open her mouth against it. Infinite such other. Hard impositions in my weak sense for so weak a sex. And such also as long since have been deplored by Syra in the Comedian:

> Alas we women live in servile awe,
> But men enjoy a freedom of the law.
> For if a husband serve in Venus pay
> Apparently, the wife must nothing say.
> Yet if a wife chance steal her wantonness,
> The law is open for the man's redress.
> But were the laws equal to both the same,
> We soon should see who most deserveth blame.[22]

If the adultery of a wife be a wrong unto the husband, why not the adultery of a husband an injury unto the wife? Or if suspicion only may discharge a man of his wife, who is more happy than the jealous husband, who as often as his mind changeth may therewithal change his wife? Or if all the luster and glory of wedlock descend only from the husband unto the wife and none reflect again from the wife unto the husband, it is hard to be conceived how there can be a true society or a fit match. The like may be said of the rest. But all are so palpably against reason that there is no reasonable man who will seem to reason for them.

Now, the rigor and severity of these and the like laws against women are supposed by some to have proceeded from the lawgivers' not hate but ignorance. Who for the most part (altogether the Canonists) being single and unmarried men knew not so well the estate and mystery of marriage. And so conceiving perchance no better of a wife than as a man's best servant, ranked them in a degree of too low servility. Neither is there reason improbable. For who can discern the sun's brightness that never saw the light? Who can judge of a pure scarlet who never was acquainted with difference of colours? Who can give a true censure in scholarship who never was so much as baptized at the Muses' font? Right so, who can rightly estimate the rites of marriage who never knew the happiness thereof?

But I accuse not the law. For these former positions are for the most part but deductions from thence. Neither reprehend I these Law-givers, for they were ancient trophies of yet-living glory. Yet needs must I find some fault with some interpreters of the law, who fit the square unto the timber not the timber unto the square, working the law as a waxen nose hither and thither as the tide and tempest of their brainsick fancy drives them. Which nowhere is more apparently seen than in the case we have now in hand. For in the whole body of either Law, Canon or Civil, I have not yet found (neither, as I think, hath any man else) set down in these or equivalent terms, or otherwise passed by any positive sentence or verdict, that it is lawful for a husband to beat his wife. But whatsoever is cited thence are either far-fetched conclusions or unfriendly sequels, which hang as well together being touched in judicial trial as the joints of a rotten carcass engibbeted, being tossed with a violent wind.

There being nothing then directly against us in the substance of the law, let us see what the shadows thereof, I mean the Interpreters, please to determine. Whose opinions I find as various as they make the subject of their opinion inconstant. And therefore I must place them in their several ranks.

In the first, such who peremptorily hold it lawful. But finding themselves o'erpressed with contrary reasons, as men altogether desperate use such turnings and windings, such evasions and contradictions, such poor shifts and trivial sophisms, as the learned may well laugh at, the ignorant perchance admire. If you have seen a mill-horse passing his circle or a spaniel turning round after his tail, you may justly conceive how those men tread the maze of their uncertain opinion. Some of them, and amongst this bad the best, hold it lawful but not convenient. Silly men, not knowing that good laws are never the direct authors of inconvenience. Some, a little more frantic than the first, think it lawful and convenient too, but it must be but a little forsooth,[23] slightly and but seldom. Having indeed forgotten or else having never learned that circumstances can but lessen a fault, never, of an action absolutely evil, convert it into good. Some other there are, the overgrown monsters of tyranny, who proclaim it from out the top of folly that a husband may beat his wife much or little according to his pleasure and as the occasion is. Nay more, that he may publicly shame her and if he lists imprison her too. Men who seem to have banished all humanity, of an iron heart, of a brazen brow, and both so cankered with vice that virtue can get no impression. For what is it that letteth loose the reins unto fury and gives madness its whole scope? What is it that violates the holy rites of marriage? What is it that infringeth the sacred bonds of love? What is it that breeds horrid and domestical massacres? What is that abolisheth all virtuous and matrimonial society if this do not?

In the second rank are those who out of a staid judgment and upright mind hold it not only unlawful but an odious, unmanly, and unseemly thing. Odious in respect of the breach of their faith given in wedlock. Unmanly in regard of woman's weakness and imbecility. Unseemly for example's sake. And therefore, in consideration of all, is altogether unlawful. Learned and virtuous men,

> Whose praise the sacred Goddess of eternity
> Keeps hallowed in the eternal shrine of fame.
> Virtue doth build them trophies; Dignity

Crowns their desert and waits upon their name.
And worthy are they of a marble stone,
Made blessed by a Homer's pen or none.[24]

In the third are such who, though they have written whole tracts and large volumes concerning the estate of wives, of their dowries, of their inheritance, of their portions, of their vows, of their divorcements, and like infinite circumstances, yet have not a word of this question nor vouchsafe to grace it with a graceful term. Perchance because they thought it so heinous and ugly a paradox as unfit to be matched with so many honest and goodly precepts of the law, or else so vile a position as unworthy to be affirmed by a Lawyer.

These are the opinions. So disagreeing you see and altogether contrary that whosoever weigheth them in the true scales of an upright judgment can by them but hardly rest satisfied in them. For where truth seemeth to have taken up her seat there authority disguiseth her, and where she cannot be found there fancy would needs descry her. Every man making an Idol of his own conceit and partially impairing another man's judgment. Not finding therefore in them the certainty we seek for, let us compare reason unto reason, oppose Lawyer unto Lawyer, confer opinion with opinion. And drawing from the law itself certain grounds and foundations in this point, by the full clearing of them we shall give a fair light unto our intended purpose.

My first ground shall be the superiority of husbands over their wives, whereunto answereth the reverence of wives towards their husbands. This superiority appeareth first in the manner of their first wedlock, wherein the woman was made of man and for man, and given intuition by God unto man. Secondly, in the difference of their sex, because Nature and the God of Nature in every kind hath given pre-eminence unto the male. Thirdly, in man's universal sovereignty, which he received over all creatures when God installed him his viceroy over all the world (Gen. 1.28 and 2.20-23). And howsoever it was not so absolute a prerogative in regard of his fellow-woman as it was in respect of others, because she was joined in commission with him. Yet such it was as might well bear the title of superiority for the man and of the woman require a duty of reverence. But neither is the one so predominant nor the other so servile as that from them should proceed any other fruits but of a royal protection and loyal subjection.

My second ground shall be the power or command of husbands over their wives, whereunto answereth the obedience of wives towards their husbands. And here I need not to weary out my pen in deciding the controversies touching the authority of husbands concerning their wives' goods, possessions, lands, dowries, and the like. Only pertaining to my purpose is the command over their persons, which the law determines to consist partly in imposing on them convenient labors for the supportance of their estate, chiefly in exacting the rights of marriage for the procreation of children and avoidance of lust. To the former, as much as in her lieth the wife must yield obedience. To the latter (unless on some restrictions which modesty refers unto my margins[25]), she is legally bound to give contentment. Nevertheless in both, hard it is to be judged whether the husband should command with greater obeisance[26] or the wife obey with greater command. Both so unitedly strive to express the effects of so perfect a union. Both so interchangeably labor for the building up of the Temple of love.

My third ground shall be the correction lawfully used by husbands against their wives, whereunto answereth the submission required of wives unto their husbands. This correction, being a punishment, must (according to the rule of law) be proportioned unto the fault punished. The faults of wives towards their husbands are all comprised under three several degrees, and therefore the punishments likewise must be of three several sorts.

In the first and highest degree are faults altogether unexcusable, never committed by any virtuous or modest wife, never endured by any loving or honest husband. Such are the defiling of his marriage bed, or against his life and person any treacherous exploit. For these the law sets down direct punishments. For the former divorce from the bond of marriage, for the second expulsion from the community of wedlock.[27] And in neither case are the husbands engaged for payment of their dowry or any ways bound for relief of their poverty. Mistake me not. I only intend that the prosecution hereof lieth in the husband's power not the execution. For that must be consummate in lawful manner: the fact proved by lawful witness, the verdict given by a lawful judge. So that the jealousy of husbands touching their wives' inconsistency or suspicion otherwise concerning their disloyalty before they come into actual proof are no actual faults of the wife but to be adjudged as the brainsick fancies of their fond husbands. Be the suspicion of the one vehement, it beareth indeed the better color and deserveth the sharper trial. But for the jealousy of the other it is a common ill humor, and therefore in wisdom nothing at all to be esteemed. Jealousy is a child conceived of self-unworthiness and of another's worth, at whose birth fear made it an abortive in nature and a monster in love. For the jealous man, unworthily loving a worthily beloved object, stands in fear of communicating his good unto another more worthy. So that neither is his love perfect because mixed with fear which love abhorreth, nor his fear medicinable because conjoined with love which fear empoisoneth. But of both ariseth this mongrel kind of jealousy, a loving fear or a fearful love. Wherein (contrary to all other actions of man) we bend all our diligence and carefulness to obtain the full sight and perfect assurance of our own misery.

We would needs forsooth know ourselves to be such Beccoes[28] as we fear to be. For of prevention there is no hope. Our English worthy can tell us:

> Sure 'tis no jealousy can that prevent
> Whereto two persons once be full content.[29]

Being then that these imaginations of husbands are not in law the faults of a wife, and when it chanceth that such great faults are they are determined of their lawful punishments, whatsoever other corrections are added in this case are done besides the law.

In the second degree are faults of another nature, far inferior to the former and yet of some moment also. Such may be their backwardness in the religious service of God, carelessness in managing their household affairs, ill behavior towards their neighbors and friends, misdemeanor in regard of themselves and husbands. These I confess to be as so many roots of weed planted in the fair garden-plot of a woman's mind, spreading into many crooked branches and bearing much bitter fruit. In these, therefore, the law alloweth husbands to use reprehension either sharper or milder, according as the quality of the fault requireth and as their own modest discretion findeth convenience. Yet nevertheless, these faults are not so absolutely evil but that they might admit some kind of excuse. Insomuch as they may thereby be somewhat extenuated though perchance not peremptorily defended.

For the first, there is no man so irreligious but commends a religious woman, especially a religious wife in whom religion is especially needful both for instruction of her family and education of her children. But if in such an imagination of religion fall into some peevish zeal through ignorance, or through some small measure of knowledge amount unto a womanish resolution, it had been better they had been less studious in those points, where the best fruit of their labors is a plentiful sheaf of errors. Wherefore for my part, I could never approve those too too holy women gospellers, who wear their testament at their apron-strings and will weekly catechize their husbands, citing places, clearing difficulties, and preaching holy sermons too if the spirit of their devotion move them. For sure I am, antiquity held silence to be a woman's chiefest eloquence and thought it their part to hear more than to speak, to learn rather than to teach. As well then too much curiosity of religion as too much neglect is a fault in women. So that if their frailty lead them into either extreme the husband hath the bit of reprehension in his power to keep them in the golden mean.

Again, if a wife be over-frugal it may be supposed it is for the augmenting of her husband's estate and benefit of his children. If she be very bountiful, it may be thought she intends her husband's credit and supportance of his estimation. Likewise, if others mislike her carriage it may be her modesty seemeth pride unto them or her familiarity otherwise breedeth contempt. Lastly, if through infirmity she fall into any inconvenience, some things are to be given to the weakness of her sex, some matter of excuse there is in the rareness of such offence. In all or either of these aggrievances, the husband hath always the reins in his own direction. And what more sovereign medicine than a husband's tender reprehension? What is there that can more effectually move than a word from his mouth? What sooner enforce allegiance than a frown of his countenance?

In the last and lowest degree are some small and trivial faults. Indeed virtues in their own nature but in their practice perchance are tainted with some savor of vice. Such may be the nimbleness of women's tongues, which although may sometimes be employed to their husband's disturbance yet for the most part are busied in their good. In merchandizing for their profit, in refreshing their wearied spirits, oft times in entertaining their friends with courteous compliment, commonly in the usual performance of other such offices as usually belong to such a quality. Of this sort likewise are women's affected curiosity of apparel, their over-nice standing on preeminence, their womanish dislikings, and their fond longings, with other such slender errors, obliquities[30] rather of nature than faults in manners. All which a husband might easily reform, either in his wisdom not stooping so low as to take notice of them or from out his love mildly to touch them. Howsoever, his allowance in these points is only admonition. Which as it is the fairest kind of correction so it taketh the best effect in any good nature. You know that many sorts of soft waters will pierce deeper than the dint of hardest steel. And many things by mildness have been accomplished which through violence could never. Policy goeth beyond force in martial actions, wisdom beyond rigor in domestical affairs. And far safer is the obedience yielded up on fair terms than that which is constrained on foul conditions. For the one proceeds from love and is even filial, the other cometh of fear and is only servile.

Now, that there cannot be thought any misdemeanor of a wife towards her husband not comprised under one of these three is by discourse plainly manifest. And that there ought not to be used by a husband towards his wife any other correction besides these three shall evidently be proved.

Concerning the former. Our haters of women have indeed well imitated the old Tragedians, whose use it was when they would set forth any odious scene to pluck the ears of their auditors down into hell, to invocate the furies, to muster up cursed spirits and whatsoever was most ugly to the eye of their understanding, to the end they might make their expression more vehement and leave a deeper impression behind them. They likewise are well-skill'd in this excellent art of railing. They conjure up whole catalogs of vices, they number out numberless obliquities, and rake together as many sins as the world is guilty of, fastening them on women as on the authors and actors of them all. Pride (say they) and greater than another pride, the pride of self-worth in unworthiness, avarice, anger, luxury, gluttony, slothfulness, envy are the usual inhabitants of a woman's mind. It much offendeth not that they are ungrateful to their friends, impatient in their choler, babblers of their tongue, witty in their deceits, willful in their resolutions, ambitious, flattering, lustful, dissembling, but that they will needs also prove the cutthroats of friendship and yet seem to be our friends. A punishment for man and yet an inevitable punishment. A temptation of man and yet a natural temptation. A calamity to man and yet a desired calamity. An absolute and yet a necessary evil. Infinite are their reproaches. And I should forget the nature of an apology if I spake any farther in their foul language.

First, then, let me give these Cynics to understand that their trade is not now so good as they could wish it were, for their chief ware, detraction, is held but for children's rhetoric. And Invectives are counted the poorest share in learning. They are but the froth of an apish invention, the purge of an idle brain, the falling-sickness of a giddy wit, flat heresies in true scholarship. For when you have spoken all that malice can speak against woman, what yet have you spoken that may not be applied unto men? Sin (you may remember) is of the neuter gender, and therefore neither hateth the one sex nor cleaveth unto the other but is too familiarly acquainted with both masculine and feminine. Was Lais a whore?[31] She was but one. Many men in Athens were her minions, but I strain not the comparison.

All women (you say) are altogether evil. Of men you are sure there are some good. And are they evil all? Why then, O grave Plutarch, how came it to pass thy wisdom so failed thee? Ancient Hesiod, who corrupted thy mature judgement? Caelius, who beguiled thy wits? Chaucer, how miscarried thy golden pen? Learned and most holy Saints, St. Jerome, St. Gregory, St. Cyprian, St. Chrysostom, who deceived you all?[32] For deceived you all are (if this position be received) who have severally written several tracts in honor of honorable women. Are they all evil? How came the whole world then to be so besotted as to record a famous memory of many millions of them? Of canonized Saints, of constant Martyrs, of grave matrons, of chaste virgins, of most virtuous and unspotted wives? Neither are such as I speak of Phoenixes, rare and but seldom found. Search all histories, travel with the sun round about the earth, recall the former days even from the world's minority, and compare them with the latter times unto this present age, you shall find that the number of virtuous women may well equalize the number of men that have been virtuous. And howbeit I cannot say that there is any woman, such an absolute paragon of virtue, who is void of all vice. Venus had her mole, the brightest sun suffers an eclipse, the purest gold is not without some dross, nor the best of women free from all reproof. Yet thus I say, to object all vices whatsoever have been in all women in general unto every woman in particular is most injurious. Were such a conclusion of any force, I would thus dispute Catiline was a traitor, Verres a thief, Nero a murderer, Aegistus an adulterer, Machivell atheistical, Jovianus heretical, Battus a fool, others other such.[33] These all were men; Misogynes is a man; therefore Mysogynes is a traitor, a thief, a murderer, an adulterer; he is atheistical, he is heretical, he is a fool, or what else you please. The form of argumentation is your own. Which if you dislike, you clear women of whatsoever is here spoken against them. If approve, you have all this while traveled with the Pelican, and the birth of your own child will be your own (if not destruction) yet discredit.

By this time perchance your heat is qualified, and you think them not as before you did, absolute evils, but refining your phrase term them in the last edition, Necessary evils. This indeed is the common tenure, and most men think they have judiciously spoken when thus they have defined the case. That they are necessary therefore I will easily grant since he that made man saw it was not good that man should be without them. That they are evils I utterly deny since he that made woman saw that all he made was good. Is woman good then in the judgment of God and in your conceit also necessary? Then once again you must alter your style, and henceforth write her a Necessary good. For these very terms Necessary and evil are incompetent. They are at dissension amongst themselves. They cannot stand peaceably together. All things that are necessary for man are good: food is necessary, it is good; apparel necessary, it is good. The fire, the air, the earth, the water necessary, they are good. Women necessary, and therefore good. For else if we suppose that God hath bound man in so hard a condition that some things are left necessary for him yet evil, we both impair the wisdom of God and detract from his goodness. But to satisfy some chief authors of this received opinion, I answer that some women are less good than others and thence they incur the name of evil. And nature requiring a necessity of them, thence they receive that title of necessary. And from both they are branded with the infamy of Necessary evils, an attribute yet not appropriate unto them but usually also applied unto men. Alexander Severus, an Emperor of Rome, called his counselors necessary evils, his provincials necessary evils, the officers in his court necessary evils. Hybicus in like sort called Euthydemus his friend his necessary evil. Varro, his testy brother his necessary evil. Martial, his angry companion his necessary evil, with whom (saith he) I can neither live well nor yet live without him.[34]

But to break of this idle cavilation, which hath too long withheld me from my purposed course. Let Mysogynes steep his quill in the gall of Invection, let him speak with as open a mouth as ever Satire did, yet all that can be alleged as offences of wives against their husbands are only such as either are expressly mentioned or else directly may be reduced unto my three former heads.

Secondly, then, that the corrections lawfully used by a husband unto his wife ought to be no other than I have prescribed remains as yet to be more amply proved. For the first, that divorcements in cases prefixed are the sole and only lawful punishment, the law itself affords so fair testimonies and the practise of all Lawyers hitherunto have given so full confirmation, that now it is too late either to be denied or gainsaid. For the two other Marcus Aurelius, a Consul sometimes and Counselor shall speak for me: "A wife (saith he) is often to be admonished, to be reprehended, but seldom, never, to be dealt withal with violent hands."[35] Where you see not only a flat denial of any rigorous sort of correcting wives, but withal a plain assertion of my prescribed punishments, admonition and reprehension.

Admonition it is that with a tender hand bendeth up the wound of a friend, and therefore most needful in marriage, the nearest of any friendship. Hence the law enjoins us to deal with our wives in mild terms, in loving talk, in gentle and fair speech. That whereas by nature women are mild, loving, gentle, and fair, they might not choose but best accept that from others which is most like unto themselves. Mercury (saith Plutarch) was seated the next God unto Venus because in marriage there is always need of settled reason and a fair language. Mars was then ushering of Jupiter in a place remote because that wars are only fit for kings and states.

Reprehension we have added in the second place, that where admonition with its smooth carriage prevailed not there reprehension with sharper entreaty might take effect. Hence the law counseleth that overmuch lenity is to be mixed with some few grains of severity, and of them both to be made a third temperature or golden compound called Mediocrity. By which all our reproofs we shall be so guided as, neither using too much exasperation or indulgence, we may soon reform whatsoever offence. God commanded that in the Ark of the Tabernacle, directly over his two Statute-tables, should be Manna preserved, but together with Moses rode.[36] Papirius set up before the Senate house in Rome the image of Mercy but placed Justice therewithal.[37] Jupiter,

> To his entreaty and his fair persuasion,
> Adjoined threatenings in his princely fashion.[38]

What God himself prescribed in matters legal, Papirius in civil, Jupiter in Imperial, the like may we likewise follow in managing of domestical and uxorial affairs. If the Manna allured not, the rod should constrain; if commiseration prevailed not, justice should succeed; if prayers were rejected, threatenings should terrify; and if a husband's admonitions be not esteemed, his reprehension then should not be spared.

In both which kinds of correction our success shall be the far more effectual if we lead the way before by our example, which by our words we persuade our wives to follow. For the abbreviary[39] of a husband's words and actions is, as it were, the chamber-glass whereby a wife should address herself. At his tongue she should learn to speak, by his carriage she should compose her behavior. And a thousand times safer way it is (as, in a case not much different, Pacatus told Theodosius[40]) to govern by example than by severity. Every good example is a most pleasing invitation unto virtue, where the eye is guided unto present action not the ear fed with feigned speculation. And hereupon was Petrarch his opinion grounded, that a mimical[41] husband will make a lascivious wife, a riotous husband a voluptuous wife, a proud husband a proud wife, a modest and honest husband a modest and honest wife.[42] Wherefore it is St. Augustine's counsel that such as we would have our wives appear unto us, the same we should first approve ourselves unto them. Would we have them chaste of their body, civil in their carriage, pure and unspotted of the world? We then must walk before them as the patterns of chastity, of civility, of irreprehension.[43] For what reason have we to expect more of them than we can perform of ourselves? It is a silly master that offendeth in those faults for which he is offended with his pupil. So is it an impudent and impious fellow (saith Seneca) who of his wife requireth an undefiled bed, yet he himself defiles it. By our virtuous demeanor then we must direct them in the way of virtue, for there are none of them vicious who will stick to tell us that we are their masters. It is reported by esteemed authors that in some places the husbands are punished only for the faults of their wives. In Catalonia, whosoever is cuckolded payeth a sum of money. In Paris he rideth in disgrace through the city, the crier proclaiming these words before him, "So do, so have." In some parts of England I have seen a custom not much different. All which though they now are well near worn out of date, yet their primary intent was virtuous, being to restrain husbands to the loving and living with their own wives, so that neither should need any other company but by their mutual example one should be a precedent unto the other of true chastity.

Thus then (to draw myself unto an end), and only thus, may a husband lawfully correct his wife. Admonition is his first degree for smallest faults. This must proceed from a patient love or a loving patience. The next is reprehension in greater offences. This must aim at the amendment of the fault, not offending of the faulty. Both of these must be seconded by our good example, that the world may see us do those things which we would have done by others. Lastly, in the last and highest degree is Divorce, in such cases as before are alleged. Now for farther satisfaction, to prove that the laws allow not any verberal correction,[44] I have added these few words.

First, if a husband may lawfully beat his wife, then is the wife legally bound to endure his beating. For the law gives not authority to the punisher but the therewithal enjoins obedience on the punished. But the law binds not a wife to such blockish patience. For in such a case it allows her to depart from her husband, and of her husband in time of her absence to obtain sufficient maintenance. Neither doeth it limit her any time to return if she fear his tyranny, nor yet constrains her to live again with him unless for her good usage be given her good security.

In answer whereof, that shift will not serve to say the Law authorizeth a man to beat his wife but slightly and not in such sort as may cause her departure. This is too coarse a salve for such a sore. For a little beating unto some women is more than much unto others, and therefore in them it will breed the same or worse effects. And how little so ever it be, they are not bound to take it.

Secondly, the law decrees that he less grievously offendeth who killeth his mother than he who killeth his wife, though both be most heinous and execrable sins. Hence by rule of disputation I conclude, therefore also he less grievously offendeth that beats his mother than he who beats his wife. But what a horrid and barbarous fact it is for a man to beat his mother judge you, and then also judge what the other is which is worse than that.

And whatsoever is said amongst Lawyers of the first proposition, some plainly affirming it, others mincing it with distinction, availeth nothing. For if (as many do) you hold the offence only greater in respect of the greater punishment allotted it by the law, but less in itself and of his own nature, I would demand you whether the law does not proportionate every punishment to the quality of every offence? To small offences, light punishments; to the greater, punishments of greater torture; to those that are most heinous, most exquisite torments? Which if you grant you must necessarily acknowledge the truth of the first proposition. If you deny, you accuse the law of injustice. Or otherwise, if your reply be (as most men's is) that herein the law was especially heedful, and because men are more prone to injure their wives than their parents (as lamentable accidents most visually do testify), therefore for greater terror to such offenders and more evident example to other spectators, the law more severely punished the one than the other. If thus you plead I then join hands with you and in the present case give the same sentence. Because men are more prone to beat their wives than their parents, therefore in law the act should be held more heinous, because by law the punishment must be more grievous.

Thirdly, the name of the wife is a name of dignity. The law styles her thy familiar friend, thine equal associate, the Mistress of thy house; to speak at once, the same person and *Individuum* (as it were) together with thee. If therefore she bear the name of dignity, she is to be respected. If thy familiar friend, she is to be embraced. If thy equal associate, she is equally to be regarded. If thy Mistress, she is to be honored. If thy very self, she is dearly to be beloved. All which duties of a husband are necessarily intended by the law, and are as contrary to the rough and unkind usage of a wife as fire unto water, heaven unto earth.

And for the mitigation which is here by some men interposed in way of answer unto this objection (which is, that in the strictness of law for a husband to beat his wife is lawful, but it is inconvenient in the decency of manners), it is a plain and peevish contradiction and injuriously robbeth the law of the end of the law. For the end of the law is the happy government of a commonwealth, which happiness is in nothing more eminently seen than in the decent conformity of manners and orderly behavior in all estate. And hence it is that the Lawyer, as a laborious traveler, goeth through all estates to bring all unto decency. He ordereth the estate of Monarchs and princes, of peers and nobles, of Magistrates and subjects, of parents and children, of husbands and wives, of Masters and servants. And in the whole body of a commonwealth whatsoever is out of decent temper must by the law be ordered, as a sick part in a body natural by physic cured.[45] So that then an absolute indecorum in manners (as they confess the beating of a wife to be) is an absolute breach of the law.

Lastly, correction by way of beating (say the best you can say of it) is merely servile, and in many men's judgments so inhuman as that a wise man, whose actions flow from discreet premeditation, will not exercise it upon his slaves or swains. But servility is only to be imposed on such as are servile, and therefore not on wives who are in the law free burgesses of the same city whereof their husbands are free, and free denizens in the same land wherein their husbands are free, both participating the same rights, both enjoying the same liberties.

But here again ariseth a cavil touching the precepts of the law and permissions of the law. They answer that though indeed the law commandeth not a man, yet it permitteth him to beat his wife. Their reason is because it setteth down no precise penalty in such a case, and whatsoever the law doth tolerate is not unlawful, and therefore this action also is lawful, though not by precept of the law yet by permission of the law. Whereunto my reply is, first, to say that the law setteth down no precise punishment in this case is a proposition not simply true, for the reasons before in my first reason alleged. Again, that whatsoever the law doth tolerate is lawful, I hold it to be a position absolutely false. The law herein shall be judge of the law, which saith that those things are not without vice (therefore unlawful) which are permitted or pardoned by the law and not commanded. The law omitteth some things in some good respects, and those things which we omit (saith St. Chrysostom) we unwillingly permit, and what we unwillingly permit we by no means would have committed, but this only we do because we cannot as we would restrain the unbridled affections of the many. Many things therefore are permitted by the law upon necessity, many things pardoned by the law upon indulgency, which yet are directly against good manners and simply sins in themselves.

I will instance the cause. A widow that remarrieth within her year of mourning is by the law free from infamy but by the law also adjudged unworthy of matrimonial dignity. A virgin that espouseth her self without her parents' consent is by the law lawfully, yet by the law also unhonestly espoused. A husband taking his wife in adultery might lawfully kill her, yet not without the guilt of heinous offence. Lastly, the Jews might lawfully crave a bill of divorce and put away their wives upon any mislike, but Christ tells them it was granted by Moses for the hardness of their heart, being yet a thing most unlawful and therefore not so from the beginning. In which, and all other cases of like nature, though an evil custom or a peculiar permission may save a man from the punishment of the law, yet it can never clear him from the unlawful act.

And here I purposely omit many eminent and pregnant proofs which hereafter upon occasion may be added. For what need I to light so many torches to the noon day, or propose such multiplicity of reasons to prove a truth so manifest? Let it suffice that hitherto I have made plea in mine adversaries' faculty, and through the firmness of the cause confirmed mine assertion. It is now time to remove the tents and gather myself within the confines of mine own profession. Not fearing to be tried herein by any trial, especially this the highest of all trials, where God is the judge, his word the law, his Saints and Angels the witnesses, and eternal verity, which never doth deceive nor can ever be deceived, attends upon the sentence.

****

My conclusion therefore shall only be an earnest request unto such as are married, that as they are bound by the word of God and as they have impledged their faith unto the church of God, they seek to honor this honorable estate. Husbands, that they love their wives as Christ loveth his church. His love unto his church is the dearest of all dear loves, such should yours be unto your wives. Resolve your consciences of what due authority you have over your wives. Try the utmost of your lawful bounds. Never step over into the thorny field of tyranny, to which the world hath proclaimed a shame and God hath denounced a curse. Wives, love your husbands as the church again loveth Christ. Its love unto Christ is its greatest glory, so should yours unto your husbands. Be you subject unto them in things lawfully commanded. Show obedience unto them where it is due. Both husbands and wives, live together, one in the unity of souls and consents as your are pronounced one in the unity of body and flesh. My last wish is that this my short treatise may prove such as the temple of the goddess *Viri-placa* in Rome, unto whom (as Livy reports[46]) whatsoever man and wife, dissentiously living, came to sacrifice, they returned home again in love and amity. If my persuasions work such effect, my labor is amply requited and their sacrifice of a little reading time not idly bestowed.

NOTES

1. Gordius, ancient king of Phrygia, tied a knot that could be undone only by Asia's future ruler. Alexander the Great cut it with his sword.
2. In a side-note Heale cites *Aeneid* 1, but the reference should be to *Georgics* 4.
3. Heale cites the *Satyricon* of Petronius.
4. Outcome.
5. Heale's antagonist, Gager.
6. Penthesilea: queen of the Amazons in Virgil's *Aeneid*; Parthenia: mistress of Argalus in Sidney's *Arcadia*; Livia: second wife of Roman emperor Augustus.
7. Vulcan's nightcap: like horns, the sign of a cuckold.
8. Nero, A.D.37-68, notorious Roman emperor, and Silvanus, Roman tribune during first century A.D., both reputed to have murdered their wives, Pompeia and Apronia.
9. Gorgias: famous sophist and teacher of rhetoric, c. 483-376 B.C.; Melanthius: tragic poet at Athens. Their clash is recounted in Plutarch's *Conjugalia Praecepta* or *Advice to Bride and Groom* in the *Moralia*. All but one of Heale's references to Plutarch, "the best moralist," are to this work (see n. 11).
10. Virgil, *Eclogues* 5; Leda's twins: Ovid, *Metamorphoses* 6; Plato, *Republic* 1.
11. Isocrates: Athenian orator and teacher of rhetoric, 436-338 B.C.; Seneca: Roman philosopher and playwright, d. A.D. 65; Cato: Roman statesman, 234-149 B.C., cited from Plutarch's *Life of Marcus Cato*.
12. In Valerius Maximus, *Acts and Sayings of Ancient Romans* 6.2.
13. Martial: A.D. 40-104, cited from *Epigrams* 6.
14. Cited from Juan Luis Vives (1492-c.1541), *The Office and Duty of a Husband* (1538).
15. Ethics.
16. A market built by Thomas Gresham in 1566 and named the Royal Exchange by Queen Elizabeth in 1570.
17. Jet, a black stone.
18. "The master has said it."
19. *Economics* 1.3.
20. Athenian statesman, 527-460 B.C.
21. Canon Law: a body of Roman ecclesiastical law compiled in the medieval period; Civil Law: Roman civil law promulgated under emperor Justinian in the sixth century A.D.
22. From Plautus, *The Merchant* 4.6; cf. Emilia's speech in *Othello* 4.3.85-102.
23. In truth.
24. Translated from the *Silvae* of the Roman poet Statius, c. A.D.40-96.
25. In a sidenote, Heale lists Latin terms for menstruation, pregnancy, infection.
26. Deference.
27. The distinction is between annulment of marriage and formal separation "from bed and board." The legitimacy of the former was much debated, as illustrated in the following text by John Rainolds.
28. Italian for goats, cuckolds.
29. Sidney, *Arcadia* 3.
30. Moral failings.
31. An Athenian courtesan in the fourth century B.C.

32. Hesiod: early Greek poet in eighth century B.C., Heale cites his *Catalogue of Women*; Caelius Aurelianus: Greek physician in second century A.D., Heale cites his *Reflections of the Ancients*; Chaucer: Heale cites *The Legend of Good Women*; Saint Jerome: c. 342-420, ascetic hermit and spiritual counselor; Saint Gregory: 335-95, bishop and theologian in Asia Minor; Saint Chrysostom: c. 345-407, Bishop of Constantinople.

33. Catiline: 108-62 B.C., a Roman politician and conspirator; Verres: b. 112 B.C., Roman despot who pillaged Sicily; Aegisthus: legendary seducer of Clytemnestra, the wife of his cousin Agamemnon; Machivell, or Niccolò Machiavelli: 1469-1529, Florentine political theorist; Jovianus: A.D. 332-64, Roman emperor who protected Christians and heathens; Battus: legendary butt of Hermes' tricks.

34. Severus: ruled A.D. 222-35; Euthydemus: Greek sophist, in fifth century B.C.; Varro: Roman poet b. 82 B.C.

35. Marcus Aurelius, A.D. 121-80, Roman emperor and religious philosopher, his *Meditations* were first printed in 1550.

36. Perhaps a reference to Exod. 16.33.

37. Lucius Papirius: Roman consul and dictator of the fourth century B.C.

38. Ovid, *Metamorphoses* 2.

39. Compendium.

40. Pacatus: a Roman rhetorician who wrote a panegyric on Theodosius, emperor during the fourth century A.D.

41. Histrionic or hypocritical.

42. Francesco Petrarch, 1304-74; Heale cites his *Remedies for Fortune Fair and Foul*.

43. Irreproachability.

44. Correction by beating.

45. Heale cites Plato, *Republic* 1.

46. Livy: Roman historian, 59 B.C.-A.D. 17, author of *History of Rome*. *Viriplaca*: "goddess who soothes man's anger," the surname of the goddess Juno, restorer of peace between married couples.

CHAPTER 4

Of the Lawfulness of Marriage
Upon a Lawful Divorce
John Rainolds

The role of Henry VIII's divorce from Katherine of Aragon in the course of the English Reformation has long been debated: "Protestant writers have tended to dismiss it as a mere 'occasion' rather than a genuine cause; Catholics have sometimes regarded the divorce as the chief cause of the cataclysm and supposed that, had it not been pressed, England might well have remained a Catholic nation" (Dickens 128). The divorce contributed powerfully but ambiguously to the Reformation, triggering neither Protestantism and anti-papal beliefs nor English nationalism in themselves, yet focusing and spurring royal and popular opposition toward the papacy. That the political and religious effects of the royal divorce cannot be precisely defined does, however, suggest its polemical significance in subsequent debates between Catholics and Protestants. Divorce becomes a trope whose meanings are disputed, contested, and, when claimed by one side, used to underwrite the truth of Catholic or Protestant theology and ethics.

Such is the rhetorical weight that divorce holds for the eminent Oxford don John Rainolds in *A Defence of the Judgment of the Reformed Churches: That a man may lawfully not only put away his wife for her adultery, but also marry another*. For Rainolds is not only contributing to a long religious dispute over the meaning of Christ's response to a question put by the Pharisees on the legitimacy of divorce (Matt. 19.7-9). He is also deliberately attacking the intellectual, ethical, and theological authority of a number of Catholic figures who had written on this and related issues, as the remaining lines of his title page assert: "Wherein both Robert Bellarmine the Jesuit's Latin treatise and an English pamphlet of a nameless author maintaining the contrary are confuted by John Rainolds. A taste of Bellarmine's dealing in controversies of Religion: how he depraveth Scriptures, misallegeth [church] fathers, and abuseth reasons to the perverting of the truth of God and poisoning of his Church with error." The obvious corollary of such an attack is that Rainolds' English, Protestant perspective is raised to religious and intellectual truth.

The Reformation introduced a changed conception of marriage and divorce: "Marriage was no longer a sacrament, a symbol of Christ's relations with his Church, but reverted to being a covenant or contract between two individuals" (Macfarlane 224). Adultery could then be considered a breaking of the contract, rendering the marriage dissoluble. This interpretation was accepted in England from 1552, when Protestant doctrines in the *Reformatio Legum Ecclesiasticarum* began to be practiced by the church courts, though the law itself was not amended. Then from 1603, Macfarlane claims, after changes to canon law under the new king, it became nearly impossible to divorce and remarry (255), though various forms of separation were permitted. Rainolds' text, when written in the 1590s, thus reflected current practices but, when published in 1609, is opposed to the position of the Anglican church.

Born in 1549, Rainolds arrived at Oxford University as a boy of eight and began studying there five years later. An uncle and two brothers also at Oxford were punished for their Catholic sympathies, but Rainolds himself had apparently accepted the Protestant faith by 1566 when elected a probationary fellow at Corpus Christi College. Having taken his MA in 1572 Rainolds was appointed Reader in Greek and soon became famous for his lecturing. In 1576 he was licensed to preach and became increasingly involved in religious issues; while studying toward a doctor of divinity degree he emerged as a leader of radical Protestant thought at Oxford (Green 29). By the early 1580s he had attracted the notice of leading Protestant politicians and on behalf of the government participated in polemics against Catholics, including the Jesuit Robert Bellarmine. By the end of the decade, he was considered the pre-eminent theologian at Oxford.

In the 1590s Rainolds engaged in various controversies, presenting lines of argument that were often adopted by Puritan groups. His argument with William Gager and Alberico Gentili over the legitimacy of stage plays is well-known in literary and dramatic history. The text on divorce and remarriage derives from his polemic against Bellarmine's views: "He wrote a treatise on the subject, but it was suppressed by Archbishop Whitgift for being too controversial, and was only published after his death and outside of England" (Green 35). Manuscript versions of the text circulated, and when in 1603 the position allowing divorce was being overturned, it was used in efforts to counter those moves.

Lawrence D. Green suggests that Queen Elizabeth recognized Rainolds as a potentially disruptive figure for the official state religion she wished to impose (36-37); and when James I came to the throne, Rainolds presented the Puritan case for reforms to various church issues and practices. In his final years Rainolds, president of Corpus Christi College, worked on what would become the King James version of the Bible but resisted subscribing to the crown's new ecclesiastical rules. He died in 1607.

The treatise on divorce and remarriage has four chapters. The first, reprinted below, introduces the issue and seeks to prove Rainolds' position through discussion and interpretation of the Bible. The next chapters argue against Bellarmine's interpretation of biblical and patristic source, while the final chapter disputes the logic of the opposing case. Rainolds' method is overtly controversial. He engages in polemical close reading of Bellarmine's text and passages from the Bible and other authors cited in it. In effect, he attempts to subvert Bellarmine's case by pointing out its inconsistencies and contradictions and by constantly verging on personal invective. At times the imagery used by Rainolds aims to imply that Bellarmine uses a kind of licentious or adulterous logic: "the whorish filth of his own fancying," "he handleth it so lewdly and perversely," or that Bellarmine's argument is driven by his own lust. In its intensity, Rainolds' attack on his opponent's sophistry also anticipates the controversy that would explode around Jesuitical casuistry in the 1606 trial of Father Garnet for complicity in the Gunpowder Plot against James I (Muir xv-xviii). In short, the text exemplifies the ways in which issues of marriage and sexuality might significantly interrelate with other social and religious concerns of the period.

As noted above, Rainolds' *Defence* was published twice, in 1609 and 1610 in Dort, Holland. The extract below is taken from the 1609 edition (*STC* 20607; Reel 726).

OF THE LAWFULNESS OF MARRIAGE

The State of the Question Being First Declared, the Truth Is Proved by Scripture: That a Man Having Put away His Wife for Her Adultery May Lawfully Marry Another
The duty of man and woman joined in marriage requireth that they two should be as one person and cleave each to other with mutual love and liking in society of life until it please God, who hath coupled them together in this bond, to set them free from it and to dissociate and sever them by death (Gen. 2.24, Matt. 19.5). But the inordinate fancies and desires of our corrupt nature have so inveigled Adam's seed in many places that men have accustomed to put away their wives upon every trifling mislike and miscontentment. Yea, the Jews supposed themselves to be warranted by God's law to do it, so that whosoever put away his wife gave her bill of divorcement (Deut. 24.1, Matt. 5.31). This perverse opinion and error of theirs our Saviour Christ reproved, teaching that divorcements may not be made for any cause save whoredom only. For "whosoever (saith he) shall put away his wife except it be for whoredom and shall marry another doth

commit adultery, and who so marrieth her which is put away doth commit adultery." Now, about the meaning of these words of Christ, expressed more fully by one of the Evangelists (Matt. 19.9), by others more sparingly (Mark 10.11, Luke 16.18), there hath a doubt arisen and diverse men, even from the primitive church's time, have been of diverse minds.

For many of the fathers have gathered thereupon that if a man's wife committed whoredom and fornication he might not only put her away but marry another. Some others, and among them namely St. Augustine, have thought that the man might put away his wife but marry another he might not.

The School divines of latter years and the Canonists,[1] as for the most part they were addicted commonly to St. Augustine's judgment, did likewise follow him herein and, the Popes maintaining their doctrine for Catholic, have possessed the church of Rome with this opinion. But since in our days the light of good learning both for arts and tongues hath shined more brightly by God's most gracious goodness than in the former ages, and the Holy Scriptures by the help thereof have been the better understood, the Pastors and Doctors of the reformed Churches have perceived and showed that if a man's wife defile herself with fornication he may not only put her away by Christ's Doctrine but also marry another. Wherein that they teach agreeably to the truth and not erroneously, as Jesuits and Papists do falsely and unjustly charge them.

I will make manifest and prove (through God's assistance) by express words of Christ, the truth itself. And because our adversaries do ween that the contrary hereof is strongly proved by sundry arguments and objections which two of their newest writers, Bellarmine the Jesuit and a nameless author of an English pamphlet,[2] have diligently laid together, for the farther clearing therefore of the matter and taking away of doubts and scruples, I will set down all their objections in order, first out of the Scriptures, then of fathers, last of reasons, and answer every one of them particularly. So shall it appear to such as are not blinded with a fore-conceived opinion and prejudice that, whatsoever show of probabilities are brought to the contrary, yet the truth delivered by our Saviour Christ alloweth him whose wife committeth fornication to put her away and marry another.

The proof hereof is evident if Christ's words be weighed in the nineteenth Chapter of St. Matthew's gospel. For when the Pharisees asking him a question, whether it were lawful for a man to put away his wife for every cause, received answer that it was not and thereupon said unto him, "Why did Moses then command to give a bill of divorcement and to put her away," our Saviour said unto them, "Moses suffered you because of the hardness of your heart to put away your wives. But from the beginning it was not so. And I say unto you that whosoever shall put away his wife, except it be for whoredom, and shall marry another, doth commit adultery;

and who so marrieth her that is put away doth commit adultery" (Matt. 19.7-9).

Now in this sentence, the clause of exception, "except it be for whoredom," doth argue that he committeth not adultery who, having put away his wife for whoredom, marrieth another. But he must needs commit it in doing so unless the band of marriage be loosed and dissolved. For who so marrieth another as long as he is bound to the former is an adulterer. The band, then, of marriage is loosed and dissolved between that man and wife who are put asunder and divorced for whoredom (Rom. 7.2-3). And if the band be loosed the man may marry another, seeing it is written, "Art thou loosed from a wife? If thou marry thou sinnest not" (1 Cor. 7.27-28). Therefore it is lawful for him who hath put away his wife for whoredom to marry another.

This argument doth firmly and necessarily conclude the point in question if the first part and proposition of it be proved to be true. For there is no controversy of any of the rest, being all grounded on such undoubted principles of Scripture and reason that our adversaries themselves admit and grant them all.

The first they deny, to wit, that the clause of exception in Christ's speech, "except it be for whoredom," doth argue that the man committeth not adultery who, having put away his wife for whoredom, marrieth another. And to overthrow this proposition they do bring sundry answers and evasions. The best of all, which as Bellarmine avoucheth, is that those words, "except it be for whoredom," are not an exception. "For Christ (saith he) meant those words, 'except for whoredom,' not as an exception but as a negation. So that the sense is whosoever shall put away his wife except for whoredom, that is to say, without the cause of whoredom, and shall marry another doth commit adultery. Whereby it is assumed that he is an adulterer who, having put away his wife without the cause of whoredom, marrieth another. But nothing is said touching him who marrieth another, having put away his former wife for whoredom." Indeed, this evasion might have some color for it if these words of Christ, "except it be for whoredom," were not an exception. But neither hath Bellarmine ought that may suffice for the proof hereof, and the very text of the Scripture itself is so clear against him that he must of necessity give over his hold. For the principal pillar wherewith he underproppeth it is St. Augustine's judgment, who hath so expounded it in his first book touching adulterous marriages.

Now, of that treatise St. Augustine saith himself in his *Retractations*, "I have written two books touching adulterous marriages, as near as I could according to the Scriptures, being desirous to open and loose the knots of a most difficult question. Which whether I have done, so that no knot is left therein, I know not. Nay, rather I perceive that I have not done it perfectly and thoroughly, although I have opened many creeks[3] thereof, as whosoever readeth with judgment may discern." St. Augustine, then, acknowledgeth that there are some wants and imperfections in that work which they may see who read with judgment. And whether this that Bellarmine doth allege out of it deserve not to fall within the compass of that censure I appeal to their judgment who have eyes to see. For St. Augustine thought that the word in the original of St. Matthew's gospel had, by the Proper signification of it, imported a negation rather than an exception. As he showeth by saying that, "where the common Latin translation hath 'except for whoredom' in the Greek text it is rather read 'without the cause of whoredom.'" Supposing belike (whether by slip of memory or rather oversight) that the same words, which were used before in the fifth Chapter of St. Matthew's Gospel to the same purpose, were used also in this place. Whereas here they differ and are well expressed by that in the Latin by which St. Augustine thought they were not so well. Howbeit, if they had been the same with the former yet neither so might Bellarmine allow his opinion, considering that the common Latin translation (which Papists by their Council of Trent[4] are bound to stand to under pain of curse) expresseth those likewise as a plain exception.

Which indeed agreeth to the right and natural meaning of the particle,[5] as the like writers use it in like constructions even then too when it hath, as it were, a link less to tie it unto that meaning.[6] Wherefore, St. Augustine's mistaking of the word and signification thereof is no sufficient warrant for Bellarmine to ground on that they must be taken so. As for that he addeth that, albeit both these particles be taken exceptively often times, yet may they also be taken otherwise since one of them is used in the Revelation "as an adversative not an exceptive."[7] This maketh much less for proof of his assertion. For what if it be used there as an adversative, where the matter treated of and the tenor of the sentence do manifestly argue that it must be taken so? Must it therefore be taken so in this place whereof our question is? Or doth Bellarmine prove by any circumstance of the text that here it may be taken so? No. Neither saith he a word to this purpose. Why mentioneth he, then, that it may be taken otherwise and is, in the Revelation, for an adversative particle? Truly I know not, unless it be to show that he can wrangle and play the caviling sophister,[8] in seeming to gainsay and disprove his adversary when in truth he doth not. Or perhaps, though he durst not say for the particular that it is taken here as an adversative, which he could not but most absurdly, yet he thought it policy to breed a surmise thereof for the general, that shallower conceits might imagine another sense therein, they knew not what. And they, whose brazen faces should serve them thereto, might impudently brabble[9] that our sense is not certain because another is possible, even as if a Jew, being pressed by a Christian with the place of Isaiah, "Behold a virgin shall conceive and bring forth a Son" (Isa. 7.14), should answer that the Hebrew word translated "virgin" may be taken otherwise since that in the Proverbs it signifieth a married woman, at least one that is not a Virgin indeed though she would seem to be (Prov. 30.19). But as the Jew cannot conclude hereof with any reason that the word signifieth a married woman in Isaiah, because the thing spoken of is a strange sign and it is not strange for a married woman to conceive and bring forth a Son, so neither can the Jesuit conclude of the former that the particle in Matthew is meant adversatively, because the words then do breed no sense at all. In which sort to think that any wise man spake were folly, that Christ, the word and wisdom of God, were impiety. Nay, if some of Bellarmine's scholars should say that words must be supplied to make it perfect sense rather than their master be cast of as a wrangler, they would be quickly forced to pluck in this horn or else they might chance to leap (which is worse) out of the frying pan into the fire. For adversative particles import an opposition and contrariety unto that sentence against which they are brought in.

Now, the sentence is that "who so putteth his wife and marrieth another, doth commit adultery." Wherefore, he by consequence committeth not adultery who doth so for whoredom if the particle be adversative, and must have words accordingly supplied and understood to make the sense perfect. Thus the shift and cavil which Bellarmine hath drawn out of the double meaning of the Greek word is either idle and beateth the air, or if it strike any it striketh himself and giveth his cause a deadly wound. Yea, that which he principally sought to confute he hath confirmed thereby.

For since the word hath only two significations, exceptive and adversative, neither durst he say that it is used here as an adversative. It followeth he must grant it to be as an exceptive. And so the place rightly translated in our English (agreeable to the other in the fifth Chapter of Matthew), "except be for whoredom," which as in their authentical Latin text also doth out of controversy betoken an exception.

Having all passages therefore shut against him for escaping this way, he fleeth to another starting hole. To wit, that if the word be taken exceptively yet may it be an exception negative.

"And this (he saith) sufficeth for the maintenance of St. Augustine's answer. For when it is said, 'whosoever shall put away his wife, excepting the cause of whoredom, and shall marry another doth commit adultery,' the cause of whoredom may be excepted either because in that case it is not adultery to marry another, and this is an exception affirmative, or because nothing is presently determined touching that cause whether it be sufficient to excuse adultery or no. And this is an exception negative, which in that St. Augustine embraced he did well." I would to God Bellarmine had St. Augustine's modesty. Then would he be ashamed to charge such a man with embracing such whorish filth of his own fancying, as in this distinction of negative and affirmative exception he doth. For he handleth it so lewdly and perversely by calling that affirmative which indeed is negative, and by avouching that to be negative which is not, as if he had made a covenant with his lip to lie, treading in the steps of those wicked wretches of whom it is written, "Woe unto them who say that good is evil, and evil good" (Isa. 5.20). For the proof whereof it is to be noted that an exception is a particular proposition contradictory to a general. So that if the general proposition be affirmative the exception is negative, and if the proposition be negative, contrariwise, the exception is affirmative.

As for example's sake, "He that sacrificeth to any Gods save to the Lord only shall be destroyed," saith Moses in the law (Exod. 22.20). The proposition is affirmative, "He that sacrificeth to any Gods shall be destroyed," the exception negative, "He that sacrificeth to the Lord shall not be destroyed."

"There is none good but one, even God," saith Christ in the Gospel (Mark 10.18). The proposition is negative, "There is none good," the exception affirmative, "One is good, even God." "I would to God that all (sayth Paul to Agrippa) which hear me this day were altogether such as I am, except these bonds" (Acts 26.29): the proposition affirmative, "I wish that all which hear me were such as I am altogether"; the exception negative, "I wish not in bonds they were such as I am." "No Church did communicate with me in the account of giving and receiving, giving you only," sayth the same Paul to the Philippians (Phil. 4.15). The proposition negative, "No church did communicate with me in the account of giving and receiving"; the exception affirmative, "You of Philippi did."

Likewise, in all the rest of exceptions adjoined to general propositions, though the marks and tokens as of generality sometimes lie hidden in the proposition, so of denying or affirming do in the exception. Yet it is plain and certain that the proposition and exception matched with it are still of contrary quality, the one affirmative if the other negative, and negative if the other affirmative. Which thing being so, see now the Jesuit's dealing, how falsely and absurdly he speaketh against truth and reason. For since in Christ's speech touching Divorcement for whoredom, the proposition is affirmative, "Whosoever shall put away his wife and marry another, doth commit adultery," it followeth that the exception which denieth him to commit adultery, "who putting away his wife for whoredom, marrieth another," is an exception negative. But Bellarmine sayth that this were an exception affirmative. Yea, which is more strange in a man learned and knowing rules of logic (but what can arts help when men are given over by God's just judgment to their own lusts and errors), he entitleth it an exception affirmative, even then and in the same place when and where himself, having set it down in the words going immediately next before, had given it the mark of a negative thus, "It is not adultery to marry another." And as no absurdity doth lightly come alone, he addeth fault to fault, saying that this is an exception negative, "When nothing is presently determined touching the cause, whether it be sufficient to excuse adultery or no." So first to deny with him was to affirm, and next to say nothing now is to deny. Yet there is a rule in Law that he who saith nothing denieth not. Belike, as they coined us new Divinity at Rome, so they will new Law and new Logic too.

Howbeit, if these principles be allowed therein by the Jesuit's authority, that negative is affirmative and to say nought is negative, I see not but all heretics and ungodly persons may, as well as Jesuits, maintain what they list and impudently face it out with like distinctions. For if an adversary of the Holy Ghost should be controlled by that we read to the Corinthians, "The things of God knoweth no man but the spirit of God" (1 Cor. 2.11), his answer (after Bellarmine's pattern) were ready, that this proveth not the spirit of God to know those things because it might be a negative exception, importing that St. Paul would determine nothing presently thereof. If one who despaired of the mercy of God through conscience of his sins and trespasses should be put in mind of Christ's speech to sinners, "Ye shall all perish except ye repent" (Luke 13.3), he might reply thereto that the exception is negative and this, though not in the former point, yet here were true. But to make it serve his humor, he must expound it with Bellarmine that Christ doth not determine what shall become of the repentant. If a usurer should be told that he is forbidden to "Give forth upon Usury" (Lev. 25.37) or "to take increase" (Ezek. 18.13), and a thief that he is commanded "To labor and work" (Ephes. 4.28), and "so to eat his own bread" (2 Thess. 3.12), they might (if they had learned to imitate Bellarmine) defend their trades both, the one by affirming that to forbid a thing is to say nothing of it, the other that to command betokeneth to forbid.

In a word, whatsoever opinion were reproved as false or action as wicked out of the Scriptures, denouncing death eternal and pains of hell thereto, the seduced and disobedient might shift the Scriptures of by glozing[10] thus upon them that false is true and wicked holy, life meant by death and heaven by hell. Or if the papists themselves would condemn this kind of distinguishing and expounding places as senseless and shameless, then let them give the same sentence of Bellarmine's that negative is affirmative and to say nothing is to deny. Which whether they do or no, I will, with the consent and liking (I doubt not) of all indifferent judges and Godly minded men who love the truth and not contention, conclude that these lying glozes of the Jesuits do not become a Christian. And seeing it is proved that an exception negative is not a preterition or passing over a thing in silence (which if Christ had meant he could have done with fit words, as wise men are wont) but a flat denying of that in one case which the proposition affirmeth in all others, it remaineth that Christ, having excepted out of his general speech them who for whoredom put away their wives, denieth that in them which in all others he affirmeth, and thereby teacheth us that the man who, putting away his wife for that cause marrieth another, doth not commit adultery.

The next trick of Sophistry, whereto as to a shelter our adversaries betake them, is that the exception ought to be restrained to the former branch of putting away the wife only. To the which intent, they say that there are some words wanting in the text which must be supplied and perfected thus, "Whosoever shall put away his wife (which is not lawful except it be for whoredom) and marrieth another doth commit adultery." This device doth Bellarmine allow of as probable, though not like the foresaid two of negation and negative exception. But our English Pamphleteer preferreth it before all. And surely, if it were lawful to foist in these words "which is not lawful," the Pamphleteer might seem to have showed greater skill herein than Bellarmine. But men of understanding and judgment do know that this were a ready way to make the Scripture a nose of wax and leaden rule (as Pighui[11] doth blasphemously term it) if everyone may add not what the circumstances and matter of the text showeth to be wanting but what himself listeth, to frame such sense thereof as pleaseth his conceit and fancy. The sundry interlacings of words by sundry authors into this very place and the wrestings of it thereby to sundry senses may (to go no further) sufficiently discover the fault and inconvenience of that kind of dealing.

For the Bishop of Avila[12] supplieth it in this manner, "Who so putteth away his wife, except it be for whoredom, though he marry not another, committeth adultery, and who so putteth her away in whatsoever sort, if he marry another, doth commit adultery." Friar Alphonsus[13] checketh and controlleth this interpretation, partly as too violent for thrusting in so many words, partly as untrue for the former branch of it, since he who putteth away his wife not for whoredom, although he cause her "to commit adultery, yet doth not himself commit it unless he marry another." Whereupon the Friar would have it thus supplied rather, "Whoso putteth away his wife, not for other cause but for whoredom, and marrieth another, doth commit adultery." But this, though it have not so many words added as the Bishop of Avila's, yet in truth it is more violently forced against the natural meaning and drift of the text. For by adding these words, "Not for other cause," his purpose is to say that whoso putteth away his wife for no cause but for whoredom yet committeth adultery if he marry another, much more if he marry having put away his wife for any other cause. And so is Christ's speech made in effect clean contrary to that which his own words do give, he saying "Whosoever shall put away his wife except it be for whoredom," and the friar forcing him to say, "Whosoever shall put away his wife although it be for whoredom, and shall marry another, doth commit adultery."

Nicolas of Lira,[14] being as in time more ancient than the friar so more sincere and single in handling the Scripture, saith that other words must be interposed, to the supplying of it thus: "Whoso putteth away his wife except it be for whoredom, sinneth, and doth against the law of marriage; and whoso marrieth another doth commit adultery." Wherein, though he deal less violently with the text than do the friar and the Bishop, yet he offendeth also in their licentious humor of adding to the Scripture where nothing was wanting and making it thereby to speak that which he thinketh, whereas he should have learned to think that which it speaketh. Yea, Bellarmine himself acknowledgeth that they all were overseen herein, albeit censuring them with gentler words as he is wont his favorites and friends. For, "the explications (sayth he) which the Bishop of Avila, Alphonsus a Castro, and others have devised are not so probable."

But why should these be noted by him as improbable, yea, denied unworthy the rehearsal, and that of his own, though adding in the like sort "which is not lawful," be allowed as probable, yea, magnified as most true by the pamphleteer? The reasons which they both or rather which Bellarmine (for the pamphleteer doth no more here but English him, as neither elsewhere for the most part, though he brag not thereof), the reasons then which Bellarmine doth press out of the text to breed a persuasion in his credulous scholars that this interposition is probable and likely are pressed indeed according to the proverb, "The wringing of the nose causeth blood to come out." For he sayeth that Christ did not place the exception after those words, "And shall marry another," but straight after those "'whosoever shall put away'; and likewise when he added, 'and whoso marrieth her that is put away committeth adultery,' he did not join thereto, 'Except it be for whoredom,' to the intent that he might show that the cause of whoredom doth only make the putting away to be lawful and not the celebrating of a new marriage too." And how doth he prove that Christ did so place the exception in the former clause to this intent, or to this intent did omit it in the latter? Nay, he proveth it not. It is but his conjecture, like a sick man's dream. Unless this go for a proof, that Christ did not so place it before without cause nor omit it afterward without cause. Which if he meant it should, it was for want of a better. For "Christ did not these things without cause," I grant; "Therefore he did them for this cause," it followeth not.

St. Paul, having occasion to cite a place of Scripture doth set it down thus, "Come yet out from among them, and separate yourselves saith the Lord, and touch no unclean thing" (2 Cor. 6.17). Herein he hath placed the words "saith the Lord" not after "touch no unclean thing" but after "separate yourselves." This did he not without cause. What, for this cause therefore, that he might restrain the words, "sayeth the Lord," to the former branch as not pertaining to the latter also? No, for it appeareth by the Prophet Isaiah that they belong to both (Isa. 52.5). It is to be thought, then, that the spirit of God, who doth nothing without cause, did move Paul for some cause to place them so. Perhaps for perspicuity and commodiousness of giving other men thereby to understand the rather that both the words going before and coming after were qualified with "sayth the Lord," which is to be likewise thought of the exception placed by our Saviour between the two branches of his speech. And that with so much greater reason, in my judgment, because if he had placed it after the latter "And shall marry another," the words "Except for whoredom" might have seemed to signify that it were lawful for a man, having put away his wife for any cause, to marry another if he could not contain. As it is written, "because of whoredom, let every man have his wife" (1 Cor. 7.2), where now the exception being set before, the Pharisees, whose question Christ therein did answer, could gather no such poison out of his words to feed their error, but they must needs acknowledge this to be his doctrine, that a man may not put away his wife for every cause and marry another, but for whoredom only.

As for Christ's omitting of the exception afterward, Bellarmine himself will quickly see there might be another cause thereof if he consider how St. Paul, repeating this doctrine of Christ, doth wholly omit the exception which nevertheless must needs be supplied and understood. For why doth St. Paul say that "to married persons the Lord gave commandment: Let not the wife depart from her husband, and let not the husband put away his wife" (1 Cor. 7.10) without adding to either part "except it be for whoredom," which the Lord did add? Bellarmine's greatest Doctor[15] saith that he omitted it because it was very well known, most notorious. If, then, St. Paul had reason to omit it wholly because it was so well known, how much more justly might Christ in part omit it for the same cause, having mentioned it immediately before and made it known thereby? Chiefly seeing that as he framed his speech to men's understanding so did he follow the common use of men therein. And if I should say upon the like occasion, "Whosoever draweth his sword, except he be a magistrate, and killeth a man committeth murder; and whosoever abetteth him that killeth a man committeth murder," what man of sense and reason would not think I meant that the exception set down in the former sentence touching man-quellers pertaineth to the latter of these abetters also, and uttered once must serve for both? Yea, even in the former too, who would not think that my meaning were the exception should reach unto both the branches of drawing the sword and killing a man, not to be abridged and tied up unto the first as if I had said, "whosoever draweth his sword (which none may do except he be a magistrate), and killeth a man, committeth murder"? Yet one who were disposed to play the Jesuit's part might thus expound my speech and say I taught thereby that Peter indeed was justly reproved for drawing his sword though he killed not. But magistrates are authorized to draw it and no more, not to put men to death and to take vengeance on him that doth evil. Neither should he do me greater wrong therein by making me to speak contrary to Scripture than Bellarmine doth Christ by the like depraving of the like sentence.

But if all these reasons will not persuade his scholars that in Christ's speech the exception of whoredom is to be extended to both the points jointly of putting away and marrying, and that Bellarmine, adding these words which is not lawful, did unlawfully sow a patch of human rags to the whole garment of God's most precious word, behold, their own doctrine, allowed and established by the Council of Trent, shall force them, will they, nill they,[16] to see it and acknowledge it. For if the exception be so tied only to the former point, then a man may not put away his wife for any cause save for whoredom, no not from bed and board as they term it,[17] that is, from mutual company and society of life, although he marry not another. But the Council of Trent pronounceth and defineth that there are many causes for the which a man may put away his wife from bed and board, wherefore the Papists (no remedy) must grant that the exception cannot so be tied unto the former point only. And therefore, whereas Bellarmine sayeth further that he thinketh it is "St. Thomas of Aquinas's opinion that Christ's words should be expounded so, and St. Jerome seemeth somewhat to be of the same mind," the Papists peradventure will be fain to say that Bellarmine was deceived herein. For else, not only Jerome, of whom they reckon less, but Thomas of Aquinas, the saint of Saints and chief light of the Church of Rome, shall be convinced of error, even by the Council of Trent's verdict.

And these considerations do likewise stop the passage of another shift, which is cousin german to the last entreated of, and Bellarmine prayeth it alike. To wit, "that the words 'committeth adultery' must be supplied and understood in the former part of Christ's sentence thus: 'Whosoever putteth away his wife, except it be for whoredom, committeth adultery, and whoso marrieth another committeth adultery.'" Solomon did wisely judge that she was not the mother of the child who would have it divided, but she who desired it might be saved entire (1 Kings 3.26-27). Surely, the Jesuit hath not those bowels of kind and loving affection towards Christ's sentence that a Christian should, who can find in his heart to have it divided, and of one living body, namely, "whosoever putteth away his wife, except it be for whoredom and marrieth another, committeth adultery," made, as it were, two pieces of a dead carcass: the first, "Whosoever putteth away his wife, except it be for whoredom, committeth adultery"; the second, "whoso marrieth another committeth adultery." Which dealing, beside the inconvenience of making the Scripture a nose of wax and leaden rule if men may add what pleaseth them, specially if they may also mangle sentences and chop them in sundry parts, but beside this mischief here it hath a greater, that Christ most true and holy is made thereby to speak an untruth.

For a man may put away his wife for other cause than for whoredom and yet not commit adultery himself. Yes, he committeth it (sayth Bellarmine) "in his wife's adultery, whereof he was the cause by putting her unjustly away." But I reply that it is one thing to cause his wife to commit, another to commit it himself. And Christ, when he was minded to note these several faults, did it with several words expressing them accordingly (1 Cor. 7.27). Moreover, understanding the term "to put away" not as the force thereof doth yield and Christ took it for loosing of the band of marriage, but for a separation from bed and board only, as Bellarmine understandeth it, he cannot allow the sentence which he fathereth on Christ, though so expounded, without either condemning of the Trent Council or being himself condemned by it.

For if whosoever separateth his wife from him but for whoredom doth commit adultery in causing her to commit it, then is it a sin to separate her for any cause save for whoredom? If it be sin, the Church of Rome erreth in holding and decreeing that she may be separated for sundry other causes. But whosoever sayth that the Church erreth herein is accursed by the Council of Trent. The Council of Trent therefore doth consequently curse Bellarmine if he say that Christ spake his words in that sense in which he construeth them. And doth it not curse Augustine also, and Theophilact,[18] whom Bellarmine allegeth as saying the same? At least it declareth that in the Council's judgment the fathers misexpounded the Scriptures sometimes, even those very places on which the Papists cite them as sound interpreters of the Scripture. Now, the speech of Christ being cleared and saved entire from all cavils, the meaning thereof is plain as I have showed, that he who, having put away his wife for whoredom marrieth another, committeth not adultery. For so much importeth the exception negative of the cause of whoredom, opposed to the general affirmative proposition wherewith our Saviour answered the question of the Pharisees touching divorcements used by the Jews, who putting away their wives for any cause did marry others.

The only reason of adversaries remaining to be answered, stood upon and urged by them as most effectual and forcible to the contrary, is an example of like sentences. From which, since the like conclusion (say they) cannot be inferred as we infer of this, the inference of this is faulty. And faulty (I grant) they might esteem it justly if the like conclusions could not be drawn from the like sentences.

But let the examples which they bring for proof hereof be thoroughly sifted, and it will appear that either the sentences are unlike or the like conclusions may be inferred of them. For of three sentences proposed to this end, the first is out of Scripture in St. James' Epistle, "To him that knoweth how to do well, and doth it not, to him there is sin" (Jas. 4.17). A sentence, though in show unlike to that of Christ's for the proposition and exception both, yet having indeed the force of the like if it be thus resolved: "To him that doth not well, except he know not how to do well, there is sin." And why may it not be concluded hereof that there is no sin to him who knoweth not how to do well and doth it not? "Because there are sins of ignorance (saith Bellarmine) and he who knoweth not how to do well and doth it not sinneth, though less than he that offendeth wittingly." I know not whether this be a sin of ignorance in Bellarmine or no, that when he should say (if he will check the conclusion) "there is sin to ignorant," he saith (as if that were all one), "the ignorant sinneth." Between which two things there is a great difference in St. James his meaning. For St. James in these words, "there is sin to him," doth speak emphatically and noteth in that man the same that our Saviour did in the Pharisees, when (because they boasted of their sight and knowledge) he told them that they had sin (John 9.41), meaning by this Phrase, as himself expoundeth it, that their sin remained, that is to say, continued and stood firm and settled. The custom of the Greek tongue, wherein St. James wrote, doth give this Phrase that sense, as also the Syriac (the language used by Christ) translating Christ's words after the same manner. And the matter treated of doth argue that he meant not generally of sin, but of sin being and cleaving to a man in special and peculiar sort. For, as "the servant that knew his Master's will and did not according to it shall be beaten with many stripes, but he that knew it not and yet did commit things worthy of stripes, shall be beaten with few" (Luke 12.46-47), likewise in transgression whereto the punishment answereth, "he that knoweth how to do well, and doth it not, sin is to him, he hath it, he offendeth notably. But he that knoweth not how to do well, and doth evil, hath not sin sticking to him, his sin remaineth not, he sinneth not so greatly and grievously." Wherefore, when Bellarmine draweth out of that sentence such a conclusion as if St. James, in saying there is sin to him, had simply meant he sinneth, Bellarmine mistaketh the meaning of the sentence, which if the text itself cannot inform him, his doctors well considered may.

But take the right meaning and the conclusion will be sound: "Whosoever doth not good and honest things, except it be of ignorance, he sinneth desperately and mainly. Therefore whoso of ignorance omitteth to do them, he sinneth not desperately." And thus our conclusion, drawn from Christ's sentence, is rather confirmed than prejudiced by this example. Yea, let even St. Augustine, whose authority Bellarmine doth ground on herein, be diligently marked. And himself in matching these sentences together bewrayeth an oversight, which being corrected will help the truth with light and strength. For to make the one of them like the other, he is fain to fashion Christ's speech in this sort: "To him who putteth away his wife without the cause of whoredom and marrieth another, to him there is the crime of committing adultery." Now, Christ hath not these words of emphatical property and strong signification whereby he might teach, as St. Augustine gathereth, that whosoever putteth away his wife for any cause save for whoredom and marrieth another committeth adultery in a high degree, and so imply by consequence that whoso marrieth another, though having put away his former wife for whoredom, yet committeth adultery too, a less adultery.

But that which Christ saith is simple, flat, absolute: "he committeth adultery." And therefore, as it may be inferred out of St. James that he who omitteth the doing of good through ignorance sinneth not with a lofty hand in resolute stiffness of a hardened heart, so conclude we rightly out of Christ's words that he who having put away his wife for whoredom marrieth another committeth not adultery in any degree at all.

The first sentence then alleged by St. Augustine, and after him pressed by our adversaries out of the Scriptures, is so far from disproving that it proveth rather the like conclusions from the like sentences. The second and third are out of their own brains. The one of Bellarmine's forging, the other of the Pamphleteer's. Bellarmine's, "He that stealeth, except it be for need, sinneth"; the Pamphleteer's, "He that maketh ale, except it be for a vantage, doth willfully sin." Whereof they say it were a wrong and bad inference that "He sinneth not, who stealeth for need," and "He who lieth for a vantage, sinneth not willfully." A bad inference indeed. But the fault thereof is in that these sentences are not like to Christ's. For Christ's is from Heaven, full of truth and wisdom; these of men, fond, and imply untruth. They might have disputed as fitly to their purpose and proved it as forcibly if they had used this example: "All four-footed beasts except Apes and Monkeys are devoid of reason," or this, "All long-eared Creatures except asses are beasts." For hereof it could not be concluded justly that Asses are not beasts, and Apes are not devoid of reason. No. But this perhaps might be concluded justly, that he had not much reason, nor was far from a beast, that would make such sentences. Considering that all men who write or speak with reason mean that to be denied in the particular which they do except from a general affirmed. And therefore, since he sinneth who stealeth though for need, as the wiseman showeth (Prov. 30.9), and he that lieth for a vantage doth willfully sin, yea, the more willfully sometimes because for a vantage, as when these scribes belied Christ, it were a very fond and witless speech to say that "Whosoever stealeth, except it be for need, sinneth," and "Whosoever lieth, except it be for a vantage, doth willfully sin." Wherefore these sentences are no more like to Christ's than copper is to gold or wormwood to the bread of Heaven.

Neither shall they ever find any sentence like to his indeed, of which the like conclusion may not be inferred as we infer of that. And so the main ground of my principal reason, proposed in the beginning, remaineth sure and clearly proved: that he, by Christ's sentence, committeth not adultery, who having put away his wife for whoredom marrieth another. Whereof, seeing it followeth necessarily that he who hath put away his wife for whoredom may lawfully marry another, as I there declared, it followeth by the like necessity, of consequence, that the popish doctrine maintained by our adversaries denying the same is contrary to the Scripture and doth gainsay the truth delivered by the Son of God.

NOTES

1. Medieval theologians and ecclesiastical experts.
2. Saint Robert Bellarmine, 1542-1621, Italian cardinal and theologian; his tract is titled, *Refutation of the Discourse Touching the Lawfulness of Marriage after Divorce for Whoredom*. Edmund Bunny's *Of Divorce for Adultery and Marrying Again*, which argues against Rainolds' position, was published in 1610 at Oxford (*STC* 4091).
3. Narrow or winding passages.
4. Council of the Roman Catholic Church, which met at Trent in Italy between 1545 and 1563 to condemn the Reformation and define Catholic doctrine.
5. A small word of functional or relational use, such as a preposition, article, or conjunction.
6. Rainolds cites supporting examples from Acts 26.29, 1 Cor. 15.27, 1 Sam. 21.9, 1 Kings 3.18.
7. Words expressing opposition and exception (e.g. *but, unless*).
8. A specious reasoner who raises trivial points.
9. Dispute obstinately.
10. Explaining away, glossing over.
11. Albert Pighui, 1490-1542, Dutch reformist theologian.
12. Juan de Avila, c. 1494-1569.
13. Alphonsus a Castro, d. 1558, Portuguese Jesuit missionary.
14. 1300-40, author of controversial anti-semitic texts.
15. Saint Thomas Aquinas.
16. If they want it to or not.
17. The basic form of marital separation granted by the church courts.
18. Archbishop of Achrida (Albania) in the twelfth century.

CHAPTER 5

A Treatise
Against Painting and Tincturing of Men and Women
Thomas Tuke

In the classical tradition, attacks on make-up and elaborate dressing, which first emerged among Cynic philosophers including Diogenes, were more fully developed in the Stoic philosophy of figures such as Epictetus and Seneca, and in the satirical writings of Persius and Juvenal (Colish 4-6). This tradition combined with biblical denunciations of lavish appearance to produce a "cosmetic theology" which, under the influence of a number of early Christian authors and church fathers including Tertullian, St. Cyprian, and St. Ambrose, assumed anti-feminist values (Colish 12). As R. Howard Bloch has shown, this line of misogynist attack persisted throughout the medieval period and into the Renaissance. It supplied a series of authoritative commonplaces or *topoi* to be reiterated in treatises and plays, and the specific subject matter for a number of tracts which dealt with the dangers of cosmetics, fashion, and, on some occasions, any concern with physical appearance. Thomas Tuke's attack on painting and tincturing falls into the second category, and while it purports to deal with excessive make-up used by men and women, like the *Homily on Apparel*, it soon concentrates exclusively on and against women.

The charges made by these texts are that women's use of cosmetics disrupts secular and religious hierarchies. Most significantly, women are seen to threaten the cosmic and natural order, challenging the perfection of God's creation and claiming their own powers of self-fashioning and creation (Dolan 229). They are also accused of seeking to lead men astray, alluring them to sensual destruction, while at the same time trying to avoid the inevitability of aging and death. These sorts of criticisms are voiced by characters in numerous Elizabethan and Jacobean plays and poems (Drew-Bear), sometimes as part of a wider social attack made by malcontent figures but always, as noted above, with a misogynist twist.

From the thirteenth century on cosmetics were increasingly used in western Europe, with products and ingredients being imported from

Mediterranean countries, India, and the Americas (Garner 131). As her portraits vividly show, Queen Elizabeth used make-up and hair coloring as did other court figures, male and female. While Elizabeth's motives combined personal vanity with the "political necessity of maintaining a stable and vigorous image of the Queen" (Cerasano and Wynne-Davies 12-13), the exoticism and prestige of such courtly and foreign habits, which increased at the Stuart court, provided further evidence of immorality and corruption to many English writers.

Tuke's treatise conforms to these moralistic patterns. He approvingly cites the views of many religious authorities, linking the church fathers to a number of Reformation and Calvinist theologians. Occasionally the focus of his attack switches from women to the decadence of Catholicism, suggesting that cosmetic theology might form part of the bridge between Protestantism and the primitive church. At other times, the anti-feminist and anti-Catholic positions coalesce, recalling Spenser's portrayal of Duessa in *The Faerie Queen*, and misogynistic imagery is used to validate the righteousness of English Protestantism.

A conservative minister, Tuke remained loyal to the royalist cause and was imprisoned during the civil war years. He died in 1657, having published a number of other religious works on topics including predestination and the doctrine of election, Christian duties, the Eucharist, and death and dying. *A Treatise against Painting and Tincturing* was published twice in London in 1616. The text below is taken from the second printing (*STC* 24316a; Reel 1191), and includes a broadside pamphlet, "The Picture of a Picture," giving "the character of a painted woman" in the style of Thomas Overbury's characters of social types. The "picture" was initially printed separately and may not be by Tuke. Its colloquial style contrasts with the learned tone of Tuke's work, but despite their different registers the two texts attack women and cosmetics with equal vehemence.

A TREATISE AGAINST PAINTING AND TINCTURING

Though these times and places in which we now live are stained with fouler faults than this of which I have taken upon me here to entreat, yet because it was (as I suppose) never so common as it is now amongst us, and seeing by connivance or silence it still dilates itself and now at length findeth some friends which stick not in corners either to defend it or to extenuate the villainess of it, I have therefore singled it out alone from many other vanities against which many have bent themselves by word and writing, purposing to declare unto the world what I am able to say against it, entreating all with judgment to ponder what I write and, if they shall perceive my reasons sound and good, to join together with me in the persecution and banishing of this evil from amongst us of whom better things are looked for and desired. And I humbly beseech Almighty God to direct my heart and hand that I may think and write that which shall be pleasing to him, and to prosper and bless it unto all that shall read or hear it, that it may find friendly entertainment in their hearts and produce fruits answerable to it in their lives and practice.

Saint Paul, inspired with the Spirit of Christ, gives a golden precept, to which if we will yield obedience as we should, we shall willingly abstain from this artificial facing. "Whatsoever things (saith he) are true; whatsoever things are venerable; whatsoever things are just; whatsoever things are pure; whatsoever things are lovely; whatsoever things are of good report, if there be any virtue, and if there be any praise, think on these things" (Phil. 4.8). These things he would have us to delight in and to do, the contrary he would have us decline and abandon. But a painted face is a false face, a true falsehood, not a true face. "That picture (or painting)," saith St. Ambrose, "is of corruption and not comely, that painting is deceitful and not of simplicity, that painting lasteth but a while, it is wiped off either with rain or sweat. That painting deceiveth and beguileth, that it can neither please him whom thou desirest to please, who perceiveth this pleasing beauty to be none of thine but borrowed. And thou dost also displease thy maker, who seeth his work to be defaced."[1]

Or is this painting venerable, or venerous[2] and abominable rather? Do men of worth and judgment respect and favor it as a thing honest and worthy to be esteemed? Did ever Patriarch, Apostle, or Father of the Church approve it? Hath it not been ever scorned of sage and grave men? A painted face is not much unlike an Idol: it is not that it would be taken for, and they that make it are like unto it, and so are all they that do delight therein and worship it.

Shall we say the painting of hair or face is just? Doth the law of God require or favor it? Or doth reason uncorrupted teach it? Or have the laws of any wise and understanding heads endured or enjoined it? Or rather is it not altogether injurious? Sure there is a wrong done to God whose workmanship they would seem to mend, being discontented with it. St. Jerome saith, "She paints herself by a glass, and to the contumely of her Creator laboreth to be fairer than she was born."[3] And in an Epistle to Laia concerning the institution[4] of her Daughter, where he relateth a story of a certain woman grievously smitten for painting of her daughter, he calleth those that do such things, "violators of the Temple of Christ." Saint Origen[5] likewise taxeth painted women by sundry places of Scripture, amongst other things for daubing their living face with dead colors, and affirmeth that they do these things to the disgrace of their Creator. Saint Ambrose also thus writeth to the same effect: "Thou art painted, O man, and painted of the Lord thy God. Thou hast a good Artisan and Painter. Do not deface that good picture, sinning not with deceitful stuff but with true colors. O woman, thou defacest the picture if thou daubest thy countenance with material whiteness or a borrowed red. Tell me, if after one workman hath done thou usest the help of another to overlay the work of the former with his new devices, doth he not take it in ill part who sees his work to be disguised? Do not take away God's picturing and assume the picture of a harlot, because it is written, 'Shall I take the members of Christ, and make them the members of a harlot? God forbid' (1 Cor.6.15). If any man adulterate the work of God he committeth a grievous offence. For it is a heinous crime to think that man can paint thee better than God. It is a grievous thing that God should say of thee, I see not the image, I see not the countenance, which myself have formed. I reject that which is not mine. Seek him that hath painted thee, deal with him, take grace of him to whom thou hast given a reward. What answer wilt thou make him?" Of the same mind also is Tertullian, who saith, that they "sin against the Lord which besot their cheeks with red colors and dye their eyes. The workmanship of God surely doth displease them. They blame and find fault with the workmaster of all things in themselves. For they reprehend him because they mend his work, because they put unto it, taking these additions from the adversary Craftsman, that is, the devil."[6] To all these ancient Doctors of the Church I will add the judgment of a modern Writer, by name Dannaeus, who saith that "the painting of the face is a deforming of the very work in us, and damnable."[7] God then is injured by this kind of painting. Now, let us see if man also be not wronged by it.

Doubtless these Painters are injurious to themselves and others. Saint Ambrose, who terms these devils "torments rather than ornaments," thus somewhere writeth: "While she studies to please another, she displeases herself. O woman, what truer image of thy deformity do we require than thyself, who seekest to be seen? If thou be fair, why art thou hidden? If ill-favored, why dost thou counterfeit beauty, having no regard of thine own conscience nor of another body's error? For he loves another, and thou wouldst please another. And thou wilt be angry if he should love another, who yet doth learn by thee to commit adultery. Thou are an evil teacher of thine own wrong."[8] It is injustice with feigned shows to endeavor to cozen[9] others, laboring to make them think they be that they are not. St Augustine doth not stick to say it is vicious.[10] And if it be not just to deceive men with counterfeit wares, much less lawful is it to deceive them with a disguised countenance. Besides, this borrowed beauty doth sometimes steal away the praise from that that is natural. Yea, and because this evil craft is so much in use, it comes to pass sometimes that they that use it not are suspected and said to meddle with it. And whereas everyone should be careful of their name, they do much wrong themselves herein that use such Arts, causing thereby their modesty, humility, wisdom, and continency to be called into question and suspected. And what wrong do they to themselves in provoking God against them to punish them for their pride and vanity?

Sir Thomas More, one not meanly learned, was wont to say of such that there were very many which purchased hell unto themselves in this life with that labor with the one half whereof they might have gained heaven. Clemens Alexandrinus saith "They are not once but thrice worthy to perish, which daub their brows and wear their cheeks with their painted stuff."[11] Saint Cyprian hath a notable speech full of sting and terror, where he thus writeth: "If some cunning Painter should set forth the countenance and shape of a woman, having ended his work, another should take upon him as being more skillful to reform and mend it, the first workman might justly seem to be wronged and offended. And dost thou think (O woman) to escape unpunished, presuming with the like audacious rashness to offend God? Doth sincerity and truth continue when those things that are sincere are polluted with counterfeit colors, and those things which are true are changed into falsehood with deceitful tricks? The Lord doth say, 'Thou art not able to make one hair white or black' (Matt. 5.36), and thou, to put down his saying, wouldst thou be stronger? By audacious endeavor and sacrilegious contempt thou colorest thine hairs. With an ill presage of future things thou beginst with flaming hair and offendest in thine head, that is, in the better part of thy body. Oh detestable act! Fearest thou not, I pray thee, who art thus disguised, lest the workman that made thee should not acknowledge thee. And lest he should say, 'This is not my work, this is none of our image, thou hast polluted thy skin with deceitful art, thou hast changed thine hair with a counterfeit color, thy face is falsified, thy shape is defiled, thy countenance is borrowed.' Thou canst not see God, having not the eyes that God hath made but which the devil hath marred. Thou hast followed him, thou hast imitated the red-shining and painted eyes of the Serpent. Being trimmed up in thine fashion, thou art to burn also in like manner with him. Ought not these things, I pray thee, to be considered of the servants of God? Are they not to be dreaded always, both day and night?"[12] But to proceed, "Whatsoever things are pure or chaste," saith Saint Paul.

Is that pure or to be deemed the fruit of a chaste mind which is so common amongst the impurest of women, and altogether contemned of those that are most grave and pious? "All those things," saith Tertullian, "are refuted as idle, and enemies to chastity. Where God is, there is chastity, there is gravity, the helper and companion of it. How then shall we practice chastity without the instrument thereof, that is, without gravity? And how shall we use gravity for the service of chastity if there be not a certain severeness both in the face and in apparel, and in the whole main round about?" Saint Jerome likewise thus writeth, "What makes this purple and white stuff in the face of a Christian women the inflamers of youth, the nourishers of lust, and tokens of an unchaste soul?"[13] Clemens Alexandrinus makes this painting a sign of a sick soul. "For as he (saith Clemens) that hath some salve applied to him, or his eyes anointed, doth by the very sight give cause to suspect that he is diseased, so painting, tinctures, and affected dressings do signify, that the soul is sick within." St. Ambrose saith boldly that "By the adulterating of the countenance they meditate the adulterating of chastity."

But I may not pretermit[14] another speech of Clemens in the place quoted already, where he saith that the Egyptian Temples were fair and sumptuous, but instead of God, who was not to be found within them, there was a Cat, a Crocodile, or some serpent of the country, or some other beast, beseeming a cave or hole or the mud and not a Temple. "So (saith he) the women which are exercised in frizzing their hair, in anointing their cheeks, in painting their eyes, and dyeing their hair, and following other wantonness with unlawful arts, do seem to me to draw on unhappy lovers. But if any man shall open the veil of the Temple, I mean their dressing, coloring, dying, and those things that are plastered on them, thinking to find true beauty, I wot well he will grow into a loathing and detestation. For he shall not find the image of God dwelling within but instead thereof a fornicatress and adulteress occupy the temple of the soul. He shall discern a painted Ape, and that seducing Serpent, through the desire of glory, doth possess the soul instead of a hole, transforming women into whores, discharging the office of a bawd." And that renowned and holy Bishop of Milan, whom before we cited, calleth this painting which of women is so much usurped, "the picture of a harlot." Plutarch also showeth that Lycurgus banished tincture out of Sparta as a flatterer of the sense, and forbad the City to all that used the arts of painting and tricking the body because evil arts corrupted men's manners.[15] And the said Author writeth that women were at that time so chaste and so far from the lightness of those that followed after that "the crime of adultery with them was counted a thing incredible." And as one said to his guest, "How could there be an adulterer in Sparta, where luxury and painting are deemed ignominious, and where shamefastness, modesty, and obedience domineer?"

But Saint Paul proceedeth, "Whatsoever things (saith he) are lovely." Doth a painted face procure love, or loathing rather, if it be perceived? "Nothing counterfeited doth afford contentment," as Saint Ambrose speaketh.[16] Who is pleased with counterfeit money, with counterfeit friendship, with counterfeit stuff? Who loves hypocrisy in religion? And what is a woman painted but a certain kind of hypocrite, resembling that in show which she is not truly? Is deceit and falsehood lovely? And what is this artificial facing but a true deceit, or a deceitful truth? "To color the face with artificial devices, to make it look red or lovely, is a counterfeit and base deceit," saith Saint Augustine, "with which I am persuaded, husbands would not be deceived."[17] And another saith, "When the face is painted with a false color, it becomes an abomination."[18] And if the painting of the face and borrowing of complexion beseem none (as Saint Cyprian saith) but whores and dishonest women, why should any one delight therein as in things pleasing or worthy love? Or if it be such a lovely thing, what reason had Saint Jerome to say, "Let a Christian woman blush for shame, if she force favor, if she take care of the flesh unto concupiscence, in which they are which cannot please God," as the Apostle speaketh?[19] Or why should he say that dressing void of curiosities became Christian matrons, and forbid Laeta to color her daughter's hair and to begin in her anything of the flames of hell?

No, no, these arts and actions are not to be loved but hated rather. Doubtless nature and art are both good and to be beloved, but the abuse of both or either is evil, is of the devil. And is not art abused when it is made an organ and slave to pride, wantonness, and vanity? And that I may speak a little by digression to her that exercises herself in these unlawful and unlovely arts: Tell me, how canst thou desire that another should not loathe thee, seeing thou loathest thine own self? For as Peter Martyr speaks out of Saint Ambrose, they that seek by these devices to please others do testify that they have disliked themselves first: "For had they not disliked themselves, and desired something in themselves, they would not have sought to have mended their faces with painting." Their very bravery, wherein they glory, bewrays their wants. Or dost thou love thyself artificial and like an Idol, and loathe or dislike thyself natural and in thy native colors? O woman, great is thy pride and folly, foolish pride and proud folly. What folly is it to fall in love with a picture? What madness is it (saith a forenamed Father) to change nature's shape and to seek a picture? Doubtless thou deservest to be loathed of others because thou dost loath thyself and, being displeased with the pleasure of God, doest please thyself in that that is displeasing to him.

But I have digressed. The Apostle addeth, "Whatsoever things are of good report." And in another place he saith, "Provide things honest in the sight of all men" (Rom. 12.17). Say now, is this painting of good report? Do all or the wisest and honestest of all account it honest? Divers of the Fathers, as we have seen, have condemned it in that name. It was ignominious in the days of Lycurgus. Peter Martyr out of Saint Chrysostom saith it is very pleasing to see such a face as God created whereas, on the contrary, a countenance full of red and white colors, otherwise than natural, is disallowed. Deformity is no point of dishonesty but painting, being discerned and known, is branded always with reproach and infamy. Saint Jerome to Marcella saith that those women are matter of scandal to Christian eyes which do paint their faces and eyes with certain artificial colors, whose faces (saith he), being plastered and deformed with too much brightness, are counterfeits of Idols. And such old women as use those and the like vanities he calls in mocking "trembling girls." And unto Furia he saith that this furniture is not the Lord's, this covering is of Antichrist. Sure it is not for Christ but rather against Christ, and ill beseems chaste and godly Christians, suiting fitter with the favorites and lovers of that Mother of harlots, arrayed in purple and scarlet colors and full of allurements (Rev. 17.4-5). Platina writeth that Paulus Secundus, Bishop of Rome, used to paint himself, a thing not much to be found fault with in such a friend unto the Whore, though very ill beseeming one that counts himself the Vicar of Christ.[20] It seems the Church's Head hath been once a painted one.

But to return, the Apostle would have us delight and think on those things that are of good account, and he will have us do it in the sight of all men, according as our Saviour says, "Let your light so shine before men, that they may see your good works" (Matt. 5.16). It is not enough to be good, but she that is good must seem good; she that is chaste must seem chaste; she that is humble must seem humble. She that is modest must seem to be so and not plaster her face that she cannot blush upon any occasion (though she would) so as to be discerned of another. It is very pat which Tertullian writeth: "It is not enough for Christian chastity that it be but that it be also seen." And good counsel which he gives to Christian women: come forth now furnished with the medicaments and ornaments of the Apostles, taking from simplicity brightness and from chastity redness, your eyes painted with modesty, for an earring having the word of God, and the yoke of Christ for a chain unto your necks. Subject your head unto your husbands, and ye shall make show good enough. Array yourselves with the silk of honesty, the fine linen of sanctity, with the purple of chastity. Being so painted and tricked up, ye shall have God your lover.

But Saint Paul hath not yet ended his speech. "If (saith he) there be any virtue." But dare any say it is a virtue or act of virtue to paint the face or hair? St. Ambrose saith this painting is of vice or vicious. And Clemens Alexandrinus commends one Caeus who fitly described virtue and vice in two images. For, "he made virtue standing simply clothed with a white-shining garment and pure, adorned only with bashfulness. But vice with superfluous and changeable apparel, and glorying in borrowed colors." But that it may appear plainly that this kind of painting and coloring is vicious, let us inquire into the cause of it. Tertullian saith expressly it's from the devil. "For who (saith he) would teach to change the body but he that hath changed the soul of man through malice? He out of doubt hath stirred up such wits that so he might, after a sort, in us lay hands on God. That which is natural is the work of God; therefore that which is counterfeit is of the devil." Saint Cyprian likewise saith as much in effect, affirming that the Apostatical Angels taught women to paint their eyes and cheeks and to alter their hair with counterfeit colors and, as he saith, to drive out all the truth of their face and head. If these things be of the devil, God is little beholding to those that use them. "What wickedness is it (saith Tertullian) to bring in Satan's devices after God's work? Our servants borrow nothing of our enemies; soldiers ask nothing of the enemy of their commander. And shall a Christian receive help of that evil one? I wot not whether this name (Christian) should belong any longer to him. For he shall be his, with whose instructions he longs to be instructed."

And as the exterior Author of these devices is evil, even no other than the devil, so the interior grounds thereof are also evil, as pride, wantonness, and lack of judgment or else rebellion of affections against judgment. What a pride it is that thou canst not be content to appear in thine own likeness, and to seem that to others which thou art in thyself? The bird appears in her own feathers, the Peacock shows himself in his own colors, the sheep is seen in her own fleece and likeness, white or black. The tree hath her own rind, appears in her own blossoms and fruits, and shall it be horrible to a woman to seem to be as she is indeed, displeasing to her to appear in her own likeness, her own hair, her own complexion? She was born in her own, nature would show itself in her proper colors. She was not born painted in this world (unless perhaps so, as is expressed in the Prophet), neither shall she rise painted in the next world (Ezek. 16), and I think she would be loathe die painted. Why then should she live painted, why should she love it? "I would I, poor wretch (saith Tertullian), might see in that day of Christian exultation whether ye shall rise again with your white, red, and yellowish paintings, and those strange dressings of your head, and whether the Angels shall lift you up so pictured to meet Christ. O ye women, let God see you such now as he shall see ye then." Is not this also a point of pride, by such deceitful shifts to gain the praises of men and to desire to be reputed fairer or younger or better favored than one is indeed? And doth not God hate pride and reward humility? Doth he not resist the proud and give grace to the humble (Jas. 4.6)? What a contempt of God is this to prefer the work of thine own finger to the work of God? What impiety is it to go about to have that thought God's which is thine own? What injustice to conceal his work and ostent thine own, and indeed to spoil his with thine own? Innocentius saith, "An artificial form is drawn over and the natural face is painted, as if the artifice of man exceeded the art of God."[21] And is not this a trick of a wanton, to use these arts to procure and tie the eyes of people to thee, or to gain some unfortunate servant?[22] Is it not a foolish wiliness and a certain wily kind of folly by these lime-twigs, these painted lime-twigs, to labor to think or labor to catch a Woodcock or a Wild-goose? Are these devices allowed, as stales[23] or snares, to take men in them? Dost thou deem men as simple as those birds that were deceived by the Painter's artifice, flying to grapes that were but painted?[24] Because Lycoris pleases herself being painted, being otherwise as black as an overripe Mulberry, doth she therefore think to gain a husband, who knows an ill face well-painted is but as a piece of counterfeit silver or as a fair carpet over an unhandsome table?[25]

Tell me, are all men born rich or noble (though all these are born men yet all men are not born these)? Now, shall he that is base and needy, and not yet promoted nor made wealthy, make fare as if he were some noble or rich man? It were intolerable vanity. Say, is every man truly virtuous and religious? No, no more than every Angel is good and holy. Now, shall he that is profane and impious make show of piety and true devotion? Were it not damnable hypocrisy in him? If he be not, let him not seem to be. For not being, his very seeming is a sin unto him. And dost thou think it lawful for thee to make show of favor and beauty or of another complexion and temper than thou art of by thy daubing, painting, and borrowing, God and Nature, which is his Handmaid, having withheld beauty or a lovely complexion from thee? Virtue is one gift of God and beauty is another. Now, as a man may not counterfeit virtue being vicious, so he may not counterfeit beauty being destitute of it.

Doubtless, unthankfulness to God hath a great stroke in this ungodly exercise. For were we thankful to God, as indeed we should be, would we loathe and despise his work upon us and love our own? Would we not care how we corrupt and mangle his with ours? If we were thankful to him for our complexions and favor, how mean so ever, we would humble ourselves before him and not go about to cozen the world with our borrowed feathers or show ourselves altogether unpatient of his handy-work. Yea, we would labor to supply the want of good outward parts by inward virtues and by the offices of piety, charity, and humility, things which (fear me) are seldom and little thought of amongst the Painters who, if we may believe the speeches of the world (and they say, "Market men use to speak as the market goes"), are too many of them not much unlike ill cloth of a good dye, or to a Letter fairly written and with good ink but not without some false English or ill contents.

But let us see how the Apostle ends his exhortation. "If there be any praise (saith he) think on these things." Now is a painted face worthy to be praised? Is a borrowed beauty or fresh-colored hair with women's skill to be commended? Shall we bestow our praises on what we may not spend our love? Shall we laud that that is not worthy one good look? Shall that be praised that is vile and vain? "What more vain," saith Innocentius, "than to dye the cheeks and anoint the face?" True it is that God hath given a man oil to make him have cheerful countenance (Ps. 104.15), but this is by refreshing and cheering the blood and not by daubing or dyeing the countenance, which is to be discommended in all that use it whatever they be. "Fucation (saith Saint Chrysostom), being espied, is ever marked with ignominy."[26] "More ornament is not to be given to the body than is profitable for the soul," saith Saint Basil the Great. "For to a generous man, and one truly worthy of this name, it were no less reproach to be wantonly decked or to take superfluous care of the body than to be affected with some other note of disgrace and evil affection through slothfulness."[27]

Consider also the judgment of Heathen men. Chius, a certain old man, came upon some business of state to Lacedaemon, and having dyed his gray hairs he came before Archidamus, the Lacedaemonian King, who seeing the old man disguised rose up and said, "What good thing can this fellow say, whose not only the heart but head also is stained with deceit?" And so exploded whatsoever he said, reprehending his disposition by the deceit he used with his hair.[28] Questionless there is lack of truth in the heart when false hair is worn for deceit. Doubtless falsehood is in his or her heart whose face or hair is falsified to deceit. Falsehood uttered in the face or hair is first conceived and coined in the heart. Wantonness, pride, and vanity are conceived inwardly before they are expressed outwardly. The hand doth but what the heart bids it. Of the abundance of the heart, the mouth speaketh and the hand worketh. King Philip of Macedonia made one of Antipater's friends a Judge, but understanding that he used to color the hair of his head and beard he displaced him saying, "He which would not be true in his affairs was not worthy to be trusted in an office."[29] He used deceit in dyeing his hair, whereof no great lucre could arise; doubtless he will be much more deceitful in the affairs of his office where deceit sometimes is very gainful. The natural form and color is not laid to a man's charge but only that which is counterfeit and ascititious.[30]

"Nature's form and favor is right and good, / But Belgick colors becomes no Roman blood."[31] That is to say, the waste of France and such painting stuff are disgraceful in an Italian. If an old woman painted herself, they used to say *Lecythum habet in malis*, which is a certain enigmatical and biting by-word used against old wives, that they cloaked their wrinkles with their artificial daubings. Festus Pompeius[32] saith that common and base whores used daubing of themselves though with the vilest stuff. Diogenes said to one that had anointed his hairs, "Beware thy sweet head make not thy life stink."[33] So may it well be said to those that buy and borrow their favor and their color: "Beware lest this borrowed grace bring ye not into disgrace both with God and his children, and that the counterfeiting of form do not deform you." Surely, the Lord did most terribly threaten the proud and wanton Dames of Israel for their pride, wantonness, and vanities (Isa. 3.16). And may it not be said of these painted faces, as the Lord said of that people, "The show of their countenance do witness against them" (Isa. 3.9)?

Doubtless, this kind of favor finds no favor, no one word of praise in all the word of God. "In Jezebel who painted her eyes is propounded (saith Piscator) an example of a proud woman."[34] "It is no good face (saith Martyr) which seeks these helps. Let us in the meanwhile, consider the impudency of a wicked woman, who being in extreme danger, yet shows no token of repentance, yea, she bestows her time in painting of her face."[35]

And on the Prophet Jeremiah, where mention is made of painting the face or eyes (Jer. 4.30), Saint Jerome in his Comments saith, "He speaketh under the figure of an adulterous woman." In like manner, Calvin thus writing on the said place saith, that the Prophet hath respect to the furniture of whores, "Because the people was like an adulterous woman. And whores (saith he) to entice adulterers are wont to paint their faces and by such allurements to entangle and catch men.[36] And whereas Ezekiel also doth once make mention of this painting (Ezek. 23.40), Saint Jerome (others likewise consenting with him) saith upon the same place, "Thou hast fulfilled all the habit of an adulterous woman."

This painting, therefore, being no better entertained in the word of God, and being (as we have heard before) a work of Satan, there is no reason at all why Christian women should be addicted to it. I would think women should beware of the Serpent (who hath an oar in this boat, as Clemens showeth), seeing their mother was beguiled with him of old, and that they all fear the worse for him still. Neither do I read that ever any grave and discreet woman used these deceits. Some write of some barbarous people which delight in painting their skin. Saint Jerome writes that Maximilla, Montanus his Prophetess, a woman devil-driven, did use to paint.[37] And there is also mention in the Ecclesiastical history made of one Prisca, who practised the same arts. Caesar likewise writes that the Britons used to color their faces with their Woad, but this was not out of pride or wantonness but to strike a terror in their enemies with whom they were to fight.[38] But methinks Christians should not only be but seem so. The children of wisdom should not only be such but seem such. They that profess modestly and humility, or which have promised it in their Baptism, should not only be modest and humble but appear to be so by their shows. And to use the words I find in Peter Martyr: "As Paul said, 'There is a difference betwixt a married woman and a virgin' (1 Cor. 7.34). So may we say there should be a difference between the handmaidens of Christ and the handmaids of the devil. The handmaids of the devil, because they are unchaste, do use these pictures. Wherefore the handmaids of Christ should fly from them, that they might show themselves to be unlike to them. In good sooth if Christian women will so color and paint themselves, I pray you what doth a matron differ from a harlot?"[39] I remember Saint Ambrose saith that "Modesty is to be kept even in the motion, gesture, and gait," and shall it be banished out of the face? "For (saith he) the condition of the mind is discerned in the state and behavior of the body."[40]

Without doubt, then, a deceitful and effeminate face is the ensign of a deceitful and effeminate heart. "Say not (Saint Augustine) that you have modest and chaste affections if ye have unchaste and wanton eyes."[41] So I say, say not that thou hast the heart of a chaste and humble woman if thou hast the face and favor of a proud dame or wanton minion. And to use the words of Tertullian, "How far from our disciplines and professions, how unworthy the name of Christians is it to have a feigned face, to whom all simplicity is commended; to lie with the countenance, who may lie with their tongue; to desire that which is not granted, who should abstain from that which is not theirs; and to practice the making of shows and faces whose study is to be chaste and modest?" These arts make those that use them too like the devils who, though they be Angels of darkness, yet to work some feat they will now and then transform themselves into Angels of light. They are one thing, but to deceive they will seem another.

And in truth, I wonder how they dare pray to God with such impure faces? How shall they look up to God with a face which he doth not own? How can they beg pardon when their sin cleaves unto their faces and when they are not able for to blush? "How can she weep for her sins," saith Jerome, "when her tears will make furrows in her face? With what confidence doth she lift up her countenances to heaven, which her Maker acknowledges not? Youth is in vain pretended, and girlish age alleged for excuse." What hope is there that God will hear whilst her heart is set on vanity and pride, on wantonness and deceit. David saith, "If I regard iniquity in mine heart, the Lord will not hear me" (Ps. 66.18). "We know (saith one in the Gospel) God heareth not sinners. But if any man be a worshipper of God and doth his will, him he heareth" (John 9.31). Doubtless these curiosities are not things indifferent, as some imagine them to be. It is well said by Calvin somewhere, "Too much fineness and superfluous brightness, and finally all excess ariseth out of the corruption of the heart. Moreover, ambition, pride, luxury, affectation, and such like are not (saith he) things indifferent."[42]

But what need I throw water into the sea or set up a candle in the Sun? But by the doctrine and judgment of Saint Paul, as is observed by Peter Martyr, men must beware not only of evil but "abstain from all appearance of evil" (1 Thess. 5.22): "But in these painting practices, the show of evil is so perspicuous as it cannot be denied. Truly (saith he) in God's Book, this painting is never taken in good part." And the greater the persons be that use these arts, the worse it is. For, "The greater the man is that sins, the greater is his sin."[43] It is more scandalous and hurtful. And the more that any man hath received of God, the more he owes unto God. The higher a man is the more humble he should be. The greater he is the better he should be. When high trees and steeples fall, there is much looking. And be men never so higher, yet there is one high before whom and under whom they must humble themselves and bewail their pride and vanities, or else they must not look to be exalted of him.[44]

And if these borrowed faces and painted locks be ridiculous and odious in a woman that is poor and base, as in a Kitchen-wench or such like, how much more discommendable is it in such as God hath advanced? What poor thanks do they pay him for those benefits of wealth and greatness which, without their merit, he hath conferred and cast upon them? Even a little stain is noted in fine Lawn, a little blot or blur is discerned in white paper. Honorable and rich persons stand as upon hills, all men's eyes are on them. They should be patterns of piety, examples of virtue. For by their examples they do either much good or much hurt. If it would please them to consider what the Apostle saith unto the Corinthians, I am persuaded they would not meddle with these vanities. Read and weigh what is said in 1 Corinthians 7.29-31. Surely they that abuse the world, that abuse their greatness, that abuse their wealth and wit, they lose a blessing of the world, of their greatness, wealth, and wit. These things are theirs whilst well used, but being abused they are not theirs, but their enemies rather; they make not for them but against them. Oh, how happy had it been for them if they had not known what wit, what wealth, what the world, what greatness meant! A man must be poor in riches, little in greatness, humble in honor, virtuous in beauty, meek in authority, modest and not self-conceited in all his ornaments, else all is nothing and he is nothing or a certain something worse than nothing.

Think we not that all Christian women, how great soever, are bound to those two speeches of their Apostle Saint Paul? "Whatsoever ye do, do all to the glory of God." And again: "Give none offence, neither to the Jews, nor to the Gentiles, nor to the Church of God" (1 Cor. 10.31-32). But do they paint their faces or dye their hair to the glory of God? Is God honored by these exercises or disgraced rather, as we have seen before? Saint Cyprian saith, "Women lay hands on God when they seek," by such counterfeit devices, "to reform and transfigure that which he hath formed. None knowing that that is God's work which is born and the devil's whatsoever is changed." And do they think that this their painting is offensive unto none. Some they displease and grieve, others they poison by this ill example, which is as a match to give fire to them that are as capable of it as tinder, flax, or gun-powder. And besides, they give the enemy occasion to disgrace the Church and that Gospel of Jesus which we profess and boast of.

Let us all therefore remember that golden rule which the Apostle there doth give us, which as Hemmingius speaketh, "Whosoever doth willingly and wittingly violate, he without doubt dishonoreth God and is made guilty of eternal anger, until he shall repent."[45] But if the respect of men cannot prevail whose eyes are offended with such vanities, yet let the reverence of God's holy Angels that tend upon you dissuade you from them.[46] For they cannot but be offended as oft as they shall see men pervert nature itself and the order that God hath appointed, and contumaciously to tread it under foot. And is not this the Ordinance of God that every man should appear in his own likeness, every woman be seen in her own face? Is not this an inversion of nature to dissemble and hide the natural visage with an artificial, and to offer one for another? Now, shall we offend our good Angels, our keepers, our protectors, who can as ill endure a painted face and counterfeit hair as any man can endure a sluttish face or nitty locks? And why should a man be so fond on beauty? "Modesty is sufficient beauty" (Propertius). Truly, virtue is the best beauty, which is indeed so beautiful and bright that were it to be seen with eyes it would draw and hold all men's eyes unto it. A virtuous woman needs no borrowed, no bought complexion, none of these poisons. For so Victor calls them when he saith, "What do this white and red paint and a hundred other poisons of colors in an honest body?"[47] The time, labor, and cost which thou wastest on these superfluities bestow and spend in getting, keeping, and exercising virtue, which is even beauty's beauty, which as Saint Ambrose speaketh, "no age shall extinguish, no death can take away, no, sickness can corrupt."

But this borrowed beauty is a vanishing beauty or beautiful vanity. A little wet, a little sweat, a little breath will mar it. Perhaps thou wilt say it is an ornament. An ornament? A torment it is, saith the said Father: "The true ornaments of Christians (saith Saint Augustine) are not only no counterfeit and lying painting, no nor so much as the pomp of gold or garments, but good manners." "An ornament (saith Crates) is that which doth adorn, and that adorneth which makes a woman more honest. But painting," either of face or hair, "performs not this, but those things which show gravity, moderation, and shamefastness."[48] Democritus likewise said that "sparingness of speech adorned a woman, and that the paucity even of an ornament is an ornament to her." I may not omit what Saint Gregory Nanzianzen hath written of the true ornaments of women, where he saith: "There is (saith he) one flower to be loved of women, a good red which is shamefastness. This our Painter painteth. We will give thee, if thou desirest, a second. Thou maiest draw a paleness unto thy beauty, spent with the labors of Christ with prayers, sighs, and restless night and day. These are the medicines both of unmarried and married people. To tarry much at home, to confer of God's word, to set the maids their tasks, to be delighted only in their husband, to bind up their lips, and not to stir forth a-doors, these manners are precious things for women."[49] So the prime of the Apostles, Paul and Peter, having shown their dislike of some things which by some foolish women are made even idols of, show that the true ornaments of Christian women, young and old, high and low, are shamefastness, modesty, and good works together with the incorruption of a meek and quiet spirit, which is of great account with God (1 Tim. 2 and 1 Pet. 3). On the contrary, painting of the face, coloring of the brows, litting[50] of the hair, and such superfluous curiosities are abominations in his eyes.

But thou wilt say that the Apostle forbids not painting of the cheeks or hair. It is true by name he doth not, but in effect he doth, and as

Theophylactus speaketh, "If the Apostle forbid those things that belong to wealth, then much more those things which, with a certain unnecessary care and study, are composed only for vain trimming, as the daubing of the cheeks and face, and some ointments put to the eyes to make them beautiful, and the rest of this rabble."[51] But tell me one thing, for food and raiment, for strength and health, for natural favor, form, and beauty, a man is bound to praise the Lord, and a good man will not forget to do it. But dare any wanton thank God for her colored hair, her borrowed beauty, her artificial facing. I remember Saint Paul saith, "In everything give thanks" (1 Thess. 5.18). Now, I demand of thee, if thou wilt give thanks in this thing (I demand again, why wilt thou live in that state in which thou wouldst not die)? Surely, they forget death and those days of darkness that are dead alive in these toys and vanities. A serious and sad remembrance of death and of the judgment, wherein everyone must receive of the Lord according to that he hath done in his body whether it be good or evil, would deter and keep us from these abuses and vain expense of time (which is not ours if we do abuse it) and would make us think of better things than these (2 Cor. 5).

It is worth the noting which Isidorus Clarius, a most eloquent Preacher as Stapleton calls him, saith in this argument: "If some man (saith he) should promise a woman that if she would leave of her painting and bodily bravery for a year she should appear for a hundred years after the most beautiful of all women that ever should be, without doubt she would most willingly accept the condition. Again, if it should be told her that she hath leave for one year's space to all kinds of painting and coloring and all manner of ornaments, but with that condition that she should be the ugliest of all women all her life long after, there is no question but that she would refuse the offer of that year's bravery for fear of ensuing deformity. But all these things shall come to pass, and those things which are of so much the more moment by how much eternity surpasseth a little time, and yet so sluggish are they in a matter of so great importance. For it shall come to pass that those women, which in this life have lived modestly and without paintings and idle ornaments, shall have bodies bright as the Sun and that for ever. But such as would needs appear conspicuous and beautiful" by borrowed bravery, "here, shall possess eternal deformity with the Devil and his Angels."[52] Calvin writing on these words of Hosea, that is, "Let her take away her whoredoms from her face, and her adulteries from between her breasts" (Hos. 2.2), saith, "What meaneth this? For women play not the whores with their face, nor breasts. It is well known (saith he) that the Prophet alludes to the dressing of harlots. Because Whores, that they may allure men, dress themselves up more costly, and paint their faces curiously and garnish their breasts. Immodesty therefore is seen as well in the face, as in the breasts." Tremellius also, and Junius commenting upon the said Scripture, understand thereby in like manner, *Adulterinos fucos*, paintings and such counterfeit devices, by the which (as one hath well observed) a woman doth not become more beautiful but rather takes away somewhat from natural favor.[53]

Master Thomas Hudson writing of a Painted woman saith accordingly, "She surely keeps her fault of sex and nation, / And best alloweth still the last translation. / Much good time lost, she rests her face's debtor, / For she has made it worse, striving to make it better."[54] Holinshed, in his description of Scotland, tells how the Picts used to "paint over their bodies."[55] And some write that Medea, a notable Sorceress, devised these arts. And sure it is that the Heathen and Infidels did first and most usurp them. Seeing therefore we have cast off their Barbarism and Infidelity, let us also lay aside their other vanities and adulterous devices. But if for very shame, let not these heathen images be brought into the houses of God. They do ill become the bodies of Saints, which are the Temples of the holy Ghost (1 Cor. 6.19), but the Congregation of Saints worse, who are assembled in God's house not to show vanity but to learn humility, not to draw down wanton eyes to themselves but to lift up their eyes and hearts unto God, not to deal with vain and idle people but with Jesus Christ, whose holy eyes are offended with such sights. Master Barnabe Rich his complaint may here not unfitly be inferred, who thus somewhere writeth: "You shall see (saith he) some women go so attired to the Church, that I am ashamed to tell it aloud they are so bepainted, so beperiwigged, so bepowdered, so beperfumed, so bestarched, so belaced, so beembroidered, that I cannot tell what mental virtue they may have, that they do keep inwardly to themselves. But I am sure to the outward show, it is a hard matter in the Church itself to distinguish between a good woman and a bad."[56] I would to God our painters would consider what Saint Jerome writes of Paula who, when he prayed her to spare her eyes for the reading of the Gospel which she marred with weeping for her sins, returned this answer to the holy Father: "That face is to be fouled, which I have often painted against God's commandment. I must afflict my body, which I have pampered with many pleasures. Long laughing must be recompensed with continual weeping."

I will end this present Treatise with the words of that golden-mouthed Teacher of the Greek Church, I mean Saint Chrysostom, who writeth much about this argument I have in hand. His words, as many as concern our purpose, I will turn[57] as faithfully as I can, which yet by turning will lose some grace as wine being turned out of one vessel into another.[58] "Thou hast (saith he) a wife too much loving the bravery of the body painted, wantonizing daily in delights, given to babbling. For though all these things cannot befall one woman, yet in our speech we will feign that they have all met together. But thou wilt say, 'Why was it your pleasure to speak of women rather than of men?' Doubtless there are men corrupter than such a woman. But because government is granted unto men by nature therefore we have described a woman, and not because more faults may be found in women than in men. For you shall often find among men many which women never or but very seldom do commit, as are murder, the eversion of sepulchres,[59] and unprofitable fighting with wild beasts and the like. Do not therefore think that we do these things in contempt of the sex (let this be far from me) but because it is now more commodious to make our description after this manner.

"Be it therefore there is such a woman as we have described, and her husband would reform her by all his care and industry. By what means then shall he effect it? Namely, if he does not command all things to her at once but the more easy things, and those things first which she doth seem to care less for. For if thou wouldst mend all at first thou shalt do nothing. Thou shalt not therefore by and by deprive her of her golden ornaments. Let her have them a time and use them. For that seems to be a lesser evil than a painted and counterfeited face. First therefore, take away her painting, and do not that with terror and threats but with a gentle and sweet persuasion. Let her ever and anon hear thee say that the painted face of women do displease thee and that they cause such a loathing in thee that thou canst not endure them. Allege also the judgment of others that are of thy mind and tell her that that gear uses to mar them that are comely without it, that by this means thou mightest weed this evil out of her. In the meanwhile as yet, speak not a word of hell or heaven, but make her believe that it will glad thine heart to see her with such a face as God hath made, but that a face corrupted and altered from its nature and filled with artificial reds and whites is commonly disliked amongst good men.

"After thou hast wrought her with these words then speak to her also of hell and heaven. Be not slack to discourse of these things not once but again and again, not spitefully or in anger but with love and pleasantness, sometimes speaking fair and sometimes turning away thine eyes with dislike, and sometimes again making much of her. Dost thou not see that painters, when they go about to make a fair picture, do now apply these colors and then others, wiping out the former? Be not thou more unskillful than painters. They being to paint the shape of the body on tables do use so great pains and care, and is it not meet that we should try all conclusions, use all means, when we desire to make souls better?

"If by degrees thou shalt thus reform thy wife's mind, thou shalt be the best painter, a faithful servant, an honest husbandman. With these also make often mention of illustrious women which either have excelled for beauty or which have not been so fair, as of Sarah, Rebecca, and the like. All which it is certain have condemned such vanity, which may appear in that Leah, the wife of the Patriarch Jacob, though she was not fair nor so well loved of her husband and besides bred among the Gentiles, did yet devise no such trick nor altered her natural complexion but constantly kept the lineaments of nature uncorrupted (Gen. 29-30). And wilt thou whose head is Christ, who art a believer, wilt thou allow of the inventions of Satan? Wilt thou not remember that water that was sprinkled upon thy face, nor the Sacrament which beautified thy lips, nor the blood which made red thy tongue? All which things if thou wouldst keep in memory, though thou lovedst bravery very well, thou wouldst not dare, thou couldst not ensure to put any powder or paint upon thy face.

"Remember that thou art made fit for Christ, and thou wilt abominate this deformity. For he joys not in these colors but requireth a more noble branch, to wit, of the soul, which also he loveth greatly and which is to be greatly esteemed, as the Prophet showeth where he saith, 'and the King shall greatly desire thy beauty' (Ps. 45.11). Let us not therefore put any idle and superfluous thing upon us. For there is nothing wanting unto any of the works of God, neither is there ought which needs thy mending. No man presumeth to put any thing to the image which is made according to the similitude of a King, and if he shall presume yet he shall not scape unpunished. Thou addest therefore nothing to the workmanship of men, and dost thou strive to amend that which God hath wrought? Neither dost thou think of hellfire nor fearest the desolation of thy soul, which then lies altogether neglected, when thou settest all thy mind, care, and study on thy body. Why say I the soul is neglected, seeing that it falls out otherwise with the body than thou wishedst? Which hence appeareth, because whereas thou studiest by this thing to seem fair, in truth with this thou appearest deformed. By this thou thinkest to please thy husband which in truth causeth him no little sorrow. Neither doth he only but others also blame thee. Wouldest thou seem a young woman? But that artifice doth bring an oldness. Through this thou imaginest that thou mayest glory as being fair, but it works thee no small disgrace. Thou maist blush[60] when thou seest not only thine equals and friends but thy maids and servants that are privy to it, and much more when thou seest thyself in a glass.

"But why do I heap up so many of these things, passing by those greater things? To wit, that thou offendest God, overthrowest modesty, kindlest the flame of jealousy, and imitatest prostituted harlots. All which considering, contemn these devilish dressings and unprofitable arts, and leaving this beauty, indeed deformity, get ye that beauty in your hearts which the Angels desire, which God doth love, which pleaseth your husbands, that having lived here honorably, ye may also obtain future glory. Unto the which I would we might come by the grace and mercy of our Lord Jesus Christ. Amen." Thus far Chrysostom.

The Picture of a Picture, or The Character of a Painted Woman
She is a creature that had need to be twice defined, for she is not that she seems. And though she be the creature of God as she is a woman, yet is she

her own creatress as a picture. Indeed, a plain woman is but half a painted woman, who is both a substantive and an adjective and yet not of the neuter gender, but a feminine as well consorting with a masculine, as Ivy with an Ash. She loves grace so well that she will rather die than lack it. There is no truth with her to favor, no blessing to beauty, no conscience to contentment. A good face is her god, and her cheek well-dyed is the idol she doth so much adore. Too much love of beauty hath wrought her to love painting, and her love of painting hath transformed her into a picture. Now her thoughts, affections, talk, study, work, labor, and her very dreams are on it. Yet all this makes her but a cinnamon tree whose bark is better than her body, or a piece of guilded copper offered for current gold. She loves a true looking-glass but to commend age, wants, and wrinkles, because otherwise she cannot see to lay her falsehood right. Her body is (I ween) of God's making, and yet it is a question for many parts thereof she made herself. View her well and you'll say her beauty's such as if she had bought it with her penny. And to please her in every of her toys would make her maid run besides her wits if she had any. She's ever a-mending as a beggar's a-piecing,[61] yet is she for all that no good penitent for she loves not weeping. Tears and mourning would mar her making, and she spends more time in powdering, pranking, and painting than in praying. She's more in her ointments a great deal than in her orisons.[62] Her religion is not to live well but die[63] well. Her piety is not to pray well but to paint well. She loves confections better a great deal than confessions, and delights in facing[64] and feasting more than fasting. Religion is not in so great request with her as riches, nor wealth so much as worship. She never chides so heartily as when her box is to seek, her powder's spilt, or her clothes ill set on. A good Bed-friend, she's commonly delighting in sheets more than in shoes, making long nights and short days. All her infections are but to gain affections, for she had rather die than live and not please. Her lips she lays with so fresh a red as if she sang, "John come kiss me now."[65] Yet it's not out of love, excepting self-love, that she so seeks to please but for love, nor from honesty but for honor. 'Tis not piety but praise that spurs her. She studies to please others but because she would not be displeased herself. And so she may fulfill her own fancy she cares not who else she doth befool. A name she prefers to nature and makes more account of fame than faith. And though she do affect singularity yet she loves plurality of faces. She is nothing like herself save in this, that she is not like herself. She seldom goes without a pair of faces, and she's furnished with stuff to make more if need be. She says a good archer must have two strings to his bow, but she hath hers bent both at once. Yet you must not say she wears two faces under one hood for that she's left long since to the hawks and hath got her headgear that pleases her better, not because better but newer. Her own sweet face is the book she most looks upon. This she reads over duly every morning, specially if she be to show herself abroad that day. And as her eye or chambermaid teaches her, sometimes she blots out pale and writes red. The face she makes in the day she usually mars in the night, and so it's to make anew the next day. Her hair's seldom her own, or if the substance then not the show, and her face likes her not if not borrowed. And as for her head, that's dressed and hung about with toys and devices like the sign of a tavern, to draw on such as see her. And sometimes is written on her forehead, as on the Dolphin at Cambridge in capital letters, *epíthi è àpithi*, like or look of.[66] She's marriageable and fifteen at a clap, and afterwards she doth not live but long. And if she survive her husband his going is the coming of her tears, and the going of her tears is the coming of another husband. 'Tis but "in dock, out nettle."[67] By that time her face is mended her sorrow's ended. There's no physic she follows as face physic, and but assure her she'st never need other while she lives and she'll die for joy. Rather than she'll leave her yellow-bands[68] and give o'er her pride, she will not stick to deny that Mistress Turner[69] spake against them when she died. Her devotion is fine apparel dear bought, and a fine face lately borrowed and newly set on. These carry her to Church and clear her of Recusancy.[70] Once in she unpins her mask and calls for her book, and now she's set. And if she have any more devotion she lifts up a certain number of eyes towards the Preacher, rises up, stands a while, and looks about her; then, turning her eyes from beholding vanities (such as she herself brings with her), she sits down, falls a-nodding, measures out a nap by the hour-glass, and awakes to say Amen. She delights to see and to be seen, for her labor's more than half lost if nobody should look upon her. She takes a journey now and then to visit a friend, or see a cousin, but she never travels more merrily than when she's going to London. London, London hath her heart. The Exchange is the Temple of her Idols. In London she buys her head, her face, her fashion. O London, thou art her Paradise, her Heaven, her all in all. If she be unmarried she desires to be mistaken that she may be taken. If married to an Old man, she is rather a Reed and a Rack unto him than a Staff and Chair, a trouble rather than a friend, a corrosive not a comfort, a consumption not a counselor. The utmost reach of her Providence is but to be counted Lovely, and her greatest Envy is at a fairer face in her next neighbour. This, if anything, makes her have sore eyes. She is little within herself and hath small content of her own, and therefore is still seeking rather than enjoying. All is her own you see, and yet in truth nothing is her own almost you see, not her head, her hair, her face, her breasts, her scent, nay, not her breath always. She hath purchased lips, hair, hands, and beauty more than nature gave her, and with these she hopes to purchase love. For in being beloved consists her life. She is a Fish that would fain be taken, a Bird that had rather a great deal be in the hand than a bush. These purchases she uses to make are not of lands but looks, not of hues but loves. Yet usually the love she meets with is as changeable as her face and will not tarry on her though she die for it. She spends more in face-physic and trifles than in feeding the poor. And so she may be admired herself she cares not though all her neighbors round about her were counted Kitchen-stuff.[71] A good housewife takes not more pleasure in dressing her garden with variety of herbs and flowers than in tricking herself with toys and gauds. Here she is costly if anywhere. 'Tis her grace to be gay and gallant. And indeed like an Ostrich or bird of Paradise, her feathers are more worth than her body. The worst piece about her is in the middest. For the Tailor and her Chamber-maid and her own skill, even these three, are the chiefest causes of all her perfections. Not truths but shadows of truths she is furnished with, with seeming truths and with substantial lies. Yet with all her fair shows she is but like a piece of coarse cloth with a fine glass,[72] or *fairo die*,[73] or as the herb Molio, which carries a flower as white as snow but is carried upon a root as black as ink. Her first care in the morning is to make her a good face, and her last care in the evening is to have her box and all her implements ready against the next morning. She is so curious and full of business that two such in a house would keep the nimblest-fingered girl in the Parish she lives in from making herself one cross-cloth[74] in a twelve-month. She is so deep in love with toys that without them she is but half herself, and half oneself, you know, is not oneself. She loses herself in herself that she may find herself in a Picture. Her trade is tincturing, and her luster is her life. You kill her if you will not let her dye. The Hyacinth or Heliotropium follows not the Sun more duly than she Vanity. Pride, which is accidental to a woman and hateful to a virtuous woman, is essential to her. Her godliness is not to do well but to go well. Her care is not to live well but to look well. And yet if she live well she'll give you leave to chide her if she look ill. She so affects the titles of illustrious and gracious that she carries them always in print about her. Her imagination is ever stirring and keeps her mind in continual motion, as fire doth the pot a-playing or as the weights do the jack in her kitchen.[75] Her devices follow her fancy as the motion of the Seas do the Moon. And nothing pleases her long but that which pleases her fancies, with one of which she drives out another as boys do pellets in Eldern guns.[76] She thinks 'tis false to say that any woman living can be damned for these devices, and it may be true she thinks. For so long as she live she cannot, but if she die in them there's the question. She's ever busy yet never less busy than when she's best busy. She's always idle yet never less idle than when she is most idle. Once a year at least she would fain see London, though when she comes there she hath nothing to do but to learn a new fashion and to buy her a periwig, powder, ointments, a feather, or to see a play. One of her best virtues is that she respects none that paint, and the reward of her painting is to be respected of none that paint not. If she be a

Maiden she would fain be rid of that charge. If a Widow, she's but a counterfeit relic, 'twere too gross superstition but to kiss or touch her. Old-age still steals upon her unawares, which she discerns not by increase of wisdom but of weakness, nor by her long-living but by her need of dying. To conclude, whosoever she be she's but a Guilded Pill, composed of these two ingredients, defects of nature and an artificial seeming of supply, tempered and made up by pride and vanity, and may well be reckoned among these creatures that God never made. Her picture is now drawn out and done.

NOTES

1. Saint Ambrose, 339-97, Bishop of Milan. Tuke quotes from his *Hexameron*, a treatise interpreting the first chapter of Genesis, as cited by Peter Martyr in a commentary on the church fathers.
2. Libidinous, lustful.
3. Quoted from Jerome's *On the Perpetual Virginity of the Blessed Mary against Hebridius*.
4. Participation in the Eucharist.
5. Alexandrian theologian and scholar, c. 185-253.
6. From *On the Dress of Women*.
7. Quoted from *Christian Ethics* (1577) of Lambert Danean, 1530-95, Calvinist theologian.
8. Quoted from *Concerning Virgins, to Marcellina, His Sister*.
9. Trick or cheat.
10. In his *Letter to Possidius*.
11. Clement of Alexandria, the first to apply Greek philosophy to the exposition of Christianity, b. A.D. 160; Tuke cites his *Paedagogus*.
12. Quoted from *The Dress of Virgins*. Tuke inserts a sidenote on the phrase "flaming hair": "He means, I think, they may justly fear that these counterfeit flames, or fire-like and yellowish hairs, shall be punished with the true flames of hell fire."
13. *To Furia, on the Preservation of the Estate of Widowhood*.
14. Let pass without notice, disregard.
15. Cited from *Sayings of Spartans* in the *Moralia*. Lycurgus: reputed founder of the Spartan constitution in the ninth century B.C.
16. In *The Duties of the Clergy*.
17. In *Letter to Possidius*.
18. Quoted from *On the Worthlessness of the Human Condition*, a tract by Francis Junius, 1545-1602, Reformist theologian.
19. Quoted from Jerome's letter *To Marcella on the Death of Lea*; the biblical reference is to Rom. 8.8.
20. Pope Paul II, 1417-71; Baptista Platina, 1421-81, Italian historian whose most famous work was *A History of the Popes* (1479).
21. Pope Innocent I, pope from 401-17.
22. Lover.
23. Lures or baits.
24. The painter in question is Zeuxis; Pliny recounts the anecdote in his *Natural History* 25.36.
25. Martial, epigram 73.
26. In his *Homilies on the Gospel of St. Matthew*.
27. Bishop of Caesarea in Asia Minor, 329-79.
28. Quoted from *Varia Historia* by Claudius Aelianus, A.D. 170-235.

29. Quoted from Plutarch's *Sayings of Kings and Commanders* in the *Moralia*.
30. Assumed, adopted from without.
31. Quoted from Propertius, *Elegies* 2.18
32. Latin grammarian in the second or third century A.D.
33. Quoted from Diogenes Laertius, *Lives of Eminent Philosophers*, 6.2.
34. Johann Piscator, 1546-1626, German professor of divinity and writer. Tuke quotes from his commentary on the two books of Kings (2 Kings 9.30).
35. Tuke cites Peter Martyr's commentary on the two books of Kings (2 Kings 9.30).
36. Jean Calvin, 1509-64, French theological writer and Reformer, based in Geneva.
37. Montanus was the leader of a heretical Christian group in Asia Minor in the second century A.D.
38. Cited from Book 5 of Julius Caesar's *Gallic War*; woad: a blue dye extracted from the leaves of a plant of this name.
39. Quoted from Martyr's commentary on the letters to the Corinthians.
40. From *The Duty of the Clergy*.
41. From *On Christian Doctrine*.
42. In his commentary on 1 Pet. 3.
43. Quoted from Juvenal, Roman satirical poet, A.D. c. 60-130.
44. In a sidenote Tuke cites Jas. 4, 1 Pet. 5, and Luke 18.
45. Referring to comments on 1 Cor. 10.31 by Nicholas Hemmingius, 1513-1600, Danish theological professor, many of whose works were translated into English and published in London during the sixteenth century.
46. Tuke cites comments on 1 Cor. 11 by Heinrich Bullinger, 1504-77, the Swiss Reformer and author of many theological texts.
47. Possibly Vitensis Victor, Bishop of Utica in the fourth century A.D.
48. Crates of Thebes, cynic philosopher of the late fourth century B.C.
49. Quoted from Saint Gregory's *Adversus mulieres ambitiosius se adornantes*, published in 1600.
50. Dyeing.
51. Theophylactus or Theophilact, Archbishop of Achrida (Albania) in the twelfth century. Tuke quotes from his commentary on the first epistle to Timothy.
52. Quoted from Isidore Clarius, 1495-1555, a German theologian. Stapleton: Thomas Stapleton, 1535-98, English Roman Catholic polemicist.
53. Emanuel Tremellius, 1510-80, an Italian born Hebrew scholar, who became father-in-law to Junius.
54. English poet of the late-sixteenth and early-seventeenth centuries, his chief work is *The History of Judith* (1584).
55. Raphael Holinshed, d. 1580; quoted from his *Chronicles* 5.14, "The Description of Scotland."
56. Barnabe Rich, 1540-1617, author of romances, reminiscences, and social satires such as *The Excellency of Good Women* (1613) and *My Lady's Looking Glass* (1616).
57. Translate.
58. The following is quoted from Chrysostom's commentary on the book of Matthew.
59. Stealing goods and bodies from graves.
60. Tuke adds the sidenote, "It may better translate it 'be ashamed,' for a painted face cannot blush."
61. Patching or mending.
62. Prayers.
63. The first of a number of puns on "die" and "dye."
64. Putting on make-up.

65. The title of a ballad in two versions, one by William Byrd (1542-1623) and one by John Tomkins (1586-1638).

66. Tuke adds the sidenote, "'Drink or be gone,' as the Persians used to say at their drinkings."

67. A proverbial expression for changeableness, derived from a charm to help cure nettle stings.

68. Probably a flat strip or strap used to tie a dress in at the waist; the color yellow may connote foolish pretension, as in Malvolio's yellow stockings in *Twelfth Night* or Thomas Overbury's remark on a country gentleman that, "If he go to court it is in yellow stockings," in *Characters* (1616).

69. Anne Turner, 1576-1615, was an accessory to the murder of Thomas Overbury and was hanged.

70. Recusancy, or refusal to attend Anglican church services, was illegal under a number of Elizabethan statutes.

71. Requisites for the kitchen such as vegetables, or kitchen refuse such as dripping; can also be used of kitchen staff.

72. Superficial luster or deceptive appearance.

73. Meaning uncertain.

74. A linen cloth worn on the forehead.

75. A machine for turning the spit to roast meat.

76. Pop guns made from hollow Elder shoots.

CHAPTER 6

The Answer of a Mother
Unto Her Seduced Son's Letter
Ez. W.

In the first quarter of the seventeenth century a number of women's advice books, often addressed from mothers to children, were published in England. They dealt with what were considered "female" topics, including religion, maternity, or domestic advice (Crawford 220-21), though such choices have been analyzed more as "responses to an ideology and culture that denied women self-expression" (Krontiris 23) than confirmations of the authors' instinctive interests. The situation is perhaps more complex than one of enforced restrictions. On the one hand, conservative pressures did place limits on which subjects women might write about. On the other, since pious subjects were regarded as legitimate concerns for women, they provided stimulation and opportunity for female authors to enter the public realm of print.

Such motives appeared to be strongly at work in books which offered religious counsel, with "writing mothers describing themselves as teachers seeking salvation for their children" (Beilin 247). The mutual religious bond between parents and children (and also servants and apprentices) was emphasized in the Catechism included in the Elizabethan *Book of Common Prayer*, in both the Fifth Commandment reproduced there, and the injunction that "all Fathers, Mothers, Masters, and Dames shall cause their Children, Servants, and Prentices...to come to the Church at the time appointed, and obediently to hear and be ordered by the Curate, until such time as they have learned all that is here appointed for them to learn." While being part of this broad responsibility, the mother-son relationship is also a highly potent symbol in the Christian tradition, and its emotive power is exemplified in "Ez. W."'s *Answer of a Mother unto Her Seduced Son's Letter*, in which a grieving mother pleads for her son to return to England, by freeing himself from the snares of a French harlot.

The mother's letter combines personal and religious advice, for she all but states that the harlot is the Catholic church, a Fidessa who has tricked the son into worshipping her sensuous self-image. The text actually commences with a letter from the son to the mother in which he tries to calm and convert her to his new faith. She rejects his misguided efforts, her response filled with biblical allusions to mothers and children and images of the soul as a building or temple which must be carefully constructed and preserved (by parents, it is implied). She reiterates a warning to other parents not to rejoice overmuch in their children, a form of vanity or presumption of worth that transgresses a fitting subjection before God. At the end of the letter, despair converts to joyful optimism and thanksgiving in a vision of God who "canst in mercy to him [the son], cause him to come out of Sodom before the brimstone and fire shall fall."

A passionate energy runs through the text, giving its religious and familial concerns a sensual fervor. The mother's loathing for the harlot suggests a bitter, almost sexual rivalry for the son, while he remains captivated by faith's pleasures and pains, now physically experienced rather than merely spoken or read about. There is a battle of religious sensibilities and sensations, suggesting that the "impassioned religious partisanship of the time" (Travitsky 63) involved powerful conflicts of body and soul.

The identity of the author, "Ez. W.," is not known. There are two editions of the text. The first, from which the extract below is taken, was published in Amsterdam in 1627 (*STC* 24903; Reel 1087). A second edition was published in London in the same year, an enlarged version, retitled as *A Mother's Tears over Her Seduced Son: or, A Dissuasive from Idolatry* (*STC* 24903.5).

THE ANSWER OF A MOTHER UNTO HER SEDUCED SON'S LETTER

"And in her forehead was a name written, a mystery, Great Babylon, the mother of whoredoms and abominations of the earth. And I saw the woman drunken with the blood of Saints, and with the blood of the martyrs of Jesus. And when I saw her, I wondered with great marvel."

(Apoc. 17.5-6)

"Be not unequally yoked with the infidels, for what fellowship hath righteousness with unrighteousness? And what communion hath light with darkness? And what concord hath Christ with Belial? Or what part hath the believer with the infidel? And what agreement hath the Temple of God with idols? For ye are the Temple of the living God. As God hath said, I will dwell among them and walk there, and I will be their God and they shall be my people. Wherefore come out from among them and separate yourselves, saith the Lord. And touch none unclean thing, and I will receive you. And I will be a father unto you, and ye shall be my sons and daughters, saith the Lord Almighty."

(2 Cor. 6.14-18)

A Letter Written from Douai,[1] 6 of March 1627, by a Seduced Son unto His Mother

Dear Mother,

It is not the first time since my departure that I have writ unto you, neither shall it be the last. Nature will find a way to vent her duty were she never so hard oppressed. Out of sight is not out of mind, for were you but as mindful of yourself as I am of you, I doubt not but by the effects you should find me a dutiful son. But as the blind who see not themselves think all other not to see them likewise, so you forgetting yourself think me forgetful of you too. God knows, before whom one day I am to give an account of my duty towards you, how that there passeth not a day or night either when you and yours take your rest, wherein there is not intercession made for you. If I knew what else in this my state, a child's natural obligation could effect on the behalf of a mother, I would with what endeavor I could accomplish it. But alas Dear Mother, when your request is unreasonable, nay unnatural, as the forsaking my religion, God's Church, his truth, nay himself, it stands not with the duty of a son any way to yield in the least to so unjust demands of a Mother. O, that your desires were but of that nature of that good Mother we read of in the Maccabees' war who did encourage her children to suffer even to death for God.[2] I doubt not but God would so strengthen me with his grace that you should find my duty as ready to obey as your piety would be willing to command. Though it be not common for a son to teach his mother but rather to follow her in what she should direct him, yet when parents, misled from the way of truth, shall without knowledge command what is contrary to God's will and their children's conscience, it may be, nay, it is the part of a dutiful son to remember that their command is amiss and cannot be followed. All I here now do is no more. I do but inform you that the happiness you wish me is not true and real happiness. That not longer I now, but your own soul might be the object of your thoughts. That you would from henceforth no longer be a stranger from the truth but submit yourself to her who, as a loving Mother, would receive and embrace you with all affection within the arms of verity.

First, be instructed by her, Dear Mother, and then shall you learn to govern and guide your own children in things that are good. And then I am sure they will be ruled and guided by you. And this is all. Should I do less, I should think with the Apostle that I were far worse than an infidel (1 Tim. 5.8). For how can I behold wolves which pray not for you but prey upon you and hold my tongue. Where were my duty? I perceiving you tossed up and down in the waves of heresy, as you are, and your self ready to suffer shipwreck, and I not so much as offering you my hand to draw you into the Ark. Which of all those blind guides that now pervert your poor soul dare or will affirm that the foundation on which your salvation, purchased so dearly by the blood of your Saviour, your faith, is built is infallible? If infallible, why do you hazard your salvation, purchased so dearly by the blood of your Saviour, upon sand?

Dear Mother, I, as a poor child of your own bowels, as upon my bended knees in all duty of a son, do desire you consider your own declining age, your life to come, your last judgment, and if you do not now here in time work a prevention of that fearful sentence which otherwise must pass upon you. That so you may avoid the wrath to come, endeavor somewhat to examine whether all be true your false prophets preach unto you, or at least whether they practice what they preach. First try and then trust. And because your capacity cannot master a better argument than to examine the lives of your professors of your own sect, there begin. See first whether your new upstart ministers do not, like stage players tricked up in their neat apparel, only and barely act and talk and practice nothing. They will tell you of Christ's passion, his poverty, his want, his hunger and thirst, his humility, his patience, his labor and travel, his ignominy in being apprehended, scourged, spit on in bearing his cross. They will also tell you of the Apostles' poverty, their sufferings, their wrongs and afflictions. But who is he either of your Ministry or Laity will follow your Saviour in these his passions? Who is there among you that in yourselves allow either of fasting, or watching, or voluntary poverty, or good works, or afflicting yourselves for God's sake? To be despised to forsake the world, and to live for ever austerely in penance for sins? They can commend these things in Christ and his Apostles, and yet forbid to be practiced by themselves. They will tell you that our Saviour paid the price for us, whereby we are become heirs of God, Co-heirs with Christ, and being heirs we shall inherit though we suffer nothing. For Christ both suffered and satisfied for us, but they will not see what followeth. For where the Apostle calleth us heirs of God etc., he addeth immediately, "if ye suffer together with him" (Rom. 8.17), signifying that we are heirs with Christ upon condition that we suffer with him, to the end we may be glorified with him. For we are not freed by our Saviour's passion from suffering but the more invited or rather obliged thereunto. Witness our Saviour himself, "He that will come after me, let him deny himself and take up his cross and follow me" (Matt. 16.24, Mark 8.34).

But contrary, if you will but look into God's Church you shall not only find Christ spoken of but truly followed. You shall see those whose only joy is in afflictions for Christ's sake, whose soul is that of the Apostle, "God forbid I should rejoice in anything, but in the cross of Christ" (Gal. 6.14). Who have forsaken all and given their whole Estate to maintain the poor, and so committed themselves to the providence of God. We have not those who barely commend virtues in our Saviour but follow them indeed. Also they are such that talk little, fast hard, pray much, suffer continually, they are in want and that willingly to help others. Poor they are in means but poorer in spirit, and theirs only is the Kingdom of heaven. I will add no more lest I should seem rather to preach you a sermon than to write you a letter.

Dear Mother, see and be acquainted with those who both of this faith and life lives amongst you. I am sure their good ways will better inform you in this kind than my letters. And that you may be the surer satisfied, let the travels of any of my brethren make trial, and let them not doubt but that they may be as safe and as well for their calling and travel here as in England. I live in Douai, a half week's journey from you. Trust my brotherly love towards them for their safety. At one of the English houses in Douai you shall find me. I could rather wish to see any of my brethren here at Douai, but I pray you if you will not take so hard a journey for my sake, at least let me hear from you. Direct your Letters to one Mr. Wetwood's house in Douai, who is an English Gentleman. What I have wrote unto you, Dear Mother, is likewise written to my poor brethren and sisters whom, with yourself, I commend in my most earnest prayers unto the safe protection of God almighty, who I hope hath brought me hither to provide for your poor deceived souls. In our Lord and Saviour farewell. Be mindful of yourselves, that your souls perish not in that heavy day of the Lord.

Your ever obedient and dutiful Son,
I. MADD.

The Answer of a Grieved Mother to Her Seduced Son's Letter
Thy letter came to my hands, my dear Child, like Joseph's particolored coat to his father Jacob. In many things there holds much proportion. "This is my Son's coat," saith the good old man, "a wicked beast hath devoured him. Joseph is surely torn in pieces" (Gen. 37.33). I cannot say so altogether, "But this is my son's letter," doth your poor aged Mother say. "I know it is the great beast hath set his mark upon him, and appointed him for the prey. I shall be robbed of my Son. Oh! I shall be robbed of my Son. At the best, the Ishmeelites[3] have carried him into Egypt, a place of gross idolatry, where he is." For his letter tells me it left him at Douai, and there must mine find him.

What there my Son? Now, let her who is acquainted with the dear name of a child say whether there holds not much proportion between Jacob's sorrow and mine. I go down to the grave mourning; I shall lie down in sorrow. Your old Father, and as full of griefs as years since thou wentest away, is not, and thou art not, and I am a poor distressed Mother. Thus hath the Lord shown me much bitterness. These things are against me, even all these. But I am robbed of my child. That, that hastens to bring my gray hairs with sorrow to the grave. Oh, come again my dear child, come again that I may see thy face with comfort once more before I make my bed in the dark. It is now almost night with me, and I shall be seen no more. O return my son; return my Son; return my Son, my Son.

Return. How readily should a dutiful child come when a dear mother calls? How soon would he do what the Mother bids? Were it of the same nature with hers in the Maccabees, how willingly would I embrace the stake and give up my breath in the flame. But alas! my Mother's request is unreasonable, nay unnatural, as the forsaking my Religion, God's Church, his truth, himself.

And is it so my Son, an unreasonable request indeed and unnatural? O, but harken my child, and if it be so let thy own Mother be hated! O harken my child, I beseech thee, even by the throes of thy first birth harken! And the Lord give thee an open ear while the true Mother pleads with the harlot for her Son, and he that is wiser than Solomon be judge betwixt us, even he be judge (1 Kings 3.16-28). He ease me of my adversary. Even he ease me of my adversary who vexeth me very sore and makes me go heavily all the day, troubling me and breaking my heart. The Lord look on the trouble of his handmaid, and remember her and give her her Son again as I have desired (1 Sam. 1), and to my power labored to give him to the Lord again all the days of his life by keeping his Religion, his Church, and his Truth. And rather than forsake these or any of these, to lie in the fetters until the iron enter into his soul (Ps. 105.18), and after to give up his breath in the flame, to resist even unto blood. O, my child consider! It is neither the chain if not Paul's, nor the prison if not Silas's,[4] nor the flame if not Bradford's,[5] that makes the Martyr, indeed child it is not. But is it Paul's chain? No reason the bearer should be ashamed (2 Tim. 1.16). A prisoner in the Lord? Sure there is a cause of rejoicing. At the stake for a good cause? Now there is cause of singing, of clapping the hands.

But the body may be given to the fire (my child) and love may be wanting. The cross may be taken up, yet not Christ's nor he followed. The body may be stripped and whipped, pinched, nay, almost starved, and yet who required these things at your hands? But let the cause be such as these Saints' were, and then let the sufferers glory. For to such is it given not only to believe but also to suffer for the name of the Lord JESUS (Phil. 1.29). And now let the harlot speak, for I know she told thee what thou shouldest say. What could I have done unto my son that I have not done for his better keeping of these, even all these? Yet would I not seem a proud Justiciary,[6] for how few are those Hannahs, who give their children back to the Lord, who present them first in the Temple (1 Sam. 1-2)? Who breed their children as they ought, as they are bound to do, as the Grandmother Lois and the Mother Eunice bred Timothy (2 Tim. 1.5, 3.15)? I cannot say I did. In how many things might I fail? I know in many. But let the Harlot accuse me. Child canst thou speak nothing for thy Mother? My good child speak, I know thou canst. Whereunto hath the dear affection of thy parents tended? Whitherto all their care, their pains, their cost, their prayers, their fears, their hopes? Their hopes! Here it was indeed, here it was, I think. I know we offended, for surely we doted upon thee, child. Forgive us that wrong. We thought thee our possession, the son of our right hand, the staff on which our old age might lean. But how often do parents' hopes deceive them? How soon may a hopeful blossom die in the bud? A forward spring be nipped with a cold wind or a sharp frost? Do not parents, I pray you, do not dote upon your children or think of them above what is meet. There are many months yet unto your harvest, and a little time makes great alteration! I tell you parents, and I tell you weeping, our extraordinary expectations on earthly things ordinarily disappoints us, sometimes our ordinary but that doth less trouble us. Mark this I pray you. It falls out many times that a beloved Rachel proves barren and hated Leah fruitful (Gen. 29). I pray you mark it, there is much use in it. It falls out so with me, and I am sure I was not the first, neither can I be the last, we have so many doters. My possession is become vanity, my Benjamin a Bennoni,[7] the Lord hath knapped[8] my staff asunder. But why should my adversary boast against me? I think he will not lest his Rachel also prove barren. So the Lord can make him or her, when we bottom[9] ourselves upon them or set our affection on them too much. But come, what would the Harlot say? I know she would speak.

Harlot: "Why, he sucked in heresy with his very milk, and his stronger meats was mingled with it. And when you sent him to the fountain and, as you thought, to the spring-head, you were quite mistaken, for they are but bitter waters, unclean and muddy."

Mistaken indeed I was, and much deceived, for had not the fountain been impure, or had not the Beast's foot mudded it, I had not been robbed of my child nor at this time been pleading for him. But there was a bad herb in the good pottage,[10] a dead fly in the sweet ointment,[11] a subtle Serpent in the pleasant garden. Thus we parents, drunk with our own hopes, little foresee our children's danger, how soon they may fall upon a shelf, and there make shipwreck of faith and a good conscience and all. A parent art thou, when will thy doubts, thy fears have an end?

And now what shall I say to thee, my adversary? I must not, I dare not, give thee revealing words, but the Lord rebuke thee, even he rebuke thee, and be judge betwixt us whether in that way which thou callest heresy, we do not worship the GOD of our father's believing, etc. (Acts 24.4).

Harlot: "What? And not to submit to our holy Church? Not come within his arms for instruction? What is this but to be as a dove without the Ark? To be tossed up and down upon the waves of heresies, still ready to suffer shipwreck? Let your son then have your hand, mother, who so piously reacheth forth his whereby to draw you into our Ark." I thank my good child knowing his simple heart and tender child-like affection, for I bear him witness that he hath a zeal though not according to knowledge. The time of his ignorance, O Lord remember not, and find out a time to take away the scales and be merciful to all such as sin not of malicious wickedness, that are in some error of judgment not of practice. And now my Son, I dare not give thee my right hand of fellowship, no I dare not, child. We have a better card whereby to sail, a more sure direction whereby we fetch our compass, a more certain and infallible Oracle whereunto all the Prophets and Apostles give witness. We know Churches may err and men may be mistaken as men. Peter was so, whereupon Paul resisted him to the face for he was to be blamed (Gal. 2.11). Alas my Child! Paul and Peter may and did take upon them the care of the Churches. The care of them is one thing, the weight of them is another that's too heavy for man's shoulders. They were but stones (child) in that spiritual building. But hear my voice, and I will tell thee.

We acknowledge (the Scriptures teach us so) that the Church of the living God (I call it neither ours nor yours, but blessed is the man that hath his name written therein) is the pillar and ground of truth (2 Tim. 3.15). No foundations whereon the building must rely but as it is built upon the foundation of the Prophets and Apostles, JESUS CHRIST himself being the chief corner-stone, in whom all the building coupled together groweth to a holy Temple in the Lord (Eph. 2.20-21).

Harlot: "Why, but all this while you are but upon the sand, no true foundation nor infallibility of supporting. Will you have a Son's soul hazarded upon sand?" Hazard my child's soul, Harlot! O precious thing! O rich Jewel! O inestimable treasure! Why it is amidst the things of the world, like David among the people (1 Sam. 18.8), worth ten thousand of them and much more of all the things in the world (my dear child). Run not the hazard of that. Hazard a foot thou maiest and yet thou wilt not; thou hast another. A leg, thou hast another; a hand, thou hast another; an arm, thou hast another; an eye, thou hast another. Here are no pairs (my child). Lose one and lose all. O, invaluable loss, and unrecoverable! The redemption thereof must cease for ever. What would not a parent now do to put a child's soul out of hazard?

Then hear me my son, son of my bowels harken. Is that soul in danger that is in the Ark, made by God's own appointment both for the matter and the manner, directed by him to that morning star from which it hath a certain course. Listen my child, child of my bowels listen. Is that corner-stone a sandy foundation? Can the weight of men and angels press it? Can the gates of hell remove it? Indeed, my child, if that stone fall upon thee or me we are crushed in pieces. So are we if we fall upon it heedlessly, carelessly, presumptuously (Matt. 21.44). But come unto it in the whole obedience of thy heart. Stick, cleave unto it, as Ruth to Naomi (Ruth 1.16-

18). Be not entreated to leave it or to depart from it, and thou canst not miscarry. Harken my son, son of my bowels harken. Can the blowing of the wind, can the beating of the storm, remove that house which the wise builders hath founded upon a Rock (Matt. 7.25, Luke 6.48)? Thou doest, my Son, believe CHRIST'S words, I know thou doest believe them. Then harken my Son this once, Son of my bowels harken. He that layeth a foundation diggeth deep, certainly so did this wise builder, beyond all human traditions. Here was no settling. Beyond all will-worship, a counterfeit ground, beyond all satisfaction of his own, this was not solid; beyond the intercession of Saints and Angels, this was not safe; beyond the righteousness of his best works, here he would fain stay but it would not hold the weight. Still he digs further, for the soul that seeketh the Lord is not satisfied until he find him. "Where have ye laid my LORD (saith MARY) let me find him or all is nothing" (John 20.15). Well, he digs deeper even as he that seeks a treasure or as a thirsty man after a spring or water. Or like those three mighty he will through the whole host of the Philistines (2 Sam. 23.16), but he will dig through those sandy bottoms and get to the rock.

And now upon it he is, and by it supported and from it refreshed. For behold here is strength to hold him up. Here are waters, living waters, to comfort him, for this rock is CHRIST. It is good being here; here will he set up his rest; here will he abide for ever. If the Rock fail not he cannot fail. Blessed is the man that hath this foundation. Thrice blessed is he that hath this water to drink. He will never dig it in broken pits. Can the rain or hail fall now upon this man as upon a wilderness? To whom that man (so Christ the Rock is called, and observe the number) will be as a hiding place from the wind and as a refuge from the tempest, as rivers of water in a dry place and as the shadow of a great rock in a weary land (Isa. 25.4). Now the rain may fall, and the floods come, and the winds blow and beat upon this house, and behold it stands for it is grounded upon a rock. See (child) a mount Sion now which stands for ever, and the blast of the mighty shall be as a storm against the wall. Oh my child, though my eyes be shut up yet am I, as it were, in Balaam's rapture (Num. 22-23). Who can tell the strength of this man? For as the rock is such is his strength, as the strength of an Unicorn (Num. 23.22). No poison shall hurt him, no sorcery shall make against him. He hath a refuge from the storm, a shadow from the heat, a strength in distress. Who can now tell the joys of this Jacob, or number the fourth part of the comforts of this Israel? Let my strength be as this man's strength, and let my last end be like his.

Dear child, I as an affectioned mother to my own bowels, by my sorrows in thy first birth, by those since wherewith I travail with thee till Christ be formed in thee, by that solemn vow thou madest to God in Baptism, by that strong bond of nature and dear name of a Mother, I do desire, nay, she that might command doth beseech thee to consider by what hath been said, and the Lord make it profitable, whether my requests that thou wouldest return be unreasonable or unnatural. Whether my reasons for it are any way dangerous or hazardous. Or rather whether the one be not pious, the other safe and certain, directing thee unto that church which is guided by a certain course. It may float, it cannot sink. Setting thee upon a fine foundation, it may shake, it cannot fall, no more than the corner-stone which cannot be removed. Entreating thee to put away those lies which are in thy right hand. All those Idols which cannot help, all those sparks with which you may compass yourself and yet lie down in sorrow too (Isa. 50.11), persuading thee to put away all those vanities (they are too long to name) which, weighed in the balance, will be found too light, and also to dig to the Rock which cannot fail.

Oh my child, consider! It is not for any of your good works that you are condemned. No, my child; they are amiable and they are commended, yea, cherished. Whither we hear of them there or see them here, nay, we confess you have them, who go beyond the works of many amongst us who carry a great show of holiness. Go on in them my child, go on in them. Yet I know thou wilt consider that there are many circumstances belonging to every action from which the work ever receives its true estimate. Thou maist hear somewhat more of this anon, because thou doest not walk uprightly according to the truth and purity of the gospel. I would drive this nail to the head now. Why consider child, whether your rock be as our rock. Even our enemies being judges, what will become of their Gods, their rock in which they trusted (Deut. 32.27)? Let them rise up and help you, and be your protection.

But see my child, this rock is he, even this is he which I have pointed out unto thee, and there is none with him, only Christ (my Son), only Christ. Can there be hazard my child? Can here be danger? Canst thou thirst at the fountain? Canst thou sink upon the rock? In thy own righteousness thou maist; the intercessions of Saints and Angels may deceive thee. Baal may be busied (my child), peradventure he may be sleeping (1 Kings 18.27). Abraham may be ignorant of thee, and Israel may not acknowledge thee. I say that it may be that thou maist see plainly how at the best here is adventure, here is a hazard. But he that keepeth Israel neither slumbereth nor sleepeth, and this is he which I point out unto thee. There can be no hazard here. This rock is a mighty redeemer, he will sustain thee alone, he must have no helper. Whom wilt thou join with him whose name is everlasting? I tell thee (child for the sum of all is this), there is nothing, though never so lovely, in thine eyes which can make thee the righteousness of God but that which was made sin for thee. Tell me, then, were any of these things crucified for thee? How long shall vain thoughts which separate from God lodge within thee? Return, then, my Son, return my Son. Or in case thou doest halt between two opinions, surely the Lord, the jealous God, who will not give his honor to another nor suffer Dagon to stand by him (1 Sam. 5.1-5), will have this controversy against thee. And what Saint or Angel shall plead for thee? Thou hast committed two great evils: thou hast forsaken the fountain of living waters, and hewed thyself out cisterns broken, cisterns that can hold no water (Jer. 2.13). Return, then, my Son, return my Son, my Son.

Son: "O my Dear Mother, you have almost persuaded me to return." Almost, my Son? Why not altogether? What, a cake half-baked? Altogether, my Son, or it is nothing. Thou must make straight step and cast off that which hangs on so fast, lest that which is halting be turned out of the way (Heb. 12.13). The Lord calls for thy heart. Give it him my Son and follow him wholly, or else thou shalt never with Caleb and Joshua come into that good Land.[12] Oh, my bowels do yearn upon my son! The Harlot shall rather have him than I will have him divided. Come away from her my Son, come away. What, hath the Harlot more to say. . . .

Notes

1. Near Lille in present-day France. Cardinal William Allen opened a seminary in Douai for English Roman Catholics, and many of the English Catholic gentry were educated there.

2. The last two apocryphal books recount the war of independence waged by the Jewish Maccabees against Syrian kings.

3. Palestinian traders who buy and then sell Joseph (Gen. 38.25-28).

4. Silas is considered possibly to have been an assistant to Paul, who was placed in prison with him (Acts 16.24-40).

5. John Bradford, a Protestant martyr, was executed during Queen Mary's reign in 1555 as a seditious heretic.

6. Judge, administrator.

7. Possibly, St. Benno (Bennonis), 1010-1106, the Bishop of Meissen, canonized in 1523.

8. Broken.

9. Base or found.

10. See 2 Kings 4.39-40.

11. See Eccles. 10.1.

12. Caleb was a leader of the Hebrews (Num. 13.6ff.); Joshua was the successor to Moses (Exod. 17.9).

CHAPTER 7

The Honor of Chastity:
A Sermon
John Featley

Classical virtues of chastity and temperance, depicted in Plato's *Symposium* as leading to the transcendence of earthly existence, were further exalted in the Christian world by worship of the Virgin Mary. Notwithstanding differences between classical and Christian societies, in both traditions chastity could connote ideal physical, ethical, and spiritual states. In the Middle Ages, the Virgin Mary was seen as incarnating key moral qualities for women, although her perfection could never be duplicated or attained. She represented an ideal conception of womanly virtue rather than a model of behavior (Maclean 23). After the English Reformation this kind of intense virgin worship was proscribed as a corruption of the pristine church, but the symbolic potential of virginity and chastity was continually used throughout the rule of Elizabeth I, and again in the reign of Charles I and Queen Henrietta-Maria, at the time when John Featley published *The Honor of Chastity*.

In her first years as queen, virginal imagery was used to glorify Elizabeth's youth and sex, and support her "self-image [as] a patroness of the Gospel" (Haigh 27). As the decades passed and Elizabeth remained the central exception in a social and political system dominated by males, her unmarried state was idealized "as the unattainable *object* of masculine desire. . .in an assimilation of Petrarchan and Neoplatonic attitudes" (Berry 62). In her final years, Elizabeth continued to be portrayed as a fusion of love and chastity, "the just virgin of the golden age returned" (Strong 52). While virginal and Neoplatonic imagery was used little during the reign of James I, it was revived during Charles's time in a court aesthetic which personified ideals of love and government in the royal couple: "About the Queen revolved all passion, controlled and idealised by her Platonic beauty and virtue, as about the King all intellect and will" (Orgel and Strong 1:55). Of course, throughout this period chastity and virginity were also represented and characterized in literary and dramatic texts, but as many critics have noted their significance was frequently informed by such royal references.

Featley's sermon, published in 1632, celebrates chastity as a central principle of social and personal conduct. Perhaps influenced by the Neoplatonic imagery of the Caroline court, he expands its reference to men and women. Chastity preserves crucial social relationships: master-servant, mistress-servant, male-female, parent-child, and husband-wife. It is also represented as vital to spiritual, moral, and physical self-preservation. While praising chastity, Featley also engages in vivid denunciations of various forms of unchaste behavior, at times describing their consequences in dramatic detail and hinting that he knows that readers have indulged and sinned themselves. While at times Featley refrains from describing vices to avoid "teaching by reproving," a veiled attraction to what is condemned may sound in such passages. The key paradox that develops in the sermon is of chastity's power, which is conceived not as abstinence but as a positive ethical and spiritual force. In this sense, Featley's sermon shows interesting (though simpler) parallels to some of Milton's writing, including the masque *Comus*, originally staged in 1634. The key to chastity for Featley is that it is tested but remains constant.

Featley was born in 1605. He studied at Oxford and was there ordained as a priest. He served for a time in the West Indies (and refers to his experiences there near the end of the sermon) before returning to work as an assistant to his uncle, Daniel Featley, a controversial cleric who defended the Church of England against Catholics and Puritans in numerous polemical pamphlets (the sermon's attack on zealots is a sign of this influence). In 1639 Featley was appointed chaplain to Charles I but left England as civil war intensified in the 1640s. After Charles II came to the throne, Featley was again appointed chaplain and then held a sequence of clerical posts until his death in 1666.

Featley published three of his sermons as well as *A Fountain of Tears* (1646), a guide to godly self-examination for women (Mendelson 186-88). *The Honor of Chastity* is similarly marked by a strong didactic tone. It was published only once, in London in 1629 (*STC* 10741; Reel 793).

THE HONOR OF CHASTITY

"How can I do this great wickedness, and sin against God?"
(Gen. 39.9)

Human policy is the life of the unsanctified, but religious is the life of the regenerate. The former plotting for the deceitful riches of this World, the latter rewarding with a Crown immortal. 'Tis no task then of impossibility to determine which of the two shall best deserve our approbation. For the one (just like a Parenthesis) giveth light only to the sentence of the other. The same supports with a bladder only, exposed to the hazard of the smallest flaw. The other is an Ark which carrieth us safely to the cape of felicity. *Dignori detur*: Let the honor, then, be given not to Pan but to Apollo, not to human devices but to religion. And let each indifferent Judge censure that gross-ear'd Midas, whose impiety or ignorance devotes him to error.

Joseph[1] (in my Text) shall be the just delegate and arbitrate the matter (contrary to custom) without any sinister corruption. Had not he been as pious to his God as just to his Master, he might (peradventure) have stolen a fall through impiety, to deprive him at once both of chastity and honor. But 'twas the plot of his religion to preserve him honest that he might remain fortunate. He that was at first rejected by his brethren was received by the Ishmeelites, and 'twas the chance of chance to make him happy when he expected misery. His bondage (instead of servility) became a freedom. His slavery was soon converted into liberty. And (as if the Sea of his afflictions deemed him too good to be drowned in infelicity) even that helped him to float in the height of applause. None so great as Joseph now, in the love of the vulgar, in the talk of the greater, or in the heart of his Master. Durst we to attribute this change unto Fortune, we might (with the Poet) justly deify her. But the great Jehovah disdains such a nothing should prove injurious to his Majesty, and hates as much the Epicure's deity[2] as this sacrifice. Joseph was not more highly promoted than religiously disposed, and renders therefore his best thanks to the God of honor.

Yet behold a strange alteration. That which before exalted him is now as ready to cry him down. His Mistress loves him, so doth he her. Nay, she lusts after him, but so will not he her. His conscience swears him to obedience to the King of Kings, teaching him observance to his Mistress but only in things lawful. Yet cannot he be bolder in refusing than she in wooing. The redoubt[3] which he had to repair to for an excuse was the infidelity to his Master, which would have ensued upon it. And (lest he should be taken off from that) he retreats to another of far greater strength, in the words of my Text: "How then can I do this great wickedness, and sin against God?" (Gen. 39.9).

The words are an interrogative objurgation[4] to avoid a more impious temptation, and contain:

1. The Author refusing, I Joseph.
2. The action refused, aggravated,
   1. by the name, Wickedness.
   2. by the extension, Great.
3. The reason of the refusal.
   1. in respect of the offence, Sin.
   2. in respect of the object, or party offended, God.

Of these in their order. And first of the Author refusing, I Joseph.

When God distills his grace into the heart, 'tis sin's antidote and works effectually. Divine virtues elevate the soul and disdain as much a willing consent to as the act of sin. The purity of the Operator contemns a corrival in the heart, solely possessing that chair of estate. But (if once the malice of temptation purchaseth entertainment) the former peace was not more delightful than the succeeding war proves terrible. The Almighty becomes a suitor who (not intending to work by his power) woos by entreaty. And (as if that Virgin, that chaste soul of man were not worth acceptance if won without opposition) the devil likewise aims at the purchase of it too. Happy is that person whose reason (despising the false allurements) yields a consent to the God of Gods. Thus was Joseph won by the deity, and his heart was found as constant as the opposer turbulent. Had his education nuzzled[5] him up in error, or his parents instructed him in Idolatry; had his brethren played with wickedness, or his companions dallied with disobedience, then the mist of ignorance might (peradventure) have bred a Cataract, or drawn a Curtain over the eyes of his understanding. But such excuses must need be silent because his education was virtuous, his life religious. *Quo semel est imbuta recens*, etc.[6] Teach a child the trade of his youth (says Solomon) and he will not forget it when he is old (Prov. 22.6). Joseph had learned the principles of Religion of his parents and therefore must not (nay, cannot) forget them among the Egyptians. That Court (which in some kind was the school of villainy) could never prove guilty of so bad a proficient in such ill and uncivil ways.

But "What dost thou here Elijah" (1 Kings 19.9)? What hath Joseph to do that he dances attendance at the Court? "Let him desert the court who would be pure."[7] Methinks that a Cottage in the Country or a lodge in the Wilderness of rustics should have better suited with his religious life. He knows that company may allure a man by subtlety to what they cannot entice him by entreaty. And where did the Devil employ his servants more than among King Pharaoh's household, where wickedness was (with some) become their religion, and iniquity their common devotion? But (alas) he was a servant and must obey. Yet where the misery of bondage shall command him to impiety, the uprightness of his conscience may repeal the act. It was the Divine providence which raised his decayed estate and now ravished his Master with the love of his slave. He that before was sold by his brethren is now redeemed from bondage by the hand of his Father. For (behold) God suffers him not to live in obscurity but gives him success in his endeavors to usher him to promotion. So that now his Captain begins to take especial notice of him and rewards his fidelity with the command of his house. Where before his honor goeth humility, for he is humbled to his God before he dares venture upon command. 'Twas his obedience to God which advanced him, and 'tis the service of that God which his thoughts entertain.

Thus shall it be done to the man whom God will honor. The envy of fraternity shall be the means of promotion where loyalty to the Divinity petitions for it. Though the hatred of a brother (upon unjust terms) may seem to entreat, yet it can never persuade the Almighty to curse when the malice of the one takes a daring[8] from the devout Religion of the other.

Though the strictness of unfeigned zeal receives the daily alms of Joseph's brethren even in these wretched times (I mean nothing but opprobrious calumnies), yet the God of that Zeal will burn up those reproaches with fire unquenchable. He that fights under the Colors of pure Religion and sanctity shall be shot-free when he is level'd at by any real injury. Enemies may spit the fire of wrath against him; yet it shall prove as an *ignis fatuus*,[9] to lead themselves to destruction.

To Joseph's brethren (then) in this Age, I wish as much religion as their neglected brother can teach them, and let the bond of Nature rectify their minds when the presumption of anger would swell into revenge.

And to Joseph himself I wish as much constancy in obedience as honor in observance, that his divine graces may promote him to happiness and his resolute perseverance in his duty to his God may teach him both to know and shun every small and trifling mistake in the eyes of the world, because Religion will write it wickedness, which is the subject of the second general: the action refused, aggravated, first by the name, Wickedness.

The excellency of a curious Picture is the misty shadowing of it. Our Saviour's Espouse (in the Canticles) is fair though black, and the night is best shaped to its property when 'tis muffled with its wonted darkness.[10] But (alas) miserable man in this only becomes wretched, being shadowed with corruptions, black with sin, and dark with wickedness.

Disobedience is the nature of an unregenerate person, which foils that grace that seeks to wound it. And the devil proves destructive to the man upon whose ground they fight. Had God been pleased as well to forbid the nature of Adam as his person sinning, the strength of his authority would have challenged the weakness of the other resistance and (without contradiction) have overcome by power where it would not by entreaty. But (behold), lest we should grow too happy by obedience, our forefather (through unadvisedness) hurried us into misery by an ignorant knowledge. Yea, and (lest mischief should want[11] a mistress to work by) Eve was the Serpent's hand to offer up to Adam the petition for disobedience. The Devil (as needing the wit of a woman to plot our ruin) became humble to work upon her pride, whereby the temptation drew on our destruction. "The female sex (saith St. Ambrose) grows strong only in allurements, and takes off the edge of man's goodness by a sharper edge of temptation." Yet (lest the observation should prove too general, that the weak sex are continually guilty of the victory) Joseph steps in here to triumph over the intended conqueror. His Mistress, wanting the power of command, dissolves herself into sick entreaties. But the sweetness of her lovely compliments discovers the ugliness of her foul intents. The grace of his Protector burns in his heart and lights him to the knowledge of her intended mischief. He that (before) seemed to be the object of her love is (now) possessed with the hatred of her lust, and instead of consenting construes it wickedness.

When I read the variety of ways the Devil hath projected to seduce us to this wickedness, I lose myself in the Labyrinth and (struck dumb with admiration) strange at the wretchedness of human frailty. Let me crave your audience and wonder at once when I name the many filthy ways of purging this wickedness by unclean physic. Eight several Monsters present themselves unto you, under these titles, viz.:

1. *Fornicatio.*
2. *Adulterium.*
3. *Stuprum.*
4. *Incestus.*
5. *Raptus.*
6. *Mollities.*
7. *Sodomia.*
8. *Bestialitas.*[12]

1. The first of these receives denomination from persons not matrimonially engaged to a civil conversation.

2. The second is, but not to know is better. I would describe these deformed Fiends in our Mother tongue, but I hold it fitter to draw Timanthes' veil over such a bed of snakes, lest I should teach by reproving.[13] My desire is that each of these enormities might prove like the herb Anonymos in Pliny, which got a name by retaining the nature thereof in obscurity,[14] rather than the name of the vice should teach the crime.

Happy was Joseph (then), who (knowing the malice of his corruption to project a farther mischief if once he had consented) neglects the opportunity of yielding to Adultery, (the second kind), and terms that wickedness which his Mistress would have judged happiness.

I doubt not (beloved) but that Joseph's example (in my Text) shall work powerfully in you against your provocations to uncleanness. And where destruction shall crave entertainment (being painted over with a seeming pleasure), the GOD of Joseph shall tell you 'tis wickedness.

Who knows not the weakness and willfulness of them which Saint Paul terms silly and laden with divers iniquities (2 Tim. 3.6)? Who skills[15] not the cunning of those delicate imposters in their wretched devices? As their arms embrace the necks of their enchanted captives, so doth vengeance their souls. They are sad Ditties which their melodious voices warble out though the notes be harmonious. And that destruction which they bear about them is as full of deceit as allurement.

I fear (beloved) I shall not need to go farther than to your own guilty consciences for examples of men seduced to this impiety. Yet (rather than I will condemn before I can accuse, or accuse you without a credible information) I will search the Scriptures, where (I am sure) I shall find Reuben entangled with Bilhah, his Father's Concubine (Gen. 35.22), David with Bathsheba (2 Sam. 11), Herod with his brother Philip's wife (Mat. 14.3), and the Corinthians, as Saint Paul had been informed, in his first Epistle to them, Chapter Five, verse one.

As saith Saint Ambrose, Samson excelled thee in strength, David in holiness, and Solomon in wisdom, yet they suffered by these enticing vanities. Let it be your pious industry to be taught both by examples and precepts that ye may be crowned with the glory of celestial bliss.

Yet let not him expect the Diadem which justifies himself, being preserved from the act of this wickedness only by compulsion. For (as Saint Jerome gravely adviseth us), necessity is a faithless preserver of Integrity, and he only is truly termed chaste who may fall and will not. Thus doth Joseph stand excused, for he leaves (in a manner) the possibility of sinning by a religious resistance.

To every Joseph here (then) let me prefer the example of him in my Text. If superiors entice you, refuse them; if inferiors, disdain them; if equals, shun them. Let not the complexion of the vice steal credit to the Lie, but correct the fury of it by a pious reneging.

And to Joseph's Mistress, here, I must in all humility tender this advice to her petulant disposition. Let her neither ensnare the righteous by her painted hypocrisy, nor her Jezebel's face entrap the ignorant. Let not her Siren songs steal to the ears of any on whom she desires to surfeit with incontinency. But let her prayers rather crush those desires and her devotion repel them. Religion is the best remedy against such swelling tumors of impiety. And the very remembrance that it is wickedness, nay, great wickedness, may control the vice, if every one in particular determine with Joseph in my Text, "How can I do this great wickedness," etc. Which is the second part of my second General: the action refused, aggravated, secondly, by the extension, Great.

The habit of sinning removes the sense of sin (saith the divine Philosopher).[16] He that sells himself to the custom of disloyalty to his Creator becomes ignorant of his offence, and instead of correction proves unskillful in the knowledge of his sin. The gluttonous satiety of our swelling Gulists[17] argues their necessity of offending by forgetfulness. And their own abundance bars them from the just weighing of the poverty of the distressed. The common drunkard cannot be taken with a due thanksgiving for that superfluity which he corrupts, from whence many thirsty souls might suck a reasonable supply for necessity. How, then, can we determine of any Religion to be found in him who (inclined to this great wickedness mentioned in my Text) borrows his provocations from newfound compositions?

We are all beleaguered by our homebred enemies, but especially by Saint Paul's three squadrons: the lust of the flesh, the lust of the eye, and the pride of life (1 John 2.16). He that loseth but the least ground upon necessity to either of these suffers in the retreat, and (unless he gathereth strength by the power of grace) can never recover what he hath lost. Amongst all the contests of Christians, only the battles of chastity are difficult or hard, when the fight occurs daily and victory is rare etc., as Saint Augustine speaketh to the same purpose.

Ye may be pleased to observe both the entry and progress of this sin. 'Twas begun in Paradise inclusively, though not actually, by the fall of Adam. 'Tis hereditary to all of us the offspring of him, for by a certain law of nature desire results in wickedness as Jerome hath it. And (without repentance) it must be punished in Hell. The first enticing is grounded either upon necessity or pleasure, or sometimes upon both. At which present (if GOD be not pleased to guide the heart), the sin is purchased though not yet acted. Then is the Devil for the most part rhetorical, and persuades by insinuating arguments for his own advantage. Trifles seldom break friendship between the enticer and the allured, and what in itself is impious he persuades to be a very slight (or rather no) sin. Thus if the heart consent, the Devil's proselyte is won. And (lest he should know what destruction he plunges himself into) he's kept in ignorance by that "God of this World, who blinds the eyes of his understanding, lest the light of the glorious Gospel of CHRIST, which is the Image of GOD, should shine unto him" (2 Cor. 4.4).

But oh, that ineffable and most dreadful sequel which ensues upon the first consent! That which Joseph here accompts[18] a great wickedness, the forlorn creature either not knows or not values. While he was tottering, he halted (as it were) between two opinions, for the grace of his Protector withstood the opposer. But so soon as the weak understanding had surrendered to the will, the sin was entertained, yet that 'twas a sin or a great wickedness was kept concealed. 'Tis then an easy matter to hasten to the pit of destruction when the Devil drives a man by his hourly provocation.

But alas, miserable wretch, shall the fire of thy lust burn within thee and not the fire of hell burn for thee? Shalt thou cast thyself into that deep ditch, as Solomon calleth an adulteress (Prov. 23.27), for thy pleasure and not expect a deeper ditch of destruction for thy pain? Shall the flashes of this great wickedness dazzle thine eyes and not the flashes of hell terrify thy conscience? Earthly pleasures (methinks) in reason cannot or (at least) should not delight us because they are of no continuance. Before they come we consume ourselves with a longing desire and expectation of them. When they are present, if they continue long, they cloy us; if they fly suddenly, they torment us. And when they are past, we may hang down our heads with the consideration of Saint Paul's question, "What profit had ye then in those things whereof ye are now ashamed? For the end of them is death" (Rom. 6.21).

Diseases (ye know) are the common rewards of the flesh in this life. And for the understanding, there shall not want the terrors and gnawings of a guilty conscience. Oh, the hideous screeches which the heart vents in unmeasured sobs! Oh, the dismal affrights which the darkness of the night presents to the fancy of an impious adulterer! Oh, that ill-boding noise and fearful croaking which this creature hears yet knows not how or where or whence! His conscience is sick of the worms, his understanding stifled in clouds of mist, his will rushes him headlong to the whirlpool of destruction. And lest his body should be forgotten behind, that crawls upon the very diseases which it hath gotten and so stalks to confusion.

Err not then, my beloved brethren, as St. James saith (Jas. 1.16), neither fall into the talons of your untutored lusts. Subject not yourselves to the slavery of temptation but determine with the Father that the smallest and finest-spun thought of sinning is an offence. What, then, Joseph (in my Text) hath termed great, call not thou small. What he hath determined to be styled wickedness, do not thou boast of with impudence, but correct thy libidinous motions with the words of my Text. These sins (peradventure) may seem small to thee, yet they are many, saith St. Augustine, and will oppress thee as much by their number as others by their weight.

That this offence then (which belongeth chiefly to our purpose) is not wickedness, who dares affirm? Or that 'tis great, who can deny? Thomas Aquinas is so sensible of the greatness of it that he proposeth a question touching a branch thereof, seeming very trivial in appearance yet of greater consequence than a common judgment will censure it: whether a mortal sin may not couch itself under our common greetings? And he resolves the question thus: those kind of compliments (of themselves) suffer not the name of sins, but if their aim be luxurious, their end is pernicious. If, then, our very salutations and common greetings (standing only in impure vessels) may gather dregs and so be turned into corruption, what are those more impious acts which, swelling in our hearts, break forth into wickedness? Might not Joseph, upon grounds sufficiently warranted, aggravate the offence by the extension of it and conclude it a great wickedness?

Great, indeed, in the first place on his own part if you consider him, first, merely as a man, should he have thus trespassed with any of the least, the worst, the poorest of women. Secondly, as a man in honor, in the same house. Justly might his fidelity have been stained with infamy, had his Captain's courtesy been rewarded with such an injury. And thirdly, as a child of Grace, whose fall (had he yielded) might have proved more destructive to his soul than his former honor could gain him affection. But indeed (as if his integrity grew too wise to forget the danger of such an error), he could not easily fall lest his example should teach his inferiors to be guilty of the like or the noise of the fact[19] command the people to scorn him. For whom we suspect guilty of so great an offence we rather crush with our blushes than maintain by our industry.

Great, again, on her part too. If his Master's wife should have prostituted herself to her servant, her vassal, the censure of her crime would freely have passed, and each common inferior would have become her Judge. Secondly, if to one whom she loved, the sin had been the greater. For who knows not that God, in his Justice, hath punished the fact here on earth, at least, with a mutual hatred between the delinquents. So that (like to that of Tamar and Amnon[20]) the future hatred wherewith she would have hated him might have been greater than the love wherewith she had loved him.

Thirdly, great in respect of her greatness also, by the Poet's censure, "Vice glares more strongly in the public eye, / As he who sins in power or place is high."[21] Enormities are built up higher and grow more eminent when their foundation is the error of an eminent person. And Isidore[22] renders the reason of it. For the fault (says he) increaseth and the lofty Cedars are viewed by all when they are shaken, whilst the neglected shrubs are not regarded.

Great, again, not in respect of Joseph, the favorite of his Master, only, or his Mistress the wife of his Master, but also in respect of the offence, chiefly considered in itself, that it is a sin. Which is the first part of my third General, the reason of the refusal. First, in respect of the offence, Sin: "How can I do this great wickedness, and sin" etc.

This part of my Text commands me to extract something out of nothing. For my discourse must be of a privation, and that which only hath gotten a name must teach us our proper nature. I am fallen here upon sin, yet without offence (I hope), and shall entreat thereof without trespassing on your patience. My Text gives me not authority to be tedious in the generality, lest I should neglect this which it doeth chiefly particularize. Curious School distinctions I could but will not trouble you with, lest the time deny me your attention and the niceness your acceptance. Let it suffice that I walk in the vulgar tract and divide sin only into original and actual. The former includes both a falling from God in the loins of Adam and the evil which followed it, which is as well the defect of original good in the soul and body as the succession of evil instead of that original good in both.

The second, which is Actual, is either internal or external, spiritual or carnal, of omission or commission, infirmity or presumption, etc., as your daily Sermons instruct you.

To our purpose, then, I must confine myself to the intention of my Theme. Where I find that if Joseph had sinned according to his temptation, it might have been a great actual sin, committed (perhaps) with presumption and severely to be punished by the rod of Heaven. It was (therefore) the mercy of our jealous God to vouchsafe him assistance in his greatest temptations. Thus a man, being in honor, was of understanding that he might not be compared to the beasts that perish (Ps. 49.20).

Had he himself been the tempter and she denied, his sin had been entertained by the first extravagancy of his words (Eph. 5.4). Had he wooed and she consented, the mischief had doubled itself by the act. Had he secretly desired her and not discovered[23] the fire, yet Athanasius would censure him in his "He that desires the beauty, yet not fully enjoying it, hath committed a sin, though without a witness."[24] Or (if you please), the Scripture shall better English it in that "Whosoever looketh upon a woman to lust after her hath committed adultery with her in his heart" (Matt. 5.28).

Here (peradventure) I have only as yet awakened the conscience of Joseph's Mistress, whilst the rest applaud themselves in their seeming integrity. But (alas beloved) I must summon you all to the Court of Conscience, and (it may be) find them guilty which are most confident in their justification. For I must distinguish of a twofold adultery, both Carnal and Spiritual. The former ye have heard me hitherto treat of. The latter is twofold.

First, metaphorical, which is any sin of what nature and condition soever, because our souls are espoused to Christ, which the Scripture termeth spiritual whoredom.

The second consisteth in the abuse of any holy thing, which is adultery by way of sacrilege, as Thomas Aquinas will have it.

Not to enter into a strict examination of your hearts or common application, which your guiltiness (I suppose) hath already prevented me of, let me keep to the purpose of this word as it is in my Text.

Ye have hitherto seen the diversity of sin and the monstrous birth of this we treat of. Let Isidore now have leave to present you with the ladder by which this impious vice climbs up to heaven to call for vengeance. "Evil thoughts (saith he) beget delight; delight a consent; consent the act; the act custom; custom necessity; and necessity death." Saint James makes but three rounds to this Ladder: "Lust, when it conceiveth, bringeth forth sin; and sin, when it is finished bringeth forth death" (Jas. 1.15). But he that hath a desire to walk more leisurely to his destruction and (in spite of the Spirit of grace) will follow his own unbridled lusts may travel in those eight by-paths of iniquity mentioned formerly, and so build up the mighty Babel of his own confusion.

But traveler, stay a little, as Minucius Felix speaketh in another kind.[25] Stay thou that walkest in those uncouth paths, while I question thee with St.

Bernard, "Why doest thou sin thus, O, thou unjust creature? Why doest thou offend, O, thou miserable wretch?"[26] The all-seeing providence espies out all thy ways, and the darkest Cells and foulest caverns of thy sooty heart lie open and manifest to his piercing eyes. Plead not the unchaste allurements of lascivious women which tempt thee for an excuse. For our age returns itself guilty of such hellish inventions, such Philters and Diasatyrions,[27] such powders and potions to cherish this abortive brat of uncleanness, that they seem even to justify the several allurements of the weaker sex by more horrid and devilish enchantments. Desire is fed by feasts (says Saint Ambrose), nurtured by delicacies, kindled by wine, and inflamed by drunkenness. This is not to learn of St. Paul to beat down our bodies and keep them in subjection (1 Cor. 9.27), nor of Joseph in my text to contend with the temptation, because to consent is to sin.

Again, he that seeks to excuse himself by the superfluous humors of a pampered body should rather (with Lazarus) live by the crumbs than fare so deliciously with gluttonous Dives (Luke 16.19-31).

Plutarch reports of Antiochus, King of Asia, that when he was invited to perform a visit to the fair Panthea by the various reports of her admired beauty, refused to go, replying, "If (says he) I should repair unto her now my leisure serves me, perhaps she will so take me by her alluring form that when I should follow the affairs of my Kingdom I should spend my time with her when I have no leisure."[28]

I read that Dionysius disinherited his son, which was heir to his Kingdom, for defiling himself with another man's wife.[29]

The Egyptians punished the adulterer with a thousand stripes, and the adulteress with the loss of her nose. A punishment continued since to divers, not by Egyptian edict to the women only, but by the Indian disease,[30] even many times, to both the delinquents.

If these examples, which are fetched from profane Authors, want the power and efficacy of persuading you to shun this sin in my Text, let then the Word of God (which is sharper than any two-edged sword) divide between the joints and the marrow of him that runs on still in this wickedness (Heb. 4.12).

Who so committeth adultery with a woman (saith Solomon) lacketh understanding. He that doth it, destroyeth his own soul (Prov. 6.32). By the Levitical Law, the adulterer and adulteress were both put to death (Lev. 20.10). Zimri and Cozbi were both thrust through by Phinehas, even in the tent (Num. 25.8). Yea, and twenty-and-five thousand of the Benjamites were slain in battle by the Israelites (Judg. 20.46).

What shall I say then? Think ye (my beloved) that either Zimri and Cozbi or those twenty-and-five thousand of the Benjamites were greater adulterers than any of our age? I tell ye nay, but except ye repent, ye shall all likewise perish. The Canon of the Law runs, those must equally share in their punishments which have been equally guilty of an offence. If those, before mentioned, suffered for their lusts in so high a degree, 'twere but justice in God to punish us in the like nature as (or rather worse than) them.

Go then, thou guilty conscience, "sin no more, lest a worse punishment than these happen unto thee" (John 5.14). "As thou hast yielded the members' servants unto uncleanness and to iniquity unto iniquity, even so now yield thy members' servants to righteousness unto holiness, and thy end shall be everlasting peace" (Rom. 6.19). Learn of good Joseph here to shun this spiritual Adder which stings thy soul and then hisses at thee for thy folly. Let God be the object of all our desires, the moderator of our thoughts, and the controller of our actions, so whatsoever rebellious thought steals into our fancies, he will correct it by discovering it unto us to be sin against his sacred Majesty. When the Sun shines into a Chamber through any crevice the smallest atoms are discerned by it, saith St. Chrysostom; so when the grace of the Sun of glory shines into our hearts we shall easily discover the smallest allurements to this impurity. And suddenly, then, may we seek for help when we find it to be a sin against God. Which is the last part of my last general, the reason of Joseph's refusal in respect, secondly, of the object or party offended, God. "How can I do, etc.?"

To question a Deity is to wound it. Nay, to suspect it only is to deny it. The hearts of men are the Book of God, wherein his Majesty is written (for the most part) in so small a character that it dazzles the eyes of their understandings which attempt to pry into it. He that sits in the high and holy places hath commanded all to the knowledge and service of himself. Ignorance, therefore, of his sacred Majesty (although it may seem to plead an excuse in some, yet it) can be at the most but *a tanto* not *a toto*,[31] as the Schoolmen speak. "For he hath not left himself without witness, in that he doth good, and giveth us rain from heaven and fruitful seasons, filling our hearts with food and gladness" (Acts 14.17). Whatsoever, therefore, is endued with a reasonable soul cannot choose but determine of a supernatural power. "See how widely the very heavens are stretched, how rapidly they turn, etc.," as Minucius Felix hath it. And the Psalmist shall be the interpreter: "The heavens declare the glory of God; and the Firmament showeth his handiwork" (Ps. 19.1).

I will not labor your ears with the many and vulgar arguments to prove a God, as if I were to catechize a congregation of Infidels. Let me only present you with one of the same Author, which (I hope) shall command your attention and approbation. Let us consider ourselves as we are men, and view the variety of faces (which we daily behold) with a reasonable eye, and observe how we are lost in the admiration of so much dissimilitude in our likenesses: "We seem all (among ourselves) like one the other, and yet are we found (in something or other) each unlike the other." Which demonstrates unto us the wonderful work of a superior Power to be magnified in this variety.

The Heathens, in ancient times, were confirmed in the *Quod sit*[32] in the positive determination of a divine Commander, although they erred in the *Quid sit* as well as the *Quis sit*, what he was, as who he was. And I can justify by mine own experience that the Salvages[33] in the Western Indies (at this present) have a general tradition received from their Ancestors, which teaches them as far in Divinity as some of the former Heathen had learned, even that there is a great Controller above who doth never injure them. Yet they sacrifice to the Devil because they feel his frequent correction.

I tax not our times for a worse (than salvage) ignorance, although (with sorrow I speak it) I fear here are some, even among us, which are not ignorant of the name but the attributes of God. Let it not then be accounted a digression if I give the same Minucius leave to instruct such ignorant Christians in the properties of their unknown GOD: "'Tis he (saith he) which commandeth all things which are by his Word, orders them by his reason, and perfects them by his virtue. He is such a GOD as cannot be seen (to convict the worshippers of beasts and the like) because he is clearer than our sight. Nor can he be comprehended (to confute our Labans with their stolen gods) because he is too pure to be touched. Nor can he be sufficiently valued (to convince our Libertines which serve him after their common, trivial, and irreligious manner) because he is greater than our senses can determine him to be. He is infinite, immense. Yea, what he truly is is only truly known to himself. So that we esteem him most when we conclude him inestimable."

But this way to discourse of God is not directly commended by my Text. We are here to look upon him with the eyes of our minds more directly, either as a sin-revenging GOD, and so learn to avoid uncleanness because 'tis a sin against GOD who will "wound the heads of his enemies, and the hairy scalp of such a one as goeth on still in his wickedness" (Ps. 68.21); or else as an indulgent Father, and so learn to shun all appearance of this evil because it is a sin against GOD who is so loving to us and requires no requital at all but our reciprocal love (in our obedience) to him.

Should not Joseph, then, have been justly questioned if (in this conflict) his Mistress's temptation had overswayed his religion to tax him with ignorance or forgetfulness of the Lord his Maker? If neither a filial nor a servile fear of this GOD could have reigned his unbridled appetite? To the prevention whereof (ye see) 'tis the only spell which he charms the fiery devil in his Mistress with, "How can I do this great wickedness, and sin AGAINST GOD?"

Let not us then (beloved), who know the GOD of Joseph by his attributes, yea, and are trained up in the ways of his service, subject ourselves to the bondage of our corruptions. Let not the affectation of nor the smallest consent to the least sin rob us of our service to the greatest GOD. But let us reason with our temptations in the words of my Text.

Paula the Matron is commended by St. Jerome that she did so bewail her smallest sins, that she seemed (by her zealous repentance) to be guilty of the greatest.[34]

Servants we are to GOD. "Let us therefore (as Saint Paul commandeth) be obedient to our Master in all things" (Eph. 6.5). Sons we are of GOD. Let us tender, therefore, our duties to him as he himself requires and enables us to perform it, lest he question us in his own words: "If I be a Father, where is mine honor? If I be a Master, where is my fear? saith the Lord" (Mal. 1.6).

"Subdue, then, thine affections; direct thy actions; and correct they steps," as saith Bonaventure,[35] that thou maist not tread out of this path which Joseph hath led thee in, checking thine opposer upon all assaults with "How can I do this great wickedness, and sin against GOD?"

Hitherto, have I endeavored to handle each particular part of my Text severally.[36] Your attention hath now given me assurance of your acceptance, and (to gratify you) I must crave your patience a second time. I am engaged to look back upon my Text once more before I can leave it. And in the first part (which is the Author, Joseph) I must beseech you to consider his place of honor, from a low estate; his place of justice, guided by discretion; and his place of providence, to store for a future necessity. Here is true honor, begot by wisdom, born by observance, and maintained by honesty.

Again, here's the form of envy from his brethren, wiped clean off by the love of his GOD. Moreover, here's poverty and bondage (without repining) climbed up into riches and freedom (yet without pride or ambition). Besides, here's patience in adversity and faithfulness in servility. Here is humility in honor and piety in plenty. If his example win us not in any of these, we'll proceed to the second part, the action refused. Here (I am certain) none can want admonition.

None of the eight sorts of uncleanness write our Joseph guilty. He denies though his Mistress entreats. Here's GOD and the Devil contending for a soul. The woman (who first tempted man) exercises her authority again in Potiphar's wife. But GOD (who is greater) commands by his supremacy. Here's the wickedness of a woman and the goodness of a man positively. And again, here's the goodness of a woman (as some will have it) and the wickedness of a man inclusively. Here Virtue and vice are at contention. Here's the sulphurous fire of Hell burning in lust, and the power of Heaven quenching the flame. Here's a conflict between Chastity and Adultery, but Religion becomes the Judge. Here's a controversy in Law, but Piety is the

Umpire. And (lastly) here's fire and water meeting together in a strong contention, but the spirit of God breathes upon the water (Gen. 1.2).

See here how opposition adds glory to the triumpher. Had not Joseph been tempted, he had not been proved. But (being tempted) had he consented, he had not been accepted. How knew he but that it might be policy in his Mistress to allure him to wickedness not intended to be acted, that she might depose him from honor whom perhaps she hated?

To prevent an injury (therefore) in his repute, he disdained the power of his Mistress's temptation. 'Twas enough that he knew her a woman and therein her infirmities, although he remembered she was his Mistress and therefore instructs her.

A virtuous Woman is like the Jewel in the field, mentioned in the Gospel.[37] Or as the sun in the Heavens, dazzling the eyes of the weak spectators and giving luster to the rest of her sex, the smallest stars. Yea, a Woman in honor (invested with the Ermines[38] of Religion) is all white and goodness of herself, though not without some black spots of malice and corruption. But (on the other side) a Woman in honor, supported by power, leaning upon command and yet bending double with vice is witty in her revenge, dangerous in her malice, contemning the virtuous and (in a furious rapture) plotting for mischief on those who sell not their very souls to content her humor. Do but observe the wife of Potiphar and ye may find it her truest character.

But (on the other party) Religion is predominant though contemned. For great wickedness, ready to be performed by great persons (if it had not been controlled by piety), would have broke out into destruction. Had she only loved him it had been her courtesy. Had she loved his Religion only it had been her goodness. Had she loved only his integrity it had been her discretion. Had she loved only his humility it had been her honor. But in her love (which was but the counterfeit of her lust) she discovered her willful impurity. "The sparks of love are honest but the flames are dangerous," saith Jerome. If any here have been scorched with them, let the tears of contrition quench the fire and the GOD of that contrition accept the repentance.

Hitherto, I have only touched upon that Adultery which is carnal, mentioned formerly. I must now look back upon that which is spiritual also. St. Cyprian, speaking of some Virgins that were Votaries, says they were adulteresses before they were wedded to that austere life, although they were Virgins. And he explains himself presently after, saying, "Not to any husband, but to CHRIST."[39] O, that we could once be free from this whoredom, and become like the King's Daughter in the Psalms, "All glorious within!" (Ps. 45.13). O, that our souls were clad in white robes of innocence and not in the monstrous rags of our natural corruptions! O, that a feared conscience might not persuade us to a drowsy security in a seeming honesty, when these Tabernacles of flesh cannot be truly freed from impiety.

Whatsoever sin we commit is in itself a great wickedness, and the Apostle tells us that the wages thereof is death (Rom. 6.23). Our mortality, then, teacheth us the punishment of our disobedience; much more therefore ought our lives to instruct us in repentance. Our sins are committed against a mighty Jehovah, the LORD strong and mighty, and yet our GOD. Which puts me in mind of my third and last part.

Quarrels among men may be taken up by the amity of friends, but sins against God only by enmity with ourselves. If, then, Joseph refused to admit of a conspiracy against reason and put it off divinely, lest he should sin against GOD, how much more ought we, whose slackness in righteousness condemns us to be less religious. The least here hath not Joseph's command, nor the greatest (I fear) his goodness. Let all contend for his honesty. What vice soever begs for entertainment will be best answered in the words of my Text, if each particular person reply, "How can I do this great wickedness, and sin against God?" To which God, the Father, Son, and Holy Ghost, be all praise, honor, etc.

NOTES

1. The son of Jacob, and the servant to Potiphar during the episode with which Featley deals (Gen. 39).
2. That is, pleasure.
3. Refuge.
4. Chiding or scolding.
5. Nurtured or reared.
6. The sense of the Latin is taken up in the following quotation from Solomon; it translates literally as "Because once something is recently learned."
7. From Lucan, *Pharsalia* 8.492
8. Courage.
9. Something misleading or deluding.
10. See Canticles or Song of Solomon 1.5 and 1.15.
11. Lack.
12. The terms can be translated as fornication, adultery, rape, incest, ravishment, effeminacy, sodomy, bestiality.
13. Timanthes: Greek painter c. 400 B.C. His masterpiece of the sacrifice of Iphigenia had Agamemnon hiding his face in his cloak.
14. See Pliny's *Natural History* 27.4
15. Perceives, realizes.
16. A reference to Seneca's *Moral Letters*.
17. Gluttons.
18. Accounts.
19. Deed.
20. See 2 Sam. 13.
21. Juvenal, *Satires* 8.140.
22. Possibly, Isidore of Seville, 560-636, Spanish archbishop and author.
23. Revealed.
24. Saint Athanasius, 296-373, Bishop of Alexandria.
25. Minucius: Christian apologist of the third century A.D.

26. Saint Bernard of Clairvaux, 1090-1153, French monk, preacher, and mystical writer.
27. Love potions.
28. *Moralia* 3.183-84.
29. *Moralia* 3.175.
30. Syphilis.
31. "By a lot not by all."
32. "Because there was."
33. Savages.
34. In the letters of Saint Jerome.
35. Saint Bonaventure, 1221-74, Italian scholastic theologian.
36. Separately.
37. Possibly Matt. 13.44.
38. Ermine-trimmed, ceremonial robes.
39. Cyprian in a letter to his brother, Cornelius.

Marriage and Household Manuals

CHAPTER 8

The Order of Household:
Described Methodically out of the Word of God, with the Contrary Abuses Found in the World
Dudley Fenner

Written at the end of the English Renaissance, in many ways Milton's *Paradise Lost* sums up numerous opinions and beliefs of preceding years. None is conveyed so vividly as the range of attitudes on marriage, with the poem appearing in some lights as a "transcendent conduct book," celebrating "the apotheosis of 'conjugal love'" (Collinson, *Birthpangs* 69). Milton presents many facets of the marriage relation in pre- and postlapsarian conditions, but apart from intimations of Eve's resistance to Adam's governance prior to her wandering from him in Book 9, she is consistently depicted as his subordinate. In early books she seems to embrace this position: "My author and disposer, what thou bidd'st / Unargued I obey; so God ordains. / God is thy law, thou mine; to know more / Is woman's happiest knowledge and her praise" (4:635-38). Later, her submission is first enjoined, "Lament not, Eve, but patiently resign / What justly thou has lost. . .with thee goes / Thy husband, him to follow thou art bound" (11: 286-91), and then somberly accepted, "But now lead on. . .thou to me / Art all things under heav'n, all places thou" (12:614-18). In short, Milton depicts the mythical emergence of views on marriage that prevailed in the many conduct books and household manuals that were published in the 1500s and 1600s.

In the early-sixteenth century, figures such as Erasmus, Martin Luther, and Juan Luis Vives authored various texts on family and gender relations which emphasized the importance of the family under paternal authority, thereby setting aside the medieval "scholastics' grudging justification of marriage as a cure for concupiscence. . .and lay[ing] greater emphasis on its comfort and companionship" (Maclean 19). Their work set precedents and patterns for many of the later English texts (O'Day 39-41), which were also influenced by Reformation treatises such as *The Christian State of Matrimony*, by the Swiss Reformer Heinrich Bullinger. It is not surprising, then, that many of the manuals were written by Puritan preachers who sought to demonstrate their learning and their religious and moral virtue through constant reference to the Bible and, to a lesser degree, classical authors. Citing such authoritative sources was the accepted logical and rhetorical method of developing the body of an argument. It granted the author's persona, as well as the text, intellectual, ethical, and spiritual substance.

Dudley Fenner's *Order of Household* illustrates many of these features. Fenner, a Puritan clergyman, was born in 1558 and died in 1587. His short life was quite controversial, as staunch convictions placed him in conflict with Elizabethan church and political authorities on a number of occasions. Due to his reputation as a Puritan preacher, he was forced to leave Cambridge University before completing his degree. He moved to Holland and was there ordained into the Reformist ministry. In the early 1580s he returned to England but was soon embroiled in a religious controversy. Along with sixteen other ministers from Kent, Fenner refused to accept three new articles of religious conformity introduced by Archbishop Whitgift in 1583. He was interrogated and imprisoned for a few months in 1584, before subscribing to the new articles. After being released from prison he took charge of a Puritan church in Middleburgh in Holland, dying there in 1587.

Fenner is credited with being one of the originators of English Puritan theology (Collinson, *Godly People* 293). He wrote a number of works which explained reformist beliefs and attacked opposing views. He also published some texts on other topics, including *A Short and Profitable Treatise of Lawful and Unlawful Recreations* (1587), and *The Arts of Logic and Rhetoric* (1584), the first English translation of the French philosopher Peter Ramus's logical method, which proposed analyzing any subject by using dichotomies or opposites to move from general to particular cases. Fenner's philosophical interests supplemented rather than contradicted his religious beliefs, for he contended that "method" was prescribed by God (Ong 74). The translation of Ramus was initially published together with *The Order of Household*. The analytical approach of binary definitions is employed throughout the latter, and the influence of Ramism sounds in Fenner's use of words such as "order" and "methodically" in the title and subtitle.

Fenner married and had four children. He was one of the introducers of the fundamentalist practice of baptizing children with "peculiar names" having godly significance (Collinson, *Godly People* 423). His own children were named Freegift, Morefruit, Faintnot, and Wellabroad. *The Order of Household* endorses this practice, but overall it does not have a strongly personal tone. Its views are traditional, based on repeated reference to the Old and New Testaments. One of the distinctive features of *The Order* is its use of the Bible as a definitive source of authority. The gospels provide powerful evidence and instruction on all aspects of contemporary family life. Fenner's approach suggests a timeless conception of the family, with relationships between husband and wife, parents and children, master and servants reproducing biblical ideals.

A second distinctive feature of the text is, as noted earlier, Fenner's attempt to divide and order all aspects of family life into significant parts, which can be defined and explained. While this feature derives from his interest in Ramism, it also represents an important contrast to conduct and marriage books written earlier in the sixteenth century. Such works as those of Erasmus and Vives used numerous images to portray rather than define the qualities of marriage and gender. Fenner's dialectical method aims to limit the meanings of these qualities, and effectively introduces a "sexual division of behavior and labor" in its "representations of ordered family life" (Newman 25).

At times Fenner appears to quote the Bible from memory, and occasional errors in citation or typesetting have been corrected. *The Order* is also filled with many direct biblical quotations. Where a quotation is incorporated into Fenner's own sentences, it has been retained in the text; where the quotation functions as an illustration of a point Fenner is making and is entirely freestanding, it has not been included though the citation is. Occasionally, short quotations are used to introduce new sections of the text, and these too have been retained.

The Order of Household was republished posthumously in a 1592 collection of *Certain Godly and Learned Treatises*, testifying to the popularity of Fenner's work at least in parts of Britain (the place of publication was Edinburgh). The version below is based on the first edition of 1584 which was published in Middleburgh (*STC* 10769; Reel 224).

THE ORDER OF HOUSEHOLD

The order of a household called *Oiconomia* is an order for the government of the matters of a household, according to the word of God: "which governeth his house well and excellently" (1 Tim. 3.4); and "I will walk in the perfect way, in the uprightness of my soul in the midst of my house" (Ps. 101.2). Which declareth there is a perfect way which cometh from God only, as all perfection doth, wherein is required the uprightness of one's soul, and whereof he setteth down some part afterward: "By wisdom the house is built, and established by understanding, and by knowledge the rooms shall be filled with all precious and pleasant substance" (Prov. 23.3-4).

Now the wisdom meant in this book is that which is allowed of God's word, especially when he joineth such blessing unto it.

The household order hath two parts: the first of these which concern the governors of the family; the second of those which are governed in the same.

"If one care not for his own, especially those of his house" (1 Tim. 5.8), which showeth an especial rule of mutual duty between these two. Also, the wisdom of the holy Ghost in setting down mutual duties unto them (Prov. 31, Eph. 6.2-6, Col. 3.18-24).

Those which govern the family are those superiors who have authority in the same. Their general and common duty is to order their house according to the former rule. Yet one may (being urged by the great care of Magistracy or for such like) have a steward, that is, one to govern his household according to the rules he prescribeth. Contrary to this is the common and whole casting off of this care, unless in worldly matters. The first part of this rule is proved by these places: "I will have the younger women to marry, and govern their household" (1 Tim. 5.14); "If one rule not his household well how shall he care for the church?" (1 Tim. 3.5); the examples of David (Ps. 101.4-7), and Solomon's mother (Prov. 31).[1]

The second part of this rule is proved by the example of Abraham who had his elder servant in his house, who was over all that he had, and to whom he committed the weighty duty of providing a wife for his son (Gen. 24.2-4). So Joseph in Potiphar's house.[2]

This government must be performed with all comeliness fit for the household, which is that agreeable fitness or convenience which worthily becometh the diversity of persons in the family, as superiors, inferiors, equals; of sex, male, female; of age, childhood, youth, ripe age, old years; of matters, as some concerning God, some man; of time, the day, the night. For all these have not one and the same Rule of decency. Therefore the Apostle saith: "Which ruleth his house which keepeth his children in subjection, with all comeliness" (1 Tim. 3.4). Now as there is comeliness peculiar to the subjection of children, so of servants. And as there is comeliness for subjection, so for equality. And as for behavior of those of the house, so to those not of the house, and so likewise in all other the former respects, as shall appear by the shining light or eye of this general rule in every part of household government.

Of the duties of ordering the household by the chief of the same, there are two sorts: the first regardeth those in the household; the other, strangers or guests coming into the same.

"If she have brought up her children well, if she have been given to hospitality" (1 Tim. 5.10). "If the men of my tent have not said: O that some would give us of this flesh: we are not satisfied, because the stranger did not lodge abroad, I opened my doors to the wayfaring man" (Job 31.31-32). So he caused servants to give place to strangers, which showeth this diversity of duties.

Now both of these are in regard of: Christian holiness; the things of this life.

"She openeth her mouth in wisdom, and the doctrine of mercy is on her tongue. And rising while it is yet night, she giveth meat to her house, and a task to her maids" (Prov. 31.26 and 15). And in Exodus 18.5-18.[3]

And this ariseth from a double respect: the commodity they receive, and the duty they owe to the common state wherein they are. That as they have of their children, servants, guests, not only bodily service and friendship, but that which is of conscience and cometh from their faith and religion and their prayer and the blessing in them (Matt. 10.41), so they must give them this double recompense.

Also to the common state they are bound by covenant, not only as much as in them lieth by their household government to further the peace and tranquillity of the commonwealth, but also of religion and true holiness (2 Kings 11.17). Contrary to this is their best care to be most exquisite in the latter and wholly negligent in the former, which is the chiefest. So that their administration of household matters is altogether civil not religious.

For the family, the duty which regardeth them is to keep them in subjection, for the performance of all duties of holiness and religion, and for the diligent performance of works and labors which are fit for everyone (1 Tim. 3.4, Tit. 1.6, Ps. 101.1-8).

Now for the performance of this general duty, two sorts are required, which are: such as where they must commonly go before them and direct them; such as they must perform unto them.

Gen. 35.2-4, where we see that Jacob doth both instruct them what to do and in the doing of these things directeth them.

Such as wherein they must only go before them and direct them are those which only ought to be done jointly of the whole family, and then the superiors must be there the chief directors of them. Otherwise when they are absent they must cause them to be done, as in prayer before and after their labor, in thanksgiving before and after meals (Jas. 5.13, Ps. 127.1-2, Ps. 55.18, 1 Tim. 4.4, Luke 22.17, Gen. 24.12 and 48, Est. 4.16, Neh. 1.4-6). For as it is their duty in their own private fast to do this by themselves, so to direct others in the same when they do it with them. Contrary to this is the unchristian profaneness in such cases, also the unchristian shamefastness[4] of some and common negligence in others in these duties.

Such as they must perform unto them are duties: of instruction; reforming.[5]

"He which keepeth back his rod, hateth his son, but he which loveth him, doeth give him instructions betimes" (Prov. 13.24). "He which withdraweth himself from instruction, despiseth his soul: but he that hearkeneth unto rebuke, possesseth his soul" (Prov. 15.32).

The duties of instruction are that by a familiar and most plain manner of teaching, they may grow in the knowledge of that truth which is according to godliness (Gen. 18.19, Gen. 14.14, Deut. 20.21).

They are for: continual daily instruction; that which respecteth the public ministry.[6]

Duties for daily instruction are: instruction out of the Scriptures; instruction drawn from God's works.[7]

Instruction out of the Scripture is by the daily reading of the same with them, both to make them acquainted with the course of them, so that they may mark the same for their better profiting, by the allegations[8] of the public ministry, and also to refer those things which are plain and easy or which they have learnt from the public ministry unto such plain instruction as, they instructed, may understand and know how to bring it in use. "Thou hast known the Scriptures from a child" (2 Tim. 3.15), which cannot be spoken of a through knowledge,[9] no, nor such as belongeth to the old men who should be sound in faith, much less such as belongeth to a Minister. But such as this, in being made acquainted with it and caused to mark, as he was able, the course of it, and to learn for use and practice, such as his parents were able to note unto him, and he fit to receive by daily practice (Deut. 6.6-9).

Contrary to this is, first, that they are utterly negligent and ignorant how they should do this. Then, that some presume above this rule and go beyond their calling, and especially that their household is not trained by this means, nor made fit for the public ministry and to amend their lives by such Christian exercises.

Instruction drawn from God's works is by applying the works of God, past or present, to move them the better to confidence and truth in God, by works of his mercy; to fear to offend God, by works of his justice; and so to sow the very seed of true religion and good conscience in them (Gen. 18.19).

The duty which respecteth the public ministry [is] Double: first, concerning the obtaining of it; the second, concerning the use of it.

First, concerning the obtaining of it, they must (if it be possible) in their place and calling adjoin them to a set ministry, if not, to bestow at least the Sabbath days, yea, other also, in seeking to the Ministers and prophets of God to hear the word of God. This is manifest, first, because we must first seek the kingdom of GOD, whereof this is a part: "Behold a King shall rule justly, and excellent ones shall govern according to the rule, the eyes of them who see shall not wink, but the ears of them who hear, shall hearken: the mind of the hasty shall understand knowledge, and the tongue of the stutterer, shall readily speak shining things" (Isa. 32.1-4).[10] Secondly, it is the ordinary means to beget and nourish faith to us: "How can they believe except they hear: how can they hear without a Preacher: how can he preach without he be sent?" (Rom. 10.14-15).[11]

[Thirdly], because it is the greatest blessing to have it and the greatest plague to want it. Jeremiah 23, having threatened them that they feed not the people, he saith after, "I will gather the rest of my sheep but of all the land whither I had driven them, and I will bring them back unto their sheepcotes, where they shall multiply and increase, and I will set over them Pasters, which shall feed them: so that they shall fear no more, nor shall be wanting, saith the Lord" (Jer. 23.3-4).[12]

"But when he saw the multitude he had compassion on them, because they were dispersed and scattered abroad as sheep having no shepherd: Then he said, Surely the harvest is great, but the Laborers few," etc. (Matt. 9.36-37), which showeth how miserable they are which want this benefit. It alloweth also this duty of seeking: "And he said, wherefore wilt thou go to him (meaning the Prophet) today? It is neither new Moon or Sabbath day" (2 Kings 4.23), which showeth that in the scarcity of the preaching ministry, they went on those days to the Prophets to hear the word of God.

The second duty is to cause them to do that which is commanded them in the third Commandment to that purpose. Which although it be not proper to this place, yet for the simpler sort it is thus set down. First, to prepare themselves to the preaching of the word, by consideration of God's ordinance and promise and their corruption. So that, laying aside all superfluity of evil, that they may with meekness receive the word (Jas. 1.17, Luke 8.18). And for the Sacraments, to consider God's institution, their ministry, his mercy in Christ, their faith, their repentance, and their wants. And so seeking the assurance of grace, of reconciliation and comfort, to come unto the table of the Lord (1 Cor. 11.28, Isa. 1.16, Isa. 66.2, Matt. 5.23-24).

Secondly, in the works themselves, with reverence and understanding to hear and receive the word, to be touched according to the matter, and, with joy and assurance of faith, receive solace and increase of grace by the right use of the Sacraments. And after to call to mind and try by the Scripture things delivered, and so hold fast the good and to apply the comfort of the Sacraments unto all temptations afterward (Ps. 78.1, Neh. 8.10, 1 Thess. 1.5, Matt. 26.30, 1 Thess. 5.20).

For obedience of life it behoveth them to teach them, call on them, and see them do this which they learn, that the public ministry and private use of the word be not contemned, neglected, unprofitable unto them, and so God provoked not only against their family but also the Church of which they are. Contrary to this is that men, both themselves and their families, go to the public ministry as to a common matter, let it fall after to the ground, without any looking into the certainty of doctrine, the power and practice of it. And some with the ministry of the word become worse, both they and their households, than those which never heard it. "And declare unto thy son in that day, saying: For this hath the Lord done these things unto me, when I went out of Egypt. So shall it be unto thee for a sign upon thine hand, and for a monument between thine eyes, that the doctrine of the Lord may be in thy mouth: to wit, that the lord with a strong hand brought thee out of Egypt" (Exod. 13.8-9). Which with the rest of the law showeth that at those times this must be done, and that so thoroughly, that this work by this means may be a lively sign, and the doctrine be so understood that it may more fruitfully and lively be communicated by conference one to another. Also Acts 10.24.[13]

Job the first chapter, verse 5: "After it came to pass, when they had finished the days of the banquet that Job sent and sanctified them, and rising early, he offered a sacrifice according to the number of them all." For Job said, "Peradventure my sons have sinned, or cursed God in their heart. So Job did every of those days." Which showeth he called on them to do their duties, in sanctifying themselves and their families, and preparing them according to the manner prescribed.

The duties in reforming are those duties whereby they must labor to reform everything amiss which is espied for God's glory and their good, and lest it creep further. Contrary to this is that many corruptions are not accompted of,[14] that they are winked at.[15]

The rule of this must be the meaning of the ten commandments, which because it is necessary for the simple, though not so proper for this place, it is briefly set down. They shall suffer none in their house unreformed, who either in Judgment is known to err from the truth of the word of God, or in manners from the practice of the same.[16] But if any delight in the ignorance of God, be careless to approve himself as one that wholly dependeth on him, loveth him, feareth him, reverenceth him, laboreth to approve all his ways before him; if any be given to Idolatry, superstition, etc., and careth not in every part of the worship of GOD to follow his revealed will; or, if in the parts commanded, he appear negligent and cold, or to put them to any other use than is commanded, or be given to images, superstitious monuments, customs, occasions, or such like; if any dishonor the Name of God, either in the unreverent using or abusing, or perverting and not using with that preparation before, feeling at the present time and fruit after which is prescribed his titles, words, Sacraments, works; and if any profane his Sabbath by vain pastimes, going to plays, or give not himself to the exercises appointed on that day, out of the word; if any neglect especial duties towards their equals, superior or inferior in years, gifts, authority, as Masters, Parents, Magistrates, Ministers, servants, children, or people; if any declare not a conscience to flee evil, anger, malice, contention, quarrelling, fighting, or any hurting of the person of a man, either in soul or body, not being careful to succor the same according to his calling; if any be found unchaste in body, words, countenance or gesture, intemperate in diet, in apparel dissolute, not caring to maintain the contrary holiness in himself and others; if any care not for the goods of another man, but by falsehood, flattery, oppression, etc. diminish the same; if he be negligent in increasing of his own by honest and lawful means; if he misspend it in cards, dice, gaming, etc.; if any care not to maintain the good name of others, but be given unto unnecessary blazing[17] of other men's infirmities by lying, slandering, backbiting, taunting, etc.; if any show himself careless to restrain the motions and enticements unto sin, and the lusts of the same, then they shall use the means following to redress them.

The duties which are to be applied to this rule are these: those which they must do by themselves; those which they must procure to be done by others.

"And the prayer of faith shall save the sick, and the Lord shall raise him up: and if he have committed sins, they shall be forgiven him" (Jas. 5.15). As this must be done for him in sickness, so in health; and as in this cause so in any other of the like nature.

The duties they must do by themselves must have two properties: they must be done with wisdom fit for those duties; patience fit.[18]

Wisdom is that the causes may be thoroughly sifted and soundly reproved out of the word of God. According unto this wisdom also, until a fitter occasion this duty may be let pass and, with keeping the authority of the chief of the family, be winked at for a time (Eccles. 7.21, Prov. 20.21).

Patience fit for it is, with keeping the authority of the chief of the family, to hear what can be alleged, and by equity also to allow or disallow the same. Contrary to which is hastiness without discretion and making the matter plain, that the conscience may be touched for the fault. Also, pride not to hear any excuse or defence delivered in duty, submission, and obedience of child or servant. Finally, bitterness, which may provoke wrath rather than cause amendment (Col. 3.21, Job 31.13-14, Num. 22.26-28, Eph. 6.9).

And these are the properties of those duties. The diverse sorts are: rebuke; correction (Prov. 22.15, Prov. 23.13, Prov. 20.30, Prov. 29.15).

Correction is when, with a sharp rebuke of instruction, punishment is inflicted or laid upon the offender, according to their discretion, consideration being had of the fault and all circumstances of the same. Yet if this at any time for some causes be omitted, a greater is to be threatened and performed when they shall next deserve the same (Prov. 19.19). Contrary to this is too much lenity, also immoderate correction (Prov. 29.15, 17 and 19).

That which they must procure to be done by others is that, when the former means will not serve, they do according to St. James his rule. Send for the elders of the Church, that they may by new admonitions, rebukes, and censures of the Church draw them to repentance. And if that serve not, to bring them to the Magistrate and so (those which they may) to discharge them from the family unless they amend. And those which they may not, to keep them in such order till God or the commonwealth cut them off (Jas. 5.15, Matt. 18.16, Deut. 21.18-21, Ps. 101.7).

And hitherto of the first sort of duties concerning Christian holiness in the family.

The other concerning the things of this life is conveniently to provide the necessary things of this life, as that they have convenient clothing, food, rest, and (if on certain causes need be) recreation (1 Tim. 5.8, Prov. 31.21, Prov. 12.9).

And then, much more the master must care for the servants, that they may have even that refreshing and ease which are meet.[19] And thus much for the general duties and of their special duties towards those who shall be continually or ordinarily under their government in the family.

Now followeth the other which is the entertainment of strangers, whose property is the love of entertaining of Guests. "Therefore a Bishop must be unreprovable, the husband of one wife, watching, sober, modest, given to hospitality, etc." (1 Tim. 3.2). "Be not unmindful of entertaining guests: for hereby certain unawares have entertained Angels" (Heb. 13.2). "Be harbarous[20] one toward another, without grudging" (1 Pet. 4.9).

The first duty required of this work is a liberal and cheerful ministering of protection and all things which serve for the necessity and comfort of this life, as is meet for the ability of them who receive and the condition of those who are received (Gen. 18.2-8, Gen. 19.1-8, 1 Tim. 5.10, Judg. 19.16-18).

The other is as occasion serveth mutually to edify one another, by calling to mind God's works, mutual instructions, and exhortations. Also, by bringing them to the public service of God, and causing them to keep with them the Sabbath, as appeareth by the example above.[21] And Romans, the first chapter, the tenth [and eleventh] verse, "Always in my prayers be seeking, that (if by any means) at length a prosperous journey by the will of God might be given me to come unto you. For I long to see you, that I might impart unto you a spiritual gift, that you may be established."

Contrary to this is niggardliness, such as was in Nabal in receiving of guests.[22] Also suffering God to be dishonored, his word or Sabbath neglected, or any such abuse to be committed by their guests, and not labor by good means to amend them or remove them from the family.

And hitherto of the chief of the family, and their duties as are general to all.

Now for the most part, the chief of the family are married folk, and so in common the governors of the house. They are called married folks because of the band of Marriage. Marriage is that joining of one man and one woman together by the covenant of God, that they may be one flesh until they end their life (Gen. 2.24, Prov. 2.17, Matt. 2.14, 1 Cor. 7.30, Rom. 7.1-3).

To be one flesh, by a part put for the whole, is that most near and holy society, with the power and use of the bodies one of another in purity, whereby the man in an especial manner is become the head of the wife, and the wife another help unto the husband likewise (Gen. 2.18, Prov. 2.17, Matt. 19.6, Eph. 5.31).

Therefore in the whole government of the family: the husband is the chief or foregovernor; the wife is a fellow helper.

To be a foregovernor is in the whole administration of household government to be over all persons and matters in the house, and even the wife: "For if any man knoweth not how to govern his own house, how shall he care for the Church of God?" (1 Tim. 3.5). And to look, as the chief honor, to all revenues and the estate of the good things of this life, especially to care for the keeping and increasing of it (Prov. 27.23).

To be a fellow helper is to yield help to her husband, especially at home in all the matters of the family (1 Tim. 5.14, Tit. 2.5, Judg. 5.24, Prov. 31.5, Gen. 18.6-8).

Contrary to which is that we keep not the authority and chiefdom in all matters; that women usurp any part of it; that they be given to gadding and to meddle with matters not fit for their labor and travel: "They will go from house to house," etc. (1 Tim. 5.13); "Her feet dwell not in the house" (Prov. 7.11).

The duties of married folk in the family are of two sorts: first, mutual; then, towards others (Prov. 31.10-15).

Mutual duties are those which are to be performed one to another of them. They are: common to both; proper to each (Exod. 21.10, Tit. 2.3-5).

Common to both is that which both owe to each other. And it is: dwelling together; mutual good proceedings from thence (1 Cor. 7.12-13).

Dwelling together is to be ordinarily in a dwelling place for the better performance of each other's mutual duties (Matt. 1.18, 1 Cor. 7.10-13, 1 Pet. 3.7, Ruth 4.11-12).

Yet the Scripture alloweth upon necessary occasion of warfare, service to the common wealth, Church, or necessary affairs of their own, sometimes a long absence (Deut. 20.7-9, 2 Sam. 11.11, Prov. 17.19)

Contrary to this is ordinary abuse and negligence of this duty, which bringeth manifold inconveniences.

The mutual good proceeding from dwelling together is that which consisteth in a sweet communicating of the persons and goods, for the mutual necessity and consolation one of another (1 Cor.7.3-5, Gen. 2.18).

Here also must be considered the parts of this duty. First, due benevolence which is the honorable possession of their vessels[23] in holiness one towards another, for avoiding of sin, bringing forth a seed of God, and the honest and proper delight which ought to be between the man and wife (Heb. 13.4, Mal. 2.14, Isa. 62.5, Gen. 26.8, Prov. 15.18-20).

Contrary to this is the abuse of their liberty between themselves, communicating that which is proper to the husband to others in whoring, dancing, uncomely familiarity with another.

The second is their mutual help or labor one towards another, in word, deed, and communicating of good things, for the mutual nourishing one of another (Eph. 5.29, Prov. 31.28-29).

And these are the common duties of one towards another. The proper do follow; they are the duties one of them in several to another. They are of the: husband to the wife; wife to the husband.

"But also you particularly every one so love his wife as himself, and let the wife fear the husband" (Eph. 5.33).

The proper duties of the husband are: a proper care for his wife; the applying of the general duty of all men towards women to his wife.

"Likewise let men dwell together with them: giving honor unto the woman's vessel as unto the weaker, seeing that ye are heirs together of the grace of life, that your prayers be not hindered" (1 Pet. 3.7).

The proper care for the wife is to cover her, that is to provide all things meet for a mate so nearly joined in full blessing to him; and thus according to their condition, to give honor to her as the fittest for him, in heaven and in earth, with a patient covering or bearing of her infirmities (1 Pet. 3.7, Exod. 21.10, Gen. 30.16, Ruth 3.9, Isa. 3.28).

The applying of the general duty of all men in regard of care towards his wife is when, in an especial manner, the image of God's glory and wisdom doth shine in the government of the husband towards his wife, and the glory which God hath in the same shineth in the honor and glory which the man in all things taketh from the wife (1 Cor. 11.3 and 7-8).

Contrary to this is when men are indiscreet, childish, fond, lose their authority, or keep it not, but also their hardness, bitterness, want of wisdom in framing them to perfection in obedience.

The proper duties of the wife are: recompense of her husband's care; and the applying of that general duty of all women in regard of men in a peculiar manner to him, who is called to have him, that covering of her eyes before all men.

The recompense of the husband's care is by obeying him in all good things, and by her advice, sweet counsel, labor and travel, to be a comfort or help unto him (Prov. 31.11-17).

The labor is double: either in matters of this life; or Christian holiness.

"She openeth her mouth wisely, and the doctrine of mercy sitteth on her tongue. She beholdeth the ways of her family, and eateth not the bread of slothfulness" (Prov. 31.26-27).

The matters of this life are her labor: in regard of her family; and her own work.

For the family, she must oversee all the ways of them, and both set them work and task, and also give them their meat and other necessaries in due season (Prov. 31.15-21).

Her own work is to labor diligently, early and late, in something of profit for the family (Prov. 31.13-22).

Her labor for Christian holiness is to see all duties accomplished at the commandment of her husband. For which Christian watchfulness proper to a Mistress of the house is required even to be his eyes, foot, and mouth, when he is away, in espying, looking, admonishing, rebuking, and also giving alms to the poor (Prov. 31.20 and 26).

The second especial duty of the wife, so called by the sign of it, is to be an image of the authority and wisdom of her husband in her whole administration, and so to be his glory and honor. And from a meek and quiet spirit in all her behavior of words, deeds, apparel, countenance, gesture, etc., to signify plainly she hath feeling of him in her heart as of the image of God's Majesty, glory, and perfection (Gen. 24.63-65, Gen. 20.16). "As Sarah obeyed Abraham, calling him Lord, whose daughters ye are made as long as ye do well even when ye are not terrified with any fear" (1 Pet. 3.6).

Where Sarah speaking of her husband but in her heart, the Apostle sayth she did it as of her Lord. Contrary to this is the pride and untamed affection of the wife, their uncomely gestures, their hot and chiding answers towards their husbands, their unshamefast or equal-like looks. Finally, whatsoever is contrary to the former rules.

And hitherto of the duties which are between themselves.

Now follow the duties towards others.

They are double: as they are parents; as they are masters and mistresses.

"Fathers, provoke not your children to wrath, lest they be discouraged" (Col. 3.21). "Ye Masters, give right and equality unto your servants, knowing that you have a master in heaven" (Col. 4.1; Tit. 2.4).

The duty of parents must be performed moderately of the Father, with great gravity and authority (Gen. 22.7, Prov. 4.3-5). Of a Mother, with that cheerful easiness of a mother which keepeth her authority (Prov. 31.1-3).

The duties are: common to both; proper to each.

Common to both, from the first conception of children to take care of them, even to the end of their lives, as appeareth by the parts following.

The especial parts of this duty are these, which respect: their tender age; youth.

"This I say, the heir as long as he is a child, differeth not from a servant though he be Lord of all. But is under tutors and governors until the time appointed of the father" (Gal. 4.1-2).

The duty in their tender age is, according to their years and ability, to nurse them up in discipline fit for children, and admonitions of the Lord (Eph. 6.4, Prov. 22.6).

Discipline fit for children is when by enticements, allurements, corrections, etc., fit for them, they are framed to good. The giving of the admonitions is by little and little, by often repetitions, in greatest plainness which may be, to make them understand some chief grounds and seeds of religion, of good manners, and behavior towards all, and so to begin some conscience in them (Isa. 28.10, 2 Tim. 3.15, Heb. 5.12-13, Prov. 20.11).

Contrary to this is to let them have their will from the beginning, to discourage them by severity, to let the common ignorance of the word to be rooted in them, and not in this care to frame them to truth and goodness and to prepare them to be apt to receive profit from the public ministry.

Their duty towards them in their youth is: either in the entrance of their youth; or in their ripe age.

Their duty in the entrance of their youth is, according to their gifts and diversity of them, to prepare them unto some profitable calling in the church by applying them unto it, beating into them the gifts and conscious use of the gifts which is required (1 Chron. 28.9-11, Prov. 31.1-3).

Here the Church may not be deprived for honor, gain, or such fleshly respects of meet Ministers.

In their ripe age, their duty is to give their children that which may help them in this life and also, if they have not the gift of continence, to counsel them, to govern them unto a fit and religious wife, such as is fit for the duties aforenamed (2 Cor. 12.14, Gen. 24.2-3, Ruth 3.1, 1 Cor. 7).

Contrary to this is the neglect of their life to come, to make matches only for carnal respects, suffering them to live wantonly and uncleanly, and not seeking the remedy appointed.

The proper duties of both is commonly towards them in their infancy. The Father's duty is with all convenient speed that may be, according to the assembly of the congregation, to present the Child for the first Sacrament, and there to give a name in the mother tongue, which may have some godly signification fit for that work.

Contrary to this is deferring of that work for trifles or unmet causes, a giving of a name in another tongue, a profane name (Gen. 25.25-26, Luke 1.59-63, Gen. 4.25, Gen. 19.11 and 15). So the Greeks in Greek, as Timothy, the fear of God (Acts 16.1). And the Latins in Latin, as Tertius (Rom. 16.22).

The proper duty of the mother is to nourish it up, if she be able, with her own milk, and to wean it and perform all such motherly care and duty (1 Tim. 5.10, Gen. 21.7-8, 1 Sam. 1.29, Luke 2.12).

Contrary to this is the tenderness of many mothers, who bring on them the threatening of the prophet willingly, of barren breasts, which should go only with a barren womb.[24]

Hitherto of their duties as they be parents.

Now followeth their duties as they be masters and Mistresses, where besides these, common both to children and servants, this is proper in regard of servants, that not only according to justice they pay them their due wages, but also otherwise help them, comfort them, liberally reward them, as far as Christianity, liberality, inequality shall bind them.

Contrary to this is to retain their wages, to exact of them, to oppress them, or only reward them strictly, according to the exact deserving. "Ye masters, do unto your servants that which is just and equal, knowing that ye also have a master in heaven" (Col. 4.1). And these are the duties which they must perform in their lifetime. All which must be shut up with setting order for all things at their death, with especial exhortations and prayers for religion, for uprightness in their calling, for peace and order after them (Isa. 31.1, 1 Kings 2.1-10, Gen. 49.30).

Hitherto of the first part of householders, which concerneth the government of the same by the Superiors in it.

Now followeth the duties of the inferiors.

The inferiors are those who are under the rest in the household, and are called of Peter, those of the household or household fellows.[25]

Their duties are towards: the household governors; or others (Tit. 1.6).

Toward the household governors: to be helpful to them in outward behaviour; be in subjection and obedience (Luke 2.51).

The first is by outward behavior to acknowledge their authority such as shall be prescribed unto them, as of cap, leg,[26] manner of speaking.

Contrary to this are unmannerliness, answering again, giving cutted[27] answers, etc. (1 Tim. 6.2, Tit. 2.9-10, 1 Pet. 2.18).

The second duty of obedience is in all commandments, concerning the forenamed duties of the Superiors towards them, willingly to perform them, and to submit themselves to rebukes, to admonitions, corrections and such like with meekness (Prov. 4.1-2 and 20, Numb. 12.14).

The duty to be helpful is by their example and persuasions one to another and, by revealing things which by admonition will not be amended, to be helpful to the Superiors in the former duties.

Contrary to this are evil example, evil persuasions, hiding things which ought to be revealed (Gen. 37.2, Gen. 27.44).

The duty towards others is: amongst themselves; towards other besides themselves.

Amongst themselves that with peace and quietness. They have their mutual equality, bear with one another and help one another as far as is lawful. Contrary to which is unquiet minds, pride, jars,[28] lifting up above others, not keeping the place of difference made by the chief of the family.

Towards others is that they so order themselves towards all as they are taught out of the commandments, and towards Guests and strangers, rich and poor, high and low, as they be taught out of the fifth commandment. And thus of the common duties of all inferiors of the family, and this is proved by the commandments and sentences going before (Gen. 45.24).

Inferiors in the family are: children; servants.

Children's duty is from their beginning to their ending to be subject, obedient, and helpful to their parents.

Contrary to this is the rejecting of these duties at some years (Luke 2.51, John 19.26, 1 Kings 2.19, Gen. 47.29, Gen. 49.29-30).

The proper or especial parts of this duty is in their proper: obedience; recompense which they must make.

The proper obedience is that which springeth from a cheerful, natural, continual, and childlike love and reverence.

Contrary to this are disobedience, unnatural behaviors or affections, etc. (2 Tim. 3.2, Col. 3.20, Eph. 6.1).

This obedience must show itself especially in being governed by them in the matter of calling[29] and marriage, according to the rules prescribed in the word of God, and all such matters of weight and moment. Chiefly until by the father's authority and consent more full power be given to their children, because of their years and discretion (Num. 30.3-5, 1 Cor. 7.36-38). "Behold Ribkah is before thee, take her and go thy way, that she may be a wife unto the son of thy Lord, as the Lord hath spoken" (Gen. 24.51).

Laban, the son, having the government of his father being old, was the thief in this business (Gen. 24.55-57).

Their especial recompense is to relieve and maintain them, or any other, who is knit unto them in any especial care and duty, as far as their ability or duty towards the wife and care of the family will suffer.

Contrary to this is contempt of your parents, grieving of them, neglecting to help and succor them, etc. (1 Tim. 5.4, Matt. 15.4-6, Gen. 47.12).

The especial duties of servants is to do all things which their master shall, according to God's will, give them in charge (Col. 3.22, Luke 17.7-9).

Contrary to which is that some will do one thing only at this time, and which pleaseth him.

The manner of doing this hath two parts: diligence; faithfulness.

"Let servants be subject to their master, and please them in all things, not answering again, neither pickers, but that they show all good faithfulness, that they may adorn the doctrine of God our Saviour in all things" (Tit. 2.9).

Their diligence is in a single heart, as to the Lord, not only by labor and travail,[30] but prayer, religious care, and all good means to perform the things laid on them.

Contrary to this is eye-service: "Servants be obedient unto them that use your master according to the flesh in all things, not with eye-service as men pleasers, but with singleness of heart fearing God. And whatsoever ye do, do it heartily as to the lord, and not unto men" (Col. 3.22).[31]

Faithfulness is in their labor and charges to seek, the uttermost they can, the commodity and benefit of their masters.

Contrary to which is picking, turning another way, in banqueting, feasting, riot, etc.

This appeareth most lively in the description which Jacob doth make of his faithful service to Laban (Gen. 31.38-40).

And thus much for the order of Household, which is prescribed by the word of God.

NOTES

1. Fenner writes Solomon, to whom the book of Proverbs was ascribed, instead of Lemuel, King of Massa.
2. Potiphar was Joseph's first master in Egypt; the story of his house and wife is told in Gen. 39. See John Featley's sermon, *The Honor of Chastity*.
3. In these verses, Moses greets his father-in-law Jethro, and Jethro observes Moses judge his people on the basis of God's statutes.
4. Modesty.
5. Along moral and religious lines, in terms of Fenner's reforming Puritanism.
6. Fenner here cites at length Exod. 12.25-26 and 13.14.
7. Here Fenner cites Ps. 78.1-8.
8. Assertions.
9. That is, a knowledge of the whole Bible.
10. Fenner goes on to quote Obad. 21, 1 Cor. 12.5, and 2 Cor. 5.20.
11. Fenner then quotes Eph. 4.11-14 and 1 Tim. 4.13-16.
12. Fenner then quotes Jer. 3.15 and Isa. 30.20.
13. Fenner then quotes Neh. 8.13 and 1 Kings 13.31-33.
14. Taken account of.
15. Fenner cites Job 1.5 and quotes Ps. 101.3-5.
16. In the ensuing discussion of the wide range of sins and vices that people may commit, Fenner includes a vast number of biblical references but no quotations. Fenner's emphasis on reform again reflects his Puritan point of view.
17. Proclaiming.
18. That is, suitable patience.
19. Suitable or appropriate.
20. Hospitable.
21. In Gen. 18.
22. Nabal, a prominent landowner, churlishly refused David's offers of help (1 Sam. 25).
23. Bodies and souls.
24. See Prov. 30.11-16.

25. This may in fact refer to Paul's remark to the Ephesians that they are "fellow citizens. . .of the household of God" (Eph. 2.19).
26. Taking off one's cap and bowing, as signs of respect.
27. Sarcastic or insulting.
28. Quarrels.
29. Vocation or station in life.
30. Work.
31. Fenner goes on to quote Eph. 6.5, Gen. 24.9-11, 26, 33, and 56.

CHAPTER 9

A Godly Form
Of Household Government:
For the Ordering of Private Families
Robert Cleaver

The Form of Solemnization of Matrimony, included in *The Book of Common Prayer*, contains the basis for most of the precepts and views which authors of Elizabethan and Jacobean marriage and household manuals presented to their readers. Such texts were extremely popular; many were written and many went through numerous editions. Robert Cleaver's *Godly Form*, for example, came out in nine editions between 1598 and 1624, including a version "newly perused, amended, and augmented" by Cleaver and John Dod in 1610.

The words of the marriage ceremony cover the key points raised in these texts as well as setting out the different stages of the ceremony. The banns were the first step. For three Sundays prior to the wedding, during the morning or evening service, the curate was to announce the impending marriage and ask if those present knew of any cause or impediment why it might not proceed. On the day itself, the priest explained first the symbolic and religious value of the union, "an honourable estate, instituted of God in the time of man's innocency, signifying unto us the mystical union that is betwixt Christ and his Church"; and next, the motives for matrimony, ordained "for the procreation of children. . .for a remedy against sin, and to avoid fornication. . .for the mutual society, help, and comfort, that the one ought to have of the other, both in prosperity and adversity." Then he conducted the ceremony itself, following with either a sermon on "the duties of Man and Wife" or a summary of Saint Paul's and Saint Peter's pronouncements on these duties, and concluded with communion for "the new-married persons." These explanations and quotations are expanded in many of the manuals, for in Elizabethan society, it has been suggested, Christian teaching offered "the only comprehensive synthesis of thought concerning the family" (Houlbrooke 22).

Historians and critics have debated the extent of changes to conceptions of marriage introduced by the Reformation. On one side, it is argued that

Protestantism instituted a major revision in the cultural valuing of marriage. Rather than celibacy, "the married state now became the ethical norm for the virtuous Christian" (Stone 135), replacing any idealization of unmarried chastity "with the glorification of marriage" (Rose 3). In addition, a "heavy responsibility [was] placed by Protestantism upon the head of the household to supervise the religious and moral conduct of its members" (Stone 154). On the other side, it is claimed that the Reformation was not a change but "a phase of intensified effort in a long struggle to inculcate Christian beliefs and attitudes," and that "heads of families on *both* sides of the religious divide found themselves confronted by the religious dissidence of wives and children" (Houlbrooke 31). It is also argued that the driving force behind developments was not Protestantism but "a common European heritage of Christian humanist thought and scholarship" (O'Day 39). One indisputable change, however, was in the source of orthodox advice on marriage and the family: "in the past, counsel on marital and domestic matters had been dispensed within the pastoral and penitential office by celibate priests. Now advice was given by preachers who were themselves family men, typically in sermons preached at weddings" (Collinson, *Birthpangs* 68).

Cleaver's *Godly Form* is one of the major conduct books of the period. Its structure and contents are outlined on the title page: the duties of husband to wife and wife to husband (from which the following extracts are taken); parental duties to children and children's duties to parents; masters' duties to servants and servants' to masters. The emphasis in the sub-title is noteworthy, "For the Ordering of Private Families." As in Fenner's *Order of Household*, the notion of order is used intellectually and ethically, as a means of structuring the household (along with texts on the household) and organizing the kind of structure it is to have, one based on authority and hierarchy. Whereas the husband's duties derive from affection and rule, the wife's are based on subjection and submission. Here, as in similar guides, "women are urged not merely to chastity, obedience, and silence; they are admonished to repress even gestures and facial expressions, *any visual sign* of opposition to their husbands" (Newman 9).

Cleaver's date of birth is uncertain. He was a Puritan divine and a member of a group of Puritan preachers based in the town of Banbury, itself "a byword for Puritanism" (Collinson, *Godly People* 484). In his play *Bartholomew Fair*, Ben Jonson's caricatured Puritan divine, Zeal-of-the-land Busy, is described as a "Banbury man." Many of these preachers presented views which contradicted official church doctrine. Cleaver was suspended from preaching at one point and had to take refuge in Northamptonshire, a county where Puritanism had become strongly established in the Elizabethan period. Eventually he was removed from his position as rector of Drayton in 1606 and died three years later.

Works written by the Banbury preachers were popular and sold widely. The preachers published prolifically, the texts usually being based on sermons that had been well-received. It seems that there was a degree of collaboration, even rivalry, among the preachers which spurred on their productivity; historian Patrick Collinson writes of "the mutual pressures of a fraternity" and a "benevolent pressure to publish" (*Godly People* 496). Cleaver published numerous texts, largely comprising sermons and pamphlets on religious topics such as the sabbath and infant baptism. He collaborated extensively with another, more famous "Banbury man," John Dod (1549-1645). Indeed, they were "the most successful co-authors of the century" (Collinson, *Godly People* 496), with their best-known work (apart from the revised version of *Godly Form*) being a commentary and explication of the Ten Commandments. As noted above, *A Godly Form of Household Government* was republished nine times. The following extracts are taken from the second edition which, like the first, was published in London in 1598 (*STC* 5383; Reel 317).

A GODLY FORM OF HOUSEHOLD GOVERNMENT

The Duty of the Husband towards His Wife

This duty consisteth severally in these three points. First, that he live with his wife discreetly, according unto knowledge. Secondly, that he be not bitter, fierce, and cruel unto her. Thirdly, that he love, cherish, and nourish his wife even as his own body, and as Christ loved his Church and gave himself for it to sanctify it. But before we shall speak of these three points we will a little touch the original and beginning of holy Wedlock: what it is, when, where, how, and of whom it was instituted and ordained.

Wedlock or Matrimony is a lawful knot, and unto God an acceptable yoking and joining together of one man and one woman with the good consent of them both (Matt. 19.5-6, Gen. 1.27, 1 Cor. 6.16, Ephes. 5.31, Prov. 5.18-20). To the end that they may dwell together in friendship and honesty, one helping and comforting, the other eschewing whoredom and all uncleanness, bringing up their children in the fear of God. Or, it is a coupling together of two persons into one flesh, not to be broken according unto the ordinance of God, so to continue during the life of either of them (Gen. 2.24, Mal. 2.14, Rom. 7.3).

By yoking, joining, or coupling is meant not only outward dwelling together of the married folks, as to be ordinarily in a dwelling place for the better performance of each other's mutual duties (Matt. 1.18, 1 Cor. 7.10-13, 1 Pet. 3.7, Ruth 4.11-12), but also a uniform agreement of mind and a common participation of body and goods. For as much as the Lord saith that "they two shall be one flesh" (Gen. 2.24), that is, one body, this is to be remembered, that Matrimony or Wedlock must not only be a coupling together but also it must be such a coupling together as cometh of God and is not contrary to his word and will. For there be some marriages made whom God coupleth not together but carnal lust, beauty, riches, goods and lands, flattery and friendship. In such marriages God is not thought upon, and therefore they sin the more against him.

These and such like marriages be disliked and condemned in the Scripture (Gen. 6.12, Ezek. 10.1ff., Matt. 24.38-39). God did appoint and ordain Matrimony himself in Paradise, so that he is the author of the same (Gen. 2.20). Yea, and our Saviour Christ himself who, being the very natural son of God, was born in wedlock, although of a pure virgin, did honor and commend Matrimony while he did vouchsafe to show his first miracle at a marriage (John 2.1). Whereby he did declare that the Lord is able to make the bitterness of marriage sweet and the scarcity thereof to abound with plenty. And the Apostle giveth this excellent title to marriage, saying that it is "Honorable among all" (Heb. 13.4), that is, among all estates and all nations. The institution of Matrimony is an indissoluble bond and knot, whereby the husband and wife are fastened together by the ordinance of God, and is straighter than any other conjunction in the society of mankind.[1] Insomuch that it is a less offence to forsake father and mother and to leave them succorless (which, notwithstanding, ought by God's commandment to be honored), than it is to do the like toward his lawful married wife. Wherefore, let them look well what they do that are ready for light and small causes to separate man and wife, seeing that Christ himself saith that whosoever is separated from his wife saving for whoredom and marrieth another committeth adultery (Matt. 19.9).

This is a thing worthy to be remembered, both on the behalf of the Suitor and Wooer, as also on her part that is wooed. Namely, that they deal plainly and faithfully one with the other and not guilefully and craftily go about to deceive one the other in body or goods. For so doing, they shall never use one the other so lovingly and commodiously as they hoped and desired they might, when the one hath fraudulently and deceitfully enticed and beguiled the other either in body or substance. For naturally we hate him or her that doth beguile us. Neither is there anything that displeaseth a man or woman more than to lack and fail of the thing they both hoped and looked for. And therefore it were convenient and also much better that both parties should disclose the one to the other such imperfections, infirmities, and wants in either of their bodies, as also the mediocrity and meanness of their goods and substance as in truth it is. Yea, though it should be with the peril and loss one of the other, rather than the one to obtain and get the other with fraud, guile, and discord.

But before we shall come to speak of the causes of marriage, we purpose (God so willing) briefly to show how everyone that intendeth to marry should choose him a meet, fit, and honest mate (Gen. 2.18). For there lieth much weight in the wise election and choice of a wife. As he that will plant anything doth first consider the nature of the ground in the which he mindeth to plant, even so much more ought a man to have respect to the condition of the woman out of whom he desireth to plant children, the fruits of honesty and welfare.

The first thing that is to be remembered of such a one as mindeth to marry is that he do not choose his wife within such degrees of consanguinity and affinity as are by God's law forbidden (Levit. 18.6ff). Secondly, Religion and faith must be considered, lest he make divorce of the true faith or bring it into peril (Deut. 7.3). For although he think himself as wise as Solomon (1 Kings 11.4) and as strong as Samson (Judges 16.17-18), yet may he be overcome as they were. Therefore, great advisement beforehand is to be taken on this behalf, lest afterwards with much grief and sorrow of heart he do too late repent.

Now, if any that hath matched himself with a wife that is an infidel, irreligious, or of a corrupt religion, and would put her away for this matter, herein he deceiveth himself as the Apostle manifestly proveth (1 Cor. 7.12ff.). For we must put a difference between that marriage that is made and done already and it that is yet to do (1 Pet. 3.1). Wherefore he that is snared and matched with such a wife as is either froward, wayward, or else is poisoned with superstition and popery, in such a case he must call upon God and live in his fear, in faithfulness, in patience, and with discretion and godly counsel labor to win her from the same. For like as that Husbandman doth with great labor and diligence till that ground which he hath once taken to farm although it be never so full of faults, as if it be dry if it bring forth weeds, brambles, or briars, or though the same ground cannot bear much wet, yet through good husbandry he winneth fruit thereof. Even so, in like manner, he that hath married a wife that is irreligious or froward, if he shall use like diligence to instruct and order her mind, if he diligently and courteously apply himself to weed out by little and little the noisome weeds out of her mind, both by wholesome and godly precepts and by Christian conversation, it cannot be but in time he shall feel the pleasant fruit thereof to both their comforts. For as it is commonly said, a good Jack maketh a good Jill.[2] Everyone, therefore, that purposeth to marry ought also to remember that there be three manner of riches in man: 1. the riches of the mind; 2. the riches of the body; 3. the riches of temporal substance. The best and the most precious are the riches of the mind, as without which the other two are more hurtful than profitable.

The riches of the mind are the fear of God, faith, God's glory, knowledge of his will, soberness, liberality, chastity, silence, humbleness, honesty, and such like virtues. These virtues lie not still, neither hide themselves wheresoever they be, but will break out divers ways so that they may well be spied and discerned. As a traveler hath marks in his way that he may proceed aright, so likewise the man or woman that intendeth to marry have also marks in their ways by which they may make a right choice. There be certain signs of this fitness and godliness both in the man and in the woman. So that if the man be desirous to know a godly woman, or the woman would know who is a godly man, then let them observe and mark these six points: 1. the report; 2. the looks; 3. the speech; 4. the apparel; 5. the companions; 6. and lastly, the education and bringing up, which are like the pulses that show whether a man be sick or whole, well or ill.

1. The report, name, or fame he or she hath had and yet have, and what opinion honest folks have of them. Because as the market goeth, so the market-men will talk. A good man and a good woman commonly have a good name, because a good name is one of the blessings which God promiseth to good men and good women (Prov. 10.7 and 22.1, Ps. 112.6). But a good name is not to be praised from the wicked, and therefore our Saviour Christ saith, "Woe be to you when all men speak well of you" (Luke 6.26), that is, when evil men praise and commend you. For that is a plain argument that you are ambitious, vainglorious, and of the world, "For the world liketh and praiseth her own" (John 15.19). Nevertheless, it is convenient that every Christian should so live in the world that, though he cannot say as Christ said, "Which of you can rebuke me of sin?" (John 8.46), yet in truth he with a good conscience may boldly say, which of you can accuse me of lying, swearing, whoring, dissembling, dishonesty, deceit, covetousness, or such like. Which, though no man can clear himself in thought before God of these and other notorious vices, yet everyone before men should avouch it and approve it in their doings, and live so uprightly, holily, justly, and unblameably that none could justly charge them with any open sin (Luke 1.6 and 15, Job 1.1, 1 Thess. 2.10 and 3.13, Tit. 2.12, 1 Pet. 1.15).

2. The next sign is the look, for as Solomon saith, "The wisdom of a man doth make his face to shine" (Eccles. 8.1), that is, procureth him favor and good liking. So also godliness is in the face of a man or woman, and so likewise folly and wickedness may many times be seen and discerned by the face of a man or woman. And therefore it is said in Isaiah, "The trial of their countenance testifieth against them" (Isa. 3.9), as though their looks could speak. And therefore we read of proud looks and angry looks and wanton looks because they bewray pride and anger and wantonness. It is truly said that a modest man dwells at the sign of a modest countenance and an honest woman dwelleth at the sign of an honest face. Which may fitly be compared to the gate of the Temple that was called Beautiful, showing that if the entry be so beautiful, within is great beauty (Acts 3.2).

To show how a modest countenance and womanly shamefastness do commend a chaste wife, it is observed that the word *Nuptiae* which doth declare the manner of her marriage. For it importeth a covering because virgins which should be married, when they came to their husbands, for modesty and shamefastness did cover their faces, as we read of Rebecca which, when she saw Isaac and knew that he should be her husband, she cast a veil before her face (Gen. 24.65), showing that modesty should be learned before marriage, which is the dowry that God addeth to her portion.

3. The third sign is her talk or speech or rather her silence. For a man or woman's talking is the mirror and messenger of the mind, in the which it may commonly be seen without in what case the man or woman is within, according to the common proverb, "Such as the man or woman is such is their talk." Now, silence is the best ornament of a woman, and therefore the law was given to the man rather than to the woman to show that he should be the teacher and she the hearer. And therefore she is commanded to learn of her husband (1 Cor. 14.34-35). As the Echo answereth but one word for many which are spoken to her, so a maid's answer should be in a word. For she which is full of talk is not likely to prove a quiet wife. The eye and the speech are as the Glasses of the mind, "For out of the abundance of the heart (saith our Saviour) the mouth speaketh" (Matt. 12.34), as though by the speech we might know what aboundeth in the heart. And therefore he saith, "By thy words thou shall be justified, and by thy words thou shalt be condemned" (Matt. 12.37). That is, thou shalt be justified to be wise or thou shalt be condemned to be foolish; thou shalt be justified to be sober or thou shalt be condemned to be rash; thou shalt be justified to be humble or thou shalt be condemned to be proud; thou shalt be justified to be loving or thou shalt be condemned to be envious. Therefore Solomon saith, "A Fool's lips are a snare to his own soul" (Prov. 18.7). Snares are made for other, but this snare catcheth a man's self because it bewrayeth his folly and causeth his trouble and bringeth him into discredit. Contrariwise, "The heart of the wise (saith Solomon) guideth his mouth wisely and the words of his mouth have grace" (Prov. 16.23).

Now, to show that this should be one mark in the choice of a wife, Solomon describing a right wife saith, "She openeth her mouth with wisdom and the law of grace is in her tongue" (Prov. 31.26), for that she delighteth to talk of the word of God. A wife that can speak this language is better than she which hath all the tongues. But as the open vessels were counted unclean (Num. 19.15), so also account that the open mouth hath much uncleanness.

4. The fourth sign is the apparel. For as the pride of the Glutton is noted in that he went in purple every day (Luke 16.19), so also the humility of John is noted in that he went in haircloth every day (Mark 1.6). For doubtless, by a man or a woman's apparel, excessive laughter, and going, they may partly be discerned of what disposition they are of. It is convenient that he that will be a suitor to a woman, that he mark what

apparel she customably useth to wear, whether it be vain, whorish, wanton, light, or comely, modest, and mannerly, and beseeming her estate and condition, to wit, honest and sober raiment. For apparel doth give often a certain and sure testimony of pride, lightness, wantonness, inconstancy, unshamefastness, filthiness, or uncleanness and other vices or virtues that be either in the man or the woman. For a modest man or woman are for the most part known by their sober attire, as the Prophet Elijah was known by his rough garment (2 Kings 1.8). So that we are to look for no better within than we see without, for everyone seemeth better than they be. If the face be vanity, the heart is pride. He that biddeth us abstain from the "show of evil" (1 Thess. 5.22) would have us to abstain from those means, husbands or wives, who have the shows of evil. For it is hard to come in the fashion and not to be in the abuse. And therefore the Apostle saith, "Fashion not yourselves like unto this world" (Rom. 12.2), as though the fashions of men did declare of what side they are.

5. The fifth sign is the company, by means whereof much may be perceived. For as whole and sound eyes with beholding and looking on sore eyes be annoyed and hurt, even so good and honest folks be often times stained and hurt with the company of the wicked and ungodly according to the common proverb: "Such like is everyone as the company is with whom they keep." For birds of a feather will hold together, and fellows in sin will be fellows in league, even as young Rehoboam chose young companions (1 Kings 12.8). The tame beast will not keep with the wild, nor the clean dwell with the leprous. If a man can be known by nothing else then he may be known by his companions. For like will to like, as Solomon saith; thieves call one another (Prov. 1.11 and 13.20). Therefore when David left iniquity he said, "Away from me all ye that work iniquity" (ps. 6.8), showing that a man never abandoneth evil until he abandon evil company. For no good is concluded in this Parliament. Therefore choose such a companion of thy life as hath chosen company like thee before. For they which did choose such as loved profane companions before in a short time were drawn to be profane too.[3]

6. The last sign is education, which giveth also great testimony. Namely, by whom and how everyone is brought up, whether the man or the woman were conversant among virtuous or vicious persons, and whether the parties have continued in the nurture of the virtuous and showed themselves obedient to them under whom they were brought up, or whether either of the parties have broken out of this discipline and followed his or her own willfulness. For it is a small matter for either of them to have dwelt among or with virtuous and religious folk. But rather herein lieth the force and weight: how far and how much either or both the parties have followed those and profited under them, and were dutiful and obedient unto them. For Judas was among and accompanied with the Apostles, brought up

certain years under Christ. But for all this he was never the better, for he left not his wicked pranks, neither was he obedient. Nevertheless, good education and discipline formeth good manners. Men and women commonly favor most of those good or evil things which in youth they learned. Therefore, to prove good, honest, and virtuous, it emporteth and forceth much from the infancy to be well-governed and christianly brought up, for we retain much more of the customs wherewith we be bred than of the inclinations wherewith we be born.

All these properties are not spied at three or four comings and meetings of the party. For hypocrisy is spun with a fine thread and none are so often deceived as lovers. He therefore which will know all his wife's qualities, or she that will perceive her husband's dispositions and inclinations before either be married to them, had need to see one the other eating and walking, working and playing, and talking and laughing and chiding too. Or else it may be the one shall have with the other less than he or she looked for or more than they wished for.

Here is to be remembered a thing adjoined to marriage and going before it, namely, Betrothing being a solemn and laudable custom of God's children (as is proved, Deut. 20.7 and 22-24). This Betrothing is a covenant between the parties to be married before fit witnesses appointed thereto. Whereby they give their troth that they will and shall marry together, except some lawful unmeetness[4] and disliking of each of other do hinder it in the meantime. The practice of it we see where the Virgin Mary being betrothed to Joseph, yet they had not met together, to wit, to accompany together according to the end of marriage (Matt. 1.18, Luke 1.27). This custom, noted and marked in divers places of the Scripture, hath divers good grounds to be observed, which prove that there ought to be a Contract before marriage. And for the better understanding of this point of Betrothing, it shall not be amiss in some plain and short manner to make known the holy doctrine hereof, with the doctrine also of marriage and marriage duties.

First, then, we must know that every marriage that hath been well and orderly used, either of the heathen (which were only enlightened with the law of nature) or of the people of God, who also were to be directed by his word, was perfected by two solemn actions: that is, by an apparent and open Contract, and by public marriage, the true and unfeigned confirmation thereof. Whereof we will first speak of a Contract (which is also called espousing, affiancing, betrothing, or handfasting), then of marriage itself.

And for betrothing or espousals, we read in the writing of ancient Philosophers, Histories, Orators, Poets, and others that they be of great antiquity, of necessary use, and have been ordinarily practiced. Insomuch as the users thereof are highly commended, the neglecters and abusers hereof sharply rebuked and condemned. Which seeing they could not do but upon knowledge and judgement, it doth manifestly declare that they did it by nature's law, written and bred in their breasts. And therefore that even nature itself, though in some matters stark blind and in many of very dim sight, yet she hath in all ages bewrayed the lawfulness, the necessity, and the use of espousals to be the first step and degree to a lawful and comfortable marriage.

But to omit this law and to come to the written word, let us further consider what allowance we find in the same, and consequently what it is not only to marry, not only according to the direction of nature, but also in the Lord. First, it is certain that the Lord approveth them as his own sacred ordinance, for we read in Exodus 21.7-11 how carefully he provideth by sundry and many straight commandments for the Maidservant that is betrothed. First, that she shall not go out of her service as the Menservants do. Secondly, that her Master shall have no power to sell her to a strange people. Thirdly, that being betrothed unto his son he shall deal with her as with his own daughter. Fourthly, if another wife be taken with her, that neither her food, her raiment, nor recompense of her Virginity shall any whit at all be diminished. Fifthly, that whensoever she goeth out of her service she shall pay no money at all. None whereof the Lord would have done (much less all of them) unless espousals had been his own ordinance, instituted, ordained, and commanded by himself to be used even of the Maidservant that was bought and sold.

Again, it is written in Deuteronomy 22.23ff. how the Lord by like commandment provideth for the espoused maid being inoffensive yet being guilty, he punisheth with less punishment than if she had been indeed married. First, then, he commandeth that if any man shall abuse a betrothed virgin in the City both shall be stoned to death, the Maid because she cried not, the man because he hath humbled his neighbor's wife. Whereby the way is to be remembered how God calleth the betrothed a wife. If then such wickedness by justice deserveth death, and if betrothed persons be truly to be termed man and wife only in regard of the precedent espousals, we may then plainly see how highly the Lord doth esteem and honor them. The breach whereof he punisheth with the punishment of adultery, and the persons betrothed he honoreth with the names of man and wife. If, indeed, he had not ordained and allowed them but that they had been of human institution alone, he would not have honored them with such titles or have imposed death by stones for the breach of man's ordinance. Again, if a man abuse a betrothed maid in the field he saith that the man shall die, but unto the maid thou shalt do nothing because there is in the maid no cause of death.

Now, imposing death upon this man and not upon him that abuseth a maid not betrothed, the Lord doth hereby evidently teach that espousals are a principal degree in marriage. And therefore the unlawful breach thereof deserveth death. For what else should the Lord grace them with such great privileges and punish the breach thereof with severe punishment?

Further, the faithful in all ages, instructed by these and such commandments, approved and practiced these espousals not only by themselves but also by their children. Samson, liking and loving a woman of the Philistines in Timnah, desired his Father and Mother to give her to him to wife, and so they did, at which time Samson made a feast according to the custom of the young men (Judg. 14.1ff). Albeit, her father afterward would not suffer him to marry her but gave her to another, for which injury Samson revenged himself of the Philistines by burning up the ricks of standing corn, vineyards, and olives. For which the Philistines burnt both the Father and the daughter. So David begged Michal of her father Saul, who gave her to him to wife with condition that he would bring him a hundred foreskins of the Philistines (1 Sam. 18.15, 26-27). And therefore, when Saul was dead he required her of Ishbosheth, Saul's son, who sent her unto him. Also, Joseph and Mary, the mother of Christ, were betrothed, which God would never have permitted if it had not been of his own ordinance and agreeable to his own will, or if he might any manner of way have stained either Joseph's honesty or Mary's virginity. Nay, if he had not much more graced and adorned both then the want of espousals could have done.

And to avoid tediousness in so plain a truth, seeing the Scripture giveth power and authority to Parents to give and not to give their children in marriage, saying let him do what he will (1 Cor. 7.36-38).

Again, he that giveth her in marriage doth well and he that giveth her not to marriage doth better (whereof we shall speak more at large anon). There must needs be before the public act of marriage some special time appointed, wherein both Parents and parties may testify and signify their mutual liking and consents, unless they despise to marry in the Lord.

Wherefore, if the law of nature, the law of God, the practice of the Heathen, the custom of Faithful, especially of the Parents of Christ; if the punishment of the espousal-breakers and the rewards and privileges of the espoused; and finally, if the fatherly authority over children do approve and require the continual use of this ordinance of God, it must needs be confessed to be both lawful and necessary. Yea, being the first principal part of marriage itself, it must needs be honorable in his kind as well as marriage itself is. Now then, in the next place, let us see and learn what a Contract is, to the end that upon sound knowledge and right judgment we may always use it well and never ill for want of good understanding.

A Contract is a voluntary promise of marriage, mutually made between one man and one woman, both being meet and free to marry one another, and therefore allowed so to do by their Parents.

This short sentence showeth the whole nature, quality, property, use, and abuse, with all other things that are to be observed or eschewed in a right Contract, as shall appear by the unfolding of every word contained therein. For as there is none vain and idle, void of his proper signification, so every one hath his proper weight serving for special and necessary use.

1. First, we call a Contract a promise, and so it is indeed. For what is a promise but a speech which affirmeth or denieth to do this or that, with purpose and words of testimony to perform and accomplish the which is affirmed or not to do that which is denied? And what other thing is indeed a marriage Contract but this? So that it must be in nature a true and right promise, not the vow of a promise in time to come but a present promise in deed. For if one party do say I will promise to marry thee, this is no promise in deed but a promise of a promise, and consequently no Contract but a promise of a Contract. And therefore tieth nor bindeth neither parties nor Parents to keep the same, for it is not in nature any Contract at all. Again, if a Contract be a promise it is not only a purpose of the heart, nor a dumb show or doubtful signification of promise, but a plain promise, uttered and pronounced in a right form of speech, as when one saith I do promise to marry thee or I do espouse, affiance, or betroth myself to thee in marriage, or such like, wherein all ambiguity and doubtfulness of speech is to be eschewed, that as the meaning of the heart is simple and plain so likewise the words of the tongue might be simple and plain void of all deceit.

Secondly, we call a Contract a promise of marriage because it is not a promise of everything, neither of honor or inheritance of riches or of any other thing else, saving only of marriage. Now, we mean by marriage not only the parties married but all conjugal and marriage duties and offices that peculiarly belong to this honorable estate and are necessarily to be performed mutually of both. For this promise touching persons themselves is of such force and weight that it tendeth to the alienation of the property of bodies. For so it is written the wife hath not the power of her own body but the husband, and likewise also the husband hath not the power over his own body but the wife (1 Cor. 7.4). For although this is not perfectly done till the act of marriage be ended, yet this promise is the principal beginner and worker thereof, because they that promise marriage do necessarily thereby promise that two shall become one flesh and that they will always give mutual benevolence one to another.

Touching the peculiar duties of husbands and wives which likewise are promised by this Contract, we will here only recite them leaving the doctrine thereof to another place and time.

The husband, his duty is first to love his wife as his own flesh. Then to govern her in all duties that properly concern the state of marriage in knowledge, in wisdom, judgment, and justice. Thirdly, to dwell with her.

Fourthly, to use her in all due benevolence, honestly, soberly, and chastely (1 Pet. 13.7, 1 Cor. 7.45).

The wife, her duty is in all reverence and humility to submit and subject herself to her husband in all such duties as properly belong to marriage. Secondly, therein to be a help unto him according to God's ordinance. Thirdly, to obey his commandments in all things which he may command by the authority of a husband. Fourthly and lastly, to give him mutual benevolence. As for the rest of mutual duties, as they may be all comprehended under these so there shall be a fitter occasion to speak thereof.

Thirdly, we call this promise of marriage voluntary because it must not come from the lips alone but from the well-liking and consent of the heart. For if it be only a verbal promise without any will at all (and so mere hypocritical and dissembled), though it bindeth the party that promiseth to the performance of his promise made before God and man, yet if the Parents afterwards shall certainly know this and that there was no will nor unfeigned meaning at all in the party, neither yet is but rather a loathing and abhorring of his spouse betrothed, though he be not able to render just and sufficient cause thereof, they may upon this occasion either defer the day of marriage the longer to see if God will happily change the mind of the party, or utterly break and frustrate the promise if all good means and occasions having been used none will prevail, but that the party rather groweth worse and worse. For a Contract being a willing and a voluntary consent there is no cause why the Parents and such as have authority and power in such cases, when they shall undoubtedly know that the promise was altogether unwilling and therefore made in mere hypocrisy and dissimulation, neither can be by tract of time or any other good means used be bettered but rather (waxeth worse and worse), may not break and frustrate the same.

For why did Rebecca's Parents deny her to Isaac, neither would send her with Abraham's servant to be married before such time as they had asked her consent? Yea, when as they said, "We will call the maid and ask her consent" (Gen. 24.57-58), do they not plainly show that both the law of Nature and the law of God taught them that this consent was of great moment and absolute necessity? And when the Apostle doth command men and women to marry in the Lord, how can that marriage be in the Lord when the one party doth not only not love but hate the other? And how can such two become one flesh lawfully when as there wanteth the union and conjunction of the heart, the true natural mother of all marriage duties? Wherefore this promise must be in this respect at least willing and voluntary. For albeit it is not necessary, neither yet possible, that there should be such great measure of true holy and sanctified love at that time as afterward (for that groweth by little and little, according to the blessing of God and the faithful performance of other duties afterward even to their lives' end), yet if it be voluntary and unfeigned it is enough and fully sufficient to make a true Contract in the Lord. So, as no man ought to separate those whom God hath thus joined.

Secondly, we call it voluntary in respect of constraint and compulsion contrary to a free consent. For if either party be urged, constrained, or compelled by great fear of their Parents or others, by threatening of loss of preferment, of health, of limb, of life, or of any such other like, or by any other violent manner of dealing whatsoever to yield their promise clean contrary to the motion of good liking of their hearts. This kind of promise, as it doth not bind the party to keep it, so it ought to be frustrated and broken by the Parents themselves or by such masters as may and ought to command and rule them in such cases. If this were not so how could the parties keep the commandments of God giving them direction whom to marry? First, that they should marry only in the Lord.

Again, that they should not be unequally yoked with the infidels, neither whereof they can keep if their parents might compel them or Contract and marry. It becometh rather the Parents to persuade their children by all good means to yield their consent rather than to draw them by wicked sleight and cunning drunkenness or any other wicked and violent means. For as that is not to marry in the Lord, so all such forced Contracts may be broken and frustrated by the Magistrate, who is God's Lieutenant to redress such intolerable enormities among the societies of men. For if Parents may deny marriage to such as have not only by force and violence obtained the word and body of their child, much more may the Magistrate deny marriage where only a verbal promise hath been gotten by violent compulsion. And so for these causes, and in this sense and meaning alone, we conclude that Contract must be voluntary.

Fourthly, it must be a mutual promise, that is, either party must make it to other, not the man only, nor the woman only, but both the man and the woman, though decency and order require the man to do it first and then the woman because he is her head and she his glory, and ought to lead and guide her in all things wherein the Lord hath put a pre-eminence. For if this promise be not mutually made of them both but of one alone, it is no true and perfect Contract. And therefore may be broken by Parents and such as have authority herein, because the party unpromising is not bound by word nor deed but is free, insomuch that such a Contract is rather so termed than for that it is any true Contract indeed. But if it be mutual then it doth mutually and inviolably bind both, so that in this regard neither Parent, Magistrate, nor any other can or ought to break it. For this, being fully performed and accomplished, is one principal cause of making two one flesh, in such sort as it is written. Therefore shall man leave his father and mother and shall be joined to his wife, and they two shall be one flesh etc. (Gen. 2.24). Also, that the man hath not power over his own body nor the woman over hers. And so to be short, hence ariseth all mutual benevolence between them, and therefore a point of great weight and necessity, in no wise[5] to be omitted in Contract.

Fifthly, we say it must be between one man and one woman. Where, first, it is to be noted that it may not nor ought not to be between any other creatures but mankind, nay, neither among brute beasts nor Angels. For God hath not ordained nor instituted marriage for them, neither can it be between man and man or woman and woman. If any such Contract be either voluntary or by fraud and deceit, by ignorance or error, it is no Contract at all, but a mere wicked profanation of God's ordinance, who gave only woman to man not woman to woman nor man to man. Likewise it cannot be between Angels, good or bad, and woman because God hath set no such ordinance in the nature of these creatures. If therefore there hath been any such matter or shall be attempted by Satan with any woman (as some stories report), it is nothing else but a mere illusion and devilish practice to draw and deceive superstitious persons into the kingdom of darkness and to entrap them in the chains of condemnation. Against which and all other diabolical illusions we ought to watch and pray continually.

Secondly, it is to be observed that between one man and one woman, and not two men and one woman or two women, not between two women and one man or more. By which is condemned, as mere nullities and profanations, all Contracts whatsoever made between more than two. For it is written, "And they twain shall be one flesh" (Matt. 19.5), to which Mark addeth, "So that they are no more twain but one flesh" (Mark 10.8).[6] Wherefore, seeing that Christ and his Apostles expound the first institution of marriage of two only and not of any more, it is certain that the Contract or promise thereof ought to be of two alone and no more. So the holy Ghost saying, "Let every man have his own wife and every woman her own husband" (1 Cor. 7.2), and not let every one have his own wives or own husbands. It is therefore plain and questionless that he would have a Contract and marriage to be only between one and one. Again, saying his own and her own doth he not plainly insinuate every other person and persons not to be their own but mere strangers with whom they ought to have nothing ado in respect of marriage duties, especially considering that the Greek word *Idio* can import no less?[7] Now then, if there be at any time or in any place a promise between more than two, as it is a wicked and mere profanation of the holy ordinance of God, so it may and ought to be broken, yea, severely punished by Parents and Magistrates.

If against this it be objected that many of the Patriarchs and good men under the Law had many wives or at least more than one, we answer it was their secret sin and great infirmity, though proceeding from ignorance of the first institution of marriage of the Law and the holy Prophets (or else they had warrant from God, which we have noted). Of the institution, because

Christ interpreting it sayth, "From the beginning it was not so" (Matt. 19.8), proving that Moses permitted divorcement of the first wife and marriage of the second, not moved or warranted by the authority of God's institution but by a fearful and timorous consideration of the hardness of the people's hearts whom he ruled, lest they should have rebelled against him if he had not so done. Of the law, because there was by this means great injury done to God's truth and to the wives divorced. Besides, the law itself, well understood as Christ expoundeth it (Matt. 5.32), admitteth no divorcement except it be for fornication.

And that the Lord did disallow and hate all other kinds of divorcement made without the cause of fornication, it is evident in that he condemneth the second marriage after the first divorcement, affirming that the woman so divorced is defiled by her second husband (Deut. 24.4), which could not be true if their marriage had been lawful and warrantable by the commandment of God. For where the marriage is lawful and honorable, there the bed is undefiled (Heb. 13.4). Of the Prophets, "Because the Lord hath been witness between thee and thy wife of thy youth against whom thou hast transgressed, yet is she thy companion and the wife of thy covenant. And did not he make one? Yet had he abundance of the spirit. And wherefore one? Because he sought a godly seed. Therefore keep yourselves in your spirit and let none trespass against the wife of his youth. If thou hatest her, put her away (sayth the Lord of Israel). Yet he covereth the injury under his garment (sayth the Lord of Hosts). Therefore keep yourselves in your spirit and transgress not" (Mal. 2.14-16). Than which words what can be more plainly spoken against this sin of having more wives than one? For doth not the Prophet plainly say that God is witness that they have transgressed against the wife of their youth and covenant? Doth he not call them to the first institution when God made but one, and that because he would have a godly seed and not an adulterous generation? Doth he not further say that in putting away the wife they did nothing else but cover injury under pretence of his law as with a garment? And finally, doth he not give a clean contrary commandment to that wicked custom of divorcement and marrying of others, when he saith, "Keep yourselves in your spirit, and let none transgress against the wife of his youth, and of his covenant?" Surely, none can be so blind but reading this portion of scripture he must needs plainly see and acknowledge the same. . . .

What the Duty of a Wife Is towards Her Husband

This duty is comprehended in these three points. First, that she reverence her husband. Secondly, that she submit herself and be obedient unto him. And lastly, that she do not wear gorgeous apparel beyond her degree and place, but her attire must be comely and sober according to her calling. The first point is proved by the Apostles Peter and Paul, whereby they set forth the wives' duties to their husbands, commanding them to be obedient unto them although they be profane and irreligious, and that they ought to do so much the more that, by their honest life and conversation, they might win them to the obedience of the Lord (1 Pet. 3.1, Ephes. 5.22, Col. 3.18, 1 Cor 7.3).

Now, for so much as the Apostle would have Christian wives that are matched with ungodly husbands and such as are not yet good Christians to reverence and obey them, much more they should show themselves thankful to God, and willingly and dutifully perform this obedience and subjection when they are coupled in marriage with godly, wise, discreet, learned, gentle, loving, quiet, patient, honest, and thrifty husbands. And therefore they ought evermore to reverence them and to endeavor with true obedience and love to serve them, to be loath in any wise to offend them. Yea, rather to be careful and diligent to please them that their soul may bless them. And if at any time it shall happen that the wife shall anger or displease her husband by doing or speaking anything that shall grieve him, she ought never to rest until she hath pacified him and gotten his favor again. And if he shall chance to blame her without a cause and for that which she could not help or remedy (which thing sometimes happeneth even of the best men), yet she must bear it patiently and give him no uncomely or unkind words for it, but evermore look upon him with a loving and cheerful countenance, and so rather let her take the fault upon her than seem to be displeased.

Let her be always merry and cheerful in his company, but yet not with too much lightness. She must beware in any wise of swelling, pouting, lowering, or frowning, for that is a token of a cruel and unloving heart, except it be in respect of sin or in time of sickness. She may not be sorrowful for any adversity that God sendeth, but always to be careful that nothing be spilt or go to waste through her negligence. In any wise, see that she be quick and cleanly about her husband's meat and drink, and to prepare him the same according to his diet in due season (Gen. 27.9). Let her show herself, in word and deed, wise, humble, courteous, gentle, and loving towards her husband and also towards such as he doth love. And then shall she lead a blessed life. Let her show herself not only to love no man so well as her husband, but also to love none other at all but him, unless it be for her husband's sake. Wherefore let the wife remember that (as the Scripture reporteth), she is one body with her husband, so that she ought to love him none otherwise than herself (Gen. 2.23-24, Matt. 19.5, 1 Cor. 6.16, Ephes. 5.31). For this is the greatest virtue of a married woman, this is the thing that wedlock signifieth and commandeth, that the wife should reckon to have her husband for both father, mother, brother, and sister, like as Adam was unto Eve, and as the most noble and chaste woman Andromache said her husband Hector was unto her: "Thou are unto me both father and mother, / Mine own dear husband and well beloved brother."[8]

And if it be true that men do say that friendship maketh one heart of two, much more truly and effectually ought wedlock to do the same, which far passeth all manner both friendship and kindred. Therefore it is not said that marriage doth make one man, or one mind, or one body of two, but clearly one person. Wherefore matrimony requireth a greater duty of the husband towards his wife and the wife towards her husband than otherwise they are bound to show to their parents. The Apostle biddeth, "to rejoice with them that rejoice, and weep with them that weep" (Rom. 12.15). With whom should the wife rejoice rather than with her loving husband? Or with whom should she weep and mourn rather than with her own flesh? "I will not leave thee," saith Elisha to Elijah (2 Kings 2.2), so she should say I will never leave him till death. "Bear one another's burden," saith Paul (Gal. 6.2). Who shall bear one another's burden if the wife do not bear the husband's burden? Wicked Jezebel comforted her husband in his sickness (1 Kings 21.5), and Jeroboam's wife sought for his health though she was as bad as he (1 Kings 14.4). God did not bid Sarah leave her father and country as he did bid her husband, yet because he bade Abraham leave his she left hers too (Gen. 12.1), showing that she was content not only to be his playfellow but his yokefellow too.

Beside a yokefellow she is called a Helper (Gen. 2.18), to help him in his labors, to help him in his troubles, to help him in his sickness like a woman physician, sometime with her strength and sometime with her counsel. For sometime, as God confoundeth the wise by the foolish and the strong by the weak, so he teacheth the wise by the foolish and helpeth the strong by the weak. Therefore Peter saith, "Husbands are won by the conversation of their wives" (1 Pet. 3.1), as if he should say sometime the weaker vessel is the stronger vessel. And Abraham may take counsel of Sarah as Naaman was advised by his servant (2 Kings 5.3). The Shunamite's counsel made her husband receive a Prophet into his house (2 Kings 4.9), and Esther's counsel made her husband spare the Church of the Jews (Esth. 7.3). So some have been better help to their husbands than their husbands have been to them, for it pleaseth God to provoke the wise with the foolish, as he did the Jews with the Gentiles (Deut. 32.31, Rom. 10.19).

Beside a helper she is called a Comforter too, and therefore the man is bid to rejoice in his wife (Prov. 5.18-19). Which is as much to say that wives must be the rejoicing of their husbands even like David's harp to comfort Saul (1 Sam. 16.23). A good wife therefore is known when her words and deeds and countenance are such as her husband loveth. She must not examine whether he be wise or simple but that she is his wife, and therefore they that are bound must obey, as Abigail loved her husband though he were a fool, churlish and evil-conditioned (1 Sam. 5.23). For the wife is as much despised for taking rule over her husband as he for yielding it unto her. Therefore, one saith that a mankind woman is a monster, that is, half a woman and half a man. It beseemeth not the mistress to be a master no more than it becometh the master to be mistress. But both must sail with their own wind, and both keep their standing.

Lastly, we call the wife Huswife, that is, housewife, not a street-wife, one that gaddeth up and down like Thamer (Gen. 38.14), nor a field-wife like Dinah (Gen. 34.1), but a house-wife, to show that a good wife keeps her house. And therefore Paul biddeth Titus to exhort women that they be chaste and keeping at home, presently after chaste he saith keeping at home, as though home were chastity's keeper (Tit. 2.5). And therefore Solomon, depainting and describing the qualities of a whore, setteth her at the door, now sitting upon her stall, now walking in the streets, now looking out of the window (Prov. 7.12), like cursed Jezebel, as if she held forth the glass of temptation for vanity to gaze upon (2 Kings 9.30). But chastity careth to please but one, and therefore she keeps her closet as if she were still at prayer.

The Angel asked Abraham, "Where is thy wife?" Abraham answered, "She is in the tent" (Gen. 18.9). The Angel knew where she was, but he asked that he might see how women in old time did keep their tents and houses. It is recorded of the Shunamite that she did ask her husband leave to go unto the Prophet. Though she went to a Prophet, and went of a good errand and for his cause as much as her own, yet she thought it not meet to go far abroad without her husband's leave (2 Kings 4.22).

The second point is that wives submit themselves and be obedient unto their own husbands as to the Lord, because the husband is by God's ordinance the wife's head, that is, her defender, teacher, and comforter (Ephes. 5.22-23, 1 Cor. 11.3 and 14.34). And therefore she oweth her subjection to her husband like as the Church doth to Christ, and because the example of Sarah, the mother of the faithful, which obeyed Abraham and called him Lord, moveth them thereunto (Gen. 18.12, 1 Pet 3.6). This point is partly handled before in the first point, as in the duty of the husband to the wife.

As the Church should depend upon the wisdom, discretion, and will of Christ, and not follow what itself listeth, so must the wife also submit and apply herself to the discretion and will of her husband (Ephes. 5.24), even as the government and conduct of everything resteth in the head not in the body. Moses writeth that the Serpent was wise above all beasts of the field (Gen. 3.1), and that he did declare in assaulting the woman that, when he had seduced her, she might also seduce and deceive her husband. Saint Paul, noting this among other the causes of the woman's subjection (1 Tim. 2.14), doth sufficiently show that for the avoiding of the like inconveniences, it is God's will that she should be subject to her husband so that she shall have no other discretion or will but what may depend upon her head. As also the same Moses saith, "Thy desire shall be subject to thy husband and he shall rule over thee" (Gen. 3.16). This dominion over the wife's will doth manifestly appear in this, that God in old time ordained that if the woman had vowed anything unto God it should, notwithstanding, rest in her husband to disavow it. So much is the wife's will subject to her husband. Yet it is not meant that the wife should not employ her knowledge and discretion, which God hath given her, in the help and for the good of her husband. But always it must be with condition to submit herself unto him, acknowledging him to be her head, that finally they may so agree in one as the conjunction of marriage doth require.

Yet, as when in a Lute or other musical instrument, two strings concurring in one tune, the sound nevertheless is imputed to the strongest and highest, so in a well ordered household there must be a communication and consent of counsel and will between the husband and the wife, yet such as the counsel and commandment may rest in the husband. True it is that some women are wiser and more discreet than their husbands, as Abigail the wife of Naball, and others. Whereupon Solomon saith, "A wise woman buildeth up the house" (Prov. 14.1), and "Blessed is the man that hath a discreet wife" (Ecclus. 26.1).[9] Yet still a great part of the discretion of such women shall rest in acknowledging their husbands to be their heads, and so using the graces that they have received of the Lord that their husbands may be honored not contemned, neither of them nor of others, which falleth out contrary when the wife will seem wiser than her husband. So that this modesty and government ought to be in a wife, namely, that she should not speak but to her husband or by her husband. And as the voice of him that soundeth a trumpet is not so loud as the sound that it yieldeth, so is the wisdom and word of a woman of greater virtue and efficacy when all that she knoweth and can do is as if it were said and done by her husband.

The obedience that the wife oweth to her husband dependeth upon this subjection of her will and wisdom unto him (1 Pet. 3.6, Ephes. 5.33, Esth. 1.1-12). So that women may not provoke their husbands by disobedience in matters that may be performed without offence to God, neither to presume over him, either in kindred or wealth, or obstinately to refuse in a matter that may trouble household peace and quiet. For disobedience begetteth contempt of the husband, and contempt wrath, and is many times the cause of troubles between the man and the wife. If the obedience importeth any difficulty, she may for her excuse gently propound the same, yet upon condition to obey in case the husband should persist in his intent, so long as the discommodity importeth no wickedness. For it is better to continue peace by obedience than to break it by resistance. And indeed it is natural in the members to obey the conduct and government of the head.

Yet must not this obedience so far extend as that the husband should command anything contrary to her honor, credit, and salvation, but as it is comely in the Lord (Col. 3.18, Ephes. 5.22). Therefore, as it were a monstrous matter and the means to overthrow the person that the body should, in refusing all subjection and obedience to the head, take upon it to guide itself and to command the head, so were it for the wife to rebel against the husband. Let her then beware of disordering and perverting the course which God in his wisdom hath established. And with all let her understand that going about it, she riseth not so much against her husband as against GOD, and that it is her good and honor to obey God in her subjection and obedience to her husband. If in the practice of this duty she find any difficulty or trouble through the inconsiderate course of her husband or otherwise, let her remember that the same proceedeth not of the order established by the Lord but through some sin afterward crept in, which hath mixed gall among the honey of the subjection and obedience that the woman should have enjoyed in that estate wherein, together with Adam, she was created after the image of God. And so let her humble herself in the sight of God and be well assured that her subjection and obedience is acceptable unto him. Likewise, that the more that the image of God is restored in her and her husband through the regeneration of the holy Ghost, the less difficulty shall she find in that subjection and obedience, as many in their marriage have indeed tried to their great contentment and consolation.

Further, there is a certain discretion and desire required of women to please the nature, inclinations, and manners of their husbands, so long as the same imports no wickedness. For as the looking-glass, howsoever fair and beautiful adorned, is nothing worth if it show that countenance sad which is pleasant or the same pleasant that is sad, so the woman deserveth no commendation that (as it were), contrarying her husband, when he is merry showeth herself sad or in his sadness uttereth her mirth. For as men should obey the laws of their cities, so women the manner of their husbands. To some women a beck[10] of her husband is sufficient to declare that there is somewhat amiss that displeaseth him, and specially if she bear her husband any reverence. For an honest matron hath no need of any great staff but of one word or one sour countenance. Moreover, a modest and chaste woman that loveth her husband must also love her house, as remembering that the husband that loveth his wife cannot so well like of the sight of any tapestry as to see his wife in his house. For the woman that gaddeth from house to house to prate confoundeth herself, her husband, and family (Titus 2.5).

But there are four reasons why the woman is to go abroad. First, to come to holy meetings, according to the duty of godliness. The second, to visit such as stand in need, as the duty of love and charity do require. The third, for employment and provision in household affairs committed to her charge. And lastly, with her husband when he shall require her (Gen. 20.1ff.). The evil and unquiet life that some women have and pass with their husbands is not so much for that they commit with and in their persons, as it is for that they speak with their tongues. If the wife would keep silence when her husband beginneth to chide, he should not have so unquiet dinners, neither she the worse supper. Which surely is not so, for at the same time that the husband beginneth to utter his grief, the wife then beginneth to scold and chafe. Whereof doth follow that, now and then, most unnaturally they come to handy gripes,[11] more beastlike than christianlike, which their so doing is both a great shame and a foul discredit to them both.

The best means, therefore, that a wife can use to obtain and maintain the love and good liking of her husband is to be silent, obedient, peaceable, patient, studious to appease his choler if he be angry, painful and diligent in looking to her business, to be solitary and honest. The chief and special cause why most women do fail in not performing this duty to their husbands is because they be ignorant of the word of God which teacheth the same and all other duties. And therefore their souls and consciences not being brought into subjection to God and his word, they can never until then yield and perform true subjection and obedience to their husbands, and behave themselves so every way as Christian wives are in duty bound to do. But if wives be not so dutiful, serviceable, and subject to their husbands as in conscience they ought, the only cause thereof for the most part is through the want and neglect of the wise, discreet, and good government that should be in the husbands, besides the want of good example that they should give unto their wives both in word and deed. For as the common saying is: such a husband such a wife; a good Jack maketh a good Jill. For so much as marriage maketh of two persons one, therefore the love the husband and wife may the better be kept and increased and so continued, if they remember the duties last spoken of, as also not forget these three points following.

1. They must be of one heart, will, and mind, and neither to upbraid or cast the other in the teeth with their wants and imperfections anyways, or to pride themselves in their gifts. But rather the one to endeavor to supply the other's wants, that so they, both helping and doing their best together, may be one perfect body.

2. It doth greatly increase love when the one faithfully serveth the other, when in things concerning marriage the one hideth no secrets nor privities from the other, and the one doth not utter or publish the frailties or infirmities of the other. And when of all that ever they obtain or get they have but one common purse together, the one locking up nothing from the other. And also when the one is faithful to the other in eating, drinking, and so in all their necessities and affairs. Likewise, when the one harkneth to the other, and when the one thinketh not scorn of the other, and when, in

matters concerning the government of the house, the one will be counseled and advised by the other. And always the one to be loving, kind, courteous, plain, and gentle in words, manners, and deeds.

3. Let the one learn ever to be obsequious, diligent, and serviceable to the other in all other things. And this will the sooner come to pass if the one observe and mark what thing the other can away withal or cannot away withal, and what pleaseth or displeaseth them. And so from thenceforth to do the one and to leave the other undone. And if one of them be angry and offended with the other, then let the party grieved open and make known to the other their grief in due time and with discretion. For the longer a displeasure or evil will rageth in secret, the worse will be the discord. And this must be observed that it be done in a fit and convenient time, because there is some season in the which, if griefs were showed, it should make greater debate. As if the wife should go about to tell or admonish her husband when he is out of patience or moved with anger, it should then be no fit time to talk with him. Therefore Abigail, perceiving Naball her husband to be drunk, would not speak to him until the morning (1 Sam. 25.36-37). Both the husband and wife must remember that the one be not so offended and displeased with the manners of the other that they should thereupon forsake the company one of the other. For that were like to one that being stung with the Bees would therefore forsake the honey. And therefore, no man may put away his wife for any cause except for whoredom, which must be duly proved before a lawful Judge.[12]

But all godly and faithful married folks are to commend their state and marriage to God by humble and fervent prayer, that he, for his beloved son's sake, would so bless them and their marriage that they may so christianly and dutifully agree between themselves that they may have no cause of any separation or divorcement. For like as all manner of medicines (and specially as they that go nighest death as to cut off whole members, etc.) are very loathsome and terrible, even so is divorcement indeed a medicine, but a perilous and terrible medicine. Therefore every good Christian husband and wife ought with all care and heedfulness so to live in marriage that they have no need of such medicine. As the holy Scripture maketh mention of many wives and women that were wicked and ungodly, as partly may be seen by these quotations (1 Kings 11.1-2, Prov. 21.9,14,22, 25.24, and 27.15, Eccles. 7.28-30), so contrariwise, the same sacred Scripture also commendeth unto us many women that have been devout, religious, and virtuous, as partly is manifest by that which hath already been said, and also by these places of Scripture (Ruth 3.11, 1 Sam. 25.3, Prov. 14.1 and 31.10, Matt 28.1,8-10, Luke 8.2-3, 14.1, and 23.55-56, Acts 1.14, 9.36-39, 16.14-15, and 17.4, 2 John 1, 2 Tim. 1.5). And whosoever shall observe it in the reading of the word of God shall find that it speaketh of the praise of as many, and more, good women as men. Yea, and we are persuaded that if at this day a due survey should be taken of all men and women throughout her Majesty's dominions, that there would be found in number more woman that are faithful, religious, and virtuous than men.

Now, if a wife be desirous to know how far she is bound to obey her husband the Apostle resolveth this doubt where he saith Ephesians 5.22, saying, "Wives submit yourselves unto your husbands as to the Lord." As if he had said: wives cannot be disobedient to their husbands but they must resist God also, who is the author of this subjection, and that she must regard her husband's will as the Lord's will, but yet withal, as the Lord commandeth one that which is good and right, so she should obey her husband in good and right or else she doth not obey him as the Lord but as the tempter. The first subjection of the woman began at sin. For when God cursed her for seducing her husband when the Serpent had deceived her, he said, "He shall have authority over thee" (Gen. 3.16). And therefore, as the man named all other creatures in sign that they should be subject to him, as a servant which cometh when his master calleth him by his name, so he did name the woman also, in token that she should be subject to him likewise. And therefore Ahasuerus made a law that every man should bear rule in his own house and not the woman (Esth. 1.20-22). Because she sinned first therefore she is humbled most. And ever since, the daughters of Sarah are bound to call their husbands Lord, as Sarah called her husband (1 Pet. 3.6), that is, to take them for heads and governors (Judg. 19.26).

Amongst the particular duties that a Christian wife ought to perform in her family, this is one: namely, that it belongeth to her to nurse[13] her own children, which to omit and to put them forth to nursing is both against the law of nature and also against the will of God. Besides it is hurtful both for the child's body and also for his wit. And lastly it is hurtful to the mother herself, and it is an occasion that she falleth into much sickness thereby.

First, Nature giveth milk to the woman for none other end but that she should bestow it upon her child. We see by experience that every beast and every fowl is nourished and bred of the same that did bear it. Only some women love to be mothers but not nurses. And as every tree doth cherish and nourish that which it bringeth forth, even so also it becometh natural mothers to nourish their children with their own milk (1 Tim. 5.10).

Secondly, the example of the Scriptures are many that prove this. As Sarah who nursed Isaac though she were a Princess, and therefore able enough to have had others to have taken the pains (Gen. 21.7), as also having been a beautiful woman even in old age, being of great years, yet she herself nurseth and giveth suck to her son. Also Anna, whom the holy Ghost hath left it recorded as a commendation unto her, for that she nursed her own son Samuel (1 Sam. 1.23). So when God chose a nurse for Moses he led the Handmaid of Pharaoh's daughter to her mother, as though God would have none to nurse him but his mother (Exod. 2.3).[14] Likewise, after when the Son of God was born, his father thought none of it to be his nurse but the virgin his mother (Matt. 2.14, Luke 27.12). It is a commendation of a good woman, and set down in the first place as a principal good work in a widow that is well reported of, if she have nursed her children (1 Tim. 5.10). And therefore, such as refuse thus to do may well and fitly be called nice and unnatural mothers. Yea, in so doing they make themselves but half-mothers, and so break the holy bond of nature, in locking up her breast from her child and delivering it forth like the Cuckoo, to be hatched in the Sparrow's nest.

Again, the children's bodies be commonly so affected as the milk is which they receive. Now, if the Nurse be of an evil complexion, and as she is affected in her body or in her mind or have some hidden disease, the child, sucking of her breast, must needs take part with her. And if that be true which the learned do say, that the temperature of the mind follows the constitution of the body, needs must it be that if the nurse be of a naughty nature the child must take thereafter. Yet if it be that the nurse be of a good complexion, of an honest behavior (whereas contrariwise, Maidens that have made a scape[15] are commonly called to be Nurses), yet can it not be but that the mother's milk should be much more natural for the child than the milk of a stranger. As by experience, let a man be long accustomed to one kind of drink, if the same man change his air and his drink he is like to mislike it. As the eggs of a Hen are altered under a Hawk. Nevertheless, such women as be oppressed with infirmities, diseases, want of milk, or other just and lawful causes are to be dispensed withal, but whose breasts have this perpetual drought? Forsooth it is like the gout, no beggars may have it but Citizens or Gentlewomen. In the Ninth Chapter of Hosea, verse fourteen, dry breasts are named for a curse. What a lamentable hap have Gentlewomen, to light upon this curse more than other? Sure, if their breasts be dry (as they say) they should fast and pray together that this curse might be removed from them.

And lastly, that it is hurtful to the mothers themselves, both Physicians can tell and some women full oft have felt how they have been troubled with sore breasts, besides other diseases that happen to them through plenty of milk.

The wife is further to remember that God hath given her two breasts not that she should employ and use them for a show or of ostentation, but in the service of God and to be a help to her husband in suckling the child common to them both. Experience teacheth that God converteth her blood into the milk, wherewith the child is nursed in the mother's womb. He bringeth it into the breasts, furnished with nipples convenient to minister the warm milk unto the child, whom he endueth with industry to draw out the milk for his own sustenance. The woman, therefore, that can suck her child and doth it not, but refuseth this office and duty of a mother, declareth herself to be very unthankful to God, and (as it were) forsaketh and contemneth the fruit of her womb. And therefore the brute beasts, lying upon the ground and granting not one nipple or two but six or seven to their young ones, shall rise in judgment against these dainty half-mothers who, for fear of wrinkling of their faces or to avoid some small labor, do refuse this so necessary a duty of a mother due to her children.

The properties due to a married wife are that she have gravity when she walketh abroad, wisdom to govern her house, patience to suffer her husband, love to breed and bring up her children, courteous towards her neighbours, diligence to lay up and to save such goods as are within her charge, a friend of honest company, and a greater enemy of wanton and light toys. So then the principal duty of the wife is first to be subject to her husband (Ephes. 5.22, Col. 3.18, 1 Pet 3.1). To be chaste and shamefast, modest and silent, godly and discreet. To keep herself at home for the good government of her family, and not to stray abroad without just cause.

Here it is not to be pretermitted[16] but that we must say somewhat touching men and women that be twice married, and so become Stepfathers and Stepmothers. Such husbands and wives as marry again, after the death of their first wives or first husbands, are carefully to remember that they do not displease their wives or their husbands which they now have by overmuch rehearsing of their first wife or first husband. For the course and condition of the world is such that husbands and wives do account and recover things past better than things that be present. And the reason is because no commodity or felicity is so great but it hath some grief and displeasure and also some bitterness mingled with it. Which so long as it is present grieveth us sore, but when it is once gone it leaveth no great feeling of itself behind it. And for that cause, we seem to be less troubled with sorrows and discommodities past than with those that are present. Also, age stealeth and cometh on apace, which causeth both men and women to be the less able to sustain and endure troubles and griefs now than before. Therefore, such men and women as be twice married and be wise and religious ought not to esteem their wife or husband which is dead better than her or him which they enjoy now alive, remembering the common proverb that we must live by the quick and not by the dead, and that we must make much of that we now have.

Let the name of Stepfather and Stepmother admonish and put them in mind of their duty towards the children of the one and the other. For Stepfather and Stepmother doth signify and a stead-father and a stead-mother, that is, one father or one mother dieth, and another succeedeth and cometh in their stead and room. Therefore, to the end that both their loves may be settled towards the children of the one and the other they must remember that they are stead-father and stead-mother, that is, instead of their own father and mother. And therefore they ought to love them, to tender them, and to cherish them as their own father or mother did. They must not look upon them like Rehoboam, who told his people that he would be worse unto them than his predecessor (1 Kings 12.13-21), for then the children will dislike of you and turn from you as his subjects did from him. But ye must come to them as David came to the people after Saul's death, who said, "Though your master Saul be dead, yet I will reign over you" (2 Sam. 2.7). So ye must say to them, though your father be dead or though your mother be dead, yet I will be a father, or I will be a mother unto you. So the children will love you as much as their dead father or dead mother did. For that man and that woman that are led with discretion, reason, and consideration will reckon himself and his wife all one, and likewise, she will account herself and her husband as one.

And therefore they ought to account both the children of the one and of the other as common to them both. For if friendship make all things common among friends, insomuch that many have loved and favored their friend's children as their own, how much more effectually and perfectly ought marriage to cause the same, which is the highest degree not only of friendships but also of all blood and kindred.

But Stepmothers do more often offend and fail in this duty than men, by reason that their affections be stronger than men's and many times overrule them. And therefore they are earnestly to be admonished and warned that they show themselves to those motherless children no stepmother's friendship but a right motherly kindness. Let the stepmother advisedly consider that God hath ordained and appointed her (instead of their own mother) to be to them a right true mother, and not only to regard them as children but as orphan children, and requireth her to love them and to do them good as to her own. What a grief would it be to her heart if she should know now that her own children, whom she hath borne in her own body, should (after her death) have a stepmother that would be rigorous, churlish, and unkind unto them? Doubtless, those children's mother that dead is had upon her deathbed no less care for her children. Let her therefore always have in mind this saying of our Saviour Christ, "As you measure unto other, so it shall be measured to you again" (Matt. 7.2), that is, as the stepmother doth entreat the children of her predecessor, so another wife may come after her and entreat her children. For he that took away the first mother and sent her can take away the second mother and send a third, which will not be like a stead-mother to hers unless she be like a stead-mother to these.

Verily, a good woman will be unto her husband's children that which she may hear them call her so often, that is, Mother. For what Christian woman is so far from all humanity and natural affection that will not be moved and mitigated with this word Mother, of whom soever it be spoken? And chiefly of children, which cannot flatter but speak even so from their heart, like as they would to their own mother of whom they were born. How sweet is the name of friendship? How many injuries, hatreds, and displeasures doth it hide and put away? Then how much more effectual ought the sweet name of mother to be, which is full of incredible love? Therefore, every religious and loving wife will be mollified and moved in her heart and mind when she shall hear herself named mother by any of her husband's children. Otherwise she shall show herself to be more unnatural and unkind than the wild savage beast. For there is no beast so outrageous and cruel but if any other young beast of her own kind fawn upon her she will by and by show kindness and mildness unto it. And shall not her husband's children make her kind and loving unto them when they call and speak unto her by the loving and sweet name of mother?

The third and last point that appertaineth to the duty of wives is that they do not wear gorgeous and sumptuous apparel or broidered hair, trimmed with gold. But that after the example of holy women which trusted in God, they be sober in outward apparel and ought to be garnished and decked inwardly with virtues of their minds, as with gentleness, meekness, quietness, and chastity, which indeed are most precious things in the sight of God. This point is so plainly spoken of by the Apostle to Timothy 2.9-10, in which place he so flatly condemneth both the excess and pride of apparel, as also the pomp, curiosity, and wantonness which women use in trimming their heads by plating, crisping,[17] broiding, curling, and curiously laying out, that no man can say more against it in so few words as he hath spoken to the utter dislike thereof. For if a man should occupy himself and give liberty to his pen to write of the horrible abuse and excessive pride that many women commit on this behalf, he should rather want time to write than matter to speak. Therefore such women as will not reform themselves herein we leave them to the Lord who (no doubt) will, in his appointed time, not only severely punish them but also their husbands for suffering this great wickedness and dissoluteness in their wives, as he did the Jews for the same sin, as plainly may be seen in Isaiah 3.16ff.

For so it falleth out according to the common proverb, that pride goeth before and shame and destruction cometh after (Prov. 16.18). And on the contrary part, we hope that such women as be true professors of Christ and his religion will both attire and dress their heads so decently, and also content themselves with such comely apparel as best beseemeth their calling and degree (Tit. 2.3). So as, by their good example, they may draw on other women to reform themselves in this behalf, and so rather to come short of that which their ability and place would serve to maintain than any ways to exceed herein to the slander of their profession. And let them not so much regard what thing they would fain have, but rather what they cannot well be without. So that whatsoever they have no need of is too dear of a farthing.

NOTES

1. In support, Cleaver also cites Gen. 2.24, Matt. 19.5, Mark 10.7, 1 Cor. 1.16, and Ephes. 5.31.
2. That is, a good husband makes a good wife. The saying can also be applied to the relationship between a male master and a female servant.
3. On this point Cleaver cites Num. 16.26, Josh. 23.12, 2 Chron. 19.2, 2 Cor. 6.14, and Ephes. 5.7.
4. Unsuitability.
5. In no way or respect.
6. Cleaver also cites Ephes. 5.31 and 1 Cor. 6.16.
7. From *Idios*, own, personal, private.
8. Homer, *Iliad* 6.429-30.
9. Cleaver also cites Prov. 18.22, 19.14 and 31.
10. Beckoning gesture.
11. Grabbing or wrestling with each other.
12. Cleaver cites 1 Cor. 7.10-16, Matt. 19.6-9 and 5.32, and Luke 16.18.
13. Breastfeed.
14. Cleaver also cites Judg. 13.24, Cant. 8.1, Ps. 22.9.
15. A slip, that is, borne a child while unmarried.
16. Omitted.
17. Plating: plaiting or braiding; crisping: curling.

CHAPTER 10

A Discourse
Of Marriage and Wiving
Alexander Niccholes

Apart from authorship of this tract, there seems to be no record of Alexander Niccholes, which is possibly a pseudonym. Niccholes' work is lighter and more "literary" in tone than many of the marriage manuals printed in the period. He cites a number of poets and seems to imitate or echo some of the prevailing literary conventions used in writing about women. There is a presumption of male address and camaraderie between author and reader, the kind of rapport assumed by Joseph Swetnam's appeal to his "friend Reader" (193), or in John Donne's elegies on his mistress, where the male persona labors to construct "the illusion of his own mastery" (Fish 229). Potential flaws in this masculine self-image are not acknowledged by Niccholes; however, there is a constant concern throughout the *Discourse* that men will lose rational control in choosing a marriage partner, and at times a kind of general despair at human nature is voiced, echoing the cynicism of much late-Elizabethan and Jacobean satire.

Rather than relying on moral and religious authority, Niccholes adopts a satirist's role as detached observer. The title page tells us that he is a "Bachelor in the Art he never yet put in practice," whose outlook is captured in the couplet, "He that stands by, and doth the game survey, / Sees more oftimes than those that at it play." The *Discourse* reveals "How to choose a good Wife from a bad. An Argument of the dearest use, but the deepest cunning that a man may err in. . . . Pertinent to both Sexes and Conditions, as well those already gone before as shortly to enter this honest society." The text is prefaced by a dedication to Thomas Edgworth, undertreasurer of Windsor, who is about to marry, and by a poem addressed "To the Youth and Bachelory of England, Hot Bloods at High Revels." It then begins by considering the godly origins of marriage and the duties of men and women, in an opening "motivated," as Catherine Belsey contends, "by the newfound valorization of marriage in the course of the century following the Reformation rejection of the celibate ideal" (271). As the text proceeds, its critical focus increasingly rests on women and the problems they cause for men. Women's moral weakness and their susceptibility to the temptations of life in London and at court are both blamed.

Niccholes' "humorous" tone reflects a distinctive stylistic trait of Renaissance attacks on women through which comical allusions defuse apparently violent attitudes without actually contradicting them (Woodbridge 31). The *Discourse* was published in 1615, the same year as Swetnam's contentious *The Arraignment of Lewd, Idle, Froward, and Unconstant Women*, and though its tone is less directly acerbic it echoes many of Swetnam's sentiments, including the deceptiveness of women's appearance; the way they trick unwary men into marriage, "women have a thousand ways to entice thee and ten thousand ways to deceive thee" (Swetnam 201); and the trouble ahead for the new husband of a widow, "For thou must unlearn a widow and make her forget her former corrupt and disordered behavior, the which is hardly to be done" (Swetnam 210). The echoes between anti-feminist texts in the period may have a double influence for readers, as both "an authenticating discourse which validates the misogynistic enterprise by aligning it with what is always already apparent, and a displacing move which is supposed to make it impossible to read an individual male writer as the author of misogyny" (Purkiss 72). Pseudonyms and anonymity afford the authors of such tracts rhetorical power and an atmosphere of male solidarity.

A Discourse of Marriage and Wiving was first published in London in 1615, and a second edition came out in 1620. The extracts below are taken from the earlier edition (*STC* 18514; Reel 967).

A DISCOURSE OF MARRIAGE AND WIVING

Of the First Institution and Author of Marriage

It is not good for man to be alone, saith the alone and absolute Goodness of all goodness itself. "Let us therefore make him a helper meet for him" (Gen. 2.18). So the creation of the woman was to be a helper to the man not a hinderer, a companion for his comfort not a beration to his sorrow. For Company is comfortable though never so small, and Adam took no little joy in this his single companion, being thereby freed from that solitude and silence which his loneness would else have been subject unto had there been no other end nor use in her more than this her bare presence and society alone. But besides all this, the earth is large and must be peopled, and therefore they are now the Crown of his Workmanship, the last and best and perfectest piece of his handiwork divided into Genders, as the rest of His creatures are, Male and Female, fit and enabled to bring forth their like, to accomplish his will, who thus blessed their fruitfulness in the Bud: Increase and multiply, and replenish the earth (Gen. 1.28).

Well might St. Paul say, observing this, "Marriage is honorable amongst all men, and the bed undefiled" (Heb. 13.4), since God himself was the Author and Institutor thereof even in Paradise, who gave the woman to the man. Before in his sleep Adam lost a Rib, but now being awake he hath his Rib again with interest and increase, branched into many Veins and Ribs, and Bones and Arteries, of wonderful use and admirable quality. So the creation of woman, as it was for man so was it out of man. Adam was made of the slime of the earth, and were it not to make woman proud, I would tell her she was of that better substance, of that well-husbanded workmanship and refined matter, refined and purified by the touch of his hands, in molding to so excellent a proportion as man, of a bone taken out of his side (which that side ever wanteth since as Anatomists observe), to make him the more pliable towards her. Not of a bone of his foot that she should be so low or contemptible, or of his head, so high or ambitious, but of his side, a middle part, that she might be of a middle condition, his fellow and companion not his servant or slave, for they are fellows that walk side by side. Of a bone near to his heart to put him in mind of dilection[1] and love, from under his arm of protection and defence, etc.

Now, the Author of this creation we find here to be the Author of this Mystery. He, who made the woman of the man, gave her to the man. Even God himself who, as Cassianus[2] saith further, in the very prime and beginning of the world, gave this one woman to one man, and no more than one, although for the increase and peopling of all the yet-unhabited Regions and Kingdoms of the earth. In which, no doubt, the Divine Wisdom had a respect to the love not to the lust of man, aiming hereby to advance the one and suppress the other. For where love is divided there it is weakened, can never be strong. And, as we see by experience, he who loves many formally never loves any fervently, for unity is love's number, cannot transcend. And God would have an entire affection between the husband and the wife, which he himself in person thus vouchsafed to honor by conjunction that, as their bodies were then not two, so their desires should be but one. And withal, to insinuate by this, his proper institution, the more respect and reverence to that holy ordination which had so high a beginning and so holy an end, honored by his Person, by his Prophets, by his Miracles, and which should so generally be exercised throughout all estates and conditions, ages and times, to the end of the world and desistency of all things. Which, by this means (ere that eternal dissolution), should run a long and continued race in despite of grave and death.

****

Worldly Choice, What It Is, or How for the Most Part Men Choose Their Wives

It is a fashion much in use in these times to choose wives as Chapmen[3] sell their wares, with *Quantum dabitis*, what is the most you will give? And if their parents or guardians shall reply their virtues are their portions and others have they none, let them be as dutiful as Sarah, as virtuous as Anna, as obedient as the Virgin Mary, these (to the wise man, every one a rich portion and more precious than the gold of Ophir[4]) shall be nothing valued or make up where wealth is wanting. These may be adjuncts or good additions, but money must be the principal of all that marry, and (that scope is large) there are but few that undergo it for the right end and use. Whereby it comes to pass that many attain not to the blessedness therein.

Some undergo this curse instead of blessing merely for lust, choosing their wives most unfitly as Adulteresses. And such are said to marry by the eye, looking no further than a carnal beauty is distinguished, which consists in the outward shape and lineaments of the body, as in gate, gesture, countenance, behavior, etc. And for such a one, so she be fair and can kiss, she hath portion enough for such a Pirate. But when this flower withers, as it is of no continuance, for diseases blast it, age devours it, discontent doth wither it (only virtue is not soiled by these adversities), what shall continue love as then to the end? Their Winter sure shall be full of want, full of discontent, that thus grasshopper-like respected their Summer.

There are others that marry to join wealth to wealth, and those are said to marry by the fingers' ends. Some others there are that take their wives from the report or good liking of others, and those are said to take their wives upon truth, and such I hope are seldom deceived in their venture. There are some that marry for continuance of posterity, and those come nearest to the true intent, for the end of marriage is issue. It was the primal blessing, "Increase and multiply" (Gen. 1.22). God hath given and bequeathed many Precepts and Commandments to mankind, yet of all that ever he delivered, never was there any better observed (for the letter) than this. Nay, the most part are so ready to accomplish his Will herein that for haste, many times, they overstep the true circumstances thereof, doing it for the sake of intention more than virtue. For God requires children not bastards, and those that thus increase it do it more for the manner than the end, more for lust than for love.

How to Choose a Good Wife from a Bad

This undertaking is a matter of some difficulty, for good wives are many times so like unto bad that they are hardly discerned betwixt. They could not otherwise deceive so many as they do, for the devil can transform himself into an Angel of Light the better to draw others into the chains of darkness; so these, his creatures, themselves into the shape of honesty, the better to entangle others in the bonds of repentance. If therefore the yoke of marriage be of such perpetuity and lasting even all the way to death, and the joys or grievance thereon depending of equal continuance therewith either to make a short heaven or hell in this world, is not therefore to be undergone but upon the duest regard and most advised consideration that may be. And because it is such a sea wherein so many shipwreck, for want of better knowledge and advice upon a Rock that took not better counsel in the haven, I have therefore in some sort, to prevent this danger, erected (as it were) certain Landmarks and directions in the way, to give aim to such passengers as shall hereafter expose themselves to the mercy of this fury. And the rather because our age is so adventurous, whether boldness or blindness be their guide, that mere children dare undertake with vessels scarce capable to hoist up sail and adventure those passages that former times in their nonage, near precedent us in the like, would have thought scarce navigable. But many times this calm that leads them forth in a sunshine with pleasure brings them home in a tempest with sorrow. And therefore (as I said) he that would not repent him afterwards let him be advised before, for wise foresight for the most part is crowned with happy success. Therefore say not hereafter (for it is a weak remedy), would God I had been better advised, but be so.

The first aim that I would give to him that would adventure this voyage (for marriage is an adventure, for whosoever married adventures: he adventures his peace, his freedom, his liberty, his body, yea, and sometimes his soul too) is that, in his election, after he hath made choice of his wife, which ever I would have grounded upon some of these promising likelihoods. See that she be of a sober and mild aspect, courteous behavior, decent carriage, of a fixed eye, constant look, and unaffected gait, the contrary being oftentimes signs of ill portent and consequence. For as the common saying is, an honest woman dwells at the sign of an honest countenance, and wild looks (for the most part) accompany wild conditions. A rolling eye is not fixed but would fix upon objects it likes, it looks for, and affected nicety is ever a sign of lascivious petulancy.

Next, regard, according as thine estate and condition shall best instruct thee, the education and quality of her thou hast so elected, her personage not being unrespected. For love looks sometimes as well with the eye of the body as with the mind, and beauty in some begets affection, and affection augmenteth love, whereas the contrary would decrease and diminish it and so bring thee to a loathed bed, which must be utterly taken heed of for the dangerous consequences that follow. Therefore, let thy wisdom so govern thine affection that as it seize not up deformity to thine own proper use for some sinister respect to be shortly after repented of. So likewise (for the mean is ever best) that it level not at so high and absolute endowment and perfection that every carnal eye shall bethink thee injury, that every Goatish disposition shall level to throw open thy enclosures, that thy wife shall be harder to be kept than the Garden of the Hesperides.[5] For as the Italian proverb is, "Whose horse is white, and wife is fair, / His head is never void of care."

Next, after thou hast thus elected thy choice and considered her in herself, with the aforesaid circumstances and this one more (not being of his mind that merrily said, speaking of his wife, since he was to make choice out of things that were evil, he thought it most wisdom to choose the least), to regard that she be not of too dwarfish a size and kindred, to store thee with a generation of Pygmies, dwarves, half-men, that want the Majesty and power of height and strength and the comeliness a good stature is for the most part wedded unto. After this, a little look back to the stock from whence she sprung, for as Ezekiel saith, "Like mother, like daughter" (Ezek. 16.44). And experience and nature approves it, that the fruit will relish of the Tree from whence it sprung, as the Rose is not gathered from the Hawthorne. And as his Majesty well observed, if men be so careful to have their horses and dogs of a good breed and race, which are only for external and superficial uses and pleasures, how much more should they then wives of their own bosoms, from whom they expect to raise and continue their own generations and posterities upon earth, to represent and preserve alive their own image and virtues behind them, from generation to generation all the way to the distant future.[6]

****

What Is that Chief Moth and Canker[7] that Especially Undermineth and Fretteth the Marriage Bed

Pride, Ambition, equality with others, the Example of others, variety of Appetite, the unrealishness[8] of that which is lawful, desire of that which is restrained, is unlawful. And then the oratory of the devil of darkness, in the shape of an Angel of light, working upon these advantages, hath overthrown and betrayed to this vulture and his merciless talon that fort and Citadel, with as easy resistance as a Bower of glass. That should be so unspotted but more impregnable than a Bulwark of stone, admitted treason to the heart of the City, copt[9] with the most dangerous enemy in the world, opened those gates with weakness. And this stratagem, that an Engine should not assail with strength and might, broke down the door that struck dead the owner, laid open those enclosures that have bondaged the Lord of the soil[10] perpetually till death to enclose his own supposed interest and use.

Ambition and pride, you twin-born sisters, you, you it is, and the dependency of your estate (you true and indulcitate[11] issues of Lucifer) that have broken down this hedge of the greatest consequence and site that ever was erected, and which else had kept out the assailing and seducing enemies that batter and undermine the very supportance, root, and life-blood of chastity itself. Letting in at these casements evil conceits and motives more blasting thereto than the breath of lightning, made the vows of marriage of less stability than the oaths of drunken men. Ambition, equality, example, you forementioned evils, you football players which short-heeled[12] creatures, it is you that are arraigned and found guilty in this trial.

The Country Damsel under the thatched roof of her natural habitation, where she scarce ever thought of so much pride as handsomeness, never beheld her how otherwise presented than in a bowl of water, that dreamed more devoutlier under that innocent covering being asleep than others pray in their lofty Palaces being awake, who can scarce there remember marriage but she blushes to think what a shame it is to lie with a man. Yet afterwards bring her to the City, enter her into that school of vanity, set but example before her eyes, she shall in time become a new creature, and such a strong mutation shall so strangely possess her that she shall have new thoughts, new purposes and resolutions, and in the end so shoulder out her modesty that she shall not blush to do that unlawfully which before she was bashful to think on lawfully. Come to the City, there you shall have some good amongst many bad, but should have many more were it not for this sickness of this ill Example. Therefore, well were it with the world if what were most done were most good.

Such a one could be content (for any desire of novelty or change, or for any heat in her blood more than might be lawfully allayed) to be honest, but that she knows such a friend and such a Gentlewoman her Gossip[13] have their variety of Gowns, of gifts, of favors, and variety of pleasures too, interchanging with variety of persons. And in this regard she will be no longer her own foe, to keep herself longer without such a friend. She sees the world takes notice of no more than it sees, and they are accounted most chaste that can best seem so. In this resolution she pulls up the Floodgates, where her tide of vanity is swelled to the brim, which immediately overflows and drowns her therein, extinguishing all former sparks of virtue and respect which before this conquest she debated with, and bears her along with the perishing multitude, for these brittle respects that here she is ensnared with.

The Court, the very Element and Center of these sins, the *ne plus ultra*[14] for any example beyond that, being the pattern to itself and to others. The respects that join there are the respects of pleasure not of profit. The highest ambition of theirs is to be most allured, most desired, to have most servants, most friends, most favors, and these should presage most falls. Whose open outsides bosoms, were their insides so displayed, it would be found a poor and idle sin had not there been harbored. Whose satin outsides and silken insides, soft raiment and sweet feeding, so stroke the skin and persuade the blood that it will not be persuaded.

There is a Text in woman that I would fain have woman to expound, or man either. To what end is the laying out of the embroidered hair, embared breasts, vermilioned cheeks, alluring looks, fashion gaits, and Artful countenances, effeminate, entangling, and ensnaring gestures, their curls and purls[15] of proclaiming petulancies, bolstered and laid out with such example and authority in these our days, as with allowance and beseeming conveniency, such apish fashions and follies, that the more severer, outworn ages of the world, deceased and gone, should they have but lifted up their head and in their times would have hissed out of countenance to death. But as to please woman hath much starched up man from his slovenry,[16] so to delight man (or rather his enemy) hath the woman thus increased in prices. Doth the world wax barren through decrease of generations and become like the earth, less fruitful than heretofore? Doth the blood lose his heat or the Sunbeams become more waterish and less fervent than formerly they have been, that men should be thus inflamed and persuaded on to lust? Or hath this age of sin usurped such a seeming purity or thought that the most licenced lust hath the original from concupiscence or some taint of sin, and therefore must be thus dragged up to this anchor like a Pitcher by the ears, by these blood near-touching witcheries and inducements.

No, rather the contrary. Witness the superfluity and increase of these our times, of this our Kingdom that hath more people than pasture, more bringing forth than breeding, for that it is compelled to empty itself into far distant Regions and Kingdoms. Is it not rather the contrary when the youth of both sexes are daily cropped in the blossom by this forward motion or rather head-strong devil, and unripely pressed to that action, forestalling maturity and fitness, where a Vestal should be more pointed at in a Cloister than a Comet in the Air? Is it not rather the contrary when lust is grown so unbounded, so headstrong, that it will not be hemmed nor encircled within any Laws or limits of God or man? When it will garbage[17] without all respect or control upon Adultery, fornication, possessed, the unpossessed, the bound, the free? Where care shall more possess a man to keep his fair wife from foul play when he hath her than jealousy did to lose her when he first rivaled for her? Where virtue shall not so disguise itself in any habit but vice will trace it out and betray it?

The ignorant Papists or other sectaries of Heresies most commonly give no other reason for their seduced errors than example of multitude, of parents, progenitors, or friends that went before them. So the example of this evil, so common, so much made of, so cockered,[18] so thriving, so bedecked, so admired, so dandied on the lap of Greatness, of Authority, draws millions to perdition after it. For the greatest part never look further than the example of the greatest number. The Coach easily runs that is drawn with many horses. Soon follows one where thousands lead the way. These have disjoined in chambers by the devil that were conjoined in the

Church by God. And yet it must be ingenuously confessed, it is but a cold comfort to go to hot hell for company.

Lust, that boiling, damned putrefaction of the blood, that raging, ruling, headstrong sin of this age, that is too apt to break out though it went clothed in Sackcloth and Haircloth and fed only (as saith an Author) with the Capuchin[19] diet of grass and herbs and such like, and suppressed with all the subjection can be imposed to subdue it, that yet like lime it would flash and fly out throughout all these impositions. But on the contrary, we are so far from subduing that passion and keeping it under, by any such means, that it is attired and set out in the most Artful bewitching and enticing temptation that may be devised, whole days and nights, and thoughts and studies, and costs and cares cast away thereon, for the better success therein though the worse ill thereby, for the end thereof is but repentance and sorrow.

Another main enemy to open this breach is impatience of restraint and limitation. For that which is most forbidden is most desired. He is the old devil that still tempts in that likeness that came to Eve in Paradise and persuaded her to eat the forbidden fruit of the Tree of knowledge of good and evil. Upon whom he obtained such a victory and conquest in that first battle that ever was fought, that never since hath he distrusted the force of that stratagem. Every woman is an abridgment of all womankind, contains the shape, the proportion, the lineaments, the members, the use[20] of all the women in the world, and likewise so of man. Why should not desire, then, being so linked in the most sufficient and wisest allowance that God and man thought meet, couch and submit itself to these ordinances but that concupiscence and lust enkindle desire, and it findeth not delight in that it hath but in that it would have, according as the Poet verifieth: "Lust ne'er takes delight in what is due, / But still leaves known delights to seek out new."

It looks out of the window where fuel is administered, where temptation entereth in, edgeth itself upon one for respects that it can conceive but not utter, upon another for something it likes but knows not what. It makes choice of a third, for modesty baits his lust in that flame to think with what looks it could in conclusion that is so fired with blushes in but proffered, concerning circumstances though far distant and remote from either time or action. Upon a fourth for her quaint conceit, and discovers by debating how she could use it, being put to her "no more" in the bare point of trial. With the beauty of a fifth, to conceive what a large fruition it were to be inflamed on the promontory of the Hill, when the demesnes and adjacent Valleys, to that fuller surfeit, restrained not their shades nor fountains. And indeed, to conclude, there is none so ugly, none so deformed, but Lust will find argument to make use of it, may it but have means to enjoy it.[21]

Advice for Choice, and Whether It Be Best to Marry a Widow or a Maid

He that marrieth a Widow hath but a reversion in tail,[22] and if she prove good may thank death for his aim if evil upbraid him and not unjustly for his occasion. He that takes her thus half-worn makes account she hath that will pay for new dressing. She seems to promise security in her peace yet invites many times to a troublesome estate, when the conquest achieved scarce countervails the wars. The principal of her love is perished with the use, for what is once firmly set on can never be cleanly taken off, and he must ne'er look to be enriched that way that hath her. The end of her Marriage is lust and ease more than affection or love and, deserve what thou canst, the dead shall upbraid thee by the help of her tongue, flattered behind his back the more to vex thee to thy face. The best is, though the worse for thee, they are navigable without difficulty, more passable than Virginia and lie at an easier Road, as unsatiate as the sea or rather the grave, which many times the sooner presents them thither.

At the decease of their first husbands, they learn commonly the tricks to turn over the second or third, and they are in league with death and coadjutors with him, for they can harden their own hearts like iron to break others that are but earth. And I like them the worse that they will marry, dislike them utterly they marry so soon. For she that so soon forgets the flower and Bridgegroom of her youth, her first love and prime of affection (which like a color laid on in Oil, or dyed in grain, should cleave fast and wear long), will hardly think of a second in the neglect and decay of her age.

Many precedents we have against these sudden, nay, against these second Marriages derived from former times, the ages of more constancy and shame of these latter. The daughter of M. Cato, bewailing a long time the death of her husband, being asked which day should have her last tear, answered the day of her death (not the end of a month or year). "For (saith she) should I meet with a good husband, as I had before, I should ever be in fear to lose him; if with a bad one, I were better be without him." In like manner, Portia, a young and honorable Lady, having lost her husband, answered, solicited by another, "A happy and chaste Matron never marries but once." Valeria, having lost her husband, importuned by another, answered, "My husband ever lives in my thoughts."[23] Arthemesia, the wife of Mausolus, King of Corinth, could not be brought to any such action but still answered, being mindful of her husband deceased, "Upon thy pillow shall never second rest his head." She died a widow and, in memory of her husband, erected that Monument or Tomb, the cost and fame whereof hath overspread the world.[24] Which Wife and Monument, Lucinus[25] thus further commendeth:

> There was a King, of whom it may be read
> In ancient Stories, sepulchred ere dead.
> More wrong you'll say they did him, to deprive
> Him of his Kingdom thus he being alive.
> No he had all his rights, more than Kings have
> That rul'd a Kingdom, and reigned in his grave.
> A Kingdom, nay a little world and more,
> A great world, and respected as before.
> Nay, even a Regiment that hath disturbed,
> The ablest health and policy to curb.
> A woman's heart and mind, and which more strange
> Free from variety of thought or change:
> So willingly subjected to his blood,
> Ne'er to depose him whilst her Empire stood.
> Of whom all loves and Laws did firm remain
> In force, till one stone did enclose them twain.
> Of whom it may be said, now she is gone,
> There's few such Tombs erected, women none.

Such a Widow couldst thou marry she were worthy thy choice. But such a one she could not be, because she would not then marry.

Compare the loyalty of our times with those of more ancient, and see how they equal thy conscience and carcass-breaking. How with thy piled up chests, they build monuments of remembrances to thy name and memory after death. Nay, rather observe but how their ambition, thus heated, makes them forgetful of themselves as well as thee. Knowing this, who would not with these distracted times to leave the purchase of a Ladyship to his wife, glide like a shadow in his life upon earth with a shrinking inside and penurious outside and sleep with broken thoughts and distracted dreams, to gather with pain and forbear with want that which his living enemy may afterwards spend with pleasure and surfeit with fullness? Who can love those living that he knows will so soon forget him being dead, that are but Summer Swallows for the time of felicity, that will hang about one's neck as if they had never arms for others' embracing, or as though extreme affection without control could not but this manifest itself and break out?

Yet decease, and such a lethe[26] of forgetfulness shall so soon overtake thee as if thou hadst never been. Nay, so little a quantity of time shall confine it that she shall not lie in her month but she shall be Churched again and open to another all thy fruitions, with as fresh and plenteous an appetite as the harlot to her next sinner. Younger brothers and poor Knights may sometimes to these monsters make use of their births and Titles, making them pay dear (as it cost) for their dubbing and release of Purgatory. They are in with old rank and fashion to their new Elysium and installment. And it must be confessed, unwise they were, but with good boot and addition, to refuse a Virginity to accept a Widowhood. And yet many times with a Turkish[27] fate we pay dear for our *Credo quod habemus*, that article of

Belief we too fondly build upon, when we pay for the jewel that another hath stolen and in hope of treasure embrace that ransacked casket. Yet they are to blame that have thus been to blame, and for their easy punishment their first night shall discover them.

Be not sudden, therefore, upon thy resolution in this point, because deceit many times lurks in a modest face. But let long acquaintance or inquiry the more secure thee. The Country deceives the City, and the City again returns it with interest, and lust so reigns in both that there is scarce the quantity of virgins to be found in either to match the Parable in the Scripture.[28] They have faces more fairer than men but hearts more deformed than devils. It is ill building upon a broken foundation. Amendment may skin the sore, but the scar will long after retain a blemish. Yet no doubt free thought, which is free, and dreams and wishes, which are but shadows, though the rifling ruffians that break through all bosoms and superficially ravish all womankind, from eight to eighty; and no doubt from actual transgressions many may be found free, for there was never infection so general but it spared some, never battle so great that all were wounded, some of Eve's offspring have withstood the temptation, all have not tasted the forbidden Tree.

And such a one if thou canst pray to prey upon, she hath portion enough without other portion if she thus continue it. For she shall make thee a father of undoubted children. She shall not wrinkle thy thoughts with distracting jealousies, nor upbraid with a former husband thy unkindnesses. Her Maiden thoughts shall receive from thee a more perfect impression of love and duty, and return it back more legibly endorsed and written, free from all former character, inscription, or soil. Her affection shall be strong, not allayed by former wearing. She shall be such a one as it is a heaven to live withal, a misery to mourn without. She shall be to thy senses and delight as the budding Rose in the youth of the spring, nay, shall be such a one that He that walks by thy door shall point at her, and he that dwells by her shall envy him that hath her, and every man shall admire his hap. But he must fully rejoice and be glad that hath her, and all generations shall call such blessed.

****

The Difference between Love and Lust

Lust, the destroyer of Love, the supplanter and underminer of chastity, the Spring-frost of beauty, the tyrant of the night, the enemy of the day, the most potent matchmaker in all Marriages under thirty, and the chief breaker of all from eighteen to eighty. That professed that in a hot blood that it ne'er performs in a cold. A regarder only of the present, and to that effect will with Esau sell a birthright for a mess of pottage (Gen. 25.29-34). No longer esteeming the object than the use, which in like example is thus further followed according to a more common observance:

> Friend, Soldiers, Women, in their prime
> Are like to Dogs in Hunting time:
> Occasion, Wars, and Beauty gone,
> Friends, Soldiers, Women, there are none.

More dangerous when it roves without limits than the Lion without the verge of his grate, for he but only would deprive the body of life, but this both of life and soul and fame. Subject to more opposite immediate passions and contradictions in itself than any sense or humor in the nature of man. As now well-entreated, fairly spoken, lodged where it best likes; anon hated without enduring, cursed out of charity, thrust out of doors. And yet not only, though all this, more immediately opposite than preposterously fondly headlong, that for a minute's toy will incur a month's sorrow, that for one drop of water will mud the whole fountain that gave it, for one sweet fruit will blast the whole Tree that bare it.

Whereas the effect and force of love is contrary, oppressing folly, suppressing fury, aiming to preserve not to destroy, and to that end, regards the end by subduing passions and motives that would seem to oppose the tranquility thereof. And in conclusion, rejoiceth in the true fruition without discontent, without satiety, having captivated and subdued, though with some difficulty, those passions that sense for a time would have been best pleased with. To triumph at last in more full fruition to that purpose that one thus writeth:

> Love comforteth life sun-shine after rain,
> But lust's effect is tempest after sun.
> Love's golden spring doth ever fresh remain,
> Lust's winter comes ere summer half be done.[29]

In love there is no envy, no jealousy, no discontent, no weariness, for it digesteth and maketh sweet the hardest labor, and of all things doth the nearest resemble the Divine Nature, for God is Love. It hath in it unity without division, for true love hath not many objects. It is a fire much water cannot quench.

Now Lust contradicteth all these. For whereas Love is bounded with easy limits, Lust is more spacious, hath no mean, no bound but not to be at all. More deep, more dangerous than the Sea, and less restrained, for the Sea hath bounds but it hath none. Not woman but all womankind is the range thereof, and all that whole sect not able to quench it neither. Full of envy it is, for it envies all without his reach and envies its own nature that it cannot be satisfied, walking for the most part in similitude of an old Goat, in the shape of an incontinent man.

In Love there is no lack, in Lust there is the greatest penury. For though it be cloyed with too much, it pines for want. Ambitious it is, for where it treads it puffs up and leaves a swelling after it, turns low flats into little Mountains, down which precipitate folly tumbles headlong to confusion. A hasty breeder of disinheritable sinners it is, such as have more pleasure in the begetting than comfort in the bringing forth. Best contented when it loseth most labor. To conclude, though Love and Lust in a half brotherhood dwell both under one roof, yet so opposite they are that the one most commonly burns down the house that the other would build up.

The Best Way to Continue a Woman Chaste
Is not the Magician's Ring, nor the Italian's Lock,[30] nor a continual Jealousy ever watching over her. Nor to humor her will in idle fancies, adorn her with new fangles, as the well-paid folly of the world in this kind can witness. But for him that would not be basely mad with the multitude, would not bespeak folly to Crown him, would not set that to sale that he would not have sold (for who sets out his ware to be cheapened and not bought), that would not for his Shop have his Wife for a relative sign, is to adorn her decently not dotingly, thriftily not lasciviously, to love her seriously not ceremoniously, to walk before her in good example (for otherwise how canst thou require that of thy wife that thou art not, wilt not be thy self? Wouldst thou expect thy wife a conqueror when thou thyself liest foiled at the same weapon?), to acquaint her with and place about her good and chaste society, to busy and apply her mind and body in some domestic, convenient, and profitable exercises, according to her education and calling. For example, to the frailty of that whole sex hath a powerful hand as it shall induce either to good or evil.

There are of opinion that there is in Marriage an inevitable destiny not to be avoided. Which is either to be Actaeon'd,[31] or not to be. If it be not, as is the opinion of some damned in the error of Predestination, then let him take a house in Fleet Street, divide it like an Inn into as many several lodgings as rooms, make his wife Chamberlain to them all. Attire her like a sacrifice, paint her out like a Mayor's posts or May-pole, let her have fresh youth and high feeding, lustful company to incite her, her husband absent. All these opportunities present, yet notwithstanding, this destiny shall preserve him to wear his brow as sleek as he that near fetched again the left rib to his side, as unbunched as the front of a Bachelor. But if the contrary, be she the most pure in seeming, a very sister of that Sect, the opinion of Brownists[32] shall so near cleave to her skin that she shall beset thy forehead in thy sleep, kill thee dead in that image of thy grave. Be thee Papist, absolution shall so resolve her that she shall sin upon presumption. Nay, though thou hadst Argus eyes thou shalt not escape it, for "No policy, they say, can prevent, / Whereto two parties give their full consent."

Be she what she will in this case, it shall be all one for to restrain or to give liberty where thou dwellest or what thou doest. For thy destiny is so allotted and it shall be accomplished. The rash opinion and careless security of either is worthy the reward which, for the most part, it doth deservedly receive.

It was an error in religion that one Ludovicus had, who had given himself over to this damnable opinion and security of the devil that if he were ordained to be saved he should be without any enquiry or diligence of his. If otherwise, though he toiled to death in his best endeavor, it would not help or reserve him. In this conceit, settling himself in the most Epicurean and dissolute course of living that might be, he continued till upon a time he fell into a most grievous extremity of sickness. When sending for a Physician who, beforehand acquainted with his damnable error, came not but sent him word that he needed not his help. For if his hour were come he could not preserve him, if otherwise he should recover though never anything were administered unto him. By which easy application he understood himself, and that he must use the best means and endeavors, as well for the safety of his soul as the preservation of his body, not knowing the event of their concealed ends. And so at once (by that means) was happily cured both in mind and body.

In no less palpable error are those that so wittingly and violently are carried on either side in this dangerous stream of a corrupted judgment to the apparentest spectacle and certainest shame that woman may do them, making that unquestionable their dishonor by this consequence which a sober course might have directed to a more certain end.

Therefore, who ever thou art that wouldst not wink at such a shame, that so profit doth succeed wouldst not regard whether hand brought it in, use a good endeavor, such foresight and wariness as may provide for competency, prevent indigence and want, two great allayers of affection and a main inciter of impatient bearers to this folly and abuse. And above all seek to plant in her Religion. For so she cannot love God but withal she must honor thee, increase her knowledge in good things and give her certain assurance and testimony of thy love, that she may with hers again the more reciprocally equal thy affection. For true love hath no power to think, much less act amiss. And these, discreetly put in practice, shall more preserve at all times and temptations than Spies or Eyes, Jealousy or any restraint. For these sometimes may be deluded, or overwatched, or prevented by opportunity, but this never.

Certain Precepts to Be Observed Either in Wiving or Marriage

1. Woo not by Ambassador.
2. Make not thy friend too familar with thy wife.

3. Conceive not an idle jealousy, being a fire once kindled not easily put out.
4. Affect him not that would ill possess thee.
5. Blaze not her beauty with thine own tongue.
6. If thy estate be weak and poor marry far off and quickly; if otherwise firm and rich, at home and with deliberation.
7. Be advised before thou conclude, for though thy error may teach thee wit it is uncertain in this whether thou shalt ever have the like occasion to practice it.
8. Marry not for Gentility without her support, because it can buy nothing in the Market without money.
9. Make thy choice rather of a virtuous than a learned wife.
10. Esteem rather what she is of herself, than what she should be by inheritance.
11. You seek a virgin, let her be a virgin.
Be that example to thy wife thou wouldst have her to imitate.
For he that strikes with the Point must be content to be beaten with the Pommel.[33]
12. She whose youth hath pleased thee, despise not her age.
13. That thou maist be loved, be amiable.
14. Sail not on this Sea without a good Compass, for a wicked woman brings a man to repentance sooner than a surfeit, sooner than suretyship.[34]
15. 'Tis the greater dispraise to children to be like to wicked parents.
16. 'Tis more torment to be jealous of a man's wife than resolved of her dishonesty.
And the more misery that a man may be assured of her vice that way but cannot be of her virtue.
17. True chastity doth not only consist in keeping the body from uncleanness but in withholding the mind from lust. And she may be more maid that hath been unwillingly forced thereto in body than she that hath barely consented in heart.
18. A true wife should be like a Turquoise stone, clear in heart in her husband's health and cloudy in his sickness.
And like a Tortoise under her shell, ever bearing her house upon her back.
19. Defer not thy Marriage to thy age, for a woman out of her own choice seldom plucks a man (as a Rose) full blown.
20. Marry so thy body that thou maist marry thy mind; which that thou maist the better do, thus meditate.
21. That if thou hadst in variety of woman out-paralleled Solomon, thou shouldst in the end give up thy verdict with his: "That all is but vanity and vexation of Spirit" (Eccles. 1.14).
22. That it is in lust as in riches, where to desire nothing and to enjoy all things is but one. To uncover more several nakedness than the Turk from

his Decimary Seraglio[35] hath authority for with an insatiate, illimited appetite, and to desire none, at leastwise no variety, is the same and with advantage.

23. That if thou shouldest, thus seeking to please thine appetite, enjoy a thousand and but want one thou desirest, thou shouldst more grieve for that little want than rejoice in all thy former plenty.

24. Then since what thou canst enjoy (consume thy oil to the socket and thy substance to a morsel) will not be one to thy pleasure for ten thousand that escape it, the variety so large never to be gathered into one bundle of thy fruition to set up thy rest, but the more thou pursuest it the more thou art distracted. Content thy self within thy lawful limits, and destroy not thyself to run after that thou canst ne'er overtake, which the farther thou followest it the swifter it flies from thee.

25. That it were a grief to die for the full pleasure of any sense, but a torment for a taste to a greater distemper, like to him that should purchase at a dear rate saltwater to quench his thirst, which the more he should drink should but the more increase it.

26. That if beauty, or wisdom, or any other portion of the body or mind assail thee, refill them with this thought, that they are but shadows of that substance which should the more allure thee. But pictures which, if they please, are but that the pattern should be the more desired.

Think that as each day is an abridgment of all time, presents the same light, the same use, the same Sun and Firmament, and the ending of this renews but the same tomorrow, so each woman an abridgment of that whole sex and infirmity, how mean so ever, expresseth the same substance, the same mould and metal, proportion, quality, and use of all other in the world. Who then would be so mad against sense, though they would persuade otherwise by Title, by Trapping, by copious adulterating all parts, to believe (as they would be thought) that they are other than what they are, other than the same, unless worse than other? The same way and the same fashion, leading to the Harbor of the same site, of the same condition and quality, though a little more circumstances (in some than other) beats the Bush and ushers it on.

Know this, that the end of all such variety is no more than one dish, dressed and presented by a several Cook, and fashion the same in all one but in circumstance and carriage. Who would thus be mad without reason to toil after the whole Alphabet of woman, when the least letter in the row expoundeth all that Text and Coverture?[36] And for Title or Tomb-like bravery, well may they work upon the eye of folly but never beseige the heart of understanding. And as it was lately well observed by one who, to that effect, thus further noted their vanity, "Things were first made, then call'd, woman the same, / With or without false Title, or proud name."

And if this be not yet enough, take with thee besides for a conclusion and bar to all the rest, this Motto or Sentence to lead thee home; that, "Since all earth's pleasures are so short and small, / The way to enjoy most is to abjure them all."

NOTES

1. Affection.
2. Saint John Cassian, 360-435, first abbot of Saint-Victor abbey in Marseille.
3. A merchant or trader, or an intinerant pedlar.
4. Anna: see Luke 2.36-38; Ophir: the place from which Solomon obtained gold and jewels (1 Kings 10.11).
5. Legendary garden, at the edge of the world, in which grew golden apples.
6. James I, in Book 1 of *Basilikon Doron*.
7. A canker worm, or striped green caterpillar.
8. Impracticality.
9. Coped: encountered, come to blows with.
10. Man. The text also glances at the prolonged controversy over land ownership, in the enclosure or fencing of common lands for private use (often agricultural land taken over to graze sheep).
11. Sweetened.
12. Short-heeled can mean "wanton," which as a verb suggests to play with idly or amorously.
13. Female companion.
14. The most extreme instance.
15. Frills.
16. Being slovenly.
17. Make foul.
18. Pampered.
19. An order of Franciscan friars.
20. Habits.
21. Niccholes echoes the literary convention of using nature imagery to figure the female body; Donne's "Elegy 19" is a well-known poetic example.
22. The right of the new husband or his heirs to succeed to the widow's estate at her death may be limited.
23. Daughter of M. Cato: Portia, wife of Brutus; Portia: possibly Cato's sister; Valeria: the wife of Lucius Sulla.
24. The Mausoleum, one of the seven wonders of the ancient world, erected in 353 B.C.
25. Lucian, A.D. 120-180, Greek rhetorician and satirist; the quotation is an adaptation of his *Dialogues of the Dead* 431.
26. Oblivion.
27. Cruel.
28. The parable of ten virgins in Matt. 25.
29. Shakespeare, *Venus and Adonis* 799-802.
30. Chastity belt.
31. Actaeon was torn to pieces by his own dogs.
32. An independent Puritan sect, started by Robert Browne in the early 1580s.
33. Point: tip of a sword or dagger; pommel: hilt of a sword or dagger.
34. Indebtedness.
35. Harem.
36. Covering or disguise, with a possible pun on "coverture" as the status of a married woman under her husband's protection and authority.

CHAPTER 11

The Mother's Blessing:
Or, the Godly Counsel of a Gentlewoman, not Long since Deceased, Left behind for Her Children
Dorothy Leigh

Dorothy Leigh's *The Mother's Blessing* is a wide-ranging advice book filled with "many good exhortations and godly admonitions," as the title page states. It is addressed to the author's three sons and instructs them on personal, domestic, and social behavior, from private prayer, religious thanksgiving and observance, to choosing a wife, raising children, and managing a household. The text thus introduces a number of issues dealt with in other household manuals but places them in pious terms which are related to Leigh's religious convictions and her roles as mother and author.

The Reformation emphasis on individual spirituality enabled some women to "claim their right to speak independently from men" (Krontiris 10), especially on religious themes. Adopting a public voice, however, remained an unconventional step, contravening cultural commands to be silent and strongly imposing on female authors a "consciousness of defying a prescribed role" (Hannay 1). In response to these pressures, Leigh's preface and opening chapters strive to redefine the mother's role "to include an authorized public voice" (Beilin 275) as mother and teacher, through which she may redeem her sons and, more generally, mankind. In this connection, the image of Mary as Christ's mother is particularly important, for her chastity and solicitude provide a model of sanctified yet engaged motherhood. Leigh's elevation of these qualities over Mary's transcendent virginity is at once a means of exalting and justifying her public duty while marking the consonance of her convictions with Protestant doctrine. Motherly spirituality and chastity combine to offer redemptive advice.

Leigh's dedication of her work to Princess Elizabeth, the daughter of James I and wife of the embattled European Protestant leader, the Count Palatine, is a further endorsement of Reformist viewpoints. She begs Elizabeth to be the protectress of her book, just as Elizabeth is to safeguard the reformed faith in Europe, and just as Leigh herself is to secure the souls of her sons and their descendants. At the same time, Leigh emphasizes that in doing this duty she is remaining loyal to the wishes of her deceased husband, helping to fulfill his role as religious head of the family (sig. A5). Her explanation accepts submission to the male while subtly asserting intellectual equality (Houlbrooke 114). As has been argued, "the shift from a valorisation of virginity to married chastity still depended on women's sexual control" (Wayne 173), and Protestantism did not radically alter the social situation of women. Yet Leigh's text reveals that from within such control, simultaneously adhering to and adapting its rules, some women might redefine and reshape their subordination as they exercised influence over the people around them.

While it echoes a number of concerns with family life that sound in other Protestant manuals, *The Mother's Blessing* registers subtle shifts in tone and address. Like many of the tracts, it is addressed to males; even where these texts do not specify a male reader but seem to anticipate being read by husbands and wives, they rehearse principles of masculine authority and control, which readers are assumed to accept. In one sense, Leigh's work recognizes such dominance. Yet it also uses a position of maternal privilege and respect to pressure the "sons" to rethink presumed rights to treat women as they please. In chapters twelve and thirteen, on choosing a wife, Leigh discusses the way women may be taken advantage of by men. Though her readers are positioned as male, the author insinuates a female perspective on marriage. Any textual premise of masculine rapport is broken; and women's, rather than men's, experience is established as the basis for personal relations.

Leigh's work was very popular. First published in 1616, it was reprinted seven times in the same year, and another ten editions came out up to 1640. The opening thirteen chapters are reproduced below. They deal largely with family issues rather than with the religious and moral themes raised in the remaining thirty-three chapters. The fourth edition, printed in London in 1618, has been used (*STC* 15403; Reel 1729).

THE MOTHER'S BLESSING

The Occasion of Writing This Book Was the Consideration of the Care of Parents for Their Children

My Children, when I did truly weigh, rightly consider, and likewise perfectly see the great care, labor, travail, and continual study which Parents take to enrich their children, some wearing their bodies with labor, some breaking their sleeps with care, some sparing from their own bellies. And many hazarding their souls, some by bribery, some by simony, other by perjury, and a multitude by usury. Some stealing on the Sea, others begging by Land, portions from every poor man, not caring if the whole Commonwealth be impoverished, so their children be enriched. For themselves they can be content with meat, drink, and cloth, so that their children by their means may be made rich, always abusing this portion of Scripture: "He that provideth not for his own Family is worse than an Infidel" (1 Tim. 5.8). Ever seeking for the temporal things of this world, and forgetting those things which be eternal. When I considered these things, I say, I thought good (being not desirous to enrich you with transitory goods) to exhort and desire you to follow the counsel of Christ, "First seek the Kingdom of God, and his righteousness, and then all these things shall be administered unto you" (Matt. 6.33).

The First Cause of Writing Is a Motherly Affection

But lest you should marvel, my children, why I do not, according to the usual custom of women, exhort you by word and admonitions rather than by writing. A thing so unusual among us, and especially in such a time when there be so many godly books in the world that they mold in some men's studies, while their Masters are marred because they will not meditate upon them. As many men's garments moth-eaten in their Chests, while their Christian Brethren quake with cold in the street for want of covering. Know therefore that it was the motherly affection that I bare unto you all which made me now (as it often hath done heretofore) forget myself in regard of you.

Neither care I what you or any shall think of me if among many words I may write but one sentence which may make you labor for the spiritual food of the soul, which must be gathered every day out of the Word, as the children of Israel gathered Manna in the wilderness (Exod. 161.5). By the which you may see it is a labor, but what labor? A pleasant labor, a profitable labor, a labor without the which the soul cannot live. For as the Children of Israel must needs starve except they gathered every day in the wilderness and fed of it, so must your souls except you gather the spiritual Manna out of the word every day and feed of it continually. For as they by this Manna comforted their hearts, strengthened their bodies, and preserved their lives, so by this heavenly Word of God you shall comfort your souls, make them strong in faith, and grow in true godliness, and finally preserve them with great joy to everlasting life through faith in Christ. Whereas, if you desire any food for your souls that is not in the written Word of God, your souls die with it even in your hearts and mouths, even as they that desired other food died with it in their mouths (Num. 11.33), were it never so dainty. So shall you, and there is no recovery for you.

The Best Labor Is for the Food of the Soul

Oh my Children, is not this a comfortable labor? Our Saviour Christ saith, "Labor not for the meat that perisheth, but for the meat that endureth to everlasting life" (John 6.27). And yet I see and fear you shall see how many there be that cross Christ in these words, nay, rather cross themselves. For contrary to our blessed Saviour's counsel, they labor for the meat that perisheth, and in the meantime they lose the food of everlasting life. This, my beloved sons and dear children, this is the cause that maketh me so much to fear you and those who hereafter shall come of you, because I see so many that regard not the words of our Saviour Christ, who came from the high Throne of God (Gal. 4.4), and preached to us and prayed for us, and took our flesh upon him and kept it without sin, refusing no company, healing every sickness and disease (Matt. 4.23), fed the hungry, gave pardon to every sinner that would but ask it, died for us, endured the pains of hell for us, yea, more than this, even in our own flesh he overcame sin, death, and hell (Rom. 4.25).

Yea, and more than this also, he carried our flesh into Heaven in the sight of many and there keeps it, and is become a Mediator for us in it. He joined himself to us in our flesh, as it is written, "He took our flesh upon him" (Heb. 2.14). He taught us to join our flesh unto him by Faith, that "where he is, there we might be with him also" (John 17.24). And if we will not follow him that hath done all this for us and much more than I can write or declare, how unthankful shall we show ourselves?

My dear Children, have I not cause to fear? The holy Ghost saith by the Prophet, "Can a Mother forget the child of her womb?" (Isa. 49.15). As if he should say is it possible that she which hath carried her child within her, so near her heart, and brought it forth into this world with so much bitter pain, so many groans and cries, can forget it? Nay, rather will she not labor now till Christ be formed in it? Will she not bless it every time it sucks on her breasts, when she feeleth the blood come from her heart to nourish it? Will she not instruct it in the youth and admonish it in the age and pray for it continually? Will she not be afraid that the child, which she endureth such pain for, should endure endless pain in hell? Could Saint Paul say unto the Galatians, that were but strangers to him concerning the flesh, only he had spent some time amongst them to bring them to the profession of the truth from which he feared they would fall. And could he, I say, write unto them, "My little Children, of whom I do travail again in birth, until Christ be formed in you" (Gal. 4.19)? And can any man blame a Mother (who indeed brought forth her child with much pain) though she labor again till Christ be formed in them? Could Saint Paul wish himself separated from God for his brethren's sake (Rom. 9.3)? And will not a Mother venture to offend the world for her children's sake? Therefore, let no man blame a Mother though she something exceed in writing to her children, since every man knows that the love of a Mother to her children is hardly contained within the bounds of reason.

Neither must you, my sons, when you come to be of judgment, blame me for writing to you, since Nature telleth me that I cannot long be here to speak unto you and this my mind will continue long after me in writing. And yet not my mind but I seek to put you in mind of the words of our Saviour Christ, which saith, "Labor not for the meat that perisheth, etc." (John 6.27), where you see that the food of the soul is to be gotten by labor. Why stand you here (sayth Christ), here is no time to be idle. They that will rest with Christ in heaven must labor to follow him here on earth. "Blessed are the dead which die in the Lord, for they rest from their labor" (Rev. 14.13). Thus you see, if you will go to the place which Christ hath bought for you, you must labor to follow Christ. He labor'd to get it for you, or else all your labor would have been as nothing. And now you must labor to lay hold on him or else all your labor will be worth nothing. Many there be that labor the clean contrary way, for they leave Christ and take hold of traditions.[1] And a number loiter and by that means never get hold on Christ. And this is the cause why I write unto you, that you might never fly from him with the one nor yet loiter with the other, but that you might learn to follow him and to take hold of him in the written Word of God, where you shall find him (as Christ himself witnesseth) and nowhere else. "Search the Scriptures," saith he, "for they testify of me" (John 5.39). Labor therefore that you may come unto Christ.

The Second Cause Is to Stir Them up to Write

The second cause, my sons, why I write unto you (for you may think that had I had but one cause I would not have changed the usual order of women) is needful to be known and may do much good. For where I saw the great mercy of God toward you in making you men and placing you amongst the wise, where you may learn the true written Word of God which is the pathway to all happiness and which will bring you to the chief City, new Jerusalem, and the seven liberal sciences,[2] whereby you shall have at least a superficial sight in all things. I thought it fit to give you good example, and by writing to entreat you that when it shall please God to give both virtue and grace with your learning, he having made you men that you may write and speak the Word of God without offending any, that then you would remember to write a book unto your children of the right and true way to happiness, which may remain with them and theirs forever.

The Third Cause Is to Move Women to Be Careful of Their Children

The third is to encourage women (who, I fear, will blush at my boldness) not to be ashamed to show their infirmities but to give men the first and chief place. Yet let us labor to come in the second, and because we must needs confess that sin entered by us into our posterity, let us show how careful we are to seek to Christ to cast it out of us and our posterity, and how fearful we are that our sin should sink any of them to the lowest part of the earth. Wherefore let us call upon them to follow Christ, who will carry them to the height of heaven.

The Fourth Cause Is to Arm Them against Poverty

The fourth cause is to desire you that you will never fear poverty, but always know it is the state of the Children of GOD to be poor in the world. Christ saith, "Ye shall have the poor with you always" (John 12.8). It may be he hath appointed you or yours to be of this poor number? Do not strive against Christ. "It is as hard (sayth he) for a rich man to enter into heaven as for a Camel to go through the eye of a needle" (Matt. 19.24). Saint James sayth, "Woe be to you that are rich" (Jas. 5.1). Saint Paul saith, "The desire of money is the root of all evil" (1 Tim. 6.10). Which if it be true, as it is not to be doubted of, and you fear poverty, then doth it necessarily follow that you will desire the root of all evil, which is money, and so become good for nothing?

The fear of poverty maketh men run into a thousand sins which nothing else could draw them to. For many fearing the cold storms of poverty, which never last long, run on to the hot fire of hell, which never hath an end. This matter requireth many words, for it is hard to persuade the nature of man from the fear of poverty. Wherefore I will speak more of that afterwards, only I now say fear not to be poor with Lazarus, but fear a thousand times to be rich with Dives (Luke 16.19-31).

The Fifth Cause Is not to Fear Death

The fifth cause is to desire you never to fear death. For the fear of death hath made many to deny the known truth, and so have brought a heavy judgment of GOD upon themselves. A great reason why you should not fear death is because you can by no means shun it. You must needs endure it, and therefore it is meet that you should be always prepared for it and never fear it. "He that will save his life," saith Christ, "shall lose it, and he that will lose his life for my sake and the Gospel's shall find it" (Matt. 16.25). Do not fear the pains of death in what shape soever he come. For perhaps thou shalt have more pains upon thy bed and be worse provided to bear them by reason of some grievous sickness than thou art like to feel when God shall call thee forth to witness his truth.

The only way not to fear death is always to be provided to die. And that thou maist always be provided to die, thou must be continually strengthening thy faith with the promises of the Gospel, as, "He that liveth and believeth shall not die. And though he were dead, yet shall he live" (John 11.25-26). Meditate in the Law of the Lord day and night, as the Psalmist saith (Ps. 1.2), and then thou shalt be fit to bring forth fruit in due season. Then thou shalt be fit to serve God, thy King and country, both in thy life and in thy death, and always shalt show thyself a good member of JESUS Christ, a faithful subject to thy Prince, and always fit to govern in the Christian commonwealth. And then thou mayest faithfully and truly say, "Whether I live or die, I am the Lord's" (Rom. 14.8).

But without continual meditation of the Word this cannot be done. And this was one of the chief causes why I write unto you, to tell you that you must meditate in the Word of GOD. For many read it and are never the better for want of meditation. If ye hear the Word and read it without meditating thereon, it doth the Soul no more good than meat and drink doth the body, being seen and felt, and never fed upon. For as the body will die although it see meat even so will the Soul, for all the hearing and reading of the Word, if that ye do not meditate upon it, and gather Faith and strengthen it, and get hold of Christ. Which if ye do, Christ will bring you to the Kingdom of his Father, to which you can come by no means but by faith in him.

The Sixth Cause Is to Persuade Them to Teach Their Children

The sixth reason is to entreat and desire you, and in some sort to command you, that all your children, be they Males or Females, may in their youth learn to read the Bible in their own Mother tongue. For I know it is a great help to true godliness. And let none of you plead poverty against this, for I know that if you be neither covetous, prodigal, nor idle, either of which sins will let no virtue grow where they come, that you need not fail in this. But if you will follow the Commandment of the LORD, and labor six days and keep the seventh holy to the Lord, and love him with all your heart, soul, and strength, you will not only be willing but also able to see them all brought up to read the Bible.

Solomon, that was wise by the Spirit of GOD, said, "Remember thy Creator in the day of thy youth" (Eccles. 12.1). And ye are also commanded to "write it upon the walls of your houses and to teach it your children" (Deut. 11.19-20). "I know (sayth GOD) that Abraham will teach his Children and his children's children to walk in my Commandments" (Gen. 18.19).

Also, I further desire you because I wish all well, and would be glad you should do as much good as could be in the wilderness of this world, that if any shall at any time desire you to be a Witness to the baptizing of their Child, that then you shall desire the person so desiring to give you his faithful word that the child shall be taught to read so soon as it can conveniently learn, and that it shall so continue till it can read the Bible. If this will not be granted, you shall refuse to answer for the child. Otherwise do not refuse to be a witness to any, for it is a good Christian duty. Moreover, forget not, whether you answer for the child or no, to pray that the child baptized may receive the Holy Ghost with all other children of the faithful, especially when you are where a Child is baptized. For it is your duty to pray for the increase of the Church of God. "Pray for the peace of Jerusalem (saith the Psalmist): let them prosper that love thee" (Ps. 122.6).

The Seventh Cause Is that They Should Give Their Children Good Names

The seventh cause is to entreat you that though I do not live to be a witness to the baptizing of any of your Children, yet you would give me leave to give names to them all. For though I do not think any holiness to be in the name but know that God hath his in every place and of every name, yet I see in the Bible it was observed by GOD himself to give choice names to his children, which had some good signification. I think it good therefore to name your children after the name of the Saints of GOD, which may be a means to put them in mind of some virtues which those Saints used, especially when they shall read of them in the Bible. And seeing many are desirous to name both their own Children and others after their own names, this will be a means to increase the names of the Saints in the Church, and so none shall have occasion to mislike his name since he beareth the name of such a Saint as hath left a witness to the world that he lived and died in the true faith of Jesus Christ.

The names I have chosen you are these: Philip, Elizabeth, James, Anna, John, and Susanna. The virtues of them that bore those names and the causes why I choose them, I let pass, and only mean to write of the last name Susan,[3] famous through the world for chastity, a virtue which always hath been and is of great account, not only amongst the Christians and people of God but even among the Heathen and Infidels. Insomuch that some of them have written that a woman that is truly chaste is a great partaker of all other virtues, and contrariwise that the woman that is not truly chaste hath no virtue in her. The which saying may well be warranted by the Scripture. For who so is truly chaste is free from idleness and from all vain delights, full of humility, and all good Christian virtues. Who so is chaste is not given to pride in apparel nor any vanity, but is always either reading, meditating, or practicing some good thing which she hath learned in the Scripture. But she which is unchaste is given to be idle, or if she do anything it is for a vain glory and for the praise of men more than for any humble, loving, and obedient heart that she beareth unto GOD and his Word. Who said, "Six days thou shalt labor" (Exod. 20.9), and so left no time for idleness, pride, or vanity. For in none of these is there any holiness. The unchaste Woman is proud and always decking herself with vanity, and delights to hear the vain words of men in which there is not only vanity but also so much wickedness that the vain words of men, and women's vainness in hearing them, hath brought many women to much sorrow and vexation, as woeful experience hath and will make many of them confess.

But some will say had they only lent an ear to their words they had done well enough. To answer which, I would have every one know that one sin begetteth another. The vain words of the man and the idle cares of the woman beget unchaste thoughts oftentimes in the one, which may bring forth much wickedness in them both.

Man said once, "The woman which thou gavest me, beguiled me and I did eat" (Gen. 3.12). But we women may now say that men lie in wait everywhere to deceive us, as the Elders did to deceive Susanna. Wherefore let us be, as she was, chaste, watchful, and wary, keeping company with maids. Once Judas betrayed his Master with a kiss and repented it. But now men, like Judas, betray their Mistresses with a kiss and repent it not, but laugh and rejoice that they have brought sin and shame to her that trusted in them. The only way to avoid all which is to be chaste with Susanna and, being women, to embrace that virtue which being placed in a woman is most commendable.

An unchaste woman destroyeth both the body and the soul of him she seemeth most to love, and it is almost impossible to set down the mischiefs which have come through unchaste women. Solomon saith that "her steps lead to hell" (Prov. 2.18). Wherefore bring up your daughters as Susanna's Parents brought up her. Teach them the law of the Lord continually, and always persuade them to embrace this virtue of chastity.

It may be that some of you will marvel since I set down names for the imitation of their virtues that bore them why I placed not Mary in the first place, a woman virtuous above all other women. My reason was this. Because I presumed that there was no woman so senseless as not to look what a blessing God hath sent to us women through that gracious Virgin, by whom it pleased GOD to take away the shame which Eve our Grandmother had brought us to. For before men might say the woman beguiled me, and I did eat the poisoned fruit of disobedience and I die. But now man may say, if he say truly, the Woman brought me a Saviour and I feed of him by faith and live. Here is this great and woeful shame taken from women by GOD, working in a woman. Man can claim no part in it. The shame is taken from us and from our posterity for ever. "The seed of the woman hath taken down the Serpent's head" (Gen. 3.15). And now whosoever can take hold of the seed of the Woman by faith shall surely live forever. And therefore all generations shall say that she was blessed who brought us a Saviour, the fruit of obedience, that whosoever feedeth of shall live forever. And except they feed of the seed of the Woman, they have no life (John 6.53). Will not therefore all women seek out this great grace of GOD that by Mary hath taken away the shame which before was due unto us ever since the fall of man?

Mary was filled with the Holy Ghost and with all goodness, and yet is called the blessed Virgin, as if our God should (as he doth indeed) in brief comprehend all other virtues under this one virtue of chastity. Wherefore I desire that all women, what name soever they bear, would learn of this blessed Virgin to be chaste. For though she were more replenished with grace than any other and more freely beloved of the Lord, yet the greatest title that she had was that she was a blessed and pure Virgin. Which is a great cause to move all women, whether they be maids or wives (both which estates she honored), to live chastely. To whom for this cause God hath given a cold and temperate disposition and bound them with these words, "Thy desire shall be subject to thy husband" (Gen. 3.6). As if God, in mercy to women, should say you of yourselves shall have no desires, only they shall be subject to your husbands.

Which hath been verified in Heathen women so as it is almost incredible to be believed. For many of them, before they would be defiled, have been careless of their lives, and so have endured all those torments that men would devise to inflict upon them rather than they would lose the name of a modest Maid or a chaste Matron. Yea, and so far they have been from consenting to any immodesty that if at any time they have been ravished, they have either made away themselves or at least have separated themselves from company, not thinking themselves worthy of any society after they have once been deflowered, though against their wills. Wherefore, the woman that is infected with the sin of uncleanness is worse than a beast, because it desireth but for nature and she to satisfy her corrupt lusts.

Some of the Fathers have written that it is not enough for a woman to be chaste but even so to behave herself that no man may think or deem her to be unchaste. We read that in the Primitive Church, when there were wars between the Christians and the Pagans, if at any time the Pagans had gotten the victory that then they would seek to deflower the Virgins. To the which sin before the Christians would yield they would continually lay violent hands upon themselves, insomuch that the Doctors of the Church were often times constrained to make divers Sermons and Orations to them to dissuade them from that cruelty which they inflicted upon themselves rather than they would suffer themselves to be deflowered. Such a disgrace did they think it to have but one spot of uncleanness. And yet none of these were so holy as this Mary, this pure and undefiled Virgin.

Some godly and reverend men of the Church have gathered this, that there were five women of great virtue in the time of the Law, the first letters of whose name do make her whole name, to show that she had all their virtues wholly combined in her, as namely: **M**ichal, **A**bigail, **R**achel, **I**udith,[4] and **A**nna.

She was as faithful to her husband as Michal, who saved her husband David from the fury of Saul although he were her father and her King, not preferring her own life before the safety of her husband (1 Sam. 19.12). She was as wise as Abigail, who is highly commended for her Wisdom (1 Sam.

25.3). Amiable in the sight of her husband, as Rachel (Gen 29.17). Stout and magnanimous in the time of trouble, as Judith. Patient and zealous in prayer, as Anna (1 Sam. 1.10-11). Seeing then, that by this one name so many virtues are called to remembrance, I think it meet that good names be given to all women that they might call to mind the virtues of those women whose names they bear. But especially above all other moral Virtues, let women be persuaded by this discourse to embrace chastity, without which we are mere beasts and no women.

Reasons of Giving Good Names to Children

If ye shall think me too tedious about the naming of your children, I tell you that I have some reason for it. And the first is this, to make them read in the Bible the things which are written of those Saints, and learn to imitate their virtues. Secondly, because many have made a God of the Virgin Mary, the Scripture warranting no such thing, and have prayed to her (though there they shall find that she was a woman, yea, and a comfort to all women, for she hath taken away the reproach which of right belonged unto us, and by the seed of the woman we are all saved), it was therefore fit I should speak largely of that name.[5] Thirdly, seeing many have heretofore and now do make Images of Saints to put them in mind of the Saints, and so by little and little have at last worshipped the works of their own hands and for fear of forgetting the Saints have forgotten the Second Commandment, I thought it better to have you remember them by hearing their names and by reading what they taught us in the Scripture and how they led their lives than by looking upon a painted piece of paper or a carved stone. And this, by the way, may be marveled at, that they which love to worship Images never love to name their Children after the names of the Saints. For if they had so done, by this time we should have had no other names but Matthew, Mark, Luke, John, Timothy, and such as followed Christ faithfully. Then Moses and his mildness would be more talked of, Samuel and his obedience would be more sought after, Abraham and his faithfulness would be more followed. Lastly, this I will tell you, that there is no man but will be ashamed to do anything which shall disgrace the good name after which he is called. As if one should say: is this a Moses? Is this an Elias, and hath such qualities as these?

Children to Be Taught Betimes and Brought up Gently

I am further also to entreat you that all your Children may be taught to read, beginning at four years old or before, and let them learn till ten. In which time they are not able to do any good in the Commonwealth but to learn how to serve God, their King and Country by reading. And I desire, entreat, and earnestly beseech you and everyone of you that you will have your Children brought up with much gentleness and patience. What disposition so ever they be of, gentleness will soonest bring them to virtue. For frowardness and cursedness doth harden the heart of the Child and maketh him weary of virtue. Among the froward thou shalt learn frowardness. Let them therefore be gently used and always kept from idleness, and bring them up in the Schools of learning if you be able and they fit for it. If they will not be Scholars, yet I hope they will be able, by God's grace, to read the Bible, the Law of God, and be brought to some good vocation or calling of life. Solomon saith, "Teach a child in his youth the trade of his life, and he will not forget it nor depart from it when he is old" (Prov. 22.6).

Choice of Wives

Now for your Wives, the Lord direct you, for I cannot tell you what is best to be done. Our Lord saith, "First seek the kingdom of God, and his righteousness and all things else shall be ministered unto you" (Matt. 6.33). First, you must seek a godly wife, that she may be a help to you in godliness. For GOD said, "It is not good for man to be alone, let him have a helper meet for him" (Gen. 2.18). And she cannot be meet for him except she be truly godly. For God counteth that the man is alone still if his wife be not godly. If I should write unto you how many the Scripture maketh mention of that have been drawn to sin because they married ungodly wives, it would be tedious for you to read.

The world was drowned because men married ungodly wives (Gen. 6.2-3). Solomon, who was not only the wisest man that ever was but was also mightily endued with the Spirit of God, by marrying idolatrous women fell for the time to idolatry (1 Kings 11.4). Never think to stand where Solomon fell. I pray God that neither you nor any of yours may at any time marry with any of those which hold such superstitions as they did or as some do now, as namely, to pray to Saints, to pray in Latin, to pray to go to Purgatory, etc. Let no riches or money bring your posterity to this kind of tradition. The beloved Apostle of Christ sayth: "Love not the world, nor the things that are in the world" (1 John 2.15), for he knew well that a little that a man loveth not would suffice him. A little with a godly Woman is better than great riches with the wicked. Rebecca saith, "I shall be weary of my life if Jacob take a wife of the daughters of Heth" (Gen. 27.46), as if she should say, if my Son marry an ungodly wife then all my comfort of him and his is gone, and it will be a continual grief to me to see him in league and friendship amongst the wicked. If such a shame and sin cometh upon my Son as can by no means be helped nor by no means comforted, what availeth me then to live?

"Be not unequally yoked," saith the Holy Ghost (2 Cor. 6.14). It is indeed very unequal for the godly and ungodly to be united together that their hearts must be both as one, which can never be joined in the fear of

God and faith of CHRIST. Love not the ungodly. Marry with none except you love her, and be not changeable in your love. Let nothing after you have made your choice remove your love from her. For it is an ungodly and very foolish thing for a man to mislike his own choice, especially since God hath given a man much choice among the godly. And it was a great cause that moved God to command his to marry with the godly, that there might be a continual agreement between them.

It Is Great Folly for a Man to Mislike His Own Choice
Methinks I never saw a man show a more senseless simplicity than in misliking his own choice when GOD hath given a man almost a world of women to choose him a Wife in. If a man hath not wit enough to choose him one whom he can love to the end, yet methinks he should have discretion to cover his own folly. But if he want discretion methinks he should have policy, which never fails a man to dissemble his own simplicity in this case. If he want wit, discretion, and policy, he is unfit to marry any woman.

Do not a Woman that wrong as to take her from her friends that love her, and after a while to begin to hate her. If she have no friends, yet thou knowest not but that she may have a Husband that may love her. If thou canst not love her to the end, leave her to him that can.

Methinks my Son could not offend me in anything if he served GOD, except he chose a Wife that he could not love to the end. I need not say if he served God. For if he served God he would obey God, and then he would choose a godly Wife and live lovingly and godlily with her, and not do as some man who taketh a woman to make her a Companion and fellow and, after he hath her, he makes her both a servant and drudge. If she be thy wife, she is always too good to be thy servant and worthy to be thy fellow. If thou wilt have a good Wife, thou must go before her in all goodness and show her a pattern of all good virtues by thy godly and discreet life and especially in patience, according to the counsel of the Holy Ghost, "Bear with the woman as with the weaker vessel" (1 Pet. 3.7). Here GOD showeth that it is her imperfection that honoreth thee, and that it is thy perfection that maketh thee to bear with her. Follow the counsel of GOD therefore and bear with her. God willed a man "to leave Father and Mother for his Wife" (Gen. 2.24). This showeth what an excellent love God did appoint to be between Man and Wife. In truth, I cannot by any means set down the excellency of that love.

But this I assure you, that if you get wives that be godly and you love them, you shall not need to forsake me. Whereas if you have Wives that you love not, I am sure I will forsake you. Do not yourselves that wrong as to marry a Woman that you cannot love. Show not so much childishness in your sex as to say you loved her once and now your mind is changed. If thou canst not love her for the goodness that is in her, yet let the grace that is in thyself move thee to do it. And so I leave thee to the Lord, whom I pray to guide both thee and her with his grace, and grant that you may choose godlily and live happily, and die comfortably through faith in JESUS CHRIST.

NOTES

1. The unauthentic practices of some churches.

2. Grammar, rhetoric, logic, arithmetic, geometry, astronomy, and music, the disciplines of the traditional university curriculum.

3. Leigh adds the following sidenote, "The story of Susanna, though it be not canonical nor to be equalled to those books that are, yet it may be true and of good use as many other histories written by men are." It is told in the apocryphal Book of Susanna.

4. Judith; the "j" sound continued to be symbolized by "I" through to the early-seventeenth century. She is the heroine of the apocryphal book named after her.

5. Revaluation of Mary as a chaste matron was a significant issue in the context of Protestant views on marriage and the family. All of Leigh's reasons for giving "good names" to children are based on Reformation contrasts to Catholicism.

CHAPTER 12

A Bride-Bush:
Or, a Direction for Married Persons
William Whately

In the *Homily against Disobedience and Willful Rebellion*, rebellion is depicted as "both the first and the greatest and the very root of all other sins." To counter the possibility of universal anarchy, God not only commanded obedience to his own "Majesty" but "ordained that in families and households, the wife should be obedient unto her husband, the children unto their parents, the servants unto their masters." This view of the divine necessity of family order underpins William Whately's "Direction for Married Persons," known as *A Bride-Bush*, in which God provides the model for authority as "commander of a general subjection."

Along with Cleaver's *Godly Form of Household Government*, and *Of Domestical Duties* (1620) by William Gouge, minister in the London parish of Blackfriars, Whately's work is the most famous of the seventeenth-century conduct books. Like the other two manuals, it reveals a particularly strict view of the importance of patriarchal power in the running of family and society: "The family was central to social order; disciplined families were therefore a prerequisite of that order" (Amussen 38). A politically marked rhetoric is used to affirm the reciprocal duties of authority and submission which structure all relations within the family unit, especially between husband and wife. Whately does not examine in detail the notion that the family is a symbol for society, but he readily assumes that the family can best be represented through the structures and imagery of political rhetoric: "the Protestant defense of marriage gave new importance to family relations but it shaped these relations according to a newly elaborated theory of patriarchalism," which inculcated a "grammar of Puritan obedience" (Jones 59-60). These texts sought to establish a way of thinking and writing about the family and one's place in it.

Whately provides a rigorous account of subservience to the husband-father figure. *A Bride-Bush* begins with softer celebrations of married bliss but then turns to "the uncompromising doctrine that the authority of the husband is paramount and absolute" (Collinson, *Birthpangs* 72). The wife is to monitor and restrain every aspect of her behavior, from dress and posture, to how she speaks to and of her spouse, to how she looks at him. While entirely regulating her own conduct, she must accept all aspects of her husband's. Most striking to later readers is Whately's endorsement of wife-beating: she either deserves it or should accept it unquestioningly, with faith in God's order.

It can, however, be difficult to assess the way in which such ideas were received by congregations and readers. In the preface to later editions of *Of Domestical Duties*, William Gouge admitted that his ideas on female subservience, though supported with Biblical authority, might not reflect people's everyday lives and opinions. As has recently been noted, "These prescriptions should not be confused with the lived experience of families in these societies; the extent to which they were the expression of reality as opposed to ideology is debatable" (O'Day 63). Exhortations reinforcing men's power in marriage may signify that masculine privilege was being questioned by women who, if rarely able to produce overt and extensive change in gender relations, still disturbed any naturalization of the period's sexual politics (Howard 439). The many church-court records of cases where women attacked men verbally (and sometimes physically) can suggest that masculine authority was constantly challenged but with ambiguous effects. Reactionary responses, which might include Whately's work, could be prompted while pressure built for change to women's social and personal situations: old systems being renewed even as they changed into something different (Davis 151). It is probably because they capture the conflict and play of attitudes and beliefs on family and gender issues that the period's household manuals were so popular.

Whately seems to epitomize the character of the Puritan preacher. Born in 1583, he grew up in Banbury (his father was the mayor) before studying at both Cambridge and Oxford and entering the ministry in 1602. In 1610 he was appointed vicar of Banbury and soon won renown for his powerful and theatrical preaching style, being nicknamed "the Roaring Boy of Banbury." His views were considered too Puritan by church officials, but his popularity afforded some protection until his justification of divorce for adultery in *A Bride-Bush* led to interrogation by the Church of England's High Commission. In 1621 Whately renounced this view and went on to note his "error" in the 1623 edition of his work. He died in Banbury in 1639.

Whately published a number of sermons on topics including redemption, avarice, charity, and the Ten Commandments. He also wrote another text on marriage, *A Care-Cloth: or, A Treatise of the Cumbers and Troubles of Marriage* (1624). *A Bride-Bush* was his most popular work, being published in London in three editions, 1617, 1619, and 1623. The extracts reproduced here are taken from the second edition (*STC* 25297; Reel 1419).

Of a Man's Keeping His Authority

The husband's special duties are all fitly referred to two heads: he must govern his wife and maintain her; and, as our Lord Jesus is to his Church (for with that comparison is the holy Ghost himself delighted), so must he be to his wife a head and savior. As for government, two things also be required of him: one, that he keep his authority; the other, that he do use it.

First, then, be it known that every man is bound to maintain himself in that place in which his Maker hath set him, and to hold fast that account, reverence, and precedency which both God and nature have assigned unto him. Nature hath framed the lineaments of his body to superiority and set the print of government in his very face, which is more stern and less delicate than the woman's. He must not suffer this order of nature to be inverted. The Lord in his Word hath entitled him by the name of head, wherefore he must not stand lower than the shoulders. If he do, doubtless it makes a great deformity in the family. That house is a misshapen house and (if we may use that term) a crump-shouldered or hunch-backed house, where the husband hath made himself an underling to his wife and given away his power and regiment to his inferior. Without question it is a sin for a man to come lower than God hath set him. It is not humility but baseness to be ruled by her whom he should rule. No General would thank a Captain for surrendering his place to some common soldier. Nor will God a husband for suffering his wife to bear the sway. It is dishonorable to the Prince if subordinate officers yield the honor of their places to the overtopping of meaner subjects. And the contempt redounds upon God which a man is willing to take upon himself by making his wife his master. It is God's authority invested in his person. He must not permit (unless he will wrong God) that it be trodden down and despised. For this Saint Paul hath given us a rule, saying, "Let every man abide in the place wherein he is called" (1 Cor. 7.20). It must be understood as well of the place for order and government as for means and conditions of life.

But here, perhaps, some weak-spirited man may interrupt me and say, "The thing you speak is reasonable, and happy were it if a man could do it. But experience shows it is sooner said than done, unless you can give us some good direction how to do it." But for himself, he hath met with such a virago that will be governor or will overturn all, and against such a disordered, froward, and sturdy-spirited dame, who can preserve his authority? To such objector I answer that most men do falsely cast the blame (of losing their authority) upon their wives, when in very truth it is wholly and only due unto themselves. For it is not extorted from them by the wives' violence but lost and cast away by their own folly and indiscretion. It is not indeed in any man's power to restrain a violent-spirited woman from assailing his authority but from winning it. Whether she shall break forth into carriages of contempt, he cannot choose; but whether he will prostitute himself unto contempt, yea or no, that he may and must choose. Many a city is fiercely assaulted and not taken. Many a woman strives to break the yoke but is not able. So long as the husband's behavior is such that the wife's soul (after that she hath recovered herself out of the drunkenness of passion) is enforced to blame her own rudeness and rebelliousness and in her conscience to acknowledge him worthy the better place, so long hath he duly preserved his authority against all her rude and disloyal resistance.

Know ye therefore, all ye husbands, that the way to maintain authority in this society is not to use violence but skill. Not by main force and by strong hand must a husband hold his own against his wife's undutifulness but by a more mild, gentle, and wise proceeding. Here, we must take up the words of Solomon, the excellency of a thing is wisdom (Prov. 4.7). We wish not any man to use big looks, great words, and a fierce behavior (as it were of a mankind mastiff over some silly little cur), but we advise you to a more easy, certain, and artificial course which (that you may practice), this it is.

First, let the husband endeavor to be garnished with all commendable virtues and to exceed his wife as much in goodness as he doth in place. Let his wife see in him such humility, godliness, wisdom, as may cause her very heart to confess that there is in him some worth and dignity, something that deserveth to be stooped unto. Let him walk uprightly, Christianly, soberly, religiously in his family, and give a good example to all in the household. Then shall the wife willingly give him the better place, when she cannot but see him to be the better person. No inferior can choose but, in his soul, stoop to that superior in whom grace and God's image do appear according to his place. A virtuous man shall be regarded in the conscience of the worst woman, yea, in the behavior also of any that is not monstrous and void of all womanhood. To be worthy esteem will make one esteemed. It is no burden to any to yield themselves to such a one as is apparently better than themselves. A godly, wise carriage will draw on good respect and allure to willing subjection. Neither can any man produce an example of a husband, thus qualified, that is trodden down in contempt.

If a Prince commend a coward to the place of a Captain, his soldiers soon find it and scorn him. But if he have courage and sufficiency for the charge, though they may be mutinous, yet he shall hold his respect amongst them. It is true that (in a mad fit) the wife of the best husband may fling forth and be undutiful, but when that fit shall be past and she is returned to herself again, her self shall condemn herself and justify him. And so instead of losing his authority, he recovers his own with good advantage. Be you, therefore, all assured that you shall find virtuous and good carriage the best preservatives of good account. These awe the heart, these command reverence, these offer themselves to the mind with an honorable kind of gravity and will not suffer the man (in whom they be) to be long spurned at. Take pains to make thyself good, and that is the most compendious way to make thyself reverenced.

But as in general we prescribe a good conversation for the best preserver and maintainer of a man's authority in the family, so specially must all husbands be counseled to shun and abandon three special and disgraceful evils that are never separated from this effect of making every man to seem base and vile in the eyes of those that see him so disordered.

The first of these is bitterness, as the Apostle Paul terms it in giving all husbands warning of it, saying, "Be not bitter to your wives" (Col. 3.19). An outrageous, sharp, tart, violent carriage, consisting of railing, reviling, striking, and other furious words and gestures, he fitly calleth bitterness because it is as contrary and offensive to the mind and affections as gall and wormwood and coloquintida[1] be to the taste or palate. Who ever kept a bitter thing for any other purpose than to make a medicine? And is not that a bad husband that is good for little but to be his wife's purgation? Doubtless, he must needs be ill-respected that doth no good but by accident and against his purpose. If he be gall and aloes[2] in her mouth, is it any wonder though she strive to spit him out? This bitterness shows folly and works hatred, and therefore must needs be a great underminer of authority. They will hate whom they fear, saith one well of a tyrant.[3] A tyrannical husband, as well as a tyrannical Prince, shall thrust himself besides his place. In violent and furious words and deeds, he proclaims himself a fool, "for anger rests in the bosom of fools" saith Solomon (Eccles. 7.9). And having enforced his family to take him for a fool, can it but follow that they shall be weary of his government? Such demeanor bewrayeth great impotency of affection and great want of wisdom, whence will ensue want of reverence. Wherefore, if thou beest a husband and wouldst be respected by thy wife, tumble not thyself in those dirty and stinking guzzles[4] of cursing, railing, swearing, and the like madnesses of serious wrath, the savor of which will smell so loathsomely in thy wife's nostrils that she shall hardly keep herself from first hating thee and after despising thee. But make thyself loved by not being causelessly and excessively offensive.

Secondly, he that would retain the pre-eminence of his place must avoid unthriftiness (another great enemy to reverence) that (as a worm) rotteth and consumeth it. This is often termed folly by Solomon,[5] and a fool must needs inherit hatred and contempt. Drunkenness, gaming, ill-company keeping be the three parts, as I may call them, of unthriftiness. The first drowneth wit, the second consumeth wealth, the third eats out the heart of all good conditions. And he that hath neither wit in his head, nor money in his purse, nor good qualities in his person, how can he be but loathed and despised? When drink hath banished reason, gaming providence, ill company good conditions, the carriage must needs be foolish, wicked, beast-like; the person base, contemned, loathed. This vice, he that follows must needs forfeit at once his wit, his wealth, and his estimation. Contempt will come upon him as swiftly and irresistibly as poverty that ruinateth at once his soul, body, name, family, posterity, by seeking to please his inordinate appetite and burying his reason in sensuality.

Never did unthrift keep his place no more than his money. Honor and wealth run from him both at once. For who can regard him that will needs make himself worth nothing. Our English calls thriftiness good husbandry, and a thrifty husband a good husband, as if it were the chief part (from which the whole might worthily receive its name) of a good husband's duty to be thrifty. Wherefore, away with drinking, gaming, and following riotous companions, if thou wouldst not be cast at once out of the hearts of all thy family and all thy neighbours and of thy wife also, both for love and reverence.

Thirdly, lightness must be avoided by husbands. Foolish, childish, unstayed[6] tricks, that have no stamp nor impression of gravity or discretion seen upon them but savor strongly of a kind of puerility and boyishness. Such contemptible things must needs expose a man to contempt. If the husband put a fool's coat upon his back and take up a bauble into his hands (and what else be these toyish and odd and boyish words and behaviors, which are common with some, but badges and recognizances of folly?), can he blame his wife though she take up a loud laughter at him? The bitter man is like a frantic head, very troublesome; the unthrifty man as a scald[7] head, very fulsome; the light man, the jester, like a giddy head, very ridiculous. Such men will soon displace themselves though no man strive to undermine them. But let every godly man abhor and cast from him all these base evils and strive for holiness and gravity of conversation, that so he may be indeed a governor and that his superiority (supported by such pillars) may stand upright and unshaken, and not be cast down flat into the dust of contempt and disreverence.

Of Maintaining One's Wife

As our Lord Jesus Christ, the husband of his Church, hath been in nothing wanting to her spiritual welfare, but doth clothe her with the pure and white linen of his own righteousness and with the rich and precious graces of his good spirit, whereby she is all glorious within as the royal Princess, the Spouse of Solomon, attired in gold and needle-work,[8] so must every good husband afford his wife allowance of all necessary comforts for this present life, for attire and food, for necessity and delight, that she may live a cheerful and a well-contented life with him. Before a man do allure a woman into copartnership of life with him for his own comfort, he should consider of means to maintain both himself and her that their lives may indeed be comfortable. For how it should stand with love and duty to pull so near a companion into the troublesome fellowship of misery and want (that she shall have cause to remember with anguish and abhorring the time of their first acquaintance), I cannot in reason conceive nor I think any man else. Doubtless, it is a man's wanton passion that spurs him forward to run blindfold into this estate and not the good hand of God leading and calling him unto it, unless he be this way furnished in some measure with things fit to maintain the charge of a wife and family.

When the Lord by his good allowances go before us and wisheth us to follow him into any estate, he is so suitable to himself in all his courses that he gives us wisdom to look beforehand that we have all things necessary in some degree to perform the duties of this estate. But when our own passions thrust us forward into any course, they make us run headlong after our own appetite, not troubling ourselves with any such wise and serious and pertinent considerations. I think, therefore, I may say that the Lord is author to no man of wedding a wife to misery and distress. Before he do call him to marry he will let it appear unto him in reason how (at least by the diligent painfulness of his hand) he may yield to his wife a comfortable living in marriage. Not but that a poor man also may have both need of marriage and also allowance to marry. For God forbid that violence should be offered to the consciences of those of meaner estate by laying such a snare upon them, as if they might not lawfully enter into Matrimony because they be poor. But this we say still, that they must have some honest calling and will and ability to walk in the same faithfully, that reason may tell them, through God's blessing, there shall be something gotten to maintain a wife though not richly yet sufficiently and according to that rank. For it was never God's meaning that all should be rich, neither yet would he have any beggars that become penurious through their own folly, rashness, or idleness. Surely that counsel of Solomon, wherein he directeth a man first to prepare his business in the field and after to build his house (Prov. 24.27), must also be pertinent to the point we have in hand that, first, a man prepare how to maintain a wife, and after take her to him to build up his house. Otherwise the old proverb will prove true, that bare walls will make giddy housewives.[9]

Let not any man, through distrust of God's providence, deny himself the benefit of God's ordinance when his need requireth it for the subduing of otherwise unsubduable passions. But remember the words of the Apostle that it is better to marry than to burn (1 Cor. 7.9). Neither yet let any man so easily condescend to the desires of his own heart as hastily to adventure on matrimony till he have used all other due means of repressing such passions (watchfulness, abstinence, praying, fasting, and all earnest oppositions), when in reason he can give no sufficient answer to this demand (if his wife or her friends[10] should propound it to him, as they will if they be not foolish), how should we do to live when we be married?

I know that the over-covetous desire of elder people doth many times stand too much on such matters and cares not to thrust the younger upon miserable inconveniences, yea, mischiefs, through an unbelieving distrust and carnal fear of poverty. And I see on the other hand that the younger are apt to cast themselves upon such rocks for want of a due considering of such matters, as make them often times to make shipwreck of peace and quietness and a good conscience too. Wherefore let a due and indifferent course be followed here. Thou mayest please God in a poor estate and mayest afford a wife comfort in a meaner condition of life. But still somewhat there must be to live of, some calling, some trade, some labor, something that may promise that which God promiseth to the diligent, viz. that you shall be satisfied with bread (Prov. 20.13). So this duty must take up a good part of a man's thoughts before he be married that he may not bring his wife to the poor case of the silly hen that then likely hath her nest to seek when she should lay her first egg. And (after the contract of marriage) he must still continue to enlarge his mind with these thoughts, often looking to it that his wife may want nothing needful for her. Is it not a sign of an improvident head when the body goes naked and is half hunger-starved? Surely, we may say well that there is but little wisdom in the head that takes no better order for the body's content and comfort. And doubtless one may with as much truth conclude that there is as little love and wisdom in that husband who (to save charges) regards not how miserably his wife doth live with him, or (for fear of being poor, by using what God hath given him) will force a poverty upon himself without cause and make his wife at least needy (as it were) whether God will or no. Wherefore let each husband's heart be convinced that it is his duty to allow his wife all convenient maintenance, and not to think himself so absolutely Lord of all but that his wife must also enjoy the comfortable use of all.

It is one of the good housewife's praises that she doth give her portion to her maids. And shall the husband be worse to her than she should be to her maidservants? Yea, it is said that her servants shall not need to fear the cold of winter because they are clothed with double attire, and shall he suffer her to be in fear of the cold of winter or any other like misery for want of due clothing and other provision. Doubtless, brethren, it ought not so to be. No heart is able to justify (before God and its own serious considerations) such carelessness or such niggardice. Nay, rather, we must all take counsel of Solomon in this case, who speaking (it seemeth) to the husband minds him of his duty with this exhortation, saying, "Give her of the fruit of her hands" (Prov. 31.31). You will say, perhaps, that Solomon speaks of good housewives that will take pains and use diligence, but your wives are idle and ill housewives. I answer that I would be loath to plead the cause of waste-goods and slow-backs that give themselves to idleness and misspending. But first I say unto thee, take heed that thou beest not a slanderer of thy yoke-fellow, by seeking to justify thy niggardice with casting false imputations of idleness and unhousewifeliness upon her, as I am sure many a man doth. Is she not sickly, is she not weak? Hath she not breeding and bearing and looking to thy children to employ her? Are these no works? Is this no service? Must she over and above earn her living and make account of her gettings? And shall she be intwitted[11] with idleness if she do not? Thou art an unreasonable man and a false accuser to lay so heavy burdens and so untrue accusations upon thy poor wife's back. And assure thyself that now thou shalt answer to God for a double fault, one for denying thy wife her fit allowance, another for becoming her unjust accuser and her rigorous taskmaster.

But secondly I say unto thee, if she be not over-housewifely what hath been the cause of it? Hath not thine hard usage discouraged her? Hath not thine unreasonableness put her out of heart? Wilt thou tire a body with over-hard exactions and make them unable to do anything through grieving and lamenting at thine hoggishness, and then complain that she is idle? God will never brook these wicked and hard proceedings of a husband towards a wife, and thou shalt not wind thyself out of his hand by giving out such trifling excuses. Wherefore turn thy thoughts back to Solomon's words and give thy wife of the fruit of her hands, that if she be painful she may be encouraged to continue, if not she may be induced to begin, and that her heart may not prompt her with that desperate objection, as good play for nothing as work for nothing. For whatever she do or save, thou art almost still in one tune.

But we must also direct the husband in this part of his duty by showing him three necessary things: first, the measure; secondly, the manner; thirdly, the times and seasons of this his allowance. For the first, two things must measure out her expenses as well as his own, and those are his place and his means. So far as his calling requireth and his ability will bear, so far and no further must he extend his cost in attire and other necessaries for his wife. Not either of these but both these must be advised withal. For sometimes a man's place, in regard of his blood or birth or function in the commonweal, would well brook more than his decayed estate (perhaps by some cross, perhaps by his own former indiscretion, perhaps by the thriftlessness of his predecessors, pulled lower than it needed to have been) will well suffer. Here now, it should be a sin in a man to strive to maintain his wife to the utmost of his place and a sin in her to require such maintenance. For if God do empty Naomi of former blessings, she must willingly embrace the name of Mara and let the fairer name of Naomi go (Ruth 1.20).

Indeed, the wealthiest in any place ought to keep in the rearward (for one fool in this case, according to the proverb, will make many), and all should learn to equal themselves with them of the low sort. But the poorest in any place should (most of all) take heed of making a bragging show of abundance when they have little. Yea, rather, by abating somewhat of that their place would call for, they should help to provide timber, as it were, to build up the decayed places of their estate. For this let every man be sure of, the back and the belly are the worst borrowers for they will never repay; all is lost that they owe to any man. But they be the best lenders for they will never arrest a man, nor exact a repayment; all is clearly given and gained that is borrowed from them.

Again, sometimes a man's means can bear the cost of far exceeding his place, God having increased his wealth beyond the common condition of those of his rank, as many a Yeoman is far wealthier than some Justices of the Peace that dwell near him. Yet neither here is it lawful for him to lay it on upon his wife according as his purse would bear, but he must moderate his ability by his place. For doubtless, one principal end of the difference of attire is to represent the differences of men's callings. And even as in eating a man must not fill his belly according to the fullness of the dishes that stand on his table and according to the store and variety of food provided, but proportion his food to his stomach and to his health, so for attire also a man must not frame his costs about it to the quantity of money that is in his purse, but make it suitable to the calling and place wherein the Lord hath set him. I confess, that those which in any rank are of the most wealthy may be more abundant than those that in the same rank are more penurious. And yet doubtless it shall be more commendable for them to give a pattern of due parsimony and moderation than to go before others in costliness, because of the danger that may ensue through the unwarrantable imitation of some that will be apish (because they be not reasonable). But they must still remember to contain themselves within their places and not to make ostentation of their wealth by raising themselves higher, as if a man should go upon stilts to make his body seem taller.

Now, according to these rules, must every loving husband afford his wife that that she desires. She must be made an equal partner of that which God hath given to both, and if her own understanding will serve her (as the proverb hath it) to cut her coat according to her cloth, she must not be scanted by niggardice, neither must the husband deny her her lawful liberty. But if her fondness and vanity be such that she will needs exceed either one or both of these, either going a hunting after the fashion, or vying with some other (as indiscreet a body as herself) who shall be finest or the like, then doubtless the authority and discretion of the husband must sound retreat to her pride and lavishness. He must neither weaken his own estate, nor discredit his own name, nor give an offence to other, nor suffer her to pull reproach upon herself and misery upon her family by over-pranking her carcass, or over-much care to satisfy a sweet tooth and a disorderly appetite.

You see now in what quantity the wife's allowance must be given. Consider also in what manner, and that must be most willingly, cheerfully, readily. Before she asketh he must answer, and offer before she request. The greatest commendation of a gift is the giver's cheerfulness, and the surest sign of cheerfulness is speed and expedition. One gift quickly and willingly bestowed is worth ten long waited for and (by violence of importunate entreaties) extorted at last. Our Saviour's exceeding promptness to give all spiritual things unto his Church must be a pattern to husbands of the like promptness to bestow necessaries on their wives. Love is bountiful, and bounty is a habit that frameth a man to give with ease and with facility. We see in what fashion the head and heart do communicate the vital and animal spirits unto all the members of the body. The passages betwixt are always open, and there is no need of violent drawing for the matter, they flow willingly and of their own accord. Doubtless, in such sort should the loving husband communicate all things unto his wife. And if obstructions grow betwixt the head and body to hinder such conveyance of spirits betwixt them, we know that great distempers will ensue in the body. So must the family needs grow very sick and ill at ease when the conveyance of bounty betwixt the husband and wife is hindered or stopped up.

The Scripture saith that if the Lord do give his son for us, how shall he not with him give us all things (Rom. 8.32). May not we say likewise that, if the husband give himself to his wife, how shall he not with himself give her also all other things? Unless perhaps he account himself less worth than other things, and therefore is willing to give himself, unwilling to give other things. The ungracious whoremaster is over-frank to the lewd woman that pleaseth his eye. She may command his money to the consumption of his estate that he may the better command her body to the destruction of both their souls. Shall not a husband shame to begrudge his wife things comfortable when neither his state shall be impaired, nor his soul endangered thereby? O, let matrimonial love be as able to command liberality as whorish and adulterous affections to procure prodigality. Let not thy wife be forced to beg and entreat, and beseech and crave, and (by many and importunate suits) to batter down the walls of thine unwillingness afore her words can enter to obtain her desires. It is a sign of enmity where no entrance is granted except it be forcibly procured. Yea, rather let her speeches find thine heart open to entertain them as the gates of the City to receive friends. Let her not, as it were, wrestle with thee to pull things fit for her out of thine hands, as if a man were to wrest weapons out of Samson's hands or (rather) as if one were to beat water out of a rock. But let her first word prevail, let her half motion be sufficient. Yea, let thy desire of gratifying her (without any further motion) serve the turn to make thee willing to show thine own love and to nourish hers. Do to her as God to his Saints, and willingly and abundantly give her all things to enjoy. And this do both whilest you live together and at thy decease also, if it fall out that thyself depart this world first. For so (which is the third thing I intended to speak of) there are two seasons in which the husband's bounty should declare itself: the first, during life; the second, after it.

The love of a husband must not die before himself, no nor with him. But the effects of it must survive him, and when himself is departed his bounty must be present with her, even after death. As the band of their matrimony is extended to the bounds of their natural life, so must the practice of liberality. Some husbands be rich in kindness towards their wives for a month or two or for a year or two. But their love is soon changed into a slight esteem of their wives by reason of satiety, so it ceaseth to be able to yield forth the fruits of a liberal maintenance. Let it not be so with any of you. Let not your younger times upbraid your elder with having been better than they. All virtues should grow in the growth of years, and chiefly charity, and charity to a man's wife most of all. The more service she hath performed, the more comfort she hath afforded, the more sons and daughters she hath travailed for, the more abundant should his affection be to her and the more open his hand. True virtues will strengthen themselves by exercise, and they be none other than counterfeits that grow weaker and weaker till at last they be not at all to be found. If one's liberality towards his wife be sincerely virtuous, it must needs be constant and increasing, and the longer he hath showed the more ready he must needs be to show because he hath taken pleasure and delight in showing it.

But as I said also, it must outlast death. When a man is now to leave this world he must not leave the care of his wife, but remember in the disposing of his goods to bequeath so full a part to her as may make it appear that he thinks not himself wholly dead so long as she (the one half of him) is alive. His love must not disgrace itself in the close of all. Friends show most kindness at parting, so should the husband if he be a true friend. Else what allowance he gave her all his lifetime shall not so much commend him as his niggardliness in the conclusion of his life will reproach him. It may well be thought that what he yielded then was rather for vainglory sake (in love of his own credit, or through her mere importunity and resolution to take a part whilst somewhat was stirring) than out of any love to his wife and true desire of her comfort, if in this last act he be not suitable to himself. Let no man therefore bequeath to the world a testimony of his own unloving affection to his wife by making his bequests to her scant and niggardly. If she be not an honest woman and a true wife, how can he think that the children of her body be his? If she be, can he forget the root and remember the branches?

You will say where doth the Scripture commend me to leave my wife a good portion when I die? I answer, so oft as you read of a dowry, so oft you have proofs of this point. For the dowry was a portion for the wife's maintenance whatever occasion should fall out. And when Solomon saith, "Give her of the fruits of her hands," do you think he meaneth so long as he liveth only? Must she not be thought to have interest into a liberal portion at his death also, seeing her need of things doth not end with his life? But in very deed the disposition of many husbands in this case is not alone blameworthy but also most ridiculous. Were it not that the provision of jointures and such like unalterable conveyances[12] do tie something to their wives, they should be very poor at the decease of their husbands. Their over-fond affection to their children eateth up the love of their wives, and in remembering too much that they be fathers they forget almost that there was a wife also, by whose means they were fathers. Therefore all is accounted too little that the children have, all too much that the mother of the children hath.

The objections of men in this case are fond and frivolous. I see (saith one) that widows misbestow themselves, and so shall some unthrifts come and spend what I have labored for? I answer, dost not thou see also some wise and discreet widows that so match themselves as their husbands' kindred receive credit and their husbands' children benefit by their second husbands? Why, then, wilt thou mistrust thy wife without cause and think that she will prove fond and indiscreet with some, not wise and prudent with others? Is it not a wrong to suspect the worst by another without a cause? But I answer again: seest thou not as many young men and women play the unthrifts and wastegoods as widows married to unthrifts and wastegoods? Seest thou not as many daughters for their portions' sake mismarried as widows? Shall a fear of thy wife's ill-doing hinder thee from showing thy love to her rather than fear of thy children's to them? To the fruit of thy wife's body thou art so charitable as to hope the best. Why shouldest thou not be so to her, whose fruit they be?

Wherefore, learn thou to commit future things to God's providence. He that will trouble himself about what may be done by his wife or children when he is dead shall show a great deal of folly in affecting the praise of too much wisdom. Do thou thy duty to both according as love and the bonds of matrimony do tie thee unto both, and let God dispose of both as seems good to him. It shall be one means of procuring his blessing if (ceasing to use such suspicious forecast) thou seek to do his will and put thy confidence in his goodness to order thy wife as well as thy children. Be therefore mindful that thou art a husband as well as a father, and leavest a mother of thy children as well as children of thy body. And let thy wife, even after thy death, enjoy such a part of thy substance as that she need not stand beholding to her children (that in all reason should have them beholding to her), and that she may live as becometh the widow of a husband of such an estate. Neither let thy wife's insinuations make thee sparinger[13] to thy children than is fit, nor let thy fondness to thy children make thee more regardless of thy wife than is fit. But be sure as thine estate is to let her have wherewithal to live like a mother, they like children. For doubtless, the wife hath wrong if her husband do not provide so for her that the children shall want occasion to despise her in her age.

And thus at last I am come to the end of the man's peculiar duties also, wherein you see how long I have been and that for two reasons. First, because more is required of him to whom the greater pre-eminence is given. And secondly, because his disorders are more hurtful, as the diseases of the head and the unframedness of the main wheel of the clock. But now I proceed to declare the wife's duty also, requesting the women amongst you to attend now with your best diligence.

Of the Wife's Peculiar Duties

The wife's special duty may fitly be referred to two heads. First, she must acknowledge her inferior tie. Secondly, she must carry herself as an inferior. First, then, every good woman must suffer herself to be convinced in judgment that she is not her husband's equal (yea, that her husband is her better by far), without which it is not possible there should be any contentment either in her heart or in her house. Where the woman stands upon terms of equality with her husband (much more if she will needs account herself his better) the very root of all good carriage is quite withered and the fountain thereof utterly dried up. Out of place, out of peace, and woe to those miserable aspiring shoulders which will not content themselves to take their room below the head.

Whosoever, therefore, doth desire or purpose to be a good wife or to live comfortably, let her set down this conclusion within her soul: mine husband is my superior, my better. He hath authority and rule over me. Nature hath given it him, having framed our bodies to tenderness, men's more to hardness. God hath given it him, saying to our first mother Eve, "Thy desire shall be subject to thine husband, and he shall rule over thee" (Gen. 3.16). His will I see to be made by God the tie and tether not of mine actions alone, but of my desires and wishes also. I will not strive against God and nature. Though my sin have made my place tedious, yet will I sure confess and hold the truth: mine husband is my superior, my better.

Unless the wife learn this lesson perfectly, if she have it not without book and at her fingers' ends (as we speak), if her very heart do not inwardly and thoroughly condescend unto it, there will be nothing betwixt them but wrangling, repining, striving, and a continual vying to be equal with him or above him. And so shall their life be nothing else but a very battle or a trying of masteries, a woeful living. And so much the rather should the woman yield the truth of this point, by how much it is more plainly proved by the word of God. For so sufficient, evident, and undeniable is the manifestation of God's will on this behalf that nothing but mere willfulness can oppose itself against it. It is obstinacy not ignorance and the peremptoriness of pride and stomach, not the weakness or insufficiency of judgment, that causeth any woman to make any question of this truth, viz. that her husband is the superior, she the inferior.

Is he not termed by the Apostle in this place, "the wife's head" (Eph. 5.23)? What can that metaphor import but an evident superiority? Is she not required to be subject unto him? How can that be demanded of any but an inferior? Little it is that may be said to the contrary, yet something willfulness will have to allege. "I am (thinketh some woman) of as good birth and parts as himself, perhaps better. My wealth, wit, parentage, before I met him, did equal or surpass him. And why should I count myself his inferior to whom I am no way inferior in gifts or sufficiencies?" First, I say unto thee, O woman, that a woman's chiefest ornament is lowliness of mind, which should cause her to maintain in herself a mean account of herself and of her own abilities. Self-love is a very partial Judge and easily over-prizeth things in oneself. It is not good trusting too much to one's own opinion of himself, seeing that the knowledge of our own wants is one most commendable part of our knowledge.

But let us grant for the time that in gifts thou art his better, having more wit and understanding, more readiness of speech, more dexterity of managing affairs, and whatsoever other good quality may be incident to a woman. Yet understand for answer that so may thy servant exceed thee as much as thou dost him. Hath not many a servant in the house more wit and understanding (and often times also more grace too) than master and dame put both together? Yet loath would the wife be (I think) that the servant should deny both her husband and herself the name of betters. Know, then, that a man may be superior in place and power to one to whom he is inferior in gifts and sufficiencies. And therefore know also that thou dost wickedly abuse the good parts that God hath given in seeking thence to infringe thine husband's superiority over thee. And better were it for a woman to be of mean capacity and slow wit, and every way simply qualified (so that she can put upon her the spirit of subjection), than to be adorned with all the good qualities of nature (for those of grace she cannot have so long as her pride is so predominant that it will not suffer her to see and confess this truth) and thereby be made self-conceited against her husband.

Wherefore, O thou wife, let thy best understanding be to understand (that, that makes for thy peace) that thine husband is by God made thy governor and ruler and thou his inferior, to be ruled by him. Though he be of meaner birth and of lesser wit, though he were of no wealth nor account in the world before thou didst marry him, yet after the tying of this knot

God will have thee subject, and thou must put upon thyself a willingness to confess thyself so to be. If thou demandest what reason is there for that, I answer there is no reason in that person that cannot see reason to stand to God's appointment in the ordering of higher or lower places. Hast thou any religion in thee if thou see no reason in this reason? It is fit it should be so because the Lord hath so appointed. This duty had so much more need to be pressed because though it be so plain as it cannot be denied, yet it is withal so hard that it can hardly be yielded unto. But unless the judgment be truly informed and soundly convinced of this point, the will and affections will never be kept in good order. Set it down therefore as a conclusion, not so much as once to be called into question: my husband is my better.

Secondly, the wife, being resolved that her place is the lower, must carry herself as an inferior. For it boots little to confess his authority in word if she frame not herself to submission in deed. Now, she shall testify her inferiority in Christian manner if she practice those two duties of reverence and subjection which are appropriated to the place of inferiors. First, for reverence, the wife owes as much of that to her husband as the children or servants do to her, yea, as they do to him. Only it is allowed that to her it be sweetened with more love and more familiarity. All inferiors owe reverence alike, neither must the wife be so erroneously conceited of her place as if she were less bound to reverence her husband than are the rest of the family. This alone is the difference: she may be more familiar not more rude, as being more dear not less subject than they.

And this reverence of hers must be both inward and outward. First, the heart of the wife must be held under, inwardly, with a dutiful respect of her husband. She must regard him as God's deputy, not looking to his person but to his place, nor thinking so much who and what a one he is as whose officer. This the Apostle strictly enjoyeth, saying, "Let the wife see that she fear her husband" (Eph. 5.33), as if he had said, of all things let her most carefully labor not to fail in this point of duty. For if she do, her whole carriage otherwise must needs be rude and unbeseeming. Now, you must know that the Apostle's meaning is to prescribe a fear (not slavish but loving) such as may well stand with the nearest union of hearts, as is to be seen betwixt Christ and his Church. This fear of the wife is, when (in consideration of his place) she doth abhor and shun it as the greatest evil than can befall her, next to the breach of God's commandments, to displease and offend her husband. We stand in due awe of God's Majesty when we loathe the breach of his commandment and grieving of his spirit as the greatest of all evils. And the wife doth duly fear her husband when, next to the former evil, she shuns the disobeying, grieving, and displeasing of her husband, who is next to God above her in the family. Such regard must her heart have of her head that it may keep her hand and tongue and all from disorder. A man fears a Bear lest he should do him mischief, and this fear is always joined with a desire of the ruin and hurt of the thing feared. But the reverence of inferiors is a fear mixed with love that rather flieth from the offence of the husband than from any hurt to be received from him.

I know this is not customable among the greater number of women. Yea, they scarce esteem it a seemly or a needful thing that it should be so. Yea, they care as little for their husbands as their husbands for them. Nay, they do altogether despise them, not regarding whether they be pleased yea or no. And some (instead of observing) have inverted the Apostle's precept, causing their husbands to stand in fear of them. This impudency and unwomanhood doth track the way to the harlot's house, giving all wise men to understand that such rude creatures either have or would or soon will cast off the care of honesty as well as of loyalty. But if thou wilt ever prove a virtuous wife, take much pains with thine heart to make it stand in awe of thine husband, and know that God hath not for naught given the former precise caveat unto women. As a woman grows in this inward respect, so may she look to get the better of all other infirmities; as she is careless herein, so shall she be pestered with all other enormities. Where the heart sets light by any, the words and actions will be contemptuous. If the fountain be muddied with contempt, so shall the streams also.

But how shall a woman bring her heart to this regardful disposition? I answer, by looking through her husband to God the author of marriage, and putting herself often in mind not of his deserts but of God's ordinance. If one consider an inferior officer (in himself), he cannot sometimes but disdain him for his meanness and evil qualities. If he consider him as the King's officer (entrusted with a part of that royal authority which is originally in the Prince), his great reverence to his Prince will produce also some reverence to his officer for his sake. The husband is to the wife the image and glory of God. The power that is given to him is God's originally and his by God's appointment. Look not therefore on the gifts and qualities of thine husband but upon his place, and know that thou canst not neglect or despise him but that the contempt redoundeth unto God's dishonor, who hath ordained him to be thine head. So if religion have seasoned thine heart with the fear of God, thou shalt fear thine husband also for his commandment sake.

But as the wife's heart must be affected with this loving fear, so must her outward carriage also savor thereof and show it forth, and that in two special things. First, in her words; secondly, in her gestures and behavior. Her words are either to himself in person, of him behind his back, or to others before him. All must have a taste of reverence. First, her speeches to himself must neither be cutted,[14] sharp, sullen, passionate, tetchy, nor yet rude, careless, unmannerly, and contemptuous, but all such as carry the stamp of fear upon them, testifying that she well considers who herself is and to whom she speaketh. The wife's tongue toward her husband must neither be keen nor loose, neither such as argues rage nor neglect, but savoring of all lowliness and quietness of affection that if another should stand by and hear them he might perceive (though he knew not otherwise) that these are the words of an inferior to her better. Look what kind of words thyself wouldest dislike from thy servant or child, those must not thou dare to give unto thine husband. For the same duty of fear is in the same words and in the same plainness commanded to thee that unto them.

Herein Sarah once faulted. She was aloft and in the boughs (as we speak). "Thou dost me wrong (saith she), and God be judge between me and thee" (Gen. 16.5). Herein also Rachel offended, that came to her husband fuming, and in a pelting chafe[15] must needs chide with him for children, saying, "Give me children or else I die." Though Jacob loved Rachel tenderly, yet (you know) he could not brook this rudeness without anger (for his wrath was kindled) and he said, "Am I in God's place, that hath denied to thee the fruit of the womb" (Gen. 30.1-2). Herein also Michal, Saul's daughter and David's wife, though a Queen yet was much out of the way. For she came scoffing and flouting to the King her husband (a thing of the two less tolerable than wrath and rage, because it shows a more allowed contempt) and, "How glorious (saith she) was the King of Israel this day, etc." (2 Sam. 6.20), when her husband, in her conceit[16] (though not indeed), had carried himself somewhat unfittingly for the place of a King. She cannot tell him of it in good and respective fashion but, with a bitter taunting, must needs break a jest upon him.

These examples tend to show how subject women are to disreverent passages of speech, and withal how loathsome and unwomanly they be. Yet for all these examples and warnings, we want not women (if the name of a woman be not wronged in giving it to such shameless creatures) that chase and scold with their husbands, railing upon them and reviling them, and shaking them up with such terms as were nothing sufferable towards a neighbor or towards a servant. Stains of womankind, blemishes of their sex, monsters in nature, botches of the family, rude, shameless, graceless, next to harlots if not the same with them. Let such words leave a blister behind them, and let the canker eat out such tongues.

And what remedy a husband should use for such a festering sore, we delivered you before. If patient forbearing and admonitions will not bring them to reformation, let the words of Solomon be harkened unto, "a rod is for the fool's back" (Prov. 26.3), and strike a scorner. Why this precept should be limited with any limitation tending to safeguard a scornful, foolish, graceless woman from the execution of it I can verily see no reason. Neither (I think) can any man render any. But besides these notorious ones, women, otherwise virtuous, must be content to be told of a fault in this behalf. They can sometimes take up their husbands with quick speeches sharply set on, they can set them down short with a cutted answer, and weary their ears with tumultuous brawling. Is this seemly for a Christian woman? Should a daughter of Sarah govern her tongue no better? Why wilt thou teach thy children to be rebellious and show thy servants the trade of swelling, fuming, and rudeness? Thinkest thou that such behavior is not infectious? Shall not they use it to thee when they see thee use it to thine husband? Or is it more tolerable in them to thyself than in thee to thine head? Set not those of thy family so bad a copy. Teach them rather that reverent and dutiful carriage which thou wouldst have them practice to thyself. For be sure the woman shall make herself vile that sets her husband at naught. And those that abuse their superiors do but embolden their inferiors to pay themselves home with the like abuse.

Yea, do not you good women alone forbear these fumish speeches, savoring of passion, which cannot stand with reverence, but beware also of words that through their overfamiliarness may bewray contempt, seeing the proverb saith true, that too much familiarity will breed contempt. I told you before that it was the privilege of a wife (because of her dearness) that she may be familiar. But yet I have observed an excess of familiarness that in my conceit deserveth to be blamed. For why? It seems to bewray a forgetfulness of reverence and inferiority. A woman of sixty or seventy years old could be well content to have her married daughter (now made the mother also of children) to be familiar with her, yea, she desireth her familiarity and would not have her strange. But yet she could not choose but count it stranger than all strangeness if her daughter should speak to her in such a familiar language as this, "Good Besse," or "Good Nell," or "Good Meg, do such or such a thing for me." And why then should a woman bear herself so overbold of her husband's kindness as to nickname him with those nicknames of familiarity, Tom, Dick, Ned, Will, Jack, or the like, as I have heard good wives do, but (I confess) with a manifest distasting of their rudeness in that behalf. For could a woman speak otherwise to her child or servant (if she would speak in a phrase that should show herself well pleased) than in such kind of abbreviated names as these are? Certainly, any woman's love must be tempered with fear, and those speeches of hers which would show kindness must also have a print of reverence upon them, or else they be not allowable. Wherefore, let good wives be taught (in speaking to their husbands) to learn of her that called her husband by an honorable name. Leave Tom and Dick to call thy boy by, and call thine husband, husband or some other name of equal dignity to that. And thus must a woman's tongue be ordered towards her husband when she speaks to him.

She must also look to her speeches directed to others in his presence, that they be such and so framed as may witness a due regard of him. His company must make her more respective of her behavior to any other before him than otherwise she need to be. Her words to children and servants in his sight and hearing ought not to be loud and snappish. If she perceive a fault in them she must yet remember that her better stands by and therefore must not speak but upon necessity, and then utter that reproof in a more still and mild manner which, in his absence, she might set on with more roundness. No woman of government will allow her children and servants to be loud and brawling before her, and shall she herself be so before her husband? What then is become of the remembrance of inferiority? Nay, verily, this reverence doth enjoin the woman's silence when her husband is present. I mean not an utter abstinence from speech but using fewer words (and those mild and low), not loud and eager. The Apostle commands the woman to be in silence or in quietness, wherein he enjoins not alone a public but a general silence to hold in the house and other private meetings (1 Tim. 2.11-12). For why should that place of Scripture be needlessly restrained which is fitly capable of a larger interpretation. The reason of which duty is grounded even upon the consideration of the two sexes. For even as youth is inferior to age, and young folk to the aged (that is to say, such as do so far exceed them in years that in course of nature they might be parents unto them, for otherwise two or three years difference of age doth not make this distinction), so likewise is the male sex preferred before the female in degree of place and in dignity, as all will yield that consider the words of the Scripture in that behalf. For the woman was made for man and not man for the woman. He is the image and glory of God, she is his image and his glory. And nature hath given her her hair for a covering, as a natural badge of this her inferiority to the man, whom also God made in the first place that he might thereby make known his mind of giving that sex the first place (1 Cor. 11.3-15).

I confess that in differences of this kind (which are not joined with power of ruling and obeying), other respects may fall out to overbalance that difference which ariseth from age, sex, gifts, or the like. As a younger man may be in authority, an elder man may be in a private estate, and then is this inferiority after a sort shadowed and obscured, yet not so but that some respect must be had to it though not so much. And so a woman, in other respects preferred before a man, may, in regard of such incidental considerations, take leave to be less heedful of that inferiority which comes unto her with her sex and in regard of it (as a mistress in her carriage to her manservant), but yet still there must be some respect had to this difference, which God and nature have made. And if in anything this inferiority be to be acknowledged, then doubtless in this particular whereof we are speaking, than which there cannot be a less nor yet a fitter demonstration of it, and which is also required of younger people towards their ancients (if other things do also agree) to abstain from many and high words, and to speak little and low before them.

Wherefore, let women either excuse chat and loudness in youth before their ancients, or in their children and servants before them. Or else let them condemn it in themselves before their husbands, and not alone so but before men in general. I know this duty goes against the hair,[17] and there are but a very few women that can persuade themselves to show their thoughts of inferiority by fewness of words. For where is suddenness of wit and scarcity of wisdom (as in the greater number of this sex comparatively), there is likely forwardness to speak and multitude of words. But at all times, amongst all wise folks, the talkativeness of women before men (chiefly their husbands and most of all when it comes to loud and earnest speaking) hath gone in the reckoning of a fault and a sign of self-conceitedness and indiscretion. And contrarily, silence hath been highly accounted of as a comely ornament to that sex, who then are best like and most worthy to be liked when they show least liking of themselves by not loving to hear themselves speak. You know of what woman it was of whom Solomon saith, "She is loud and stubborn," and again, "She is clamorous" (Prov. 7.11. and 9.13).[18] Doubtless, a simple woman holding her peace shall have more honor than one of more wit if she be full of tongue. Wherefore let womankind learn silence (this is one part of the quietness of spirit commended to them by Peter [1 Pet. 3.4]), and suffer the due and reverent esteem of their husbands to work in them a special moderation of speech whilst they be in place.

And thirdly, the woman's speeches of her husband behind his back must be dutiful and respective. She must not talk of him with a kind of carelessness or slightness of speech, much less with despiteful and reproachful terms. Herein the godly fact of Sarah is commended to our imitation and must be put in practice. When she but thought of her husband in the absence of all company she did reverently entitle him by the name of "my Lord" (1 Pet. 3.6). If in her private she gave him so good and honorable a title, what should she have done in company? What in his own presence? What unto himself? So must women inure themselves to submissiveness in thoughts and speeches in their husbands' absence, that they may the better practice the same in their presence. For great is the force of custom in this matter. Who would brook a child speaking disgracefully and murmuringly against his own father, though behind his back? And shall it be thought sufferable in a wife? By how much there is more certain trial of her inward affection and disposition in such case, by so much ought she to be more attentive to her words. Very dread may force a woman to give good words unto her husband, because neither will he brook, neither doth she dare to do any other. But this demonstrateth a right conscionable respect, when she will not think or speak of him (though he be far from hearing or knowing it) without some note of good regard, that those which hear may perceive she doth account him her governor and better. He that allows not an evil thought of the Prince will not allow evil speeches of the husband in private talk between neighbors. For he is the

Prince of the household, the domestical King. Wherefore, though thine husband be far from thee, yet let thy fear of him be present with thee, that in mentioning of him to others thou bewray not a contempt of him in thyself. And thus must a woman's words be ordered towards her husband.

Something also must be spoken of her gestures and countenances, which as well as her words must be mixed with reverence and have a taste of fear. Both good and bad dispositions have more ways of uttering themselves than by the tongue. Solomon speaketh of an eye that despiseth the mother (Prov. 30.17). Surely, then, the eye also of the wife may be a despising eye, and her whole behavior with the gestures of her whole body may proclaim contempt though her tongue be altogether silent. Now, these also must be looked unto that they may not discover a base esteem of the husband. And as the bar of reverence must hold the tongue so fast in that no speeches may have licence to go abroad but those that are clad in the livery of dutifulness, so likewise must the other parts of her body, the eye, the brow, the nostrils, the hands, the feet, the shoulders, be kept in so good order by the governance of the same virtue that they may not prove as injurious and harmful as almost the worst words could do. To swell and pout, to lower and scowl, to huff and puff, to frown and fume, to turn the side towards him and fling away from him in a mixture of sullenness and disdain, be things that do break the bridle of fear and tread down the mounds of reverence so plainly that far should it be from a virtuous woman, and one that would have her conscience bear her witness that her chaste conversation is coupled with fear, so much to misdemean herself towards her husband upon any occasion. These rude and contemptuous behaviors are no less uncomely in an inferior, and do no less displease and discontent a superior to whom they are practiced than the most fierce and outrageous speeches would do. Wherefore, as herself will condemn these in her children or maidens towards herself, so let her by no means allow them in herself against her husband, towards whom the Lord hath bound her as well to practice reverence and fear as any of her inferiors unto her. For still it must be pressed upon the hearts of wives that familiarity is allowed them but no rudeness. And of reverence, the woman's first duty, so much.

Her second special duty is subjection, of which it followeth to speak. Now, that hath also two parts. The first is obedience to her husband's commandments; the second is submission to his reproofs or corrections. For the first, the Apostle doth plainly give it in charge to women, saying, "Let the wife be subject to her husband in all things" (Eph. 5.24). What need we further proof? Why is she his wife if she will not obey him? And how can she in his name require obedience of the children and servants, if herself refuse to yield it unto him? For doubtless she can exact it none otherwise than as deputy and a substitute under him. But the thing itself will not be so much questioned as the measure. Not whether a wife must obey, but how far her obedience must extend is usually called into question. To which doubt the Apostle hath yielded us a most plain and satisfactory resolution, saying, in all things in the Lord (Col. 3.18). Obedience (you see) must be general alone, so that it be in the Lord. In whatsoever matters a woman's yielding to her husband shall not prove a rebellion against her maker, in that matter she is bound in conscience to yield unto him without any further question.

For, indeed, it were better for the husband that she were left at her own liberty in all things than not in all things tied to obedience. This service will be troublesome and thankless if it be not universal. To be obsequious alone in things that please her own affections is not to obey her husband but herself. The true touchstone of obedience is a thing commanded that crosseth her desires. For what praise can it be to do what he biddeth if she would have done it though he had never bidden. But this evinceth hearty and conscionable subjection, when she crosseth her own desires to fulfill his and chooseth to do what herself would not because her husband wills it. And seeing she requireth a like largeness of duty from the servants in his name, herself shall be judge against herself if she do not readily give what she earnestly looketh to receive.

And doubtless, it were much more troublesome to have authority over a wife, otherwise than so limited or straitened, than to have no authority at all over her. If a husband might not command his wife in all lawful things, it were more for his peace and for hers and for all the family's that he might command her in nothing. For seeing there is no umpire at hand to decide the controversy betwixt them (in what things he may command, in what not), the very doubtfulness will make her bold to gainsay in anything wherein she is not willing of herself to obey. Thus more words should be spent and more labor and time bestowed in disputing the question whether in this and this she be bound to obey than all her obedience may possibly be worth. For this cause, the Lord of heaven, whose wisdom foresaw that his authority would be worth nothing if it were not of this extent, hath pleased to put it out of all controversy by giving him as great a largeness of power as might be, so that his own royal prerogative of being Lord of all and above all might not be crossed and impeached thereby.

I confess, a man is bound to look to more points than the lawfulness of the thing by him commanded, but this is the only thing to which the wife must bend her thoughts. In lawful things she may gently dissuade if she perceive them otherwise inconvenient, but in nothing may she refuse his commandment unless it be unlawful. Neither yet sufficeth it that her obedience do reach to all lawful things, unless it be also performed willingly, readily, quietly, cheerfully, without brawling, contending, thwarting, sourness. A good work may be marred (you know) by an ill manner of doing it, as good stuff maybe spoiled by the bungerly[19] making.

The wife shall utterly disgrace and disfigure her obedience if she repine and hang off, and grow impatient and show choler, and will not till she cannot choose. Needs must, needs shall (saith the proverb). Thankless is all obedience if it be compelled. Nay, indeed, it is not obedience if force do draw alone the outward man, and the will itself do not of itself submit itself. Such yieldance declareth no reverence, nor deserveth any praise. But then is obedience laudable and becomes a note of a virtuous woman and a dutiful wife when, of her own accord in a conscionable acknowledgment of her duty, she comes on herself voluntarily and without urging, even as a well-broken horse that seems to have but one soul with the rider, so readily doth he stop or turn or go with the hand of him that moves the bridle. Wherefore, if you will have your obedience worth anything, make no tumult about it outwardly, allow none within.

And thus now you have heard the first part of subjection, obedience, a duty which (I doubt not) seemeth hard enough to womankind. For it is a yoke laid upon them in their creation, which also since their fall hath been made cumbersome and so they are ever loath to bear it. But the second part of subjection is yet more hard and withal equally, if not more, needful, that is, submission in receiving reproofs and (if need be also) corrections from their husbands. As she must willingly obey all his lawful commandments, so must she patiently suffer all his reprehensions and corrections. Is not this duty plainly required in those words, "As the Church is subject to Christ, so must also the wives to their own husbands in everything" (Eph. 5.24)? Doubtless, to brook reproofs and corrections is a necessary part of the Church's subjection unto Christ, neither shall it discharge its duty in striving to obey unless, where it faileth, it be content to be chidden. And if the failings be (as oft they be) palpable, to be chastised also. Wherefore, it is impossible for women to lose their consciences from the bond of this part of subjection unless they could show (which they shall never be able to show) some other text of Scripture, limiting and abridging this generality and exempting them from suffering.

Indeed, this is an uncouth point, and that which scarce one woman of a thousand will grant to be needful for her or required of her. For corrupt nature hath no more ready means of pulling their necks from under the yoke of difficult duties than by a bold and crafty denying them to be duties. But it shall be in vain to cavil against evident proof. It is most undeniably plain that patient suffering is one part of subjection to authority, and therefore ties the conscience of every woman towards her husband as well as doth the other part, (I mean) obedience. With as much safety and reason may she refuse the one as the other, whatever be said to the contrary by some men also, who strive to nourish women in this error of thinking that they be not bound to patience, as if they knew not how of themselves to be careless enough of their duty. Nature is full of pride, and pride aboundeth in impatiency. We would not seem to be faulty and therefore cannot endure to be told of a fault in any fashion. But with authority to be reprehended for it, which properly we call chiding, who can brook it? By how much it is more difficult, by so much it is more praiseworthy. We must not dispense with ourselves in hard and troublesome duties but show that we make more account of God our Maker than of ourselves, by bowing under the heaviest burdens and buckling ourselves to the toughest labors that he doth call us unto.

And yet, perhaps many women may be content to yield that it is their duty to submit themselves to sharp words and not to think scorn to be chidden by their husbands. Only for corrections, for blows, here will be a world of gainsaying. What woman will be persuaded to think that it is her duty to take them at her husband's hands? Yet, doubtless, she cannot say she hath followed the Apostle's direction of being subject in everything, if she frame not herself to be subject also in this thing. I confess that the nearness of this society is such as maketh women to expect all kindness and nothing but kindness. And hence it is that she cannot away with anything that may savor of unkindness. But if her expectations be crossed and she meet with that that she doth not look for, the God of heaven (the commander of a general subjection) will never allow her to cast off this yoke of subjection. I confess also that a good wife should even promise herself freedom from blows at her husband's hands. For why? She should resolve never to break forth into such exorbitant carriage as may justly challenge blows. But yet withal she must be of this mind: if mine husband have just cause through my rudeness and unwifelike behavior to strike me, I will take it well and see and mend my rudeness. Yea, if he strike me causelessly and in mere passion, I will take it quietly and not suffer myself to break forth into rebellious and contemptuous words and gestures.

For this also must be diligently considered of, that some reproofs and corrections are just and causeful, even such as the faultiness of an inferior doth deserve and call for. Some again are causeless and unjust, such as the superior's passion and distemper doth give without any fault at all of the inferior, or any so great fault as deserveth so much sharpness. Now, the former kind of reproofs and blows if the wife receive, she must thank herself, and not alone be patient under them but careful also to receive them fruitfully, making conscience to reform the faults that have procured them. For to be of so desperate a mind in evil doing as to resolve that chiding and striking shall never mend her, but that she will prove worse rather than better by such means, is a thing that declareth so great a predominancy of sin as whosoever nourisheth herself in that resolution doth utterly forfeit the name of a true Christian wife. The sore is uncurably deadly that grows sorer by fit plasters, and that woman's soul is stark naught and sold under sin that will wax more sinful because she is used for her sins according to her deserts.

But if any wife have met with a husband so foolish and passionate that he will give her reproofs or chastisements of the latter kind, yet must she determine to bear them meekly and quietly without allowing herself to break forth into any sour, froward, and undutiful behavior. For she is to remember that Saint Peter saith, "A woman of a meek and quiet spirit is much set by of God."[20] And that meekness and quietness is not worthy the name of meekness and quietness which can only then be quiet when no cause is offered unto it of unquietness by hard and unjust usage. A sleeping Lion will not roar, a sleeping Bear will not bite. But this is meekness to keep the soul calm when passions are, as it were, stirred and wakened by wrongful and unjust usage. And surely Saint Peter is plain in this point. If we be beaten for our faults and do bear it patiently, that, in his judgment, is scarce praiseworthy. But if we suffer for well-doing and take it patiently, this is a matter of true commendation (1 Pet. 2.20).

It must be granted to be a thing full of difficulty, to endure patiently the rage of a furious husband that will brawl and fight without cause, and carry himself like a mad man, and perhaps add drunkenness to his passionateness to make him more passionate. But still we must remember that this is no more difficult than divers other duties in other cases required of a Christian, and that it is no excuse from our duties, in any case, to say it is hard and who can do it? God giveth liberal wages and therefore may well call for hard works. Most times women are ready to think in such cases that they may lawfully take leave to depart from their husbands. But Paul saith plainly, no, let not the woman depart from her husband, speaking of the believing wife of an unbelieving husband, who no doubt did many of them receive much hard measure and like enough also stripes and blows from their infidel husbands (1 Cor. 7.10). Wherefore, if a woman be so yoked, she must keep her place and show patience. It is not for a prisoner to break prison at his pleasure because he hath met with a rough Jailer. If God have made thine house thy dungeon, thine husband thy Jailer, yet thou must not seek to make an escape till he deliver thee out that put thee in.

You will say (perhaps) that then a wife's case is most miserable. I answer that so it is indeed, but yet no more miserable than of a godly child living under the roof of a tyrannical and wicked father, and of a godly bondman being under the yoke of a wicked and furious master, and of Christian subjects living under the yoke of an unchristian and persecuting tyrant, which yet must none of them save themselves by rebellion, nor some of them by flight. It is yielded that a woman may herein use the help of her friends, by their means to bend her husband to more mildness. Yea, she may crave aid of the Magistrate, and seek to them that must rule both in public to compel him (by fit means) to rule her better in private. But to run away from him, or to strike again, or to chide and scold, that she may not do, for that can never agree with subjection which God requireth at her hands.

If it be said that some men are so violent as the wife may be in danger to have her brains knocked out, and may she not refuse to dwell with such a one? The answer is she may decline the present brunt but she may not forsake the matrimonial society. She may fly to the Magistrate and seek safety with a purpose of returning upon such security. But she may not flee quite away from him, with a purpose of not returning. For as it is no warrant for a soldier to quit his standing because the case falls out so that he must either die or leave it, so neither must a Christian in any place depart from his place for fear of death. For how can one spend his life better than in keeping the place where God hath set him, or die with more comfort than when he knows that in losing his life he shall find it, because he chooseth rather to lose it in doing his duty than to save it by omission thereof. If any take up the objection of the disciples on this occasion, saying for the woman's part as they did for the man's upon another occasion, that then it were better for a woman never to marry (Matt. 19.10), I answer that I think so too than to marry with such a husband.

Wherefore, it should teach both maidens and parents great wariness in making their choice. But when the choice is made, it is evil redressing the inconveniences of an evil choice by sinning against God in impatiency or desertion of the place. Yea, this one argument of patient bearing should be earnestly pressed upon the consciences of women fearing God, because there is no surer means of winning their husbands from such fierceness nor of procuring to themselves an excellent measure of favor from God here and glory hereafter than by such quiet enduring of causeless hardness. For if an unbeliever may be won from infidelity to Christianity by the wife's chaste behavior united with fear, how much more may she hope to win him from unreasonableness and violence to reason and justice by the like carriage? And doubtless if that follow not, yet shall she find that Peter did not say in vain, "A woman of a quiet spirit is much set by of God." But as for the other courses of setting hard to hard and resisting violence by violence, or of departing from him with whom she lives so weary a life, the former of these shall but more exasperate him and God too against her, causing that she shall have a raging conscience as well as a raging husband. The latter shall leave her in the case of one that hath broken prison, whom the Magistrate will pursue and take and put him in a harder prison, with more gyves[21] after than before. So shall she bring a heavier hand of God upon her by not accepting the chastisement wherewith he pleaseth to try her. And so you have heard the duties of man and wife, principal and less principal, mutual and special, both to him and also to her. Now, though I have been long already, yet I shall take leave to make some use of all, but very briefly.

Containing Some Application of All

And first, this ministers a good instruction to young and unmarried people, that they do not unadvisedly rush into this estate. A thing of such difficulty should not be lightly undertaken. They shall have their hands full of duty if they get not their hearts full of grace and their heads full of wisdom. They shall find a house full of trouble and a life full of woe, meeting with gall instead of honey and gravel instead of nourishing morsels. Wouldst thou be married? See what wisdom, what patience, what grace fit to govern or fit to obey thou findest in thyself. Get these against thou come to use them, or else marriage will not yield thee such contentment as thine imagination promiseth. Vain youths grow wanton and fall in lust, and must marry before they have any power to practice, any understanding to know their duties. So they trouble themselves and discredit their estate both at once. He that leaps over a broad ditch with a short staff shall fall into the midst. And he that enters upon matrimony without care to attain great grace shall be mired and doused in disquietment and vexation. Let unmarried people think of this and be wise.

Secondly, I must advise all married persons to grow acquainted with these duties and to mark their failings in the same. But mistake me not. I would that the wife should know hers, the husband his, and both the common duties. I desire that they should observe each their own, not so much each other's failings. Indeed, it may be feared that divers hearers now will be worse for hearing because they heard amiss. The husband may perhaps ring his wife a peal of her duty when he comes home and tell her how her faults were ripped up, and yet never consider or meditate of his own duties or faults. The wife also may likely tell him of his own at home, when she hath little or nothing to say to herself. Thus both shall be worse when they seek to upbraid each other, not to amend each one's self.

Thou, husband, didst listen attentively when the woman's duties were handled and thoughtst, "There he met with my wife. Such a time she showed little reverence, less obedience." Thou, wife, hadst the like thoughts concerning thine husband: "There he told him home of his duty. It is not long since he showed himself neither wise nor gentle. I would he would see to amend." Unwise man, unwise woman. Why hadst thou not most care of thine own soul? Couldst thou mark what was good for another's disease, not what for thine own? Wilt thou grow skillful in his way and not know one foot of that wherein thyself must travel?

Brethren, sisters, let this be altered in us. If thou be a Christian husband, have more care to know that and be more frequent in considering that for which thine soul must answer than what lies to the accounts of another. So do thou that art a Christian wife. And that man or woman that sees not more faults and failings in him or herself than the yoke-fellow bewrays wondrous great pride, ignorance, and hypocrisy, if he or she be not matched with one too too notorious for ill demeanors. If the heart were well touched its own sins would be more grievous, the husband's or wife's less. Contend, therefore, not how short thy yoke-fellow comes but not to come short thyself. Pass by the other's failings more easily, be more censorious towards thine own. This were to deal as a Christian, even to judge thyself. He never yet learnt to work well in any work that would cast his eye more upon his neighbor's fingers than his own. Neither was he ever good scholar that would con[22] his fellows and not regard the task imposed upon himself. And that makes husbands and wives such ill paymasters one to another, because they look often what is owing to them not what they owe.

I doubt not but experience will back my speech if I pronounce that they be not the best husbands and wives which are heard to complain much of their yoke-fellows' defects in duty, little of their own. And yet is not this ordinary? Every man would be a good husband if his wife were not so bad, and she a good wife were not he so excessively faulty. All the accusations, all the judgings, are darted at each other. What folly is this? Understand, idle man and woman, that it is not the requiring or receiving of duty from others but the knowing and performing of what pertains to thyself that will prove thee a Christian, comfort thee in temptation, rejoice thee in death, and stand for thee in judgment. And yet art thou so loud and much in calling for duty, so mute and dumb and ignorant in yielding it?

To conclude, therefore, know thine own duty best, mark most thine own transgressions of duty. Then shalt thou be free from brawls with thy yoke-fellow if thou be taken up with pains about thyself. And there is no better means of peace in families than that everyone should learn and ply his own work, see and labor to mend his own faults. Have you then been, both or either, unchaste, unloving, unfaithful? Repent both, and strain not courtesy who shall begin. But let either set other a copy of goodness. And if you will needs strive, let it be which shall be the best, which mend first. Hast thou been a foolish, passionate, unjust husband, full of bitter words, perhaps also (which is monstrous) of blows given causelessly and in anger, seeking and serving thyself alone, and not regarding thy wife's good so thou mightest go away with thine own will? Dive not into her faults, cry not out, she hath been thus and thus to me. But repent of thy bitterness, unthriftiness, folly of all sorts. Confess it to God. Beseech him to make thee a better husband that thy wife may be better. Hast thou been a disdainful, contemptuous, brawling, impatient, discontented, and disobedient wife? Ask thine heart before God and dissemble not. If yea, clamor not against thine husband's folly, exclaim not of his rashness and hardness, but condemn thyself before, and call upon God to make thee fear and obey thine husband as a

Commander under him. Entreat him of mercy to make thee better that thy husband also may be better. Follow the Proverb, and let every of you mend one, I mean himself, and contention will cease. Pray for each one's self first, then for each other. Where you have offended, labor to see it, confess, bewail it, and call for power to reform, and be not skillful to cast the fault upon another but to cast it out of thyself. So shall your loves be sure, your hearts comfortable, your example commendable, your houses peaceable, yourselves joyful, your lives cheerful, your deaths blessed, and your memories happy forever.

NOTES

1. Gall: bile; wormwood: a plant proverbial for its bitter taste; coloquintida: a type of bitter apple.
2. Plant with bitter juice.
3. Seneca, quoting Accius, in *On Anger* 1.20.4.
4. Gutters, drains.
5. For example, Prov. 14.24.
6. Unceasing.
7. Burnt or infected (inflamed).
8. The comparison combines references to Ps. 45.13-14 and Song Sol. 4.1-5.
9. Cited from *Remains of a Greater Work Concerning Britain* (1614) by William Camden.
10. Relatives.
11. Reproached, upbraided.
12. Jointures: estates settled on a woman during marriage arrangements, to be hers after the husband's death; conveyances: documents effecting property transfers from one person to another.
13. More sparing.
14. Insulting or sarcastic.
15. Petty temper.
16. Conception or viewpoint.
17. Against the grain.
18. First, of a harlot, and then of a foolish woman.
19. Bungled.
20. Whately seems to be slightly misquoting 1 Pet. 3.1-4.
21. Fetters.
22. Study.

Midwifery

CHAPTER 13

The Birth of Mankind
Eucharius Roesslin

The Elizabethan *Book of Common Prayer* included a service for women to offer thanksgiving after childbirth. The ceremony, called the "churching of women," was held some weeks after the delivery and required the mother to "give hearty thanks unto God" who had given "safe deliverance" and "preserved [her] in the great danger of Childbirth." At the end of the service, the congregation likewise offered thanks "for that thou hast vouchsafed to deliver this woman thy servant from the great pain and peril of Child-birth." The dangers alluded to in the churching were symbolic and physical. The trials of giving birth and raising a child might strain one's faith, while the hazards of delivery and recovery could be life-threatening, with the maternal mortality rate possibly as high as twenty-five per thousand through the sixteenth and seventeenth centuries (Eccles 125).

Medical knowledge in the sixteenth century was based on the work of classical writers, with Galen, Hippocrates, and Aristotle being considered the chief sources. Woman was broadly regarded as an imperfect version of man: "Because of lack of heat in generation, her sexual organs have remained internal, she is incomplete, colder and moister in dominant humours, and unable to 'concoct' perfect semen from blood" (Maclean 31). As the following sections from two popular midwifery books show, the views of the ancient writers continued to be rehearsed in medical texts. The emphasis on tradition was only beginning to change during the sixteenth century, with increasing value applied to anatomical observation and study of dissected bodies "as a site of discovery rather than a means of confirming past authority" (Sawday 120). The excerpts below are an amalgam of reliance on classical texts, the benefits of personal observation and experience, and the influence of cultural beliefs and folklore about gender on scientific "facts": "What we call sex and gender are in the Renaissance bound up in a circle of meanings from which escape to a supposed biological substratum is impossible" (Laqueur 128). The weight of social attitudes to gender roles and relationships bore heavily on the understandings of male and female bodies, and to some modern historians it has appeared that "Seventeenth-century gynecology was a combination of ignorance about internal medicine, bias against women, and an almost total reliance on the ancients" (Smith, "Gynecology" 99).

The human body was regarded as operating through the mixture and relative balance of four humours which were based on the elements of earth, air, fire, water, and the qualities of cold, heat, dryness, and moisture: blood, yellow bile or choler, black bile or melancholy, and phlegm. As noted above, the male body was accepted as the norm, and women were considered to be in constant danger of experiencing an imbalance of humors requiring diagnosis and cure. The aim of treatment was to restore natural harmony, and to this end various therapies were used to reduce or supplement humors through techniques such as bleeding, purging, enemas, sweating, and vomits, and diets, complex medicines, and herbs. All the treatments included in the midwifery texts adopt this approach, and the extracts represent the sorts of regimens applied to women's bodies. (The other main component of such texts, not included below, is to explain how to perform deliveries of babies, with great detail being given on handling irregular or abnormal births which were almost always life-threatening for mother and child.)

Humoral medicine involves endless decoding of physical signs. In these treatises, women's bodies emerge as complex texts which are interpreted in terms of natural balance or unnatural disruption. In themselves these bodies are considered mysterious or reticent (Maus 271-72), and they require a learned gaze to uncover their secret meaning. Treatment both restores nature and asserts the correctness of expert (usually) male readings of the female body.

The Birth of Mankind is the earliest printed midwifery textbook in English. It was translated from a 1532 Latin translation of Eucharius Roesslin's German work, which was first published in 1513. Roesslin was the state physician at Worms and Frankfurt-am-Main. His work was extremely popular in England, appearing in thirteen editions up to 1654 (Eccles 11-12). Its success was followed up, especially in the seventeenth century, by a number of other works on gynecology and midwifery including Guillimeau's *Childbirth* (in the next chapter), Jacob Rueff's *The Expert Midwife* (1637), Nicholas Culpeper's *Directory for Midwives* (1651), Nicholas Fontanus's *The Woman's Doctor* (1652), and Culpeper's *The Complete Midwife's Practice Enlarged* (1659). The following excerpts are taken from the first English edition of Roesslin's work, published in London in 1540 (*STC* 21153; Reel 142).

After What Manner and Fashion the Birth Lieth in the Mother's Womb, and How Many Cauls It Is Compassed and Wrapped in

In so much as our intent is in this book following to entreat and speak of the birth of mankind and of such things which happen and chance to the mother in her labor and travail in the deliverance of the same, it shall be first very necessary to show after what manner and fashion the infant lieth in the mother's womb and in how many cauls the same is lapped and wrapped. To the farther knowledge and perseverance of such things the which we shall entreat of hereafter.

Wherefore, ye shall understand that the birth lieth in the mother after this manner. First, it lieth round in manner as a bowl, the hands being between the knees and the head leaning on the knees, either of the eyes joining upon either of the knees, the right eye upon the right knee and the left upon the left, the nose depending[1] between the knees so that the face and forepart of the infant is toward the inward parts of the woman, lying in manner upright in the mother's matrice.[2]

Farther, ye must understand that there be three covers or cauls in the which the birth is contained and lapped. Of the which the one compasseth and embraceth round about the birth and the other two cauls also. And it is called the secundine, second birth, or the after-birth, the which defendeth the birth from noisome and ill humors increasing in the matrice after conception by retention of the flowers,[3] otherwise wont to pass and issue further once in the month. The which ill humors, if they should touch or come near to the birth, would greatly perish and hurt the same. But after the deliverance of the principal birth these humours, also with the foresaid caul or secundine, issue further and is called the after-birth.

The second caul with the which the birth is covered compasseth the same birth from the navel downward, covering all the inferior parts of the infant. And this skin or caul is as it were full of pleats and wrinkles. And through this caul the birth is defended and kept from ill and sharp humors as urine or piss issuing from the infant, and sweat, etc. For so long as the child is in the mother's womb it sendeth further urine not by the due members but by the vein which proceedeth out of the navel.

The third suiting or caul likewise containeth all the birth in it, defending also the same from humors and urine and from the boisterousness of the secundine or first caul, and this is called the armor or defence of the birth.

This is the manner of the situation and lodging of the infant in the mother's belly, and these be the three cauls containing and enclosing in the birth. Now will we speak of the time of birth.

Of the Time of Birth and Which Is Called Natural or Unnatural

And when the time of birth approacheth near, most commonly these signs following come before, by the which the time of labor is known to be at home.

First, certain dolors and pains begin to grow about the guts, the navel, and in the reins[4] of the back, and likewise about the thighs and the other places being near to the privy parts, which likewise then beginneth to swell and to burn and to expel humours, so that it giveth plain and evident token that the labor is near.

But ye shall note that there is two manner of births, the one called natural, the other contrary to nature. Natural birth is when the child is born both in due season and also in due fashion. The due season is most commonly after the ninth month or about forty weeks after the conception, although some be delivered sometimes in the seventh month and the child proveth very well. But such as are born in the eight month, either they be dead before the birth or else live not long after, as the noble medicine Avicenna[5] doth testify.

The due fashion of birth is this, according as witnesseth Albert the Great.[6] First, the head cometh forward, then followeth the neck and shoulders, the arms with the hands lying close to the body toward the feet, the face and forepart of the child being towards the face and forepart of the mother, as it appeareth in the first of the birth figures.[7] For as Albertus writeth, and as we have rehearsed before also, before the time of deliverance the child lyeth in the mother's womb, the face and breast being towards the back of the mother. But when it should be delivered it is torn clean contrary, the head downward, the feet upward, and the face toward the mother's belly, and that if the birth be natural. Another thing also is this, that if the birth be natural the deliverance is easy without long tarrying or looking for it.

The birth contrary to nature is when the mother is delivered before her time, or out of due season, or after any other fashion than is here specified before. As when both legs proceed first or one alone, with both the hands up or both down, or else the one up and the other down, and divers otherwise as shall be hereafter more clearly declared.

Of Easy and Uneasy, Difficult or Dolorous Deliverance and the Causes of It, with the Signs How to Know and Foresee the Same

Very many of the perils, dangerous and strong, which chance to women in their labor which ensue and come in divers ways and for divers causes such as I shall here declare.

First, when the woman that laboreth is conceived over-young, as before twelve years or fifteen years of age, which chanceth sometime though not very often, and that the passage be over angust,[8] strait or narrow, other[9] naturally. Or else, for some disease and infirmity which may happen about that part as apostumes, pushes,[10] piles, or blisters and such other, through the which causes nature cannot (but with great dolor and pain) open and dilate itself to the expelling and deliverance of the child. And sometimes the vesica or bladder or other entrails being about the matrice or womb be also apostumate and blistered, which being grieved the matrice or womb likewise is grieved with them, and that hindereth greatly the deliverance. Also sometimes in the fundament are hemorrhoids or piles, and other pushes, chappings, or chimes[11] which cause great pain, also hardness and difficulty or binding of the belly. Which things, for the grief and pain that ensueth of them, can see the woman to have little power to help herself in her labor.

Furthermore, if the party be weak and of feeble complexion, or of nature very cold, or too young, or very aged, or too gross and fat, or contrariwise too spare and lean, or that she never had child before, or that she be over timorous and fearful, diversely wayward, or such one as will not be ruled, removing herself from one place to another, all such things causeth the labor to be much more painful, cruel, and dolorous than it would otherwise be. Also, ye must understand that generally the birth of the man is easier than the birth of the female.

Item, if the child be of a fuller and greater growth than that it may easily pass that narrow passage, or contrariwise, if it be so faint, weak, and tender that it can not turn itself or doth it very slowly, or if the woman has two children at once; other else, that it with the which she laboreth be a monster as, for example, if it have but one body and two heads, as appeareth in the seventeenth of the birth figures, such as of late was seen in the dominion of Werdenberg.

Again, when it proceedeth not in due time or after due fashion, as when it cometh forth with both feet or both knees together, or else with one foot only, or with both feet downward and both hands upward. Other else (the which is most perilous), sidelong, arse-long, or backlong; other, having two at a birth, both proceed with their feet first or one with his feet and the other with his head, by those and divers other ways the woman sustaineth great dolor, pain, and anguish.

Item, if the woman suffer aborsment,[12] that is to say, bring forth her child in the fourth or fifth month after the conception, which is before the due time. In this case it shall be great pain to her, for so much as (according to Galen's[13] saying) in that time the entrance of the womb is so firmly and strongly enclosed that scarce the point of a needle may enter in at it.

Also, if the child be dead in the mother's belly, it is a very perilous thing for so much as it cannot be easily turned, neither can it wield or help itself to come forth; or if the child be sick or weakened, so that it can not for feebleness help itself. The which thing may be foreseen and known by these tokens: if the woman with child has been long sick before her labor; if she have been sore laxed[14]; if after her conception she have had daily and unwontly her flowers; if straight after one month upon the conception her breasts yield any milk; if the child stir not nor move at such time as is convenient for it. These be tokens that it should be very weak. By what tokens ye shall know it is dead, I shall show you in the ninth chapter hereafter.

Also, there is greater peril in laboring when the secundine or latter birth is over firm or strong, and will not soon rive or break asunder so that the child may have his easy coming forth. And contrariwise, when it is over weak, slender, or thin, so that it breaketh asunder before that the child be turned or apt to issue forth, for then the humors which are collected and gathered together about this secundine or second birth pass away sooner than it should do, and the birth shall lack his due humidity and moistness which should cause it the safelier to proceed and with less pain.

The birth also is hindered by over much cold or over much heat. For in over much cold the passage and all other powers of the laboring woman be coacted[15] and made narrower than they would otherwise be. Likewise over much heat debilitateth, weakeneth, and fainteth both the woman and the child, so that neither of them in that case can well wield or help themselves for faintness.

And further, if the woman have used to eat commonly such meat or fruits which do exicate or dry and constrain or bind, as medlars, chestnuts, all sour fruit as crabs, chokepears, and such other, with over much use of verjuice[16] and such like sour sauces with rice meal and many other things, all this shall greatly hinder the birth.

Also, the use of cold baths after the fifth month following the conception or to bathe in such water where aloin[17] is, iron or salt or any such things which do coact and constrain, or if she have been often times heavy and mourning or ill at ease, or if she have been kept over hungry and thirsty, or have used over much watch and walking. Other, if she used, a little before her labor, things of great odor, smell, or savor, for such things attract and draw upward the mother or matrice, the which is great hindrance to the birth.

Also, if the woman feel pain only in the back and above the navel and not under, it is sign of hard labor. Likewise, if she were wont to be delivered with great pain in times passed is a sign of great labor always in the birth.

Now, signs and tokens of an expedite and easy deliverance be such as be contrary to all those that go before. As for example, when the woman hath been wont in times passed easily to be delivered and that in her labor she feel but little throng or dolor, or, though she have great pains, yet they remain not always in the upper parts but descend to the nether parts or bottom of the belly.

And to be short, in all painful and troublesome labors these signs betoken and signify good speed and luck in the labor: unquietness; much stirring of the child in the mother's belly, all the throngs and pains tumbling in the fore-part of the bottom of the belly; and when the woman is strong and mighty of nature and such as can well and strongly help herself to the expelling of the birth. And again evil signs be those when she sweateth cold sweat, and that her pulses beat and labor over sore, and that she herself in the laboring faint and swoon. These be unlucky and mortal signs.

Of Conception and How Many Ways It May Be Hindered or Letted

There is nothing under heaven which so manifestly and plainly doth declare and show the magnificent mightiness of that omnipotent living god as doth the perpetual and continual generation and conception of living things here in earth, by the which is saved, prorogued, and augmented the kind[18] of all things. And where that this almighty lord and creator hath so instituted and ordained that no singular thing in itself (here upon the earth) should continually remain and abide, yet hath he given from the beginning and instincted such a power and virtue unto these mortal creatures that they may engender and produce other like things unto themselves and unto their own similitude in the which always is saved the seed of posterity. Were not this provision had by almighty god the nature and kind of all manner of things would soon perish and come to an end. The which virtue and power of generation many times doth halt and miss by defect and the contrary disposition in the parts generative.

As ye may evidently see in the sowing of corn and all other manner of seed, so that there be in all manner of generation three principal parts concurrent to the same: the sower, the seed sown, and the receptacle or place receiving and containing the seed. If there be fault in any of these three then shall there never be due generation unto such time as the fault be removed or amended. The earth unto all seeds is as a mother and nurse, containing, clipping, and embracing them in her womb, feeding and fostering them as the mother doth the child in her belly or matrice, until such time as they come unto the growth, quantity, and perfection due unto their nature and kind.

But if this seed conceived in the bowels of the earth do not prove or fructify, then be thou sure that either there is let in the sower, in the seed, or else in the earth. The earth may be over waterish, dank, or over hot and dry, or else full of stones, gravel, or other rubbish, or full of ill weeds which may strangle and choke the good corn in his growing. Also, the seed may be putrefied or otherwise vitiate and corrupted, and so the life and spirit of it vanished away and destroyed. The sower may inordinately strive and cast the seed on the earth, etc. So that if there be let in none of these three parts concurrent to generation, or that the lets be removed and done away, then doubtless will ensue multiplication and increasement of that kind of the which the seed cometh, according to the natural inclination the which almighty god hath implanted and set in the kind of all things.

How Many Ways Conception May Be Letted, and How the Causes May Be Known

Everything, then, the which doth increase in his kind must first be conceived in the womb and matrice of the mother which is apt and convenient for the recreation of such seed. And as I said before, as there may be defect and lack in the mother receiving the seed, so may there be fault and defect in the sower and in the seed itself also.

And in woman there may be four general causes by the which the conception may be impedite[19] and let: over much calidity or heat of the matrice, over much coldness, over much humidity or moistness, and over much dryness. Any of these four qualities exceeding temperancy may be sufficient causes to let due conception.

Wherefore the right excellent physician Hippocrates, in the fifth book of his *Aphorisms*, sayeth, "All such women, the which have cold and dense matrices, cannot conceive. Nor such as have moist and waterish matrices can conceive, for the power of the seed is extinguished in it. Also having dry matrices conceive not, for the seed perisheth for lack of due nutriment and food. But that matrice the which hath all these qualities in temperancy, that is fruitful."[20] This is Hippocrates' saying, the which thing also may be well perceived by a familiar example of the sowing of corn.

For if it be sown in over cold places, such as be in the parts of a country called Scythia, and in certain places of Almaine,[21] or in such places where is continual snow or frost or where the sun doth not shine, in these places the seed or grain sown will never come to proof nor fructify but, through the vehement coldness of the place in the which it is conceived, the life and quickness of the grain is utterly destroyed and annihilated.

And farther, as concerning over much humidity: if ye sow your grain in a fen or marish[22] and watery ground, the seed will perish through the over much abundance of water, which extinguisheth the liveliness and the natural power of the grain and seed.

Likewise, if it be sown in such a country or place where is over great heat, not tempered with water and rain, or if the year be so dry that there came no rain at all to allay the extreme and fervent heat of the sun, then shall the seed sown wither and dry away and the power of it be consumed and burnt.

Also, if it be sown in dry places where never cometh rain, or on the sand and gravelly places, in such a place the grain can never take nor prove, nor be conceived in it to come to any fruit or profit.

Wherefore, if the matrice be distempered by the excess of any of these four qualities, then must ye reduce it again to temperancy by such remedies as I shall show you hereafter. Likewise, may there be defect and lack in the man as if the seed be over hot, the which the woman shall feel as it were burning hot; or too cold, the which she shall feel as it were in manner cold as ice; or too fluey[23] or thin, etc. Divers other ways also it may be letted which shall not need here to be rehearsed.

Now, if the woman cannot conceive, the cause coming of over much frigidity and coldness in the matrice, that shall she know by these tokens: she shall feel great cold about the sides, the reins of the back, and the matrice. Her urine shall appear white and thinnish, and sometimes also somewhat spiss[24] and thick, and all manner of cold things shall annoy her, hot things shall greatly comfort her.

But if it come by over much humidity of the matrice, that shall she know by these signs: if the body of her be of a fat and gross disposition; if with her flowers issue forth at the beginning and the latter end of them certain viscous and watery substance, and that her urine be white, thick, and sometime, as it were, milky. Also, that she feel great cold and pain about the matrice and privy parts, and much dolor in her sides and in the reins of her back.

And when over-much heat or dryness in the matrice is cause of the hindrance of conception, then is the urine high-colored red or yellow, being thin with certain motes appearing in the water, the woman hath great thirst and bitter rising or belching out of the stomach into the mouth. And many times they that are in this case are very spare and lean in all their body, having also but small quantity of flowers, the which thing may happen other by over-much watch or over-much fasting, labor, travel, sorrow, sickness, etc. But such women, which naturally are thus spare and lean, may very hardly be brought to a temperancy again and be made apt to conceive. And this shall be sufficient for this time to know which quality by his excess causeth sterility. Now will we show how it shall be known whether lack of conception be in the woman or else in the man, and how to know whether the woman be conceived or not, according to the mind of right expert doctors of physic.

How to Know Whether Lack of Conception Be of the Woman or of the Man, and How It May Be Perceived Whether She Be Conceived or No

If ye be desirous to know whether the man or the woman be hindrance in conception, let each of them take of wheat and barleycorns and of beans, of each seven, the which they shall suffer to be steeped in their several urine the space of twenty-four hours. Then take two pots, such as they set gillyflowers[25] in. Fill them with good earth, and in the one let be set the wheat, barley, and beans steeped in the man's water, and in the other the wheat, barley, and beans steeped in the woman's water. And every morning, the space of eight or ten days, let each of them with their proper[26] urine water the said seeds sown in the forenamed pots and mark whose pot doth prove and the seeds therein contained doth grow. In that part is not the lack of conception. But see that there come no other water or rain on the pots.

Item, according to Hippocrates' writing, if ye will know whether the fault be in the woman or no, then let the woman receive into her body underneath, being well and closely closed round about, the fumes of some odoriferous perfume as laudanum, storax, calamint, lignum aloes, musk, amber and such other, and if the odor and savor of such things ascend through her body up into her nose, ye shall understand that sterility cometh not of the woman's part; if not, then is the defect in her.

Item, if she take garlic, being pilled[27] out of the husks and convey of it into the privy parts, and if the scent of it ascend up through the body unto the nose, the woman is faultless; if not, then is there lack in her. These are signs to know whether the lack be in the man or the woman.

Whether she be conceived already or no, ye shall know by these signs: first, the flowers issue not in so great quantity as they are wont but were less and less, and in matter nothing at all cometh from them. Also, the breasts begin to wear rounder, harder, and stiffer than they were wont to be. The woman shall long after certain things otherwise than she was used to do before that time. Also, her urine waxeth spiss and thick-like by retention of the superfluities. Also, the woman feeleth her matrice very fastly enclosed and shut in, so much that as Hippocrates saith, the point of a needle may scarce enter.

Item, to know whether she be concerned or not. According to Hippocrates' mind, in the fifth book of his *Aphorisms*, give unto the woman when she is going to bed a quantity of melicratum to drink, and if after that drink she feel great pain, gnawing and tumbling in her belly, then be ye sure that she is conceived; if not, she is not conceived. This melicratum is a drink made of one part wine, another part water, sodden together with a quantity of honey.[28]

But if ye be desirous to know whether the conception be man or woman, then let a drop of her milk or twain be milked on a smooth glass, or a bright knife, or else on the nail of one of her fingers. And if the milk flow and spread abroad upon it by and by, then is it a woman-child. But if the drop of milk continue and stand still upon that the which it is milked on, then is it sign of a man-child. Item, if it be a male, then shall the woman with child be well-colored and light in going, her belly round, bigger toward the right side than the left. For always the man child lyeth in the right side, the woman in the left side.

Of Certain Remedies and Medicines which Shall Cause the Woman to Conceive

All sterility, then, for the most part ensueth and cometh of the distemperancy of one of these four forenamed qualities. Wherefore, the remedy and cure of the same when it chanceth must be done by such things the which have contrary power and operation to the excessive quality. For by that shall it be reduced to his temperancy again.

As, if that coldness and moistness exceeding temperancy in the matrice be occasion of sterility, then must she apply such things to that place the which be of nature hot and dry, the which may calify and warm the place, and also dry up the ill moisture and humors contained in the same, hindering conception.

Wherefore, take of savine, bay tree leaves, the flowers of camomile, melilot, marjoram, caprifolium, herba paralysis, citron leaves, and such other things of aromatical and hot nature. And seethe these in water together and let the woman receive the vapor and fume hereof underneath, into her body through some conduit or pipe made for that purpose, her clothes being close about her that none of the vapor or air issue out. And over this, let her sit all a night, if she may, receiving ever the fume hereof into her body. And in the morning let her accompany with her husband, and she shall conceive.

A bath also for the same purpose. When the time of her flowers, about the end of the last quarter of the moon, is almost finished, let her bathe herself in a bath wherein is decoct[29] and sodden caprifolium, mallows, French mallows, hollyoak, roses, juniper berries, paritary, wild mints, bay leaves, myrtles, savine, camomile, pinpernell, mints, marjoram, citron leaves, basil, pennyroyal, and such other. But before that she bathe her in this water, it shall be best for her to be purged and cleansed from the cold humors with the odoricon or with benedicta, or with the pills which be called *sinequib esse nolo* to be had at the apothecary's, and then let her enter into this foresaid bath. And when she cometh forth of the bath again, then let her take of diamargariton or of muscat, to the quantity of a nut, drinking it with good and odoriferous or well-smelling wine. Other else, let her take of this electuary[30] following, which is very excellent for that purpose.

Take of spike, nutmeg, cloves, zedoarium, galingale, long pepper, dry roses, storax, alipta muscata, of each of these like much, then take of the root of tormentil as much as of all the other forenamed things together, and beat all these to powder, tempering them with a sufficient quantity of clarified honey, to the which also add a little of pure musk. Of this electuarium, both evening and morning the space of ten days, let the woman take to the mountenance[31] of a nut with good odoriferous wine, bathing herself also every day the space of the said ten days. At her coming forth of the bath, receiving of the foresaid electuary, then also let her perfume her privities with the savor and fume of laudanum, frankincense, xiloaloes, storax, amber, alipta, xilobalsamum, and such other things. And after this let her make a suppository anointed with magna trifera or esdra, with the powder of olibanum and the oil of bays mixed and tempered together. And let her retain this suppository in her privities all the day time the foresaid space of ten days. And then at the ten days' end, the man and woman accompanying together, god willing, she shall be conceived. And these be the remedies of the defect and lack of conception come by reason of coldness and moistness.

But if it come by distemperance of the matrice in hot and dry, first let the humor which is cause of it be purged by convenient medicines. And then every night, the space of ten days, let her bathe herself in warm water, nothing else being put unto it. And in this bath let her remain not long. And at her coming forth give her to drink of trifera magna with watered wine, and after this receive she the vapor and fume of the decoction of these herbs underneath into her privy parts: take violets, bearsfoot, paritary, and pennyroyal. Seethe them in water, and then convey into the same place a suppository of trifera magna with the powder of olibanum.

Item, a suppository which is wonderful good in expelling and dowing[32] away such things which let conception. Take of silver montanum beaten to powder, two drams; of the rennet[33] of a hare, the fourth part of a dram; and temper these together with clarified honey and the oil of bays and anoint herewith a suppository, the which let the woman retain in her secrets the space of a day and a night.

Item, a suppository made of hare's dung and honey tempered together is very excellent for the same purpose. But let the woman abstain from all manner of salty and sharp meats, and use to drink good odoriferous and pleasant wines allayed with water.

Also, to drink of the wine in which is dissolved musk, or else viscus quercinus[34] is good to help to conception. Also the heart bone of a hart and the scraping of ivory is very good for the same.

Item, a suppository for the same which hath been many times well proved for that purpose: take garlic pilled and cleansed from the husks, and seethe it in the oil of roses or else the oil of marjoram unto the time that it be dissolved and that all the moistness be departed from it. Then take it out of the oil again and stamp it, and then wrap it in wool and convey it suppository-wise into the privy parts, and there keep it the space of a day. This thing is marvelous good for conception and hath been well proved.

Divers other lets of conception and remedies for the same might here have been declared which for brevity and shortness we for this time do let pass, making here an end of this treatise, the which we have composed and translated out of Latin, to the honor of God, the utility and profit of all honest matrons.

NOTES

1. Hanging down.
2. Womb.
3. Menses.
4. Kidneys.
5. Avicenna, 980-1037, Arab physician and philosopher; medicine: doctor.
6. Albertus Magnus, 1193-1280, German philosopher.
7. Illustrations accompanying the text.
8. Tight or narrow (from Latin *angustus*, narrow or strait).
9. In other cases.
10. Apostumes: abscesses; pushes: pimples or boils.
11. Chafed or dried skin.
12. Miscarriage.
13. Claudius Galen, A.D. 130-200, Greek physician and writer on medicine.
14. Incontinent.
15. Constrained.
16. Medlars: type of sour apple; crabs: crab-apples; verjuice: acidy sauce made from crab-apples and unripe grapes.
17. Bitter purgative derived from the aloe plant.
18. Species; prorogued: prolonged.
19. Impeded.
20. Hippocrates, 46-357 B.C., Greek physician, considered to be the founder of medicine; the reference is to his *Aphorisms* 5.82.
21. Germany; Scythia was the ancient name for the region north of the Black Sea, where southeastern Europe runs into the western edge of Asia.
22. Marshy.
23. Fluffy.
24. Dense.
25. The clove pink or carnation.
26. Own.
27. Peeled.
28. *Aphorisms* 5.41.
29. Boiled down.
30. Medicines usually made of powder mixed with syrup or honey.
31. Amount.
32. Pressing or squeezing.
33. Part of the stomach.
34. Oak oil.

CHAPTER 14

Childbirth, or the Happy Delivery
Of Women: Wherein Is Set Down the
Government of Women
Jacques Guillimeau

Although formal training for midwives was not introduced till the late-eighteenth century (Harley 28), it has recently been proposed that midwives in sixteenth- and seventeenth-century England received effective training through an unofficial apprentice system, which involved observing and being instructed by experienced midwives (Evenden 9). Midwives were licenced by church authorities on the basis of testimonials which verified their skill and moral standing. Their role was seen as culturally crucial, for by aiding in the birth of new lives they were centrally involved in the continuity of family lines, inheritance, and social order itself. This role as "custodian to reproduction and the cultural codes governing it" (Harvey 82) could make midwives controversial figures, who seemed to hold the power to safeguard or disrupt the social fabric, and it was not unknown in cases of disputed births and deaths for suspicions to link midwives to infanticide, abortion, bastardy, and even witchcraft (Wilson 131).

Part of the controversy around the midwife's role was due, then, to the fact that many were women not fully under the control of a medical community dominated by men. The seventeenth century was to see a gradual removal or limiting of women's role in medical practice, with male midwives and physicians beginning to officiate more frequently at births (Smith, "Gynecology" 108-9). Male authors produced the majority of medical and midwifery textbooks (an exception is Mrs. Jane Sharp's *The Midwives' Book* published in 1671), while classical authorities were exclusively male. An officially educated, male medical community was thus opposed to female midwives trained through oral means and first-hand knowledge (Harvey 90). The antagonism to female midwives was often voiced in advice to seek a male midwife or physician if delivery of the baby seemed difficult and to ignore various superstitious techniques advocated by women (Eccles 117).

This opposition is evident in Jacques Guillimeau's *Childbirth, or the Happy Delivery of Women*. Guillimeau was a surgeon at the French courts of Charles IX and Henri IV and also the pupil and son-in-law of the famed French doctor and author Ambroise Paré. As he notes through his text, his experience and treatments are related to women of upper-class and courtly backgrounds, often being very elaborate and expensive. He also contrasts his recommendations to those of female midwives and attendants, whom he sees as liable to cause problems before, during, and after the birth. The subtitle of the text, "The Government of Women" suggests that along with their salutary goals, the endorsed regimens and procedures seek to impose control over women's experience. On the other hand, the text is marked by an earnest concern with the well-being of mother and baby. In effect, it suggests the way that in the field of medicine benevolence and power are tightly intertwined.

Guillimeau was a very well-respected medical figure. A number of his other works were translated into English, including *A Worthy Treatise of the Eyes* (1587 and 1624) and *The French Chirurgery* [Surgery] (1598), while his collected works were printed in Paris in 1598 and 1612. *Childbirth* was published in France in 1609, the year of his death, and the translation was published in London in 1612 and again in 1635. The following excerpts are taken from the first English edition (*STC* 12496; Reel 838).

CHILDBIRTH

What Diet and Order a Woman with Child Ought to Keep

That a woman with child may enjoy her perfect health, she must diligently observe that which consisteth in the use of the six things not natural, which are the Air, Meat and Drink, Exercise and Rest, Sleeping and Waking, Fullness and Emptiness, and the Passions of the Mind.

First, therefore, she must dwell and live in a good and well-tempered Air, which is neither too hot nor too cold or waterish, not subject to any foggy mists or winds, and especially the South wind. For (as Hippocrates saith), when those winds do blow upon every light occasion, women miscarry. The North wind also is hurtful unto them, for those winds breed thin rheums,[1] distillations, and troublesome Coughs in great-bellied women, causing them oftentimes to abort or be delivered before their due time. Likewise, such winds as bring with them ill smells and vapors which, being drawn in together with the Air we breathe into the Lungs, do many times breed very dangerous and troublesome diseases. Aristotle saith that the smell of a Candle put forth may cause a woman to abort or lose her fruit, wherefore she must beware of all ill Air and make her abode in houses well and pleasantly seated, shunning as much as may be possible all bad savors.

Concerning her Diet, she must use meats which be of good nourishment and breed good juice, moderately drying. The quantity must be sufficient both for herself and for her child, and therefore they are to be dispensed withal from fasting at any time. For sometime too much abstinence makes the child weak and sickly and causeth him often to be born before his time, seeking after nourishment which he cannot find within his Mother's body. As also, the too-great quantity of meat his Mother takes may often stifle him or else make him grow so big that he cannot keep himself in his place, which constrains him either to come forth or else makes him sickly, seeing that those meats are corrupted wherewith he is nourished and fed. Hippocrates writeth in *Epidemics* that the sister of Caius Duellius, after she had eaten her fill, aborted.

All meats which are either too hot, cold, or too moist are to be avoided, and chiefly in the beginning of meals, as also those which are too salt or over-much spiced. And likewise all baked meats are utterly forbidden. Aristotle and Pliny write that if a woman with child eat much salt meat, her child will be born without nails, which shows that he will not be long lived. Her Bread must be of good Wheat, well-kneaded, light, and also well-baked. For her meat she may use Hen, Chicken, Capon, young Pigeons, Turtle, Pheasants, Larks, Partridge, Veal, and Mutton. And for Herbs, let her take Lettuce, Endive, Borage, Bugloss, and Sorel, abstaining from all raw Salads. She may close her stomach after meat with Pears or Quinces, baked or preserved, as likewise with Cherries or Damsons. She must shun all diuretical things which provoketh either urine or the natural courses,[2] and such as are windy as Peas and Beans.

Notwithstanding, women with child have oftentimes such disordinate appetite, by reason of some salt or sharp humor which is contained within the membranes of the stomach, that they desire to eat Coals, Chalk, Ashes, Wax, Salt-fish raw, yea, and unwatered, and to drink Verjuice and Vinegar, yea, very dregs, so that it is impossible to hinder them from eating and tasting them. But yet they must refrain and overmaster themselves therein as much as they can since that such food may much hurt and hinder both their own and their child's health. Nevertheless, if they cannot forbear suffer them a little, and let them have their longings for fear lest it should prove worse with them. For I have seen many women, which being hindered and forbidden from using such trash, have presently fallen into travail, and in others their children have carried the marks of some of the things they so earnestly desired and longed after. Beside, although that such meats for the most part are very bad and contrary, yet for the desire they have to eat them they are digested commonly without hurting the party at all. Meat and drink (saith Hippocrates) is better and fitter, though it be somewhat worse, than that which is better and not so agreeable and pleasing.

For her Drink she may use Claret wine, mature and not too strong, which she must allay very well. For this Wine hath power to comfort and strengthen the stomach and all the other parts serving for nourishment and generation. And if she cannot away with Wine, let her drink Hydromel[3] or Barley-water well boiled.

Her sleep must be in the night, the better to digest the meat she hath taken. For watchings do engender crudities[4] and diseases, which cause untimely births instead of fair and goodly children. And chiefly, she must avoid sleeping after dinner. But in the morning she may take her ease as she shall think best, yet not turning (as some great Ladies do) the day into night and the night into day.

She may use moderate exercise, but violent motion looseneth the Cotyledons or vessels of the Matrice whereby the child receives his nourishment. They must be forbid riding in Wagons or Coaches, especially in the three first months. For as upon a small occasion we see the fruits and flowers of trees do fall (as by some little wind that shakes the tree or the like), so many times through a light cause women great with child, in stirring or moving themselves, yea, or but setting their foot awry, may be deliver'd before their time.

It was not without good cause that the Romans forbad their Wives to ride in Coaches, the which also ought to be observed in these days, especially by those who are subject to take hurt. And, therefore, let them walk gently, taking an especial heed and care to themselves the first three months.

She must shun all great noise and sounds, as of Thunder, Artillery, and great Bells. Galen, in his book *De Theriaca*,[5] sayth that many women with child have died with the very fright they received by a clap of thunder. And when she is afraid of hurting herself or falling into travail, let her be carried in a Chair or Litter between two strong men and chiefly two hours before meals. For as a woman may easily lose her burden the first month, because her child (though he be but little) is not yet firmly fastened and tied to the womb; so likewise, being great or big through his weight, he may fall down and come forth. Wherefore, all violent exercise and too much labor is hurtful and dangerous for her, as also to fret, chide, or laugh immoderately. The fourth, fifth, and sixth month she may use more liberty; the seventh and eighth she must keep herself still and quiet. But when she is in her ninth month, then may she use more stirring and exercise. And therefore is it that Aristotle in his *Politics* appointeth that women with child should not be sedentary nor live too nicely, but that since God hath blessed them to bear children they should daily visit the Temples of the Gods for their exercise.[6]

The which Plato expressly commandeth in his Common-wealth, and by a kind of devotion and religious piety.[7] But Aristotle in that place speaketh like a Physician, as he sheweth in his book *De Generatione*. In the Country (saith he), where women accustom themselves to labor, they are brought abed more easily and with less pain. In brief, where women exercise themselves they are sooner delivered, for their exercise consumes the excrements which idle and slothful women gather and heap together.

In the first four months she must likewise abandon Venus for fear of shaking the child and bringing down her courses, which must also be observed in the sixth and eighth months. But in the seventh and ninth she may boldly use it, especially toward the end of the ninth month, which some are of opinion will help and hasten the delivery.

Aristotle is of this opinion, though herein he contradicts the authority of Hippocrates. The woman with child (saith he) ought not to have the company of her husband. But Aristotle and Hippocrates may easily be reconciled. The Philosopher meaneth that they should not embrace their wives all the time of their being with child, but only toward the time of their lying-in, thereby to shake the child and make him come the more readily forth. For coming into the world after this act he is commonly enwrapped and compassed with slime, which helpeth his coming forth.

It is also requisite that her belly be loose, not retaining her excrements, and that she have (if it be possible) every day the benefit of Nature which, if it be not done naturally, it must be helped, taking every morning some broth of Damask-Prunes; also Apples stewed with Sugar and a little Butter is very fit and good. She may use Broth wherein Borage, Bugloss, Purslane, Lettuce, Patience, and a little of the herb Mercury hath been boiled. She may likewise take Suppositories so they be not too sharp. Clysters[8] made of a Calf's head or of a Sheep's head, boiled with Aniseed and Fennel-seed, wherein some coarse Sugar and oil of Violets is dissolved, are very convenient, using them nevertheless with discretion, leaving out all manner of ingredients which might cause a flux of the belly for fear of Abortion or being delivered before their time, as Hippocrates saith.

Notwithstanding, the same Hippocrates is of opinion that women with child, in cases of necessity, may be purged from the fourth to the seventh month. But before and after those times he admits it not, nay, he forbids it directly. Which, for all that, the Physicians of our time observe not in cases of danger because the Medicines we use in these days, as Rhubarb, Manna, Cassia, and Tamarinds, are not so violent as those that were used by our Ancients, which were Hellebore, Scammony, Turbith, Coloquintida, or the like. And we must take especial care of giving them any opening things which may either provoke urine or their natural courses. For as the same Author saith, it is impossible for the child to be healthful if the mother have her natural sickness.

Blood-letting is forbid them unless it be very needful, especially if the child be grown anything big, because he hath more need of food and nourishment than at the beginning when he was little. For take away his sustenance and he will wax lean and feeble, being often times driven for want thereof to seek a passage forth. Notwithstanding, there are some women so sanguine and full of blood that we are forced to take some of it away lest the child be stifled with the over great quantity thereof, or when they fall into diseases where it is necessary to open a vein. The fittest time (if it be not in case of necessity) is from the fourth to the seventh month. I have seen a woman with child who for a Pleurisy was let blood eleven several times, and yet stayed her full term and was well delivered.

Now, concerning the passions of the mind, a woman with child must be pleasant and merry, shunning all melancholy-like and troublesome things that may vex or molest her mind. For as Aristotle saith, a woman with child must have a settled and quiet mind. Which Avicenna also counseleth, that those which have conceived ought to be preserved from all fear, sadness, and disquietness of mind, without speaking or doing anything that may offend or vex them. So that discreet women and such as desire to have children will not give ear unto lamentable and fearful tales or stories, nor cast their eyes upon pictures or persons which are ugly or deformed, lest the imagination imprint on the child the similitude of the said person or picture. Which doing, women shall be sure to be well and happily delivered, and that (with the help of God) they shall bear their burden to the full term, which shall be sent into the world without much pain, promising them a happy and speedy delivery. To conclude, they must leave off their Busks[9] as soon as they perceive themselves with child, not lacing themselves too straight or crushing themselves together for fear lest the child be misshapen and crooked or have not his natural growth. And their garments must be rather light and thin, than heavy and cumbersome.

How a Woman Must Govern Herself the Nine Months She Goeth with Child

Now I have prescribed what manner of life a woman ought to lead while she is with child, she may observe (if it please her) this that followeth, though not so necessary yet commodious and profitable both for the maintaining of her health and preservation of her beauty. To the end, then, that her breasts after her delivery be neither too big and puffed up, nor yet hanging down like bags, and to prevent the danger that might happen unto her by the too great quantity of blood that is turned into milk (which may be curdled and so suppurate and putrefy). As soon, therefore, as she knows herself to be with child (as in the second or third month), let her wear a chain of gold about her neck. Some prefer a chain of steel or else a little gad of steel put between the two breasts, as likewise to put a piece of cork there and to wear under her arm-pits two little pieces more of the same. This Fomentation[10] also is very good.

Take of Periwinkle, Sage, and ground-Ivy, of each a handful; Hemlock, half a small handful. Boil them in wine and water, and when you have taken it from the fire put thereto a little rose-vinegar. And with this decoction warm, bathe your breasts in the morning with a cloth or sponge dipped therein a quarter of an hour, wiping and drying them afterwards with reasonable warm cloths. The like may be done with the waters of the same herbs. And about the third or fourth month, when she feels herself quick, about which time her belly begins to swell and grow big, she must wear a Swathe (made fit for the purpose) to support her belly, being first anointed with this Liniment or Pomade,[11] which she shall continue till the ninth month to keep her belly from being full of knotty and broken veins, furrowed and wrinkled, making it grow deformed, unseemly, and hanging down lower than is fit, which happeneth by reason of the great burden and weight of the child that stretcheth and enlargeth the skin thereof and causeth them to endure great pain in their belly and groin.

Take of Kid's suet and the fat of a Sow, of each three ounces; of Capons and Goose-grease, of each an ounce and half. Cut them small and melt them in an earthen pot, putting thereto as much water as will suffice. Then strain them through a cloth and wash them in water till they wax very white and have lost their savor. Afterward, melt them again in a double vessel, adding thereto an ounce of the marrow of a Hart or Stag. Then wash it again with Rose-water or other sweet-smelling water, mingling therewithal (if you think fit or that it will not be hurtful to the womb) two or three grains of Musk or Civet.

Some use this ointment: take dog's grease and the fat about a sheep's kidney, of each two ounces; Spermaceti,[12] one ounce; oil of sweet Almonds, an ounce and a half. The fats must be melted, prepared, and washed as before, then melted again with the rest and washed with rose or sweet water.

Some take good store of Sheep's-feet, well bruised and broken in pieces, to the number of thirty or forty, and boil them well in water. Then taking off the fat and marrow that swimmeth on the top, which they wash well in common water. And take thereof two ounces; of Duck's grease as much; Spermaceti, one ounce; white Wax, six drams. Melt them all together in a double vessel and wash them in the above-named waters.

Some Ladies and Gentlewomen which love not to rub their bellies every morning with any of these liniments, wear thereon a Dog-skin or some other, well-prepared and dressed as followeth, and change it every fifteen days or according as it will last and continue, not taking it off except it shrivel and grow wrinkled.

Take a Dog-skin or some other skin ready dressed to make gloves of. Wash it often in common water, afterward in Rose-water, and dry it in the shade. And being thus dressed and dried, lay it in soak in these oils and fats following:

Take of Mesues ointments of Roses, an ounce and half; oil of Saint John's wort and of sweet Almonds, of each an ounce; fresh Butter and Spermaceti, of each half an ounce. Melt all these together in a double vessel, and let the skin lie and soak in it three or four days, moving and stirring them together daily. Then take it forth and spread it in the air, and let it lie there two or three days till it have soaked in all the oil and become dry. Then cut it to the form and bigness of the belly, and so apply it.

Dainty and curious may use the former liniments and skin. They that have not the means to do either, let them take of fresh Butter, well washed in common water and then in Rose-water, three ounces; oil of sweet Almonds, one ounce; Spermaceti, half an ounce. And with these melted together, rub their belly.

These ointments must be kept in a gallipot[13] and covered with Rose-water to keep them from being musty.

When the Woman is come to the ninth Month, having been in good health all the time of her going with child, she must continue the use of the aforesaid Ointments, and must begin to use more exercise than she did before, walking gently before meals the first twelve or fifteen days. And then afterward it will be good to use stronger exercise.

It will be very profitable for her (especially after the ten or twelve first days of the ninth month be passed) to sit in the decoction following, after the manner of a half Bath, some quarter or half an hour in the morning. And then being well dried and laid to bed, let her be anointed behind, all along the lower part of her back and before, from the Navel downward and chiefly upon Mons Pubis and the groin, with the ointment following.

Take of Mallows Althaea with their roots, Motherwort, of each two handful; white Lily roots, three ounces; Camomile and Melilot flowers, of each a good handful; Linseed, Quince seed, and Fenugreek, of each an ounce. Boil them all in sufficient quantity of running water for the Bath.

Take of Hen's fat, three ounces; Duck's fat, an ounce and a half; fresh Butter, two ounces; Linseed oil, an ounce and a half. Melt them all together, then wash them very well in Paritary and Mugwort water, adding thereto two ounces of the Mucilage[14] of Althaea Roots. In which space, let her take this drink every morning fasting. Take of Oil of sweet Almonds, newly drawn without fire, an ounce; white Wine, half an ounce; Paritary water, one ounce; mingle them together. Some have found good by taking the yolk of an Egg, and drinking a draught of Hippocras[15] after it. Others take a little Wine and water, wherein Linseed hath been steeped.

Let this or the like order and government be observed for a Woman that is of a good habit of body, and who in her going with Child hath not been subject to any sickness or accident of moment, bearing her Children well and without much pain.

Of the Disordinate Longing Called Pica

We commonly say the appetite is depraved when, beyond measure, we covet to eat and drink too much in respect of what hunger naturally requireth. Or when we desire or long after meats which are unusual and offend in quality, and are not dressed and prepared as they ought.

Of this depraved Appetite there be divers sorts. The first is called *Boulimos* of the Greeks, and of the Latins *Fames vaccina* and *appetitia immodica*, when they eat more than is requisite, not being able to satisfy themselves. And if hunger urge them farther and grow greater, then it is called of the Latins *Appetitus caninus* or *Fames insatiabilis*, and the party eats till he be full even to the throat, that he is constrained to vomit, his stomach being so overcharged. But then presently he is driven to eat again and then to vomit. From whence the Proverb is taken, "He is returned like a Dog, to his vomit" (Prov. 26.11).

The like happeneth for drinking as for eating, which the Latins call *Sitis immodica*, which is so great that the tongue cleaves to the roof of the mouth, not being able to eat or speak except the mouth be first moistened and the tongue wetted. This accident is very hard, yea, even insupportable to endure, the sick party taking no other delight but in drinking, and that often and in great draughts. Men are more subject to this drought than women.

Contrariwise, Women, and chiefly those with child and such as have not their Courses, or Wenches that are subject to the Green sickness,[16] are more troubled with this depraved or immoderate appetite called *Malacia* or *Pica*, having this name given it either because Pies[17] are troubled with this disease or else for that their feathers be of divers colors, black and white, according to the variety of things which Women long after. This sickness happeneth when they desire to eat or drink things that are wholly contrary to Nature, as eating of raw or burnt flesh, yea, even to long after Man's flesh, Ashes, Coals, old Shoes, Chalk, Wax, Nutshells, Mortar, and Lime. As Fernelius[18] witnesseth of a man who, being a long time desirous to eat unslaked lime, at last devoured thereof the bigness of one's fist, which helped him without doing him any harm either in the stomach or guts. Notwithstanding, not long since the daughter of M. Forges died with eating the plastering of walls.

Sometimes custom, which is a second Nature, makes us covet to eat such contrary things as we desire, and the rather because we have commonly eaten thereof in our youth. There is found the contrary hereof in some who abhor and loathe good meats, which is imputed to the Idiosyncrasy or particular constitution of the person. Others have observed that there are such malignant humours sometimes bred in us that they are turned into poison and make both these depraved appetites. As it is seen by poisons taken inwardly and applied outwardly which make the like effect. The biting of the serpent Dipsas doth testify the same, which breedeth an intolerable and unquenchable thirst in him that hath been wounded by it.

Now, therefore, leaving all these kinds of vitiated and depraved Appetites, we will only speak of that wherewith great-bellied Women are troubled, which is called Pica.

Some impute the cause of this sickness to certain Crudities and ill humors which are contained in the whole habit of the body and imparted to the mouth or orifice of the stomach. But the soundest opinion is that the sides and tunicles[19] of the stomach and orifice thereof are infected and stuffed with divers excrements and ill humours. And according to the quality they have, the Woman with child longeth after the like. As if Melancholy abound, not burnt or adust,[20] she longeth after sharp things, as Vinegar, Citrons, and Oranges. If the Melancholy be adust, she desireth Coals, Ashes, and Plastering. If the humor be salt, she coveteth salt meats, and so of the rest. And surely, it often happens that they long for the like things as are in their stomachs.

This malign and bad humor is engendered (as we have said) through the retention of the natural Courses in women with Child, which flow back into the stomach. In some it beginneth the first weeks, yea, the very first day; in others the thirtieth or fortieth day and continues even till the fourth month and then ceaseth. Which cometh so to pass because the Child is grown bigger, and having need of more Nourishment draws to him a greater quantity of blood, the which he consumes, and so by consequent it returns back no more into the stomach. Besides also, this humor hath been much spent and voided by the often vomitings which Women have during the first months. And also because the Child's hair is bred and grown great, which some hold to be partly a cause of this sickness. Pliny writes that women with Child feel themselves worse when their Child's hair begins to come, and chiefly about the new of the Moon.

Now, that we may preserve them from this infirmity or at least diminish it as much as may be, she must chiefly use meats that breed good juice, and that in little quantity, increasing it nevertheless as her bigness augmenteth and the child groweth. Which at length, waxing stronger and greater, will consume part of this great quantity of blood, and the rest may be put into the membranes which wrap and enfold the child and to the mass of blood which is called the after-birth which is, as it were, the liver of the Matrice.

Now, concerning their meat and drink. Considering that they are sick of this disease and so infinitely distasted that often times they do even loathe and abhor good meats, therefore we must set an edge (as it were) on their appetite, varying their meats in as many fashions as may be possible thereby to make them the more pleasing and desirable. Olives and Capers, as likewise salads a little parboiled, are very good for them. All meats that are either too fat or too sweet be naught because they stir up a desire of vomiting. For their sauces, they may use Verjuice, Oranges, Citrons, Pomegranates, and good Rose vinegar, all very moderately taken.

Avicenna commendeth toasted cheese and Amylum dried, which Aetius and Oribasius[21] do allow, and especially to those that desire to eat earth and plastering of walls or the like. Paulus Aegineta[22] allows them the use of mustard, pepper, and cloves to make sauce thereof, for the stirring up of their appetite and to help to digest the crudities contained within the stomach. After meals she may eat bak'd quinces and roasted filberts. For her drink, she must use good claret wine, well allayed; but if she long for white, you may give her leave to drink some, so that it have a little astriction.[23]

True it is that the overgreat quantity of drink is hurtful for her, by reason of the great washing which it might make in her stomach. She may take every morning a draught of Wormwood-wine or a little strong Hydromel, with a toast of bread. . . .[24]

The Ancients, as Paulus and Oribasius, exceedingly commend the decoction of Polypody and Aniseed with sugar of Roses. They may use gentle fomentations to their stomachs, made of Wormwood, Balaustine, Cumin, Citrus, and Fennel-seed, wherewith likewise may be made Cataplasms for the same use. For these medicines will comfort and strengthen the concoctive faculty of the stomach, the better to digest the meat; the retentive, to retain and keep that it hath received; the expulsive, to thrust that forth which troubleth the stomach; and the appetite, to covet and long for meat. . . .

Concerning general purgations which may evacuate downward part of this superfluity, they must not be administered when a woman is young with child but with very great care and good advice, not using any strong purgers. But if there be need and that the disease ceaseth not by light medicines, then may be given a little infusion of Rhubarb and a gentle decoction of Senna, taking the advice of the learned Physician. And therefore we must only have a regard to their vomiting, which at these times doth commonly molest and trouble them, taking heed of staying it except it be immoderate (as Avicenna saith) or too violent. For other ways it helpeth to cure this disease, evacuating part of those ill humors whereby it is nourished and increased. And if we perceive she hath a desire to vomit and that the expulsive faculty be not strong enough to help it, let her take a little Hydromel warm. And if the matter in the stomach be tough and clammy, add thereto a little vinegar the better to attenuate and cut it. I have been the longer in this Chapter because it is an accident that doth much annoy women with child. Thereby the better to instruct the young Surgeon, when there is no Physician near at hand.

****

What Diet a Woman Must Keep that Is Newly Delivered
Heretofore we have spoken of the care that must be taken of a Woman so soon as she is brought a bed and delivered of her after-birth. Now we will treat of the diet she is to keep while she lies in, and of the accidents that may befall her in that time.

First, she must be kept reasonable hot, for too much heat doth weaken and dissolve the strength. But above all, she must be kept from the cold air because it is an enemy to the spermatical[25] parts, and being very piercing it may get into the Matrice which is now empty and there procure great pains and torments, as also puff it up and the whole belly. And therefore the doors and windows of her chamber in any wise are to be kept close shut.

Her diet must be thus. First, she must live temperately and not fill herself with too much meat, and that must be of the same kind that is prescribed for them that are wounded. And indeed, in some women there happens a great *Solutio continui*,[26] and not that only which they call simple but also that which hath a contusion joined with it. For in that great striving and passing of the child many membranes are not only bruised and hurt but also broken and torn, as it happeneth in young women and in others that are far in years and never had any child before. Nay, sometimes in these the passage of the Matrice and that of Anus are brought into one. Yea, and some suffer great excoriations and hurts in those parts which, being neglected in some, have come to putrefication and Gangrenes.

And here I must admonish women in childbed not to regard the words of their nurses or keepers which continually preach to them to make much of themselves, saying that they had need to fill their bellies which have been so much emptied, telling them how much blood they have lost and do daily lose, and that at last they will grow so weak that they will not be able to help themselves.

But these are frivolous reasons, for the greatest part of the blood which a woman voideth then and all her month is but superfluous blood and is good for nothing. Which hath been kept in the body a long time, even the nine months that she hath gone with child. It being now necessary for her health to have it voided out of her Matrice that so her belly, which is swollen and puffed up with the abundance of blood (like a sponge that is full of water), may be quitted and discharged and return to the natural proportion and bigness. And therefore, for their health's sake they must not feed so plentifully the first days as the vulgar think, that by this abstinence may hinder the Ague which may happen unto them and likewise keep down the abundance of blood which would flow to their breasts and be converted into milk and by reason of the store thereof grow clotty and curdle, and in the end apostumate.

Wherefore, the five first days let her use Broths, panades,[27] new eggs, and jelly, not glutting herself (as commonly they do) either with flesh or Almonds. In the morning, let her take a supping[28] or broth, and so likewise at dinner with a couple of new laid eggs and some panade. And again at supper, let her have the like, closing her stomach with a little jelly. But yet if she mean to nurse her child herself she must feed more plentifully. Let her drink barley water, wherein a little Cinnamon and a few coriander seeds have been boiled. The great Ladies of Italy do use a water made of Capons, which is this.

Take two Capons ready pul'd[29] and dressed. Boil them in an earthen pot, with a sufficient quantity of fair water, till they be half sodden. Then take them forth and cut them into small pieces to be used as followeth. Take of Bugloss, Borage, and Balm, of each two good handfuls. Whereof you must make a lay[30] in a glass Limbeck, and upon that another of the said Capon's flesh, and so upon that a lay of leaf gold with a dram of the powder of pearl. Then pour in some of the broth on the top, which you shall do until all be bestowed in the same manner. This being done, you must distil it in a double vessel or Balneo Mariae,[31] and draw a quart of water or thereabouts, which must be reiterated so often till you think that you have enough to serve the woman in childbed for ten or twelve days. But this Curiosity is for Princesses and great Ladies. The said water must be drawn six weeks or two months before it be used and set in the sun in summer and over an oven in winter, to take away the rawness that remains in it.

If the woman have not an ague, in my opinion she may drink a little white or claret wine with twice as much boiled water. But there be some women that cannot endure wine, and therefore let them drink water and honey boiled together or else boiled water. If they desire to drink in the daytime between their meals or else in the night, give them a little syrup of Maidenhair with boiled water, or any other syrup so it be not astringent because of their purgings. When her pains, the fear of the ague, and the burning of her breasts be passed, then may she feed more liberally and then she may eat at dinner a little meat with her broth, as Capon, Pullet, Pigeon, or a bit of Veal. And at supper, beside her broth, a slice of Veal, Mutton, Chicken or any other good meat.

The eighth day being past, about which time commonly the womb is well purged and cleansed, it will not be amiss to nourish her better, giving her more solid meat and in greater quantity, that she may grow strong again the sooner. All the which time she must keep herself very quiet, not much moving or stirring herself, nor so much as once looking into the Air. Let her speak as little as may be and have no noise made about her, nor suffer her to be much visited but by her friends and kinsfolks, excluding all such tattling Gossips as may tell her anything to trouble her or make her sad. Let her sleep rather in the night than in the daytime. Yet if she have not rested in the night by reason of some pains, then let her sleep whenever it comes upon her. And because most women in that case are Costive and cannot void their excrements, therefore it will be very fit to give her some such gentle Clyster. . . . If she dislike Clysters, let her take a little broth or decoction of Senna.

I am of opinion that the Athenian women, while they were in Childbed, did take the broth of Cabbage or Coleworts rather to be loose-bellied than to drive away witchcraft as Athenaeus[32] would have it. For heretofore the Cabbage was Cato's Physic and all his household. And therefore, when the Romans banished the Physicians Cato said that the Cabbage alone was Physic enough to cure all their diseases, and besides he made a little Commentary upon that subject.[33]

Let her banish all grief and heaviness, having regard only of her health and to be merry, praising God for her delivery.

What Must Be Done to the Woman's Breasts, Belly, and Nether Parts that Is Newly Delivered

Now I have set down the manner of diet a Woman in Childbed should observe, it will not be amiss to show what is fit to be done unto her before she sit up or rise, endeavoring herein to bring all parts of her body which have been strained and, as it were, quite changed through a long and painful travail to their former state, that they may be recovered and grow strong with as much speed as may be possible.

If our French Ladies were (in this point) like unto those which Vesputius Florentinus[34] doth write of, it would then be needless to prescribe so many medicines for the restoring them to the same state they were in before their being with child. There are women (saith he) that dwell beyond the Antarctic Pole, whose bodies are entire and Virgin-like even after often child-bearing, and in whom there is perceived no difference from them that are Virgins, as they that have opened them, having made diligent search, do testify. But since there be no such women found in our quarters (though I dare boldly say, there be some not much different), therefore will it be very necessary to have a care what is to be done to their belly, breasts, and nether parts. Wherefore, after the sheep's skin or hare's skin hath stayed on four or five hours, let it be taken away and the woman's belly and groin anointed with the liniment following. And then applying the Cerecloth of a just bigness, which must be continued the first seven days, dressing it every morning and turning the said Cerecloth sometimes on the one side and sometimes on the other. . . .[35]

And when three weeks of her time are expired, she having been neither troubled with Ague, pains, or grippings, nor any other accident extraordinary, and being likewise well-cleansed from all her after-purgings, before she go abroad it will be very good for her to bath, cleanse, and wash herself, being first gently purged with some easy medicine, according to the Physician's direction.

NOTES

1. Pernicious moisture or humors secreted by nose, eyes, and mouth; distillations are discharges of rheum.
2. Menses.
3. A liquor of honey and water.
4. Undigested or indigestible matter in the stomach; watchings: wakeful nights.
5. *On Antidotes*.
6. *Politics* 7.16.
7. *Laws* 784a.
8. Enemas.
9. Corsets.
10. Flannels, soaked in hot medicated water, applied to the skin.
11. Scented ointment.
12. Fatty substance from sperm whale.
13. Small, glazed pot, used by apothecaries.
14. Pulp.
15. A drink of wine flavored with spices.
16. An anemic disease which gives a pale or green tinge to the complexion.
17. Magpies; *pica* is the Latin word for magpie.
18. Jean Francois Fernel, 1497-1558, French physician and mathematician.
19. Lining.
20. Scorched or burnt.
21. Aetius of Mesopotamia: a Greek physician and medical writer from the sixth century A.D.; Oribasius: Greek medical writer from the fifth century A.D.; amylum: starch or fine flour.
22. Celebrated Greek medical writer, specializing in obstetrics. His works were published in the sixteenth century.
23. Binding effect.
24. Various complex prescriptions for lozenges and ointments, given in the next few pages, are omitted.
25. Generative or reproductive.
26. Continuous splitting or tearing.
27. Bread boiled to pulp and flavored with sugar or nutmeg.
28. Food that can be supped by spoonfuls.
29. Plucked.
30. Layer; limbeck: an alembic or apparatus used in distilling.
31. A tray that holds hot water, in which other pots are placed to heat food.
32. Athenaeus of Attaleia practiced medicine in the first century A.D. in Rome, during the reign of emperor Claudius.
33. Cato, *On Agriculture* 156.1.
34. Possibly the Byzantine writer of the tenth century A.D., author of *Geoponica*.
35. There follows another series of complex prescriptions and recipes for various liniments and fomentations to be applied to the stomach, breasts, and "nether parts."

Ballads and Chapbooks

CHAPTER 15

Ballads

It is estimated that in the second half of the sixteenth century approximately three thousand separate ballads were published in England. Depending on the size of print runs, they may have been circulating in as many as three to four million copies (Watt 11). This great surge in publication and distribution was linked to a number of factors: the continued development of mechanical means of printing; the growth of urban populations, especially that of London; increased participation in schooling, popular education, and literacy. The ballads were cheap to buy and easily available. They were sold on city and town streets and at fairs and markets by ballad sellers, while chapmen or wandering dealers traveled the countryside selling ballads along with other books and items. The character of Nightingale in Ben Jonson's *Bartholomew Fair* is an example of an urban ballad seller, one who advertises his wares by singing them, while the roguish Autolycus in Shakespeare's *The Winter's Tale* represents the traveling chapman. Early in the sixteenth century ballads could be bought for a halfpenny each, and over the next hundred years their price increased more slowly than inflation to an average price of a penny. They were bought by all ranks of English society, from lower classes through the middle ranks of yeomen, farmers, and tradespeople, to members of the gentry, providing "stories, images and values [that] permeated the multiple tiers of English society" (Watt 5).

Many of the ballads were presented in broadside format, that is, printed on one side of a large single sheet of paper. They were often adorned with woodcut pictures across the top, which presented in cartoon-like fashion the main characters in the ballad's plot. Broadsides were frequently pasted up on walls in public places such as shops and taverns, and even in private homes. The combination of images, public display and singing meant that even people who could not read had opportunity to hear ballads being sung aloud. While greater numbers of people were learning to read if not to write, literacy was not a prerequisite to enjoying a public rendition of a ballad.

The subject matter of ballads and other popular works was quite varied, including moral and religious themes (often arising from the treacherous ways of city life), historical or chivalric episodes, and tales of courtship and sexual encounters. Often these subjects were intertwined, so that a tale of sexual betrayal would end by affirming a moral lesson. The main characters in such ballads were usually "drawn specifically from both the urban and the rural poor" (Spufford 50). Urban audiences would be amused by the confused ways of country visitors to town. Ballads on courtship and sexual imbroglios were especially favored, representing up to one-fifth of such publications as "a subject that was guaranteed to sell well, and was known to be a popular preoccupation" (Spufford 157). The ballads may thus be read as indicating some of the period's central outlooks on sexual and gender relations, including the value of romantic love, courtship rituals, pleasures and anxieties over sex (Spufford 157-71).

The following three ballads represent prevalent topics and attitudes. Steven Peele's *Warning to All London Dames* starts as a celebration of the superiority of English women to others but then turns to musings on the transience of life. The comparison of the dames to fair flowers triggers this change of tone, and with its simple form, pastoral imagery, and concerns with mortality, the ballad seems to reflect a popular source and tradition for the more complex poems of writers such as Herrick and Marvell. Peele's ballad was set to the tune of "The Black Almain" which was used in up to three other sixteenth-century ballads (Simpson 42). The almain was a courtly dance, and the melody would have been written as instrumental accompaniment (Watt 58). *London Dames* was printed in 1571, and in the same year Peele published two more ballads, both anti-Catholic satires, *A Letter to Rome* with its sequel of the Pope's furious response.

The Contented Cuckold deals with themes of women's inconstancy, deceptiveness, and sexuality. It is one of three cuckold ballads listed in the STC (the others are titled *Cuckold's Haven, or the Marry'd Man's Misery* and *The Merry Cuckold*). This ballad combines sexual themes with the motif of the outsider in London, for the cuckold travels from Newcastle to reclaim his wife. The third ballad, *A Merry Dialogue betwixt a Married Man and His Wife*, pits its main characters against each other in a dispute as to who has the harder life, due largely to the other's faults. This ballad was evidently popular as it was twice published in the period 1628-29. Neither *The Contented Cuckold* nor *A Merry Dialogue* names its melody; the first is set to a "new," the second to an "excellent tune."

Taken together, such ballads reveal that concerns about sexuality and gender relations raised in more formal texts were being addressed and debated in everyday language and situations. If Peele's ballad suggests that the kinds of cosmic and cultural disruption attributed to female behavior in sermons might be broadly recognized, then *A Merry Dialogue* shows women challenging such depictions. A final note of reconciliation in the latter may only half conceal that the wife has had the better of the argument (a result possibly endorsed by a postscript which states that the ballad was printed for "M. Trundle, Widow"). Similarly, though *The Contented Cuckold* ends with the couple living together again in Newcastle town, the husband's gladness "that he had got his wife home" is offset by his reputation as a cuckold and the silence concerning his wife's view of the outcome. Through simple style and narrative the ballads draw out the ambiguity and contest which may mark everyday interactions.

These three ballads were all published in London: *A Warning to All London Dames* (*STC* 19551; Reel 387); *The Contented Cuckold* (*STC* 6100.5; Reel 1922); *A Merry Dialogue* (*STC* 6809.2; Reel 1922).

A PROPER NEW BALLAD EXPRESSING THE FAMES, CONCERNING A WARNING TO ALL LONDON DAMES
Steven Peele

You London dames, whose passing fames
Throughout the world is spread,
In to the sky, ascending high,
To every place is fled.
For through each land and place,
For beauty's kindly grace,
You are renowned over all,
You have the praise and ever shall.
What wight[1] on earth that can behold
More dearer and fairer dames than you!
Therefore to extol you I may behold,
Your paces and graces so gay to view.

For virtue's lore, and other things more
Of truth you do excel,
I may well guess, for comeliness,
Of all you bear the bell.[2]
As trim in your array
As be the flowers in May,
With rosette new so bravely dight[3]
As twinkling stars that shineth by night.
For curtesy in every part
Not many nor any resemble you can,

In lady Nature's comely art
So gravely and bravely to every man.

And oft when you go, fair dames on a row,
In to the fields so green,
You sit and view the beautiful hue
Of flowers that there be seen.
Which lady FLORA[4] hath
So garnished in each path
With all the pleasures that may be
(Fair dames) are there to pleasure ye
Till frost doth come and nip the top,
And lop them and crop them, not one to be seen
So when that Death doth hap to your lot,
Consider and gather what beauty hath been.

For as the flower doth change in an hour,
That was so fair to see,
Consider and gather (fair dames) the weather
May change as well with ye,
And turn your joys as soon
As frost the flowers hath done.
So sudden Death may change as well
Your beauties that now doth excel,
And turn your sweets to bitter and sour
When death in his breath comes stealing near.
Such haps may hap to come in an hour
Which ever or never you little did fear.

Wherefore, I say, fair dames so gay
That Death is busiest now,
To catch you hence, where no defence
May make him once to bow.
Experience well doth try,
You see it with your eye
How quickly some are taken hence
Not youthful years may make defence.
And strange diseases many are seen
Increasing and preacing[5] to bear us each day,
But sure the like hath ever been
May hove[6] you and move you to God to pray.

And learn to know, as grass doth grow
And withereth in to hay,
Remember therefore, keep virtue in store
For so you shall decay.
And pity on the poor
With some part of your store,
Look that your lamps may ready be
The dreadful day approacheth nigh,
When Christ shall come to judge our deeds.
No fairness nor clearness can help you then,
The corn to separate from the weeds
Fair dames, when cometh the day of doom.

Now that I have said, let it be weighed
It is no festing toy,
Not all your treasure can you pleasure,
It is but fading joy.
Therefore remember me
What I have said to ye,
And thus the Lord preserve the Queen
Long space with us to live and reign,
As we are all bound incessantly
To desire with prayer both night and day,
God to preserve her majesty
Amen, let all her good subjects say.

THE CONTENTED CUCKOLD, OR A PLEASANT NEW SONG OF A NEWCASTLE MAN, WHOSE WIFE BEING GONE FROM HIM, SHOWING HOW HE CAME TO LONDON TO HER, AND WHEN HE FOUND HER CARRIED HER BACK AGAIN TO NEWCASTLE TOWN

"Come hither, thou seaman brave."
"Sir, what do you require?"
"I prithee tell me, if thou can,
the thing that I desire.
Seest thou not my true Love,
seest not my Lover go down,
And seest thou not my true lover then
come through Newcastle Town?

"And meetest thou not my true Love
by the way as you came?"

"How should I know your true Love,
that have met many a one?"
"She is neither white nor black
but as the heavens fair.
Her looks are very beautiful,
none may with her compare.

"She hath falsied[7] her word
and left me here alone.
And seest thou not my true lover then,
go through Newcastle Town?
She hath left me here alone,
alone here as you see,
And seest thou not my true lover then,
since she hath forsaken me?"

"Sure, I saw your true love,
or else I saw such a one
In a gown and petticoat gay,
go through Newcastle Town.
She went toward the sea,
O thitherward did she bend,
And with a very brave Coal ship
to London she is wend.[8]

"For when she went aboard
she mickle[9] was and merry.
Sure I did wish then verily
she had been in my wherry.[10]
'Tis now just two days since
that the ship went away,
That now a very great way off,
they're fleeting on the sea."

"O, that was my true love,
O, that was my lover true,
Though she hath now forsaken me,
and change me for a new.
I never gave her cause
why she should me forsake.
But now, alas, she is gone to sea,
and another course doth take.

"But sure the winds and fates
did both together agree,
Thus to carry away my love
that hath forsaken me.
But though the winds
did with the fates agree,
Yet will I never forsake my love,
though she hath forsaken me."

"Why hath she left you alone,
another for to take,
That sometimes did love you so dear
and her joy did you make?"
"I loved her all my youth
But now am old you see.
Love liketh not the falling fruit
nor yet the withered tree.

"She is like a careless child
forgets her promise past.
She's blind, she's death, when as she list[11]
and in faith never fast.
Her desires is fickle found
and a trustless joy.
I won her with a world of cares
and lost her with a toy.

"But since I have her long,
I vow her for to follow,
Be it by land or else by sea
or yet through deep or shallow.
And if I do her find
I'll count her for mine own,
O, then I'll bring her back again
unto Newcastle Town.

"Then sailor rig thy ship,
and thy tackles do provide.
I tell you true that I do mean
for to go the next tide.
Spread forth your sails abroad,
and drive into the main.

I pray you for to make great haste,
weigh anchor thou Jolly boatswain.

"For I think every hour
for to be seven year,
Until that I do find my love.
I shall be in great fear,
For I go her for to seek,
I know not which way nor whether,
But I would the winds and fates,
would grapple our ships together.

"For many a boisterous blast,
here do I abide for thee,
Tossing and tumbling on the sea,
though thou hast forsaken me.
Yea, greater pains I will
Five hundred times endure,
So I may win thy love again,
and thereof be made sure.

"But when that thou dost hear,
the pains that I do take,
For to find thee out again,
thou wilt never me forsake.
And now to see the seas,
how smooth they are and plain,
Sure they do Calculate that I
shall find my love again.

"And now at Gravesend town,[12]
we are arrived at last.
Let us with hearty prayers to God
give thanks for dangers past.
Now, farewell seamen all,
adieu, nay, twice adieu,
And if I chance to find my love,
I'll carry her back with you.

"For I will go down this tide,
although that it be late."
Where all the way he slept until,
he came to Billingsgate.[13]

But ere that he came there,
t'was early in the morning,
Then he went up and down the street
as one that was forlorn.

First went he into Cheapside,[14]
thinking his lover to find,
And after that to London-town,
to satisfy his mind.
So straight through Tower Street
he passéd all along,
Where it was his chance to meet,
his love with a seafaring man.

But when the man espied
her husband was so nigh,
Then he made no more ado
but ran away presently.
Which when her husband spied,
unto his wife he came,
And kissed her there most lovingly,
who blushed for very shame.

"If that you will me forgive,
and count me for your own,
I would go back again with you,
unto Newcastle town."
At which words he was full glad,
that she so soon was won.
"Then prithee, sweet, go back again,
unto Newcastle Town."

Thus were they both agreed,
to go together home,
Where we will leave them for a while
going to Newcastle Town.
Thus was the poor man glad,
that he had got his wife home,
But he for a cuckold ever went,
in fair Newcastle Town.

A MERRY DIALOGUE BETWIXT A MARRIED MAN AND HIS WIFE CONCERNING THE AFFAIRS OF THIS CAREFUL LIFE

"I have for all good wives a Song.
I do lament the women's wrong,
And I do pity them with my heart
to think upon the women's smart.
Their labors great and full of pain,
yet for the same they have small gain."

"In that you say cannot be true,
for men do take more pains than you.
We toil, we moil,[15] we grieve and care.
When you sit on a stool or chair,
Yet let us do all what we can,
your tongues will get the upper hand."

"We women in the morning rise,
as soon as day breaks in the skies.
And then to please you with desire,
the first we do is make a fire.
Then other work we straight begin,
to sweep the house, to card,[16] or spin."

"Why men do work at Plough and Cart,
which some would break a woman's heart.
They sow, they mow, and reap the corn,
and many times do wear the horn.[17]
In praise of wives speak you no more,
for these were lies you told before."

"We women here do hear the blame,
but men would seem to have the same.
But trust me, I will never yield.
My tongue's my own, I thereon build.
Men may not in this case compare,
with women for their toil and care."

"Fie, idle women, how you prate,
'tis men that gets you all your state.
You know 'tis true in what I say,
therefore you must give men the way,

And not presume to grow too high,
your speeches are not worth a fly."

"You men could not tell how to shift,[18]
if you of women were bereft.
We wash your clothes, and dress your diet
and all to keep your minds in quiet.
Our work's not done at morn nor night,
to pleasure men is our delight."

"Women are called a house of care.
They bring poor men into despair.
That man is blest that hath not been
injured by a woman's sin.
They'll cause a man, if he'll give way,
to bring him to his life's decay."

"If we prove women were as bad
as men report, being drunk or mad,
We might compare with many men,
and count ourselves as bad as them.
Some oft are drunk and beat their wives
and make them weary of their lives."

"Why women, they must rule their tongues.
That brings them to so many wrongs,
Sometimes their husbands to disgrace,
they'll call him knave and rogue to's face.
Nay, worse than that, they'll tell him plain
his will he shall not well obtain."

"We women in childbed take great care.
I hope the like sorrow will fall to your share.
Then would you think of women's smart,
and seem to pity them with your heart.
So many things to us belong,
we often times do suffer wrong."

"Though you in childbed bide some pain,
your Babes renews your joys again.
Your Gossips come unto your joy,
and say, 'God bless your little Boy.'

They say the child is like the Dad,
when he but little share in't had."

"You talk like an Ass, you are a Cuckoldly fool,
I'll break your head with a three-legged stool.
Will you poor Women thus abuse,
our tongues and hands we need to use.
You say our tongues do make men fight,
our hands must serve to do us right."

"Then I to you must give the way,
and yield to women in what they say.
All you that are to choose a wife,
be careful of it as your life.
You see that women will not yield,
in anything to be compelled."

"Yon Maids, I speak the like to you,
there's many dangers do ensue.
But howsoever fortunes serve,
See that my rules you do observe.
If men once have the upper hand,
they'll keep you down, do what you can."

"I will not seem to urge no more,
good wives, what I did say before.
Was for your good, and so it take,
I love all women for my wife's sake.
And I pray you when you are sick and die
call at my house and take my wife wye."[19]

"Well, come, sweetheart, let us agree."
"Content, sweet wife, so let it be.
Where man and wife do live at hate,
the curse of God hangs o'er the gate.
But I will love thee as my life,
as ever man should love his wife."

NOTES
1. Creature.
2. Are the first; gold or silver bells were given to winners of horse races.
3. Adorned.
4. Roman goddess of flowers.
5. Pressing.

6. Behove, is needful or proper.
7. Falsified.
8. Gone.
9. Great.
10. Skiff.
11. Chooses, desires.
12. A seaport on the Thames River.
13. Fishmarket in central London.
14. Central market in London.
15. Work hard.
16. To prepare wool or flax for spinning by disentangling the fibers.
17. As always, horn refers to the husband as cuckold.
18. To manage, to get along.
19. Away.

CHAPTER 16

Chapbooks

Another prevalent and diverse form of popular literature was the chapbook. The name derived from those who sold them, itinerant dealers or "chapmen," and they consisted of small pamphlets of tales and tracts as well as ballads. Chapbooks ranged from sixteen to twenty-four pages in length and a penny to sixpence in price, and often included wood-cut pictures of main characters and events. Like ballads, the subject matter ranged from the moral and historical to the romantic and sexual, and it also included a subgenre which recounted the exploits of rogues and villains. In many cases, such kinds of materials were mixed so that tales of sexual and criminal scandal invariably ended by emphasizing a moral or religious lesson.

In these accounts two types of social concerns and the connections between them were often addressed. Threats to sexual and legal norms recur as sensational signs of the decay of the contemporary world. Differences between ideals of conduct and social actions produced an "almost obsessive return to the subject of gender relations in popular literature" (McLuskie 46), while an increased sensitivity to petty crime and the actions of poor and unemployed people led to a proliferation of texts recounting nefarious practices of "cozenage" (Sharpe 113). In tales of female criminals both sets of fears combined, reinforced by traditional misogynist misgivings about cuckoldry and deceit, and couched in conventionally "hyperbolic portrayals of women [as] part of a didactic rhetoric" (Eaton 173).

The following two texts illustrate such anxieties and tropes. They stimulate the prurience of readers in order to inspire feelings of moral danger or risk in the face of others' actions and uncertainty regarding the integrity of one's own. That is, in accusing and scapegoating others for moral and social failings, these Early Modern urban myths implicate the very audience they seem to be trying to inform and reassure. Curiosity about the deviant ways of others suggests readers' own potential if not their inclination to offend.

The first pamphlet, *A Miraculous and Monstrous but yet Most True and Certain Discourse of a Woman*, tells of the mysterious growth of a horn from an apparently honest woman's forehead. The association with cuckoldry is raised and then left open, as the text proceeds to warn readers to survey their own consciences and sexual conduct. The second, *The Bridling, Saddling, and Riding of a Rich Churl in Hampshire* recounts the confidence tricks played by one woman in both the country and London. At the heart of this tale is a scene where she rides on the back of her dupe, a startling emblem (captured on the title page) of petty trickery and sexual transgression combined with the potential for social "violence and chaos" of woman on top (Davis 129). The motive of both the protagonist and her victims is greed, and readers are warned to guard against similar symptoms of "covetousness." In each tract, different kinds of disruption concentrate around female figures, marked physically and morally as aberrant.

Neither pamphlet identifies an author; in a sense each speaks in a "public idiom," presenting orthodox moral views as "part of the taken-for-granted reality of the public by translating the unfamiliar into the familiar world" (Hall et al. 62). *Miraculous and Monstrous* adds authority with a prefatory "censure of a learned Preacher," while *Bridling, Saddling, and Riding* does so by repeatedly invoking various courts and officials of the legal system. Both texts were published in London only once, *Miraculous and Monstrous* in 1588 (*STC* 6910.7) and *Bridling, Saddling, and Riding* in 1595 (*STC* 19855; Reel 349).

A MIRACULOUS AND MONSTROUS BUT YET MOST TRUE AND CERTAIN DISCOURSE OF A WOMAN (NOW TO BE SEEN IN LONDON) OF THE AGE OF THREESCORE YEARS, IN THE MIDST OF WHOSE FOREHEAD (BY THE WONDERFUL WORK OF GOD) THERE GROWETH OUT A CROOKED HORN OF FOUR INCHES LONG

The Censure of a Learned Preacher that Examined the Woman and Perused the Copy of this Book Before It Was Printed

I Have (not only) carefully perused this copy but have diligently examined the party herself. And seeing the thing to be true and not only apparent to all men's eyes but signified also by the Justices of the Country unto the Lords of her Majesty's Privy Council, I wish it to be printed that the beholders might not only satisfy themselves with the sight but the readers also take some benefit by the Discourse and Exhortation which hath been penned for that purpose.

This woman, whose name is Margaret vergh Gryffith, by her Father's name after the use and custom of Wales, was lately the wife of David Owyn, of the parish of Llhan Gaduain, in the County of Montgomry, Husbandman, deceased. With whom, as she lived many years (to the eye of the world) very quietly and honestly, having four children whereof three are yet alive, so hath she since during the time of her Widowhood maintained herself with her small portion of Land and other necessaries (for anything that is known) in very good order.

Yet notwithstanding, there appeared of late, viz. in May last, through the wonderful work of God, as the woman herself confesseth and so likewise testified by others, in the midst of her forehead a small hard knob, having on the top thereof at the first, as it were, a dry scab, which she labored by cutting and all other help of Surgery to have covered and cured. But all was in vain, for the more that she strove with it the more it grew, and although it was often pared away yet was she advised and in the end enforced to let it alone to see whereunto it would come. Since which time it hath full grown both in greatness and hardness, so that it is now become both in color, quantity, and proportion, a very Horn, much like unto a Sheep's horn, four inches long or thereabouts, most miraculously growing down out of her forehead to the middle of her nose. And there it crooketh towards her right eye and groweth so fast that she is fain to have it cut, lest otherwise the sight of her eye should be stopped therewith.

Moreover, there began to grow out of the root of this Horn another little knob, after the same manner that the Horn grew at the first, which she caused to be cut away for that she feared it would become another Horn. The Woman hath been examined by the Justices of Peace of the said county, who have also informed the Council of the Marches of Wales therewith.[1] And now lately she is sent up hither to London by the said Justices, to the end she might be seen of the Lords of the Queen's majesty's most honorable Privy Council. And yet there is no certain or natural cause known, but the handiwork of God, how this Horn should grow.

Some speeches there are, but yet doubtfully reported and not willingly acknowledged either by her or her friends, that there hath heretofore some words passed betwixt her husband and her in his lifetime, who suspecting her of some light behavior and charging her with it in these terms, that she had "given him the Horn."[2] She, then, not only constantly denied it but wished also that if she had given her husband the Horn she might have a Horn growing out of her own face and forehead to the wonder of the whole world. But how certain these speeches are I leave to him that is the searcher of secrets, and both she and every beholder of her to examine their own consciences. And by this spectacle to be warned to amend their former lives and to behave not only that they tempt not the Lord God in craving his vengeance to be seen upon them for their secret offences, but rather with penitent hearts most humbly to crave his pardon and forgiveness for their manifold sins and wickedness. Which he grant unto us all, most vile and wretched sinners, for his dear Son's sake, Jesus Christ, our Saviour, to whom be all honor and glory, now and forever. Amen.

Thus (well-beloved Christians) you may behold how the Lord our God, seeking to drive into our dull senses a reverent regard of his Majesty, a thankful acceptation of his mercy, and a dutiful care and consideration of our calling, doth not only often ring into our ears (by the ministry of his Word) the thundering threatenings of his just judgments, which yet might shake stony Rocks and cause them to tremble, but sometimes presenteth before our eyes visible and apparent tokens of his displeasure to make us fear before we feel his fierce wrath and indignation, to make us serve the Lord in fear and rejoice unto him with reverence, to make us "kiss the Son, lest he be angry, and so we perish from the right way" (Ps. 2.11), finally to make us know that GOD doth neither mock nor will be mocked (Gal. 6.7), but although he be "patient to us-ward" (2 Pet. 3.9), and therefore giveth us so long and large a time of repentance, letting us only see in others what might light on ourselves. Yet (in our sins) he will whet his Sword, bend his Bow, and shoot against us the arrows of Death, recompensing the delay of his punishment with the severity of his vengeance.

And yet so hard is man's heart that all this will not mollify or melt it. So stout are our stomachs that this will not assuage it. At least, so froward is our will and so corrupt are our affections that we take small benefit by it but, like filthy Swine of Epicure's Sty (notwithstanding all these warnings), wallow on still in the mire of our own concupiscence. And plunging ourselves into the puddles of our own pleasures, we say: "Tush, God seeth not us, his plagues shall not come near us." Insomuch that the judgments of the Lord our God, if they be common and usual we contemn them, if they be rare and strange we will not believe them. And if at anytime, driven by the evidence of the thing we see, we be forced to say with the Sorcerers of Egypt, "It is the finger of God" (Exod. 8.19), yet then fall we to the condemning of the parties on whom such tokens of God's wrath appear, as though they only were Sinners and we guiltless. Or at least as though we were privileged from the punishment, howsoever we have been partakers in the offence.

The matter indeed we can marvel at and the circumstances we can discourse and, if need be, amplify, reporting (peradventure) more than we know and telling (sometimes) more than we have heard. For reports are as light as reporters are lewd, and many things spoken in haste that are proved at leisure. But we are still in life and conversation as before, and as for repentance or amendment it is not once thought of. Carnal security lulleth us so asleep in delights and cogitations of worldly pleasure that we cannot fruitfully hear the dreadful threatenings of God's judgments fearing us from evil, much less comfortably embrace the sweet songs of his mercy alluring us to repentance.

Wherefore, as our Saviour Christ said unto Jerusalem in the Gospel, "O Jerusalem, Jerusalem, which killest the Prophets, and stonest them to death that are sent unto thee, how often would I have gathered thy children under my wings, as the Hen gathereth her Chickens, and you would not. Behold, your habitation shall be left unto you desolate" (Matt. 23.37-38). So saith he now continually unto England: "O England, England, how oftentimes have I called thee? How sundry ways have I provoked thee? How bountifully have I bestowed my benefits? And how plentifully have I poured out my blessings upon thee? How earnestly have I by the mouth of my Preachers clucked and cried unto thee as a Hen doth to her Chickens, that thou mightest awake out of thy security and, by repentance, return under the shadow of my wings, there to be safe from all these greedy Kites and Eagles that hover ready to pray upon thee. And yet thou wilt not. Therefore thy house shall come to confusion. Therefore I will remove their candlestick (Rev. 2.5). I will take the light of my Gospel from thee. And though I have of late for my own name sake, destroyed thine enemies and drowned them in the bottom of the Seas,[3] that all the world might know and confess there is neither wisdom, power, policy, force, nor fury of flesh and blood that can prevail against me, yet for thine unthankfulness my wrath shall wax hot against thee. I will pour down mine indignation upon thee. Thy enemies, yea, thy ancient enemies shall reign over thee because thou wilt not know the day of thy visitation."

The Lord open our eyes and mollify our hearts that we may in time turn unto the Lord our God, having thus fully fallen through our iniquity, that we may take unto us words and say unto him as the Prophet counceleth us, "Take away all iniquity and receive us graciously, so will we render the calves of our lips" (Hos. 14.2). That we, fearing his justice and trembling at his judgments executed on others, may be brought to a deep feeling, nay, to a due loathing and detestation of all our great and grievous sins. Especially of that sin which too generally is committed in breaking the indissoluble knot of holy Matrimony, by defiling the marriage bed with filthy adultery, many times for lack of wisdom in the husband, sometimes for want of obedience in the wife, but at all times for lack of faithful love joined with the fear of God in them both.

Which holy estate of marriage, as it hath singular circumstances to beautify it, drawn from the dignity of the ordainer, the necessity of the ordinance, the antiquity of the time, the excellency of the place, the innocence of the persons, the commodity of the thing whereby God's Church is increased, Christ's members multiplied, and mankind continued upon the face of the earth, and therefore justly commended by the Apostle to be honorable amongst all men (Heb. 13.4), so those that do or dare defile the temple of God, their own bodies, and sin against their own souls by giving over their members as servants of uncleanness, making the members of Christ the member of a harlot (1 cor. 6.15), let them know that God will judge them, nay, destroy them, without repentance.

And therefore, when thou shalt read this strange discourse following, do neither discredit it as untrue, for the Woman is ready to be seen and the matter is apparent to the eyes of all men. Neither do thou rashly condemn the party, for as I do not justify her so I think thou art not able of thine own knowledge to accuse her. And thou knowest that of things unknown charity willeth us to judge the best. At least, what have we to do to judge another man's servant. To her master she standeth or falleth.

But enter thou into thy own conscience, examine thine own soul, lament thy own sin. Take this token of God's judgment shown on her as though it had lighted upon thy self. Remember what our Saviour Christ said in the Gospel to those that brought him word of the Galileans, whose blood Pilate mingled with their Sacrifice, "Suppose you that these Galileans were greater sinners than all the other Galileans because they have suffered such things. I tell you nay, but except you amend your lives you shall all likewise perish" (Luke 13.2-3). If she have fallen help her up with "the spirit of meekness" (Gal. 6.1), considering that thou thyself mayest be tempted. And if thou stand yet remember thou mayst fall. And that if thou fall and continue in thy filthiness, howsoever thou escape the censure of Law or judgment of man, which sometime covereth that with a sheet that deserveth to be cut down with an axe, yet know then that there is a God in heaven who seeth all things in heaven and earth, and can, when he list, disclose and bring to light even the secrets not only of heart, and hath infinite means in thy chamber, but of thy store to bring sinners (continuing in their sin) both to shame in this world and everlasting punishment in the world to come.

THE BRIDLING, SADDLING, AND RIDING OF A RICH CHURL IN HAMPSHIRE BY THE SUBTLE PRACTICE OF ONE JUDETH PHILIPS, A PROFESSED CUNNING WOMAN OR FORTUNE TELLER

A True Discovery of Divers Notable Villainies Practiced by One Judeth Philips, the Wife of John Philips of Crown Alley in Bishopsgate Street, the Like Was Never in Any Age Committed by a Woman

Of all the seven deadly sins, there is none so common in this flourishing Realm of England as is the grievous sin of Covetousness. For it is the root of all iniquity (1 Tim. 6.10), the puddle of perdition, and the alluring bait of hell. And that mind which is once drowned in the depth of that sin is sold to eternal damnation, unless the mercy of God raise him up from that filthy and devouring gulf. For there is no sin committed under the cope of heaven but one branch of Covetousness is therein comprehended. As Usury, what is it but the desire of gold and hoarding up of wealth? What is Whoredom and

Lechery but lust and desire of the flesh? What is Drunkeness but Covetousness of wine? And what is Pride, Envy, Fury, Theft, Murder, but the desires of the wicked mind?

Yea, every vice is cloaked under the wings of Covetousness. The thief and robber, both by sea and land, ventureth the hazarding of his life for covetousness of wealth. Yea, all creatures which bear life in some sort covet after unlawful things. Lucifer, that once was an Angel of brightness, through his pride coveted to sit in the bright celestial throne of God, for which he was cast from heaven and made an Angel of darkness. We may read how Jezebel, for coveting poor Nabothes' vineyard, for the which by the last judgments of God she was devoured of filthy Dogs (1 Kings 21, 2 Kings 9.30-37). Therefore, the sin of Covetousness is so heinous before the face of heaven that God in his tenth commandment strictly doeth charge us to forsake all unlawful covetousness by these works: "Thou shalt not covet thy neighbor's house, thou shalt not covet thy neighbor's wife, nor his servant, nor his maid, nor his ox, nor his ass, nor anything that is his" (Exod. 20.17).

Which precept, if men would advisedly and carefully look into and with their true endeavors seek to follow it, we should not have in this our Realm of England, and especially in this famous City of London, so many bad and notorious members yearly cut off by the Queen's majesty's Laws as we continually have. Which spectacle we have once every month to see and behold, to the great hearts' grief of all her Majesty's loving subjects. But yet men are graceless and willfully minded, and will not be warned nor take example by the downfall of others. Some are so idly brought up that they can nor will endure no labor. And some are so haughty and proud-minded that they scorn to bend their necks to the yoke of others and live honestly in taking pains for their livings, but study and devise night and day how they may fraudently and deceitfully better their estates by the sweat of other men's brows.

For nowadays, theft, cozenage,[4] robberies, and unlawful practices are so common that not only men but women and children strive with studying and burst brains how to compass and bring to pass many cunning sleights and policies to deceive the world. As by an example, here following, is truly described by a woman, the mirror and map of all cozenage and deceit, whereat all modest women may blush, and every true-meaning man may smile at the folly of the world. Pardon my pen, you modest Dames and grave Matrons, it shall no way impair your honorable Sex, but truly emblazon to the world the cozening devices of a shameless woman whose name and conversation[5] hereafter followeth.

This is to let you understand that in the month of January last past, in the famous City of London, one Judeth Philips, the wife of John Philips, by occupation a Gun-maker now dwelling in Crown Alley in Bishopsgate

Street, was brought before her Majesty's Justices of Peace at the Sessions House in the Old Bailey,[6] and there was indicted upon cozenage, where she confessed the truth of all her practices before the honorable Lords of the bench. But know gentle Reader, before I undertake to explain the truth of all her practices done here in London, I will first in most ample manner set forth to the view of the world a notable villany committed by this cunning and fine-witted woman in the village of Upsborne in Hampshire, in distance seven miles or thereabouts from Winchester.

This Judeth Philips, before times having another husband named Pope, being an honest poor man of a good conversation and well-beloved amongst his neighbors. But this his wife, not contented with his poor estate of living, upon a certain time took an occasion to go away from him and purposed to seek some other course for maintenance of her living. So traveling along the West parts of England, it was her chance to remain for a certain space in the parish of Upsborne, a Town situate and being in Hampshire, and there practiced many cozening sleights and devices to deceive the ampler sort of people in the Country.

Only she betook herself to the profession of a cunning woman, a fortune teller, and those which she knew did abound in wealth, she daily sought means to bring into a fool's paradise, and by one device or other cozen them of some store of Crowns. Not far from this Town, there was dwelling a wealthy churl (whose name I here omit) that was somewhat fantastical and given to believe every tale he heard. Which Churl's wealth whetted so the desire of this woman that she devised a subtle practice to have a share out of his Coffers.

First, to bring her purpose to effect, she enquired secretly of his neighbors of what condition and conversation this miser and his wife were of, and in what state the manner of his living lay. Likewise, she understood that this Churl was in suit of law about a piece of ground with one Sir William Kingsman, a worshipful knight in Hampshire. Which being done, this Judeth Philips, one evening very late, went into the back side of this man's house, where under a hollow holly tree she buried an angel of gold and six pence in white money,[7] and then returned home to her lodging again for the night. But the next day after she walked by the Churl's house, and it fortuned that his wife sat at her door to take the fresh air. And so when this cunning-witted woman saw her time, stood still and looked very wishly[8] upon her, which made the Churl's wife to marvel much that a strange woman, whom she never saw before, should look upon her so steadfastly, which caused her to demand wherefore she looked so earnestly in her face.

"O, mistress," said this Judeth Philips, "you are the fortunatest woman I saw this many a day, for in your brows I see good fortune sit. Have you not (said she) a hollow holly tree standing near unto your house, with certain weeds growing about the root?" "We have," answered the miser's wife, "and what of that?" "O, mistress," said this woman then, "if I might speak with your husband, and if he be like you in the face, you will come to be exceedingly rich. For under that hollow tree there is great store of treasure hid." "Come in," then said she, "and thou shalt see my husband."

But when this woman came into the place where her husband was, she likewise looked him strangely in the face and told him that she knew by certain signs in his forehead that he was in suit of law with some great man of that country and how he should prevail in his suit. Also she told him, if he would be at some charage, she would bring him to great sums of gold and silver that was hidden about his grounds. To whom the man being somewhat covetous said, "If I might first see something of thy skill, I will be at any charge thou wilt. But first tell me what thou art, and from whence thou came?"

"I am," said this Judeth, "an Englishwoman born, but come now from the Pope, and knows more of his mind than any woman in the world." To confirm her words for truth, she took her oath upon the Bible how that she came from the Pope, which was true, for her husband's name as then was Pope. Which being done, she took him by the hand and led him to the root of the hollow tree, where she caused him to dig till he found some gold, which was the angel and the six pence which the night before she closely hid. This brought the covetous Churl into such a conceit that he promised to give her whatsoever she desired so that her promise might be performed. Then she demanded of him for her pains fourteen pounds, whereat he grumbled to lose so great a gub[9] at one time. Yet at last the hope of the treasure hidden under the tree made him to consent, and so with speed gave this woman fourteen pounds in ready gold and silver.

Then said this woman, "Now must I have the largest chamber in your house be hung with the finest linen you can get, so that nothing about your chamber but white linen cloth be seen. Then must you set five candlesticks in five several places in your Chamber, and under every candlestick you must put an angel of gold." All which was done as she required. And likewise said she, "You must also get a saddle and a bridle with two new girths thereunto." All which the covetous churl performed in hope to attain to great wealth.

Then this Judeth caused him and his wife to go into the yard, where she set the saddle on his back and thereon girteth it fast with two new girths, and also put a bridle upon his head. All which being done, she sat upon his back in the saddle and so rid him three times betwixt the chamber and the holly tree. Then said this cozening queen, "You must lie three hours, one by another, grovelling on your bellies under this tree. And stir not, I charge you, until I come back again, for I must go into the Chamber to meet the Queen of Fairies and welcome her to that holy and unspotted place." So this churl and his wife were left quaking in the cold, casting many a long look for the coming of this woman.

But she in the meantime took down all the fine linen clothes from the walls of the chamber and wrapped them up close in a bundle, and all the gold from under the candlesticks and put them into her purse. Then putting herself into a fair white smock, somewhat disguised with a thing on her head all white and a stick in her hand, she appeared unto him and his wife. Using some dalliance as old wives say spirits with night spells do, she vanished away and again entered the chamber where her pack lay ready, and so roundly went away, leaving the churl and his wife in this cold lodging.

But when the poor fool saw the time expired and his expected woman did not return, he got him up and cast off his saddle and bridle, being half-dead with cold, retired into the chamber where he supposed to have found this cunning woman talking with the Queen of Fairies. But when he entered his chamber and saw both his linen and his gold conveyed away, fell into such a perplexity of mind as though he had been distraught of his wits: one while grieving for the loss of his fourteen pounds, another while for the abuse of his good name, likewise for the penance and disgrace she put him and his wife unto, the base and ridiculous manner of his saddling, his cold lodging and weary time spent under the tree to his utter infamy and shame, and lastly the loss of his pure and fine linen.

But yet he dissembled his grief in such order that his neighbors had no suspicion thereof. So in all haste, he took horse and rode to Winchester, being in distance seven miles from the town where he dwelt, and there certified a kinsman of his of all the actions before happened. So betwixt this Churl and his kinsman they made hue and cry[10] after her, by which this deceitful woman was taken and conveyed to prison, where she remained until the great Assizes[11] came. And for the same was arraigned before the right honorable my Lord Anderson, the Lord Chief Justice of the Common Place,[12] under her Majesty, by his Office. Before whom, she confessed herself guilty of all these aforesaid practices, and there received such deserved punishment as the law would permit.

But this shameless woman, regarding neither her public disgrace nor the punishments of heaven inflicted upon all such graceless livers, putting off the garment of shamefastness and forgetting herself to have done any such thing, drowned herself in the sea of all vices and the gulfs of all outrageous mischiefs. For she after this, growing careless of her good name, fell into company of two certain bad-minded men, of the same condition and quality she was on, whose names I here omit. But the one of them was in his former time by trade a silk-weaver, but leaving that hope and course of living betook himself to a very wicked disposition, as to build the state of his living upon cozenage. And to blind the eyes of the world, goes in the habit of a Lawyer all in black like a civil Gentleman. The other fine-witted companion, in the attire of a Country Gentleman, I will not say he dwells at Borden in Kent, nor his wife is the owner of a few Cherry-trees, the only stay and maintenance of both their livings.

But to be plain, these two Caterpillars, P. and V., like Wolves in thieves' clothing, feeds upon the bloods of many innocent lambs who, knowing a woman, her husband being dead and she left a rich widow and in the way of marriage, would never cease pondering in their crafty brains till they were thoroughly acquainted with her, and so by one sly device or other overreach her for some part of her substance. They made her believe they could help her to a husband of mighty revenues and great wealth, where at last she found them but Caterpillars to live upon her labors. As for example, the notable piece of villainy committed betwixt these two counterfeit gentlemen P. and V. and this cozening woman Judeth Philips of a Tripe-wife,[13] lately dwelling on the back side of St. Nicholas Shambles[14] in London. As it was truly noted at the arraignment of the said Judeth Philips, the 14th of February last past, 1594, at the Sessions house in the Old Bailey, before my Lord Anderson and others of her Majesty's Justices. And likewise word by word, as the said Judeth confessed it herself in the prison of Newgate, where she now remaineth.

A Discovery of the Cozening and Ill-handling of the Tripe-wife by Judeth Philips and Her Confederates

There was of late, dwelling in London on the back side of the shambles, a very rich and wealthy man of good conversation, who dying, left his wife in such good estate of living as few of the trade of selling Tripes might well compare with her. This woman, as it was well known amongst her neighbors, had many suitors in the way of marriage and many of sufficient livings. Which woman's name for her wealth was bruited through every part of the city, so that it came at last to the ears of these two cozening companions, P. and V., who studied day and night how they might come acquainted with this rich Tripe-wife, so that at last this practice they devised.

This P., being a very comely man of personage and of a Gentlemanlike quality, went as a suitor among the rest unto this widow, whereby he learned the condition and quality of the woman and what large proffers she had in the way of marriage. Likewise, he understood how that a wealthy Citizen, dwelling upon London Bridge, had received from her in pledge of love a Ring with five Diamonds in it, being in value worth five pounds, which Ring upon some disagreement she received again. Also this P. understood that one Master Grace, a gentleman dwelling in Essex, was her dear friend, and one that was her counselor in all her actions, and how that she would not do anything without his consent, and how that sometimes he lodged in the widow's house.

Which things being well considered of betwixt these two fine-witted fellows, whose heads being never barren devised a present policy to deceive this covetous Tripe-wife. First, they made privy to their practices this Judeth Philips, before named, and told her the state, condition, and quality of this widow, and made her the Instrument of their intended drift, who was as subtle in performance thereof as they were crafty in devising. Then they made a counterfeit Letter from Master Grace, being as then in Essex, and sent as it were from him to this widow of London by this Judeth Philips, wherein was contained how that she was a wise woman and could tell fortunes, and requested her to welcome her to her house and to make much of her, for she might stand her in great stead. Which Letter, being in good manner contrived as best befitting their purposes, caused this Judeth Philips to be attired in a russet gown like a country woman and to bear this Letter home to the widow's house behind the Shambles. Where she was no sooner come and the Letter read, but was bid welcome for Mr. Grace's sake, but especially for the secret qualities the which her friend did commend her in.

But now, when this dissembling minion espied her time she requested to see the widow's hand, which she vouchsafed to do. "O, mistress," then said this woman, "I see by the Art of Palmistry in your hand and by mine own skill that you are born to good fortune. Likewise, I know you have had many rich proffers in the way of marriage." "I have had," said the widow, "indeed, knights' fellows come unto me." Then said this deceitful woman again, "A Citizen dwelling upon London Bridge hath been an earnest suitor unto you and hath received a ring with five Diamonds in pledge of love, but the ring you have again. And so there was another Gentleman loved you well, which once would have kissed you and used you harshly. By that token, in striving with him your hat fell into the Souse Tub."[15]

At which words said the Tripe-wife, "I think you know all things." "I know somewhat," replied this woman again. "Have you not, mistress, about your house a great rumbling when you are in bed?" "Sometimes," said the widow, "we have." "By that," said this woman again, "your husband in his life hid about your house great store of treasure, for which cause there are sprites now that haunt your house." When, indeed, the noise which she heard was no other but this P. and V. that late in the nights would lumber against her doors and likewise in the mornings. "But mistress if you will be at some charge, I will show you where this gold and silver is hid." "I will, good woman, be at any charge thou wilt with reason, so I may gain thereby."

Then said this cozening Dame, "You must set five Candlesticks and five candles burning in them in five corners of your house. Then must you earnestly pray in every corner a certain space." Which was performed with all speed. Thus is God's word made a cloak for all such devilish practices, only to blind the eyes of the simple and well-meaning people. But God surely in divers places of the scriptures saith that whosoever believeth in Witches and Sorcerers believe in the Devil. But yet God doth suffer the Devil and his Angels to spread abroad the world, to tempt those that be weak in faith and, like Wolves in sheeps' clothing, seek to devour us.

But now to our purpose again. This crafty creature, calling the Tripe-wife from her prayers, asked her what she saw and what she heard. To whom she answered that she heard nothing. Then said this minion again, "You must fetch as much Gold, Kings, Jewels, and Chains to the value of one hundred pounds, and put them into a purse." All which was done. Then she took the purse with the gold and wound about it a bottom[16] of woollen yarn, which being done she requested the widow to go a while from her. So in the mean space, like a crafty queen, she conveyed the gold into her pocket and took another bottom of yarn with two stones in it, in the same likeness the other was of, and gave it the woman again as though it had been the very same. To whom she said, "I pray you mistress, lock this up very sure, and look not into it until I come again. For I must go and converse with a wise man that is acquainted with the Queen of Fairies. But I request you that you will send him by me a fat Turkey and a couple of Capons, only to get his friendship in the matter. And no doubt but we shall find the hid treasure very shortly." Which woman, through covetousness of this money, went presently and bought a Turkey and two fat Capons, and sent them with this cozening cheater, by her maidservant, into Holborn. But being come near unto the place whither she intended to go, took them from the maid and so sent her back again.

Thus this dainty-witted Dame, having cozened the Tripe-wife of all her gold, Jewels, and Chains returned joyfully unto the lodging of her two schoolmasters, P. and V. Who seeing her come asked her presently if she had sped.[17] "I have," answered she, "in some sort, for here is a hundred pound to make us merry with." The which they divided into four parts. She received two for her pains and they betwixt them the other two, and afterwards made merry with the widow's Turkey and her couple of Capons. And so went with fifty pounds home to her husband John Philips, dwelling in Crown Alley in Bishopsgate Street. Who, noting her long absence and divers starts she made from him, asked where she had been and how she came by that money. To whom she gave many hard words and bad answers, insomuch that in his anger he struck her. But yet by no means he could do the crafty queen would reveal where she had it.

But now to return to the widow's maid again who, coming out of Holborn home to her mistress, told her that she suspected the queen had cozened her. With that she went presently and unwound the bottom of yarn, wherein she found nothing but two stones. The which being done, she went to one of her neighbors and discoursed to him all the manner of her cozening. But he, like a wise man, counseled her not to make hue and cry, but watch a time until she came again and then to apprehend her.

Not many days after this, these three aforesaid cozening companions met again together and consulted how they might get another booty of this Tripe-wife, which was platted[18] down in this manner. First, this Judeth Philips should repair unto the widow again and tell her that she came from the Queen of Fairies, and how that she gave her in charge (if she would attain the hidden treasure) to set twelve Candlesticks in divers places of her house, and under every Candlestick both gold and silver, and to set all her plate round about the Candles, whereby this subtle-headed woman might the easier deceive her of it. But coming to the widow's house again, she was bidden welcome as before and requested to come in. But in the mean time the Constable was sent for, and she apprehended and so carried to Newgate. Likewise for the same fact, her husband was arraigned before the bench but found not guilty and so quit[19] by the Jury.

But the law finding her guilty therein, was returned to Newgate, where she did remain till the Sessions following for judgment. Then that time being come, her judgment was to be whipped through the city. Thus have you heard the notable practices committed by this woman and her associates. And no doubt but there are more such wicked members in this land.

God, I beseech thee, root them from this flourishing Realm of England and from this thrice-renowned City of London. That all her Majesty's true subjects, may live devoid of such suspicious thoughts. And sweet countrymen of England, abhor that idle and wicked kind of life. And if God's pleasure be not to leave you honest maintenance at home, follow her Majesty's wars abroad and fight in the honor of England's red Cross. Then do you show your duty unto God, love unto your Country, and service unto your Queen. For whose long and quiet reign, let all true subjects daily pray. Amen.

Notes

1. The royally appointed council which administered the frontier districts between England and Wales.
2. Cuckolded him.
3. The remark refers to the sinking and scattering of the Spanish Armada in 1588 through a combination of a great storm and the English navy.
4. Fraud, confidence tricks.
5. Behavior, manner of living.
6. The Crown Court in London.
7. Silver coins; angel: a gold coin with the figure of the archangel Michael on it, worth up to ten shillings.
8. Intently.
9. A large sum of money.
10. A common law process of pursuing felons, using horns and voice to raise the alarm.

11. Law courts comprising two or more commissioners appointed by the Crown, which went on circuit around the kingdom to hear cases and disputes.

12. The Court of Common Pleas or Common Bench, one of the superior courts of the common law, which had jurisdiction over all cases between subjects.

13. A woman who dresses or prepares tripe for food.

14. One of the main meat-markets in London.

15. A tub used for salting and pickling tripe and other meats, also known as a powdering tub.

16. A ball of thread or yarn.

17. Succeeded.

18. Plotted or planned.

19. Acquitted.

Witchcraft

CHAPTER 17

A Discourse of the Damned Art
Of Witchcraft: So Far Forth as It Is Revealed in the Scriptures and Manifest by True Experience
William Perkins

The widespread witch-hunts which occurred across Europe in the fifteenth century did not extend to England. It was not until 1542 that the first statute against witchcraft was passed under Henry VIII. Unlike Europe, in England the "crime of sorcery was a matter of criminal, not religious, law" (Sallmann 453), and hanging rather than burning was the ultimate punishment (though burning might be used if witchcraft were linked to high treason against the sovereign, or to petty treason, the murder of a husband by a wife or of a master or mistress by a servant). Nonetheless, the penalties were very harsh: witchcraft, sorcery, conjuring, and enchantment were all punishable by death. The act was repealed in 1547, and a second witchcraft statute was enacted in 1563 under Queen Elizabeth. It decreed that causing the death of a person by witchcraft or conjuring spirits was to bring the death penalty, while less serious acts such as attempting to hurt or inflicting injuries on people or property, magically searching for treasure or provoking people to "unlawful" love were punishable, if a first offence, by a year in prison along with four appearances in the stocks. Second or repeated offences could bring life imprisonment or death. This act was reinforced by another statue passed in 1604 after the accession of James I, who had authored a text on witchcraft titled *Daemonologie*, published in Edinburgh in 1597 and London in 1603 (Sharpe 309).

The Old Testament was seen as providing indisputable justification for harsh penalties against witches: "Thou shalt not suffer a witch to live" (Exod. 22.18). Though witches could be male or female, demonic sorcery was traditionally linked to women. In England the peak periods for witch-trials were from 1563 to the end of Elizabeth I's reign and in the mid-1640s (Sharpe 310), and in both periods the great majority of those accused were female. In the county of Essex, where large-scale witch-hunts and trials occurred in the sixteenth and seventeenth centuries, over 90% of those accused were women. It seems generally to have been considered that every woman was a potential witch (Sallmann 444).

The kinds of events which might lead to accusations of sorcery comprised natural disasters affecting the populations of a village or countryside, such as epidemics, poor harvests, and bad weather, and individual or personal misfortune, including male impotence, sterility of women, the death of children, and injury to animals and livestock. Accusations were often made against older single women, who seemed to be disruptive figures living outside the norms of the local village or community. A recurring pattern was that such a woman would seek alms or charitable aid from a neighbor and, having been given only a small amount, would curse the donor. When the latter suffered some kind of misfortune, sometimes a few years later, he or she would charge the old woman who was then subject to interrogation and trial. The ensuing investigation of witchcraft was not bound by usual legal procedures. Witchcraft is a secret crime, spells are cast privately rather than publicly, and so a reduced burden of proof was permitted (Hester 127, Newman 54). There were no witnesses to the act itself, and circumstantial evidence such as overhearing curses or observing certain behaviors was admitted. The onus was on the accused to explain that such actions were not malevolent. One of the final pieces of evidence was the discovery of the witch's teat, a secret nipple used to feed the diabolic spirit who visited the witch (Willis 113). The evidence through which witches were charged and condemned thus comprised a set of verbal and visual signs whose meanings were interpreted in very specific and negative ways (Newman 66-68).

The last execution for witchcraft in England occurred in 1682, the last major trial in 1712 (Sharpe 310). The destructive violence of Early Modern witch-hunts and trials seems to have been generated by a combination of religious, gender, and socio-economic motives. As noted, accusations were often linked to economic misfortune in village life (Hester 195), and relevant factors included poverty and unemployment, which grew throughout the sixteenth century, breakdowns in village and community relations with the beginnings of rural capitalism (Beckwith 148), and political and religious tensions that reached a climax in the civil wars of the 1640s. All contributed degrees of social pressure and enmity leading to accusations against fellow residents which, in turn, were used to punish and awe whole communities by a "prosecuting class" made up of gentry and aristocratic judges, justices of the peace, clergy, magistrates, and sovereigns (Willis 104). People who were judged socially disruptive at a local or state level might be further attainted as enemies of God. Witch-hunting could combine political and religious power into a "state-enforced national ideology" (Beckwith 148).

William Perkins' *Discourse of the Damned Art of Witchcraft* explains witchcraft in religious terms as the result of a covenant with the devil.

Perkins is assured of the reality of witchcraft, seeing it as the cause of various personal and economic misfortunes, and he is also adamant about the need for harsh punishment, citing and supporting the biblical sentence of death. In placing witchcraft in a traditional, religious context, Perkins does not address immediate social or economic factors; he does, however, emphasize the likelihood of women's involvement over men's. Ironically he does so while explaining that either men or women can be witches. While both may fall into the devil's snare he "give[s] us to understand that the woman being the weaker sex is sooner entangled by the devil's illusions with this damnable art than the man. And in all ages it is found true by experience that the devil hath more easily and oftener prevailed with women than with men."

Perkins was a teacher and theological writer, who studied and lectured at Cambridge University. He was born in 1558 and by the mid-1580s had developed a reputation as a popular but stimulating preacher, admired by university intellectuals and townspeople. He was involved in religious disputes at Cambridge, standing vehemently against any traces of Roman Catholic ritual or practice in church services and siding with the Puritan lobby in theological controversies. Perkins died in 1602, having been considered one of the university's great teachers. During the seventeenth century his theological writings were very highly regarded and various collected editions were published (some edited by Thomas Tuke). He wrote treatises on predestination, the ministry, the evil of man's imagination, divine grace and free will, death, conscience and other topics, as well as numerous commentaries on sections of the Bible.

A Discourse of the Damned Art was composed in the 1590s and delivered in sermon form. It was not published until 1608 and again in 1610, well after Perkins' death. The following extracts are taken from the first edition, published at Cambridge University (*STC* 19697; Reel 725).

A DISCOURSE OF THE DAMNED ART OF WITCHCRAFT

What Witches Be, and of How Many Sorts

Having in the former part of this Treatise opened the nature of Witchcraft, and thereby made way for the better understanding of this Judicial Law of Moses,[1] I come now to show who is the practicer hereof, whom the Text principally aimeth at, namely the Witch, whether man or woman.

A Witch is a Magician who, either by open or secret league, wittingly and willingly, consenteth to use the aid and assistance of the Devil in the working of wonders.

First, I call the Witch a Magician to show what kind of person this is, to wit, such a one as doth profess and practice Witchcraft. For a Magician is a professor and a practicer of this art, as may appear where Simon, a Witch of Samaria, is called Magus or Simon the Magician (Acts 8.9).

Again, in this general term I comprehend both sexes or kinds of persons, men and women, excluding neither from being Witches. A point the rather to be remembered because Moses, in this place setting down a Judicial Law against Witches, useth a word of the feminine gender, which in English properly signifieth a woman Witch. Whereupon some might gather that women only were Witches. Howbeit, Moses in this word exempteth not the male, but only useth a notion referring to the female, for good causes, principally for these two.

First, to give us to understand that the woman being the weaker sex is sooner entangled by the devil's illusions with this damnable art than the man. And in all ages it is found true by experience that the devil hath more easily and oftener prevailed with women than with men. Hence it was that the Hebrews of ancient times used it for a proverb, "The more women, the more Witches." His first temptation in the beginning was with Eve a woman, and since he pursueth his practice accordingly, as making most for his advantage. For where he findeth easiest entrance and best entertainment, thither will he oftenest resort.

Secondly, to take away all exception of punishment from any party that shall practice this trade, and to show that weakness cannot exempt the Witch from death. For in all reason, if any might allege infirmity and plead for favor it were the woman, who is weaker than the man. But the Lord saith if any person of either sex among his people be found to have entered covenant with Satan and become a practicer of Sorcery, though it be a woman and the weaker vessel, she shall not escape, she shall not be suffered to live, she must die the death. And though weakness in other cases may lessen both the crime and the punishment, yet in this it shall take no place.

The second point in the description is "consenting to use the help of the devil, either by open or secret league, wittingly and willingly." Wherein standeth the very thing that maketh a Witch to be a Witch: the yielding of consent upon covenant. By which clause two sorts of people are expressly excluded from being Witches. First, such as be tainted with frenzy or madness, or are through weakness of the brain deluded by the devil. For these, though they may be said after a sort to have society with Satan or rather he with them, yet they cannot give their consent to use his aid truly but only in imagination. With the true Witch it is far otherwise.

Secondly, all such superstitious persons, men or women, as use Charms and Enchantment for the effecting of anything, upon a superstitious and erroneous persuasion that the Charms have virtue in them to do such things, not knowing that it is the action of the devil by those means but thinking that God hath put virtue into them as he hath done into herbs for Physick. Of such persons we have (no doubt) abundance in this our Land, who though they deal wickedly and sin grievously in using Charms, yet because they intend not to join league with the devil either secretly or formally, they are not to be counted Witches. Nevertheless, they are to be advertised in the meantime that their estate is fearful. For their present ungodly practices have prepared them already to this cursed trade and may bring them in time to be the rankest Witches that can be. Wherefore, I advise all ignorant persons that know not God nor the Scriptures to take heed and beware of this dangerous evil, the use of Charms. For if they be once convinced in their consciences and know that God hath given no power to such means and yet shall use them, assuredly they do in effect consent to the devil to be helped by him, and thereupon are joined in confederacy with him in the confidence of their own hearts, and so are become Witches.

The third and last thing in the description is the end of Witchcraft, the working of wonders. Wonders are wrought three ways (as hath been showed,) either by Divination, or by Enchantment, or by Juggling.[2] And to one of these three heads all feats and practices of Witchcraft are to be referred.

Now, if any man doubt whether there be such Witches indeed as have been described, let him remember that beside experience in all ages and countries, we have also sundry examples of them even in the Scriptures.

In the Old Testament we read of Balaam who, though he be called a Prophet because he was so reputed of men, yet indeed he was a notorious Witch both by profession and practice, and would have showed his cunning in that kind upon the Israelites if God had not hindered him against his will (Num. 23). Of the same kind were the Enchanters of Egypt (Exod. 7), the Witches of Persia (Dan. 2), and the Pythoness[3] of Endor, known for a renowned Sorcerer over all Israel. And therefore Saul's servants, being asked, could presently tell of her, as we read (1 Sam. 28.7ff).

In the New Testament, mention is made of Simon, whose name declared his profession. His name was Magus, and the text saith that he used Witchcraft and bewitched the people of Samaria, calling himself a great man (Acts 8.9). Whence it was that after his death there was a statue set up in Rome in honor of him in the days of Claudius Caesar, with this inscription, *Simoni Deo sancto*.[4] And it is not unlike but Bar-Jesus, the false prophet at Paphus, was a man addicted to the practices of Witchcraft, and for that cause was called by a kind of excellency, Elymas the Magician, that is, the great or famous Sorcerer (Acts 13.6 and 8). Lastly, the Pythoness at Philippi, "that got her master much advantage by divining" (Acts 16.16). And all these used the help of the devil for the working of wonders.

Of Witches there be two sorts, the bad Witch and the good Witch, for so they are commonly called.

The bad Witch is he or she that hath consented in league with the devil to use his help for the doing of hurt only, as to strike and annoy the bodies of men, women, children, and cattle with diseases and with death itself, so likewise to raise tempests by sea and by land, etc. This is commonly called the binding Witch.

The good Witch is he or she that by consent in a league with the devil doth use his help for the doing of good only. This cannot hurt, torment, curse, or kill, but only heal and cure the hurts inflicted upon men or cattle by bad Witches. For as they can do no good but only hurt, so this can do no hurt but good only. And this is that order which the devil hath set in his kingdom, appointing to several persons their several offices and charges. And the good Witch is commonly termed the unbinding Witch.

Now, howsoever both these be evil, yet of the two the more horrible and detestable Monster is the good Witch. For look in what place soever there be any bad Witches that hurt only, there also the devil hath his good ones who are better known than the bad, being commonly called Wisemen or Wisewomen. This will appear by experience in most places in these countries. For let a man's child, friend, or cattle be taken with some sore sickness or strangely tormented with some rare and unknown disease, the first thing he doth is to bethink himself and inquire after some Wiseman or Wisewoman, and thither he sends and goes for help. When he comes he first tells him the state of the sick man. The Witch, then being certified of the disease, prescribeth either Charms of words to be used over him, or other such counterfeit means wherein there is no virtue, being nothing else but the devil's Sacraments, to cause him to do the cure if it come by Witchcraft. Well, the means are received, applied, and used, the sick party accordingly recovereth, and the conclusion of all is the usual acclamation, "Oh, happy is the day, that ever I met with such a man or woman to help me!"

Here observe, that both have a stroke in this action: the bad Witch hurt him, the good healed him. But the truth is the latter hath done him a thousandfold more harm than the former. For the one did only hurt the body, but the devil by means of the other, though he have left the body in good plight, yet he hath laid fast hold on the soul and by curing the body hath killed that. And the party thus cured cannot say with David, "The Lord is my helper" (Ps. 54.4), but the devil is my helper, for by him he is cured. Of both these kinds of Witches the present Law of Moses must be understood.

This point, well considered, yieldeth matter both of instruction and practice.

Of instruction in that it shows the cunning and crafty dealing of Satan, who afflicteth and tormenteth the body for the gain of the soul. And for that purpose hath so ordered his instruments that the bad Witch gives the occasion by annoying the body or goods, and the good immediately accomplisheth his desire by entangling the soul in the bands of error, ignorance, and false faith. Again, this showeth the blindness of natural corruption, specially in ignorant and superstitious people. It is their nature to abhor hurtful persons such as bad Witches be, and to count them execrable. But those that do them good, they honor and reverence as wise men and women, yea, seek and sue unto them in times of extremity, though of all persons in the world they be most odious. And Satan in them seems the greatest friend when he is most like himself and intendeth greatest mischief. Let all ignorant persons be advised hereof in time to take heed to themselves, and learn to know God and his word, that by light from thence they may better discern of the subtle practices of Satan and his instruments.

For matter of practice, hence we learn our duty to abhor the wizard as the most pernicious enemy of our salvation, the most effectual instrument of destroying our souls and of building up the devil's kingdom. Yea, as the greatest enemy to God's name, worship, and glory that is in the world next to Satan himself. Of this sort was Simon Magus who, by doing strange cures and works, made the people of Samaria to take him for some great man who wrought by the mighty power of God, whereas he did all by the devil. He therefore being a good Witch did more hurt in seducing the people of God than Balaam, a bad one, could with all his curses. And we must remember that the Lord hath set a law upon the Witch's head, he must not live, and if death be due to any then a thousand deaths of right belong to the good Witch.

But the patrons of Witches endeavor to delude the true interpretation of that Law. For by a Witch (say they) we must understand a poisoner, and they allege for that purpose the seventy Interpreters, who translate the original word which signifieth a poisoner.

I answer, first, the word used by the seventy Interpreters signifieth indeed so much, yet not that only but also a Witch in general, as may appear in sundry places of Scripture. The Apostle, reckoning up Witchcraft among the works of the flesh (Gal. 5.20), useth the Greek word not for poisoning but for all Magical arts, as Jerome testifieth upon the place. And that it must necessarily be so translated it is evident because in the next verse murder is termed another work of the flesh, under which poisoning and all other kinds of killing are comprehended. And the same word is used in the like sense (Rev. 21.8, 22.15).

Again, the word which Moses useth is ascribed to the Enchanters of Egypt in the seventh, eighth, and ninth chapters of Exodus, and to the "wisemen of Babel" (Dan. 2.24), and both sorts of them were Witches and sorcerers. The kings of Egypt and Babylon used these for sundry purposes and made them of their counsel. And if they had been, according to this allegation, poisoners it is not like they would have so fitted the humors of those two Princes, Pharaoh and Nebuchadnezzar, much less that they would have so ordinarily required their presence and assistance in the business there mentioned.

Thirdly, there is a peremptory Law against the willful murderer, that he should be put to death and that no recompense should be taken for his life (Num. 35.31). In which place all poisoners are condemned because they are willful murderers. Now, if here in Exodus we should understand a poisoner, then there should be one and the same law twice propounded for the same thing, which is not like. And therefore the word used by Moses in this text signifieth not a poisoner properly but a Witch.

Of the Punishment of Witches

Hitherto, I have treated of the nature of witchcraft, both in general and particular, and have also showed what witches are both good and bad. And now I proceed to the second point considered in this Text, the Punishment of a Witch, and that is Death.

In the Judicial Laws of Moses (whereof this is one) the Lord appointed sundry penalties, which in quality and degree differed one from another, so as according to the nature of the offence was the proportion and measure of the punishment ordained. And of all sins, as those were the most heinous in account which tended directly to the dishonor of God, so to them was assigned death, the greatest and highest degree of punishment. He that despised the Law of Moses died without mercy under two or three witnesses (Heb. 10.28). The punishment of the thief was restitution fourfold (Exod. 22.1), but the murderer must be put to death (Num. 35.31). The Idolater and Seducer were commanded to be slain (Exod. 22.20, Deut. 13.5), the Blasphemer must be stoned (Lev. 29.19). And the Witch is numbered amongst these grievous offenders, therefore his punishment is as great as any other. For the text saith he might not be suffered to live (Exod. 22.18).

But why should the Witch be so sharply censured? And what should move the Lord to allot so high a degree of punishment to that sort of offenders? Answer: The cause was not the hurt which they brought upon men in body, goods, or outward estate. For there be sundry that never did harm but good only. We read not of any great hurt that was done by the Enchanters of Egypt, or by the Pythoness of Endor, or by Simon Magus in Samaria. And those divining Witches, which have taken upon them to foretell things to come, hurt not any but themselves, yet they must die the death. This therefore is not the cause. But what if these do hurt or kill, must they not then die? Yes, verily, but by another law, the law of Murder, and not by the law of Witchcraft. For in this case, he dieth as a murderer and not as a Witch, and so he should die though he were no Witch.

The cause then of this sharp punishment is the very making of a league with the devil, either secret or open, whereby they covenant to use his help for the working of wonders. For by virtue of this alone it cometh to pass that Witches can do strange things in Divining, Enchanting, and Juggling.

Now, let it be observed of what horrible impiety they stand guilty before God who join in confederacy with Satan. Hereby they renounce the Lord that made them; they make no more account of his favor and protection; they do quite cut themselves off from the covenant made with him in Baptism, from the communion of the Saints, from the true worship and service of God. And, on the contrary, they give themselves unto Satan as their god, whom they continually fear and serve. Thus are they become the most detestable enemies to God and his people that can be. For this cause Samuel told Saul that "rebellion was as the sin of Witchcraft" (1 Sam. 15.23), that is, a most heinous and detestable sin in the sight of God. The traitor that doth no hurt to his neighbour, but is willing and ready to do him the best services that can be desired, is, notwithstanding by the law of Nations, no better than a dead man because he betrays his Sovereign, and consequently cannot be a friend unto the Commonwealth. In like manner, enough the Witch were in many respects profitable and did no hurt but procured much good, yet because he hath renounced God his king and governor, and hath bound himself by other laws to the service of the enemy of God and his Church, death is his portion justly assigned him by God. He may not live.

NOTES
1. "Thou shalt not suffer a witch to live" (Exod. 22.18).
2. Conjuring tricks.
3. Witch.
4. To Simon, the sacred god; the period is A.D. 41-54.

CHAPTER 18

The Admirable History of the Possession and Conversion of a Penitent Woman
Sebastien Michaelis

Reginald Scot's *The Discovery of Witchcraft* (1584) is a sustained attack and repudiation of continental theories of witchcraft. In the final chapter of book three Scot warns readers that they may be offended by the fourth book which details the "filthy and bawdy matters," "beastly and bawdy assertions and examples" described by European works on witches. The topics include witches and devils dealing with each other "in the way of lechery," the magical removal and restoration of genitals, the bewitching of men "to use other men's wives and to refuse their own" and "to love an old hag," and the reformation of saints and clerics "which were exceeding bawdy and lecherous." The climax of this section is the tenth chapter, whose title conveys the degree of Scot's skepticism: "A confutation of all the former follies touching Incubus, which by examples and proofs of like stuff is shewed to be flat knavery, wherein the carnal copulation with spirits is overthrown."

Scot's stance reflects a tendency throughout the period of the English witch-hunts not to view sex and sexuality as inextricably linked to witchcraft. Demonic sex did not become a prominent aspect of trials until the 1640s, while accusations of magical interference in reproduction and sexual intercourse were not common (Sharpe 313). Scot's views were not, however, universally accepted, and at one point James I whose own work *Daemonologie* would emphasize links between witchcraft and appetite, especially sexual appetite (Levine 113), ordered copies of *The Discovery* to be burned. If sexuality was not an overt feature of the English conception of witchcraft, gender and sexual difference were significant elements, with prosecuting officials being almost entirely composed of men (though accusers were often female), while the great majority of defendants were women. In this light, the witch-hunts do appear as a "systematic victimisation and oppression of women" (McLuskie 58), as "Magistrates, playwrights and actors, preacher and pamphleteers, the politically ambitious and village hangers-on, all sought or built reputations on the persecution of women as witches" (Newman 64). It has been suggested that even the decline of witch-hunts, frequently explained as resulting from growing rationality and common-sense among the population, was in fact from the development of more sophisticated and powerful means of gendered authority: "the new construct of the sexually passive and domesticated woman emerged as an effective alternative to witchcraft as a means of socially controlling women" (Hester 156). In the years leading up to the household subordination of most women in English society, the witch-hunts worked to impose Christian social order, to regulate gender relations and female behavior.

The kinds of scrutiny that women's actions might be subjected to are captured in Sebastien Michaelis's *The Admirable History of the Possession and Conversion of a Penitent Woman*. The narrative covers a period of half a year, from November 1610 to mid-1611, when the woman, a religious sister, undergoes an exorcism at the hands of a Dominican father aided by a host of male clerics and assistants, and witnessed by Friar Michaelis and at times by the local townspeople as well as the woman's family. The exorcism is a protracted battle between the Dominican and the refractory will of Magdalene along with a second possessed nun, Louise, and the devils who inhabit them, Verrine and Beelzebub. On one hand, the two women are the territory over and for whom these male figures battle each other; on the other, the women are presented as the origins of evil (even the spirit Verrine regularly pleads with them to repent) and are the constant focus of various male characters, of the author Michaelis, and of readers. For most of the time this attention is registered verbally, through the pleas, laments, and quarrels waged among the characters; occasionally, however, it is depicted physically in the sufferings inflicted by both the devils and the exorcist and his assistants on the possessed. The narrative plays upon readers' voyeuristic shock at the moral and religious conflict played out upon the bodies and souls of the two women, re-staging in "the Acts" of each day the "illicit forms of theater" of possession and exorcism (Greenblatt 110) for an English audience.

Sebastien Michaelis, 1543-1618, was himself a French Dominican father, and author of various theological works. *The Admirable History* was translated within two years of its publication in French, appearing in 1613 having been printed in London. Its appeal to local readers again suggests that Scot's skepticism about European views on witchcraft are not wholly representative of English attitudes. The following excerpts are taken from a reprint of the text also issued in 1613 (*STC* 17854a; Reel 1387).

THE ADMIRABLE HISTORY OF THE POSSESSION AND CONVERSION OF A PENITENT WOMAN

The Acts of 9 December

On which day in the morning, Louise and Magdalene were by the said Dominican father exorcised,[1] and at the entrance of the same[2] Verrine began to speak in this manner: "Accursed woman, listen and be attentive unto what I shall now say unto thee. I call thee accursed because in the world there is none so impure as thou. It is true thou art most wicked and shalt be most unfortunate unless thou be converted. Never was Cain, never was Judas, never was Pilate, never was the rich Glutton[3] so horribly tortured as thou shalt be. Louise is no Philosopher, Louise hath no endowments of literature, Louise never was a student, and thou well knowest that Louise understandeth not the secrets of thy heart. But almighty God, who knoweth thy most reserved cogitations, compelleth me to say that thou hast again harkened unto Beelzebub with stronger attention (dissembling and graceless Witch as thou art) than unto thy Creator, and this thou covertly dost day by day.

"Graceless and accursed woman, I do here lay it unto thy heart that he is fearfully incensed against thee. And though it be an uncontrollable truth that thou art a thankless and proud wretch, yet doth the mother of God stand for thee. She is ever, ever, ever speaking for thee. She is ever telling her son, 'Tomorrow Magdalene will be obedient; tomorrow Magdalene will be humbled, tomorrow she will turn to goodness, tomorrow she will be converted.' O, heart of stone! O, heart of marble and of Diamond! Nothing can soften or make thee tender but the blood of the Lamb. Look to thyself Magdalene and be no more willful, else art thou everlastingly undone. O, thou a thousand and a million of times accursed! Damned shalt thou be and that more deeply than any other. The Devil shall carry thee, body and soul, to hell.

"I say unto thee, never was there, nor shall be, such a wonder as God hath now wrought for thy sake. It is true, thou ungracious and flint-hearted woman, that God could do no good upon thee neither by his inspirations, nor by preaching, nor by reading, nor by Angels, nor by all those that are in heaven, nor by so many good men as have prayed for thee. What? Must thou have a Devil to convert thee? Must thou have a Devil to be thy Physician, Apothecary, and Surgeon? This is more strange than to see a hundred and a hundred and a hundred dead bodies raised and enlivened again. The defect is nowhere but in thee, to be, if thou wilt, another Magdalene, another Thais, another Mary of Egypt, and another Pelagia.[4] Magdelene, I advise thee, resist no longer. Open the door which thou hast locked against thy God, and he will compassion thy youth and give pardon to thy transgressions."

Verrine continued on and said, "Magdalene, thou knowest well that Louise is very scrupulous and dainty of an oath and will not swear for any good. I, then, do swear by your God and by your Redeemer that it is most true which I have formerly spoken. And till this present thou didest conceive it was Louise. Is not this true? The all-powerful God, who seeth thy inmost imaginations, constraineth me to speak it."

Then he cried, "Ha, woe is me. Ha, Beelzebub thou dost threaten me. But I must not regard thy threats, for a master more potent than thou and all hell besides doth command me." Then turning to Magdalene he said, "Magdalene, renounce Beelzebub, Leviathan, Baalberith, Asmodee, Astoreth.[5] Say but I renounce thee cursed Beelzebub, and thee wretched Leviathan, and thee Baalberith, and thee Astoreth, and thee Asmodee." Then he willed the Exorcist that he would force him to make this abjuration, which he did by the mouth of Louise.

After the end of this discourse and of so terrible an invective, the Father Dominican turned to Magdalene, and commanded her to say, "Convert me Lord, and turn me to you." Then began she to weep very tenderly, and in external appearance showed marvelous great contrition for her life past, and often times kissed a Crucifix which she held in her hand.

The Dominican when he perceived in her so much compunction, after the terrible batteries of such a hammer that did so beat at the gate of her heart, asked her how she found herself. Magdalene answered, "Ha! My father, I am at the brink of desperation." To which the said Father replied, "No Magdalene, God doth not call thee to reject thee afterwards. Be confident that the gate of his mercy is opened unto thee and that his hand is stretched out to receive thee. Magdalene, resist not his motions any longer but ponder well upon them, for in them God doth offer unto thee the remission of thy sins and such abundance of grace, that if thou be willing, thou maist prove another Magdalene. What inducement leadeth thee to be distrustful of the bounty and mercy of thy Redeemer?" To which she said, "I am as it were swallowed up in the immense sea of my offences and with the foulness of my transgressions."

Then did Verrine lay hold on those words and said, "I have not spoken this unto thee to occasion thee to despair. No, no, Magdalene, although any other sinner should commit a million of impieties more than thy self, Magdalene, it is true, God would pardon him upon his coming home unto him. God cannot lie. He hath said in whatever hour;[6] he hath made no assessment of the number or enormity of sins; he desireth only unfeigned repentance. And it is most true, God receiveth a sinner as the prodigal child was received."[7] These and the like words were uttered by Verrine, so that the whole assembly was possessed with more amazement than on the day before.

The same day after Evening-song[8] were Louise and Magdalene exorcised by the same Dominican Father before the great Altar at St. Baume,[9] where there remaineth a portrait or picture of the blessed Mother of God with her son Jesus in her arms, having on one side of her the blessed Magdalene and on the other side St. Dominic.[10] At the beginning of the Exorcisms, the said Father demanded of Magdalene, "Do you acknowledge yourself to be a proud, ungrateful, and refractory woman, and to be the most miserable creature that did ever tread on earth? Do you renounce with your whole heart Beelzebub and his adherents? Are you ready to set open your heart to God, who hath created you?" To which she answered yes, and in contempt of Satan she spit three several times upon the earth.

Then presently spake Verrine and said, "Magdalene, true it is that this is the first time thou spakest from thy heart. Magdalene, now doth the whole host of heaven rejoice for thee, and all hell is in great sorrow and confusion. The Almighty compelleth me to speak it. Magdalene, take now unto thee thy God and thy Creator for thy Father and husband. Love him and him alone with all thy heart, and let neither men nor women, nor any other creature whatsoever share or have fellowship herein but for his sake. Magdalene deliver up the key of the three faculties of thy soul unto him, for he now begins to take affection unto thee.

"Magdalene, thou dost affect beauty, thy spouse is the comeliest amongst men. Hadst thou but once seen him, as hath that other Magdalene, thou wouldest nothing but languish after him. It is true," said he, turning to those that were present, "you know not this, but we know it well. Yet never saw we him in his glorious beauty, although we would endure whole millions of torments to gain the fruition of the same.

"I say, Magdalene, thy spouse is most lovely, most gracious, most perfect. He would yet be ready to die for thee and for all those that are here. He hath hands of iron for us and feet of wool for you. He that knew the greatness of his beauty would suffer millions of torments to have only a glance of him as he passed by. Yea, the very devils confess that he is beauty, goodness, and perfection itself.

"Thou lovest riches and pleasures, Magdalene. Thy Spouse is powerful to bestow upon thee Paradise and Heaven, which are replenished with all riches and pleasures that may be. Fie on devils, fie on Beelzebub, fie on all hell. True it is, Magdalene, that we Devils promise mountains and marvels, but the wages we give to those that serve and pleasure us is merely hell. But with thy Spouse there are a thousand millions of pleasures, which do never decrease nor will ever have end. The delights are so infinite, the contentation[11] so numberless, the joys so exquisite and immense withal, that though I should discourse thereof until the day of judgment, yet could I not set forth their indescribable greatness and excellency.

"Magdalene, thou lovest nobleness of blood. Thy Spouse shall ennoble thee and place thee in the rank and condition of a Queen and Princess. Only love him with all thy heart, since he loveth thee so much, and will invest thee with so much honor.

"Thou art also to take the most blessed Mother of God for thy mother. For thy natural mother here wisheth thee much good but hath not ability of performance. But the sacred Mother of God hath all power to satisfy thy desires, all knowledge to understand what is meet for thee, all goodness to grant thy requests unto thee. Magdalene, she is so amiable that she is not to be paragoned by any. We Devils neither have seen her nor shall see her; but it is in thee to behold her if thou wilt. Magdalene, the Devils will assault thee again and again, even until they tempt thee to despair. But be of good cheer, be of good cheer. God will yield thee his assistance if thou wilt but permit him to discipline and govern thy soul. And take thou no thought for anything, for the victory will remain with thee.

"True it is, Magdalene, that to enter into Paradise thou oughtest to tread in the paths of simplicity. Thou hast read many books but art little advantaged by them. The gate of Paradise is so narrow that there can enter but one at once, neither can you pass so, but you must be forced to creep upon your belly.[12] Thou art to thank Magdalene a thousand million of times, for she hath done much on thy behalf and will hereafter be thy advocate, yea, even thy sister, to be assistant unto thee in all perils and dangers.

"Thou oughtest also to render thanks unto St. Dominic (a great enemy of mine he is), for he hath mediated much on thy behalf. Thou must do the same unto the Angel that is thy Guardian, who hath begged thee of his Lord, saying, 'Lord leave Magdalene to me, suffer her to be a day longer in my custody, and she will be converted, she will repent, she will readily relinquish all the blandishments and enticings of hell.' Courage then, Magdalene, for thou hast gracious and diligent Advocates for thee unto God." Then showing her Father Romillon and the Father the Exorcist, he said unto her, "Magdalene, behold thy Gods on earth. Thou art yet as a child; suffer thyself to be governed, humble thyself, be observant of them, and follow their advice and counsel."

Verrine added, "Magdalene, tell me, didst thou never seek the Devils?" Whereunto she answered that she had. Then said Verrine, "And knowest thou not that the inferior Devil dareth not to speak in the presence of his superior. Is it not thus? Speak?" To which she answered that it was so. After this was spoken, Verrine said to Beelzebub, "I regard not at all thy threats; a greater Master than thou commandeth me. In Hell I owe thee homage and observance as one more powerful than myself, but being in this body I have nought to do with thee. For I am here by the appointment of thy Creator."

Then towards the end, he addressed his speech again to Magdalene and said, "Thou hast been served like a Princess. Thou hast had the first place at the table, and the middle, and also the last. Content thyself, and digest this remonstrance well. All these discourses are intended to thee."

When this was finished, the whole assembly thought it fit to say a *Te Deum laudamus* etc.,[13] to give thanks unto the Almighty for his manifold mercies showered down from above upon the said Magdalene. Which was done to the great joy and contentment of her own mother, who by accident was there present at St. Baume.

Te Deum laudamus etc. being ended, Magdalene cast herself at the feet of her mother and humbly craved her pardon, and performed the same to the whole assembly, who received much comfort and gladness to see the unbounded and infinite bounty of God towards his creatures.

At the same time, some advised Magdalene to take her Creator for her husband, the blessed Mother of God for her mother, the holy St. Magdalene for her sister, and St. Dominic for her father, and all the Angels for her brothers, and so to call them by these several appellations when she prayed. This being done, she directed a letter by the advice of the Father her Confessor to her blessed and gracious Mother the Virgin Mary, in this following manner.

"My most sacred, most glorious most sweet and amiable Mother, I salute you with my very heart and present myself before you, as a poor afflicted daughter before her mother, to receive some consolation. I do address myself to you (my dearest and most amiable mother) as a poor desolate girl, that is on all sides destituted and defeated of comfort, devoid of all goodness and surcharged with whatsoever is naught. I therefore in all humility pray you to take pity upon me, and do here protest that I offer and consecrate myself wholly unto you and do freely bequeath you the keys of my heart, that you may in the midst thereof implant the unstained lilies of purity and chastity, that my dearest spouse Jesus may repose himself and take his delight in the same. I give also unto you the keys of the three powers of my soul: the key of my understanding, to plant therein the laurel of perfect hope, that I may trust wholly upon my spouse; the key of my will, to plant therein the rose of fervent love, that I may above all things cleave unto him and for his love abandon all other by affection; the key of my memory, to plant therein the violet of deep humility, to put me in mind of my base and mean condition that so I may deject and debase myself to the feet of everyone, after the example of my beloved and dearest spouse. And I heartily beseech you, my dearest and best-beloved Mother, to accept these my prayers and offers. So shall I remain, now and forever, your most humble, most observant, most unworthy daughter, servant and slave, Magdalene of Jesus."

This letter Father Romillon did then approve of, but the correction thereof was on the twelfth of December, as afterward appeareth by the acts of the said day.

The Acts of 17 December

This day Verrine, for an infallible mark to discern whether this spirit came by God's permission or no, did yield very readily his obedience. And in token that he was there on God's behalf, he said he would suffer Louise to communicate without any resistance whatsoever, upon the commandment of her superior, Father Romillon. Which before this time he never did. And did dictate very distinctly unto us the disputation of the sixteenth of this present month, by the virtue of the like commandment.

Also Louise, being twice or thrice as it were ravished in an ecstasy, she recovered and came to herself as soon as her superior's command was laid upon her.

The same Magdalene was shrewdly tempted by the Devil and was depressed with a great and extraordinary sadness. And whilst Mass was saying the temptation ended, Magdalene performing all acts of humility and weeping very bitterly in St. Baume when she called to mind what had happened unto her. In the morning she was exorcised by the Dominican father, and Verrine began to speak in this manner, "Let the Luxurions live. Let those that bear false witness live. Let these and the like live for hell. But let obedience, simplicity, a good intention, pure affection, unspotted conscience, humility, and resignation of the world live for the living God, as do all they that are belonging unto the train and company of the Lamb. I say, that immaculate Lamb. He that will conquer must suffer. Peter, thou hast seen thy master in the mountain of glory and hast endured martyrdom for his sake. And thou James hast drunk of his cup, which thy mother did so little esteem of (Matt. 20.20-23).

"Surrender yourselves up into the hands of God. He knoweth what is good for you and shall be a guide unto you in all your ways.

"John the Evangelist, thou didest tell thy master *Possumus*,[14] and didest indeed afterward prove a Martyr; but it was a martyrdom of passion and grief when thou wert with thy master at the Cross. He that will go to heaven must honor God and love his neighbor as himself, and be ready to depart with his goods for his neighbor's body and with his own body for his soul. And if any shall remain obstinate, they shall fry in those unquenchable flames. It is true, many Sacrifices have been offered up unto God on the behalf of Magdalene and Lewis the Priest.[15]

"Thou Louise didest beg of God to suffer for his sake, and thou shalt suffer. And for the better support of thy patience, God will augment and double thy force upon thee. And to show that this proceedeth from God he shall make thee obedient." Then Beelzebub said that Magdalene had given up her keys unto him. Verrine answered, "Thou liest. God seeth more clearly than thyself. Thy aim is to overthrow her and make her perish, by impatience and despair. No, no, Beelzebub, this soul belongeth unto God. But put case she had made a bequest of her soul unto thee, I say that God may at any time take her home unto himself. Cannot a King enter into his own Palace at any time that pleaseth him?" Beelzebub answered, "That is true, but not against the will of the creature."

Then said Verrine unto him, "He will enter either by force or love and will have her to himself, although she had committed all the sins of those that are damned in hell. If Judas had been penitent, if Cain had craved pardon, if Adam had not stood upon his justifications and excuses, God would have forgiven them. Of such unspeakable goodness is the God of the Christians, and so well doth humility please and accord with him. The God of the Turks and the Gods of the Gentiles are all Devils. There is but one God, one Church, one Baptism. The God of the Christians is the true God, the Baptism of the Christians is the true Baptism, the Church of the Christians is the true Church. The Baptism of Turks or Jews is of no avail for the soul. The Christian shall say *In te Domine speravi*,[16] and shall never perish. It is true Magdalene, thy life shall be written and described from the first three years of thy age, and Louise shall endure much sorrow and afterwards die in pain; but the end crowneth the work.

"Think not, Magdalene, that thy God will come to thee and take thee by the hand. No, no, he will not descend in his humanity for such a purpose. Where is thy *Credo*,[17] Magdalene? Thou must now believe Magdalene; dost thou look for miracles as many others do?"

To this Beelzebub said, "I have nothing to do with that *Credo*." Verrine replied, "Ha, wicked spirit. It was not for thy sake I spake it. Magdalene shall be converted in despite of Lucifer and of all hell besides. I am true of my word." Beelzebub answered, "No, no, she shall be mine. She shall be damned, for the gate of mercy is shut against her."

Then said Verrine, "It is not so. Her will to do well [will] prove acceptable and pleasing, and thou saist this (accursed as thou art) to plunge her into despair. But the just shall say *In te Domine speravi*, and shall find the gates of Paradise opened unto them, as witnesseth St. Augustine.[18]

"The Church shall examine this whole tract, wherein is nothing contained either against God or his Church. Here shall many be illuminated, and he that shall dive into the bottom of the sack shall easily approve the same. The curious and proud shall have their abode in the pit of hell, and shall not have the power to believe." Then he said, "*Carreau*[19] cannot fill thy heart. Magdalene, thy part is set triangle-wise, and the blessed Trinity is to replenish and comfort the same."

The same day, Verrine told Magdalene roundly and rigorously of her faults, being in her chamber, and spake unto her in this sort. "Magdalene, if thou resolve not upon thy conversion between this and Christmas, thou shalt be everlastingly damned and burnt alive, and shalt not for all this escape our hands, as none have ever escaped us these hundredth ninety-nine years, because we made them all to despair. This indeed will be the Magician's confusion,[20] but shall leave no touch or taint upon the company of St. Ursula,[21] the company of the Christian doctrine, or upon thy father, whom I have pronounced innocent though Beelzebub took a false oath against him, saying that thy father had given thee unto him, which was false. For thou of thy own accord and from a full and frank will didest give thyself to Lucifer and to all his adherents, renouncing God, the blessed Trinity and Paradise; renouncing all the merits of the Passion of Christ Jesus, all the prayers of the sacred mother of God and of all Angels and Saints; taking and choosing hell; accepting the same as thy last and everlasting habitation; saying that thou hadst rather live in this world in all varieties of delights and villainies than to serve God thy Creator and thy Redeemer Jesus Christ; promising Beelzebub to be obedient unto all his commands, and that thou diddest give him with all thy heart, thy body and soul with the powers thereof, reserving nothing to thyself but hell, which those that are culpable of the like abominations do deserve, if they remain and die in their sins; making a schedule written in thy blood by thine own hand, and giving it to Beelzebub, which afterwards the Magicians got into their custody.

"It is true, she did not enter into these infernal courses herself, but was induced and by allurements drawn unto it by the thieves of her soul. But Lodovicus, seeing that dreadful wolf of hell to approach, left this silly sheep to be seized by him, yea, enticed her into the claws of ravenous wolves which are the Devils of hell.

"She was young, which will be a good plea for her because God is accustomed to compassionate youth. Witness the prodigal child, who left his father's house, as Magdalene hath done, and fed with hogs, as she did. Yet did he not die in his obstinacy, but acknowledged his fault and prostrated himself at the feet of his father in great humility. So, if Magdalene shall cast herself at the feet of the mercy of her God and shall knock at his gate, that father of pity will command her to be let in and will bid the fat calf to be killed. He will also cause new garments to be fetched and cast upon her, which signifieth a good conscience and repentance, and will put a ring on her finger to declare the faith and trust she ought to give to the words of her father, and how grateful she should be in her acknowledgments of his benefits. Then, is she to say, 'Father, father, I have sinned against heaven, and against thee, and am no more worthy to be esteemed thine. Entreat me as one of your hirelings, although most unworthy of such a place as that.' Thus should Magdalene humble herself, and should say, approaching to the seat of his mercy, 'Father, I have sinned against heaven and against thee, against thy blessed Mother, against the whole Court of heaven, and against all thy creatures. I am therefore unworthy to be called your daughter, nay, your slave; nay, I am not worthy to lift up mine eyes to heaven. But take me unto your mercy (if it stand with your good pleasure), who am the most wretched and disconsolate creature that lives under the heaven, or upon the earth.'"

Then he added further, "Magdalene, be converted and abandon thy sins. Thou hast been hitherto gently led on in calmness and in softness. Thou hast been privily reproved by secret inspirations, by preaching, by reading of good books, by many spiritual instructions which have from time to time been infused into thee, as well in the house of St. Ursula as by the fathers the Confessors and other learned and illuminated personages, who have given them unto thee both for thy practice and for a remedy against thy adversaries." He further said, "Magdalene being rebelliously bent against her God and the admonitions of his Spouse the Church, and God seeing her perdition so near and herself so obstinate in her sins, and having by all the above-named remedies profited nothing, hath permitted that an unworthy, yea, thrice-unworthy sister of the Company of St. Ursula, Louise Capelle, who of herself is less powerful than the leaf of a tree, a stone, or a pismire,[22] yea, who conceiveth herself to be unworthy of the title or style of one of God's creatures, should pronounce these things by the appointment of God almighty and a Devil named Verrine, should by her mouth dictate and deliver all these writings."

Then he made this remonstration unto Magdalene, saying unto her in a great fury and chafe[23] as if he had been mad, that God was infinitely angry with her if she were not amended, or did remain in a determinate kind of obstinacy. And he for his part did speak with as great assuredness from God as ever the Prophet Jonah did speak to the people of Nineveh, when he said unto them, "If you repent not, you shall all perish." But they were wise, as Magdalene will be, and followed the example of their King, who took ashes and cast them upon his head to appease and slake the wrath of God against them (Jonah 23).

He also said to Magdalene, "Art not thou an accursed woman, that the Witches' Sabbath is kept here? Blushest thou not, that these Sabbaths and abominable conventions are kept here for thy sake, and that Magicians, Witches, Hags, and Sorcerers do bewitch all these that are here? Yea, Father Francis himself hath taken in a charm whilest he was drinking."

Verrine further said unto sister Magdalene, "If God were capable of sadness, he would bewail, Magdalene, the great uncertainty and suspense wherein thou keepest him touching thy conversion." Then did Verrine threaten her with more absoluteness and authority than ever her Superior[24] did use towards her or any creature in the world beside. And good reason hath he for the same, because he was to execute the will of the Creator, being (as he himself said) as the King's Sergeant, who speaketh in the

King's name and authority and commandeth, saying, "If you do not put this in execution and obey the King, you shall be grievously punished because he that withstandeth his King deserveth the most severe punishment that can be inflicted. So the sinner that rebelleth and grows obstinate against his God, not keeping his commandments, nor observing his and the Churches' Counsels, he deserveth sharpe correction, yea, tortures and hell itself."

Also he said, "O, Magdalene, convert thyself. God is most gracious and full of pity. Thou art vexed, Magdalene, to contemn and set at naught the delights of this world, and yet regardest not the pleasures of eternity."

Then he said, "Miserable, accursed, and damned as thou art, art thou not truly unhappy to believe that which cometh from Lucifer and givest no heed unto me who am here from God? Art thou not unhappy to believe that Louise is the author and expresser of these things? O Magdalene, thou doest believe it, and this belief is exceedingly prejudicial unto thee. It is true Magdalene, and I must lay it close unto thee, thou didest double and hadst a false intention before God, and thy opinion was that Louise spake these things from her own head. And this is true, Magdalene. As for Louise, she is possessed, Catherine is also possessed, and so are the rest that are bewitched, but they know nothing of what is here delivered. Whereof thou, Magdalene, art the only unhappy cause. It is true, Magdalene, thou art proud and ungrateful, having a heart of stone, a heart harder than a Diamond. Thou conceivest that God is thy debtor. O, thou proud caitiff, how willing wouldest thou have been to pluck him if thou hadst been able from his throne of Majesty. But be of good courage, Magdalene, and humble thyself. Thy God is so good that although thou hadst run through all the sins of the world and of all the damned, thy God can show thee mercy, yea, and will pardon thee thy offences, if thou humble thyself and be penitent."

The same day in the evening Louise and Magdalene were exorcised by Father Francis, and Verrine spake in this manner, "Who hath ever beheld the like, that a Devil should enter the lists[25] against a Devil? We are all damned forever, and what we do we do by constraint. For there is no joy of charity dwelling in us. I aver that this woman is possessed and hath three Devils in her body, for the particular conversion of two principally and then for the conversion of many others. He that will not travel to Mount Calvary shall not ascend Mount Tabor.[26] God did intimate thus much unto the mother of the children of Zebedee.[27] Peter denied his Master, but he repented and wept very bitterly, yea, afterwards died for him and was crucified for his name's sake. Our Lord had many friends and associates that did bear him company at the Table at Easter, Whitsuntide[28] and Christmas, but there were few that received him worthily and a small number that presented themselves before him with due and serious preparation.

"I take God to witness, his blessed Mother, and all Saints, that I do now tell you, if you do not repent and acknowledge the benefits that God hath so plentifully poured upon you, you are not worthy to be partakers of any Sacrament. Nay, you deserve to die without the comfort of them.

"Those that are curious are liquorous[29] of more knowledge than is expedient for them. Which they make inquisition after in the pit of Hell, as do the Calvinists and all other Heretics who would interpret the passages in holy writ not according to God's meaning, but interpose their own giddy and private fancies, and reject the meaning and exposition of the Church.[30] Young people, be you penitent. You pamper up your flesh with such delicacies and niceness and let in all pleasures with such a full scope unto you that you stand under the arrest of high treason against God. We tempt youth and make them fall like mellow figs from a tree when they are shaken by a strong wind. Neither need we to help this wind by our breath. I am as a Sergeant and execute my commission; I say you may attain, if you will, unto heaven. Yet are you obstinate and think that God is indebted unto you, and that the way to Heaven is easy and open.

"No, no, I tell you that God cannot sin, nor lie. Ponder well upon this so fearful a sentence, 'Go ye cursed into Hell' (Matt. 25.41), and live forever in all misery in that other world, together with those whom in this life you have obeyed and harkened unto.

"We that are Devils do dandle and make much of them with a thousand varieties of torments. We bestow sights and visions upon them, but they are the visions of Devils that would at one clap strike all men stark dead to have but a sidelong glance of their horrid deformities. They do also see the souls of the damned who, having in their first creation been fashioned with much beauty, are now as hideous in their semblances as are the Devils themselves.

"You have indeed the Saints to intercede for you, saying Lord give them of the water of life (Rev. 22.1). But you are to conceive yourselves to be unworthy of that life unless you humble yourselves, believing that you are unworthy of such a place as Hell. Nay, if that God shall make ten thousand hells, yet are you to think that your deserts do surmount the torments of them all. If you fast in this world you shall feast in the world to come. The excellency of the choice delicacies of the world to come doth breed a satiety and disgust of the meats you here enjoy. And whosoever could but get a crumb or the least relish in the world of those dainties, they are so exquisitely prepared that they would cause all the viands of this world to be loathed. We may talk of them but we shall never taste them. It is too late now to repent us. That horse is not a horse of price and value that gallopeth not but when he is spurred, and he who serveth God with an ill will is of no reckoning. It is many times a greater fault to omit that thou oughtest to do than to do that which thou oughtest to omit. There are three sorts that serve God. The first serve him as slaves, and they are those that are always in

Hell. Others serve him as Hirelings, and those have regard to nothing but to the reward of Heaven and are like those that work and travel merely for their profit. And there are those that serve him more faithfully, who serve him as children out of mere love.

"A virtuous child hath no regard unto the goods of his Parents. Neither doth he murmur at those blows which for his reformation they give unto him, but is respective of his duty and is serviceable unto them merely out of affection. So do the children of God; they serve him not out of expectancy of reward but from the strength of their love. A cup of fresh water that is given unto the poor payeth a whole year's ransom in Purgatory. O great God, it is no wonder if neither beasts, Barbarians, nor Indians do know thee, for they either have no understanding or do live in darkness. But I marvel at thy children the Christians, that they do not acknowledge thee whose name and stamp they carry. For a Christian hath his appellation from Christ, as the Bride beareth the name of the Bridegroom. In the blessed baptism, God the Father taketh the soul for his daughter; the son taketh it for his sister; the holy Ghost for his Spouse; and all the blessed Trinity for their Temple.

"You do so little reckon of Baptism that when you approach to this Sacrament a man would say that you went to some May-game or dance, for you talk in the Church and do nothing but laugh, using many other scandalous misdemeanments of this nature, and do indeed anything rather than conceive of this Sacrament with reverence. St. John did not run into such an error, but when he baptized our Lord he baptized him in great fear and devotion (Matt. 3.13-15). How great an oversight is this in you thus to disesteem the Sacraments that have their institution from God himself and are the pillars on which this Church doth lean. Neither is there any Sacrament that hath not drawn blood from him." Then Verrine set his foot upon Beelzebub and said, "Beelzebub, I do adjure thee by the living God that if thou have anything to reply that what I have now said is not true, thou give answer thereunto. Speak Beelzebub, whether that which I have spoken be true or no. I do further adjure thee by Lucifer that if thou canst take me tripping thou do directly tell me wherein I lie. O cursed Beelzebub, thou canst not reply against me for I deliver the truth, and that by the appointment of God. Thou art accursed and as wretched as myself. Speak wicked spirit if thou hast anything to say."

Then Verrine began to cry. "All you here may observe (speaking to the Assembly that was there present[31]) he is my Prince, but I do not now acknowledge him to be so. It is true Beelzebub thou art my Prince, but I here renounce any superiority which thou pretendest to have over me. I also renounce thee Lucifer and the authority of all the Devils in Hell, for we are not powerful to resist the Almighty. You who take Lucifer's part can reply nothing of any moment or importance, neither have you more force than a sort of Flies." All this while did Verrine, in contempt, tread upon Beelzebub, saying, "Thou proud Spirit, and full of arrogance as myself; thou swellest and art in the height of pride. I hope there is no offence done if that these proud creatures be dejected and thoroughly disheartened."

Then Verrine said to Magdalene, "Magdalene, the gate of Heaven is opened. So is the gate of Hell, and there men may enter in at full Carroche,[32] yea, four Carroches together may have easy passage thither, and all four may enter in a front. But the gate of Paradise is so narrow that few pass in thereat, and much humiliation is expedient to enter in at the same.

"Over this gate Obedience is seated, and under it is Humility. On the one side standeth Charity, on the other Hope. And Perseverance is the Porter that letteth in those that come thither.[33] Humility represents the birth of the Son of God, and Obedience signifieth that the Son of God hath humbled himself from his birth until the time of his death.

"Sin is more ugly and deformed than the Devil. If a man had a convenient house of his own and a reasonable competency wherewith to live, and yet without cause should give and cast himself into the hands of Turks, and should from them receive hard usage and entertainment, if such a one should plain[34] himself, men would say unto him, 'Friend, you were not well advised. You lived well in your own house, and who is cause of this calamity but yourself?' I say there is no man that would compassionate such a fellow. Even so, every man hath somewhat whereby he is enabled to make opposition against the world provided that he have the grace of God. But if he will sin and invassal[35] himself to the Devil, who will pity his case? He is disabled in his brain that enjoyeth liberty and doth voluntarily render himself up to flattery." Then he confirmed this speech with a solemn oath, and after said, "To what use and purpose are wholesome waters if there be none to drink of them? You must frequent the Sacraments that you may make your profit and advantage of them. Magdalene, the judgments of God are not to be squared by the judgments of men. You are to stoop and abase yourselves in this world if you will ascend to that which is to come. This which I have spoken, Magdalene, was never hammered in the shop of Hell.

"The Devils have at sundry times preached and broached divers curiosities to the prejudice and perdition of those that entertained the same, but the things which I deliver conduce to the amendment of men's lives and conversations.

"The souls of men fall as thick into Hell as the Corn doth from the Mill. Men go to Hell by thousands but they enter one by one into Heaven, though it be not always so. At times there have gone to Heaven ten thousand Martyrs in one day and eleven thousand Virgins in another day, and many other arrive there after sundry manners, according to the good pleasure of God."

The same day Verrine was asked why Magdalene was not yet endowed with upright intention since she followed his instructions, and the day before the conception had heartily renounced Satan. To this he answered that he is perfectly possessed with upright intention that casteth no lustful wink or glance of the eye on any creature. Yet a man might have an honest heart although his intention do fleet and waver, and might be, as it were, placed in the middle, seized upon by neither party. Then he said that he was not able to speak one word before another, but as he received them from above so he spake them.

The Acts of 10 April, being Tuesday

At these Exorcisms the Devil brought up a new fashion of torments, making Magdalene to leap when she was upon her knees. And as she was kneeling he caused her to give great jumps, so that she broke the stool which was under her knees, although they had laid two cloaks upon the same. His meaning was to have broken her legs, as he afterwards declared. For Lucifer did ever feed them with new experiments.

The Acts of 20 April, being Wednesday

Beelzebub being asked and adjured to tell whether Magdalene were truly converted or no (for some made a doubt thereof), he answered that she was, and that Verrine and he did jump and agree in this: "You may easily believe it (said he) since by the commandment of God I have taken away those marks that were upon her, which is a great miracle and an infallible argument of her conversion."

Being adjured to tell whether the Magician were converted or no, he answered, "Not very soundly."

Being adjured to tell whether he would surrender up the schedules or no, he said, "Yesterday, by reason of an act of humility and obedience that Magdalene had performed, Fortitudo[36] did advertise me from God that if the Magician were converted he should surrender them himself. If not, then Beelzebub should be constrained to present them openly in the face of the Court, both Ecclesiastical and Civil, and then all Charms and possession should have an end." Then they applied a Relic unto the back of Magdalene, whereupon he cried, "Take her away from me, for she is an enemy unto the Synagogue." Being adjured to explain the meaning hereof, he answered, "The Synagogue hath three great enemies, Magdalene, for her repentance; Catherine of Sienna, for her charity towards her neighbors; and Catherine of Bologna,[37] for her purity and great humility. And the Relics do belong unto this last."

The Acts of 21 April, being Thursday

Upon this day Magdalene was seven sundry times tormented very cruelly both in the Chapel and in her chamber, and at suppertime she had some rest. But presently after supper Leviathan came and said, "Beelzebub and I cannot be here, for we are busied at the prison." Then he said, "Mistress, since you have not been made much of all supper time, we will now bestow the rack upon you." And incontinently four Devils, who she visibly saw, did give her the rack for the space of three quarters of an hour, after such a cruel manner that three men, who kept her from falling, were all in a bath with sweating and laboring about her so that they could endure the toil thereof no longer. That which most disquieted her (as she afterward told us) was the vehement temptations wherewith they did inwardly assault her, which always happened when she was not corporally tormented. So that she was incessantly assaulted either within or without.

NOTES

1. Louise is possessed by the devil Verrine, while Magdalene, the penitent woman of the title, is possessed by Beelzebub, "prince of the devils" (Matt. 12.24). Both are sisters in the convent of Saint Ursula. The exorcist is identified on the title page as Friar Francis Domptius, Doctor of Divinity at the University of Louaine.
2. Magdalene. The motive for Verrine's outburst is given in an earlier sidenote: "There was observed a great hatred betwixt the two possessed, proceeding from the devils that were contrary."
3. Luke 16.19-31.
4. Magdalene: Mary Magdalene, witness to the Resurrection; Thais: mistress of Alexander the Great; Mary of Egypt: fifth-century penitent and ascetic; Pelagia: Saint Pelagia of Antioch, died c. 311.
5. Leviathan: sea-monster (Job 41); Baalberith: god of Shechem (Judg. 8.33); Asmodee: devil in Jewish demonology; Astoreth: Phoenician and Canaanite goddess of fertility and reproduction.
6. Cf. Matt. 24.42 and Rev. 3.3.
7. See Luke 15.11-33.
8. Evensong or vespers, prayers sung at around sunset.
9. A French convent and church.
10. Saint Dominic, 1170-1221, Spanish priest and founder of Dominican order of priests.
11. Contentment.
12. Cf. Matt. 7.14.
13. "Let us praise God," an ancient Latin hymn.
14. "We are able" (Matt. 20.22).
15. Possibly Dionysius van Leeuwen, 1402-71, Belgian ascetic monk and theologian, also known as Dionysius the Carthusian.
16. "I have trusted you, Lord."
17. "I believe."
18. In a commentary on Ps. 30.
19. A small square.
20. The male witch who seduced Magdalene and made her become a witch.
21. Legendary Christian British princess, supposedly murdered at Cologne with 11,000 attendant virgins.
22. An ant.

23. Irritation, annoyance.
24. The head of the convent, Father Romillon.
25. Barriers which enclose a space for tilting.
26. Calvary: where Christ was crucified (Luke 23.33); Tabor: in Galilee (eg. Judg. 4.6).
27. Father of apostles, James and John (Mark 3.17).
28. Festival commemorating the descent of the Holy Spirit to the apostles, starting on the seventh Sunday after Easter.
29. Desirous.
30. Labeling Calvinists "heretics" (which would not have been considered at all inappropriate by members of the orthodox Anglican church) underlines the fact that Reformation and Counter-Reformation controversies were a predominant context for Early Modern witch-hunts.
31. Religious figures, villagers, and townspeople.
32. A stately coach or carriage.
33. Cf. the House of Holiness in *The Faerie Queene* 1.10.
34. Complain.
35. Enslave.
36. An attendant devil; the schedules are records of spells and of those who are or will be possessed.
37. Saint Catherine of Sienna, 1347-80, sister of the order of Saint Dominic; Saint Catherine of Bologna, 1413-63, Italian abbess.

Law

CHAPTER 19

The Law's Resolutions of
Women's Rights: Or, the Law's
Provision for Women
T. E.

In the opening chapter of *The Law's Resolutions*, the author, "T. E.," suggests that on the basis of the Biblical account of creation, "Male and female he created them," a twofold legal system developed: "of which division, because the part that we say hath least judgment and discretion be a Law unto it self (Women only women), they have nothing to do in constituting Laws or consenting to them, in interpreting of Laws or in hearing them interpreted at lectures, leets, or charges, and yet they stand strictly tied to men's establishments, little or nothing excused by ignorance" (2). It has been suggested that such a view of women's exclusion from and restriction by the law is somewhat overstated, neglecting powers held by certain women "by reason of property, wealth, or standing" (Davis, "Women" 168), and possibly diminishing the importance attributed to women as mothers "defined in terms of the patriarchal linear descent: she is a custodian of the carriers of the line" (Jardine 81). Nonetheless, women's legal rights were curtailed by tradition and precedent: "the principle of woman's inferiority is almost universal. It is to be found in the substratum of legal thought" (Maclean 81). Some room for legal maneuver was developing, however, and "T. E." aims to "handle that part of the English Law which containeth the immunities, advantages, interests, and duties of women" (3).

Women were subject to the same laws and punishments as men in regard to criminal law (though the murder of a husband was regarded as treason). Since most women's places in society were determined by fathers or husbands, their rights in many areas of civil law were weaker than men's. For example, women could not make contracts on their own or their family's behalf unless granted the authority to do by their husbands. They were not legally prevented from being heirs to the family estate, but a brother would always be chosen ahead of a sister. They were unable to participate in legal processes as lawyers or jurors or to hold legal and administrative positions. The restrictions were intensified by marriage, "which altered the status of a woman for the purposes of the law of actions, obligations and property" (Baker 391). In marriage, the woman's legal identity was subsumed by that of her husband or *baron*, who was regarded as "both her sovereign and her guardian": "She could not sue or be sued at common law without her *baron*, and this prevented her from suing him for any wrong done to her" (Baker 395). Her belongings and property became his.

One area of law which was developing and increasing women's legal power at the end of the sixteenth century, especially in regard to property, was Equity, administered by the Court of Chancery. Generally, Equity worked to offer relief where the Common Law was too rigid or obscure. The main way in which it could assist the position of married women (though only those who owned land) was in allowing them to hold estates separately from their husbands: "By creating and enforcing trusts in the later sixteenth century, Chancery was able to modify the existing law and enable a married woman to hold property independently of her spouse and to exercise the same rights over this property as a *feme sole* [unmarried woman] or a man could" (Cioni 15). The Chancery Court might also decide that poor or ignorant women, unable to run a case through the expensive and complex Common Law system, deserved financial support or rights to property from which they had been evicted. Indeed, "the motive behind the majority of [Chancery] suits involving female litigants was the need to be assured of present or future security in estates and chattels" (Cioni 282).

The Law's Resolutions discusses many such aspects of the law that affected women, and thus men, negatively and positively. Its principal concerns are with situations connected to the law of marriage, "the most important part of the English law of persons" (Baker 391). These include rights and obligations in relation to processes of betrothal and engagement, during marriage, and in cases of separation and annulment. The recurring concern within the law of marriage is with ownership of property. At times the author's tone is rather sardonic as explanations are given of how common law precedents work, in supposedly just ways, against women's interests, and it is often suggested that they ought to retain a materialistic rather than romantic attitude toward marriage and husbands. Women are also urged to move for redress and reform through parliament. The later chapters turn to the topics of rape and abduction and attack the leniency of the relevant laws in certain situations. In closing, the text suggests that the historical and interpretative complexities of the law work to reduce women's position and rights and can only be resisted if knowledge and awareness of the law are held by women themselves.

The author of *The Law's Resolutions of Women's Rights* is not known. The opening "Epistle to the Reader" is signed by "T. E." who, the *Short*

Title Catalogue suggests, might be Thomas East, a printer, or Thomas Edgar, an editor from the period. The work has sometimes been attributed to Sir John Doddridge, an eminent lawyer of the Elizabethan and Jacobean years, who wrote a number of other legal digests, such as *The Lawyer's Light: Or, a Due Direction for the Study of the Law* (1629), and *The English Lawyer: Describing a Method for the Managing of the Laws of This Land* (1631).

The Law's Resolutions was published in London in 1632 (*STC* 7437; Reel 883). It is over 400 pages in length; accordingly, only a selection of chapters are reproduced here, the title of each with relevant book and section numbers given at the start of each extract. For a non-specialist it represents a particularly complex text, filled with legal references and jargon in English, French, and Latin. *OED* definitions have been used for some of these terms, and E. R. Hardy Ivamy's tenth edition of *Mozley and Whiteley's Law Dictionary* has also been consulted.

THE LAW'S RESOLUTIONS OF WOMEN'S RIGHTS

The Creation of Man and Woman (1.2)
In the second chapter, Moses declareth and expresseth the Creation of Women, which word in good sense signifieth not the "woe of Man" as some affirm, but "with Man." For so in our hasty pronouncing we turn the preposition "with" to "woe" or "we" sometimes. And so she was ordained to be with man as a help and a companion, because God saw it was not good that Man should be alone. Then, when God brought Woman to Man to be named by him, he found straight away that she was bone of his bones, flesh of his flesh, giving her a name, testifying she was taken out of Man. And he pronounced that for her sake man should leave Father and Mother and adhere to his Wife, which should be with him one.

Now Man and Woman Are One
Now, because Adam hath so pronounced that man and wife shall be but one flesh, and our Law is that if a feoffment[1] be made jointly to John at Stile and to Thomas Noke and his wife of three acres of land, that Thomas and his wife get no more but one acre and a half, *quia una persona*,[2] and a writ of conspiracy doth not lie against one only.[3] And that is the reason a writ of conspiracy doth not lie against *baron* and *feme*,[4] for they are but one person. And by this a married Woman perhaps may either doubt whether she be either none or no more than half a person. But let her be of good cheer. Though for the near conjunction which is between man and wife and to tie them to a perfect love, agreement, and adherence, they be by intent and wise fiction of Law one person, yet in nature and in some other cases by the Law of god and man they remain divers. For as Adam's punishment

was several[5] from Eve's, so in Criminal and other special causes our Law argues them several persons. You shall find that *persona* is an *Individuum* spoken of anything which hath reason, and therefore of nothing but *Vel de Angelo, vel de homme* (154 in Dyer[6]), who citeth no worse authority for it than Calepinus's own self.[7] Seeing, therefore, I list not to doubt with Plato whether Women be reasonable or unreasonable creatures, I may not doubt but every woman is a temporal person, though no woman can be a spiritual vicar.

Of Hermaphrodites
Of Hermaphrodites I have some kind of doubts, not whether they be persons but what persons they be. If a man die seised,[8] leaving three children which be all Hermaphrodites, whether the eldest shall have all his land or that it be partible among coheirs? Also, if the eldest be a Hermaphrodite and the other two fair young Virgins, which way setteth the descent? Bracton, in his first Book, chapter seven,[9] saith it must be deemed male or female according to the predominance most inciting.

And, as I remember, I have read the like division, Bracton in his first book (30.438). . . . Now, then, if these creatures be no Monsters but are in conjunction to take on them the kind which is most ruling in them, this must needs be understood in matrimony. And consequently they may have heirs. Which, being granted, why may they not be heirs according to the prevalence which Bracton speaketh of?

If I were to furnish myself a house, I would place no picture or image in any parlor, dining, or bedchamber but it should be of good, seemly, and natural proportion. Satyrs and Centaurs should come no nearer than the post at my door. And at the threshold of this my treatise or, as it were, a little behind the door, I will leave these deformed Children of Mercury or Venus,[10] suffering them to enter no further.

The Punishment of Adam's Sin (1.3)
Return a little to Genesis, in the third Chapter whereof is declared our first parents' transgression in eating the forbidden fruit. For which Adam, Eve, the serpent first, and lastly the earth itself is cursed. And besides the participation of Adam's punishment, which was subjection to Mortality, exiled from the Garden of Eden, enjoined to labor, Eve, because she had helped to seduce her husband, hath inflicted on her an especial bane: "In sorrow shalt thou bring forth thy children, thy desires shall be subject to thy husband, and he shall rule over thee" (Gen. 3.16).

See here the reason of that which I touched before, that Women have no voice in Parliament. They make no Laws, they consent to none, they abrogate none. All of them are understood either married or to be married and their desires subject to their husband. I know no remedy though some women can shift it well enough. The Common Law here shaketh hand with Divinity. But because I am come too soon to the title of *Baron* and *feme*, and Adam and Eve were the first and last that were married so young, it is best that I run back again to consider of the things (which I might seem to have lost by the way) that are fit to be known concerning women before they be fit for marriage.

The Ages of a Woman (1.4)
The learning is 35 Henry VI 40,[11] that a Woman hath divers special ages. At the seventh year of her age, her father shall have aid of his tenants to marry her. At nine years' age, she is able to deserve and have dowry. At twelve years to consent to marriage. At fourteen to be *hors du guard*[12]; at sixteen to be passed the Lord's tender of a husband[13]; at twenty-one to be able to make a feoffment.[14] And per Ingelton,[15] there in the end of the case, a woman married at twelve cannot disagree afterward, but if she be married younger she may dissent till she be fourteen.

The age of seven years, when Bracton wrote this aid, for making the son a knight or marrying the daughter, was due by grace and not by right, and measured by the indigence of the Lord and opulence of the tenants. But Westminster 1.35, in the third year of Edward I,[16] the Law was made certain: the Lord shall have aid of his tenants, as soon as his daughter accomplished seven years' age, for the marriage of her. Viz. rents of a whole knight's fee,[17] and rents of rental land in socage[18] and so forth, according to the rate more or less.

The King shall have this aid according to this proportion by a Statute made 25 Edward III. And for this aid every Lord may either distrain[19] or bring his writ *de auxilio habendo*[20] at his election, but tenant by grand serjeanty or petit[21] shall not pay this aid. No more shall copy-holders, as seemeth by the writ both in Fitzherbert and Bracton. . . .

A Woman Compellable to Serve (1.5)
The next age of a Woman is 9 years when she is dowable. But we will stay a while with the virgins concerning whom, if they be in the power and governance of parents, masters, or close friends, or if they be poor, the Law differeth little or not much from the common form appertaining unto males, unless it be in cases of rape, which I reserve to the end of my discourse, where the poor have least need of subsidy. Only this I observe here, by a Statute made 5 Elizabeth 4. Two Justices of Peace in the Country, or the head officer and two Burgesses in Cities, etc., may appoint any woman of the age of twelve years and under forty, being unmarried and out of service, to serve and be retained by year, week, or day, in such sort and for such wages as they shall think meet. And if she refuse, they may commit her to prison till she shall be bound to serve.

Of Heirs (1.6)
But leaving this sort to the title of day laborers, come we to women wards in the custody of their lords. And take for the foundation here the Statute itself, Westminster 1.22. This Statute, expressly reciting the material point of the Statute of Merton,[22] willeth it in every of them to be observed. And the Statute of Merton is this: whosoever lay person shall be convicted, be he parent or other, to have detained, abducted, or married some child, he shall yield the value of the marriage and be imprisoned until ye have both made amends to the party damnified, if the ward be married, and satisfaction to the King for the transgression. But if any heir of fourteen years' age, or upward till twenty-one, shall marry himself without agreeing with his Lord to defraud him of the marriage, where the Lord offered him a convenient marriage and without disparagement, there it shall be lawful to hold the inheritance until and after the full age of twenty-one years, by so long time as shall suffice to reap and receive the double value of the marriage. . . .

Let us speak of heirs, and see a little in what cases a woman shall inherit. It is known to all that because women lose the name of their ancestors, and by marriage usually they are transferred *in alienam familiam*,[23] they participate seldom in heirship with males, and therefore Bracton is bold to say a woman is never named in inheritance as long as male heirs remain. But to this rule be subjoineth exception and examples, the very same which are in Littleton.[24] To wit exception of right line, right blood, and manner of giving.

The Second Book
Now that I have brought up a Woman and made her an Inheritrix, taken her out of Ward, helped her to make partition, etc., methinks she should long so be married: woman desires man, as matter desires form. And I did not mean when I begun to produce any Vestal Virgin, Nun, or nun Saint Bridget. Following therefore my first intention, I will begin to instruct Women grown, first such as are or shortly shall be Wives, and then Widows.

Of Marriage, According to the Civil and Common Law (2.1)
Marriage is defined to be a Conjunction of Man and Woman, containing an inseparable connection and union of life. But as there is nothing that is begotten and finished at once, so this Contract of coupling man and woman together hath an inception first and then an orderly proceeding. The first beginning of Marriage (as in respect of Contract and that which Law taketh hold on) is when Wedlock by words in the future tense is promised and vowed, and this is but *sponsio* or *sponsalia*.[25] The full Contract of Matrimony is when it is made by words in the present time[26] in a lawful consent, and thus two be made man and wife, existing without lying

together. Yet Matrimony is not accounted consummate until there go with the consent of mind and will Conjunction of body.

Of Sponsion or First Promising (2.2)

The first promising and inception of Marriage is in two parts. Either it is plain, simple, and naked, or confirmed and born by giving of something. The first is when a man and woman bind themselves simply by their word to contract Matrimony hereafter. The second, when there is an oath made, or somewhat taken as an earnest or pledge betwixt them, on both parts or on one part, to be married hereafter. There is not here to be stood upon the age definitively set down for making of marriage irrevocable, but all that are seven years old (betwixt whom Matrimony may consist) may make sponsion[27] and promise. But if any that is under the age of seven begin this vow and betrothing, it is esteemed as a mist and vanisheth to nothing.

Of Public Sponsion (2.3)

This Sponsion (in which, as it stands, is no full Contract of Matrimony, nor any more save only an obligation or being bound in a sort to marry hereafter) may be public or secret. Public, either by the parties themselves, present together, or by message or Letters when they be distant one from another. Neither is there herein any curious form of paction or stipulation required, but only by words, howsoever expressed, a plain consent and agreement of the parties. And, by the Civil Law (with which the ancient Canons concorded) of their parents if the Contractors were under the power of parents. The like reason seemeth to be for consent of tutors, etc. But it is now received a general opinion that the goodwill of parents is required in regard of honesty not of necessity, according to the Canons which exact necessarily none other consent but only of the parties themselves whose Conjunction is in hand, without which the conclusion of parents is of none effect. Note further that *sponsalia* may be made pure or conditional, and whatsoever is else adjected (as earnest, pledge, or such like) is but accidental.

Of Secret Sponsion (2.4)

Those Spousals which are made when a man is without witness, *Solus cum sola*,[28] are called secret promising or desponation. Which, though it be tolerated when by liquid and plain probation it may appear to the Judge and there is not any lawful impediment to hinder the Contract, yet it is so little esteemed of (unless it be very manifest) that another promise public, made after it, shall be preferred and prevail against it. The cause why it is misliked is the difficulty of proof for avoiding of it when for offence, her just cause of refusal, the one or other party might seek to go loose and perhaps cannot but must stand haltered from any other Marriage, and the Judge in suspense what to determine.

The Validity of the Desponsation (2.5)

Though this *Sponsalia* be always made with intent that Matrimony should ensue, yet the Contractor cannot thereunto be compelled unless there were another thing joined to the Contract of Spousals. Neither are they compellable to marry, though an oath accompanied the promise, unless it were made pure and without Condition. For in conditional sponsion of Marriage, the bond of performance is suspended in the Condition till that be performed, unless there follow a relinquishment of the Condition by copulation of bodies or a new consent by words of the present.

The Nature of the Condition (2.6)

And here, in the quality of Conditions, it is observed that if the Condition annexed to the promise be repugnant against the right of Matrimony, the disposition of the whole Spousals are void. As if a man promise a woman to marry her if she poison the child which she conceived, the promise is of none effect as towards Marriage. But a Condition, though it be otherwise dishonest or impossible, corrupteth not promise of Marriage if it be not adversant and against the Law of Wedlock.

How Long the Performance of Promise Is to Be Excepted (2.7)

Now, it may be demanded what time must be tarried and expected by the Law Civil and Common, for perimplishing[29] of promises made of future Wedlock. It is answered that if the limits of time prefixed when the sponsion was first made be once passed and expired, if the vow were made without limitation of time, then (where there appeareth not any weighty cause of stay) if both the parties be residing in one Province, the woman who does not wish her consummation to be frustrated for any longer may, after two years, marry to whom she listeth. But if her Spouse be commorant[30] in another Province, then she must tarry three years. Though, indeed, these times of expectance may be prolonged and lengthened by a Judge, as he shall find cause just and reasonable.

In What Case the Betrothed May Refuse One Another (2.8)

If after the Sponsion or first betrothing and before Matrimony contracted, some evil disease (as leprosy or some violent cause or casualty) make one of the parties unfit for generation, the other may repudiate and abandon him or her which shall be so diseased or unabled. Spousals are also dissolved for fornication, specially if it be committed by either of the parties with their kindred. Likewise Spousals which are made by wards may be dissolved by a bare renunciation. But by no means they are rightlier avoided than by a dissension of both the Contractors from their first consent. For by such dissent also society is or may be broken in sunder. There are other causes for which the bond of desponsation may be taken away, as divulgation of kindred unknown and opportunity of nuptials sought by detestable means, for which cause not only Spousals but Marriage itself, when it is contracted, may be dissolved.

By What Authority Spousals Are to Be Undone (2.9)
To all these causes of undoing the first vows of marriage there must be added the authority of the Bishops which hath power to absolve. Yet the Canons do, without the authority of any Bishops, make free from the obligation of only promised marriage all those which abdicate themselves to Religion. And Hortensius[31] contendeth that, without authority of any Judge, Spousals are undone by the law itself by a post-marriage made by words of the present time, but no man may be his own Judge. And it is certain that espousals ought never to be undone but by public authority, unless the cause for which we will have them undone be so well known that it needeth neither proof nor sentence, such as is fornication when it is notorious and public to all the world.

Of Matrimony Contracted in the Present Time and Who May Contract (2.10)
Those which the Latins call *puberes*, that is, they which are come once to such state, habit, and disposition of body that they may be deemed able to procreate, may contract Matrimony by words of the time present. For in contract of Wedlock, *pubertas* is not strictly esteemed by number of years, as it is in wardship, but rather by the maturity, ripeness, and disposition of body. There is further required in them which contract Matrimony a sound and whole mind to consent. For he that is mad, without intermission of fury, cannot marry. But he that is deaf and dumb may contract Matrimony because the mind's meaning is expressed not only by words but by nods and signals. And as they which are *impuberes* cannot, for infirmity of age, make any firm knot of Wedlock, so likewise they which by coldness of nature or by enchantment are impotent be forbidden to contract.

The impediments Ecclesiastical, as vows, Compaternity,[32] and spiritual kindred, I will not meddle with, but come to kindred of blood, which containeth a principal let and prohibition of Marriage.

Impediment of Marriage by Kindred and Consanguinity (2.11)
In the world's infancy, men were enforced by necessity to marry with own kindred on account of the paucity of people. But that necessity is taken away and long since, by the very voice of God, they which are in certain degrees of blood are forbidden to marry (Lev. 18). And because Marriage is an

abundant seminary of charity and love, it is wisely and profitably ordained that it should be dispersed into many families.

Therefore by Natural, Civil, and Common Law, Marriage is clean forbidden betwixt all those which are as Parents or Children one towards another *in infinitum*.[33] And betwixt those persons which are of kindred in the transverse line,[34] Marriage is forbidden till the fourth degree be passed.

The Impediment of Marriage by Affinity (2.12)

There is further a certain nigh alliance called affinity, as it were, the limits uniting the two married persons. This riseth betwixt them which are married and the kindred of one of them, as betwixt the husband and the kindred of his wife. Now, affinity prohibiteth Marriage only to the persons contracted, etc. For the Cousins or Consanguinity to my wife are of affinity only to me, and not to my brothers or children by a former Wife. And my blood and consanguinity are kindred of affinity only to my Wife, and not to her brothers or former children. Here is it that the Father and the Son may marry the Mother and the Daughter, and two Brethren may marry two Sisters in another Family. For the Consanguinity, of which one is of blood to the husband and another to the wife, are betwixt themselves in no bond of affinity. And observe that in what degree a man or woman is to one of them that are married by Consanguinity, they are accompted in the same degree to the other in affinity. As the wife's brother, who is in primary relation to his Sister, is in the same degree to her husband and their children in the second, etc. And so forth, their Children's Children, which after the fourth degree are again by all laws permitted to marry, united and related through an illicit connection.

Diversity of Religion (2.13)

Amongst the hindrances of marriage note this also, that by Constitution of holy Church marriage is forbidden betwixt persons of divers Religions, as Jews and Christians.

Of Fear and Constraint (2.14)

Also Matrimony holdeth not when it is extorted by force, or by such a fear as may fall onto a constant man, because matrimony must be free.

Of Marriage Detestable Made (2.15)

Also Marriage holdeth not when it is sought or made with wickedness. And if a man promise to a woman which he hath adulterously polluted that he will marry her when his wife dieth etc.; or, if a man have sought to abridge the days of his lawful wife to marry another, these villainies are such perpetual cankers in marriage that they do not only hinder it to be made but also rend it in sunder when it is made.

There are other crimes which dissolve the marriage contract, as Incest with knowledge and ravishment. Yet if any man ravish a Maid or other unmarried Woman, the Canons do admit him to marry with her if she consent. But otherwise she shall be rendered to her Father, upon whose suit and accusation the ravisher is put to Capital punishment.

There are by the Civil and Common Laws many other impediments of Marriage as increase of one's children, public penance, killing a priest, ecclesiastical interdiction, etc., which I will not trouble Women withal.

Marriage Forbidden by Public Constitution (2.16)

By Civil ordinance also Marriage is sometime restrained and forbidden, as betwixt him which adopteth and her which is adopted. For seeing that they which are adopted are in the place and stead of Children, there resteth a League as of kindred betwixt them and the blood of him which adopteth, by the Civil Law and Canons both.

But this Civil kindred lasteth no longer than the adopted are in the power of the adoptant. Neither is it any obstacle to a Marriage, save only betwixt the adopted and adoptant and those which are in his power. And as adoption hindereth Marriage by the Civil Law, so by the same law a man may not marry her whom he took exposed as a castaway or a foundling and brought her up as a Daughter. Marriage is also forbidden, sometime by reason of public honesty, as if a Man be divorced from his wife and afterwards she hath a Daughter by another man. This is no Daughter in Law to the husband, yet he should do impudently to marry her. Those prohibitions of Marriage that were sometime betwixt a Tutor and Pupil, betwixt a President and a Woman in his subjection, betwixt a Senator and a freed bondswoman, betwixt a Senator's Daughter and a freed bondsman, betwixt a woman Comedian[35] or one whose parents used some lascivious or light Art and a Senator, lastly betwixt free and servile, are all either by long public Custom or by Common Law taken away.

Of Polygamy (2.17)

There are examples in Scripture of Polygamy, viz. where men had more wives than one at once, as Abraham, Jacob, David, and Solomon had. And it seemeth that it was sufferable by Moses his law (Deut. 21.15). But it was said at the first, man and wife shall be one flesh, and the examples were rather permitted than lawful. The Civil Law Canons and all Christian Commonwealths do utterly condemn Polygamy, and so much did the wise Emperors of Rome detest all petulancy of Marriage that they made and ordained Laws that Women, which within the year of mourning for their husbands betake them to wedlock again, should be reputed infamous and defamed. But this also the Canons have taken away.

Contracts of Matrimony ought to be public. Nuptials *de presenti*[36] ought always to be made public at the Church, or at the least in presence and Congregation of gentlemen. Yet is it not of necessity that they which marry stipulate by themselves, or be present in person at the contract-making. But it may be well enough by Proctor, so that the Contractors themselves be willing and witting, or that they ratify it when it is done.

What Words Are Requisite (2.18)
There needs no stipulation or curious form of Contract in Wedlock making, but such words as prove a mutual consent are sufficient and it may be made by Letters. If question rise about words, reference is to common understanding and use of speech and judgment in the case of a certain marriage. For there is more doubtfulness in construing of words so that the matter prevails rather than being lost.

The Accidents of Marriage (2.19)
Those things which are of solemnity or benevolence as provision of Dower, earnest, giving pledges, nuptial benediction, etc. are not of the essence of Matrimony which is made by consent. For though Dower cannot consist without Marriage, yet Marriage may very well stand without dower. And so it is of all Donations on account of nuptials. In only one case written instruments are required in making of Marriage, and that is where a man marrieth her whom he hath holden a long time as Concubine. Here *instrumenta doralia*[37] are behoveful that the children had before Marriage may be esteemed Legitimate. But this holdeth not in England.

Wherefore Marriage Ought to Be Made (2.20)
The causes of Matrimony principally are two. The first is *susceptio sobolis*, increase of Children. For even by Plato every good man ought to desire that he may leave behind him worshippers of God and propagators of piety. The second cause is the evicting of fornication and uncleanness. Saint Paul biddeth that to avoid fornication every man have his own wife, and every woman her own husband (1 Cor. 7.2). And whosoever marrieth for beauty, age, order, splendor of birth, or for riches rather than for these two causes doth very perversely, though it be not expressly disallowed. But Marriage may be for the other things also, and the Consent may be given for them.

The Consummation and Individuity[38] of Marriage (2.21)
When to the Consent of mind there is added Copulation of body, Matrimony is consummate, the principal end whereof is propagation or procreation. But where the course after going is not observed, there riseth no lawful offspring, the Children which are had are not in power and commandment of them which beget or bear them, neither are they taken by Law for any

other, then it is to be publicly questioned. Otherwise it is in lawful Wedlock, the knot whereof is so straight and indissoluble that they which are yoked therein cannot, the one without the consent of the other (neither was it ever permitted), abdicate themselves or enter into Religion. For Saint Paul, in the above titled Epistle and Chapter, saith plainly that the husband hath not power of his own body, etc. And there cannot chance any fedity or uncleanness of body so great as that for it a man and wife ought perpetually to be segregated. Yea, so unpartible be they that law saith they may not utterly leave the conjugal life though one of them have the very leprosy itself.

And here is moved a question not impertinent. That is, whether a woman be bound to follow her husband wheresoever he goeth if he require it. Whereunto is answered by Barrall and by some other that if the wife, before she married, knew the negotiations and occasions of her husband would be such that he must of necessity ever be traveling, she is bounden and in the Contract seemeth to have consented to go with him at commandment. But if after the bargain made he take up a new trick of wandering around, she may let him go when he list and tarry at home when she will.

Of Divorce (2.22)

And as no man can be compelled by any convention of pain or penalty to contract Matrimony, so it is impossible when it is once lawfully and evidently contracted to distract it by any partition, covenant, or human traction. *Quos Deus conjunxit, homo non separet.*[39] Yet there are Causes for which divers are permitted. But Divorce that only separateth from the conjugal life taketh not away the bond of Matrimony. And therefore Divorces are sometimes perpetual, as long as the parties live, sometimes for a season limited, and sometime till reconcilement be had. And he that maketh Divorce with his wife, being only separated from *a Toro*,[40] is forbidden to take another wife.

Causes of Divorce (2.23)

The Civil Law hath many causes of Divorce, but by Divine and Common Law the only sufficient cause is adultery and fornication, which by the Canons is carnal and spiritual. The spiritual is heresy and Idolatry. They dissolve Matrimony for spiritual fornication only, where one of the parties is converted to Christian faith and the other, for hatred of his religion, will not cohabit, etc. And this is taken also from Saint Paul where he saith, "If the unbelieving depart, let him depart, a Brother or Sister is not in subjection" (1 Cor. 7.15).

Impotency or Disability of Procreation (2.24)

There is admitted also in dissolution of Marriage the complaint of impotency. And Justinian[41] very discreetly willed that in that exploration or proof of the defect there should be expected three years. But the Canons ordain that Matrimony is dissolved by probation of impotency without mention or limits of time. And this is more than a bare divorce or separation *a Toro*, for it dissolveth Marriage, avoiding it as it had never been. So that he or she whose fellow is convicted of impotency may choose a new friend and presently marry again.

But this is to be understood of impotency which was before the Marriage made. For indeed, where the impediment was so precedent there could not any Matrimony exist or have being, etc.

Otherwise it is when this disability betideth after Marriage perfected and consummate. For in that case, he or she which remaineth potent shall not leave and depart from the impotent but be compelled to bear the discommodity as well as any other ill fortune. And that which is here taught of Conjugal impotency stretcheth to all impediments of Marriage which are perpetual, so through that marriage is judged never to be extinguished.

Marriages *inter ascendentes and descendentes*[42] (2.25)

Those Marriages that are made between *ascendentes* and *descendentes* are so detestable that by the Civil law they deserve exile and confiscation of goods. And there is a gloss that would extend this to all unlawful Marriages. But by Barrall and others it is to be inflicted only upon those which are against the law of blood.

Captivity or Long Absence of One Which Is Married (2.26)

It falleth out not seldom the one of them which are married to be taken captive or otherwise so detained that it is uncertain if he live or no.

Therefore, because it is in some sort dangerous to expect long the uncertain return of an absent yoke-fellow, here the Civil Law did ordain that after a husband had been gone five years, and nothing known whether he lived or not, the wife might marry again, and so might the husband that had expected his wife, etc. But the Common Law commandeth simply to forbear Marriage till the death of him or her that is missing be certainly known.

That No Crime Dissolveth Marriage (2.27)

Of old time, some Crimes were numbered amongst the Causes of dissolving marriage. But Justinian changed the Law here in part, and the Canons, upon the saying of Christ, *Quos Deus conjunxit*, etc., will not by any means that Matrimony rightly made and consummate can be dissolved as far as the bond of matrimony, though for fornication they suffer a parting as far as the marriage bed. So that the knot of legitimate marriage is never dissolved but by death, and the wife as long as she liveth is subject to the law of her husband by Saint Paul.

Yet, saith Lagus,[43] seeing that in Contracts of Wedlock we regard as well what is decent and convenient as what is lawful, I cannot tell why we be not bound in dissolving of it to follow the like equity. And, for example, if a Wife cannot dwell with her husband without manifest danger of death because he is cruel and bloody, why may not she be separated by the preceding knowledge of regular justice.

The Authority of the Ordinary Judge,[44] etc. (2.28)

For if Spousals of future Marriage cannot be dissolved without public authority, it must needs follow that without like authority there can be no repudiation when Matrimony is fully contracted and consummate. But in pursuing of divorce the strict order of Judicial proceedings is not always severely kept. For regularly, production of witnesses before contestation of suit does not help to make them appear. Yet if Cornelia sue a Divorce against Sempronius on the grounds of consanguinity, and Sempronius being cited will not appear, if now Cornelia bring her witnesses, the Judge may receive them.

Marry, this religious observation the Canons give him ever when he cometh to point of Judgment: that the danger is less in leaving men contrary to the Statues of men than in separating (contrary to the Statutes of God) those which are lawfully conjoined.

Thus far have I run myself in debt to Doctor Conradus Lagus, of whom in the third part of his *Method*, chapter twelve, may be further learned the difference betwixt *scortum*, *pellex*, and *Concubina*.[45] Our English comprehendeth them all in one word, and I would they dwelt all in one House, beyond Seas. Concubinage has the hope of wedlock; and the benefit of legitimacy is withdrawn from those born to a concubine.

If maid, wife, or widow ask what I mean to tell them so much of Civil and Canon Law, seeing they be none of those Country women, I pray them not to look for the Regions in the map of the world, but for their own Regiment in Christian duty. The Spiritual Law is here an Oracle to the temporal, which evermore sendeth to the Ecclesiastical Judge, viz. the Bishop, for certification of lawfulness or unlawfulness of Wedlocks when Accouplements come in question.

Statutes Concerning Marriage (2.29)

For it is true that Newdigate[46] saith, 12 Henry VIII 6, that marriage and Divorcements, with the circumstances of them, be properly no parcel of Common Law's learning.

Yet it is very needful here that I shew you here what the Laws of England have needfully concerning Marriage established. 32 Henry VIII 38 declareth all persons lawfully to marry which are not prohibited by God's law. And it was ordained that all Marriages contracted and solemnized in face of the Church and consummate with bodily knowledge should remain indefeasible, notwithstanding any pre-contract, etc. Further, that neither dispensation, prescription, law, reservation, prohibition, or anything (God's law excepted) shall trouble or impeach any Marriage made without the Levitical degrees, nor any man be received in spiritual Court to process, plea, or obligation contrary to this Act.

This Statute, though it seemed to be made upon good and great considerations (because pre-contracts, too too slenderly proved and sometime only surmised, helped the Romish oppression and separated those which were at quiet in honest consummation), yet many did after the making of it, and very dissolutely, come from their first vows and, as it were, in spite of conscience and Ecclesiastical censure, coupled themselves bodily with such as they newly fancied, slipperily leaving their former Contracts. It is repealed, 2 and 3 Edward VI 3, only in the points of pre-contracts. And they are left in the validity which they were of by the King's Ecclesiastical laws immediately before the making of 32 Henry VIII, with provision that all the rest of the said Act standeth whole and in strength. So it is now again by 1 Elizabeth 1. See also 5 and 6 Edward VI 12, that the marriage of Priests and Ecclesiastical persons is lawful, their children legitimate, a Priest may be tenant by the curtesy,[47] and his wife have Dower.

It is a sport to behold how some of the Canonists and Glossographers refreshed themselves in their disputes about Nuptial questions, how clear they make it that if Adam our first father were now alive and a Widower, he could not take a Wife because all Women are his Children, and that in the right line, then what a question it is whether unlawful copulation cause any affinity or no.

In hoc articulo (saith one of them) *non parcam in soro verecundiae*; that is to say, he will handle the quiddity without shame or honesty. And then in the plainest that may be, he findeth a difference betwixt a dog's neck in the Collar and his nose in the Ring, betwixt knocking at the Barrel's head and setting it abroach. But the curious learning was that of spiritual kindred, caused either by the holy Baptism or by the blessed Chrism.[48] And this had power of impeding and breaking off the marriage contract. Yea, this was such a matter that 39 Edward III 32, Bastardy is pleaded against the plaintiff in assize,[49] and the cause was that the Father married a woman before which Marriage he had christened she which was his Wife's cousin. And for this cause, after one of them was dead, Divorce was sued and Judgment thereof given in the Spiritual Court, though indeed by Justice Thorpe[50] and the greatest opinion in the temporal Court the issue could not be bastardized unless the Parents had been called and the Nuptials destroyed by consent, which was now impossible to do for death had determined them.

Out of question, therefore, if the parties had lived a little or no kindred had marred great good acquaintance. But howsoever, by those days secular Marriage was forbidden in spiritual men, and secular men were straitly prohibited by spiritual. Spiritual kindred, the Statutes afore-going, have now welcomed Wedlock clean out of the Pope's stocks, and the eighteenth chapter of Leviticus alone doth in a manner sufficiently demonstrate with what persons Women are restrained to marry.

With What Persons Women May not Marry (2.30)

Such are her Grandfather, her Father, her Son's Son, etc., her Brother, though it be but the one part, her Father's or Mother's Brother, her Brother's or Sister's Son, or her Son's Son. Brother's or Sister's Children (saith Ramus in his *Commentaries of Christian Religion* 2.9[51]) are forbidden to intermarry, but by custom not by the Roman or religious law. Christians, he saith further, which have abrogated the Law, fifteenth chapter of Deuteronomy, whereby a Brother might be challenged to raise up the house of his deceased brother, have also constituted a prohibition within certain degrees of affinity. And therefore a man may not marry with the widow of his Grandfather or of his father, or with the widow of his own Son, or of his Son's Son, or with the widow of his Brother, or of his Brother's Son, or of his Brother's Son's Son, etc. Nor with the Grandmother, Mother, Daughter, Niece, great Aunt, Aunt, or Sister of his deceased wife.

Of Wooing (2.31)

I am afraid my feminine acquaintance will say I write as I live. I talk much of Marriage but I came not forward. Stay a while yet, I pray you. I know many an honest woman more repenting her hasty Marriage ere she was wooed than all the other sins that ever she committed. It were good reason we speak a little of wooing, but to handle that matter, *per genus et species*, would take up as much room as the Indian fig-tree: everything whereof, when it falleth to the ground, groweth to a body. I will slip by it, only observing that the giving of gloves, rings, bracelets, chains, or anything that is *ex sponsaliorum largitate* (as a man would say, of love's liberality), or as a pledge of future Marriage betwixt them that are promised, have a condition (silent for the most part) annexed unto them, that if Matrimony does not ensue the things may be demanded back and recovered. Yet there is a distinction of like, for I have authority in it, if a bridegroom gave something and the marriage is impeded by some cause, the gift is wholly rescinded unless a kiss has taken place. Marry, if he had a kiss for his money then the one half of that which was given is the woman's own good. And she hath yet more favor in the case; for whatsoever she gave, were there kissing or no kissing betwixt them, she may ask all and have all again. Inquire of this in the Consistory.[52]

The Condiments of Love (2.32)

There are with us, as well as with the Civilians, many kinds of Donations on account of nuptials and some *ex sponsaliorum largitate*. Good meats are the better for good sauce, venison craveth wine, and Wedlock hath certain Condiments which come best in season in the wooing time and serve (as Breton[53] saith) to give property as a better token of matrimonial love. A husband *per se* is a desirable thing, but Donements or Feoffements etc. better the stomach,[54] though of itself it be good and eager. And because the first Marriage made in Paradise, if you mark it well, had a Jointure,[55] I cannot but allow the circumspection which is had.

The Baron May Beat His Wife (3.7)

. . . Justice Brooke, 12 Henry VIII 4,[56] affirmeth plainly that if a man beat an outlaw, a traitor, a Pagan, his villain,[57] or his wife it is unpunishable because by the Law Common these persons can have no action. God send Gentlewomen better sport, or better company.

But it seemeth to be very true that there is some kind of castigation which Law permits a Husband to use. For if a woman be threatened by her husband to be beaten, mischieved,[58] or slain, Fitzherbert sets down a Writ which she may sue out of Chancery to compel him to find surety of honest behavior toward her, and that he shall neither do nor procure to be done to her (mark I pray you) any bodily damage otherwise than appertains to the office of a Husband for lawful and reasonable correction. See for this, the new *Natura Brevium* 80f. and 238f.

How far that extendeth I cannot tell, but herein the sex feminine is at no very great disadvantage. For first, for the lawfulness, if it be in none other regard lawful to beat a man's wife than because the poor wench can sue no other action for it, I pray why may not the Wife beat the Husband again? What action can he have if she do? Where two tenants in Common be on a horse, and one of them will travel and use this horse, he may keep it from his Companion a year two or three and so be even with him. So the actionless woman, beaten by her Husband, hath retaliation left to beat him again if she dare. If he come to the Chancery or Justices in the Country of the peace against her, because her recognizance alone will hardly be taken, he were best be bound for her. And then if he be beaten the second time, let him know the price of it on God's name.

That Which the Husband Hath Is His Own (3.8)

But the prerogative of the Husband is best discerned in his dominion over all external things, in which the wife by combination divesteth herself of propriety in some sort and casteth it upon her governor. For here practice everywhere agrees with the Theoric of Law, and forcing necessity submits women to the affection thereof. Whatsoever the Husband had before Coverture,[59] either in goods or lands, it is absolutely his own; the wife hath therein no seisin[60] at all. If any thing when he is married be given him, he taketh it by himself, distinctly to himself.

If a man have right and title to enter into Lands, and the Tenant enfeoffe the *Baron* and *Feme*, the wife taketh nothing (Dyer 10). The very goods which a man giveth to his wife are still his own; her Chain, her Bracelets, her Apparel are all the Good man's goods.

If a Woman taketh more Apparel when her husband dieth than is necessary for her degree,[61] it makes her *Executrix de son tort demesne*.[62] A wife, how gallant soever she be, glittereth but in the riches of her husband, as the Moon hath no light but it is the Sun's. Yea, and her Phoebe borroweth sometime her own proper light from Phoebus.

That Which the Wife Hath Is the Husband's (3.9)

For thus it is, if before Marriage the Woman were possessed of Horses, Neat,[63] Sheep, Corn, Wool, Money, Plate, and Jewels, all manner of movable substance is presently by conjunction the husband's to sell, keep, or bequeath if he die. And though he bequeath them not, yet are they the Husband's Executor's and not the wife's which brought them to her Husband.

Of Elopement (3.14)

Amongst the acts of a *Feme Covert*, I must not forget to admonish her that she take heed of Elopements. A woman shall not forfeit Dower by not suing appeal of her Husband's death, or by not visiting her husband, or not coming to comfort him when he is wounded or exceedingly sick in a foreign shire. But if he be in his home Country where he dwelleth, *quaere*[64]: a woman in her frenzy may cut her husband's throat and it is no forfeiture of Dower, but if she make an Elopement (which is a mad trick) Dower is forfeited. Elopement by the sound and quality of the offence might seem to be derived from a *lopex*, a fox,[65] for it is when a woman seeks her prey far from home, which is the fox's quality. But the word seemeth to be French. There is a fair Statute against Elopement, Westminster 2.34. A Woman that leaves her husband, goeth away, and abides with her adulterer, if she be convicted thereof, loseth for ever her command of Dower, etc., unless the Husband, of his own free accord without ecclesiastical compulsion, suffer her to be reconciled and to cohabit with him, in which case her action is restored for Dower.

It is commonly holden (saith Parkins[66]) that a Woman shall lose her Dower by voluntary Elopement, though her abiding be involuntary and though she make none abode at all with her Adulterer. But if she be ravished and demur[67] with the Ravisher against her will, she loseth no Dower. If, when the husband is commorant at one manor his wife depart to another of his manors and there live in adultery, this is not Elopement, for it cannot but be intended. She cannot abide there without gree[68] and goodwill of her Baron. Ye shall have a case for your erudition out of my Lord Dyer concerning this matter. Of Dower was demanded of a Manor, from the dowry of Lord Powes by R.H. and Anne his Wife. It was pleaded that the said Anne, in the life of Lord Powes,

> Frankly of her own accord,
> Left her Husband and her Lord,
> And from Bethnall Greene she ran
> With Mathew Rochlei, Gentleman,

to the parish of Saint Clements Danes, where she lived in adultery all the life long of Lord Powes, divorced. [In the case] that ever she was reconciled, the demandants pleaded a *reconciliavit et cohabitare permisit.* The rejoinder is *non reconciliavit modo et forma.*[69]

To prove the reconciliation, a lying together divers nights at divers places was given in evidence, with demeanor as *Baron* and *Feme*. Against this, it was objected that they never were restent or abiding in one house together but always in sunder, and that the woman continued in adultery with one or other continually as long as her husband lived. And it was not granted, for there may be many elopements with many reconciliations, and the Defendant at his peril must take issue upon one (1 and 2 Philip and Mary; Dyer 107).

But methinks here wanteth equality in the Law. Women go down stile,[70] and many grains' allowance will not make the balance hang even. A poor Woman shall have but the third foot[71] of her Husband's lands when he is dead, for all the service she did him during the accouplement (perhaps a long time and a tedious). And if she be extravagant with a friend, as above, this is an elopement and a forfeiture, etc. But as the saying is, men are happy by the mass. They may go where they list, I warrant ye, and because they are enforced to travel in the world, they will pay dear abroad for that which they esteem of no value at home. Their adulterous sojournings is not discerned. They may lope over ditch and Dale. A thousand out-ridings and out-biddings is no forfeiture, but as soon as the good wife is gone, the bad man will have her Land, not the third but every foot of it.

Have patience, my Scholars. Take not your opportunity of revenge, rather move for redress by Parliament. And in the mean season be persuaded that liberty or impunity in doing evil by immodest life and lascivious gallops is no freedom or happiness. No, but rather act thus far your Husband's duty of instruction, namely, to learn him to leave his incontinency abroad by your modest and chaste life at home. And if this will not produce you the comfort of your Husband, yet a far greater comfort the effect of Balaam's desires.[72] Let me die the death of the righteous, and let my end be like his.

Of Felonies (3.43)

In matters criminal and capital causes, a *Feme Covert* shall answer without her husband (15 Edward IV 1). And note, if a *Feme Covert* steal anything by coercion of her Husband, this is not felony in her (27 *Libri Assisarum* 40[73]). It was found that a woman had stolen bread to the worth of two shillings by compulsion of her husband, and awarded that she should go quit.[74] It seemeth to be all one if a woman steal by commandment of her husband, *quaere*.

If a man and his wife commit felony jointly, it seemeth the wife is no felon, but it shall be wholly judged the Husband's fact, saith Stamford.[75] Seven men and a woman were arraigned of felony, found guilty, and because the woman cried out she was wife to one of the seven the Judges sent to the Bishop to be certified of the Marriage. But a woman by herself, without the privity[76] of her husband, may commit felony to become either principal or accessory. As if she steal goods or receive thieves to her house, etc., and if the husband so soon as he perceive it waive and forsake their company and his own house, in this case the Woman's offence makes not felony in the *Baron*. But if the *Baron* commit felony, his wife, not ignorant of it, may keep his company still notwithstanding and not be deemed accessory. For a woman cannot be accessory to her husband, insomuch as she is forbidden by the Law of God to bewray him.

Note also that a woman cannot be thief of her husband's goods. If she take and give them away, the receiver is no felon (Stamford 1.19). Breton allows that the wife shall keep her husband's counsel, but yet so that if she acquit herself in trial by jury of deed and consent. For felons' wives, he saith, have often held men whiles the husband killed them, and in that case it is reason and Law that they hang together. By Bracton, the wife must not accuse the man nor disclose his theft or felony; however she must not consent to be an accessory but try to impede his crime and wickedness as much as she can.

And by him, if goods stolen be found *sub clavibus uxoris*,[77] she shall be culpable with her husband of his felony. Likewise, if the wife has joined with the man or has confessed that she provided him with a plan or help, they will be held together. For it is allowed that the wife must obey; by the same token, however, she ought not to obey him in acts of cruelty and robbery. The man can tie up and restrain, and if the wife is not compelled to kill and does so freely, then each is held for the crime (3.32). In the end he sheweth how execution of judgment shall be deferred when the woman condemned is with child whether conceived before or after the felony. He coteth[78] civil Law for it. But Stamford hath it perfecter.

If a woman be arraigned of felony, it is no plea to say she is with child. But she must plead to the felony, and if she be found guilty she may then claim the benefit of her womb, whereupon the Marshall or Viscount[79] shall be commanded to put her in a chamber and cause some women to examine and try her whether she be pregnant; which if she be not, she shall be hanged immediately. And though she be quick with child, yet Judgment shall not be delayed but only execution deferred. If after such respite when she is once delivered, she become great again and object to prolong her life, the Judge ought to command execution presently, for this benefit shall be claimed but once. If the Judge inquire further of it, it must be but to set a fine on the Marshall or Sheriff for looking no better to her (Stamford 3, last chapter). And by the books which he citeth the objection must not be anticipating pregnancy but bearing a living child.

Of Treasons (3.44)
And this objection of pregnancy is as well to delay execution for treason as for felony. A woman for committing either grand or petty treason shall be burned. The latter part of the Statute 25 Edward III 2 is that if any servant kill his Master, any woman kill her husband, or any man secular or religious person kill his Prelate to whom he owes obedience, this is treason and every Lord shall have the Escheats[80] for such treasons of his own proper fee. The Statute is but declaration of the common law *titulo Coronae*[81] in Fitzherbert. A woman compasseth with her Adulterer the death of her husband. They assailed him riding on the highway, beating, wounding, leaving him for dead, and then they fled. The husband got up, levied hue and cry, came before the Justices; they sent after the offenders, which were gotten, arraigned, and the matter found by verdict. The adulterer was hanged, the woman burned to death; the husband living, an intention will be reckoned through the deed (15 Elizabeth 2). A woman servant conspired to rob her Mistress and brought a stranger to the bedside where the Mistress lay asleep. The stranger killed her, the servant silent, nothing doing but holding the Candle. The two Chief Justices and the Crown thought the servant a Traitress and a principal (2 and 3 Elizabeth, Dyer 128). Yet "Mistress" is not *verbatim* in the Statute. Stamford was one of them against the Chief Justices' opinion in this case; yet in his own book he teacheth that abettors and procurers are within the meaning and intent of the Law. The servant and the wife conspire the husband's death; he is killed by the servant. In absence of the wife, this is petty treason in them both, by opinion of divers Justices. Otherwise it is if the murderer be no servant (16 Elizabeth, Dyer 332). For Saunders' wife, which procured Browne to kill

her husband, but barely hanged as accessory because the principal was but a murderer (8 Elizabeth, Dyer 254).

Of Divorce (3.50)

But it is time to make an end of marriage since we are come to matter of divorcement, of which I reckon this of outlawry for none.[82] 47 Edward III, in the very end of the year, setteth down five ways, *Causa professionis*, *Causa precontractus*, *Causa consanguinitatis*, *Causa affinitatis*, and *Causa frigiditatis*,[83] with an observation, that when divorce is *Causa professionis* the wife shall be endowed and the heir inherit, *contra* in all the residue. *Immaturitia* also, or minority of age at the time of espousals, may be one cause of divorce as 39 Edward III 32. John and Alice his wife brought an assize. The tenant said that Alice had sued divorce in the Archbishopric of Barwick because she was under age of consent at the time of espousals, never consenting afterward, and divorce was had judgment of brief. And Brooke 124, under the title "Guardianship," remembreth that 5 Philip and Mary, the Doctor of Law declared for divorces upon this case: that if an heir or other body be married below marriageable years, and do dissent at the age of discretion or after (before assent) to marriage, it is sufficient; and the party may be wedded to some other body without either divorce or testimony of the disagreement before the Ordinary. Who, though he may punish through judgment of the court here, yet the second espousals are good by Law of both Realm and Church. But when divorce is had for kindred, precontract, frigidity, or such like case, the Law is clean contrary. For trial of divorce, when it is pleaded in a temporal Court, must be by certificate of the Bishop and not *per pais* (5 Henry IV 2),[84] and sentence of divorce belongeth to the Bishop in his spiritual Court.

Of which there is authority (2 Elizabeth 179 in Dyer). This year, he saith, sentence of divorce was given on grounds of natural frigidity in the Archbishop's Court of Audience. And the woman was the plaintiff and complainant of sterility in the man, who was adjudged impotent by the Physicians. The same year or next year, another case and judgment happened like, and the woman which complained married to a second husband of better stuff by whom she had children, and gave him all her land by fine, etc.[85] Her first husband also was married to another woman and had children by his second wife (as it was asserted), in which case the Doctors held that the parties divorced were compellable to live again together as man and wife, because the holy Bishop was deceived. Therefore much ado was made to stay the engrossing[86] of the fine, yet the Justices made it be engrossed against the orders of the Custodian, etc. But see Sir Edward Coke,[87] 5 *Reports* 98, in Burye's case, that the Doctors were deceived; for the parties divorced *causa frigiditatis* cannot live together again, and the issue by the second wife is legitimate, for a man may be virile and impotent at different times. Again, 13 and 14 Elizabeth, Dyer 305, teacheth that right and lawfulness of marriage is ever to be judged not by the temporal but by the spiritual Judge. And therefore, in an issue of not ever accoupled in loyal matrimony, if the Bishop certify not the lawfulness of wedlock but the circumstances, he shall be amerced[88] and a *melius certiorando*[89] awarded.

Seeing, therefore, right of marriage is to be discussed by the spiritual Judge, they which are married ought in no case to sever themselves and remarry without the spiritual Judge. If they do, the second marriage is no marriage, the children had in it are illegitimate, and the woman not dowable, except in the case first specified. And generally where espousals are not merely void but defeasible,[90] if they be not avoided by divorcement the issue which is had without defeasing, that shall inherit. As, if a man marry his cousin or his sister, saith the book, and have issue by her and die before divorce had, now nothing can bastardize the issue. For though the Commissary[91] was wont in his visitation to make a kind of divorce in such cases after death of one of the parties, it was never any more than an Inquisition of office, to the investigating into sins. For the heir could not be bastardized when the parents both or one of them were dead, and therefore not citable to appear, etc. And it is holden strongly by Thorpe, 39 Edward III, and in the Parliament 24 Henry VIII (see Brooke under the title "Bastardy" 23, 37, 44, 47).

And a divorce cannot be had but of a marriage consisting and not yet by death dissolved. For there cannot well be a reversing of any divorce when the parties divorced be dead, as Brooke understandeth Conningsby, 12 Henry VII 22. For, saith he, it was adjudged in Corber's case, where the *baron* and *feme* had issue and afterward were divorced, the *baron* taking another wife by whom he had issue and died, that when the first issue sued in spiritual Court to reverse the divorce and bastardize the second issue after his father's death, a prohibition lay. But it was said that the title and descent were comprised in the libel, or else the prohibition could not have been granted. Thus saith Brooke under the title "Deraignment." But under the title "Bastardy" 47, he setteth down the same case, that a man be bastardized after the espousals wherein he was begotten and born or by death determined. See Sir Edward Coke 7, report Kennes' case, that some divorces dissolve the matrimony, that is to say, from the bond of marriage, and bastardize the issue and bar the woman of her Dower, and some from bed and board, which dissolveth not the marriage nor bar the wife of her Dower, nor bastardize the issue.

And therefore if any action be brought and divorce pleaded, the cause of divorce ought to be shown. And there it is said that a divorce may be repealed in the spiritual Court after the death of the parties, but a suit after the death of the parties to divorce them and to bastardize their issue may not be. For that the trial of bastardy or not belongeth to the temporal Court originally, if sentence do not hinder. And see Sir Edward Coke, *Institutes*, "Dower" 33, and "Estates upon Condition" 181, the derivation of the word divorce from *divertendo* or *divortondo*, because the man is diverted from the wife. And see there the several causes of divorces and how far any of them respectively do extend in power and effort. And in Littleton's time many divorces were of force, which the Statute of 22 Henry VIII 18 take away, and there see that a man may marry the sister of his first wife since that Statute.

By *Natura Brevium* 44, in the writ of prohibition, and *Natura Brevium* 129 and Dyer 28 Henry VIII 13 agree if the woman shall have the goods not spent and that detinue[92] lies for them, if goods be given in marriage with a woman, she shall recover them in the spiritual Court after divorce, and there lieth no prohibition. 26 Henry VIII 7 is that if the husband, before divorce had, have given or sold without collusion such goods as were the wife's before marriage, she is without remedy for them being divorced.

But if he aliened[93] them by collusion and bring a writ of detinue for so much of them as the property may be discerned of and, for the residue, money and such like, she shall sue in spiritual Court. If a man, which is bound to a woman by obligation, marry her and they be divorced, she hath her action again, which was suspended *ibid* by Fitzherbert and Norwich.[94] But see the book of 11 Henry VII 4, *per Curiam* contrary,[95] where the divorce is on grounds of precontract, and it is so cited (Dyer, 4 Mary 140).

If the woman divorced were an Inheritrix etc., and the husband before divorcement hath done waste, felled her woods, received her rents, granted her wards, presented to her Churches,[96] given away her goods, none of these things past in possession executed can be reversed or recalled. But if the Inheritance itself were discontinued or charged, or a release made of it, or her villains manumitted, she shall have remedy for these things by common Law.

If *baron* and *feme*, joint purchasers, be disseised, and the baron release,[97] etc., the wife shall have a moiety[98] if they be divorced, although before there were no moieties betwixt them. For the divorce convert that into moieties, which see Brooke's title "Deraignment and Divorce" 32 Henry VIII. In Sir Edward Coke 5 *Reports*, in Oland's case it was holden that if a Lease be made to *baron* and *feme* during the Coverture, and the baron soweth the land, and after there is a divorce on the grounds of precontract, the baron shall have the Corn and not the lessor. For although the baron prosecuted the suit, yet the sentence which dissolves the marriage is the judgment in Law, and an inquiry is appointed into the unpunished.

And as by divorce that which was entire may be converted or divided into moeties, so by it inheritance may be made franktenement.[99] And if *baron* and *feme*, donees in tail,[100] have issue and be divorced, now they have but franktenement and the issue shall not inherit. For it is not like here as where lands are given to two men, or to a man and his mother, or to a man and his daughter, and to the heirs of their bodies, where several heirs shall severally inherit, for it was never lawful for them to marry (7 Henry IV 16, Brooke 9, under the title "Tail"; see also 13 Edward III, under the title "Deraignment"). If land be given to *baron* and *feme* in tail, which be divorced on the grounds of precontract etc., they shall hold jointly for term of their lives, and the land go to the Survivor. But by the Reporter, if the gift were in frankmarriage,[101] the party which did not cause the divorce shall have all. And agreeing to that difference is Parkins, chapter "Feoffment" 238. And also agreeing is Sir Edward Coke 9 *Reports* in Beumont's case.

12 *Liberi Assisarum* 22, Donees in frankmarriage were divorced at the woman's suit. The *baron* continued possession till he died. And afterward, the woman died, the possession was adjudged to have remained always to the woman because she never made any debate for it, so that the man never had it by disseisin. And agreeing to that is Plowden, Wymbysses' case, 58,[102] and Dyer 3 Mary 26, 19 *Liber Assisarum* 2. The Donee in frankmarriage, wedded below marriageable years, sued divorce by the *baron*'s motive and the wife's agreement at their full age, and the woman recovered all the land against her quondam husband by assize. And under the title "Assise" in Fitzherbert 413, 442, is this case: a man of certain tenements enfeoffed his feoffor, and his wife in tail,[103] the remainder to the right heirs of the *baron*. They were divorced at the suit of her husband, which kept the woman out of the lands, and she brought an Assize whereby she recovered a moiety of the tenements by judgment presently. And on account of the difficulty it was adjoined for the other moiety to the Common pleas, where she had judgment of that also, because divorce was at the husband's suit.

As a woman may have an Assize against her companion divorced for lands wherein she claimeth inheritance or estate for life, so if he have aliened in fee, fee tail, or for life the lands which he had in fee simple, fee tail, or for term of life to a stranger, she may as soon as she is divorced bring a Writ called a *cui ante divorsium* against the Alienee. And this Writ may be in the *per*, *cui*, and *post*.[104] If she die before action commenced or before recovery, her heir may have a Writ called a *sur cui ante divorsium*, and the Aunt and Niece may join in it. But for her estate tail her heir shall be put to a formidone.[105] But note Reader, that it seemeth both the woman and her heir may enter, after the Statute of 32 Henry VIII and never bring *Cui in vita*, nor *sur cui in vita*, etc. For the opinion in Grenlie's Case, Sir Edward Coke 8 *Reports* 73, is that if the *baron* alien, and after the wife is divorced on grounds of precontract which dissolve the marriage from the bond of matrimony, the wife during the life of the husband, or after his death, may enter. For the words of the Act are no fine feoffement, etc. during the Coverture between them. And although the Statute saith, "But that the same wife, etc.," that is to be intended of her which was his wife at the time of the alienation, etc.

Note that whereas Westminster 2.3 giveth a *cui in vita* upon recovery by default against the husband, etc. She shall have a *cui ante divorsium* upon the like recovery by equity and extension of the Statute, and the process is summons, *grand cape* and *petit cape*.[106]

I will here set the bounds and limits of my third book, not because this sequel and consequence, divorce I mean, whereby the issue had is bastardized and the woman restored to her goods and lands, consorteth with the marriage so perfectly begun as I meant it. For this is not the untying of true wedlock but rather a dissipation of marriage tainted at the beginning, and in Christian Court adjudged to a nullity, as if it had never been. The *Baron* and *Feme* that I have spoken of all this while, if they were not married in their infant love and very first flowing age, yet were they not frostbitten or so blasted either of them when they were young but they might well have fructified. Neither was either of them a common Law-breaker, entangled with promise or precontract, and as for consanguinity or affinity, there was no more betwixt them than is between Jack Fletcher and his bolt.[107]

You may imagine some matter, by only imagination, perhaps more viable than it could have been being true, whereupon a public sentence of separation being published from bed and board. But then there was a monition[108] of chaste living, and prohibition to both the parties that neither of them should flow to other marriage so long as both of them were living. And the Author of separation, that is the party suing divorce, did put in sufficient caution to do nothing contrary to this prohibition. So that the holy lives of matrimony were not clean broken and pulled asunder, but within a year or two they were reconciled, voluntarily of their own accord. And soon after (so I will make it) having the Distaff, Spindle, and Shears all in mine own hand,[109] the husband's life was suddenly cut off, or else the wife had been sole executrix.

Of Rape (5.20)

Choose now, whether ye will imagine, that the widow hath agreed with him which was her husband's bane or that she hath pursued him to death. She remaineth from henceforth a widow, giving herself to alms and deeds of charity. And of this good mind are many of our widows, which purpose constantly to live out the residue of their days in a devout remembrance of their dear husbands departed, to whom perhaps they made vows never to marry again after their deaths. But to what purpose is it for women to make vows when men have so many millions of ways to make them break them?

And when sweet words, fair promises, tempting, flattering, swearing, lying will not serve to beguile the poor soul, then with rough handling, violence, and plain strength of arms, they are, or have been heretofore, rather made prisoners to lust's thieves than wives and companions to faithful honest lovers. So drunken are men with their own lusts and the poison of Ovid's false precept, "*Vim licet appellant, vis est ea grata puellis,*"[110] that if the rampier[111] of Laws were not betwixt women and their harms, I verily think none of them, being above twelve years of age and under a hundred, being either fair or rich, should be able to escape ravishing.

This is therefore a matter concerning maids, wives, widows, and women of all degrees and conditions, if either they be or possess anything worth the having. And because the ignorance of Law may here turn a mollifying heart to harm, I were to blame if I left my Scholars without warning to take heed.

Ravishments in Two Sorts (5.21)

There are two kinds of Rape, of which though the one be called by the common people and by the Law itself Ravishment, yet in my conceit it borroweth the name from *rapere* but unproperly. For it is no more but *Species stupri*, a hideous, hateful kind of whoredom in him which committeth it, when a woman is enforced violently to sustain the fury of brutish concupiscence. But she is left where she is found, as in her own house or bed as Lucrece was, and not hurried away as Helen by Paris, or as the Sabine women were by the Romans. For that is both by nature of the word and definition of the matter.

The second and right ravishment is when anyone abducts a woman of honest reputation, whether a virgin, widow, or nun against the will of those under whose power she is. It matters not if someone does it; for once she has been ravished, willingly or unwillingly, the violence done to the parents or guardians seems to be of the highest degree. It seemeth the first kind of rape deserved always death by God's Laws, unless the woman ravished were unbetrothed so that the ravisher might marry her, as you may read (Deut. 22.23), and by the Civil Law. Ravishers, in the second kind, were subject to penalty of death if the ravished woman were of free-birth. How heinous they be both, and have a long time been by the Laws of England, ye shall now perceive.

The Old Law of Libidinous Rape (5.22)

Bracton, in the eighth and twentieth Chapter of his third Book, showeth that by the antique Law of King Adelstan,[112] he that meeting a virgin, sole or with company, did but touch her unhonestly was guilty of breaking the King's Edict and will make amends according to the judgment of the Court. If against her will he threw her on the ground, he lost the King's favor; if he discovered her and cast himself upon her, he lost all his possessions; if he lay with her, he suffered judgment of life and member, yea, if he were a horseman, his horse lost his tail and main (as Stamford citeth it to be, Book 2). But the words are "His horse was shamefully adorned about the upper lip, and they must crop its tail near the rump. Likewise if he has his dog with him, etc., it will be dishonored in the same way." His Hawk likewise lost her beak, talons, and train.[113] And the virgin had in recompense all his land and money by the King's warrant. This was in King Adelstan's days, at least a hundred and twenty years before the Conquest, when corrupters of virginity and chastity were hanged and their fautors[114] also.

But in Bracton's time, it seemeth that these kind of ravishers were otherwise punished. They lost their eyes and were gelded. She that brought an Appeal was to complain herself presently to the next neighbor or to the chief men of the Hundred,[115] or to the Coroner or Viscount, showing her garments bloody and torn, and in the first County to enter her Appeal and pursue it at coming of the King's Justices. Before whom, unless the offender aid himself by exception[116] that the Appellant was still a virgin (which was tried by inspection of women), and if she were found a virgin, the Appellant was imprisoned for her slander, or that he held her before times as his Concubine, or that she consented to his embraces or some other like plea, he lost his eyes and stones, for they induced him to the heat of rape. Except the woman, before judgement given, demanded him for her husband, for that was only in the woman's election and not in the man's because of the inconvenience which otherwise might have happened if some hardy strong Lecher had ravished a Dame noble or of great birth, he should either go away unpunished or else, by means of one pollution, perpetually desire her to the disgrace of her whole stock. Thus far Bracton.

And in the Book *De Priscis Legibus*,[117] it is set down for a Law made by King William the Conqueror, "I command that from henceforth no man be hanged or put to death for any transgression, but let the offender's eyes be pulled out, or his stones, feet, or hands cut away, that the trunk or mutilate body, still left alive, may remain as a testimony of his prodition[118] and lewdness." Now, if this mangling Law of King William were still in force in Bracton's time against ravishers, was it *Magna Carta* 29? Or, what was it that made the Law so meek in Edward the First his time, that the Statute against Rape speaketh of it so mildly as if it had been at Common Law a very small trespass?[119]

The Case of Elizabeth Venor (5.37)

Now that women may learn to stand upon their own guard partly, and not trust altogether to defence or courtesy of Laws, which are not more rigorously penned than sometime put in execution against them, let them mark this case. Lands were given in tail to William Venor and to Elizabeth his wife and to the heirs of their two bodies, the remainder to the said

Elizabeth and the heirs of her body, the remainder to Robert Babbington in tail, the remainder to the right heir of T.S., father of Elizabeth. William Venor died without issue, and Elizabeth, being sole seized, was afterward ravished by John Worth which, after that he had married her, was indicted of rape and took Sanctuary at Westminster. Elizabeth his wife, being there with him, was advised to disassent and to part from him to save her inheritance, which she refused to do and was afterward brought before the Council in the Star Chamber.[120] Being there demanded if she assented or not, and she answered that John Worth was her husband and she would not forsake him, whereupon the issue of Robert Babbington (Robert being dead) entered upon her land by the Statute of 6 Richard II, which willeth (saith Brooke) if any woman assent to the ravisher that he to whom the land should descend, revert, remain, or escheat may enter. And though it were contested that there was another person, more near in blood to Elizabeth than was this issue of Robert Babbington, yet because he was next in remainder his entry was lawful. But Elizabeth did oust him, and he brought an Assize.

Then, to prove the assent, it was given in evidence that she had married him, assenting to him as well in Sanctuary as before the Council. And for Elizabeth it was alleged that the espousals and all the assentings were by duress and force and for fear of the ravisher, which might not be called assenting, for none consenteth but frankly, voluntarily, and *sans* fear, which the Statute seems to say at that place. But in the end, because she might have disagreed before the Council and did not, her assent was holden voluntary and the Assize passed for the Plaintiff. And it was agreed for Law that if title of entry into lands be given to a daughter by force of this Statute and she entereth, that she shall retain and enjoy them, notwithstanding the birth of any son Posthumous coming afterward, though he be more near or worthy of blood. And so it is generally where the entry is given by Statute. But if by Common Law a dissent be cast upon a daughter which entereth, she must give place to a son born afterward. It was remembered in this case that, in former time, a woman being ravished, after she had continued seven years with the ravisher and had borne him a child, escaped from him and sued in Parliament in the time of Henry VI against him till he was attainted.[121] And being demanded how she could now say that she never assented having conceived etc., she answered that her flesh consented to him but her soul and conscience did ever abhor him (5 Edward IV 58).

The Statute 18 Elizabeth 7 (5.38)

I am at the end of my voyage. But before I take shore I will show you how our late most excellent Law-giver, renowned Queen Elizabeth (whose vigilant care hath always been that all her people might live under her in peace and without oppression) hath given strength and perfection to the former function of other Princes to make them a firm bulwark against all manner of injurers that possibly might oppress women. And I can but marvel that when so damnable a crime as rape had given so often to the whole Realm such cause of bitter complaint, and men in sundry ages had beaten their brains so carefully in finding out remedy against it, how it was possible so long space together to leave such a privilege to him that could read the blessed Psalm of *Miserere*, etc. (Ps. 51), that though he had ravished the fairest Lady in the Land he might almost go away without touch of breath for it.

Therefore the eighteenth[122] of Queen Elizabeth, for repressing of felonious rapes and ravishments of women and of felonious Burglaries, it was enacted that they which were found guilty by verdict or by confession, or outlawed of or for such felonious Rapes or Burglary, they should suffer death and forfeit as in cases of Felony had been used by the Laws of the Realm, without allowance of privilege or benefit of Clergy.[123] Further, that they which were in other cases to have benefit of Clergy should immediately after burning in the hand, according to the Statute in that case provided, be forthwith enlarged by the Justices and not be delivered to the Ordinary. But yet that the Justices, before whom the Clergy shall be allowed, may detain such persons in prison for correction as long as they shall think convenient, so it be not above a year.

Then, because in the fourteenth year of her Majesty's reign (as you may perceive in Dyer 304), in the case of a Scot which had ravished a girl, being not past seven years' old, the Justices were in doubt whether rape could be of a child of such tender years, not yet nine years' old. And therefore they went not to judgment of the Scot, though by guidance of divers Matrons he seemed guilty. This Statute ordaineth, that if any person, unlawfully and carnally, know and abuse any woman child under age of ten years, every such unlawful and carnal knowledge shall be felony, and the offender being only convicted shall suffer as a Felon without allowance of Clergy. And as M. Lambard and M. Crompton[124] do both of them note, it is not material whether she consent or not, for the Law adjudgeth her unable to consent at so tender age. The last proviso of this Statute is that they which are admitted to their Clergy shall answer to all other manner of felonies, whereof they have not formerly been acquitted, convicted, attainted, or pardoned, as they should have done if, as Clerks convicted, they had been delivered to the Ordinary and made their purgation.

The Statute 39 Elizabeth 9 (5.39)

Lastly, because this exemption of Clergy was leveled only against Burglaries and felonious rapers by violence and of the antique Falconer's fashion, leaving unto covetous ravishers by abduction and, I might say, by insinuation the benefit of their Book, by reason whereof divers maids, widows, and wives, had of very late days been first carried away and then defiled, married, etc. It was enacted at the first Parliament begun in the thirty-ninth year of the late Queen Elizabeth that whosoever shall be convicted or attainted of or for any offence made felony by the Act above specified, 3 Henry VII 102, which, being indicted or arraigned of or for any such offence, shall stand mute or make no direct answer, or shall challenge peremptorily[125] above the number of twelve, shall in every such case suffer death, without benefit of Clergy, provided that nothing in this Act contained shall extend to take Clergy from any person or persons which are not either principals or procurers or accessories before the offence committed.

The Conclusion (5.40)

Thus have I sailed betwixt the capes of *Magna Carta* and *Quadragesima*[126] of Queen Elizabeth, collected the statutes principally belonging to women, conjoining customs, cases, opinions, sayings, arguments, judgments, and points of learning of like sort and subject dispersed in our Law books. Now, coming to take haven, God grant I may fall in at port Grace and good acceptance of all that shall read what I have gathered. They which are less learned than myself in this study (which I accompt to be those that have but newly taken acquaintance of Littleton) may spend some time here not without some fruit and profit. They that are better learned than I (into which company some may crowd that perhaps might be challenged of intrusion) will give me no thanks for my pains. Rather, I must thank them if they vouchsafe to read them without open scorn and bitter censuring. But they to whom my travels are chiefly addressed are women, so many as bear the title of honest women. How good and virtuous soever they be, I see not how they can escape the taint of ingratitude if they give not a reasonable favor and applause to my good intention and labor, whereby things behoveful for them to know are laid plain together and in some orderly connexion, which heretofore were smothered or scattered in corners of an uncouth language, clean abstruded from their sex. Which concealment, because it seemed to me neither just nor conscionable, I have framed this work, admonishing them not to take it for so strong and substantial a piece as London bridge is, whereon you may boldly set up great buildings. But I will say to you as Littleton said in his *Tenures* to his son: there be some things in these Books which are not Law, yet even those may enable you the better to understand the reasons and arguments of Law, and to confer and enquire what the Law is amongst the sage Matters thereof.

NOTES
1. Feudal term for a transfer of land with freehold ownership to a person.
2. "Because one person."

3. Reference is made to Sir Anthony Fitzherbert's *La Nouvelle Natura Brevium* 116, an authoritative legal text cited frequently throughout *The Law's Resolutions*. Fitzherbert, d. 1538, was a judge during Henry VIII's reign. (He is also known as the "Father of English Husbandry," having written a number of books on farming and gardening.)

4. "Husband and wife."

5. Separate, distinct.

6. "Either of Angel or of man." The reference to "Dyer" is to the reports (that is, histories of legal cases, with arguments used by counsel and the reasons for the court's decision) from the Common Law jurisdiction during the period 1513-81. Sir James Dyer was chief justice of the Queen's Bench during Elizabeth I's reign.

7. Ambrose Calepinus, 1435-1511, an Italian Augustine monk, renowned for his work as a lexicographer. His *Dictionary of Eleven Languages* was first published in 1506.

8. As a freehold owner of land.

9. Henry de Bracton (or de Bretton), d. 1267, a celebrated lawyer and judge of the mid-thirteenth century (under Edward III). His *De Legibus et Consuetudinibus*, a famous legal text, was first printed in London in 1569.

10. In classical mythology, Hermaphrodite was the son of Hermes (Mercury) and Aphrodite (Venus).

11. Such a citation is to an English statute: the year of the reign, the sovereign's name, and the chapter or folio number. Thus this reference is to an act passed in 1457, the thirty-fifth year of Henry VI's rule.

12. "Outside guardianship."

13. Not compelled to marry whom the feudal lord chooses.

14. To give a gift such as land and houses to another.

15. The preposition "per," when followed by a name, refers to the dictum of a judge made in giving a decision. I have been unable to identify Justice Ingelton in any detail.

16. The reference is to the Statutes of Westminster, the whole of legislation that was passed in 1275.

17. A quantity of land sufficient to maintain a knight with money, about twenty pounds during Edward I's reign.

18. Tenure of land in return for specified services (in contrast to knight-service which was unpredictable and might involve military service).

19. The taking of goods by a landlord for non-payment of rent.

20. "Concerning the having of help."

21. Petit serjeanty: the holding of lands in return for annually supplying the Crown with a war weapon; grand serjeanty: land tenure granted in return for performing an honorary personal service to the sovereign.

22. A statute of Henry III (1235), passed at Merton in Surrey.

23. "Into a different family."

24. Thomas de Littleton, d. 1487, a famous magistrate and jurist. His influential work was titled *Les Tenures, Natura Brevium, Diversité des Courtes*, first published in 1487 and frequently reprinted.

25. "Engagement or betrothal."

26. That is, in the present tense.

27. Pledge.

28. "A man alone with a woman alone."

29. Fulfilling, accomplishing.

30. Abiding.

31. Aegidius Hortensius, French author of legal commentaries in the early 1600s.

32. That is, the relationships between godparents and between the godparents and birth parents of a child.

33. "For ever."
34. Between siblings and cousins.
35. Actor.
36. "Of the time present."
37. "Formal legal documents."
38. Indivisibility.
39. "Those whom God hath joined together let no man put asunder" (Matt. 19.6, Mark 10.9). The words are also used in the marriage service in *The Book of Common Prayer*.
40. "From the marriage bed." The usual phrase for separation was *a mensa et toro*, "from bed and board."
41. The emperor Justinian ordered that an elementary treatise on Roman law be written; it was published in A.D. 533.
42. "Between forebears and descendants."
43. The French lawyer Conradus Lagus is often cited by "T. E."; his main work, *Juris Utriusque Traditio Methodica*, was published in 1552.
44. A judge who has authority to hear cases in his own right.
45. Whore, mistress, concubine.
46. John Newdigate (or Newdegate) was Serjeant at Law under Henry VIII, the highest degree in the legal profession, appointed by royal mandate to hearings exclusively in the Court of Common Pleas.
47. The widower's right to hold his deceased wife's estate till his death.
48. Sacramental anointing.
49. In court.
50. Robert de Thorpe, d. 1371, Lord Chancellor during the reign of Edward III.
51. Translated into English and published in 1573 and 1574.
52. Ecclesiastical courts, under the authority of bishops, which heard cases in their particular dioceses.
53. John le Breton, d. 1275, English judge during Edward I's reign.
54. Stomach: appetite; Feoffements: gifts of portable property or land.
55. A joint tenancy or an estate acquired by two or more persons.
56. Sir Robert Brooke, d. 1558, English lawyer, judge, and Recorder of London (1545); his Common Law reports are known as Brooke's New Cases, 1515-58.
57. Villein or feudal serf.
58. Physically harmed.
59. The condition of a married woman, under the cover, protection, or authority of her husband.
60. Right of possession.
61. Social status.
62. One who intermeddles, as though executrix but without just authority, in the estate of her dead husband. A reference to 33 Henry VI follows this point.
63. Cattle.
64. "One may ask."
65. The usual Latin word for fox is *vulpes*.
66. John Parkins, d. 1544, an English legal writer and jurist; author of *A Very Profitable Book Treating of the Laws of This Realm* (1528 in Latin, translated into English in 1555).
67. Abide.
68. Consent.
69. "He reconciled and permitted cohabitation. . .he did not reconcile by mode and form."
70. Steps allowing a person to pass over or through a fence; the phrase suggests having to confront many obstacles.

71. One-third, considered to be the widow's reasonable share of her deceased husband's estate.

72. That is, material gain.

73. The *Tabula Libri Assisarum et Plitorum Corone* or *The Table of Books of the Assizes and Crown Pleas* contains case reports from the yearbooks kept during the reign of Edward III. Abridged versions were published in 1502 and 1555, and a complete edition in 1514.

74. Be acquitted.

75. Sir William Stamford, sixteenth-century lawyer and author, whose *Exposition of the King's Prerogative* (1567) was republished many times.

76. Prior knowledge and concurrence.

77. "In the wife's possession" (literally, under the wife's household keys).

78. Quotes.

79. Attendants on the judge, in charge of prisoners.

80. A rightful obstruction to the bequeathing of estates, the land reverting to the original lord of the estate or fee.

81. "Under the title of The Crown" (referring to a chapter title).

82. The previous section has discussed the conditions when the outlawry of one spouse might extend to the other. Outlawry is when a person (usually a man) loses protection from the law, cannot bring an action to redress injuries, and forfeits goods and chattels to the Crown.

83. "On the grounds of profession, precontract, consanguinity, affinity, frigidity or impotence."

84. Trial by jury.

85. That is, land which she had recovered in the earlier case.

86. Taking into possession (by the first husband).

87. Lord Chief Justice of the King's Bench during the reign of James I. His case *Reports* and *Institutes* on the Common Law were considered highly authoritative.

88. Fined, punished.

89. An order removing the case to a superior court for review.

90. Capable of being made void.

91. Officer of the Bishop.

92. An action to recover personal property unlawfully detained.

93. Transferred the property to another.

94. Robert Norwich, Chief Justice under Henry VIII.

95. *Per Curiam*: "by the Court," implies that the decision was arrived at by the court, consisting of one or more judges.

96. Transferred minors under her control to himself or others; made gifts to the Church or, perhaps, informed the Church court of possible offences.

97. Extinguishes his right or interest in the property.

98. Half.

99. Freehold.

100. Empowered to pass, after their death, their estate onto their issue.

101. A special tenure of land, where a man gives land to another man and his wife, the latter being related to the donor, whereby the couple and their issue (for three generations) hold the land in exchange for no service.

102. Edmund Plowden, 1518-85, English judge and author of the *Commentaries, or Reports on Diverse Cases* (1571), from Edward VI to Elizabeth's reign; Plowden's work was reprinted many times.

103. Made a gift of property to the person who had given him the property, and made a limited gift to the wife (if she had no issue the property would revert to the husband and his heirs).

104. "For whom before divorce"; "in the presence of, for whom, after," i.e. regardless of whether the wife is present or alive, that is, her representatives or relatives may serve the writ.

105. A writ available to one who had right to lands by virtue of a gift in tail.

106. Grand cape: a writ issued where the tenant or defendant defaults on the day appointed for appearance; petit cape: a writ issued when the tenant or defendant defaults after the day appointed for appearance.

107. The relation between a bowman and his arrow.

108. A formal notice from a bishop or ecclesiastical court.

109. The author can play the role of the three Fates, determining the length of the man's life.

110. A slight misquotation of *Ars Amatoria* 1.673: "You may use force; women like you to use it."

111. Rampart or barrier.

112. Adelstan or Athelstan, 895-940, grandson of Alfred the Great and King of England.

113. Tail.

114. Supporters, accomplices.

115. Part of a county or shire.

116. An objection.

117. *De Priscis Anglorum Legibus Libri* (*Of the Ancient Laws of the English*), written by William Lambard, 1536-1601, keeper of the records in the Tower of London and author of a number of legal texts.

118. Treachery.

119. The following sections review statutes passed during the reigns of Edward I, Richard II, Henry VI, Henry VII, and Philip and Mary which legislated on appeals by a woman that charges of rape be laid against her attacker. In these periods, there were restrictions on time and locality which affected when and where such appeals could be made. For example, under Edward I, in some cases if the woman did not make an appeal within forty days the crown might do so; during Henry IV's rule, a married woman had to appeal jointly with her husband. Through these sections, the author is critical of the leniency of laws on rape.

120. A court comprising members of the Privy Council and two Common Law court judges, which heard trials, without a jury, on notorious offences.

121. A judgment for outlawry made against him, his property being forfeited and his blood deemed to be corrupted.

122. Eighteenth year.

123. Privilege: that which is granted or allowed to a person or people against or beyond the law as it ordinarily operates; benefit of clergy: privilege allowed to clerical figures, and later to anyone who could read, to be discharged from prosecution for felonies in a temporal court.

124. Richard Crompton, the author of numerous books on legal matters in the 1580s and 1590s.

125. The defendant objects to individual jurors without assigning cause.

126. The fortieth year.

Works Cited

Amussen, Susan Dwyer. *An Ordered Society: Gender and Class in Early Modern England*. Oxford: Basil Blackwell, 1988.
Baker, J. H. *An Introduction to English Legal History*. 2nd edition. London: Butterworths, 1979.
Beckwith, Sara. "The Power of Devils and the Hearts of Men: Notes towards a Drama of Witchcraft." In *Shakespeare in the Changing Curriculum*. Ed. Lesley Aers and Nigel Wheale. London: Routledge, 1991. 143-61.
Beilin, Elaine V. *Redeeming Eve: Women Writers of the English Renaissance*. Princeton: Princeton U P, 1987.
Belsey, Catherine. "Love as Trompe-l'oeil: Taxonomies of Desire in *Venus and Adonis*." *Shakespeare Quarterly* 46 (1995): 257-76.
Berry, Philippa. *Of Chastity and Power: Elizabethan Literature and the Unmarried Queen*. London: Routledge, 1989.
Blench, J. W. *Preaching in England in the late Fifteenth and Sixteenth Centuries: A Study of English Sermons 1450-c.1600*. Oxford: Basil Blackwell, 1964.
Bloch, R. Howard. "Medieval Misogyny." *Representations* 20 (1987): 1-24.
Boose, Lynda E. "Scolding Brides and Bridling Scolds: Taming the Woman's Unruly Member." *Shakespeare Quarterly* 42 (1991): 179-213.
Cerasano, S. P., and Marion Wynne-Davies, "'From Myself, My Other Self I Turned': An Introduction." In *Gloriana's Face: Women, Public and Private, in the English Renaissance*. Ed. S. P. Cerasano and Marion Wynne-Davies. New York: Harvester, 1992. 1-24.
Cioni, Maria L. *Women and Law in Elizabethan England with Particular Reference to the Court of Chancery*. New York: Garland, 1985.
Colish, Marcia. "Cosmetic Theology: The Transformation of a Stoic Theme." *Assays: Critical Approaches to Medieval and Renaissance Texts* 1 (1981): 3-14.

Collinson, Patrick. *The Birthpangs of Protestant England: Religious and Cultural Change in the Sixteenth and Seventeenth Centuries.* London: Macmillan, 1988.

---. *Godly People: Essays on English Protestantism and Puritanism.* London: Hambledon, 1983.

---. "The Elizabethan Churches and the New Religion." In *The Reign of Elizabeth I.* Ed. Christopher Haigh. London: Macmillan: 1984. 169-94.

Crawford, Patricia. "Women's Published Writings, 1600-1700." In *Women in English Society 1500-1800.* Ed. Mary Prior. London: Methuen, 1985. 211-82.

Davis, Natalie Zemon. *Society and Culture in Early Modern France.* Cambridge: Polity, 1987.

---. "Women in Politics." In *A History of Women in the West: III. Renaissance and Enlightenment Paradoxes.* Ed. Natalie Zemon Davis and Arlette Farge. Cambridge, Mass.: Belknap Press, 1993. 167-83.

Davis, Natalie Zemon and Arlette Farge. "Women as Historical Actors." In *A History of Women in the West: III. Renaissance and Enlightenment Paradoxes.* Eds. Natalie Zemon Davis and Arlette Farge. Cambridge, Mass.: Belknap Press, 1993. 1-7.

Dickens, A. G. *The English Reformation.* 2nd edition. London: Batsford, 1989.

Dolan, Frances E. "Taking the Pencil out of God's Hand: Art, Nature, and the Face-Painting Debate in Early Modern England." *PMLA* 108 (1993): 224-39.

Drew-Bear, Annette. *Painted Faces on the Renaissance Stage: The Moral Significance of Face-Painting Conventions.* Lewisburg: Bucknell U P, 1994.

Eaton, Sara J. "Presentations of Women in the English Popular Press." In *Ambiguous Realities: Women in the Middle Ages and Renaissance.* Eds. Carole Levin and Jeanie Watson. Detroit: Wayne State U P, 1987. 165-83.

Eccles, Audrey. *Obstetrics and Gynaecology in Tudor and Stuart England.* Kent: Kent State U P, 1982.

Evenden, Doreen. "Mothers and Their Midwives in Seventeenth-Century London." In *The Art of Midwifery: Early Modern Midwives in Europe.* Ed. Hilary Marland. London: Routledge, 1993. 9-26.

Fish, Stanley. "Masculine Persuasive Force: Donne and Verbal Power." In *Soliciting Interpretation: Literary Theory and Seventeenth-Century English Poetry.* Eds. Elizabeth D. Harvey and Katharine Eisaman Maus. Chicago: U of Chicago P, 1990. 223-52.

Garner, Shirley Nelson. "'Let Her Paint an Inch Thick': Painted Ladies in Renaissance Drama and Society." *Renaissance Drama* n.s. 20 (1989): 123-39.

Green, Lawrence D., ed. and trans. *John Rainolds's Oxford Lectures on Aristotle's Rhetorica*. Newark: U of Delaware P, 1986.

Greenblatt, Stephen. *Shakespearean Negotiations: The Circulation of Social Energy in Renaissance England*. Berkeley: U of California P, 1988.

Greene, Thomas M. *The Light in Troy: Imitation and Discovery in Renaissance Poetry*. New Haven: Yale U P, 1982.

Haigh, Christopher. *Elizabeth I*. London: Longman, 1988.

Hall, Stuart, et al. *Policing the Crisis: Mugging, the State, and Law and Order*. London: Macmillan, 1978.

Hannay, Margaret Patterson. Introduction. In *Silent But for the Word: Tudor Women as Patrons, Translators, and Writers of Religious Works*. Ed. Margaret Patterson Hannay. Kent: Kent State U P, 1985. 1-14.

Harley, David. "Provincial Midwives in England: Lancashire and Cheshire, 1660-1760." In *The Art of Midwifery: Early Modern Midwives in Europe*. Ed. Hilary Marland. London: Routledge, 1993. 27-48.

Harvey, Elizabeth D. *Ventriloquized Voices: Feminist Theory and English Renaissance Texts*. London: Routledge, 1992.

Henderson, Katherine Usher and Barbara F. McManus, eds. *Half Humankind: Contexts and Texts of the Controversy about Women in England, 1540-1640*. Urbana: U of Illinois P, 1985.

Hester, Marianne. *Lewd Women and Wicked Witches: A Study of the Dynamics of Male Domination*. London: Routledge, 1992.

Hill, Christopher. *The English Bible and the Seventeenth-Century Revolution*. London: Allen Lane, 1993.

---. *Society and Puritanism in Pre-Revolutionary England*. London: Secker and Warburg, 1964.

Houlbrooke, Ralph. *The English Family 1450-1700*. Harlow: Longman, 1984.

Howard, Jean E. "Crossdressing, the Theatre, and Gender Struggle in Early Modern England." *Shakespeare Quarterly* 39 (1988): 418-40.

---. "Sex and Social Conflict: The Erotics of *The Roaring Girl*." In *Erotic Politics: Desire on the Renaissance Stage*. Ed. Susan Zimmerman. New York: Routledge, 1992. 170-90.

Ingram, Martin. *Church Courts, Sex and Marriage in England, 1570-1640*. Cambridge: Cambridge U P, 1987.

Ivamy, E. R. Hardy. *Mozley and Whiteley's Law Dictionary*. 10th edition. Sydney: Butterworths, 1988.

Jardine, Lisa. *Reading Shakespeare Historically*. London: Routledge, 1996.

---. *Still Harping on Daughters: Women and Drama in the Age of Shakespeare*. Brighton: Harvester, 1983.

Jones, Ann Rosalind. "Net and Bridles: Early Modern Conduct Books and Sixteenth-Century Women's Lyrics." In *The Ideology of Conduct: Essays* on *Literature and the History of Sexuality*. Eds. Nancy Armstrong and Leonard Tennenhouse. New York: Methuen, 1987. 39-72.

Krontiris, Tina. *Oppositional Voices: Women as Writers and Translators of Literature in the English Renaissance*. London: Routledge, 1992.

LaCapra, Dominick. *Rethinking Intellectual History: Texts, Contexts, Language*. Ithaca: Cornell U P, 1983.

Laqueur, Thomas. *Making Sex: Body and Gender from the Greeks to Freud*. Cambridge: Harvard U P, 1990.

Levine, Laura. *Men in Women's Clothing: Anti-theatricality and Effeminization 1579-1642*. Cambridge: Cambridge U P, 1994.

Macfarlane, Alan. *Marriage and Love in England: Modes of Reproduction 1300-1840*. Oxford: Basil Blackwell, 1986.

Maclean, Ian. *The Renaissance Notion of Woman*. Cambridge: Cambridge U P, 1980.

Maus, Katharine Eisaman. "A Womb of His Own: Male Renaissance Poets in the Female Body." In *Sexuality and Gender in Early Modern Europe: Institutions, Texts, Images*. Ed. James Grantham Turner. Cambridge: Cambridge U P, 1993. 266-88.

McLuskie, Kathleen. *Renaissance Dramatists*. Atlantic Highlands: Humanities Press, 1989.

Mendelson, Sara Heller. "Stuart Women's Diaries and Occasional Memoirs." In *Women in English Society 1500-1800*. Ed. Mary Prior. London: Methuen, 1985. 181-210.

Muir, Kenneth. Introduction. *Macbeth*. London: Methuen, 1976. xi-lxv.

Newman, Karen. *Fashioning Femininity and English Renaissance Drama*. Chicago: U of Chicago P, 1991.

O'Day, Rosemary. *The Family and Family Relationships, 1500-1900: England, France and the United States of America*. London: Macmillan, 1994.

Ong, S.J., Walter J. *Ramus, Method, and the Decay of Dialogue*. Cambridge: Harvard U P, 1958.

Orgel, Stephen. *Impersonations: The Performance of Gender in Shakespeare's England*. Cambridge: Cambridge U P, 1996.

Orgel, Stephen and Roy Strong. *Inigo Jones: The Theatre of the Stuart Court*. 2 vols. London: Sotheby Parke Bernet, 1973.

Padgug, Robert. "Sexual Matters: Rethinking Sexuality in History." In *Hidden from History: Reclaiming the Gay and Lesbian Past*. Ed. Martin Bauml Duberman, Martha Vicinus, and George Chauncey, Jr. London: Penguin, 1991. 54-64.

Purkiss, Diane. "Material Girls: The Seventeenth Century Woman Debate." In *Women, Texts, and Histories, 1575-1760*. Ed. Clare Brant and Diane Purkiss. London: Routledge, 1992. 69-101.

Rackin, Phyllis. "Foreign Country: The Place of Women and Sexuality in Shakespeare's Historical World." In *Enclosure Acts: Sexuality, Property, and Culture in Early Modern England*. Eds. Richard Burt and John Michael Archer. Ithaca: Cornell U P, 1994. 68-95.

Rose, Mary Beth. *The Expense of Spirit: Love and Sexuality in English Renaissance Drama*. Ithaca: Cornell U P, 1988.

Sallmann, Jean-Michel. "Witches." In *A History of Women in the West: III. Renaissance and Enlightenment Paradoxes*. Eds. Natalie Zemon Davis and Arlette Farge. Cambridge, Mass.: Belknap Press, 1993. 444-57.

Sawday, Jonathan. "The Fate of Marsyas: Dissecting the Renaissance Body." In *Renaissance Bodies: The Human Figure in English Culture c. 1540-1660*. Eds. Lucy Gent and Nigel Llewellyn. London: Reaktion, 1990. 111-35.

Scot, Reginald. *The Discoverie of Witchcraft* (1584). New York: Dover, 1972.

Scott, Joan Wallach. *Gender and the Politics of History*. New York: Columbia U P, 1988.

Shakespeare, William. *The Riverside Shakespeare*. Ed. G. Blakemore Evans. Boston: Houghton Mifflin, 1974.

Sharpe, J. A. *Early Modern England: A Social History 1550-1760*. London: Edward Arnold, 1987.

Shepherd, Simon, ed. *The Women's Sharp Revenge: Five Women's Pamphlets from the Renaissance*. London: Fourth Estate, 1985.

Shuger, Debora Kuller. *The Renaissance Bible: Scholarship, Sacrifice, and Subjectivity*. Berkeley: U of California P, 1994.

---. *Sacred Rhetoric: The Christian Grand Style in the English Renaissance*. Princeton: Princeton U P, 1988.

Simpson, Claude M. *The British Broadside Ballad and Its Music*. New Brunswick: Rutgers U P, 1966.

Smith, Bruce R. *Homosexual Desire in Shakespeare's England: A Cultural Poetics*. Chicago: U of Chicago P, 1991.

Smith, Hilda. "Gynecology and Ideology in Seventeenth-Century England." In *Liberating Women's History: Theoretical and Critical Essays*. Ed. Berenice A. Carroll. Urbana: U of Illinois P, 1976. 97-114.

Spufford, Margaret. *Small Books and Pleasant Histories: Popular Fiction and Its Readership in Seventeenth-Century England*. London: Methuen, 1981.

Stone, Lawrence. *The Family, Sex and Marriage in England 1500-1800*. London: Weidenfeld and Nicolson, 1977.

Strong, Roy. *The Cult of Elizabeth: Elizabethan Portraiture and Pageantry*. London: Thames and Hudson, 1977.

Swetnam, Joseph. *The Arraignment of Lewd, Idle, Froward, and Unconstant Women* (1615). In *Half Humankind: Contexts and Texts of the*

Controversy about Women in England, 1540-1640. Eds. Katherine Usher Henderson and Barbara F. McManus. Urbana: U of Illinois P, 1985. 190-216.

Travitsky, Betty, ed. *The Paradise of Women: Writings by Englishwomen of the Renaissance.* Westport: Greenwood, 1981.

Watt, Tessa. *Cheap Print and Popular Piety 1550-1640.* Cambridge: Cambridge U P, 1991.

Wayne, Valerie. "Historical Differences: Misogyny and *Othello.*" In *The Matter of Difference: Materialist Feminist Criticism of Shakespeare.* Ed. Valerie Wayne. Ithaca: Cornell U P, 1991. 153-79.

Willis, Deborah. "Shakespeare and the English Witch-Hunts: Enclosing the Maternal Body." In *Enclosure Acts: Sexuality, Property, and Culture in Early Modern England.* Eds. Richard Burt and John Michael Archer. Ithaca: Cornell U P, 1994. 96-120.

Wilson, Richard. "Observations on English Bodies: Licensing Maternity in Shakespeare's Late Plays." In *Enclosure Acts: Sexuality, Property, and Culture in Early Modern England.* Eds. Richard Burt and John Michael Archer. Ithaca: Cornell U P, 1994. 121-50.

Woodbridge, Linda. *Women and the English Renaissance: Literature and the Nature of Womankind, 1540-1620.* Brighton: Harvester, 1984.

Index

Adelstan 398-399
Aetius of Mesopotamia 301, 305n.21
Ambrose, Saint 107, 109-110, 112-114, 118, 121, 149, 151
Amussen, Susan Dwyer 37, 245
Anselme, Saint 41
Aquinas, Saint Thomas 42, 101
Aristotle 22, 71-72, 277, 292, 294-296
Augustine, Saint 51, 82, 92-95, 102-104, 110, 112, 118, 121, 359
Aurelius, Marcus 81
Avicenna 280, 296, 301
Avila, Juan de 98-99

Baker, J. H. 372
Basil, Saint 116
Beaumont, Francis xv
Beckwith, Sara 342
Becon, Thomas 5
Beilin, Elaine V. 133, 231
Bellarmine, Robert 89-104
Belsey, Catherine 213
Benno, Saint (Bennonis) 139
Bernard, Saint 156
Berry, Philippa 145
Blench, J. W. 3, 5

Bloch, R. Howard 107
Bonaventure, Saint 159
Boose, Lynda E. 64
Bracton, Henry de 374-376, 391, 399
Bradford, John 138
Breton, John le 388, 391
Bridget, Saint 52
Brooke, Sir Robert 388, 394, 396
Browne, Robert 226, 230 n.32
Bullinger, Heinrich 130 n.46, 165

Caesar, Julius 41, 118
Calepinus, Ambrose 374
Calvin, Jean 119, 122
Camden, William 274 n.9
Cassian, Saint John 215
Castro, Alphonsus a 98-99
Catherine of Bologna 366
Catherine of Sienna 366
Cato 40, 69, 222, 304
Cerasano, S. P. 108
Charles I xiii, 145
Charles II 146
Chartier, Alvarus 44
Chaucer, Geoffrey 79
Chrysostom, Saint 5, 79, 84, 113, 116, 123-125, 157
Cioni, Maria L. 372

Clarius, Isidore 122
Cleaver, Robert xx, 183-211, 245
Clement of Alexandria 111, 114, 118
Coke, Sir Edward 393-396
Colish, Marcia 107
Collinson, Patrick 3, 165-166, 184-185, 245
Cooke, Richard xv, xix, 37-59
Cranmer, Thomas 4
Crates 121
Crawford, Patricia 133
Crompton, Richard 401
Cyprian, Saint 39, 79, 107, 111-112, 114, 120, 160

Danean, Lambert 110
Davis, Natalie Zemon xvii, 151, 324, 371
Democritus 22, 121
Diaconus, Paulus 46
Dickens, A. G. 4, 89
Dietrich, Veit 5
Diogenes the Cynic 49, 107, 117
Dod, John 183, 185
Doddridge, Sir John 373
Dolan, Frances E. 107
Dominic, Saint 355-357
Donne, John xv, 213, 230 n.21
Drew-Bear, Annette 107
Dyer, Sir James 374, 389-390, 392-396, 401

Eaton, Sara J. 323
Eccles, Audrey 277-278, 291
Edward VI 4
Elizabeth I xvii, 90, 108, 145, 400-402
Epictetus 107
Erasmus, Desiderius 45, 58 n.27, 165-166
Eusebius 56
Evendeen, Doreen 291

"Ez. W." xx, 133-143

Farge, Arlette xvii
Featley, John xx, 145-162, 181 n.2
Fenner, Dudley xx, xxii, 165-182
Fernel, Jean Francois 299, 305 n.18
Fish, Stanley 213
Fitzherbert, Sir Anthony 373, 375, 388, 392, 395-396, 403 n.3
Fletcher, John xv

Gager, William 63, 64, 90
Galen 277, 281, 294
Garner, Shirley Nelson 108
Gorgias 68
Gouge, William 245-246
Green, Lawrence D. 90
Greenblatt, Stephen 352
Greene, Thomas xiv
Gualterus, Rodolphus 42
Guillimeau, Jacques xx-xxi, 291-305

Haigh, Christopher 145
Hall, Stuart 324
Hannay, Margaret Patterson 231
Harley, David 291
Harvey, Elizabeth D. 291
Heale, William xvi-xvii, xix, xxii, 63-87
Hemmingius, Nicholas 120
Henderson, Katherine Usher xxiii n.4, 63
Henry VIII xiii, xiv, 4, 89
Hesiod 79
Hester, Marianne 342, 352
Hill, Christopher 3-4
Hippocrates 277, 284, 286, 292-293, 295
Holinshed, Raphael 123
Hortensius, Aegidius 379
Houlbrooke, Ralph 183-184, 232

Howard, Jean R. xvii, 246
Hudson, Thomas 123

Ingram, Martin xvi, 37-38, 64
Isidore of Seville 154
Isocrates 69
Ivamy, E. R. Hardy 373

James I xvii, 90, 145, 218, 230, 231, 351
Jardine, Lisa xxiii n.2, 371
Jerome, Saint 79, 101, 109, 111, 113, 118, 123, 159-160
Jones, Ann Rosalind 245
Jonson, Ben 184, 309
Justinian 384
Juvenal 107, 154, 161 n.21

Katherine of Aragon xiv, 89
Krontiris, Tina 133, 231

LaCapra, Dominick xviii
Lacqueur, Thomas 277
Laertius, Diogenes 35 n.47, 59 n.33
Lagus, Conradus 385
Lambard, William 401, 406 n.117
Latimer, Hugh 51
Leigh, Dorothy xv, xx, 231-244
Levine, Laura 351
Littleton, Thomas de 376, 395, 402
Livy 86
Lucian 222-223
Luther, Martin 165

Macfarlane, Alan 90
Machiavelli, Niccolò 80, 87 n.33
Maclean, Ian 145, 165, 277, 371
Magnus, Albert 280
Martial 70, 80
Martyr, Peter 48, 113, 117-119
Maus, Katharine Eisaman 278
McLuskie, Kathleen 323, 351

McManus, Barbara F. xxiii n.4, 63
Michaelis, Sebastien xxi, 351-368
Milton, John 146, 165
Minucius, Felix 155, 157
Mirandola, Pico della 52
More, Sir Thomas 111
Muir, Kenneth 91

Nanzianzen, Saint Gregory 79, 121
Newdigate, John 385
Newman, Karen 167, 184, 342, 352

Niccholes, Alexander xv, xx, 213-230
Nicholas of Lira 99
Norwich, Robert 395

O'Day, Rosemary 165, 184, 246
Ong, Walter J. 166
Orgel, Stephen xiii, 145
Oribasius 301, 305 n.21
Overbury, Thomas 108, 131 nn.68, 69
Ovid 81, 87 n.38, 398

Padgug, Robert xvi
Paré, Ambroise 292
Pareus, David Woengler de 57
Parkins, John 389, 396
Paulus Aegineta 301, 305 n.22
Peele, Steven 310, 311-313
Pelagius, Alvarius 52
Perkins, William xxi, 341-349
Persius 107
Petrarch, Francesco 64, 82, 145
Philo of Larissa 21
Pighui, Albert 98
Pilkington, James 5
Piscator, Johann 117
Platina, Baptista 114
Plato 5, 69, 145-146, 294, 374
Plautus 73, 86 n.22

Pliny 129 n.24, 150, 300
Plowden, Edmund 396
Plutarch 35 n.34, 46, 48, 69, 79, 81, 112, 117, 130 n.29, 156
Pompey 4
Princess Elizabeth (daughter of James I) 231
Propertius 117, 130 n.31
Purkiss, Diane 214
Pyrrhus 23

Rackin, Phyllis xxiii n.1
Rainolds, John xiv, xix, xxii, 89-105
Ramus, Peter 166-167, 387
Rich, Barnabe 123
Roesslin, Eucharius xx-xxi, 277-289
Rose, Mary Beth 184

Sallmann, Jean-Michel 341-342
Sawday, Jonathan 277
Scipio Africanus 40
Scot, Reginald 351
Scott, Joan Wallach xvii
Seneca 5, 82, 107, 151, 249, 274 n.3
Shakespeare, William xv, 64, 86 n.22, 225, 230 n.29, 309
Sharpe, J. A. 37, 323, 341-342, 351
Shepherd, Simon xxiii n.4
Shuger, Deborah Kuller 3-4
Siculus, Diodorus 48
Sidney, Philip xv, 64, 77, 86 n.29
Simpson, Claude M. 310
Smith, Bruce R. xv
Smith, Hilda 278, 291
Socrates 22, 33

Sophocles 22
Spenser, Edmund 108
Spufford, Margaret 310
Stamford, Sir William 391
Stapleton, Thomas 122
Stone, Lawrence 184
Strong, Roy 145
Swetnam, Joseph 213-214

"T. E." 371-406
Tertullian 19, 21, 107, 110-111, 114-115, 118
Theodoricus of Niem 52
Theophilact 102, 122
Thorpe, Robert de 386, 394
Timanthes 150
Tostatus (Tossanus) 51
Travitsky, Betty 134
Tuke, Thomas xvi, xix-xx, 107-131, 343

Udulricus (Saint Ulrich) 52
Ursula, Saint 360-361

Vesputius Florentinus 304
Virgil 66, 68
Vives, Juan Luis 64, 165-166

Watt, Tessa 309
Wayne, Valerie 232
Whately, William xx, 245-274
Willis, Deborah 342
Wilson, Richard 291
Wood, Anthony 63
Woodbridge, Linda xxiii n.4, 214
Wynn-Davies, Marion 108

Zeuxis 129 n.24

For Product Safety Concerns and Information please contact our EU representative GPSR@taylorandfrancis.com
Taylor & Francis Verlag GmbH, Kaufingerstraße 24, 80331 München, Germany